Infusing Critical and Creative Thinking into Content Instruction

A Lesson Design Handbook for the Elementary Grades

Robert J. Swartz and Sandra Parks

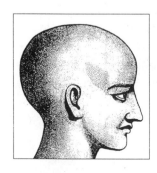

© 1994

CRITICAL THINKING PRESS & SOFTWARE
(formerly Midwest Publications)
P.O. Box 448 • Pacific Grove • CA 93950-0448
Phone 800-458-4849 • FAX 408-372-3230
ISBN 0-89455-481-6
Printed in the United States of America

These handbooks are dedicated to all of the teachers with whom we have worked, whose commitment to helping their students achieve their full potential as clear and careful thinkers has stimulated many of the ideas we have included in these handbooks.

Robert Swartz received his Ph.D. in philosophy from Harvard. He is a faculty member at the University of Massachussetts at Boston. He is Director of the National Center for Teaching Thinking. Through the Center, he provides staff development to educators across the country on infusing critical and creative thinking into content instruction. He has authored numerous articles and books on critical thinking and has acted as a thinking skills testing consultant for the National Assessment of Educational Progress.

Sandra Parks received an M.A. in Education, specializing in Curriculum Development, from the University of South Florida. She pursued doctoral studies at Indiana State University and is presently pursuing studies at Harvard Graduate School of Education. She has conducted National Curriculum Studies Institute workshops annually for the Association for Supervision and Curriculum Development and provides staff development to schools across the country. Sandra has served as co-director of the National Center for Teaching Thinking.

PREFACE

This book explores what can be accomplished when we combine effective classroom techniques for teaching students to become good thinkers with effective strategies to engage students in thoughtful learning of the regular elementary school curriculum. The technique of lesson design and instruction that results is called *infusing critical and creative thinking into content instruction.* The infusion lesson design framework and the tools that we introduce in this handbook to facilitate designing and teaching infusion lessons are powerful devices to accomplish the basic objectives of education.

Infusion has not only grown out of our own ideas and experience but also builds on previous work in the field of teaching thinking. We expand upon ideas developed by Art Costa and Ron Brandt in their important distinction between teaching for thinking and the teaching of thinking. We draw upon the insights of Art Costa, Robert Sternberg, and others on the importance of metacognition in instruction, and on those of David Perkins, Gavi Solomon, and others on ways of facilitating the transfer of thinking skills into new contexts.

The deepest roots for the concepts we employ in the framework for infusion lessons lie in two previous collaborations—the book *Teaching Thinking: Issues and Approaches* and the article "The Nine Basics of Teaching Thinking," by Robert Swartz and David Perkins—and two lesson-book series—*Building Thinking Skills* and *Organizing Thinking* by Sandra Parks and Howard Black. A number of the illustrative graphics we use in this handbook are modifications of diagrams used in *Teaching Thinking; Issues and Approaches*, and the articulation of the "ladder" of metacognition first occurred there. The idea of thinking defaults was first developed in "The Nine Basics of Teaching Thinking." Similarly, some of the graphic organizers used in infusion lessons are modifications of graphic organizers appearing in the *Organizing Thinking* series.

As important as these sources have been for the work we have done on infusion, the most significant influence on the ideas in this book has occurred in elementary school classrooms. To assure effectiveness, the model lessons included in this handbook were assessed and revised based on their implementation with elementary school students. We thank the multitude of classroom teachers with whom we have worked for their involvement in this process. This includes the group of teachers from the Provincetown Elementary School in Massachusetts who worked with Robert Swartz on lessons that were published in *Addison Wesley Science* and the teachers from a variety of other schools who worked with Robert Swartz on science lessons published in *Biology: The Study of Life*, published by Allyn and Bacon, Inc. These lessons were the prototypes for some of the science lessons in this handbook.

In particular, we wish to thank the following classroom teachers whose specific ideas and experiences have yielded some of the other specific lessons in this handbook:

- Cathy Skowron and Sandra Bostwick of the elementary school in Provincetown, Massachusetts, whose lessons developed to teach thinking using the *Henny Penny* story inspired the two lessons on this theme in this handbook.

- Elizabeth Fuller of the Brevard Elementary School in Brevard, North Carolina, whose comparison and contrast lesson designed to help her third grade students understand the relationships between triangles and pyramids inspired the version of that lesson included in this handbook.

- Mary Ann Brearton and Sarah C. Duff of the Baltimore City Schools and William W. Duff of the MITRE Corporation, whose lesson on observation instruments, originally published in *Chemistry: The Study of Matter* by Prentice-Hall, Inc., was the basis for the lesson that appears in this handbook on ranking observation instruments.

- Kevin O'Reilly of Wenham, Massachusetts, whose ideas for lessons in American history in which students learn how to make critical judgments about the reliability of sources of information by using different accounts of the first battle in the Revolutionary War led to the strategy for teaching students how to think skillfully about the reliability of sources of information used in this handbook.

We are also indebted to the keen insights of our editor Gaeir Dietrich, whose understanding of thinking instruction and the practicalities of classroom procedures helped us express our ideas clearly. Finally, we wish to thank Jennifer Swartz, whose technical assistance with inputting the manuscript in a manageable form was invaluable.

Infusion, as we describe it in this book, combines techniques that many teachers who will use this book have been employing in their classrooms for many years. If you already guide your students' thinking by prompting questions, you will not be surprised to find that asking a series of prompting questions is a key technique in guiding organized thinking in infusion. If you regularly ask your students to plan the way they think through problems and issues, you will not be surprised to find that this is a key metacognitive technique that dramatically enhances learning in infusion lessons. If you already teach students strategies for thinking in a direct and explicit way, you will not be surprised to find that this is a also key technique in infusion lessons.

However, these individual practices do not in themselves constitute infusion. The infusion framework builds upon what many teachers, to their credit, already do in their classrooms to enhance thinking. What is different about infusion is the way that these and other techniques are combined to complement each other to produce a complete and effective framework for lesson design and instruction. Any teacher at any grade level and in any content area can create infusion lessons to enhance his or her instruction using this framework.

While we are indebted to many of our colleagues who have done significant research and who have developed ways of clarifying the domain of thinking and instruction in thinking, we wish to dedicate this book to the many reflective teachers with whom we have worked over the past fifteen years and who are dedicated to helping their students realize their full potential as thoughtful learners and good thinkers. What you find in these pages may come to you from the two of us, but their voices are represented in it as well.

ROBERT SWARTZ & SANDRA PARKS

The National Center for Teaching Thinking
815 Washington Street, Suite 8
Newtonville, Massachusetts 02160
June 1994

TABLE OF CONTENTS

HOW TO USE THIS HANDBOOK

FAMILIARIZE YOURSELF WITH THE DESIGN OF INFUSION LESSONS

Acquaint yourself with the structure of infusion lessons by reading Chapter 1: What Is Infusion?

SELECT A THINKING SKILL THAT YOU WOULD LIKE TO TEACH.

If you learn better by seeing examples, read the four sections below beginning here.

If you learn better by understanding the whole structure, read the four sections below beginning here.

EXAMINE A MODEL LESSON

Review a model lesson based on the thinking skill you chose. Relate the thinking map and student responses to the questions in the lesson and to the graphic organizer. Teachers' statements are shown in bold type. Students' answers are italicized, and directions for teachers are in plain type.

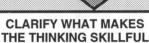

CLARIFY WHAT MAKES THE THINKING SKILLFUL

Clarify the thinking skill that you chose by reading the explanation which introduces the chapter on that skill. Examine the thinking map and the graphic organizer.

CLARIFY METACOGNITION

Read Chapter 19: Metacognition (p. 519). Familiarize yourself with the types of questions that can prompt students to think about their thinking.

CLARIFY METHODS FOR TEACHING INFUSION LESSONS

Read Chapter 18: Instructional Methods (p. 507). Clarify the types of methods that are used in all infusion lessons and those that are helpful in teaching the content.

AFTER YOU HAVE READ THE SECTIONS ABOVE, BEGIN PREPARING YOUR OWN INFUSION LESSON!

FIND AN INFUSION LESSON CONTEXT IN THE CURRICULUM YOU TEACH

Examine the lesson menus that follow the model lessons. They offer lesson ideas; also reading them may suggest other ideas. Read Chapter 20: Selecting Contexts (p. 531) for alternative methods of selecting infusion lesson contexts. Check textbooks or curriculum guides for good contexts. Identify a context in which you could teach the thinking skill or process.

DESIGN YOUR INFUSION LESSON

Use the lesson plan form (pp. 25–27) to jot down what you will ask students in each part of the lesson. Be brief. The detailed comments in the model lesson plans are intended to help readers; your plan may not be as lengthy. Fill in the graphic organizer to predict students' responses. If possible, work with a colleague.

TEACH YOUR LESSON

Try out your lesson. Save any transparencies or chart paper for review and possible revision. Plan how you will reinforce this skill with other activities as the school year progresses.

WORK ON ANOTHER THINKING SKILL

Select another thinking skill for implementation and repeat the same process of lesson design.

PART 1

THE DESIGN OF INFUSION LESSONS

Chapter 1: What is Infusion?

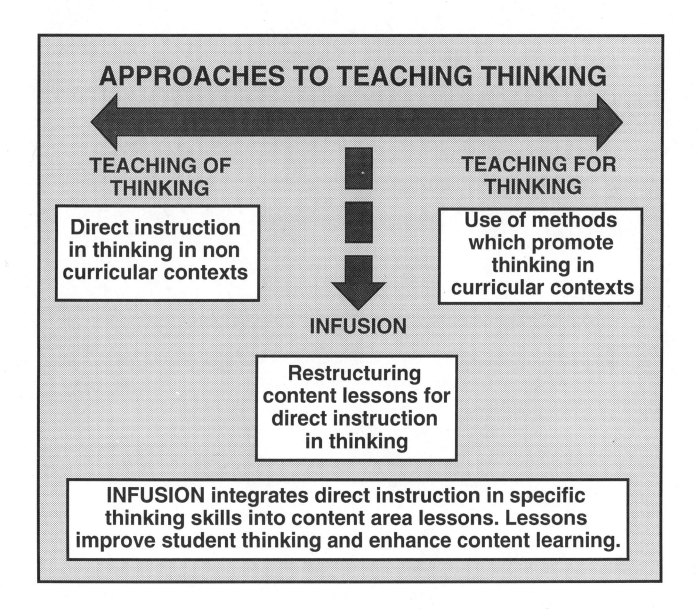

APPROACHES TO TEACHING THINKING

TEACHING OF THINKING

Direct instruction in thinking in non curricular contexts

INFUSION

TEACHING FOR THINKING

Use of methods which promote thinking in curricular contexts

Restructuring content lessons for direct instruction in thinking

INFUSION integrates direct instruction in specific thinking skills into content area lessons. Lessons improve student thinking and enhance content learning.

CHAPTER 1
WHAT IS INFUSION?

Helping Our Students Become Better Thinkers

Improving the quality of student thinking is an explicit priority of current educational reform efforts. Recommendations from groups ranging from education commissions to the nation's governors support this priority and affirm that good thinking is essential in meeting the challenge of living in a technologically oriented, multicultural world.

While these recommendations have been advanced primarily because of the projected demands of the work force in the twenty-first century, they also reflect an awareness that knowledgeable thinkers have a better chance of taking charge of their lives and achieving personal advancement and fulfillment. Our students must be prepared to exercise critical judgment and creative thinking to gather, evaluate, and use information for effective problem solving and decision making in their jobs, in their professions, and in their lives.

Making good thinking an educational goal affirms that growth in thinking is obtainable by *all students*. This goal also reflects confidence that *all teachers* can help students to become better thinkers whatever the learning level, socioeconomic background, and culture of the students may be.

Although textbooks and tests are changing to reflect this aim, it is the classroom teacher who, through day-to-day instruction, must assume the main responsibility for helping our students become better thinkers. The effort that is required to meet this goal must, therefore, be directed at effective classroom implementation. This handbook presents a teacher-oriented approach to improving student thinking that blends sound theory and effective classroom practice and can be used by every teacher.

What does it mean to emphasize good thinking as a major educational goal? Students already use a variety of types of thinking in their personal lives. They compare and contrast when choosing friends. They predict that they will soon eat when they stand in line in the cafeteria. They make numerous decisions in and out of school every day. They do not have to be taught to do thinking.

Performing such thinking tasks, however, does not necessarily mean performing them *skillfully*. For example, sometimes a person feels inclined to do something and may not think much about it before doing it. A person may purchase an automobile just because he likes the way it looks. Such hasty and ill-considered decisions may lead to disappointing and unexpected surprises, such as high repair bills. In contrast, if we think about many options, search for new alternatives, think about the significant factors in making the choice, consider the consequences of our actions, and plan how to carry out our choice, our decision may be a more effective one. It is *ordinary thinking done well* that is our goal when we "teach thinking."

How can we teach students to improve the quality of their thinking? The thinking skills movement of the '80s produced special programs and emphasized instructional methods to foster thinking. Three principles emerged from these efforts:

- The more explicit the teaching of thinking is, the greater impact it will have on students.

- The more classroom instruction incorporates an atmosphere of thoughtfulness, the more open students will be to valuing good thinking.

- The more the teaching of thinking is integrated into content instruction, the more students will think about what they are learning.

These principles provide the basic rationale for infusing critical and creative thinking into content instruction.

This process, known as infusion, is a natural way to structure content lessons. The curriculum is not a collection of isolated bits of information but the material that informed, literate people use to make judgments. We expect that information about nutrition should influence students' dietary habits. We expect that an understanding of American political history should affect how citizens vote. We expect that a deep understanding of a character's motivation and actions in a work of fiction should inform a discerning reader about his or her own conduct and responsibility.

It is essential that we teach students how to use information and concepts that they learn in school to make decisions and solve problems effectively. Infusion, as an approach to teaching thinking, is based on the natural fusion of information that is taught in the content areas with forms of skillful thinking that we should use every day to live our lives productively.

Improving Student Thinking in Content Area Instruction

This handbook spells out how we can perform ordinary thinking activities skillfully. Key questions that effective thinkers raise and answer when making sound judgements are organized into thinking plans that can be used to guide good thinking.

The curriculum offers natural contexts to teach skillful thinking. Any teacher can design well-crafted infusion lessons which dramatically enhance student content learning.

Kevin O'Reilly, a teacher from the Hamilton-Wenham School District in Massachusetts, introduces a lesson on determining the reliability of sources of information in history by staging a scuffle in the corridor outside his classroom. He then asks student witnesses to describe what happened. He draws an analogy between his students' differing accounts and the variety of accounts regarding who fired the first shot at the Battle of Lexington, the first battle of the Revolutionary War in 1775. As O'Reilly's students attempt to determine which of the eyewitnesses gave accurate accounts, they reflect on why some historical accounts may be more reliable than others. This reflection arms them with critical thinking skills that they draw on again and again in O'Reilly's classroom. These skills relate to assessing the reliability and accuracy of eyewitnesses, of observation, or of other sources of

information—skills of great importance in our lives outside of the classroom.

In the immediate context of studying the Revolutionary War, O'Reilly's students use the skills of assessing the reliability of sources to examine the context of the battle and the biases that people might have had in describing it. They then make informed critical judgments about the accuracy of various textbook accounts of the Lexington incident. Students who are simply directed to read to "get the facts" typically do not make such judgments about material in their texts. O'Reilly's students gain a deep critical perspective on the role of first-hand reports in constructing a history and learn that histories can be written from different points of view.

Infusion lessons are similarly effective in the primary grades. Cathy Skowron, a first grade teacher at the Provincetown (Massachusetts) Elementary School, uses the same technique to teach the tale of Henny Penny. Many first grade teachers use this story to help students develop listening skills and vocabulary. While fulfilling these language-arts goals, Skowron also uses the story to teach students to think skillfully about the reliability of sources of information. Prompted by her questions, students discuss whether the other animals should have accepted what Henny Penny told them. How can they determine whether Henny Penny is a reliable source of information?

Skowron restructures her lesson by including questions that students might ask about *any* source of information. Raising questions about Henny Penny as a source of reliable information helps them understand the story at a deeper level. They then grasp the "moral" of the story: *hasty and unquestioning thinking can be dangerous.*

Skowron's lesson differs from O'Reilly's in the sophistication of the content, the level of vocabulary, and students' background knowledge. However, both groups of students consider factors that are often overlooked in thinking about sources. They develop strategies for asking and researching the relevant questions about reliability.

Skillful evaluation of sources can be taught, reinforced, and elaborated in many contexts, subjects, and grade levels. Teachers may ask students to compare a variety of books on a topic and then to develop a list of questions they would need to answer to decide which sources are likely to give them accurate information on that topic. The students consider relevant factors, such as the date of the publication, the expertise of the authors, whether the account is primary or secondary, whether the account is fictional, etc. Students' interest in the topic is enhanced, and better research projects result.

The same content material can be used to teach other critical thinking skills. For example, Skowron introduces causal reasoning by prompting her students to think about whether Henny Penny had good evidence that the sky was falling. Could something other than falling sky have caused the bump on Henny Penny's head? How could we find out? In general, what do we ask in order to find out what caused something to happen?

Causal reasoning, a fundamental skill of inference, involves considering a cluster of questions different from those involved in thinking about reliable sources. These questions prompt consideration of which possible causes are reasonable in the light of the evidence.

Skowron's students engage in causal reasoning by thinking about what evidence they would need to tell what really hit Henny Penny. The students then look at the pictures in the book for clues to determine what the cause might be. They contrast *careful* thinking about causes with Henny Penny's quick conclusion that the sky is falling, identifying her thinking as hasty thinking. They use the term "Henny Penny thinking" to describe someone who jumps to a conclusion about causes. This reminds them not to do the same thing but, instead, to look for evidence. Helping students think skillfully about causes in the primary grades can make this kind of thinking second nature as they progress through upper elementary and secondary school.

Causal reasoning also clarifies human motivation and action and helps us to determine responsibility for things people do. Cathy Peabody, a high school English teacher in Groton, Massachusetts, asks her students causal questions (similar to the type asked by Cathy Skowron) as they study *Romeo and Juliet.* She recognizes that in this play chance, emotion, misunderstanding, and deliberate intent weave a tragic causal web that raises important questions about responsibility.

Peabody helps her students spell out the causal chain that led to the deaths of Romeo and Juliet by helping students to identify possible causes of the tragedy and then to select the best explanations based on the text. Recognizing that various people played a role in this causal chain, Peabody poses the question, "Who, if anyone, is responsible for the deaths of Romeo and Juliet? The feuding parents? The Prince? Friar Lawrence? The lovers themselves? On what basis do we hold people responsible for things that happen?" Through a detailed examination of the play, informed by their conclusions about the causes of the tragedy, Peabody and her students raise, and try to answer, deep questions about responsibility. There is no substitute for careful thinking to answer questions like these.

Peabody helps her students see analogies between issues in the play and issues in their own experience in which questions of blame and responsibility have arisen. Peabody helps her students test their ideas about responsibility by applying them in these personal cases. Her intention is not only to expose them to this kind of thinking but to help them to transfer and use it reflectively in a variety of appropriate contexts.

Curricular contexts for causal explanation are plentiful. Through exploring causes, students gain a richer understanding of such topics as endangered species and environmental issues, the extinction of the dinosaurs, the motivation of characters or historical figures, the causes of the Civil War, or why plants or animals in the classroom thrive or fail.

Thinking carefully about causes is crucial in almost every profession. Effective work in science, engineering, accounting, journalism, nursing, and law enforcement, for example, involves the need for well-founded judgments about causes. This kind of thinking is also crucially important in our daily lives. We make judgments about causes in getting to work on time, preventing or treating illness, preparing a tasty meal, and minimizing stress in our lives. Helping students transfer the use of skillful causal explanation to these contexts enriches any infusion lesson on causal explanation.

These examples demonstrate how the infusion of key critical thinking skills into content learning adds richness and depth to the curriculum. These examples are representative of a multitude of other lessons that are designed to help students develop a wide range of thinking skills and processes. This handbook provides the basic tools needed to construct such lessons.

Thinking Skills and Processes Featured in this Handbook

The types of skillful thinking we discuss in this handbook form a core of important thinking skills that cut across the various content areas. They fall into the three main categories: skills at generating ideas, skills at clarifying ideas, and skills at assessing the reasonableness of ideas. Generative skills are creative thinking skills: they stretch our thinking and develop our imaginations. Skills of clarification involve analysis: they enhance our understanding and the ability to use information. Skills at assessing the reasonableness of ideas are critical thinking skills: they lead to good judgment.

When we engage in natural thinking tasks, these skills of good thinking are rarely used in isolation. Many thinking tasks that we face in our lives or professional work involve decision making and/or problem solving. Thinking skills from each of the three categories blend together for thoughtful decision making and problem solving. We should try to generate original solutions to problems; we should base our decisions on relevant information; and we should assess the reasonableness of each option in order to select the best one.

These broader thinking processes are also discussed in this handbook. The strategies we present for skillful decision making and problem solving provide the link between the more circumscribed thinking skills that appear in each of the three categories and the authentic thinking tasks students must engage in both in and out of school.

The outline in figure 1.1 shows the thinking skills and processes featured in this handbook.

In figure 1.2 (p. 7), these thinking skills and processes are shown within the more comprehensive context of the thinking domain.

Figure 1.3 (p. 8) shows how various thinking skills from each of these categories are combined in decision making.

Continued on page 8.

Thinking Skills and Processes Featured in Infusion Lessons in This Handbook

THINKING SKILLS

I. **Skills at Generating Ideas**
 1. **Generating Possibilities**
    - Multiplicity of Ideas
    - Varied Ideas
    - New Ideas
    - Detailed Ideas
 2. **Creating Metaphors**
    A. Analogy/Metaphor

II. **Skills at Clarifying Ideas**
 1. **Analyzing Ideas**
    A. Compare/Contrast
    B. Classification/Definition
    C. Parts/Whole
    D. Sequencing
 2. **Analyzing Arguments**
    A. Finding Reasons/Conclusions
    B. Uncovering Assumptions

III. **Skills at Assessing the Reasonableness of Ideas**
 1. **Assessing Basic Information**
    A. Accuracy of Observation
    B. Reliability of Sources
 2. **Inference**
    A. Use of Evidence
       a. Causal Explanation
       b. Prediction
       c. Generalization
       d. Reasoning by Analogy
    B. Deduction
       a. Conditional Reasoning (if...then)

THINKING PROCESSES

I. **Goal Oriented Processes**
 A. Decision Making
 B. Problem Solving

Figure 1.1

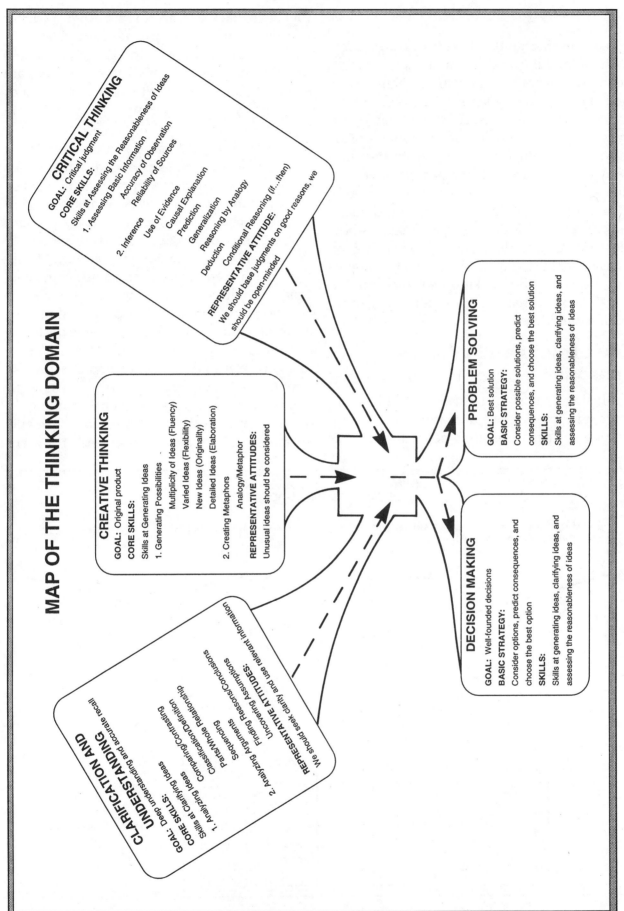

MAP OF THE THINKING DOMAIN

CRITICAL THINKING

GOAL: Critical judgment

CORE SKILLS:

Skills at Assessing the Reasonableness of Ideas

1. Assessing Basic Information
   - Accuracy of Observation
   - Reliability of Sources

2. Inference
   - Use of Evidence
   - Causal Explanation
   - Prediction
   - Generalization
   - Reasoning by Analogy
   - Deduction
   - Conditional Reasoning (if...then)

REPRESENTATIVE ATTITUDE:
We should base judgments on good reasons, we should be open-minded

CREATIVE THINKING

GOAL: Original product

CORE SKILLS:

Skills at Generating Ideas

1. Generating Possibilities
   - Multiplicity of Ideas (Fluency)
   - Varied Ideas (Flexibility)
   - New Ideas (Originality)
   - Detailed Ideas (Elaboration)

2. Creating Metaphors
   - Analogy/Metaphor

REPRESENTATIVE ATTITUDES:
Unusual ideas should be considered

CLARIFICATION AND UNDERSTANDING

GOAL: Deep understanding and accurate recall

CORE SKILLS:

Skills at Clarifying Ideas

1. Analyzing Ideas
   - Comparing/Contrasting
   - Classification/Definition
   - Parts/Whole Relationship
   - Sequencing

2. Analyzing Arguments
   - Finding Reasons/Conclusions
   - Uncovering Assumptions

REPRESENTATIVE ATTITUDES:
We should seek clarity and use relevant information

PROBLEM SOLVING

GOAL: Best solution

BASIC STRATEGY:
Consider possible solutions, predict consequences, and choose the best solution

SKILLS:
Skills at generating ideas, clarifying ideas, and assessing the reasonableness of ideas

DECISION MAKING

GOAL: Well-founded decisions

BASIC STRATEGY:
Consider options, predict consequences, and choose the best option

SKILLS:
Skills at generating ideas, clarifying ideas, and assessing the reasonableness of ideas

Figure 1.2

Continued from page 6.

Teaching the thinking skills of clarification, creative thinking, and critical thinking without helping students learn how to use them in decision making and problem solving accomplishes only part of the task of teaching thinking. Teaching strategies for problem solving and decision making, without teaching students the skills needed to use these strategies effectively, is similarly limited. If we teach lessons on individual thinking skills *and* lessons on decision making and problem solving, we can show how these thinking skills are connected with good decision making and problem solving. Students will then have the thinking tools they need to face their most challenging tasks in using information and ideas.

The Structure of Infusion Lessons

Infusing critical and creative thinking into content instruction blends features of two contrasting instructional approaches that educa-

tors have taken to teaching thinking: (1) direct instruction of thinking in noncurricular contexts and (2) the use of methods which promote thinking in content lessons. Infusion lessons are similar to, but contrast with, both of these types of instruction. The diagram in figure 1.4 (p. 9) represents this triad.

The *teaching of thinking* by direct instruction means that, in a time period designated for thinking instruction, students learn how to use explicit thinking strategies, commonly guided by the teacher. Such lessons employ the language of the thinking task and procedures for doing it skillfully. Usually the *teaching of thinking* occurs in separate, self-contained courses or programs with specially designed materials and is taught outside the standard curriculum. For example, students are guided in using the terms and procedures of classification to classify buttons, in order to demonstrate and practice the thinking skill, or they are asked to assess arguments from text books on critical thinking, in order to practice skills in logic. Since the skills are taught using examples that are not curricu-

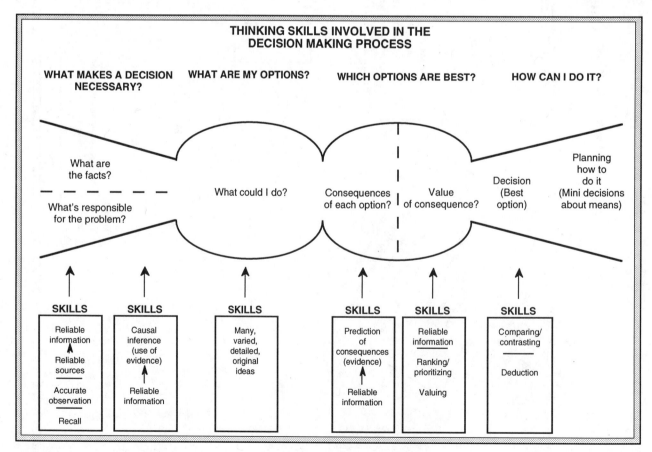

Figure 1.3

lum related, they must then be bridged into the curriculum if students are to apply them to content learning.

In contrast to this approach, infusion lessons are not taught in separate courses or programs outside the regular curriculum. They do, however, employ direct instruction in the thinking skills and processes that they are designed to improve. In infusion lessons, direct instruction in thinking is blended into content lessons.

Teaching for thinking involves employing methods to promote students' deep understanding of the content. Such methods include using cooperative learning, graphic organizers, higher order questioning, Socratic dialog, manipulatives, and inquiry learning. While students may respond thoughtfully to the content, no think-ing strategy is taught explicitly. In contrast, although infusion lessons also feature such methods, infusion lessons are characterized by direct instruction in thinking skills and processes.

Educators often confuse using methods that promote thinking with infusion. For example, many teachers employ "higher order questioning" or "Socratic dialogue" to stimulate more thinking about the content than asking standard recall-oriented questions. They typically ask "Why," "What if," and "How" questions. For example, a question like "Why did the plague spread so rapidly in medieval Europe?" is a challenging question and unlike the question "What were the dates of the plague in medieval Europe?" provides an opportunity for higher order thinking.

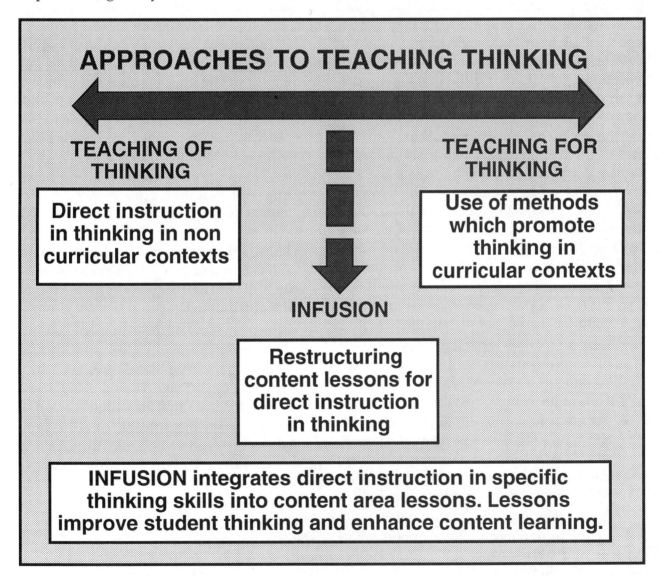

APPROACHES TO TEACHING THINKING

TEACHING OF THINKING

Direct instruction in thinking in non curricular contexts

INFUSION

Restructuring content lessons for direct instruction in thinking

TEACHING FOR THINKING

Use of methods which promote thinking in curricular contexts

INFUSION integrates direct instruction in specific thinking skills into content area lessons. Lessons improve student thinking and enhance content learning.

Figure 1.4

This kind of questioning, however, remains content oriented. Its goal is usually to yield a deeper understanding of what is being taught. When students respond by mentioning factors like lack of sanitation or lack of medical knowledge, teachers usually ask students to elaborate these responses so that the class can develop a rich understanding of conditions that could cause such a devastating epidemic. The product (student answers), rather than the process (student thinking), is the focus in these lessons.

Typically, when using such methods as higher order questioning, teachers spend little or no classroom time discussing the thinking students engage in when they respond to such questions. *How* students arrive at their responses remains implicit. While some students may respond thoughtfully, others may respond hastily and unsystematically. Some students may not respond at all. In order to yield more thoughtful responses from more students, teachers must take time to clarify the skillful thinking needed to develop thoughtful responses to the questions.

Infusion lessons are crafted to bring into content instruction an explicit emphasis on skillful thinking so that students can improve the way they think. Classroom time is spent on the thinking skill or process, as well as on the content. Infusion lessons feature a variety of effective teaching practices that characterize the way thinking is explicitly emphasized in these lessons:

- The teacher introduces students to the thinking skill or process by demonstrating the importance of doing such thinking *well*.

- The teacher uses explicit prompts to guide students through the skillful practice of the thinking as they learn concepts, facts, and skills in the content areas.

- The teacher asks reflective questions which help students distance themselves from what they are thinking about, so that they can become aware of how they are thinking and develop a plan for doing it skillfully.

- The teacher reinforces the thinking strategies by providing additional opportunities for students to engage in the same kind of thinking independently.

Conducting a lesson using this four-step strategy to teach thinking is time well spent and will maximize our chances for real improvement in student thinking

A Third Grade Language Arts Lesson That Infuses Critical Thinking

The following reading lesson serves as a model for designing infusion lessons to teach any thinking skill or process featured in this handbook. It has all the elements of infusion lessons in any content area. The lesson uses a passage from *Charlotte's Web* as a context for teaching skillful decision making.

The thinking skill objective of this lesson is to teach students to consider options and consequences in their ordinary decision making and to make sure that they have good reasons for believing that the consequences will happen.

The content objectives of this lesson include the development of characterization skills and reading for details. As you review this lesson, notice how the decision-making activity leads students naturally to read the text closely in order to determine what the characters are like.

The lesson introduction. The lesson introduction should give students a sense of the importance of the thinking process and link it to the content objective. The teacher starts this lesson by saying the following:

- **Think about a time when you had to make a decision and you weren't sure what to do. Tell your partner what you were thinking about doing.**

- **Let's hear some of the examples you just discussed.**

- **Thinking about what to do is called "decision making." The different choices you were thinking about are called "options."**

The key strategy in the lesson introduction is to make a connection between the thinking process taught in the lesson and the students' own experiences. This connection increases their acceptance of the lesson and makes it more meaningful.

Notice the emphasis on the vocabulary of decision making in the teacher's comments. This is a direct and explicit way of introducing students to the thinking process being taught. These terms serve as verbal cues as the lesson unfolds.

Talking to their partners involves students at the outset in collaborative work. More sophisticated forms of collaborative activities appear throughout this lesson.

As the introduction continues, the teacher prompts more discussion in collaborative groups:

- **Now tell your partner what you decided to do and how you figured it out. What did you think about to pick the best thing to do?**

- **Sometimes, when people are trying to decide what to do, they think about what will happen if they do what they are considering. These are called the "consequences" of their options. What were some of the consequences you were thinking about?**

The teacher may reinforce using the word "consequences" by writing it on the board then listing some of the consequences that students mention next to the corresponding option. To help students identify consequences, she prompts them with questions like, "What did you think might happen if you did what you were considering?"

Although students usually think of some consequences, they often think only of immediate ones. This lesson helps students realize that there is a range of consequences to consider in making choices.

Next, the teacher reminds students that it is important to have reasons for thinking that projected consequences will happen. Young people sometimes distort the likelihood of what they think might occur.

- **When you think about consequences, it's always a good idea to make sure you have a reason for thinking that the consequence will happen.**

- **Tell your partner your reasons for thinking that the consequences you mentioned would really happen.**

These three basic ideas about skillful decision making (options, consequences, and reasons for

their likelihood) are then summarized to guide students' thinking during the lesson:

- **After you think about which of the consequences are important, you are ready to choose the best option. Here's a thinking map which puts all of these ideas together. It tells us what we should think about when we are trying to make a decision.**

The teacher then posts on the wall or writes on the board the "thinking map" for skillful decision making (figure 1.5).

SKILLFUL DECISION MAKING

1. What makes a decision necessary?

2. What are my options?

3. What information is there about the consequences of each option?

4. How important are the consequences?

5. Which option is the best in the light of consequences?

Figure 1.5

While there are variations in the way a strategy for a thinking skill or process can be introduced, it should always be made explicit. In this infusion lesson, the teacher presents the students with the decision-making plan directly. In other lessons, the students may develop this plan themselves.

The introduction concludes by connecting decision making to the content objective of the lesson:

- **We've been thinking about our own decisions. Think about decisions that were made by characters in stories you've read. Describe some of those decisions.**

- **As we read stories, we can understand the characters better by thinking about why they made their decisions. We're going to read part of a story. As we do, we're going to think about a decision that one of the characters is trying to make and what that decision tells us about the kind of person that character is.**

This brief introduction to the content objective sets the stage for the main thinking activity in the lesson.

The thinking activity. In order to have a real impact on the way that the students think about their own decisions, it is important to guide them in skillful decision making. Simply discussing decision making is not enough. Let's see how guided practice is woven into the lesson:

- **I'm going to read the first few pages of the book *Charlotte's Web* by E. B. White. Listen for the decisions that the characters make in this passage.**

   "Where is Papa going with that ax?" said Fern to her mother as they were setting the table for breakfast.

   "Out to the hoghouse," replied Mrs. Arable. "Some pigs were born last night."

   "I don't see why he needs an ax," continued Fern, who was only eight.

   "Well," said her mother, "one of the pigs is a runt. It's very small and weak, and it will never amount to anything. So your father has decided to do away with it."

   "Do away with it?" shrieked Fern. "You mean kill it? Just because it's smaller than the others?"

   Mrs. Arable put a pitcher of cream on the table. "Don't yell, Fern!" she said. "Your father is right. The pig would probably die anyway."

   Fern pushed a chair out of the way and ran outdoors. The grass was wet and the earth smelled of spring time. Fern's sneakers were sopping by the time she caught up with her father.

   "Please don't kill it" she sobbed. "It's unfair."

   Mr. Arable stopped walking. "Fern," he said gently, "you will have to learn to control yourself."

   "Control myself?" yelled Fern. "This is a matter of life and death, and you talk about controlling myself." Tears ran down her cheeks and she took hold of the ax and tried to pull it out of her father's hand.

   "Fern," said Mr. Arable, "I know more about

raising a litter of pigs than you do. A weakling makes trouble. Now run along!"

   "But it's unfair," cried Fern. "The pig couldn't help being born small, could it? If I had been very small at birth, would you have killed me?"

   Mr. Arable smiled. "Certainly not," he said, looking down at his daughter with love. "But this is different. A little girl is one thing, a runty pig another."

   "I see no difference," replied Fern, still hanging on to the ax. "This is the most terrible case of injustice I ever heard of."

- **What decisions do the characters make in this passage?**

- **Let's think about one of these decisions— Mr. Arable's decision to kill the runt pig. Suppose that you were Mr. Arable and what Fern says makes you think again about what to do about the runt pig. Let's look at the decision-making map and ask the first question: What makes a decision necessary? Why do you think Mr. Arable feels he has to make a decision here?**

This question focuses students' attention on the background to this decision. They think about the text and have to select relevant information from it. A litter of pigs was born last night. One of them is a runt. Mr. Arable remembers how much trouble (and probably expense) this type of situation has caused in the past. But his daughter has raised questions about whether killing the pig is the best thing to do.

Asking what makes the decision necessary calls up information that the students will have to use later in choosing the best option. Asking them to provide this information and share it with the class assures that everyone is thinking about this decision from a common starting point.

- **Now let's try to answer the next question on the decision-making map: What are Mr. Arable's options? What else could he do? We will use a special diagram that can help us think more carefully about decision making. It has a box for "options."**

The teacher introduces a graphic organizer for her students to use in their thinking. She has

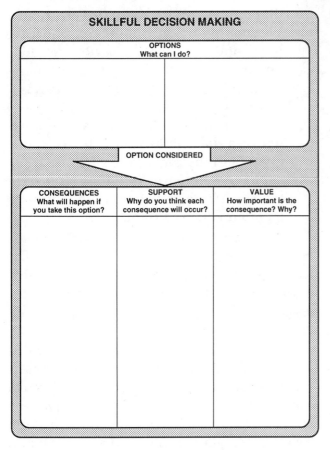

Figure 1.6

chosen a specialized one for decision making (figure 1.6).

Graphic organizers like the diagram in figure 1.6 enhance thinking dramatically. They are particularly helpful for visual learners but have benefits for all students. A well-constructed graphic organizer

- Shows important relationships in the thinking process
- Guides the students through the thinking process
- Makes it possible for users to "download" information otherwise difficult to hold in memory
- Shows important relationships between pieces of information in a clear way

Not all graphic organizers serve these multiple functions. Some, such as appointment books or Venn diagrams, only help to organize information. Those that also guide thinking processes, such as the specialized diagrams featured in this handbook, are especially useful in infusion lessons.

In this lesson a teacher may draw this graphic organizer on the board, use a transparency of it, or create a large poster. Then, when she asks the class for ideas about options and consequences, she can write their responses on the diagram. As an alternative, she may ask the students to work again in collaborative learning groups, write their ideas on a "group" diagram, and report back to the class. Whichever technique she uses, she should write suggested options and consequences on the class graphic so that all students can see the results.

As the lesson continues, the teacher asks the students to work on the first part of the graphic organizer (figure 1.6).

- **Work together in groups of three or four and try to come up with as many options as you can. Try to include different kinds of options as well as some unusual ones. Write them on the diagram.**

Notice that the students are asked to brainstorm options. Simply asking this basic question in the decision-making strategy ("What are the options?") prompts this brainstorming. Referring students to the decision-making map reinforces where this question fits in the overall thinking strategy.

The brainstorming activity can be conducted in a variety of ways. The teacher may ask each individual student to brainstorm his or her own list of options, the class may brainstorm as a group, or the class may work in small collaborative learning groups, each of which generates its own list of options.

Notice that the teacher sets standards for the brainstorming. She requests many options, asks for varied options, and encourages the students to suggest some original ones. If the students in a group are having trouble generating options, she may ask: "For example, could they give it to someone else to raise? To whom? Think of a number of different possibilities."

Like brainstorming practiced in noncurricular contexts (e.g., "Think of as many different uses of this paper clip as you can."), all student suggestions are acceptable at this point. Note, however, that this brainstorming is done in a broader context of decision making, not as an end in itself. The students will shortly think about these options critically in order to sort out which are viable.

A teacher may choose to be more directive in setting this task. She may ask students to generate at least five options or remind them to include at least one unusual option. Such prompting depends on whether, in this particular class, students typically come up with only a few or only routine possibilities when they brainstorm.

Then the teacher asks the students to report to the whole class in the following way:

- **Tell us one option from your group's list.**

By asking for one option from each group, the teacher can create a class list involving as many of the students as possible. This composite confirms the value of collaborative work in the class and gives the students an important message: *Thinking together can help us think of ideas that we might not ordinarily bring to mind.* The teacher may wish to stress to students that it is perfectly all right for them to work with the ideas of others, since they are all working together.

As the students report, the teacher again uses an explicit prompt in the language of decision making. She writes the word "options" on the board and lists students' suggested options under it. The more the teacher uses these terms, the more likely her students are to remember to think about options in making decisions.

The teacher also asks some of the students to elaborate on the options they report. Students should be able to explain ideas they generate. This dialogue makes each student's knowledge available to the rest of the class.

Students generally suggest a variety of options for Mr. Arable's decision: give the pig away, sell the pig, kill it anyway, give it to a sow who doesn't have a big litter, give it to Fern to take care of, lie to Fern and kill it anyway, take care of it himself, etc. Usually these options are spontaneous and show good thinking on the part of the students.

The teacher is now ready for the next stage of the process: to shift her students' attention to consequences. She does this in a simple and straightforward way:

- **Let's follow the decision-making map and think about the consequences of one of**

the options—giving the pig to Fern to raise. We should think about the consequences of our options so that we can decide which option is best. What might be the consequences of giving the pig to Fern to raise? Write "Give the pig to Fern to raise" under "option considered." Then list the consequences that might result if Mr. Arable gives Fern the pig. Make sure you think about consequences for others as well as for Mr. Arable and about both long-term and immediate consequences.

In this part of the activity, the whole class begins to think about one of the options. The teacher's plan is to guide students' examination of one option and then ask them later in the lesson to examine another option in their collaborative learning groups.

Notice that, in guiding her students to focus their attention on consequences, the teacher sets some standards. She asks them to think about consequences for others, as well as for Mr. Arable, and to include both long- and short-term consequences so that her students consider a balanced and comprehensive set of consequences. She phrases these requests in directions to the students: "Make sure you think about consequences for others...." She may ask questions instead: "What are some consequences for other people as well as Mr. Arable?" "What are some long-term consequences as well as some immediate ones?"

If, as the students report, the teacher notices that the students are listing consequences of the same kind, she may say: "These are all consequences for Mr. Arable. What consequences might there be for others as well, like Fern or her mother?"

The lesson continues by emphasizing the need to base decisions on *well-founded* predictions of consequences:

- **Remember how important it is to make sure that you have reasons for thinking the consequences will really happen? Let's think about the first consequence—that Fern will be relieved. What do we know about Fern from the story that is a reason for thinking that she will be happy if her father gives her the pig to raise? We'll**

write that in the "Support" column on the graphic and put a check mark next to the consequence. If you can't find a reason or if there is a reason against thinking the consequence will happen, cross out the consequence.

As students review the story for details, they continue to write appropriate responses on the graphic organizer. The group diagram may look like the sample in figure 1.7. Notice that this particular graphic organizer has the desirable features we mentioned above. Using it not only helps students organize information; it leads them through the decision-making process.

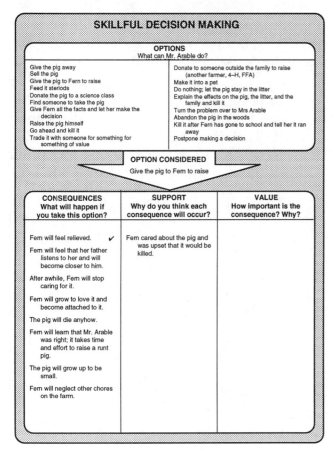

Figure 1.7

Reading for details to describe Fern's character is a key content objective in the lesson. The teacher prompts the students to reread the passage and think about what Fern's comments and actions tell us about her. At the same time, students identify this information as a reason for thinking that Fern will react a certain way in the future. They identify it as evidence for one of

the consequences. The teacher may wish to guide the students more directly if she feels that these characterization tasks are too abstract for them.

The decision-making activity in the lesson now continues in a predictable way.

- **Work in your groups now. One group should finish discussing this option and complete the diagram. Other groups should choose one of the other options. Write down what you think the consequences may be for your option. Then see if you can find reasons for thinking the consequence will really happen. You can use information from the story or what you know about animals, farms, and people. Continue to put check marks next to the consequences that you have good reasons for thinking will occur and cross out any consequences for which you can't find reasons.**

The teacher next asks students to complete their assessment of the consequences by determining whether the consequences count for or against the options and how important they are.

- **Continue working in your groups. Think about whether each likely consequence counts for or against the option you have chosen and how important the consequence is. Put a "plus" next to it if it counts in favor of the option and a "minus" if it counts against the option. Then rate the importance of each consequence in the last column, giving the reasons why after each rating. If the consequence is very important, circle it in the first column.**

After the groups report, the teacher writes their assessment of the consequences on the board so that the students can compare and contrast the options that they have considered. The students are now ready to make a decision.

- **Now choose what you think is the best thing for Mr. Arable to do. Explain why.**

Making a judgment culminates the decision making part of the activity. The students make a choice and support it with reasons. Previously, the students were guided to exercise creative thinking in generating options. In this part of the activity, the students are guided to think critically about the options based on the consequences. The sample completed graphic organizers (figures 1.8 and 1.9) from two student groups show how information and students' consideration of it is summarized and highlighted to assist them in supporting their choices with reasons. All that the students need to develop an answer to the question "Which option is best based on the consequences?" is recorded in the consequences column on these graphic organizers.

Notice how helpful using the decision-making graphic organizer becomes in carrying out this thinking process skillfully. Students need not keep all of this information in memory, where some of their ideas may slip away. The information is all recorded on the diagrams for them to take into account in order to make a well-considered critical judgment. Almost at a glance they can see that giving the pig to Fern has far better consequences than lying. The rationale for this judgment appears in the "Support" and "Value" columns.

In this case, it is hard to see how anyone could argue that lying is better than giving the pig to Fern to raise. Some options, however, may not contrast as sharply as these. Then there is more room for legitimate disagreement. In such cases, ask students to discuss any differences that they may have in the value of and support for various consequences before making a final judgment.

As reflected in these diagrams, the teacher has told the students to use a three-level rating system for importance: *Not too important, important,* and *very important*. Other rating systems can be used, developed by the teacher or the students. Time considerations and the degree to which a teacher wants to emphasize prioritizing will determine how the basis for rating is determined.

Finally, in order to think about Mr. Arable's character, this part of the lesson ends by seeing how the decision is resolved in the story:

- **We've done some decision making by thinking carefully about what Mr. Arable should do. Let's read the rest of the chapter of *Charlotte's Web* to see what Mr. Arable decides to do. When you find out, think about what Mr. Arable's decision tells us**

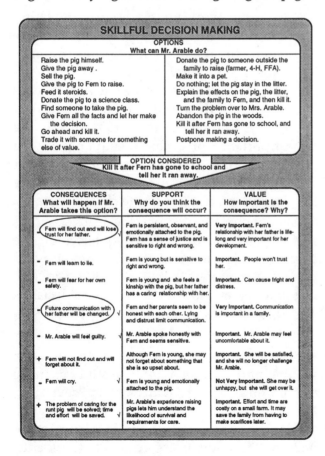

Figure 1.8

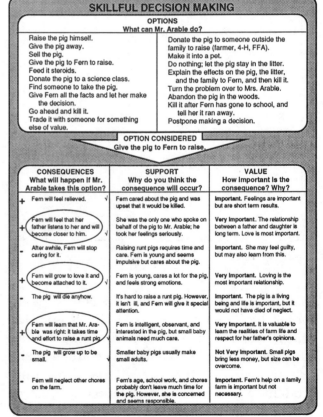

Figure 1.9

about what kind of person he is. Write down two words that describe Mr. Arable.

When students find that Mr. Arable did not kill the pig but gave it to Fern to raise, they describe him as fair, thoughtful, kind, willing to listen to Fern, and open-minded. Repeated practice in making judgments about the traits of a character prepares students for conducting more sophisticated character analyses both in curriculum contexts and in their relationships with other people.

To summarize: The thinking activity in this lesson is crafted to blend instruction in content and in thinking. When the students put themselves in Mr. Arable's place and think through one of his decisions, they get the kind of practice needed to develop better thinking habits. Using the decision-making strategy prompts students to read the text for key details that they might otherwise overlook. Reading for such details produces a deep understanding of the characters, an important reading objective.

There are two key strategies used to guide students through the thinking activity in the lesson:

- Using sequenced explicit verbal prompts (e.g., questions) in the language of the thinking skill or process;
- Using a graphic organizer that visually represents the process.

Using explicit prompts is one of the basic ways that infusion lessons differ from merely employing higher-order or Socratic questioning about the content.

Guiding students to do skillful thinking by using an organized sequence of explicit questions is a basic strategy that is common to all the lessons in this handbook. The teacher typically reinforces the thinking strategy by writing focus words like "options" on the board, emphasizing the vocabulary of the thinking process.

Throughout this book "thinking maps," like the one for skillful decision making (figure 1.5) used in this lesson, verbalize what makes the thinking skillful. Thinking maps employ the vocabulary of the thinking skill or process and provide the key organizing questions that should be incorporated into the lesson.

Prompting students to reflect on how they are thinking. Thinking about what Mr. Arable should do is the central thinking activity in this sample lesson. The goal of this thinking activity is to involve students in deliberately making a considered judgment that they support with reasons. The teacher now helps the students understand how they carried out skillful decision making so that they can guide themselves in the future:

- **How did you think about what Mr. Arable should do? What did you think about first, second, and so on?**

- **Look at the thinking map of decision making. Is that a good way to describe how you thought about Mr. Arable's decision?** (See thinking map in figure 1.5 on page 11.)

This line of questioning distances students from Mr. Arable's decision so that they can reflect on their own thinking. This type of reflection is called "metacognition." Students are *thinking about their thinking*. Thinking about their thinking has dramatic effects on students' learning and is usually not a difficult or complicated task for even primary-level children.

At first, many students find it disorienting to shift from thinking about Mr. Arable's decision to thinking about their own thinking. Teachers may have to ask questions like, "Did you think about Mr. Arable's options first?" After such a direct question, most students catch on.

Notice that the students are asked simply to *name* and *describe* how they thought. They are learning how to *monitor* their thinking, one of the key functions of metacognition. If students know *how* they think about their decisions, they can choose whether they want to continue to think about decisions in the same way or to choose some different way. Here, as elsewhere in the lesson, the language of thinking is important. The teacher expects students to describe their thinking using key terms: "options," "consequences," etc.

The next series of questions takes students to the next step in metacognition: *evaluating* their thinking. The questions that the teacher asks to prompt this reflection are simple and straightforward:

- **Is this way of making a decision a good**

one to use when you're not sure what to do? Is it good to do this even when you feel pretty confident about your choice? Is it better than the way you think about your decisions now? Why?

Teachers who have conducted this metacognitive activity usually ask students to discuss their responses to these questions. In intermediate grades it is appropriate to ask students to write their responses.

Students often say that they like this way of making choices because they think their decisions will be better. Some students say, however, that they find this way of thinking about decisions difficult. This is a legitimate reaction. If a student makes this comment, it is appropriate to ask the class how it can be done more easily next time. Students often respond to this question thoughtfully and offer good suggestions. Asking metacognitive questions helps students to take ownership of a thinking strategy that will work for them.

Finally, the students are asked to *develop a plan* for the next time they have to make an important decision. In so doing, they are employing another type of metacognition that builds on the first two: *directing* their thinking.

- **Can you write down a plan for making decisions to help you remember what you should think about? Draw your own thinking map and use some words that you learned in this lesson.**

Writing a plan for thinking clarifies what we need to think about and the order in which we may want to think about it. A thinking plan serves as a cue to remind us of the strategy that we think should be employed the next time we need to do this type of thinking.

Writing down a plan is, of course, a familiar technique for taking better control of *any* task that we undertake, like baking a cake, repairing a car, and Christmas shopping. The great insight about metacognition as a tool for good thinking is that our thinking itself is subject to our deliberate control, just as we can control our overt behavior. By taking charge of our own thinking, we can reorganize it to counter shortfalls that we detect in the way we ordinarily think.

Neither the language nor the organization in the metacognitive part of this lesson is complex. Second and third graders can understand and respond to the metacognitive questions easily.

To summarize: The metacognitive part of this lesson serves two functions:

- It brings to students' consciousness the structure of the thinking that they just did, using the language of the thinking skill. This is a retrospective function.

- It allows students to develop an explicit written plan for thinking that can guide their thinking in the future when a need for careful decision making arises. This functions to prepare students for future thinking.

Helping students transfer the use of this skill to other examples. To complete the lesson, the teacher asks the students to apply their decision-making strategy to two other examples.

This transfer activity should occur as soon as possible after students' metacognitive reflection. When the thinking activity and the students' reflection on their own thinking take a full class period, students should be asked to apply their thinking to transfer examples in the next available class period.

The teacher continues the lesson by reading more of the story and commenting:

- **In the next passage, we found out that when Fern's younger brother saw the runt pig at breakfast, he also asked for a pig to raise. Use your plan for decision making and decide what the best thing is for Mr. Arable to do.**

She also asks students to apply their decision-making strategy to a second example not related to the story:

- **Think about the decision you discussed with your partner before we started thinking about Mr. Arable's decision. Think through that decision using your decision making plan. Will your decision now be the same as the one you made? Why or why not?**

This part of the lesson provides students additional practice in using the same thinking process. It is included to teach for *transfer*. Notice that it builds on the previous activities, referring back to the thinking plan students developed in the lesson.

Notice, also, that the students are asked to guide their own thinking. This shift is deliberate and important. If they need help, the teacher can provide it. However, the more students guide themselves, the more they will develop the habit of directing their own thinking according to the plan they developed. That is the ultimate goal of this lesson.

The two transfer examples differ. The first is similar to the original lesson activity about Mr. Arable. It is a "near transfer" example. The second example is quite different. It is a "far transfer" example, applying skillful decision making to a different curricular or noncurricular situation, in this case, a personal choice. Both types of transfer are important.

The transfer component of the lesson can be conducted in a number of different ways. The teacher can vary the examples or ask students to suggest some. However the application is selected, teaching for transfer is an essential part of the lesson, helping students develop the habit of asking important questions about decisions to guide their choices.

Thinking skillfully about decisions should be reinforced regularly throughout the school year. Suggestions for reinforcement are included at the end of every lesson. For example, when the class is studying the Pilgrims, the teacher may ask students to think about the Pilgrims' decision to leave their homes in Holland. She will prompt students to use their decision-making plan to list options and consequences and to consider why it was important to the Pilgrims to practice their religion as they wanted. She may also ask students to apply skillful decision making to current problems, such as litter in the school or studying for a test. In each case, she expects her students to follow their plan for skillful decision making.

To summarize: In the transfer portion of the lesson, students are given additional practice to help them develop habits of skillful decision making. This involves

- Additional examples for decision making similar to the one students considered in the main lesson activity (*near* transfer)

- Additional examples quite different from the one considered in the main activity in the lesson (*far* transfer)
- Reinforcement of the same thinking throughout the school year

In each instance, students are challenged to guide themselves in their thinking, usually by referring to the thinking plans that they themselves developed for skillful decision making.

Overview of Infusion Lessons

The lesson as a whole. The lesson on *Charlotte's Web* is an initial lesson on decision making for elementary students. Students not only engage thoughtfully with what they are reading, but their attention is also focused on the thinking process that they are learning. Such an interrelationship distinguishes an infusion lesson from other practices to prompt thinking in content lessons.

The lesson introduction. Focusing students' attention on the thinking that they are learning is done differently in each of the four sections of the lesson. Students are introduced to the thinking skill goal of the lesson along with the content. This is achieved by a discussion or activity designed explicitly to

- Demonstrate to the students themselves what they already know about the thinking skill being taught
- Show students why this type of thinking is important
- Help them to relate its importance to their own experience
- Introduce them to the process of engaging in the thinking skillfully
- Introduce them to the significance of engaging in this kind of skillful thinking as they reflect about the content they are learning

In the sample lesson plans in this handbook, the activities listed above form the *Introduction to the Content and to the Thinking Skill/Process*. Figure 1.10 on page 20 summarizes the main emphasis in this part of the lesson.

Thinking actively. Next, students engage in an activity in which they are guided through a skillful performance of the kind of thinking

---

INTRODUCING THE THINKING

1. Importance of the thinking.

2. How do you do the thinking?

3. Importance of the content.

Figure 1.10

METACOGNITION MAP

1. What kinds of thinking did you engage in?

2. How did you carry out this kind of thinking?

3. Is this an effective way to engage in this kind of thinking?

Figure 1.11

---

being taught. In this part of the lesson, teaching the content and teaching the thinking skill are combined. Two explicit thinking prompts guide the thinking activity:

• Verbal prompts (usually questions)

• Graphic organizers.

This is called *Thinking Actively* in each of the lessons in this handbook.

Thinking maps are furnished for each of the skills and processes of critical and creative thinking featured in the lessons in this handbook. These thinking maps provide the organizing questions that teachers should ask to guide students through the main thinking activity in each lesson. Graphic organizers to reinforce these questions are also included.

Thinking about thinking. In the next part of the lesson, the teacher engages the students in a reflective activity in which they distance themselves from the lesson's content so as to consider the thinking they did. Students map out their own thinking process explicitly, commenting on how easy or hard it was, how they might improve it, whether this was a productive way to think about such issues, and planning how they will do the same kind of thinking in the future.

We call this metacognitive section of infusion lessons *Thinking About Thinking*.

The thinking map in figure 1.11 provides guidance in designing the metacognitive section in infusion lessons by providing basic question types that can be adapted to individual lesson contexts.

Using this map should not limit the teacher from asking students other important questions about the thinking that they have been doing. For example, one might also ask students how the thinking strategy in the lesson compares to

their usual way of thinking. Furthermore, including a special metacognitive section in these lessons should not preclude asking metacognitive questions in other sections of the lesson.

Applying the thinking. Finally, the teacher helps the students apply the thinking skill or process taught in the lesson to other situations. These transfer activities should occur soon after the other three parts of the lesson have been completed and should be reinforced in other activities throughout the school year. Important additional practice is offered by both "near transfer" examples (those from the same field as the thinking activity in the lesson) and "far transfer" examples (those from other disciplines or from personal experience).

This section of the lesson is called *Applying the Thinking*. In lessons throughout the handbook, the categories in figure 1.12 are used to remind readers of the importance of using different types of examples that demonstrate the versatility of the thinking skill or process.

TRANSFER MAP

1. Immediate transfer

   a. Near transfer

   b. Far transfer

2. Reinforcement later

Figure 1.12

Infusion lessons designed to teach any thinking skill or process and any content objective all have the same structure.

Figure 1.13 on page 21 summarizes the components that will be used throughout the infusion lessons in this handbook.

INFUSION LESSON

Introduction

Thinking Actively

Thinking about Thinking

Applying your Thinking

Figure 1.13

The flow chart in figure 1.14 (p. 22) details this structure. A lesson plan form incorporating these details appears in figure 1.15 (p. 23). A blank reproducible version of the lesson plan form for use in designing infusion lessons appears on page 25.

Infusion as an Approach to Teaching Thinking and Enhancing Learning

In this chapter, we have provided a rationale for infusing the teaching of critical and creative thinking into content instruction, illustrated the breadth of contexts for designing infusion lessons throughout the curriculum, and commented on the variety of instructional strategies that can be combined to give infusion lessons a powerful structure. We believe that infusion lessons bring out our students' capabilities for quality thinking and learning. These lessons are not difficult to design and teach. The learning they engender will prepare students to enter an increasingly complex and technological world with skills that they will need to use information meaningfully, to make sound judgments, and to have confidence in themselves as thoughtful people.

COMPONENTS OF INFUSION LESSONS

INTRODUCTION TO CONTENT AND PROCESS

Teacher's comments to introduce the content objectives
The lesson introduction should activate students' prior knowledge of the content and establish its relevance and importance.

Teacher's comments to introduce the thinking process and its significance
The lesson introduction should activate students' prior experience with the thinking skill/process, preview the thinking skill/process, and demonstrate the value and usefulness of performing the thinking skillfully. The introduction serves as an anticipatory set for the thinking process and should confirm the benefits of its skillful use.

THINKING ACTIVELY

Active thinking involving verbal prompts and graphic maps
The main activity of the lesson interweaves the explicit thinking skill/process with the content. This is what makes the content lesson an infused lesson. Teachers guide students through the thinking activity by using questions phrased in the language of the thinking skill/process and by using graphic organizers.

THINKING ABOUT THINKING

Distancing activities that help students think about the thinking process
Students are asked direct questions about their thinking that prompt them to reflect about what kind of thinking they did, how they did it, and how effective it was.

APPLYING THINKING

Transfer activities that involve student-prompted use of the skill in other examples

There are two broad categories of transfer activities: (1) near or far activities that immediately follow the substance of the lesson and (2) reinforcement later in the school year. Both types of transfer involve less teacher prompting of the thinking process than in the Thinking Actively component of the lesson.

Immediate transfer
Near transfer
Application of the process within the same class session or soon afterward to content similar to that of the initial infusion lesson. Decrease teacher prompting of the thinking.

Far transfer
Application of the process within the same class session or soon afterward to content different from that of the initial lesson. Decrease teacher prompting of the thinking.

Reinforcement later
Application of the process later in the school year to content different from that of the infusion lesson. Decrease teacher prompting of the thinking.

Figure 1.14

INFUSION LESSON PLAN EXPLANATION

TITLE:

SUBJECT: **GRADE:**

OBJECTIVES

CONTENT	THINKING SKILL OR PROCESS
Statement of content objectives from curriculum guide or text outline	Description of the thinking skill/process the students will learn

METHODS AND MATERIALS

CONTENT	THINKING SKILL OR PROCESS
Use of instructional methods to teach the content effectively	Use of instructional methods to teach the thinking process effectively

CONTENT		THINKING SKILL OR PROCESS
Expository methods	Using manipulatives	Structured questioning strategies
Inquiry methods	Discourse/Socratic dialog	Specialized graphic organizers
Co-operative learning	Integrated arts	Collaborative learning, including Think/Pair/Share
Graphic organizers	Directed observation	Direct or inductive explanation of thinking processes
Advance organizers	Advance organizers	
Higher order questions	Higher order questions	Learner-generated cognitive maps (diagrams and pictures)
Specialized software	Specialized software	

LESSON

INTRODUCTION TO CONTENT AND THINKING SKILL/PROCESS

Teacher's comments to introduce the content objectives
The lesson introduction should activate students' prior knowledge of the content and establish its relevance and importance.

Teacher's comments to introduce the thinking process and its significance
The lesson introduction should activate students' prior experience with the thinking skill/process, preview the thinking skill/process, and demonstrate the value and usefulness of performing the thinking skillfully. The introduction serves as an anticipatory set for the thinking process and should confirm the benefits of its skillful use.

THINKING ACTIVELY

Active thinking involving verbal prompts and graphic maps
The main activity of the lesson interweaves the explicit thinking skill/process with the content. This is what makes the content lesson an infused lesson. Students are guided through the thinking activity by verbal prompts (e.g., questions) in the language of the thinking skill/process and by graphic organizers.

Figure 1.15

INFUSION LESSON PLAN EXPLANATION

THINKING ABOUT THINKING

Distancing activities that help students think about the thinking process
Students are asked direct questions about their thinking. The metacognition map guides the composition of these questions. Students reflect about what kind of thinking they did, how they did it, and how effective it was.

APPLYING THINKING

Transfer activities that involve student-prompted use of the skill in other examples
There are two broad categories of transfer activities: (1) near or far activities that immediately follow the substance of the lesson and (2) reinforcement later in the school year. Both types of transfer involve less teacher prompting of the thinking process than in the Thinking Actively component of the lesson.

Immediate transfer

Near transfer: Application of the process within the same class session or soon afterward to content similar to that of the initial infusion lesson. Decrease teacher prompting of the thinking.

Far Transfer: Application of the process within the same class session or soon afterward to content different from that of the initial infusion lesson. Decrease teacher prompting of the thinking.

Reinforcement later Application of the process later in the school year to content different from that of the infusion lesson. Decrease teacher prompting of the thinking.

OPTIONAL EXTENSION ACTIVITIES
(Can occur at any time during the lesson)

REINFORCING OTHER THINKING SKILLS AND PROCESSES: Working on additional thinking skills/processes from previous infusion lessons which can play a role in this lesson.

RESEARCH EXTENSION: Gathering additional information which may be useful in reaching a conclusion or an interpretation in this lesson.

USE OF SPECIALIZED ASSIGNMENTS TO REINFORCE THE THINKING: Assigning written or oral tasks or projects which may further illustrate students' thinking about the content in this lesson.

ASSESSING STUDENT THINKING

Extended written or oral assignments or performance assessments of the effective use of the thinking skill or process

Figure 1.15 continued

INFUSION LESSON PLAN

TITLE:

SUBJECT: **GRADE:**

INFUSION LESSONS
Introduction
Thinking Actively
Thinking about Thinking
Applying Your Thinking

OBJECTIVES

CONTENT **THINKING SKILL/PROCESS**

METHODS AND MATERIALS

CONTENT **THINKING SKILL/PROCESS**

LESSON

INTRODUCTION TO CONTENT AND THINKING SKILL/PROCESS

INTRODUCING THE THINKING
1. Importance of the thinking.
2. How do you do the thinking?
3. Importance of the content.

THINKING ACTIVELY

THINKING ABOUT THINKING

THINKING ABOUT THINKING
1. Kind of thinking?
2. How did you do it?
3. Is it effective?

APPLYING THINKING

Immediate Transfer

Reinforcement Later

EXTENSION

ASSESSING STUDENT THINKING

PART 2

SKILLFULLY ENGAGING IN COMPLEX THINKING TASKS

Chapter 2: Decision Making

Chapter 3: Problem Solving

MAP OF THE THINKING DOMAIN

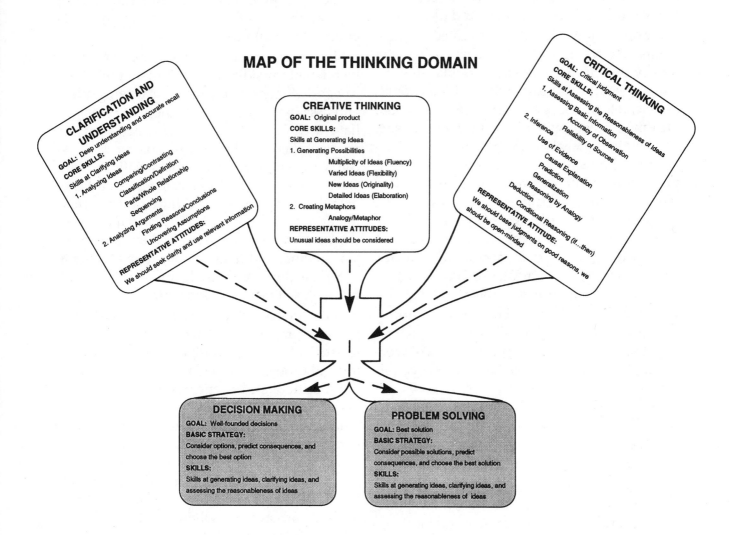

CLARIFICATION AND UNDERSTANDING

GOAL: Deep understanding and accurate recall

CORE SKILLS:

Skills at Clarifying Ideas

1. Analyzing Ideas

   Comparing/Contrasting
   Classification/Definition
   Parts/Whole Relationship
   Sequencing

2. Analyzing Arguments
   Finding Reasons/Conclusions
   Uncovering Assumptions

REPRESENTATIVE ATTITUDES:

We should seek clarity and use relevant information

CREATIVE THINKING

GOAL: Original product

CORE SKILLS:

Skills at Generating Ideas

1. Generating Possibilities

   Multiplicity of Ideas (Fluency)
   Varied Ideas (Flexibility)
   New Ideas (Originality)
   Detailed Ideas (Elaboration)

2. Creating Metaphors
   Analogy/Metaphor

REPRESENTATIVE ATTITUDES:

Unusual ideas should be considered

CRITICAL THINKING

GOAL: Critical judgment

CORE SKILLS:

Skills at Assessing the Reasonableness of Ideas

1. Assessing Basic Information
   Accuracy of Observation
   Reliability of Sources

2. Inference
   Use of Evidence
   Causal Explanation
   Prediction
   Generalization
   Reasoning by Analogy
   Deduction
   Conditional Reasoning (if...then)

REPRESENTATIVE ATTITUDE:

We should base judgments on good reasons, we should be open-minded

DECISION MAKING

GOAL: Well-founded decisions

BASIC STRATEGY:

Consider options, predict consequences, and choose the best option

SKILLS:

Skills at generating ideas, clarifying ideas, and assessing the reasonableness of ideas

PROBLEM SOLVING

GOAL: Best solution

BASIC STRATEGY:

Consider possible solutions, predict consequences, and choose the best solution

SKILLS:

Skills at generating ideas, clarifying ideas, and assessing the reasonableness of ideas

PART 2
ENGAGING IN COMPLEX THINKING TASKS: DECISION MAKING AND PROBLEM SOLVING

Often in our personal and professional lives it is important to think carefully about what we are going to do before we do it. For example, suppose there is a school holiday this week, and students need time for collaborative work and a set of field trips in order to complete projects for an exhibit next week. Making arrangements so that students can complete these projects effectively requires careful thought and planning.

We often think through complicated arrangements like these without mishap: arranging transportation, helping students plan for the kinds of equipment they will need (notebooks, cameras, etc.), making accurate predictions about the time students will need at the field trip site, and obtaining reliable information about when facilities allow student visits. Moreover, we need to keep all of this information in mind when scheduling the field trip.

The daily thinking tasks that govern our actions are not all as complex as the one just described. Most of us easily arrange to go out for an evening's entertainment, purchase items for personal or home use, and have friends over. However, even these tasks require careful thought.

In this handbook, we emphasize two overarching types of thinking that are involved in almost all our personal and professional actions. Each is crucially important to engage in skillfully:

- Deciding what to do when a choice is needed (decision making); and

- Solving the problems that arise when circumstances make it difficult to do what we want or need to do (problem solving).

Skillful decision making and problem solving require that we blend *a range of different types of thinking skills,* including skills at generating ideas, clarifying ideas, and assessing the reasonableness of ideas. In addition, decision making and problem solving require the selection and use of *available information* with a keen sense of its relevance.

Good decision makers and problem solvers also manifest key *attitudes* and *dispositions.* For example, good decision makers reserve judgment until they have appropriately explored the decision or problem. They are persistent in their thinking. They monitor and guide themselves so that their thinking is as thorough as the circumstances permit.

Since decision making and problem solving blend thinking skills from each of the other three categories (generating ideas, clarifying ideas, and assessing the reasonableness of ideas), we have a choice of the order in which we teach students these thinking skills and processes. We can work with students on the specific thinking skills in each of the three categories and then help them apply these to skillful decision making and problem solving. Or we can begin by teaching students decision making and problem solving, and later we can refine students' use of the thinking from the three basic categories by teaching those skills directly.

The order in which the thinking skills and processes are presented in this handbook favors the second of these approaches; decision making and problem solving are introduced before the specific skills of generating, clarifying, and assessing the reasonableness of ideas. However, where you start is not as important as making sure that you work with students at both levels – the complex tasks involved in decision making and problem solving and the individual thinking skills that we engage in to perform decision making and problem solving well.

In the following section, we stress the importance of managing our thinking well when we face decisions and problems. By using a plan for thinking and then following it, we can avoid the disappointments of poorly thought out actions and bring about results that we can deservedly feel proud to have organized.

CHAPTER 2
DECISION MAKING

Why is Skillful Decision Making Necessary?

When we think about decision making, we often only think of "big" choices like buying a car, choosing a college, or deciding whom to vote for. However, opportunities for decision making are plentiful. Our decisions may also be about "little" things, like which route to take on a trip or what clothing to wear to work. Whenever we want to do something and believe we have a choice, we make a decision. Recognizing the multitude of circumstances in which we make decisions is the first step in making them better.

Causes and effects of poor decisions. Whatever the circumstance, good decision making is important. Purchasing a car that breaks down frequently can be more costly than the original purchase price. Choosing the wrong street on the way to work can cause a delay that can be embarrassing and put one at risk of losing one's job.

Sometimes things beyond our control make our decisions work out poorly. A water main may break on the street we decide to take to work. A car purchase may be a one-in-ten-thousand lemon.

Sometimes the fault is ours, however. We may not consider everything that we might in making a decision. Suppose that there is readily-available information showing that a car I am considering for purchase has a very bad repair record, but I don't think to seek that information. Then, if the car needs frequent repairs and I regret having purchased it, the fault is mine. I could have taken the time to get sufficient information in order to make a better decision. We can all recall situations in which we might have thought about a choice more carefully.

Problems with the way we think about decisions. A number of common shortcomings limit our decision making. One is that we often make snap decisions—we decide to do the first thing that comes to mind. We may have more options than we realize, however. Some of these options

may work out better than others. For example, someone may say, "I stained my blouse; I'll put water on it to get the stain out." The water may set the stain; cleaning fluid may do a better job. If we don't stop to think about other options, we'll never find out whether there are any alternatives that might be better.

Sometimes we fail to consider alternatives, not because we are hasty in our decision making, but because we think that our decisions are "black or white." We sometimes hear, "I can either do x or not do x." Choices are seldom so simple. I may believe that I must either pay the asking price for a car or not buy it at all. Usually, though, "not doing x" masks a variety of other options. I might negotiate with the seller for a better price, trade in my old car, or wait for a special sale. Thinking about the different ways of *not* doing something may reveal choices we didn't realize we had.

A second common problem in decision making arises when we don't take the time to think about all the important consequences of our choices before we make them. Considering outcomes can show us whether a decision is a wise one. Often, however, we consider only the most immediate and obvious consequences. I may just think about the initial cost of the car I am interested in and not consider other important factors like gas mileage, reliability, availability of service, etc. If I find out after I purchase the car that it needs constant repair, it is too late for this consequence to influence my decision. Knowing about this consequence beforehand might have deterred me from buying the car.

These problems with decision making are instances of two common defaults (failures to think effectively) in thinking: *hastiness* and *narrowness*. There are other defaults as well.

Sometimes I may miss important options or consequences because my thinking is *scattered* and *sprawling*. I may jump from one idea to another without exploring any fully. I may think about going to the mall, and that may generate images of some of the stores at the mall. That, in turn, may make me think about how much I like to find bargains. It may not enter my mind to think about whether I have the time to make this shopping trip, whether I have other more important things to do, or whether I really need anything at the mall. I may simply not be aware that I am missing important factors.

Finally, I may make poor decisions because my thinking is *fuzzy*. I may blur together a number of quite distinct options, not being aware of differences between them. I may think that travelling to Florida means a trip to Miami because Miami is where people I know who travel to Florida always go. Thus, fuzziness in my thinking is another habit that can limit an appreciation of my range of choices and the different implications of each.

In summary, four habits of thought limit our decision making. They are listed in figure 2.1.

COMMON DEFAULTS IN OUR THINKING ABOUT DECISIONS

1. We make quick decisions without thinking much about them. (Our decision making is **hasty**.)

2. We make decisions based on very restricted information. (Our decision making is **narrow**.)

3. Our thoughts about our decisions are disconnected and disorganized. (Our decision making is **scattered**.)

4. Lack of clarity about important aspects of a decision causes us to overlook important considerations. (Our decision making is **fuzzy**.)

Figure 2.1

These defaults can affect all of the thinking we do, not just decision making. In the case of decision making, however, such defaults can lead us to be unaware of our options or miss important consequences that make a difference. Being aware of these defaults can motivate us to develop better decision-making habits.

How Do We Make Decisions Skillfully?

Good decision makers. We can all think of times when we have made poor decisions. If we

ask how good decision makers might have made decisions in those circumstances, various remedies come to mind. First, good decision makers understand why a decision is needed. Understanding what creates the need for a decision can help us set our standards for a good choice—one that resolves the problem. For example, if I am regularly late for work, I may think that I have to choose a better route to get to work in the morning. When I realize getting to work on time may depend on how early I leave, as well as the route I take, I expand my options to include leaving earlier.

Second, it is always important *to consider as many options as possible*. I might ask myself, What are some different ways to get to work? At what different times can I leave home? An effective way to answer these questions is to engage in brainstorming. We can generate many ideas by brainstorming. When we brainstorm in the context of decision making, the many ideas we generate increase our chances of finding a really good option.

There are three other matters that good decision makers attend to before they make a decision: *they consider a range of consequences of their options*, *they consider how likely these consequences are*, and *they consider how significant the consequences are*.

Considering a range of consequences prevents narrowness in our thinking. For example, it is often important to note short- and long-term consequences for ourselves and for others who might be affected by our actions. If leaving for work earlier in the morning will create a conflict because my children and I will have to use the same bathroom before they catch an early school bus, I should certainly take this into account.

It is also important to consider *how likely a consequence may be*. If I don't, I may exaggerate the significance of consequences that are unlikely, if not far-fetched. I may initially think that there will be a conflict with my children over using the bathroom if I leave for work earlier, but I remember that they usually get up early to review their homework. They are often out of the bathroom before I would want to use it. When in doubt, we should judge consequences by looking at evidence that supports or counts against their likelihood. Careful consideration of the likelihood of consequences is often missed in strategies for decision making that emphasize listing only pros and cons of our options.

We should also think about *how important the consequences are.* Are they a cost or a benefit? How serious is that cost or benefit? In leaving earlier for work, I may have to sacrifice watching the morning news. Is that serious? Should I weigh it heavily in my decision making? In thinking about this, I may realize that while I like watching the morning news, it may not be as significant as the stress of rushing to get to work on time. In addition, if continuing to be late is likely to result in losing my job, I should take that outcome even more seriously. Thinking about the significance of possible consequences—their value—is very important in good decision making.

Of course, *all of these critical judgments should be based on accurate information from reliable sources.* For example, we usually trust our watches. Most of the time they are accurate, but sometimes they aren't. Checking them periodically is a good idea, especially if it is important to be some place on time. Good decision makers make sure they only use information from trustworthy sources.

When a decision is being made in a context in which other people are considering the same question, it is important to state the reasons for our choices. If other people disagree with us, making our reasons explicit will locate specific points of disagreement. This, in turn, facilitates dialogue. We should always allow for the possibility of changing our minds in the light of such dialogue. This kind of *open-mindedness* is also an important mark of a good decision maker.

Tips for good decision making. How do people who are skillful decision makers make sure they attend to all of these issues? One way is to prompt thinking explicitly before or during making a decision. We can do this by reminding ourselves of key questions and the order in which we should answer them. Here is an organized list of questions that reflect what good thinkers ask when they make decisions.

- What makes this decision necessary? What is creating the need for a decision?

- What are my options? Are there unusual ones that I should consider in this circumstance?

- What consequences would result if I took these options? Are there long-term consequences, consequences for others, or consequences that I might not ordinarily consider?

- How likely are these consequences? Why? What evidence or reasons are there for thinking that they are likely? Is this information reliable?

- Do these consequences count in favor of or against the options being considered?

- How important are these consequences—not just for me, but for all those affected by them? Are there some consequences that are so important that they should count more in my thinking than others?

- When I compare and contrast the options in the light of the consequences, which option is best?

- How can I carry out this decision?

Thinking about our decisions in this way counters each of the thinking defaults. Organizing our thinking by following this sequence of questions prevents our decision making from being sprawling. Considering a wide range of options and consequences prevents it from being either narrow or hasty. Systematically thinking about my options and consequences prevents my thinking from being fuzzy.

Tools for good decision making. Using a thinking map (a series of guiding questions) for skillful decision making is an easy way to remember these questions. The thinking map in figure 2.2 on page 34 contains a simpler list of core questions to guide decision making. This thinking map can be elaborated, if needed, for more complex decision issues.

Supplementing these questions with a graphic organizer can be very helpful in organizing thinking and managing information in skillful decision making. The diagram reproduced in figure 2.3 on page 34 is a basic graphic organizer that serves this purpose.

The graphic organizer is designed to allow consideration of on one option from the many

SKILLFUL DECISION MAKING

1. What makes a decision necessary?

2. What are my options?

3. What are the likely consequences of each option?

4. How important are the consequences?

5. Which option is best in light of the consequences?

Figure 2.2

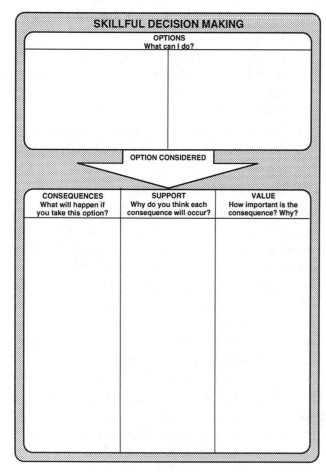

Figure 2.3

options generated. Notice that this graphic focuses on questions 2–4 from the thinking map (figure 2.2). These questions are the heart of good decision making. Question 1 on the thinking map should be discussed prior to using this diagram. Reviewing the completed graphic organizers for many different options should serve as a basis for answering question 5.

Using the graphic organizer for skillful decision making. The graphic organizer in figure 2.3 provides both structure to guide our thinking as we make decisions and space to record our thoughts. It is designed to prompt the organized use of both critical and creative thinking. The following explanation describes how it should be used:

Options. As an important first step in most decision-making situations, brainstorming techniques should be employed to generate a list of options. Record the options in the options box before giving any further consideration to any of them. Make sure to include unusual as well as ordinary options in the list. (Adding options later is perfectly acceptable.)

Consequences. Select one option to consider. The diagram guides us to project as many consequences as we believe might occur as a result of this option, again using standard brainstorming techniques. List these proposed consequences in the first column. We should make sure to include consequences for others as well as for ourselves and long-term as well as short-term consequences. If we list primarily negative consequences, we should strive to include a balance of positive ones as well.

Support for the consequences. The second column prompts a search for evidence to evaluate how realistic the consequences are. We can use either of two strategies to do this.

The first strategy is to consider each consequence, asking what evidence we have, or can find, to support its likelihood. When we find good evidence, we should write it next to the consequence. Then we should put a check mark next to the consequence as an indication that it is a reasonable one. On the other hand, if we don't find evidence in support of the consequence or if we find evidence against it, we can cross it out.

For example, suppose one of the cars you are considering for purchase is a foreign import. You have listed "Higher cost for repairs and service than U. S. made cars" as a consequence. After you acquire opinions from your friends who own foreign imports and U. S. made cars, you find that the labor and parts costs on the foreign imports have been consistently higher than the comparable work on U. S. made cars.

This information would go in the "Support" column next to this consequence, and you would check the consequence as reasonable.

To follow this strategy through, we should continue to work horizontally after we have assessed the likelihood of a specific projected consequence. We should move to the last column and ask how important that consequence is. Procedures for working in this column are outlined below.

The second way to evaluate the likelihood of the consequences is to consider specific pieces of relevant information (e.g., an article from a consumer magazine about a product we are thinking about purchasing) and ask what this information shows about each of the projected consequences. If we find that a projected consequence is well supported by the information, it should be checked. We should then note the information we base these judgments on—e.g., the magazine article—in the middle column as a reference, though not necessarily next to the consequence(s) which it supports.

In employing either of these strategies, we should, of course, make sure that the information we use to determine the consequences' likelihood is reliable and accurate.

The value of the consequences. The third column prompts us to think about the force and importance of the consequences. This, too, requires careful critical judgment.

We have a number of choices in the way we use this graphic organizer to indicate our judgments about the value of the consequences. The first question to ask is whether the consequence counts in favor of or against the option. A simple way to mark our judgment is to put a "plus" for the pros and a "minus" for the cons to the left of the consequences on the diagram. That will make it easy to see at a glance the balance of pros and cons.

Our judgments about the relative importance of certain consequences are usually based on our values. We can express these judgments of relative importance in a number of ways. We may indicate, simply, that some consequences are important and others are not. We can, however, express our judgments of priority more finely. For example, we might want to indicate whether a consequence is *very important, moderately important,* or *not too important.* Comments such as these should be placed in the "Value" column beside the appropriate consequence. Circling the consequences that are very important makes it possible to spot significant ones at a glance.

In whatever way we choose to indicate importance, the graphic organizer provides space for us to accompany our judgment with written comments about *why* we think the consequence has the importance we attach to it. Then, when we compare options, we can make sure that we have assigned values consistently.

Making a choice. Our final choice should be made after comparing and contrasting a number of these diagrams, appropriately filled in with relevant information. The balance of pros and cons—now easily discerned—should be compared from option to option. Usually, the best choice is clear. The information on the diagram can then be used to articulate our reasons for this choice.

Using a data matrix to manage skillful decision making. Some decision issues require a considerable amount of information that is not initially available. As we research an issue, we do not want to become so overwhelmed that we forget important information. In addition, we want to make sure to consider everything available that is relevant. We can follow the same strategy for decision making, represented on the thinking map (figure 2.2, p. 34), but use a different graphic organizer—a decision-making matrix—that is more suitable for complex decisions. This appears in figure 2.4 on page 36.

Before using this matrix, we should brainstorm a list of options. These options—or a smaller group that we consider the most promising options—can be recorded in the left-hand column on the matrix. Then we should ask what we need to find out about the options to make a well-thought-out decision. This will generate a list of factors to consider. These factors should be written at the top of each column. The list of factors can guide our search for data relevant to the decision we are trying to make. This data can then be recorded in the cells on the matrix.

For example, if you are carefully researching

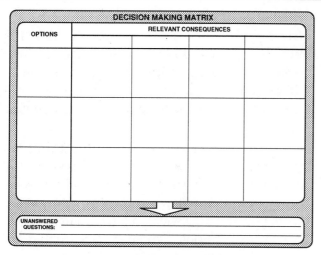

Figure 2.4

an expensive purchase, you can list the factors to consider (cost, durability, ease of use, safety, etc.) across the top of the matrix. Then you can use this list to guide your search for information. When you get the information, you can record it in an orderly and systematic fashion in the cells.

The box below the matrix provides space for writing important unanswered questions that arise about the information we are recording in the cells. For example, an advertisement for one of the items you are researching may include the comment that it is safe to use. You may write this information in the appropriate cell under "Safety." However, you may also realize that this information appears in an advertisement prepared by the manufacturer of the item and that it, therefore, may not be reliable. In this case you may record the question, "Is there a safety record for this item from independent sources that don't have a vested interest in selling this product?" Questions like this can direct further inquiry in order to make sure that the recorded information is accurate and complete.

As we continue the decision-making process, we should ask the same questions discussed above about the force and importance of the data recorded. We can add a "plus" or a "minus" to the information to indicate whether it counts for or against the decision. Similarly, we can circle the information that is especially significant. Comments about the basis for these judgments, however, should be written out separately; this graphic organizer does not provide a place to record such reflection.

The decision-making matrix provides a compact way of organizing information relevant to a decision so that we can easily compare and contrast options to make an informed choice. One addition to it that can be helpful in cases of great complexity is a summary column placed after each row for our overall appraisal of the strengths and weaknesses of each of the options. With or without such a summary column, the decision-making matrix, suitably filled in, can be used to provide the documentation we may need to explain the choices we make.

Comparing the two graphic organizers for decision making. The data matrix in figure 2.4 is primarily an information-organizing graphic. Using it in the process of decision making requires a heavier reliance on verbal prompts than is needed in using the previous graphic organizer in figure 2.3 (p. 34). If you are using the data matrix in an instructional context, for example, you will have to guide students through the decision-making process by asking more prompting questions than are necessary when you use the basic decision-making graphic organizer, where these questions explicitly appear. The virtue of using the data matrix, however, lies in its usefulness in organizing a large amount of information. The basic graphic organizer for decision making depicts less complex data but guides us through the process of decision making more explicitly than the matrix. These considerations should guide your choice of which graphic organizer to use for which decision-making issues.

How Can We Teach Students to Make Decisions Skillfully?

Teaching students to internalize the organized series of questions that guide skillful decision making can help them improve the way they think through their own decisions. Simply asking students what they think someone (e.g., a character in a story they are reading or a historical figure) should decide will not accomplish this. Such a request gives students an *opportunity* for decision making but does not *teach them how to do it skillfully*. Students who do not usually make well-thought-out decisions will continue to practice poor decision-making habits.

Teaching skillful decision making explicitly. A better approach is to teach skillful decision making explicitly. You can explain the strategy directly and ask your students to practice it on an example from the regular curriculum, or you can demonstrate it using an activity in which you guide students through such a decision. When you do the latter, you can use the thinking map to generate the structured questions or directions that guide thinking. In both cases, supplementing your verbal prompts with a graphic organizer is important.

A thinking map and a graphic organizer for the primary grades. A simplified version of the decision-making thinking map for students in grades K–2 is shown in figure 2.5.

CHOOSING

1. What are some things I can do?

2. What will happen if I do these things?

3. Which are good things to do?

Figure 2.5

The basic graphic organizer for skillful decision making and the data matrix, pictured in figures 2.3 (p. 34) and 2.4 (p. 36), are recommended for use in grade 3 and up. However, these graphic organizers are more complex than most grade K–2 students can manage. A simpler graphic organizer for primary grade students, pictured in figure 2.6, is more suitable.

Primary grade teachers who use this graphic organizer in their lessons should draw it on the board and record students' oral responses. This form can also be used with older students who do not write easily. Some teachers have enlarged this diagram so that students can draw pictures in the spaces instead of writing their responses.

The main difference between this graphic organizer and the basic graphic organizer for decision making is that it does not provide guidance or space for students to consider how realistic or likely the consequences of their options are. They simply list the consequences under

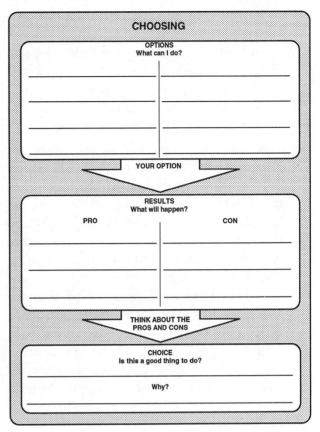

Figure 2.6

"pros" and "cons." Consequently, students will not differentiate between far-fetched consequences and those that are more likely to occur. You can, of course, supplement the use of this graphic organizer with your own questions about why students think these consequences are likely, or you can simply mention this and leave practice in sorting out likely from unlikely consequences for instruction in later grades. We do not recommend the primary level graphic organizer for use beyond second grade, except in special circumstances, unless you explicitly supplement its use by helping students make judgments of likelihood.

Contexts in the curriculum for decision-making lessons. The curriculum offers numerous opportunities to teach skillful decision making. Contexts in the curriculum in which decision is a *natural* response provide such opportunities. In general, there are two types of decision-making contexts in the standard curriculum:

- *Real or fictional characters make important decisions.* Students may reenact a historical decision (e.g., Lincoln's decision to sign the Emancipation Proclamation) using the decision-making strategy and then evaluate the actual decision made by the historical figure. Thinking through the decisions of characters like Jack in *Jack and the Beanstalk* or Huckleberry Finn give students opportunities to exercise decision making and to understand the character more deeply.

- *What students are learning has application to or generates decision-making issues.* The study of technology gives us many opportunities to infuse this strategy into science instruction. For example, students can be asked to think through issues about air pollution, nuclear power, or damming rivers. Posing decision problems about purchases can enhance students application of basic mathematical operations. Helping students choose the best way to solve mathematics problems also provides a natural context for decision making. Physical education instructors can use these techniques to help students decide which strategies to use in a football game.

A menu of suggested contexts for infusion lessons on decision making is provided on pp. 64–67.

Reinforcing the process. Your goal in teaching these lessons is to help your students develop, remember, and internalize strategies for skillful decision making so that they can guide their own thinking when they have to make a decision. This requires continued reinforcement. Make the graphic organizers for skillful decision making available in your classroom and encourage your students to use them on their own. Help them to practice skillful decision making deliberately in curricular contexts other than the one in which you introduced it. School related decisions, including behavioral issues or interpersonal difficulties, are also natural contexts in which you can help students transfer what they learn about thoughtful decision making in your infusion lessons. You will find that as the process becomes familiar, students will use it without your guidance.

Model Lessons On Decision Making

Three model lessons on decision making are included in this chapter. The first is a kindergarten/first grade lesson using a favorite Dr. Seuss story, *Horton Hatches the Egg.* The second is the lesson on *Charlotte's Web,* commented upon in Chapter One. The third is an upper elementary science lesson on alternative energy sources which can accompany most standard fifth and sixth grade science textbooks. Each of these lessons uses a different graphic organizer, selected because of its appropriateness in the specific contexts of these lessons.

As you review these lessons, think about the following key questions:

- How does the thinking skill instruction interweave with the content in these lessons?
- Can you clearly distinguish the four components of infusion lessons in these examples?
- Can you identify additional transfer examples to add to these lessons?

Tools for Designing Decision-making Lessons

The thinking maps on pp. 39–40 provide focus questions to guide students' decision making in infusion lessons. The questions may be stated as shown or expressed in students' own words. The three graphic organizers described earlier follow the thinking map. They supplement and reinforce the guidance in decision making provided by the questions from the thinking map. The first diagram is used primarily in kindergarten and the first grade. The second is used in the second grade through high school. The third—the decision-making matrix—is used in grades three through high school for complex decision-making issues.

The thinking maps and graphic organizers can guide you in designing the critical thinking activity in the lesson and can also serve as photocopy masters, transparency masters, or as models that can be enlarged and used as posters in the classroom. Reproduction rights are granted for single classroom use only.

SKILLFUL DECISION MAKING

1. What makes a decision necessary?

2. What are my options?

3. What are the likely consequences of each option?

4. How important are the consequences?

5 Which option is best in light of the consequences?

CHOOSING

1. What are some things I can do?

2. What will happen if I do these things?

3. Which are good things to do?

CHOOSING

OPTIONS
What can I do?

YOUR OPTION

RESULTS
What will happen?

PRO   CON

THINK ABOUT THE
PROS AND CONS

CHOICE
Is this a good thing to do?

Why?

SKILLFUL DECISION MAKING

OPTIONS
What can I do?

OPTION CONSIDERED

CONSEQUENCES What will happen if you take this option?	SUPPORT Why do you think each consequence will occur?	VALUE How important is the consequence? Why?

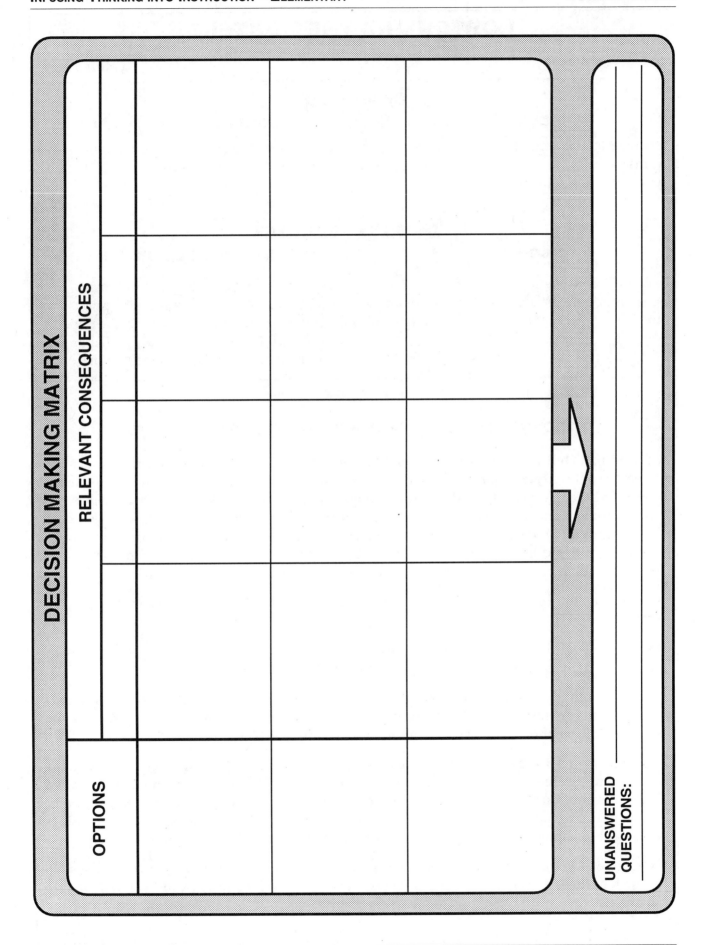

DECISION MAKING MATRIX

RELEVANT CONSEQUENCES

OPTIONS

UNANSWERED QUESTIONS:

HORTON AND THE HUNTERS

Language Arts   **Grades K–1**

OBJECTIVES

CONTENT

Students will interpret story characters in terms of their character traits and actions. They will also practice listening skills.

THINKING SKILL/PROCESS

Students will learn to think about options and the consequences of those options in making decisions.

METHODS AND MATERIALS

CONTENT

Read aloud *Horton Hatches the Egg* by Dr. Seuss. Students should repeat the refrain in the story. They will explain why the main character behaves as he does.

THINKING SKILL/PROCESS

A thinking map, a graphic organizer, and structured questioning emphasize options and consequences in decision making. (See pp. 39–43 for reproducible diagrams.) Collaborative learning in groups enhances the thinking.

LESSON

INTRODUCTION TO CONTENT AND THINKING SKILL/PROCESS

- **I'm going to tell you about a time when I had to make a decision. I wanted to take a vacation away from home, and I had to choose between going skiing where it was cold or going to the beach where it was hot. I couldn't go to both places, so I finally chose to go to the beach. Now, think about a time when you had to decide about something and weren't sure what was best. Take turns and tell your partner what you were thinking about doing.** Give students enough time for both students in each pair to relate their decisions. If necessary, prompt the class to switch roles in order to give each partner a chance to relate his or her decision.

- **Let's hear some of the examples you just discussed.** Ask for three or four examples from the class.

- **What kind of thinking helped you figure out what to do?** POSSIBLE ANSWERS: *Picking, choosing, deciding.* Write these words on the top of the board as a main heading.

- **The different things you were thinking about doing are called "choices" or "options."** Write these words on the board under the main heading. **Let's hear one of the choices or options you were thinking about when you were trying to decide.** ANSWERS VARY.

- **In order to pick the best thing to do, we usually think about what will happen if we do it. We do this to figure out the good and bad things that might happen. These are usually called "Results" or "Consequences" of our options.** Write these words on the board under options, and write "Pro" and "Con" after them. Explain that we use "pro" for things that are good, things we want to happen, and "con" for things that are bad, things we don't want to happen.

- **Pick one of your options and discuss with your partner what might happen if you chose it. Which of these consequences would you want to happen and which would you not want to happen?**

- **After we've thought about the consequences of our options, we can pick the best thing to do. The best thing will be the choice that has more pros and fewer cons than any of the other choices.** Write "Choose the best thing to do" under "Consequences—pro and con." **This thinking map shows what we need to think about when we make a decision.** Show a copy of the chart at the right.

> ### CHOOSING
>
> 1. What are some things I can do?
>
> 2. What will happen if I do these things?
>
> 3. Which are good things to do?

- **Now tell your partner what you decided to do. What did you think about in order to pick the best thing to do?**

- **When we read stories, we hear about many characters who make decisions. It's interesting to think about whether they picked the best thing to do. We're going to read part of a story. As we do, we're going to think about a decision that one of the characters makes and try to figure out the best thing to do.**

THINKING ACTIVELY

- **I'm going to read the first few pages of *Horton Hatches the Egg* by Dr. Seuss. Listen for the decisions that Horton the elephant makes. Let's try to understand why he makes them.** Read the book to the students and, when you get to the refrain, ask them to join in and repeat

> "I meant what I said
> And I said what I meant....
> An elephant's faithful
> One hundred per cent!"

Show the pictures as you read. Continue reading up to the part where Horton's friends make fun of him.

- **What decision did Horton make at the beginning of the story?** ANSWER: *To take care of the egg for the bird.* **What does that tell you about Horton?** POSSIBLE ANSWERS: *He's a nice elephant. He's helpful. He wants to do good.* **What does Mayzie's decision tell you about the bird?** POSSIBLE ANSWERS: *Mayzie is lazy, doesn't care about Horton, and tricks people.*

- **Were there any consequences that Horton didn't think about when he decided to take care of the egg?** POSSIBLE ANSWERS: *He didn't think about how wet he would get when it rained or how cold he would get when winter came. He didn't think about what would happen if the mother bird didn't come back. He didn't think about how uncomfortable sitting on the egg would be.* If students have difficulty answering this question, ask them what things happened that Horton didn't expect.

- **Was it a good decision to take care of the egg? If you had thought about the consequences before agreeing, would you have decided to stay with the egg?** POSSIBLE ANSWERS: *I would have stayed because keeping the egg warm is important even if I get wet. I would have brought my raincoat and winter jacket, but would still have stayed on the egg so that it wouldn't die.*

- **Now let's read a little farther in the story.** Continue up to the part where the hunters approach the scene. Stop reading with the following:

> "He heard the men's footsteps! He turned with a start!"

- **Let's think about the problem Horton now has. Getting wet and cold made Horton feel uncomfortable. Now what does Horton find?** *Some hunters with guns.* **What could be the** *consequence? They could shoot Horton.* **Would that be a good thing?** *No, because Horton could die and then the egg would also die.* **Is that more serious than just getting wet and cold?** *Yes. Being alive is more important than being comfortable.*

- **Suppose that you were Horton. Let's use our plan to decide what Horton should do. Remember what comes first: What are Horton's options? What could Horton do? Talk to your partner and try to come up with three or four options.** After a few minutes, ask the students to report. Get as many options as possible, one at a time, from different groups. Write the options on a transparency or drawing of the graphic organizer. POSSIBLE ANSWERS: *Fight the hunters, run away without the egg, run away with the egg, stay on the egg, talk to the hunters and tell them what he's doing and ask them to go away, hide, make himself look like a tree, give them something nice in trade for not hurting him.*

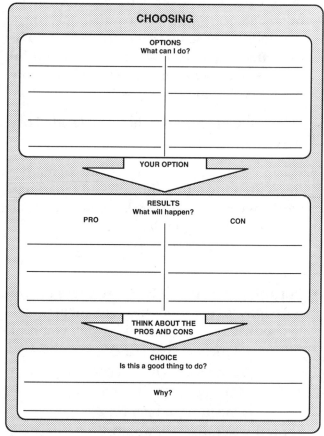

- **Now let's figure out which option is the best thing to do. Let's think about the consequences and list them as pros or cons. Let's try this first with the option "Horton runs away without the egg." What do you think might happen?** POSSIBLE ANSWERS: *Pros: Horton would escape. The hunters would be unhappy. Horton wouldn't have to be cold again.*

Cons: Horton would feel guilty because he had broken his promise. Mayzie would be angry when she returned. The egg would die.

- **Is it a good option to run away without the egg? Why or why not?** POSSIBLE ANSWERS: *No, because the egg would die and that's important. Horton would be breaking his promise and, even though he'd escape, he might feel guilty.*

- **Discuss another option with your partner. Think of some things that might happen if Horton did that. Decide whether these results are pro or con.** Assign each group a different option. On a transparency or on the board, write the consequences the students generate.

- **Let me summarize the pros and cons of each option. Discuss with your partner what you think the best option is.** Ask the students to vote on the best option. Check the one that gets the most votes. Then ask students why they voted for their option.

- **Now we are going to read the rest of the story. Let's see what Horton decides to do. Let's think about why he decides what he does.** Finish reading the story, and ask students why Horton decides to stay with the egg. Coach them by prompting them to repeat the refrain. Ask them what Horton's decision tells them about him. POSSIBLE ANSWERS: *He's brave. He loves the bird in the egg. He cares a lot about the bird in the egg. He keeps his promises no matter what.*

- **Is Horton's decision better than yours? Why?** Ask this question only if what Horton decides is different from what the class decides.

THINKING ABOUT THINKING

- When you were making your decision, you thought about Horton's options when the hunters arrived. Were Horton's options important to think about? Why or why not?

- Was it a good idea to think about the consequences of Horton's options the way we did? Why?

- If Horton had to make another decision, what would you tell him to think about? Draw a picture that can help Horton make better decisions. Accept any diagram that emphasizes options and consequences.

APPLYING THINKING

Immediate Transfer

- Use your plan for decision making to figure out what you can do next weekend.

- In the story of *Peter Rabbit,* Peter makes lots of decisions. Use your plan for decision making to decide what Peter should do when he gets to Mr. McGregor's garden.

Reinforcement Later

Later on in the school year, introduce this additional transfer activity by saying the following:

- In science we're studying what animals need in order to stay alive. Pick an animal. Use your plan for making decisions to choose something you can do to help one of these animals to live and grow.

ART EXTENSION

After your students have brainstormed options for Horton, ask them to select one option and draw a picture of Horton doing it.

ASSESSING STUDENT THINKING ABOUT DECISIONS

To assess student thinking about decisions, use a decision problem, such as what to do for the weekend or during recess. Ask students to identify each step of decision making as they think about the problem. Prompt students to use the right terms for their thinking. Determine whether they are attending to each of the steps in the thinking map for decision making that you developed. Because students in first and second grade may not write easily, you may conduct this assessment orally, either individually or in small groups.

SAMPLE STUDENT RESPONSES • HORTON AND THE HUNTERS

CHOOSING

OPTIONS
What can Horton do?

Run away without the egg.	Fight the hunters.
Run away with the egg.	Give the hunters something nice in exchange for not hurting him.
Ignore the hunters.	Make himself look like a tree.
Talk to the hunters. Tell them what he's doing and ask them to go away.	Hide from the hunters.

YOUR OPTION
Run away without the egg

RESULTS
What will happen?

PRO	CON
Horton may escape.	Horton will feel bad because he broke his promise to Mayzie.
Horton won't be afraid anymore.	If Horton falls down, the hunters would get him.
Horton won't have to get cold anymore sitting on the egg.	The egg will die.
	Mayzie will get upset when she returns and finds her egg dead.

CHOICE
Is this a good thing to do?
No
Why?
Because it's very important to keep the egg alive and Horton made a promise to Mayzie to take care of the egg.

SAMPLE STUDENT RESPONSES • HORTON AND THE HUNTERS

CHOOSING

OPTIONS
What can Horton do?

Run away without the egg.	Fight the hunters.
Run away with the egg.	Give the hunters something nice in exchange for not hurting him.
Stay and faces the hunters.	Make himself look like a tree.
Talk to the hunters. Tell them what he's doing and ask them to go away.	Hide from the hunters.

YOUR OPTION
Stay and face
the hunters

RESULTS
What will happen?

PRO	CON
The hunters might not shoot because Horton is brave.	The hunters might shoot Horton.
Horton keeps his word to Mayzie.	The hunters might capture Horton and take him away from the egg.
The hunters might miss.	The hunters might steal the egg and sell it.

CHOICE
Is this a good thing to do?
Maybe if the hunters are nice and don't hurt Horton.
Why?
Because Horton made a promise to Mayzie to take care of the egg and that's important.

MR. ARABLE AND THE RUNT PIG

Language Arts   **Grade 3**

OBJECTIVES

CONTENT

Students will learn to think about story characters in terms of their character traits and actions

THINKING SKILL/PROCESS

Students will learn to think about options and the likelihood of the consequences of those options in making decisions.

METHODS AND MATERIALS

CONTENT

Students read part of a story, use background information, work in collaborative learning groups to share information, and record it in a graphic organizer. The book *Charlotte's Web* is needed.

THINKING SKILL/PROCESS

An explicit thinking map, a graphic organizer, and structured questioning emphasize options, consequences, and reasons in decision making. (See pp. 39–43 for reproducible diagrams.) Collaborative learning in groups of four enhance the thinking.

LESSON

INTRODUCTION TO CONTENT AND THINKING SKILL/PROCESS

- **Think about a time when you had to make a decision and you weren't sure what to do. Tell your partner what you were thinking about doing.** Give students enough time for both students in each pair to relate their decisions. If necessary, prompt the class to switch roles in order to give each partner a chance to relate his or her decision.

- **Let's hear some of the examples you just discussed.** Ask for three or four examples from the class. Write each decision at the top of a column under the word "Decisions."

- **When thinking about what to do, your thinking is called "decision making." The different choices you were thinking about are called "options."** Write "Decision Making" and "Options" on the board. Under the word "options," list the alternatives that students mention.

- **Now tell your neighbor what you decided to do and how you figured it out. What did you think about to pick the best thing to do?**

- **When people are trying to decide what to do, they sometimes think about what will happen as a result of their decision. These results are called the "consequences" of their options. What were some of the consequences you were thinking about?** Write the word "consequences" on the board, and list some of the consequences students mention.

- **In making decisions, you should have a good reason for expecting particular consequences.** Write the word "reason" on the board.

- **Tell your neighbor your reasons for thinking that your decision would have the consequences you mentioned.** Ask the students to mention some reasons, and list these on the board under "reasons."

- **After you think about which of the consequences are important, you are ready to make the** best choice. Here's a thinking map putting all of these ideas together. It tells us what we should think about when we are trying to make a decision. Show a copy of the thinking map at the right.

- We've been thinking about our own decisions. Now, think about decisions that were made by characters in stories you've read. Describe some of those decisions. Get three or four examples from the class.

- As we read stories, we can understand the characters better by thinking about why they made their decisions. We're going to read part of a story. As we do, we're going to think about a decision that one of the characters is trying to make and what that decision tells us about the kind of person that character is.

THINKING ACTIVELY

- I'm going to read the first few pages of the book *Charlotte's Web* by E. B. White. Listen for the decisions that the characters make in this passage.

"Where is Papa going with that ax?" said Fern to her mother as they were setting the table for breakfast.

"Out to the hoghouse," replied Mrs. Arable. "Some pigs were born last night."

"I don't see why he needs an ax," continued Fern, who was only eight.

"Well," said her mother, "one of the pigs is a runt. It's very small and weak, and it will never amount to anything. So your father has decided to do away with it."

"Do away with it?" shrieked Fern. "You mean kill it? Just because it's smaller than the others?"

Mrs. Arable put a pitcher of cream on the table. "Don't yell, Fern!" she said. "Your father is right. The pig would probably die anyway."

Fern pushed a chair out of the way and ran outdoors. The grass was wet and the earth smelled of springtime. Fern's sneakers were sopping by the time she caught up with her father.

"Please don't kill it," she sobbed. "It's unfair."

Mr. Arable stopped walking.

"Fern," he said gently, "you will have to learn to control yourself."

"Control myself?" yelled Fern. "This is a matter of life and death, and you talk about controlling myself." Tears ran down her cheeks and she took hold of the ax and tried to pull it out of her father's hand.

"Fern," said Mr. Arable, "I know more about raising a litter of pigs than you do. A weakling makes trouble. Now run along!"

"But it's unfair," cried Fern. "The pig couldn't help being born small, could it? If I had been very small at birth, would you have killed me?"

Mr. Arable smiled. "Certainly not," he said, looking down at his daughter with love. "But this is different. A little girl is one thing, a runty pig is another."

"I see no difference," replied Fern, still hanging onto the ax. "This is the most terrible case of injustice I have ever heard of."

- **What decisions do the characters make in this passage?** POSSIBLE ANSWERS: *Mr. Arable's decision to kill the runt pig, Fern's decision to try to get her father to spare the pig, Fern's decision to grab the ax, Mr. Arable's decision to reason with Fern, Fern's decision to try to convince her father, Mrs. Arable's decision to tell Fern what her father plans.*

- **Let's think about Mr. Arable's decision to kill the runt pig. Suppose you were Mr. Arable and that what Fern says makes you think again about what to do about the runt pig. Let's look at the decision-making map and ask the first question: What makes a decision necessary? Why do you think Mr. Arable feels he has to make a decision here?** POSSIBLE ANSWERS: *A litter of pigs was born last night. One of the pigs was a runt. Mr. Arable remembers how much trouble raising a runt pig has caused in the past. It may cost a lot of money to care for the runt pig. Fern has raised questions about whether killing the pig is the best thing to do.*

- **Now let's look at the next question: What are Mr. Arable's options? What else could he do? We will use a special diagram that can help us think more carefully about decision making. It has a box for "Options." Work together in groups of three or four and try to come up with as many options as you can. Try to think of different kinds of options, including some unusual ones, and write them on the diagram.** POS-SIBLE ANSWERS: *Take care of the pig himself, give the pig away, sell the pig, let Fern take care of the pig, lie to Fern and kill it anyway, do nothing (let the pig fend for itself), advertise for someone who can take care of the pig, make it a pet, kill it anyway, abandon the pig in the woods.*

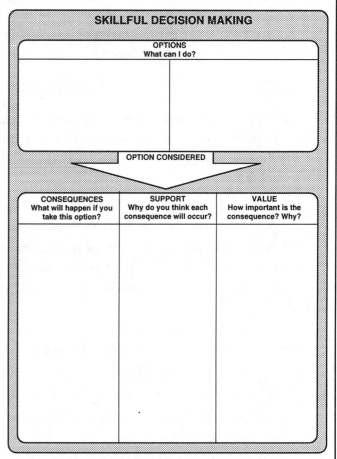

- **Tell us one option from your group's list.** As each group of students responds, write these on the board or on a transparency of the diagram under the word "Options." Then ask for volunteers to add options that haven't been mentioned. As you list responses, ask for elaboration of some by the students who offer them.

- **Let's follow the decision-making map and think about the consequences of one of the options: giving the pig to Fern to raise. We should think about the consequences of our options so that we can decide which option is best. What might be the consequences of giving the pig to Fern to raise? Write "Give the pig to Fern to raise" under "Option Considered." Then list consequences that might result if Mr. Arable did that. Make sure you think about consequences for others as well as for Mr. Arable and about both long-term and immediate consequences.** Ask the students for suggestions about the consequences, and fill in the graphic organizer as they give them. POSSIBLE ANSWERS. *Fern will be relieved. The pig will die anyhow. Fern will learn how hard it is to keep an animal alive. Fern will be able to keep the pig alive. Fern will feel that her father values her ideas. Fern will learn farm responsibility. Raising the pig will take Fern away from other chores on the farm, and pig care could become time consuming and expensive for the family. The pig* *may live and grow normally. Fern will learn about death. Fern will understand the wisdom behind her father's decisions. The parents may disagree over the decision. Pig care may come back to the parents. Mr. Arable may feel guilty about giving Fern the responsibility if the pig dies. The pig may breed other small pigs.*

- **Remember how important it is to make sure that you have reasons for thinking the consequences will really happen. Let's think about the first consequence—that Fern will be relieved. What do we know about Fern from the story that is a reason for thinking she will be relieved if her father gives her the pig to raise? We'll write that in the "Support" column on the diagram. Since we have a reason that supports it, we'll put a check mark next to the consequence. If you can't find a reason or if there is a reason against thinking the consequence will happen, we'll cross out the consequence.** Write what the students suggest on the graphic organizer. As you fill in student responses, your organizer should resemble the one at the right.

- **Now work in your groups to come up with the consequences for another option.** Assign one group to finish discussing this option and complete the diagram. Let each of the other groups pick another option. **Write down what you think the consequences might be for your option. Then see if you can find reasons for thinking the consequences will really happen. You can use information from the story or what you know about animals, farms, and people. Cross out any consequences for which you can't find support.** After five minutes, ask the groups to report by telling what the option is and whether the reasons show that the consequences are likely.

- **In your groups again, think about whether each likely consequence counts in favor of or against the option you have chosen. Put a plus next to the consequence if it counts in favor of the option; use a minus if it counts against the consequence; if the consequence is important, circle it, and explain why it is important in the last column on the diagram.**

- **Now pick what you think is the best thing for Mr. Arable to do. Explain why.** Ask each group to report. After the discussion, ask the class to vote on the best thing to do.

- **We've done some decision making by thinking carefully about what Mr. Arable should do. Let's read the rest of this chapter of *Charlotte's Web* to see what Mr. Arable decides to do. When you find out, think about what Mr. Arable's decision tells us about the kind of person he is. Write down two words or phrases that describe Mr. Arable.** Read the rest of the chapter aloud. Ask a number of students to report on their descriptions and why they chose these. POSSIBLE ANSWERS: *Fair, thoughtful, listens to Fern, kind, open-minded.*

SKILLFUL DECISION MAKING

OPTIONS
What can Mr. Arable do?

Raise the pig himself.	Donate the pig to someone outside the family to raise (farmer, 4-H, FFA).
Give the pig away .	
Sell the pig.	Make it into a pet.
Give it to Fern to raise.	Do nothing; let the pig stay in the litter.
Feed it steroids.	Explain the effects on the pig, the litter, and the family to Fern, and then kill it.
Donate the pig to a science class.	
Find someone to take the pig.	Turn the problem over to Mrs. Arable.
Give Fern all the facts and let her make the decision.	Abandon the pig in the woods.
	Kill it after Fern has gone to school, and tell her it ran away.
Go ahead and kill it.	Postpone making a decision.
Trade it with someone for something else of value.	

OPTION CONSIDERED
Give the pig to Fern to raise.

CONSEQUENCES What will happen if Mr. Arable takes this option?	SUPPORT Why do you think the consequence will occur?	VALUE How important is the consequence? Why?
Fern will feel relieved. ✓	Fern cared about the pig and was upset that it would be killed.	
Fern will feel that her father listens to her and will become closer to him.		
After awhile, Fern will stop caring for it.		
Fern will grow to love it and become attached to it.		
The pig will die anyhow.		
Fern will learn that Mr. Arable was right: it takes time and effort to raise a runt pig.		
The pig will grow up to be small.		
Fern will neglect other chores on the farm.		

THINKING ABOUT THINKING

- How did you think about what Mr. Arable should do? What did you think about first, second, and so on? POSSIBLE ANSWERS: *Options first, then consequences, then evidence about how likely the consequences were, and then what the best thing to do is.*

- Look at the thinking map of decision making. Is that a good way to describe how you thought about what Mr. Arable should do? ANSWERS VARY, BUT STUDENTS GENERALLY AGREE THAT IT IS.

- Is this a good way to make a decision when you're not sure what to do? Is it good to do this even when you feel pretty confident about your choice? Is it better than the way you think about your decisions now? Why? ANSWERS VARY.

- Can you write down a plan for your decisions to help you remember what you should think about? Draw your own thinking map and use some words that you learned in this lesson.

APPLYING THINKING

Immediate Transfer

- Later in the chapter, we found out that Fern's younger brother saw the runt pig at breakfast the next morning and asked for a pig to raise, too. Use your plan for decision making and decide what is the best thing for Mr. Arable to do.

- Think about the decision you discussed with your partner before we talked about Mr. Arable. Think through that decision using your decision-making plan. Would your decision now be the same as the one you made earlier? Why or why not?

Reinforcement Later

Later on in the school year, introduce additional transfer activities.

- In social studies, we've been studying about the Pilgrims' decision to leave Europe and come to the New World. Use your plan for decision making to think through whether or not they should leave Holland.

- We will be studying about pollution in science. Litter in the school is one type of pollution. Use your plan for decision making to think about how to keep the school free from litter.

- Think about a decision that you have to make sometime soon. Use your plan for decision making to think it through the same way. How can you remind yourself to think about decisions in this way when you have to make them? SUGGESTION: *Write a note to yourself.*

ASSESSING STUDENT THINKING ABOUT DECISIONS

To assess student thinking about decisions, ask students to consider the school littering problem, or ask them to think through a personal decision. Ask your students to make their thinking explicit as they consider the best option. Determine whether they are attending to each of the steps in the thinking map for decision making.

Sample Student Responses • Mr. Arable and the Runt Pig

SKILLFUL DECISION MAKING

OPTIONS
What can Mr. Arable do?

Raise the pig himself.	Donate the pig to someone outside the family to raise (farmer, 4-H, FFA).
Give the pig away.	
Sell the pig.	Make it into a pet.
Give the pig to Fern to raise.	Do nothing; let the pig stay in the litter.
Feed it steroids.	Explain the effects on the pig, the litter, and the family to Fern, and then kill it.
Donate the pig to a science class.	
Find someone to take the pig.	Turn the problem over to Mrs. Arable.
Give Fern all the facts and let her make the decision.	Abandon the pig in the woods.
	Kill it after Fern has gone to school, and tell her it ran away.
Go ahead and kill it.	
Trade it with someone for something else of value.	Postpone making a decision.

OPTION CONSIDERED
Give the pig to Fern to raise.

CONSEQUENCES What will happen if Mr. Arable takes this option?	SUPPORT Why do you think the consequence will occur?	VALUE How important is the consequence? Why?
+ Fern will feel relieved. √	Fern cared about the pig and was upset that it would be killed.	**Important.** Feelings are important but are short term results.
+ Fern will feel that her father listens to her and will become closer to him. √	She was the only one who spoke on behalf of the pig to Mr. Arable; he took her feelings seriously.	**Very Important.** The relationship between a father and daughter is long term. Love is most important.
- After awhile, Fern will stop caring for it.	Raising runt pigs requires time and care. Fern is young and seems impulsive but cares about the pig.	**Important.** She may feel guilty, but may also learn from this.
+ Fern will grow to love it and become attached to it. √	Fern is young, cares a lot for the pig, and feels strong emotions.	**Very Important.** Loving is the most important relationship.
- The pig will die anyhow.	It's hard to raise a runt pig. However, it isn't ill, and Fern will give it special attention.	**Important.** The pig is a living being and life is important, but it would not have died of neglect.
+ Fern will learn that Mr. Arable was right: it takes time and effort to raise a runt pig. √	Fern is intelligent, observant, and interested in the pig, but small baby animals need much care.	**Very Important.** It is valuable to learn the realities of farm life and respect for her father's opinions.
- The pig will grow up to be small. √	Smaller baby pigs usually make small adults.	**Not Very Important.** Small pigs bring less money, but size can be overcome.
- Fern will neglect other chores on the farm.	Fern's age, school work, and chores probably don't leave much time for the pig. However, she is concerned and seems responsible.	**Important.** Fern's help on a family farm is important but not necessary.

Sample Student Responses • Mr. Arable and the Runt Pig

SKILLFUL DECISION MAKING

OPTIONS
What can Mr. Arable do?

Raise the pig himself.
Give the pig away .
Sell the pig.
Give the pig to Fern to raise.
Feed it steroids.
Donate the pig to a science class.
Find someone to take the pig.
Give Fern all the facts and let her make the decision.
Go ahead and kill it.
Trade it with someone for something else of value.

Donate the pig to someone outside the family to raise (farmer, 4-H, FFA).
Make it into a pet.
Do nothing; let the pig stay in the litter.
Explain the effects on the pig, the litter, and the family to Fern, and then kill it.
Turn the problem over to Mrs. Arable.
Abandon the pig in the woods.
Kill it after Fern has gone to school, and tell her it ran away.
Postpone making a decision.

OPTION CONSIDERED
Kill it after Fern has gone to school and tell her it ran away.

CONSEQUENCES What will happen if Mr. Arable takes this option?	SUPPORT Why do you think the consequence will occur?	VALUE How important is the consequence? Why?
− Fern will find out and will lose trust for her father. √	Fern is persistent, observant, and emotionally attached to the pig. Fern has a sense of justice and is sensitive to right and wrong.	**Very Important.** Fern's relationship with her father is life-long and very important for her development.
− Fern will learn to lie.	Fern is young but is sensitive to right and wrong.	**Important.** People won't trust her.
− Fern will fear for her own safety.	Fern is young and she feels a kinship with the pig, but her father has a caring relationship with her.	**Important.** Can cause fright and distress.
− Future communication with her father will be changed. √	Fern and her parents seem to be honest with each other. Lying and distrust limit communication.	**Very Important.** Communication is important in a family.
− Mr. Arable will feel guilty. √	Mr. Arable spoke honestly with Fern and seems sensitive.	**Important.** Mr. Arable may feel uncomfortable about it.
+ Fern will not find out and will forget about it.	Although Fern is young, she may not forget about something that she is so upset about.	**Important.** She will be satisfied, and she will no longer challenge Mr. Arable.
− Fern will cry. √	Fern is young and emotionally attached to the pig.	**Not Very Important.** She may be unhappy, but she will get over it.
+ The problem of caring for the runt pig will be solved; time and effort will be saved. √	Mr. Arable's experience raising pigs lets him understand the likelihood of survival and requirements for care.	**Important.** Effort and time are costly on a small farm. It may save the family from having to make scarifices later.

ALTERNATIVE ENERGY SOURCES

Science   **Grades 5–6**

OBJECTIVES

CONTENT

Students will learn how energy can be derived from the major alternative energy sources; they will learn of the availability, renewability, and environmental impact of these energy sources.

THINKING SKILL/PROCESS

Students will learn to consider options and their consequences and the importance of these consequences in making decisions. Students will also recognize the need for reliable information in making decisions.

METHODS AND MATERIALS

CONTENT

Students will use textbook material on the subject of alternative energy. This lesson includes a research option in which students gather reliable information about alternative energy from a variety of sources.

THINKING SKILL/PROCESS

Structured questioning about options and consequences and the use of a data matrix guide students through the decision-making process. (See pp. 39–43 for reproducible diagrams.) Collaborative learning groups brainstorm options and consequences.

LESSON

INTRODUCTION TO CONTENT AND THINKING SKILL/PROCESS

- Usually when we are trying to figure out what to do, we try to choose the best thing among a number of alternatives. If your parents are planning a vacation, they may compare and contrast a number of options, such as going on a trip, going to a resort, visiting relatives, and staying home. When they think about vacation possibilities, they take account of relevant factors like cost, travel time, etc. Of course they want to make sure they are getting accurate information about these factors so that they can make a good choice. How might they get accurate information about the cost of the trip?

- As your parents think about the consequences, they usually weigh their importance. For example, going to a quiet restful spot may be more important than the cost of taking a trip. They note which consequences count in favor of (pro) or against (con) their options. If they then pick the vacation that seems to be the best one based on this process, their decision is well thought out. The thinking map for decision making (at right) provides a list of things a person should think about in making a decision.

SKILLFUL DECISION MAKING

1. What makes a decision necessary?

2. What are my options?

3. What information is there about the consequences of each option?

4. How important are the consequences?

5. Which option is best in light of the consequences?

- Good decision making is especially important when it comes to decisions our country has to make about issues that affect all of us. One such decision involves the energy source our country should rely on. This decision should be based on scientific facts. Let's think about this

issue according to our plan for making good decisions. Ask the students to review what they have studied about energy, in general, and about alternative sources of energy, in particular.

THINKING ACTIVELY

- **Why are people today concerned about energy? Can you remember a time when you heard someone discussing this question? What made them concerned about it?** POSSIBLE ANSWERS: *We use a lot of energy. We rely on oil for our main energy needs, and the supply of oil may run out sometime within the next fifty years. We depend on oil from other countries, and some of those countries have closed off our oil supply in the past. We'll be needing more energy in the future. Pollution affects our health and the environment. Oil can be use in more valuable ways. The price of oil continues to go up.*

- **What are some of our options regarding energy sources? Which should be our major source? We now rely on oil. Maybe oil should still be our dominant source. However, let's think about other possibilities and try to decide which is best. Work together in groups of four and list as many energy sources as possible. Try to include some that are unusual. Think about how energy is produced from each source.** Ask the groups to report at random but to mention only one energy source from their lists. Then ask for sources that haven't been mentioned, creating a list from as many students as possible. Write the energy sources on the chalkboard or on a transparency under the heading "Options." When uncommon sources are mentioned, ask if anyone knows how energy is produced from those sources. This taps students' prior knowledge and contributes to the collaborative nature of the activity. POSSIBLE ANSWERS: *Nuclear power, wind, water power from dams, solar power, burning garbage, ethanol from grain, the tides, heat from the earth (geothermal), magnetism, lightning, animal power, human power, wood, oil, coal, methane gas, natural gas, steam, gravity, and chemical reactions (batteries).*

- **When you are trying to make a complicated decision like this one, it's a good idea to think about what information you might need in order to decide. What would you want to know about the consequences of relying on each of these energy sources? Make a list of the things you need to know about a type of energy in order to decide whether it is a good source for our country to rely upon. Your list might include, for example, how easy it is to produce the energy. What else would you add?** The students should work in groups again and then report. Write student responses on the chalkboard or a transparency with the heading, "Factors to Take into Account." POSSIBLE ANSWERS: *Costs (production, transportation, storage, distribution, finding the source, and research), availability, safety for workers in producing the energy, environmental pollution, how long it will last, cost to convert to a new energy source, public acceptance, cost of the energy, technology needed to produce and transmit the energy, whether the source is renewable, jobs lost or created, ease of use, consumer comfort, ease of production, public acceptability.*

- **Each group should now pick two sources from its list of options. Gather information about the consequences of relying on these different forms of energy with regard to the factors you have listed. You'll use diagram called a "data matrix," which is a chart having columns and rows. Write the energy forms down the side under "options," and write the factors to consider across the top. Get the appropriate information from your textbooks or other sources to fill in the boxes. If you don't have information, if you have only partial information, or if you're not sure about its reliability, put a question mark in the cell. Write your unanswered questions on the lines below the diagram.** (See the sample matrix p. 62.)

  Allow sufficient time for your students to complete this activity. If they only use their textbooks, they can finish it within the class period. To include outside research (e.g., using resources in the school library) extend this lesson over additional class sessions.

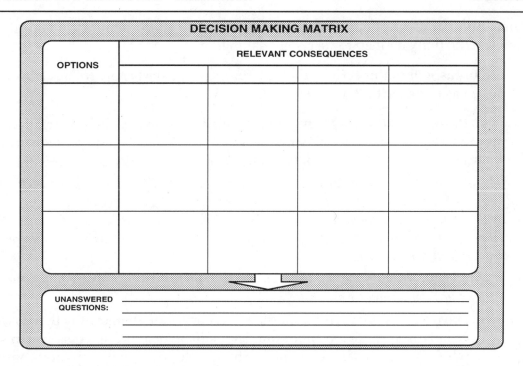

DECISION MAKING MATRIX

OPTIONS	RELEVANT CONSEQUENCES			

UNANSWERED QUESTIONS:

- **What does this information about the consequences of using these energy sources show about the options? Put a plus next to the factors that you think count in favor of choosing the energy source and a minus next to those that count against choosing it. Put a circle around the factors you think are more important than the others. For each entry, explain why you put a plus, a minus, or a circle.** ANSWERS WILL VARY. Ask each group to report its findings to the rest of the class and explain why they rated the consequences as they did. Make a "class matrix" on the chalkboard or on a large piece of poster board. Fill in the matrix based on the reports of each group. Encourage students to add information from the group matrix to their individual ones. More than one copy of the matrix can be used if students need more space.

- **Work together in your groups and decide what you would pick as the best source of energy for this country to rely upon, given the information on the chart. Discuss why it is the best energy source.** Ask students to attend to the following questions as they make their decisions:

    What important unanswered questions do you have?

    In the light of these unanswered questions, how certain are you about your decision? Why?

  Ask each group to prepare an oral or written recommendation explaining the reasons for their choices. To make this lesson an ongoing research project, students should continue to gather information to answer their unanswered questions and periodically report their findings. Ask students to think about how they might get answers to their questions and then to develop a plan for gathering this information. Sources may include libraries, governmental agencies that deal with energy, TV documentaries, etc. When they get additional information, students may add it to their diagrams and report it to the class. Encourage them to reconsider their recommendations in the light of new information. A diagram may also be kept on a bulletin board for students to fill in.

THINKING ABOUT THINKING

- **How did you go about thinking through your decision? Describe what you did first, next, etc. Draw a diagram that represents a flow chart of your thinking.** Ask students to display their diagrams. Student descriptions will vary, but their flow charts should contain the five key questions on the thinking map for decision making.

- **Were there any aspects of this activity that you found particularly hard? Why? How might you do this more easily next time?** ANSWERS WILL VARY.

- **What do you think about this way of making a decision? Is this a good way to do it? What are some of its pros and cons?** Discuss this strategy with the class and ask students whether the pros outweigh the cons or whether there is some better way to make a decision. POSSIBLE ANSWERS:

    <u>Pros</u>: *Helps us think about wider energy options, reduces narrow thinking, presents an organized way to think about a complex subject, improves confidence in choices, encourages active involvement in the topic, makes us aware of the important information in determining desirability of relying on the source, makes it possible to record relevant information in an organized way so that we won't forget it and can compare different options easily.*

    <u>Cons</u>: *Takes longer, requires that we write on the diagram the information we find, depends on the reliability of the information we are using.*

    Most students favor this approach for important decisions, though many say that it is too much trouble for decisions that are not too important. They still favor a shorter version of this strategy for even these choices—one that involves taking time to think about options and consequences prior to the decision.

- **What plan for careful decision making works best for you?** Allow students to map out their own plan for skillful decision making. If they omit one of the five attention points, suggest that they include something comparable. Students may include any points that they think will help them avoid difficulties they may have encountered with the energy activity.

- **How does this compare to the way you ordinarily make decisions? What's a good way to make sure that you follow this new plan instead?** Students sometimes suggest writing down their plan in their notebooks or thinking portfolios or posting it on the wall of their classroom.

APPLYING YOUR THINKING

Immediate Transfer

- Select a decision that you are trying to make right now or that you will have to make soon. Think it through, following the plan for decision making you just developed. List any unanswered questions that you may have so that you can continue to think about your decision making and research it after you leave class. After you reach a decision, indicate how confident you feel about it, based on the questions you've been able to answer through your research.

- Imagine that your parents are considering whether they should use alternative energy sources in their apartment or home. Help them decide by using your decision-making strategy.

Reinforcement Later

Later in the school year, introduce reinforcing activities.

- As we study the atmosphere of the earth, we will find out that it is polluted with many different particles and chemicals. Decide what to do about some types of this pollution.

- As we study endangered species, select one endangered animal and recommend what to do to prevent its extinction.

• We will be studying the way many immigrants came to this country from Europe in the early years of this century. Suppose you were a senator living at the time. What immigration policy would you support in Congress. Why? Use your decision-making strategy to decide what you think is the best thing to do. Would you support the same policy with regard to the Asians and Latin Americans who wish to immigrate to this country now? Explain why or why not.

SKILL EXTENSION: DETERMINING THE RELIABILITY OF SOURCES

Read an advertisement about nuclear power. What does it tell us about nuclear power? What would you want to find out about the advertisement and its source to help you determine whether or not the information it includes is reliable? Make a checklist of things that you might find out that would help you decide whether or not the information given in the advertisement is reliable. How could you get this information? Try to get this information so that you can judge whether the ad information is likely to be reliable.

Now think about whether the ad leaves unanswered any questions you have about nuclear power. If so, pick two of these questions. How could you get additional, reliable information to answer your unanswered questions? List some sources you think will be reliable and some that you are not sure about. Explain why you think they are or are not reliable.

ASSESSING STUDENT THINKING ABOUT DECISIONS

To assess this skill, ask students to write about any of the application questions. For example, ask them to think through a personal decision or to write about a controversial social issue, such as disposing of hazardous waste or environmental pollution. You may ask a similar question about a major historical decision, like Lincoln's decision to issue the Emancipation Proclamation (making sure that students have enough background knowledge to answer it). Their writing can be in the form of a standard essay, a recommendation to someone, or a letter to the editor of a local newspaper. Ask students to make their thinking explicit in their writing. Determine whether they are attending to each of the steps in the thinking map for decision making.

If you choose the extended form of this lesson, in which students gather additional information and periodically return to the question, you can use portfolio assessment techniques. Ask your students to state their learning and thinking goals in this activity and to include their comments in a special portfolio for this project. They should include products in their portfolios that indicate how well they are meeting these goals (filled-in matrices, notes on energy sources from their research, their written recommendations, etc.). They should comment on how well they believe they are meeting their goals, both with regard to gathering information about energy sources and in their decision making. The students should include these comments in their portfolios.

SAMPLE STUDENT RESPONSES • RESEARCH OPTION • ALTERNATIVE ENERGY

DECISION-MAKING MATRIX

OPTIONS	RELEVANT CONSEQUENCES			
	EASE OF PRODUCTION	ENVIRONMENT	COST	AVAILABILITY
SOLAR	Easy, if location, latitude, and weather conditions are favorable. Little maintenance. Limited service for repairs.	No undesirable air or water pollution. Unsightly equipment or circular fields of mirrors. Loss of trees.	Start-up is costly (could be reduced by mass manufacture). Low maintenance and repair. Operation costs are minimal.	Limited by location, latitude, and weather. Seasonal in some areas. Distribution of resulting electricity limited. Renewable.
NUCLEAR	Complex, requiring sophisticated instruments, specialized technicians, and unusual safety measures. Waste disposal is risky and requires long-term safeguards.	Radiation danger. Mining erosion, toxic tailings to secure uranium. Storage of waste may result in radioactive contamination. No atmospheric pollution when operating normally.	Protective measures in operation and start-up costs are high. Licensing, certifying, and inspecting plants are expensive. Lower costs to consumers in some regions.	Uranium is scarce. Breeder reactors are controversial and limited in number.
PETROCHEMICAL	Complex, but commonly practiced.	Oil spills may result. The oil supply may be depleted. Hydrocarbons pollute the air, damage the ozone layer, and create acid rain. Processing pollutes air.	Exploration, research, distribution and clean-up costs are high. Importing is costly and depends on international pricing. It has value for uses other than energy.	Limited regional supplies. Non-renewable.
COAL	Complex, but commonly practiced.	Strip- and shaft-mining scar the land. Use creates a grey film on surfaces. Particulate emissions pollute the air. Acid rain pollutes air and water.	Research and development of soft coal use is costly. Labor, transportation, and conversion are costly.	Diminishing supply. Soft coal underutilized.

SAMPLE STUDENT RESPONSES • RESEARCH OPTION • ALTERNATIVE ENERGY

DECISION-MAKING MATRIX

RELEVANT CONSEQUENCES

OPTIONS	EASE OF PRODUCTION	ENVIRONMENT	COST	AVAILABILITY
TIDAL POWER	Easy, if location and weather conditions are favorable. Technology not well developed.	No undesirable air or water pollution. Unsightly. Plant and animal life affected. Rivers altered.	Start-up is costly. Operation costs are minimal. Technology is not well developed; research may initially be costly.	Limited by location. Distribution of resulting electricity limited.
WIND POWER	Easy, if location and weather conditions are favorable. Use in large numbers may reduce efficiency due to interference of air between units.	No undesirable air or water pollution. Unsightly. Noisy equipment or fields of windmills.	Start-up can be costly (could be reduced by mass manufacture). Low maintenance and repair costs. Conversion costs for home or industrial use may be considerable.	Limited by geographical location and weather. Distribution of electricity limited. Large number of units required for relatively little power.
BURNING GARBAGE	Easy to make anywhere.	Reduce/recycle landfills. Air emissions with current technology undesirable.	Start-up is costly using current technology.	Raw material is available everywhere there are people to use the power.

DECISION MAKING LESSON CONTEXTS

The following examples have been suggested by classroom teachers as contexts in which to develop infused lessons. If a skill or process has been introduced in a previous lesson, it can be reinforced with transfer activities designed in these contexts.

GRADE	SUBJECT	TOPIC	THINKING ISSUE
K–3	Literature	*Jack and the Beanstalk*	What should Jack consider in these situations in the story: trading the cow for beans, stealing the hen from the giant, returning twice up the beanstalk, avenging his father by his actions toward the giant.
K–3	Literature	*Goldilocks*	What should Goldilocks think about before entering the three bears' home?
K–3	Literature	*Peter Rabbit*	What should Peter Rabbit think about to decide what to do when he arrives at the gate of Mr. McGregor's garden?
K–3	Literature	*Dr. DeSoto*	What should Dr. DeSoto take into account in deciding whether to treat the fox's tooth?
K–3	Literature	*The True Story of the Three Little Pigs*	What factors might the wolf take into account before his actions in the story? Use the same information to write another fairy tale from the antagonist's point of view.
K–3	Literature	*Three Little Pigs*	What should the pigs consider in deciding how their houses should be built (quality of construction, durability, value of time etc.)?
K–3	Social studies	Pilgrims	What should the Pilgrims take into account in deciding whether to go to the new world?
K–3	Social studies	Food	What should you consider in deciding what food should be grown locally?
K–3	Social studies	Transportation	What different means of transportation can a person use to travel from one city to another? What are the advantages and disadvantages of each?
K–3	Social studies	Communities	What should be considered in deciding whether to live in a city or a small town?
K–3	Science	Animals	What should you consider to decide the best way to keep a pet turtle alive and healthy in the classroom?
K–3	Science	Plants	Given information on various types of beans, what should be considered to decide which type of bean the class should grow?
K–3	Mathematics	Arithmetic	To set up a school store, how would you decide what to sell, how much to sell it for, and what to do with the earnings?
K–3	Mathematics	Measurement	To prepare a meal for the class, what should you consider to decide what ingredients to use, how much to use, and the amount of time needed to prepare it?
K–3	Art	Colors	How can you decide what colors to use to create a particular feeling in a picture?
K–3	Music	Instruments	How can you decide the best instruments to use to create an effect in playing a piece of music?

DECISION MAKING LESSON CONTEXTS

GRADE	SUBJECT	TOPIC	THINKING ISSUE
K–3	Health	Nutrition	What should be considered in choosing a nutritious snack?
K–3	Health	Nutrition	What should be considered in choosing a balanced meal from the basic food groups?
K–3	Guidance	Conflict resolution	How can you decide what to do when someone in your work group gets the group into trouble?
K–3	Guidance	Conflict resolution	How can you decide what to do when someone cuts in line in the cafeteria?
K–3	Guidance	Being lost	How can you decide what to do when you have become separated from your family at the shopping center or department store?
4–6	Literature	*How to Eat Fried Worms*	How should the character in the story decide what to do when he is presented with the dare?
4–6	Literature	*Tales of a 4th Grade Nothing*	What should Peter consider to decide whether to have Dribble the Turtle as a pet?
4–6	Literature	*My Brother Sam is Dead*	What should the colonists have taken into account to decide whether or not to quarter soldiers?
4–6	Literature	*Song of the Trees*	How might the family prevent being cheated on the sale of the trees?
4–6	Literature	*Sarah, Plain and Tall*	What should Sarah take into account in deciding whether to leave her home to live with a new family in the Midwest?
4–6	Reading	*Emma Lazarus*	What might Emma Lazarus take into account to decide whether to remain in her homeland or come to America?
4–6	Writing	Fiction	What would you take into account to decide how to write an opening paragraph in a mystery story?
4–6	Writing	Letter writing	Consider three or four different ways of starting a letter to a friend. What would you take into account to decide which way is the best way to start the letter?
4–6	Language arts	Reference skills	What should be taken into account in deciding what kind of reference book to use in a specific project?
4–6	Social studies	Industrial expansion	What should be considered in converting parkland for industrial use?
4–6	Social studies	Discovery of America	What might Columbus have taken into account in deciding whether to make the voyage in one ship rather than three?
4–6	Social studies	American independence from Britain	What would the colonists take into account in deciding whether to remain a part of Great Britain or become independent?
4–6	Social studies	Colonization	Suppose you were a member of a party travelling to North America to establish a new colony. What would you take into account in deciding where the colony was to be located?
4–6	Social studies	Western expansion	What should be considered in deciding what to take when travelling on foot with a wagon train from St. Louis to any city west of Missouri?

DECISION MAKING LESSON CONTEXTS

GRADE	SUBJECT	TOPIC	THINKING ISSUE
4–6	Social studies	Tobacco	What should farmers in southern states consider when deciding whether or not to continue to grow tobacco as a major cash crop? Other cash crops might be corn, soybeans, peanuts, cotton, and Chinese vegetables.
4–6	Social studies	South America	How would you decide what country in South America to visit?
4–6	American history	The Alamo	What should Santa Anna take into account in deciding whether or not to launch a destructive attack on the Alamo?
4–6	American history	Civil War	What should Kentucky citizens take into account to decide whether or not the state should secede from the union?
4–6	American history	Daniel Boone	What would Daniel Boone consider in deciding whether or not to go to Kentucky, as suggested by John Findley? Should he explore new areas or stay in the ones he had already explored?
4–6	American history	Industrial Revolution	What factors should a farm girl consider before she decides whether to move to Lowell, Massachusetts to work in the textile factories?
4–6	Geography	Family vacation	What does a family take into account in selecting a family vacation (where, what to do, mileage, climate, money, etc.)?
4–6	Geography/ mathematics	Speed/time/ distance	What should you take into account in planning a trip from Chicago to Los Angeles? Decide on the best route and how much time you should allow for the trip.
4–6	Science	Pollution	What might your family take into account in deciding how to conserve resources (treatment of waste, water and air quality, etc.)?
4–6	Science	Ecology	What should be considered in deciding what and how we should recycle? How far should we go in imposing laws?
4–6	Science	Animal rights	What should be considered in deciding which of the following animals, if any, should be harvested in over-populated areas: mammals, insects, birds, fish?
4–6	Science	Animals	What should be taken into account in deciding which animals should be protected?
4–6	Science	Environment	What should be taken into account in deciding what kind of cups should be used in the school cafeteria?
4–6	Science	Trees	What should be taken into account in deciding which fruit trees to plant in your area?
4–6	Science	Ocean ecology	How should we decide whether and how to intervene to mitigate or prevent ocean pollution?
4–6	Science	Simple machines	How would you decide which simple machine is best to lift a heavy bundle in a given situation?
4–6	Mathematics	Estimation/ distance	What is the best method to use to estimate a given distance in order to determine how long it will take to travel it?

DECISION MAKING LESSON CONTEXTS

GRADE	SUBJECT	TOPIC	THINKING ISSUE
4–6	Mathematics	Fractions	What should be taken into account in choosing which operation to use to compare fractions?
4–6	Mathematics	Measurement	How would you decide whether to choose metric or English measurement units?
4–6	Mathematics/ science	Decimals/ nutrition	Which of a given group of breakfast cereals would you pick as the best value and the most nutritious? How could you decide?
4–6	Art	Shirt design	What should be taken into account in deciding what designs and methods are best to use in designing a shirt?
4–6	Art	Sculpture	Plan a sculpture project and determine the best materials to use.
4–6	Music	MTV	What should a parent take into account to decide whether MTV is appropriate for a 10 year old?
4–6	Music	Popular music	Suppose you have to choose music to express feelings such as love, fear, happiness, or sadness. How would you decide the best music to use?
4–6	Health	Health habits	What should be taken into account in deciding whether and how to change an overweight condition?
4–6	Health	Substance abuse	What should women who smoke or take drugs consider to prevent harm to the unborn child?
4–6	Health	Diet	What should be taken into account when selecting foods that reduce the risks of heart disease?
4–6	Physical education	Sports	How should individuals decide which kind of sport is best for them?
4–6	Physical education	Exercise	How should individuals decide which kind of exercise is best for them?
4–6	Physical education	Team sports	What options do you have and what would you take into account in deciding what each student on your team should do?
4–6	Physical education	Team sports	Suppose you had to develop a strategy to score the most points in a specific football game. How would you decide on a strategy?
4–6	Guidance	Money	How should you go about deciding how to spend your allowance?
4–6	Guidance	School rules	What should be considered in making and following school rules?
4–6	Guidance	Time management	What should be considered in planning your time for doing a specific task?
4–6	Guidance	Choice of junior high / magnet school	What should you consider in picking a school (take into account results to yourself and the community)?
4–6	Guidance	Security	What should be taken into account to protect one's belongings at school?

CHAPTER 3
PROBLEM SOLVING

Why is Skillful Problem Solving Necessary?

Solving problems well is very important. Good problem solution often improves the quality of the lives it affects. In fact, many of the benefits we enjoy today would not be available to us if some problem solvers had not tackled and mastered difficulties they perceived. The cures of diseases, advances in technology, and our present standard of living are all the results of careful and successful problem solving.

Realizing that we face a problem and trying to do something about it is the first step in problem solving. If we fail to deal with problems, difficulties usually do not go away. In most cases, intervention by a problem solver is necessary for change to take place.

Success in problem solving means eliminating difficulty for ourselves or others. Problem solving has not occurred until we have succeeded in implementing the solution. This makes problem solving a somewhat more complex process than decision making. In problem solving, as in decision making, we think through and choose the best solution to a problem. However, carrying out a solution may pose a new set of problems. As important as it was to solve the original problem, it is equally important to find the best solutions to these new problems.

Sometimes the term "problem solving" refers to using mathematical operations. In trying to figure out the best way to get to work, I may have to calculate how long it will take me to get to the bus in order to decide whether taking the bus will get me to work on time. I arrive at an answer to this mathematical "problem" based on the application of certain mathematical operations using given facts (how far away the bus stop is, how fast I can walk). In typical mathematics problems of this sort, "problem solving" refers to selecting the appropriate mathematical operations and getting the right answer by doing them accurately.

Many science "problems" involve the application of science principles in analogous ways to solving mathematics problems. Learning to solve such mathematical and scientific problems well can help us to learn the mathematical and scientific principles involved but will not teach us the thinking strategies we need to carry out everyday problem solving skillfully.

Common Difficulties about the Way We Choose Solutions to Problems

Problem solving, like decision making, occurs much more frequently than we think it does. It is not just big problems, like trying to find a cure for AIDS, that engage us in problem solving. Hardly a day goes by that we do not tackle a multitude of "little" problems, often with some degree of success. Suppose, as I leave for work and get into my car, I realize that I do not have my car keys. That's a problem because I can't start my car, and I need it to get to work. This problem may be easily solved, however. I may remember that I left the keys in the house. I can return to get them.

This is not to say that we tackle every problem that we face, that finding good solutions is easy, or that we find solutions as effectively as we could. When I get to work, I may notice that it's awfully hot in my office. Unless I recognize this as a problem, I might sit there feeling uncomfortable. Often situations present difficulties, but we do not recognize a problem until it's too late to do anything about it.

Furthermore, to do effective problem solving, I should be clear about exactly what the problem is. I may realize that the heat is a problem because it makes me uncomfortable and think that to solve this problem I have to make myself comfortable. So I may change my clothes, putting on shorts and a light shirt. But that may cause more problems because informal dress is frowned upon where I work. Moreover, it's only a short-term solution. The heat may be a continual problem. Even if it were permitted, it may not be practical to wear shorts every day.

On the other hand, if I identify the problem as

getting the temperature lower in my office, there are a whole range of other solutions that may be more viable than the shorts solution. I may open the window, turn on a fan, install air conditioning, turn the heater down, have the heating system repaired, etc.

Identifying the problem in a comprehensive way opens the door to a variety of possible solutions, but it does not guarantee that we will consider them. There is a tendency in problem solving, as in decision making, to adopt the first solution that comes to mind without asking whether there are any better or more creative solutions. A quick solution like opening a window may not be the best way to solve the problem. It may reduce the temperature but may be costly since the lower temperature will surely keep the heater running (if the thermostat is causing the problem). As in decision making, many people fail to generate alternative solutions and consider consequences. This often leads to adopting solutions which have many unwanted side effects.

Choosing solutions hastily often means not considering the feasibility of carrying out the solution. I may think that installing air-conditioning in my office is the best solution because it is a long-term solution and will lead to better comfort and productivity. But in order to have air-conditioning installed, my school may have to bring in air-conditioning specialists from 250 miles away. That may be time consuming and so costly that the school's resources for programs like staff-development would have to be cut. This solution may not, therefore, be a feasible one. While this is not the direct consequence of installing air-conditioning, it is a consequence of my school's adopting this solution to the problem and should be considered along with all the other relevant consequences.

These five basic shortcomings with the way we choose the best solutions to problems are listed in figure 3.1.

What Does Skillful Problem Solving Involve?

Countering tendencies for choosing hasty or poorly considered solutions involves strategies and skills that most of us can learn easily. But, of

---

COMMON DEFAULTS IN THE WAY WE SOLVE PROBLEMS

1. We often do not recognize problem situations as problems, hence we do nothing about them.

2. We often conceive of the problem to be solved in very narrow ways.

3. We make a hasty choice of the first solution we think of; we fail to consider a variety of possible problem solutions.

4. We do not consider many, if any, consequences of adopting the solutions we are considering.

5. We do not consider how feasible it would be to undertake this solution.

Figure 3.1

course, we also need to develop the disposition to use these strategies and skills when faced with a problem.

Identifying a situation as problematic. When we become aware of circumstances that create *problems*, we become aware that these conditions conflict with our purposes, interests, or needs. Not having my car keys is a problem because I need them to start my car and get to work on time, and I need to be on time because I have planned to take my students on a field trip.

While this example is a problem for me as an individual, we can identify other situations that are problems for groups of people. Unemployment in the United States is a problem for this country. The depletion of the ozone layer is a problem for people in general. These conditions are problems because they frustrate, or otherwise conflict with, our basic needs or interests. Raising the question of whether any such conflict exists is the first step in identifying a problem. Once we have determined that there is a conflict, we recognize that the existing situation or condition creates a problem. Identifying a situation as problematic, in turn, prompts us to recognize the need for change.

A special case of this occurs when we are thinking about man-made objects and their functioning. Machines that we create, for example, are designed to serve certain purposes. Unless we recognize that they are not serving these purposes as well as they could, we will simply accept the machines as they are and not try to improve them.

For example, less than 20 years ago computers tended to be large and cumbersome, even though their capability for processing information was greater than hitherto known to man. Typically, for individuals to gain the benefits of using computers, they had to link up with large mainframe computers. Recognizing that such large computers, while serving their purpose, were by no means perfect led to creative problem solving that has yielded small personal computers that have tremendous capability. For many of us, the availability of such devices has revolutionized our lives.

Skillful problem solvers do not just ask how things function. They also consider the purposes that things serve. Then they are in a better position to devise improvements.

Defining the problem. Before we can actually engage in trying to solve a problem, it must be defined. If I do not have my car keys and define my problem as finding my car keys, I may be defining it too narrowly. I may have lost my keys yesterday and did not know it. Taking the time now to try to find them may be nonproductive. Maybe I can get my car started without the keys by bypassing the ignition. Then I am defining the problem as getting my car started. I could also try to get a spare key.

How I might get my car started, however, may also be too narrow a definition of the problem. When I realize that getting the car started and driving it to my destination serves the purpose of getting me to work, I may define my problem as getting to work. Since I usually use my car, but now I can't start it, perhaps I can get other transportation. Maybe I can catch a bus or ask my neighbor to drive me there.

These possible solutions will, of course, have to be thought through carefully. For example, I will have to find out whether I can still catch the bus. But catching the bus and having my neighbor drive me to work will occur to me as possible solutions only if I define the problem broadly, not simply as a problem about finding my keys.

Effective problem definition can be facilitated by taking the time to think about the kinds of problems generated by the unsatisfactory situation. These resulting problems can be listed, then organized into types of problems that include problems about *means*, like finding the keys, as well as broader problems about *goals*, like getting to work. Problems related to goals should be given priority over problems about the means to accomplish those goals.

Generating and Assessing Possible Solutions

Generating possible solutions. Some specialists in problem solving have described the process of skillful problem solving as accordion-like: We engage in divergent, open, thinking then converge by analyzing and evaluating; then we engage in divergent thinking again, etc. One insight this image gives us into the process of skillful problem solving is the interplay of critical and creative thinking in the problem-solving process. Once we have defined a problem, we should not, of course, jump at the first solution that occurs to us. As in skillful decision making, it is well worth the time to generate a number of different possible solutions. Expanding the range of possible solutions "moves us out" from the convergent thinking that is involved in defining the problem into open, divergent thinking. As in skillful decision making, brainstorming is a technique that works well.

In situations in which the problem is an important one and solution finding is complex, a variety of solutions, not limited to those that initially seem the most promising, should be considered. Even alternatives that seem "far out" may be worth considering in order to make sure that we conduct a thorough search for the best solution.

In many approaches to problem solving, unusual solutions, however unworkable, are valued because they are "creative." Just as in skillful decision making, it is important to generate original and unusual solutions. However, we should not prefer these solutions unless our investigation of their consequences shows them to be preferable to other, more ordinary remedies. If a routine solution to a problem works better than an unusual one, it should be chosen. It might be interesting to take the space shuttle to work, but more routine ways of getting there will, in most circumstances, be preferable.

At the same time, we often face situations in which old solutions to problems do not work too well. Then, more creative solutions are in order. One effective strategy is combining possible solutions to overcome the shortcomings of each. For example, if I decide to take the bus to work, I may miss the bus that will get me there on time and have to wait for a later one that will make me arrive late. If I ride with my neighbor, she can leave right away, but she can only take me part of the way. Walking the rest of the way may make me late. Perhaps, however, she can drop me off at the bus stop, which is on her way, and I can catch the early bus which will get me to work on time. It is well worth asking whether any of the proposed solutions can, either in whole or in part, be combined for a more creative solution than either would offer.

Assessing possible solutions. Like skillful decision making, skillful problem solving requires careful consideration of the consequences before picking the best solution. The strategy for a thorough investigation of consequences that is used in skillful decision making can also be used in problem solving. Think about consequences for others, as well as for yourself; think about both short- and long-term consequences. Weigh the important consequences more heavily than the less significant ones. Asking my neighbor to go out of her way to drive me to work may get me there on time but may strain our friendship. Our relationship may be more important to me than getting to work late.

To be more rigorous in our consideration of the consequences, we may wish to adopt a set of criteria for good solutions beforehand, setting out the factors we should consider and weighing how important they are. For example, I might note that to find a good solution to the problem with my car keys, I should consider whether a proposed solution to the problem will get me to work, whether I can arrive on time, how costly the transportation is, whether the way that I get to work offends anyone, etc. I might determine that getting to work on time is the most important consideration, indicating a willingness to pay more if necessary. These criteria can then guide me in getting information to assess possible solutions. As always, we should make sure that the information we use is accurate and reliable.

A key consideration in deciding which solution is best is whether or not a particular solution is feasible. Solutions that solve problems but are not practical are too idealistic. For example, giving everyone free medical care will solve the problem of inadequate health care for those who can't afford it. But is this solution practical? This is not a good option if implementing it will bankrupt the health-care system or if there are real obstacles to putting the solution into practice that we can't reasonably overcome.

Implementing problem solutions. The strategies we have suggested for problem solving are strategies for choosing the best solution to the problem at hand. However, problem solving involves more than deciding what to do. Many problem-solving experts have stressed two additional considerations: developing an implementation plan and convincing others that the solution is a good one (sometimes called "acceptance finding"). You do not really solve problems unless you actually put into practice the solution you think is best and it proves to be effective. Implementation often requires that the solution is acceptable to and endorsed by others whom it involves.

Developing an implementation plan and convincing others that the solution is best become new situations for problem solving. In the first instance, the problem is how to carry out the solution we have chosen. In the second, the problem is convincing others. Each of these calls for careful thinking. The thinking should be guided by the same strategy used to develop the original problem solution while considering two additional questions:

- What resources are needed to put this solution into effect?

- What obstacles are likely to be encountered in trying to implement this solution?

These strategies for skillful problem solving are useful for any problem we face, including everyday problems, like the problem about the lost key, and problems faced in more technical contexts, like in engineering, business, and communications. There are some problems, of course, which we cannot now solve. All of the possible solutions we come up with fail, and we do not have enough information to generate other workable solutions, as in the present case of the AIDS epidemic. We won't ever find a solution in the future unless we keep trying, however. Using strategies for skillful problem solving can guide us even in the most difficult cases.

Tools for Finding the Best Problem Solutions

The thinking map in figure 3.2 provides questions to ask as we go through the process of skillful problem solving.

Two graphic organizers are useful for skillful problem solving: one for problem definition (figure 3.3) and one for finding the best solution (figure 3.4, p. 74). Figure 3.3 shows the graphic organizer for problem definition.

To use the graphic organizer for problem definition (figure 3.3), write the facts of the problem situation in the first box. Write the

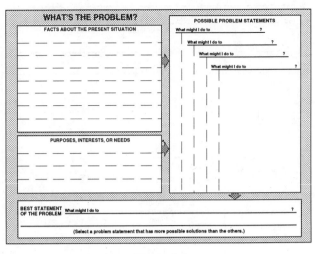

Figure 3.3

purposes, interests, or needs that are frustrated by these facts in the second box, and write the problems generated in the spaces to the right. Then the best problem statement can be selected and written in the bottom box. We should make sure that the problem we select is not too narrow and that it does not presuppose that one of the other problems identified is solved.

For example, in the first box I would list the fact that I can't find my car keys and that my job is a distance from my home. In the second box, I would note that one of the purposes of my car is to transport me to my job; I need to be at work shortly, and I need my keys to start the car. Then, on the right, I might write the following problems: "How might I find my keys?" "How might I get my car started?" and "How might I get to work?" I would then write the most comprehensive problem statement in the box at the bottom. The overriding problem to be solved would then read, "What might I do to get to work?"

The graphic organizer for finding the best solution (figure 3.4, p. 74) should be used after we have defined the problem. We brainstorm possible solutions and, as in skillful decision making, use the graphic organizer to explore one of the possibilities. We do this by first listing the different kinds of factors we should take into account in order to choose a well-thought-out solution. We might, for example, be interested in how quickly alternative means of transportation will get us to work, how much it will cost, whether it has an adverse effect on others, whether it is legal, etc. Working collaboratively

---

SKILLFUL PROBLEM SOLVING

1. Why is there a problem?

   a. What is the present situation?

   b. What purpose, interest, or need makes it desirable to improve on the present situation?

2. What is the problem?

3. What are the possible solutions to the problem?

4. What would the consequences be if these solutions were adopted?

   a. What types of consequences are important to consider?

   b. What are these consequences?

   c. How important is each consequence?

5. What is the best solution to the problem based on this information?

Figure 3.2

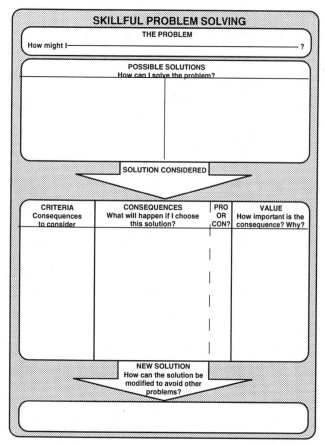

Figure 3.4

with others to define our criteria for good solutions can help us avoid bias in our selection of criteria.

Once we have thoughtfully selected a comprehensive set of criteria, they can be used to guide us in determining what to expect if we adopt a particular solution. If the projected consequence serves our purposes, interests, or needs, it should be counted as a "pro." If it conflicts with or frustrates our purposes, interests, or needs, it should be counted as a "con." For example, if taking a taxi will get me to work on time, that is a "pro." If it will cost a large amount of money, that will be a "con." Stealing someone else's car may get me to work on time; that's a "pro." However, stealing is illegal and puts me in jeopardy of punishment. That's a "con."

Finally, I can modify the solution I am considering to make it work better. Combining parts of two possible solutions is often an effective strategy for making such modifications.

As in decision making, if you compare different solutions that have been thought through

using these diagrams, it can be very easy to determine which solution is preferable.

How Can We Teach Students to Solve Problems Skillfully?

To teach skillful problem solving, it is not enough to give students problems to solve. Skillful problem solving involves asking and answering various questions that guide us through the problem-solving process in an organized and reflective way. Students usually do not attend to such questions as they solve problems. To teach students skillful problem solving, we should teach them what these guiding questions are and help them develop the habit of asking and answering them when they are faced with problems.

When teaching students this approach to skillful problem solving, it is, likewise, not enough to ask students to brainstorm possible solutions to problems and then select the best one. More articulation of the strategy for skillful problem solving is needed. Problem definition should be done thoughtfully. Careful judgment about the likelihood and weight of the consequences of the different solutions is also necessary. These considerations are sometimes overlooked in approaches to problem solving. Using the thinking map in figure 3.2 (p. 73) to guide this type of thinking, supplemented by the two graphic organizers, provides this needed articulation.

Contexts for lessons on problem solving. The curriculum already contains many contexts in which students study how various real-world problems have been solved. They are sometimes directed to solve problems themselves. Authentic problems in any curriculum area may provide excellent contexts for teaching students skillful problem solving.

Specialized problem-solving examples often found in mathematics and science texts may not provide adequate contexts to teach skillful problem solving. Such activities are intended to give students practice in applying mathematical and scientific principles, rather than grappling with problems that require definition, the selection of the best solution, and implementation. The range of thinking skills that students use in such problem solving is quite restricted.

There are two basic contexts for problem solving lessons in the curriculum:

- *Students study how important problems have been defined and the solutions that people have tried.* In history, for example, students study how the settlers in the New World tried to solve the many problems they encountered in setting up viable communities. They read how characters in stories such as *Jack and the Beanstalk* and *The Wizard of Oz* solve key problems. They also study the problem solving scientists have engaged in as science has advanced.

- *Students have to solve problems themselves as part of their academic work.* For example, when students write essays or fiction, they grapple with a variety of problems, such as how to communicate their ideas clearly and how to generate suspense and drama in a story. Students are also asked, with increasing frequency, to engage in problem solving in which they use what they are learning in science and mathematics to develop solutions to authentic problems like those connected with saving endangered species or building a tree house. In hands-on subjects like home economics, industrial arts, and physical education, students have to engage in problem solving regularly.

A menu of suggested contexts for infusion lessons on problem solving is provided on pp. 89–92.

Problem-based learning activities as contexts for lessons on skillful problem solving. *Problem-based learning* challenges students with authentic problems whose solutions require specific content knowledge and conceptual understanding that the teacher helps the students to acquire. To teach skillful problem solving in problem-based learning activities, teachers must infuse instruction in the problem-solving process into these activities.

Introducing problem-based learning is one way various subjects in the curriculum can be integrated. For example, in the elementary grades students learn about the 19th century westward movement. Material in standard textbooks gives them information about gold in California, wagon trains, American Indian tribes, the railroad, etc. When teachers teach this material through problem-based instruction, they may ask students to simulate being pioneers who were making the long trip from east of the Mississippi to the West by planning out a trip and constructing and outfitting a wagon that might be used for the trip. When students work on this problem, their learning often cuts across standard subjects like geography, social studies, and mathematics.

Problem-based learning can also be designed within specific disciplines. For example, students might engage in a measurement project to determine how much carpeting is needed for the school. A science project can involve students in determining the best way to keep plants and animals alive in their classroom. In each of these cases, the activities are designed specifically to require students to learn and use concepts and information that is part of the regular curriculum.

Practical problems like these examples provide excellent contexts for designing problem-solving lessons. The teacher creates the problem-based learning activity and then designs an infusion lesson in skillful problem solving in that context.

Teaching Students Skillful Problem Solving in the Primary Grades

A simplified approach to problem solving that preserves the fundamental outline of the problem-solving strategy is appropriate for the primary grades. Students attend to what a problem is, consider why it is a problem, generate many possible solutions, and assess each solution by considering its pros and cons. Wherever possible, students should be encouraged to combine solutions to come up with ones that are better than those they initially generate.

The thinking map for skillful problem solving in figure 3.5 (p. 76) is appropriate for the primary grades.

The graphic organizer in figure 3.6 (p. 76) is also a modification of the more complex diagram. It can be used easily in the primary grades.

SKILLFUL PROBLEM SOLVING

1. Why is there a problem?

2. What is the problem?

3. What are possible solutions to the problem?

4. What would happen if you solved the problem in each of these ways?

5. What is the best solution to the problem?

Figure 3.5

This graphic organizer omits the step in the problem-solving strategy in which students introduce the criteria for their choice of the best solution. They simply list consequences that count in favor of or against the solution. The teacher must prompt students orally to take a range of different considerations into account.

Contexts like *Jack and the Beanstalk*, the Pilgrims establishing a community, setting up a store in the classroom, and keeping classroom animals alive all provide opportunities to teach primary grade students this strategy. Skillful problem solving should, of course, be reinforced in the upper grades after students are introduced to it in the lower grades. Skillful problem solving will become second nature to our students if they start it early and it is reinforced throughout their schooling.

Model Lessons on Skillful Problem Solving

The model lesson on skillful problem solving is a second grade social studies lesson in which students supplement what they learn about food production with an activity in which they have to solve the problem of getting apples from apple trees to provide this fruit to grocers.

As you read these lessons, ask yourself the following questions:

- What are alternative ways of introducing this thinking process to students prior to the main activity in the lesson?

- How can the lesson be transformed into a hands-on lesson?

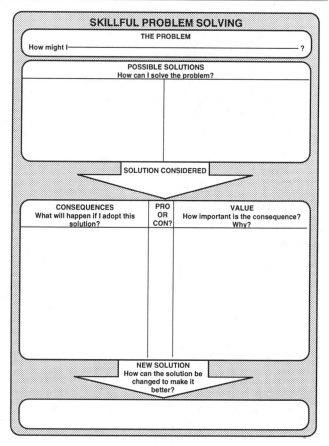

Figure 3.6

- What other contexts or activities reinforce this thinking process in other content areas in the elementary school curriculum?

Tools for Designing Problem-solving Lessons

There are two thinking maps for skillful problem solving used in this handbook: one for the primary grades (p. 78) and the other for grades above the primary level (p. 77). Similarly, there are two graphic organizers for skillful problem solving. The one on page 81 is for the primary grades, and the other (p. 80) is for grades above the primary level. Finally, a basic diagram is used for problem defining at all grade levels.

The thinking maps and graphic organizers can guide you in designing the critical thinking activity in the lesson and can also serve as photocopy masters, transparency masters, or as models that can be enlarged and used as posters in the classroom. Reproduction rights are granted for single classroom use only.

SKILLFUL PROBLEM SOLVING

1. **Why is there a problem?**

   a. **What is the present situation?**

   b. **What purpose, interest, or need makes it desirable to improve on the present situation?**

2. **What is the problem?**

3. **What are possible solutions to the problem?**

4. **What would the consequences be if these solutions were adopted?**

   a. **What types of consequences are important to consider?**

   b. **What are these consequences?**

   c. **How important is each consequence?**

5. **What is the best solution to the problem based on this information?**

SKILLFUL PROBLEM SOLVING

1. Why is there a problem?

2. What is the problem?

3. What are possible solutions to the problem?

4. What would happen if you solved the problem in each of these ways?

5. What is the best solution to the problem?

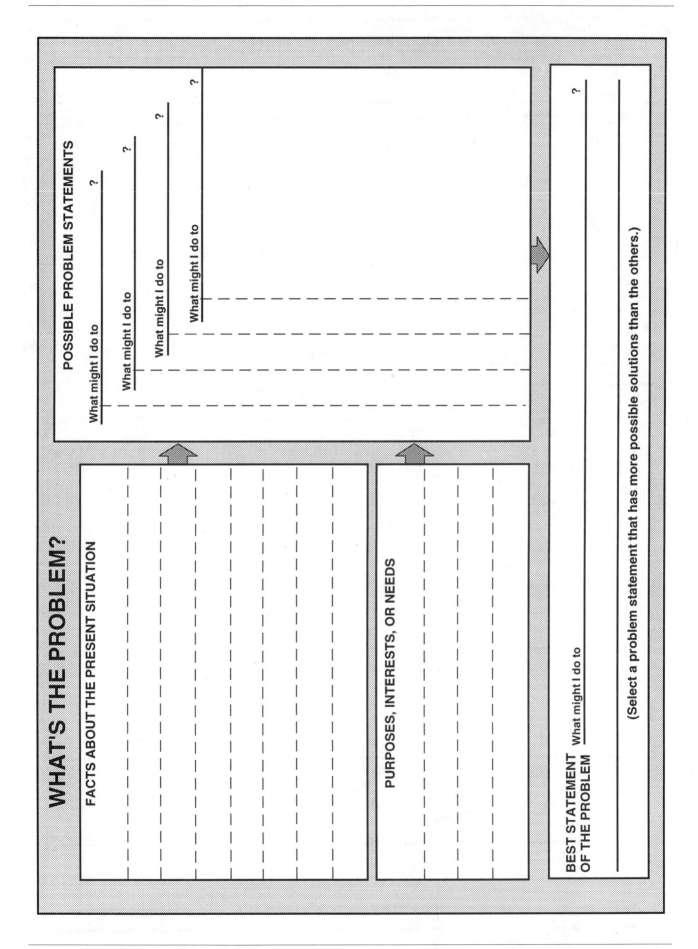

WHAT'S THE PROBLEM?

FACTS ABOUT THE PRESENT SITUATION

PURPOSES, INTERESTS, OR NEEDS

POSSIBLE PROBLEM STATEMENTS

What might I do to _____ ?

What might I do to _____ ?

What might I do to _____ ?

What might I do to _____ ?

BEST STATEMENT OF THE PROBLEM   What might I do to _____

_____

(Select a problem statement that has more possible solutions than the others.)

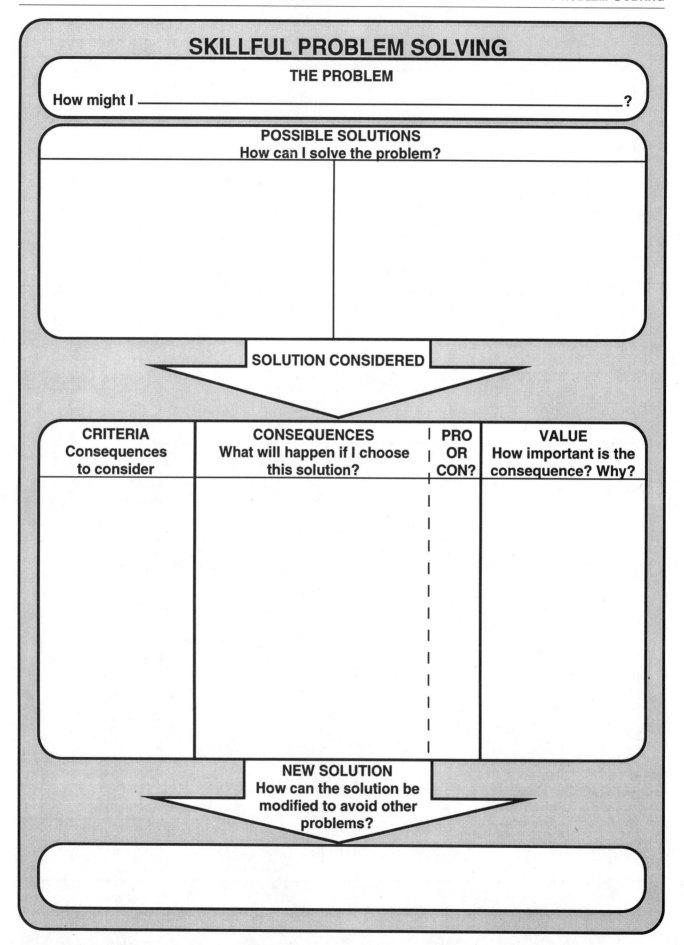

SKILLFUL PROBLEM SOLVING

THE PROBLEM

How might I _____ ?

POSSIBLE SOLUTIONS
How can I solve the problem?

SOLUTION CONSIDERED

CRITERIA Consequences to consider	CONSEQUENCES What will happen if I choose this solution?	PRO OR CON?	VALUE How important is the consequence? Why?

NEW SOLUTION
How can the solution be modified to avoid other problems?

SKILLFUL PROBLEM SOLVING

THE PROBLEM

How might I————————————————————————————————?

POSSIBLE SOLUTIONS
How can I solve the problem?

SOLUTION CONSIDERED

CONSEQUENCES What will happen if I adopt this solution?	PRO OR CON?	VALUE How important is the consequence? Why?

NEW SOLUTION
How can the solution be changed to make it better?

LOTS OF APPLES

Social Studies   **Grades 2–3**

OBJECTIVES

CONTENT

Students will learn that fruit is cultivated for food and that some fruit grows on bushes and some on trees. They will also learn how fruit is harvested.

THINKING SKILL/PROCESS

Students will learn to solve problems skillfully by determining what the problem is, by generating possible solutions, and by selecting the best solution on the basis of consequences.

METHODS AND MATERIALS

CONTENT

Students will read in their textbooks about food production, transportation, and marketing. They will discuss methods of harvesting fruit.

THINKING SKILL/PROCESS

An explicit thinking map, graphic organizers, and structured questioning emphasize a thinking strategy for problem solving. (See pp. 77-81 for reproducible diagrams.) Collaborative learning enhances the thinking. Questioning strategies for metacognition are also employed.

LESSON

INTRODUCTION TO CONTENT AND THINKING SKILL/PROCESS

- **Have any of you ever been in a situation in which you were listening to someone or to the television and you couldn't hear it because there was too much noise?** Some students will probably say that they have. **What did you do so that you could hear?** POSSIBLE ANSWERS: *I got closer to the television. I told the person I couldn't hear her because there was too much noise. I asked my brother to repeat what he said.*

- **You were trying to make things better so that you could hear. When you try to make things better, you are "problem solving." When we think that something isn't working out as we would like, we know there is a problem. When we try to make the situation better, we are trying to solve the problem. We do a lot of problem solving. Can you think of any other time when you did some problem solving?** Ask students for some examples. ANSWERS VARY.

- **We should never try to solve problems without thinking about them. If we do, our solutions may not turn out too well. We are going to practice a way to think about problems so that when you solve problems, you'll know you're thinking carefully. This thinking map for problem solving will guide us in this lesson.** Show the thinking map for skillful problem solving.

> **SKILLFUL PROBLEM SOLVING**
>
> 1. Why is there a problem?
> 2. What is the problem?
> 3. What are possible solutions to the problem?
> 4. What would happen if you solved the problem in each of these ways?
> 5. What is the best solution to the problem?

- **As we use this thinking map, we'll be trying to solve a problem about how we can get food. This is something** we've been studying in social studies. Let's think, for a moment, about the foods we've been studying. I don't mean food like hamburgers, but I mean the natural food that things like hamburgers are made from. For example, it contains beef, and the bun is made of flour, which you learned comes from wheat. Can you name some other foods that we eat as they are or that the things we eat are made from? POSSIBLE ANSWERS: *Beef, wheat, peas, apples, rice, tomatoes, peanuts, chicken, potatoes, carrots, shrimp, tuna, pork, lima beans, corn, peaches, oats, cherries, lobster, strawberries, broccoli, lettuce, plums, cod, mushrooms, walnuts, and cucumbers.* Write these on the chalkboard as the students mention them. **These foods fall into different groups. Do you remember some of these groups? Mention a group and identify some of the foods listed here that fall into that group.** Students typically identify the basic food groups: (1) bread, cereal, rice, and pasta group, (2) vegetables, (3) fruit, (4) milk, yogurt, and cheese group, (5) meat, poultry, fish, dry beans, eggs, and nuts group, and (6) fats, oils, and sweets. **Work with your partner and put all of the foods listed into these different groups. Add any others that fall into these groups.** Under the name of each group, list the different foods in columns on the board.

• In order to be able to use these foods, we have to be able to get them, when ripe, from their natural locations. We are harvesting the food. If some of these foods existed only at the bottom of the ocean, it would be hard to harvest them. **Where do the foods from these different groups appear in nature? How hard is it to harvest them?** Work with your partner again and, next to each group, write where these foods appear. Check them if they are hard to harvest. Allow a few minutes for students to work together.

THINKING ACTIVELY

• **Now let's focus our attention on one of these groups: fruit. Why do people eat fruit?** *Fruit tastes good and is healthy to eat.* **Where does fruit appear in nature?** *On bushes, on trees, on vines.* **It's easy to get the fruit off bushes isn't it?** *Yes, you just pick it off.* **Sometimes the bushes have thorns, however, so we have to do some problem solving to figure out how we can get the fruit without being pricked by the thorns. That's not too hard--maybe we can wear special gloves. But what about the fruit on trees? Consider apples.** Show the students some pictures of apple trees with the fruit on them. **Is getting the apples a problem? Why?** POSSIBLE ANSWERS: *They are usually too high for a person to reach, so you can't just pick the apples off like you can berries on a bush. If we don't get the apples off the trees, people won't have apples and won't be able to make things they like, like apple pie, apple turnovers, apple dumplings, apple sauce, and apple juice. Apples are also good to eat on their own without being cooked or squeezed into juice.*

• **What is the problem, then?** *Getting the apples from the apple tree so that people can eat them.* **I'm going to write this problem on the board after the words "How might I___" so that we can all see what the problem is. Now imagine that your job is to solve the problem of harvesting apples. We've already thought about the first two questions on the map of problem solving. Let's look at the other questions and do some problem solving to try to figure out the best solution.**

• Use the diagram for skillful problem solving and work with your partner to list as many different solutions as you can think of in the possible solutions box. After a few minutes, ask each to share one of their solutions and write these on a large graphic organizer on the board, on a transparency, or on a poster containing the graphic organizer. POSSIBLE ANSWERS: *Shake the tree. Throw rocks at the apples. Climb up the trunk and out on the branches, pick the apples, and drop them down. Cut the tree down. Climb down a*

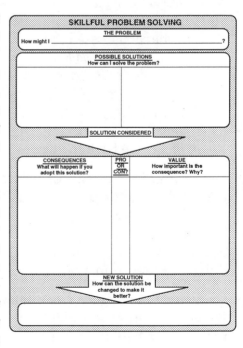

ladder from a helicopter and pick the apples by hand. Climb up a ladder from the ground and pick the apples by hand. Use a vacuum cleaner on a long stick to suck the apples off the tree.

• **In order to decide whether a possible solution to a problem is a good solution, we have to consider what would happen if we adopted this solution. If the solution is likely to cause more problems than it solves, it may not be such a good solution. Let's first think about what would happen if we did the things you have suggested. Work with your partner again. I'd like you to do several things. First, pick one of the solutions you'd like to think about, and draw a picture of it. Then, write the solution you are working on in the arrow in the middle of the page. Use your pictures to try to figure out all of the important things that would happen if you tried that solution. Finally, write these consequences on your diagram in the first column under the arrow.** After the students have completed their pictures and worked together on the consequences of the solution they are considering, ask each group to show their pictures to the class and to report on two important results that they noticed: one positive and one negative. POSSIBLE ANSWERS: *Shaking the tree: The apples would fall off the tree, but they would probably get bruised or break as they fell. Cutting the tree down: The tree would fall and we would be able to get the apples, but it would die and not produce apples next year. Throwing rocks: Apples would fall, but they would be damaged by the rocks and damaged apples don't taste good. Climbing a ladder: I could pick the apples by hand, but the ladder might fall and I would get hurt. Using a vacuum: We could suck the apples off the trees, but they would probably fall and get bruised, and it would be hard to lift the vacuum very high. Climbing down a ladder from a helicopter: We could get the apples, but we couldn't carry very many, and it would cost a lot.*

• **Those are interesting ideas about what might happen if you adopted these solutions. In each case, you thought that the problem of getting the apples off the trees would be solved, but other problems would result. What we're going to do now is to see if we can change the solutions a little bit so that we can get the apples down from the trees without the other problems. For example, how could you avoid having the apples bruised if you shook the tree? Talk to your partner and see if you can think of a way.** After a few minutes, ask for the modified solutions. POSSIBLE ANSWERS: *Maybe you could put a net under the tree to catch the apples. Maybe you could put pillows under the tree. If the apples fell into a funnel, they could roll, without bruising, down a tube connected to the funnel.* **Now work with your partners and change your solutions so that you can avoid the problems. If you can't, then the solution may not be a very good one.** After students have discussed this, ask for their ideas. *Throwing rocks: Maybe we can't avoid damaging the apples. Climbing a ladder: Someone could hold the ladder and the person picking the apples could put them in bags that are lowered to the person holding the ladder. Cutting the tree down: There is no way to save the tree for next year. Climbing down the ladder from a helicopter: It will have to be expensive if we do it this way. Using a vacuum: We could put a net under the vacuum, but it would still be hard to lift the vacuum to get the apples off the top of the tree. But we could climb up a ladder with the vacuum. It would still be heavy.* **Go back to your pictures now and add these changes.**

• **Let's think about these possibilities now. Are there some that you think aren't going to be very good solutions because you can't eliminate the problems? Are there some that you can change? Let's see how the class feels.** For each possible solution, ask for a show of hands in favor of abandoning it. Cross off possibilities if a good-sized majority thinks they should be deleted. Students usually vote to cross off throwing rocks and cutting the tree down. Often, climbing down a ladder from a helicopter is crossed off as well.

• **I'm going to ask you to work in larger groups now. I'll select one student as the group leader. For each solution, a student who worked on that possibility should show his or her revised picture and explain how this solution would work, mentioning at least one good point and** one remaining problem. It's going to be up to your group to discuss and reach agreement on the best solution. You should decide that a solution is best if it gets the job done and has fewer problems doing so in comparison to the rest. Make sure you all approach this with open minds—don't just vote for a solution because its one that you worked on. They can't all be the best. Divide the class into two groups, with one student from each pair in each group. Allow time for discussion. Appoint as the group leader a student who has good leadership skills, and ask a student who needs better speaking skills to be a reporter. Tell the groups that they should take no more than ten minutes to discuss the solutions. Ask for reports explaining why certain solutions were rejected and why the one selected is the best. After each group reports, give the students a round of applause.

Most groups decide in favor of climbing into the trees using a ladder, picking the apples by hand, and then getting the apples down to the ground in bags that can be put on trucks and transported away.

- As the final part of this activity, I'd like you to do some homework tonight. Plan how you will get the apples using the method you have decided on. What resources will you need to bring with you, who will go along, how will you get there, and what will you do with the apples after they are picked? Write your plan down, and draw whatever pictures you'd like to accompany it. On the next day, ask students to share their plans.

THINKING ABOUT THINKING

- **What do we call the kind of thinking we just did?** *Problem solving.*

- **What questions did we ask as we did our problem solving?** Students should mention at least the questions that are on the thinking map of problem solving. If they are having trouble, point to the thinking map and ask if these were questions we asked. The questions students identify are: *Is there a problem about the apples? What makes this a problem? What is the problem? How can we solve the problem? What would the results be if we solved it one way or another? How can the solutions be changed so that they are better? Which solution is the best? Why is it the best?*

- **Is the thinking map of skillful problem solving okay? If not, what would you change or add?**

- **Is it a good idea to do problem solving this way? Why or why not?** POSSIBLE ANSWERS: *We won't pick bad solutions to problems. We'll be able to tell whether or not something is a problem that we have to solve. We won't have other problems later.*

- **In this activity, you worked in groups. Is this a good way to do your thinking or would you rather work on your own? Why?** Most students say that they like to work in groups because they get ideas from other students. Some students, however, say that they'd rather work alone because other students don't let them talk or because what other students say confuses them.

- **When you have to solve a problem next time, how will you do it? Will the diagram we used help you? What will you do with it?** ANSWERS VARY.

APPLYING YOUR THINKING

IMMEDIATE TRANSFER

- We're reading the story of Dr. De Soto, a mouse who has become a pretty good dentist. In this story, Dr. De Soto is approached by a fox who loves to eat mice, and who says he has a toothache. Dr. De Soto realizes he has a problem and decides to solve it a certain way. We're going to read up to the point in the story where Dr. De Soto realizes he has a problem. Put yourself in Dr. De Soto's place, and think carefully about his situation so that you can identify the problem he has to solve. Then solve it carefully. After we've finished, we will compare your solution to Dr. De Soto's.

- One of the other things we've studied in social studies is how we use raw materials like wood to make things that we can use. Think about the many ways in which we use wood. We get wood from trees. What problem can you identify with using wood from trees, and how would you solve it?

REINFORCEMENT LATER

- We've got a number of plants and animals in our classroom. The Christmas holidays are coming up. Will this create a problem? If so, what is it? What's the best solution?

- Children often come to school with illnesses. What problem does this create? What are some ways of solving the problem?

CONTENT EXTENSION

In your classroom, make some material available on fruit growing and picking. Include material on how orchards are cultivated, the kinds of jobs people have in orchards, and the ways in which commercial orchards contribute to a community. Ask students to read this material, and have each report on how a particular fruit is grown and harvested. A resource for this lesson extension is *An Apple-Growing Community: Yakima, Washington*, prepared by the Social Science Staff of the Educational Research Council of America, from the American Communities Series (Allyn and Bacon: Boston).

ASSESSING STUDENT THINKING ABOUT PROBLEM SOLVING

Examples that challenge students to think through interesting problems, such as the transfer and reinforcement examples, can be used to assess whether students are raising good questions about problems and answering them carefully. Make sure the problems you suggest to students are authentic and open-ended and need defining in order to get the most comprehensive profile of your students' problem-solving abilities. Ask students to use a graphic organizer to record their ideas, but let them choose which one they will work with. Also ask them to write down their plan for implementing their solution. Make sure they are raising the questions on the thinking map as they try to solve the problems in the example(s) you give them.

This thinking process can also be assessed by giving students performance tasks for which you ask them to plan out their performances. This should provide some information about their problem-solving abilities. As you observe their performance, note how they identify problems, think through possible solutions, and make judgments about the best solution. If you have trouble ascertaining whether they are doing this, you can interview the students after they have completed the task. Skillful problem solvers will attend to each of the steps in the thinking map for problem solving.

Sample Student Responses • Apples

SKILLFUL PROBLEM SOLVING

THE PROBLEM

How might I _get the apples from apple trees so that people can eat them_**?**

POSSIBLE SOLUTIONS
How can I solve the problem?

Shake the tree till the apples fall off.

Throw rocks at the apples and knock them off the tree.

Climb up the trunk and out on the branches, pick the apples, and drop them down.

Cut the tree down and climb in to pick them.

Climb down a ladder from a helicopter, pick the apples, and pass them up.

Climb up a ladder from the ground and pick the apples.

Use a vacuum cleaner to suck the apples from the tree.

SOLUTION CONSIDERED
Cut the tree down and climb in to pick the apples.

CONSEQUENCES What will happen if you adopt this solution?	PRO OR CON?	VALUE How important is the consequence? Why?
You'd be able to pick the apples easily.	Pro	Very important. Apples are good to eat and they are used a lot.
You'd kill the tree.	Con	Very important. Apple trees have to be alive to produce apples.
No more apples would grow on the tree.	Con	Very important. Apples are good to eat and people use them a lot.
You could cut the tree up for firewood.	Pro	Not too important. Apple trees aren't very big and we have lots of firewood.
The tree might fall on someone.	Con	Very important. It could kill someone.
The wood could be used to make things.	Pro	Not very important. We have lots of wood.

NEW SOLUTION
How can the solution be changed to make it better?

You could cut the tree down and make sure no one is under it by yelling "timber."
You couldn't do anything to keep the tree from dying if you cut it down.

Sample Student Responses • Apples

SKILLFUL PROBLEM SOLVING

THE PROBLEM
How might I _get the apples from apple trees so that people can eat them_?

POSSIBLE SOLUTIONS
How can I solve the problem?

Shake the tree till the apples fall off.	Climb down a ladder from a helicopter, pick the apples, and pass them up.
Throw rocks at the apples and knock them off the tree.	Climb up a ladder from the ground and pick the apples.
Climb up the trunk and out on the branches, pick the apples, and drop them down.	Use a vacuum cleaner to suck the apples from the tree.
Cut the tree down and climb in to pick them.	

SOLUTION CONSIDERED
Climb up a ladder and pick the apples.

CONSEQUENCES What will happen if you adopt this solution?	PRO OR CON?	VALUE How important is the consequence? Why?
I could get all the apples off the tree.	Pro	Very important. Apples are good to eat and they are used a lot.
I might fall off the ladder.	Con	Very important. I could hurt myself.
I would have to move the ladder a lot.	Con	Important. Moving the ladder takes time.
I could eat an apple.	Pro	Important. I like apples.
I could bruise the apples if I dropped them to the ground.	Con	Very important. Bruising the apples can make them rotten; then we can't use them.

NEW SOLUTION
How can the solution be changed to make it better?

I could ask someone to hold the ladder and I could put a rope around myself. I could put the apples in a bag and lower them to the person holding the ladder.

LESSON CONTEXTS FOR PROBLEM SOLVING

The following examples have been suggested by classroom teachers as contexts to develop infused lessons. If a skill or process has been introduced in a previous infused lesson, transfer activities can be designed in these contexts to reinforce it.

GRADE	SUBJECT	TOPIC	THINKING ISSUE
K–3	Literature	*Too Many Daves*	This poem by Dr.Seuss describes a person who had twenty- three sons all named Dave. Why is this a problem? How might you solve this problem?
K–3	Literature	*Little Bear*	Little Bear keeps on saying he's cold. Why is that a problem? How can his mother solve the problem?
K–3	Literature	*Frog and Toad Together*	Toad had a lot of things to do; he wrote them down on a list so he could remember them, but the list blew away. What problem does that cause for Frog and Toad? How might you solve it?
K–3	Literature	*The Hole in the Dike*	Why does Peter think that the tiny leak in the dike is a problem? What problem does this pose for Peter? If you were Peter, what might you do when faced with this problem? Now compare what you think you might do to what Peter did.
K–3	Literature	*Franklin in the Dark*	What problem does Franklin have with dark places? How might he solve this problem?
K–3	Social studies	The Pilgrims	What problems did the Pilgrims face when they tried to set up a community in the New World? Which problems were important to solve? What might you do to solve one of these problems?
K–3	Social studies	Communities	Suppose that you have just moved into a new neighborhood. How might your parents learn the locations of businesses that they will need to use (e.g., drug store, super market, bank)? What problems could they have if they don't know where these places are located?
K–3	Social studies	Services	When you get a haircut, your parents pay the barber for the service that was performed for you. Firefighters, the police, and teachers also perform services for the community. Who should pay them? Where should the money come from? Think of ways that this problem can be solved. Which way do you think is best? Why? Compare it to what is done in your community.
K–3	Social studies/Science	Trees	People use wood from trees for many things. If they keep on doing this, what problems might it cause? How might we solve these problems?
K–3	Science	Plants	Mr. Gardner has just started a vegetable garden. He has seen birds and rabbits nearby. What problem does he have to solve? What are some ways to solve the problem?
K–3	Science	Animals	Cattle ranchers have a problem in the winter when snow covers many animals' foods. How would you state the ranchers' problem? What might they do to solve it?

LESSON CONTEXTS FOR PROBLEM SOLVING

GRADE	SUBJECT	TOPIC	THINKING ISSUE
K–3	Science	Energy	Our family believes that everyone should save energy so that our energy resources will last longer. However, we need to be able to see at night, we like to watch television, we need to keep food cold in the refrigerator, etc. How would you define our problem? What are some possible solutions? Which do you think will work the best? Why?
K–3	Science	Animals	Suppose we've got a collection of plants and animals in our classroom, including some gerbils, white mice, and turtles. What problem would school vacation cause for the plants and animals? Why would it be a problem? What do you think might be done to solve this problem? Which possible solution is the best one? Why?
K–3	Science	Simple machines	Imagine that you are helping your parents move the furniture in your house because they want to paint the walls. Some of the furniture is too heavy and won't budge. How would you state the problem? What might you use to help your parents move the heavy furniture? Why would these help?
K–3	Mathematics	Arithmetic	Suppose you and eight of your friends are having a party. Your mother has ordered a pizza, but when it comes you realize that it is cut into six pieces. What problem do you have? What are some ways of solving the problem? Which way do you think is best? Why?
K–3	Mathematics	Measurement	Suppose you want to cut out a one-foot piece of paper to make a book cover. You can't find a ruler. What problem do you have? Why is this a problem? What are some ways you might solve this problem? Which is the best way and why?
K–3	Health	Emergencies	Suppose you see smoke coming from a closed closet in your school. No one is in the area. What problem do you have? What might you do in these circumstances? Which possibility is the best and why?
K–3	Health	Disease	Sometimes children come to school sick. What problems does this cause? What possible solutions do you have for these problems?
K–3	Guidance	Social relationships	One student frequently pushes ahead in the line. Is this a problem? Why? What might we do to solve this problem?
K–3	Guidance	Family Relationships	Suppose you get a toy airplane for your birthday. Your little sister likes to play with it, but she breaks a lot of the things she plays with. What problem does this cause for you? Why is this a problem? What are some things you might do? Whuch is the best and why?
K–3	Guidance	Family relationships	Suppose one of your parents frequently blames you for things you didn't do. What problem does this cause for you? Why is it a problem? What might you do? Which possible solution is the best and why?
K–3	Art	Clay sculpture	Suppose you want to make a sculpture of a bird. What media would show the bird's features best? Which do you most like to use? Why? What problems might you have using this medium? How could you avoid these problems?

LESSON CONTEXTS FOR PROBLEM SOLVING

GRADE	SUBJECT	TOPIC	THINKING ISSUE
4–6	Literature	*Atalanta's Race*	In this Greek myth, anyone who wanted to marry Atalanta had to beat her in a race. Otherwise, he was put to death. Hippomenes wanted to marry Atalanta. How would you define the problem he had to solve? What might you have done if you were in his position? Compare this to what he actually did.
4–6	Literature	*The Big Wave*	This story, written by Pearl Buck, portrays a tidal wave that destroyed a village and killed many of its inhabitants. Jiya escaped harm, but his family was killed. What problems did this cause for Kino and his relatives? How would you solve them? How did Kino solve them?
4–6	Literature	*Lyddie*	While Lyddie worked in the Lowell mills, she also had to care for her younger sister. What problem does she have? What are some possible ways that she might solve it? Which solution do you think is best? Compare this to what Lyddie did.
4–6	Literature	*My Name is Not Angelica*	Raisha faces a serious problem when she is wounded and needs assistance. What is the problem? How might she solve it?
4–6	Social studies	Ancient civilizations	Despite the fact that the Sumerians had developed an advanced civilization, the city-states continually fought among themselves. What problem did this cause with regard to their ability to defend themselves against an external threat? How would you define the problem? If you were a Sumerian and were aware of this problem, what would you consider as possible solutions? What would you advise Sumer to do? Why?
4–6	Social studies	Rome	As the Romans conquered more of the peoples who inhabited Europe, more non-Romans either entered or were brought to Rome. Soon, non-Romans outnumbered Romans. What problems might this have caused? What might the Romans have done about these problems? Compare your suggestions to what actually happened in ancient Rome during this period.
4–6	Social studies/ personal problem solving	Economics	Most students find that they need more money than allowances or birthday gifts provide. What problem do they have? How might students solve this problem?
4–6	Social studies	"Castle," by David Macaulay	In medieval Europe, castles had to be built to provide for the security and personal needs of the nobleman, his family, and the nearby villages. Did the way castles were built serve these purposes? How? Do you think any parts of the castle described in Macaulay's book could be improved upon to better serve these purposes? How?
4–6	Social studies	"Cathedral," by David Macaulay	What problem did medieval builders have to solve in order to heighten the roofs of cathedrals? How might they have solved this problem? Now apply your strategy to another problem they faced: how to get heavy stone to the tops of cathedral vaults in order to construct the roof.

LESSON CONTEXTS FOR PROBLEM SOLVING			
GRADE	SUBJECT	TOPIC	THINKING ISSUE
4–6	Social studies	Pirates	Edward Teach, otherwise known as "Blackbeard," was described as "the fiercest pirate of them all." He terrorized those shipping off the east coast of colonial America in 1717-1718. What problem did this cause? How could it have been solved? Compare your solution to what actually happened.
4–6	Social studies	Westward movement	What problems did easterners face when they travelled in wagon trains to settle in the west? Why were these problems? Put yourself in the position of someone making this journey. Pick one of the major problems. Define it. Then consider what possible solutions would have been available to you at that time. Select what you think is the best one.
4–6	Social studies/ student government	Economics	The class undertakes a project to earn money for a class trip by gathering cans, bottles, paper, and other recyclable materials and selling them to a dealer in the community. What might the class do to make sure that the project is a success?
4–6	Social studies	The Alamo	What problem did Santa Anna perceive he was solving by attacking the Alamo? What problem did the defenders of the Alamo face? What might they do when they learn of Santa Anna's plan to attack?
4–6	Social studies	Transportation	In the1900s, horses and horse-drawn carriages were the main source of transportation in this country. After its invention, the automobile became the main source of transportation. How did the automobile improve on horse-drawn vehicles? Given their purposes and how they operate, do automobiles generate any problems? How can they be improved to overcome these problems? Pick one problem, consider what might be done to solve it, and recommend the best solution.
4–6	Science	Food chains	When prairie dogs are near farms, they eat farmers' crops. Because of this, farmers have killed thousands of prairie dogs. Black-footed ferrets eat prairie dogs. What problems do the ferrets have? What problems do the farmers have? Is there some way that you can solve both of these problems? What might you do and why? Which possible solution would probably work best? Why?
4–6	Science	Whales	Some people use whale meat for food, for animal feed, and as a source of oil. The teeth are used for carvings called scrim- shaw. The population of some whales has fallen so low that they are considered endangered. What problems does this situation create? What are some ways to solve these problems? Which do you think might work best? Why?
4–6	Science	Air Pollution	What problems does air pollution cause? What are some ways that we might solve these problems? Have any of these solutions actually been adopted?
4–6	Science	Waste disposal	Research any effort in your community to minimize waste disposal. Evaluate the current plan or suggest another one.

PART 3

SKILLS AT CLARIFYING IDEAS: THINKING FOR UNDERSTANDING

ANALYZING IDEAS

Chapter 4: Comparing and Contrasting

Chapter 5: Classification

Chapter 6: Parts-whole Relationships

Chapter 7: Sequencing

ANALYZING ARGUMENTS

Chapter 8: Finding Reasons and Conclusions

Chapter 9: Uncovering Assumptions

MAP OF THE THINKING DOMAIN

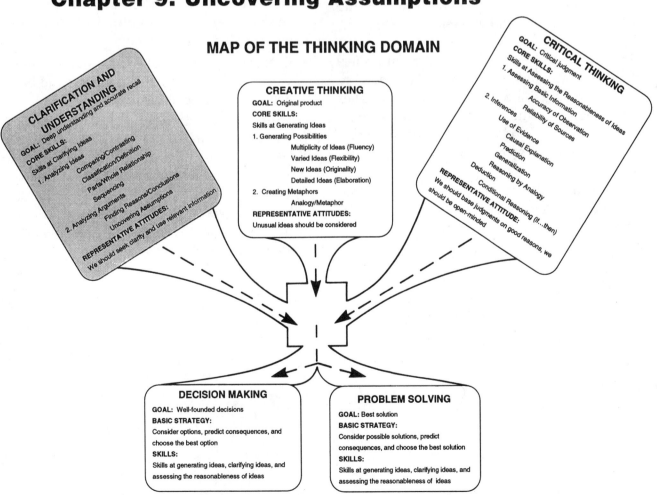

CLARIFICATION AND UNDERSTANDING
GOAL: Deep understanding and accurate recall
CORE SKILLS:
Skills at Clarifying Ideas
1. Analyzing Ideas
Comparing/Contrasting
Classification/Definition
Parts/Whole Relationship
Sequencing
2. Analyzing Arguments
Finding Reasons/Conclusions
Uncovering Assumptions
REPRESENTATIVE ATTITUDES:
We should seek clarity and use relevant information

CREATIVE THINKING
GOAL: Original product
CORE SKILLS:
Skills at Generating Ideas
1. Generating Possibilities
Multiplicity of Ideas (Fluency)
Varied Ideas (Flexibility)
New Ideas (Originality)
Detailed Ideas (Elaboration)
2. Creating Metaphors
Analogy/Metaphor
REPRESENTATIVE ATTITUDES:
Unusual ideas should be considered

CRITICAL THINKING
GOAL: Critical judgment
CORE SKILLS:
Skills at Assessing the Reasonableness of Ideas
1. Assessing Basic Information
Accuracy of Observation
Reliability of Sources
2. Inferences
Use of Evidence
Causal Explanation
Prediction
Generalization
Reasoning by Analogy
Deduction
Conditional Reasoning (If...then)
REPRESENTATIVE ATTITUDE:
We should base judgments on good reasons, we should be open-minded

DECISION MAKING
GOAL: Well-founded decisions
BASIC STRATEGY:
Consider options, predict consequences, and choose the best option
SKILLS:
Skills at generating ideas, clarifying ideas, and assessing the reasonableness of ideas

PROBLEM SOLVING
GOAL: Best solution
BASIC STRATEGY:
Consider possible solutions, predict consequences, and choose the best solution
SKILLS:
Skills at generating ideas, clarifying ideas, and assessing the reasonableness of ideas

PART 3
SKILLS AT CLARIFYING IDEAS: THINKING FOR UNDERSTANDING

We seek deeper understanding of ideas for many different reasons. For example, I may read an ad for a low-priced vacation at a seaside resort. Before I decide to go there, I want to clarify what vacationing at this site will involve. Do the benefits pointed out in the advertisement give me good reasons for choosing this resort, or do I need more information? For example, how does this resort compare to the one I enjoyed visiting last year? What kind of resort is it: a health spa, a gambling casino, a sports facility? How is the restaurant rated? What will a vacation there be like; do they have any organized activities for guests, like sight-seeing or fishing trips? In deciding to go there, am I taking anything for granted, like what the weather will be like?

Answering these questions skillfully will give me a deeper understanding of what vacationing at this resort is like and will enable me to make an informed choice. Not answering these questions may leave me with a superficial understanding that could result in an unwise decision. The difference between these two situations lies in the degree to which I attempt to *clarify* what I am considering. To clarify ideas, I use *analytical* thinking skills to provide me with insight and understanding.

Clarification involves basic analysis skills that fall into two categories. The first category involves analyzing ideas or things by

- Determining their key properties and what having these properties implies (classification / definition);
- Breaking them into their parts and determining how these parts function in relation to the whole (determining parts-whole relationships);
- Comparing them to other things in order to bring out similarities and differences (comparing and contrasting); or
- Locating them in a sequence relative to other things that have different degrees of the same properties (sequencing / ranking).

The second type of analysis involves identifying the ingredients in the thinking that people engage in when they communicate ideas:

- Finding the reasons people (including ourselves) offer to support the ideas they try to convince others to adopt (finding reasons and conclusions); and
- Detecting what we take for granted, often without knowing it, in our actions and beliefs (uncovering assumptions).

Clarification yields deeper understanding. While understanding, alone, is not all there is to good thinking, we cannot do without it if we are to think about the world around us in an informed way. Teaching students the skills of clarification covered in this handbook will improve their abilities to achieve this understanding when it is needed.

CHAPTER 4
COMPARING AND CONTRASTING

Why is Skillful Comparing and Contrasting Important?

Comparing and contrasting involves detecting a variety of similarities and differences between two or more objects, events, organisms, institutions, or ideas in order to achieve certain specific purposes. Comparing and contrasting always involves analyzing features that match and features that do not and drawing out the implications of this analysis. Comparing and contrasting is helpful to gain a deeper understanding of the things compared in order to make well-considered decisions or to clear up confusion. Comparing and contrasting is also involved in more complex thinking tasks such as classification, definition, and reasoning by analogy.

Purposes of comparing and contrasting. We compare and contrast for a variety of purposes. Many everyday decisions, like shopping or choosing a route to work, involve comparing and contrasting. A manufacturer might compare and contrast his firm with more successful firms to get ideas about improving productivity.

Our goal in comparing and contrasting may be to gain insight and understanding. We may compare and contrast a friend's new job to her old one because we notice that she is more relaxed than she was. We wonder whether her new job is contributing to this change.

Problems about the way we compare and contrast things. We compare and contrast with varying degrees of thoroughness. Sometimes we attend only to surface characteristics, like how things look, when other factors are more relevant.

Suppose I want to buy a car and am trying to decide between two models. If I attend only to how they look, I may miss important differences in their gas mileage, durability, and overall performance. Making sure we attend to all of the relevant points of comparing and contrasting is very important.

While we often make only rough comparisons and contrasts, precision may be particularly important in certain contexts. I may note that both cars I'm considering cost under $10,000, yet determining the price precisely may reveal an important difference.

In determining equality, such as the congruence of two mathematical shapes or equality in job opportunities, we sometimes make rough comparisons and contrasts. This imprecision may lead us to think that the figures are equal or that any qualified individual's chances for being hired for a specific job are comparable, when, in fact, subtle differences may result in significant inequalities.

Another problem arises when we do not realize the implications of the similarities and differences we note. I may realize that a car I am considering gets 10 miles per gallon lower gas mileage than another but may not consider what effect the better gas mileage will have on the long-term operating costs of the vehicle. In statistical analysis, difference in raw scores may seem important until we perform other procedures and find out whether or not the difference in scores is significant. Understanding the implications of similarities and differences is very important for successful comparisons and contrasts.

The four basic defaults in comparing and contrasting are summarized in figure 4.1. The first default relates to quantity, the second to depth, the third to precision, and the fourth to completeness.

How Do We Compare and Contrast Skillfully?

Comparing and contrasting can lead to more effective choices and deeper insights if we focus our attention on a variety of important similarities and differences and take the time to think about what the similarities and differences show. There are two basic ways to compare and contrast skillfully:

- Open comparison and contrast

```
┌─────────────────────────────────────────┐
│   COMMON DEFAULTS IN THE WAY             │
│   WE COMPARE AND CONTRAST                │
├─────────────────────────────────────────┤
│  1. We identify only a few similarities  │
│     and differences.                     │
│                                          │
│  2. We identify only superficial         │
│     similarities and differences.        │
│                                          │
│  3. We make rough and imprecise          │
│     judgments of similarity or           │
│     difference.                          │
│                                          │
│  4. We don't draw out the implications   │
│     of the similarities and differences  │
│     we have identified.                  │
└─────────────────────────────────────────┘
```

Figure 4.1

```
┌─────────────────────────────────────────┐
│      OPEN COMPARE AND CONTRAST           │
│                                          │
│  1. How are they similar?                │
│                                          │
│  2. How are they different?              │
│                                          │
│  3. What similarities and differences    │
│     seem significant?                    │
│                                          │
│  4. What categories or patterns do you   │
│     see in the significant similarities  │
│     and differences?                     │
│                                          │
│  5. What interpretation or conclusion is │
│     suggested by the significant         │
│     similarities and differences?        │
└─────────────────────────────────────────┘
```

Figure 4.2

• Focused comparison and contrast

Open comparison and contrast. One way to counter making too narrow a comparison and/or contrast is to use brainstorming to identify as many different similarities and differences as we can. We then select those similarities and differences that are significant or relevant to our goals, explicitly drawing out their implications. We call this broad consideration of similarities and differences *open compare and contrast.*

Suppose I am comparing two cars to decide which one I want to buy, and I prefer the color of one of them. Instead of deciding just on the basis of color, however, I then list other similarities and differences in order to make sure that I consider as many factors as possible. I then sort out which of the similarities and differences are significant, look for patterns, and ask what these significant similarities and differences show about the cars.

This broad comparison and contrast may reveal a variety of features relevant to my purchase. For example, I may find that there are certain hidden costs for one car that are not present for the other. This discovery may make a difference in my choice.

Open comparing and contrasting generates a broad consideration of what is being compared. It brings to light similarities and differences that we ordinarily might not take into account. The thinking map of open comparing and contrasting in figure 4.2 can guide us through this process.

Using a graphic organizer for open compare and contrast. The graphic organizer for open comparing and contrasting in figure 4.3 reinforces the process highlighted on the thinking map and provides spaces in which to record information.

The use of this graphic organizer is very straightforward. First note similarities and write them in the "How Alike?" box. Then note differences and write them in the two outer columns under "How Different?" For each difference recorded, clarify the kind of difference you are recording by filling in the category word in the middle column.

For example, in comparing two cars I might first notice that one costs $7,000 and the other $9,000. I would list this difference in the two columns. Then I should ask, "What kind of difference is this?" It is, of course, a difference in cost. "Cost" should be written in the corresponding space in the middle column.

We shouldn't stop with just a few similarities and differences or those of the same kind. We should search for as many varied similarities and differences as we can find. Taking time for this investigation is important, and working with someone else can be helpful. Brainstorming what to look for is a good way to assure the openness and breadth of this search.

When we categorize differences, we determine what these differences describe. This is very important in helping us articulate what the comparison and contrast shows when we later

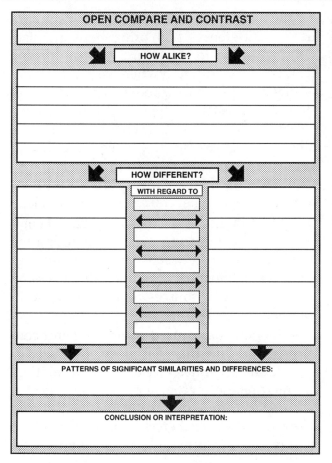

Figure 4.3

draw a conclusion. Categorizing the differences can also broaden our thinking by prompting us to consider other related differences which we may have overlooked, such as operating expenses.

The *patterns* step is important in considering complex examples. Asking whether there are important patterns revealed in the comparison and contrast prompts us to scrutinize the range of similarities and differences we've found to determine whether common themes emerge. I might notice, for example, that there is a pattern of "extras" on one car and not on the other. Since this is worth taking into account in making my purchase, I would write down "More extras on car A" in the *patterns* box. When I formulate a conclusion about the two cars, more "extras" may be a factor that I would want to mention.

Focused compare and contrast. There is a second way to compare and contrast which makes our search for similarities and differences more organized from the outset. We *first*

determine the types of similarities and differences that we should consider in order to achieve our goal. These factors then guide our search for specific similarities and differences. When we have located information about these factors, we then draw conclusions about the two things compared. This is called *focused compare and contrast.*

In the case of the two cars, instead of noting similarities and differences as I found them, I would first ask, "What factors should I consider if I need a reliable car that I can afford and that will serve me well in the hot summer and cold winter?" I might then list factors like cost, performance in cold weather, etc. Noting these factors in advance will then guide my search for relevant similarities and differences. When these similarities and differences have been taken into account, I will be in a position to make a well-considered judgment about which car will serve my purpose better.

Notice that the thinking map for focused compare and contrast (figure 4.4) organizes the questions in a different sequence from the open compare and contrast thinking map (figure 4.2).

FOCUSED COMPARE AND CONTRAST

1. What kinds of similarities and differences are significant to the purpose of the comparison and contrast?

2. What similarities fall into these categories?

3. What differences fall into these categories?

4. What pattern of similarities and differences are revealed?

5. What conclusion or interpretation is suggested by the comparison and contrast that is significant to its purpose?

Figure 4.4

Using a graphic organizer for focused compare and contrast. Notice that the graphic organizer in figure 4.5 reflects the different sequence of questions for focused comparing and contrasting. In using this graphic organizer, first state the purpose of the comparison and con-

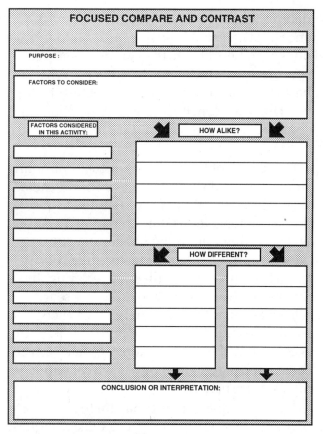

Figure 4.5

trast in the purpose box, and then in the next box, list the relevant factors to consider to accomplish this purpose.

For example, when I answer the question "What factors should I consider in making my car purchase?" I would write "cost" and "performance in cold weather" in the "Factors to Consider" box, along with any other relevant factors that I should take into account. I would use this list as a checklist to guide my search for relevant similarities and differences in the cars I am considering.

After gathering information, I write it in either the similarities or differences boxes, depending on what I find. If both cars cost $7,000, for example, then I would record this information in the similarities box and "Cost" in the corresponding "Factors Considered" box. If, on the other hand, one costs $6,000 and the other costs $9,000, I would write this information in the difference columns and write "Cost" in the corresponding box next to these columns.

Open vs. focused compare and contrast. Both the open and focused forms of comparing and

contrasting go beyond merely listing similarities and differences. Both bring more organization and depth to comparing and contrasting than we ordinarily find when we just list similarities and differences. Both generate a conclusion or interpretation suggested by the comparisons and differences. Your choice of one or the other of these two strategies depends on whether you have a specific goal in comparing and contrasting or whether you are exploring the things compared to see what you can learn about them.

Other thinking skills that supplement comparing and contrasting. It is worth noting the interrelationship between comparing and contrasting and two other thinking skills: assessing the reliability of sources and drawing well-founded inferences.

Both open and focused comparing and contrasting presume that the information used is reliable and accurate. If we use misinformation, the interpretation or conclusion that is suggested by comparing and contrasting may be distorted or erroneous. When there is a question about the quality of the information, examining the reliability of the sources should be considered to supplement comparing and contrasting.

In both open and focused comparing and contrasting, when we draw out the implications of the similarities and differences, we do not necessarily follow guidelines for inference to determine whether or not our conclusion is well-supported. In some cases, conclusions may reflect faulty reasoning. Any conclusions or interpretations drawn from the similarities and differences should, therefore, be treated as suggestions only. We underscore this tentativeness by using the phrase "Conclusion Suggested" on both graphic organizers. If you are unsure whether or not your conclusion is well-supported, or if someone challenges it, you may check it out by using appropriate critical thinking skills of inference, described in the section on assessing the reasonableness of ideas (Chapters 12–17).

How Can We Teach Students to Compare and Contrast Skillfully?

Tips for teaching skillful comparing and contrasting. To teach comparing and contrasting well, it is not enough to ask students simply to list similarities and differences between two things. We must teach students explicitly what questions to ask to generate many kinds of similarities and differences, to select relevant similarities and differences for certain purposes, and to draw out the implications of the similarities and differences they've found. The goal of this instruction is to help students internalize these questions so that they guide themselves in thinking skillfully when they compare and contrast.

The thinking maps for comparing and contrasting contain questions which can be adapted to guide students through a compare and contrast activity in any instructional area. These guiding questions can be supplemented by using one of the appropriate graphic organizers. Guided activities in which students compare and contrast what they are studying will deepen their understanding of what they are comparing and contrasting. This active-thinking component of the lesson is an important step toward students' learning how to compare and contrast skillfully.

Prompting metacognition is another important step in teaching this skill. In order to use comparing and contrasting in other contexts, students must distinguish the thinking strategy from the content. To focus students' attention on the guiding questions, you can use several techniques: prompt them to recall the process by discussing it or writing about it, show them the thinking map, or help them construct a similar one.

Make sure you give your students an opportunity to reflect on whether asking and answering these questions is a useful way to compare and contrast. Asking students for examples of things that might be compared and contrasted can enhance this kind of reflection.

Then, as in all infusion lessons, provide additional opportunities for students to practice skillful comparing and contrasting deliberately. Always strive to let your students guide themselves in this kind of thinking and to check themselves by referring to the thinking map and the graphic organizer. Repeated, increasingly self-directed practice in comparing and con-

trasting can lead your students to use this thinking skill as a matter of course.

Variations on the thinking maps and graphic organizers for the early elementary grades. Two variations on the comparison and contrast strategy are suitable for students in grades K–4. The first is a simplified form of the strategy for kindergarten and first grade students. It involves emphasizing only three of the five attention points in comparing and contrasting—similarities, differences, and drawing a conclusion. This is the core of skillful comparing and contrasting. Figure 4.6 contains the thinking map for the K–1 version of comparing and contrast.

COMPARE AND CONTRAST

1. How are they similar?

2. How are they different?

3. What does this show?

Figure 4.6

If students learn to ask and answer these questions routinely, they will build a solid foundation upon which the more sophisticated forms of comparing and contrasting can be developed. For students in grades 2–4, a more advanced thinking map (figure 4.7) can be used.

OPEN COMPARE AND CONTRAST

1. How are they similar?

2. How are they different?

3. What similarities and differences seem significant?

4. What interpretation or conclusion is suggested by the significant similarities and differences?

Figure 4.7

The simplified graphic organizer in figure 4.8 can be used in lessons based on either of these thinking maps. Notice that this diagram omits

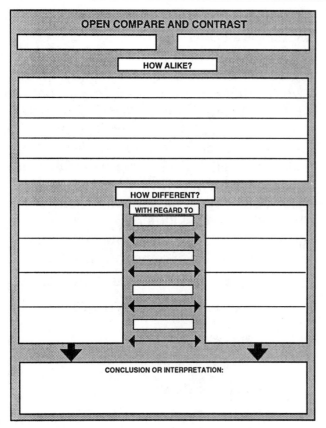

Figure 4.8

the "patterns" step found in the more advanced strategy for open comparing and contrasting.

In teaching young students who cannot write, the teacher may record students' responses in a large poster-sized version of this graphic organizer.

Contexts in the content areas for compare and contrast lessons. There are many occasions when students can compare and contrast things. Repeatedly asking for comparisons and contrasts, however, can lead to ineffective overuse. To avoid this, employ compare and contrast lessons only to serve important content objectives. It is particularly helpful to infuse instruction in comparison and contrast when

- *Certain concepts are likely to be confused,* such as breathing and respiration, the greatest common factor and the least common multiple, or myths and legends;
- *Concepts that are complex or abstract are important for students to understand and differentiate from other concepts,* such as producers and consumers, or numbers and numerals; and

- *Students will benefit from applying, clarifying, extending, or refining other key concepts.* Similarities and differences in the attitudes of Abraham Lincoln and Frederick Douglass toward abolitionism, for example, clarifies the distinction between an abolitionist and someone who generally opposed slavery.

Comparing only and contrasting only. Some content objectives can be served best by only comparing or only contrasting. Comparison is especially useful in studying poetry, such as interpreting figurative language. Generating a long list of similarities helps students understand the effectiveness of figures of speech in conveying images and attributes of items being described.

Contrasting underscores significant differences between two concepts. For example, only differences are significant in distinguishing between the rights and responsibilities of state and federal government.

Reinforcing the skill. Once you have taught comparing and contrasting, you can use a variety of examples to reinforce it. These, too, should serve your content objectives. You can, for example, make comparing and contrasting a regular habit in reviewing vocabulary words. When you introduce a new concept in mathematics (e.g., a new polygon) you can ask your students to compare its properties to other figures that they already know.

A menu of suggested contexts for infusion lessons on comparing and contrasting is provided on pp. 129–132.

Model Lessons on Comparing and Contrasting

In this chapter, we include three model lessons on comparing and contrasting: a primary lesson in mathematics, a third grade lesson in children's literature, and an upper-elementary lesson in American history. Each features one of the variations on comparing and contrasting we describe in this commentary. As you review the lessons, try to answer these questions:

- What content objectives does comparing and contrasting activities in the lessons enhance? How?

- What verbal prompts guide students through the process of comparison and contrast so that they attend to a range of similarities and differences and draw out their implications?

- How does the graphic organizer reinforce this process?

- What methods are used in these lessons to enrich students' thinking?

- Can you think of other ways to reinforce skillful comparison and contrast after these lessons have been completed?

Tools for Designing Comparing and Contrasting Lessons

These thinking maps provide questions to guide students' thinking in open or focused comparing and contrasting lessons. Versions of these maps for the lower elementary grades are also included (see p. 106). Each of these thinking maps can also be used to help students reflect on comparing and contrasting skillfully.

The graphic organizers for open or focused comparing and contrasting lessons are on pages 102–107. The simplified graphic organizer for the lower elementary grades is on page 107. Each of these graphic organizers supplement and reinforce the sequenced questions on the thinking maps.

The thinking maps and graphic organizers can serve as photocopy masters, transparency masters, or as models that can be enlarged and used as posters in the classroom. Reproduction rights are granted for single classroom use only.

OPEN COMPARE AND CONTRAST

1. How are they similar?

2. How are they different?

3. What similarities and differences seem significant?

4. What categories or pattern do you see in the significant similarities and differences?

5. What interpretation or conclusion is suggested by the significant similarities and differences?

OPEN COMPARE AND CONTRAST

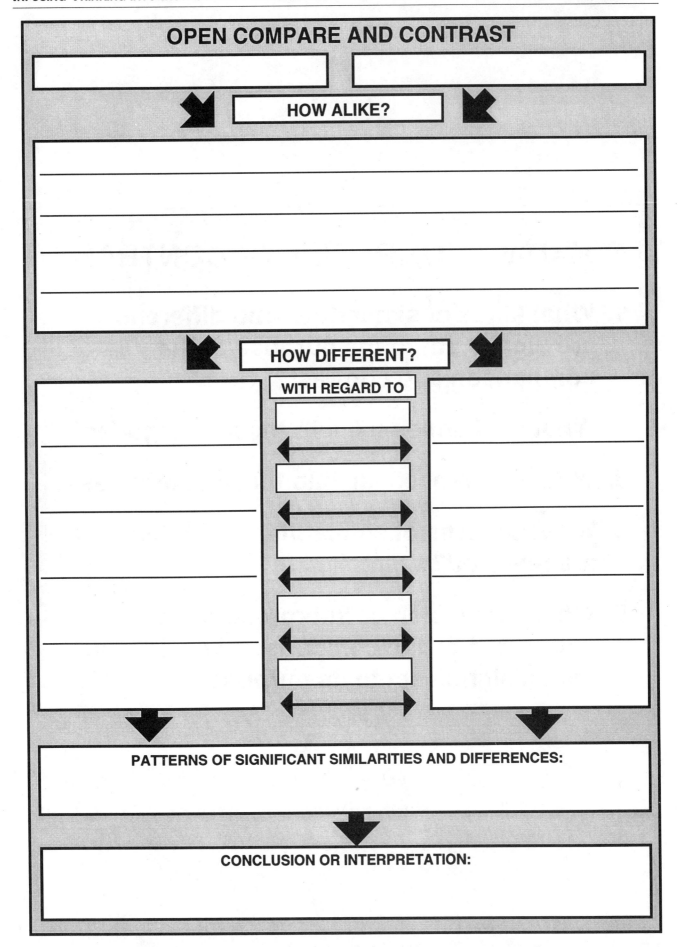

HOW ALIKE?

HOW DIFFERENT?

WITH REGARD TO

PATTERNS OF SIGNIFICANT SIMILARITIES AND DIFFERENCES:

CONCLUSION OR INTERPRETATION:

FOCUSED COMPARE AND CONTRAST

1. What kinds of similarities and differences are significant to the purpose of the comparison and contrast?

2. What similarities fall into these categories?

3. What differences fall into these categories?

4. What patterns of similarities and differences are revealed?

5. What conclusion or interpretation is suggested by the comparison and contrast that is significant to its purpose?

FOCUSED COMPARE AND CONTRAST

PURPOSE :

FACTORS TO CONSIDER:

FACTORS CONSIDERED IN THIS ACTIVITY:

HOW ALIKE?

HOW DIFFERENT?

CONCLUSION OR INTERPRETATION:

COMPARE AND CONTRAST

1. **How are they similar?**

2. **How are they different?**

3. **What does this show?**

OPEN COMPARE AND CONTRAST

1. **How are they similar?**

2. **How are they different?**

3. **What similarities and differences seem significant?**

4. **What interpretation or conclusion is suggested by the significant similarities and differences?**

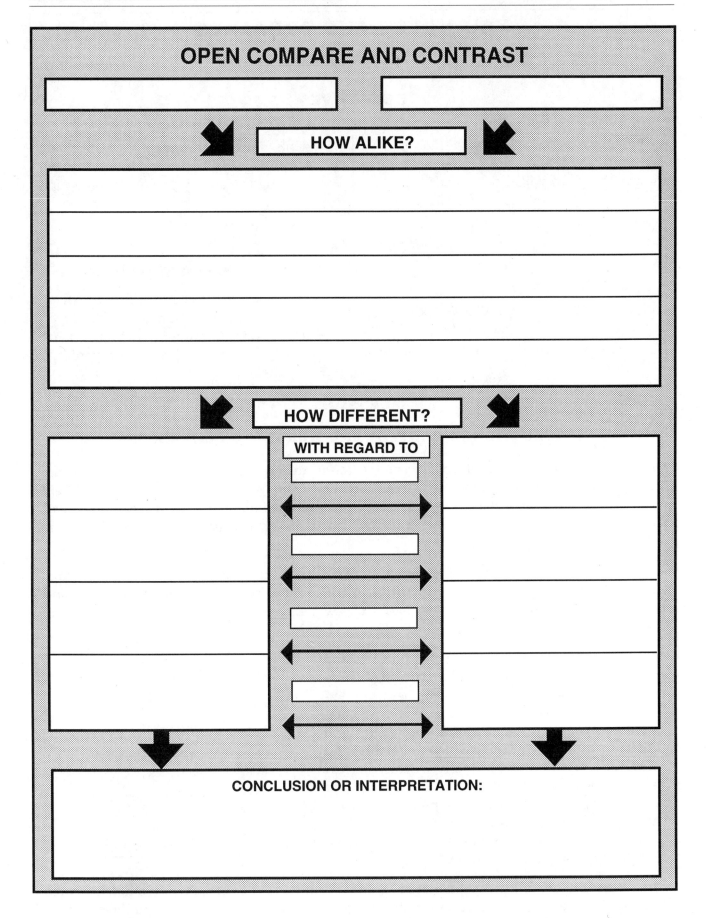

OPEN COMPARE AND CONTRAST

HOW ALIKE?

HOW DIFFERENT?

WITH REGARD TO

CONCLUSION OR INTERPRETATION:

107

TRIANGLES AND PYRAMIDS

Mathematics   **Grades 2–3**

OBJECTIVES

CONTENT

Students will learn that plane figures have two dimensions and solid figures have three dimensions. They will also recognize that solid figures can be made by putting plane figures together.

THINKING SKILL/PROCESS

Students will compare and contrast effectively by determining similarities and differences between two figures and by drawing a conclusion based on them.

METHODS AND MATERIALS

CONTENT

Students will examine models of triangles and pyramids with equal angles and sides. They utilize prior knowledge that geometrical figures have sides, angles, and faces and are described in terms of height, width, and depth.

THINKING SKILL/PROCESS

Compare and contrast is guided by structured questioning and a graphic organizer which highlights points for careful attention in using the thinking skill. (See pp. 102–107 for reproducible diagrams.)

LESSON

INTRODUCTION TO CONTENT AND THINKING SKILL/PROCESS

- Remember when we examined leaves? We found differences in their shapes, edges, the design of the veins, and the kinds of trees they came from. We found that, even though there were differences, they also had similarities. Can you remember some of these similarities? *Most leaves are flat, green, are exposed to the sun, have veins, grow on branches, have stems, and are connected to trees or plants.*

- When we find similarities and differences in things, it helps us understand these things better. How did discussing the similarities and differences in the leaves help us understand how leaves help trees grow? *Food production occurs in leaves, is activated by the sun, and nourishes the plant to which the leaves are attached.*

- Using similarities and differences to understand leaves is called "comparing and contrasting." Comparing and contrasting can help us better understand ideas that we are studying. When we compare and contrast, we first note similarities and differences. Then we decide which similarities and differences are important. Finally, we ask what this shows about the things we are comparing and contrasting. A statement that expresses what the similarities and differences show is called a "conclusion." Here's a chart that will help you remember how to compare and contrast.

> **OPEN COMPARE AND CONTRAST**
>
> 1. How are they similar?
> 2. How are they different?
> 3. What similarities and differences seem significant?
> 4. What interpretation or conclusion is suggested by the significant similarities and differences?

- In order to understand them better, we're going to compare and contrast two geometric figures that look alike. Let's compare and contrast a triangle and a pyramid. The triangle is a plane figure and the pyramid is a solid figure. We study them in mathematics and often see them

in the world around us. Draw these two figures on the chalkboard and show students pictures of each of these figures, for example, a picture of a triangular pattern of roads, of bridge supports, and of the pyramids. **Discuss with your partner other things that have these shapes.** Ask the students to report to the class about some of the triangles and pyramids that they have identified.

THINKING ACTIVELY

- **The triangle and the pyramid have some similarities and some differences. We're going to see what we can learn about triangles and pyramids and about plane and solid figures by comparing and contrasting them.** Circulate triangles and triangular pyramids constructed of dowel rods for the students to examine. **Discuss with your partner how these two figures are alike. Each time you find a similarity, write it on a line in the box under "How Alike?"** (See p. 112 for reproducible diagram.) Give the students enough time to list at least three similarities.

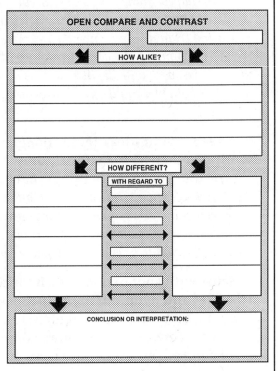

- **Now look for ways that the figures are different. Write the differences in the boxes under "How Different?" Think about what a difference means and write it on the arrow under "With Regard To." For example, the triangle has three edges, while the pyramid has six edges. What term describes that difference?** *Number of edges.* **Write the phrase on the arrow.** Give the students enough time to list at least three differences on the diagram.

- **How are the figures alike?** Randomly call on four or five student pairs to report one similarity that they have found. Record their responses on an overhead transparency or on a large diagram on the chalkboard. Draw out the student's thoughts by asking for clarification or extension of the responses—their significance, implications, etc. POSSIBLE ANSWERS: *Both have faces. Both have corners. Both have angles. Both have edges. You can flip, turn, and slide both. Both take up space. You can change the length of the edges and they will still both be triangular. The angles in both are the same.*

- **How are the figures different?** Record differences, asking what each difference describes and writing it on the arrow. Continue to ask extending questions about the significance or implications of each difference. After the class diagram is completed, encourage students to add any similarities and differences they wish to their own diagrams. POSSIBLE ANSWERS: *With regard to faces, the triangle has one face, while the pyramid has many faces (or three faces). With regard to angles, the pyramid has more angles than the triangle (or the triangle has three angles, while the pyramid has twelve). With regard to thickness, the triangle is flat while the pyramid has depth (or is three-dimensional). With regard to weight, if both are made of the same material, the triangle will weigh less than the pyramid. With regard to faces, the triangle is one triangular face, while the pyramid has four.*

- **Now let's think about the similarities and differences on your diagram. There are many true things that we could say about the two figures that may not be very important. For example, both are made of wood. We want to base our understanding of the figures on factors that are important. Are there any similarities or differences that are not really important? Draw a line through them.** Student responses will vary.

- Now think about something interesting that you have learned about the two figures based on your comparison and contrast. What do the similarities and differences you have noted tell you about the figures? In the bottom box, write one sentence that expresses a conclusion or interpretation that is suggested by important similarities and differences. Ask students to write their conclusions. After they have had time to reflect and write, ask for three or four volunteers to read their statements to the whole class. POSSIBLE ANSWERS: *Triangles and pyramids are both shapes. Plane and solid figures are both shapes. Triangles have one face; pyramids have more than one face (have four faces). While triangles and pyramids both have triangular shapes, pyramids extend into space and triangles occur just on a surface. Pyramids are made of many triangles put together to enclose a space, not just a surface. In triangles, the lines surround an area; in pyramids the triangular sides surround a space with depth as well as height and width (a three-dimensional space). You can turn, flip, and slide both plane and solid figures, and the shape remains the same. Solid figures are built out of plane figures.*

- Let's see if your ideas about triangles and pyramids fit other plane and solid figures. First, work together with a partner, draw a plane figure and then draw the corresponding solid figure. Can you think of things that have these shapes? Name a few that you know. POSSIBLE ANSWERS: *A square and a cube, a rectangle and a rectangular solid, a circle and a sphere. Objects that have these shapes include a square piece of paper, a square playground, a square box (cube), a sugar cube, a dollar bill (rectangle), a trailer (rectangular solid), a house with a flat roof (rectangular solid), a zero (circle), the letter "O" (circle), a tennis ball (sphere), and the sun (sphere).*

- Discuss with your partner which conclusions that you reached by comparing and contrasting triangles and pyramids apply to the pairs of figures you have drawn. After giving students a few minutes to discuss the figures, ask for reports. Students deepen their understanding of the difference between two- and three-dimensional figures by noting that the other solid figures also have more edges, angles, and faces than the corresponding plane figure, even though the sides and angles may be equal. You may also prompt students to recognize that there are different types of solid figures such as cubes and rectangular solids (regular and irregular solids). Students can sort the solids into these categories.

- Create definitions of a plane figure and a solid figure based on your comparing and contrasting. Answers vary.

THINKING ABOUT THINKING

- Let's stop thinking about plane and solid figures for a moment and focus our attention on what we thought about in order to learn something important about these figures. The kind of thinking we did was called "comparing and contrasting." What did we do to compare and contrast a triangle with a pyramid? What, for example, did you think about first? Next? Prompt students to recall the steps in the process. Record their strategy on the board or use a transparency of the thinking map, uncovering each step as students identify it.

OPEN COMPARE AND CONTRAST
1. How are they similar?
2. How are they different?
3. What similarities and differences seem significant?
4. What interpretation or conclusion is suggested by the significant similarities and differences?

- How was the compare and contrast process different from just identifying similarities and differences? Is comparing and contrasting in this

way helpful in thinking about things? How? POSSIBLE ANSWERS: *Comparing and contrasting asks what kind of differences were found, determines which similarities and differences are important, and draws conclusions from the similarities and differences noted.* Students comment that this allows them to think about what the similarities and differences mean and to understand more clearly what they are comparing and contrasting.

• **Was using the graphic organizer helpful to you in this process? How?** Students answer that the graphic organizer allows them to write things down that they might forget otherwise. It also helps them to reach a conclusion.

• **Do you think that this is a valuable way to think about two things? Why or why not?** Answers vary.

APPLYING THINKING

Immediate Transfer

• Describe how you might use comparing and contrasting in making purchases.

• Compare and contrast regular and irregular solids.

Reinforcement Later

• Compare and contrast two different pieces of music or two pictures.

• Compare and contrast two plants or animals that we study in science.

• Compare and contrast two characters from stories you have read recently to understand how the two characters respond differently to situations in the stories.

CONTENT EXTENSION

Show students prisms and cylinders (irregular solids made of more than one kind of plane figure), and ask them to identify the plane figures from which they are constructed. If students are having difficulty, you can clarify the plane figures by creating a silhouette of the figure on the wall. Ask students to identify other figures that are constructed out of one or more plane figures.

Ask each student to plan and construct a solid figure from plane figures. Students can use long toothpicks and gumdrops or clay. Students should describe how their understanding of the relationship between plane and solid figures helped them to do this project. Then ask them to describe three-dimensional, man-made objects that have the shapes they have constructed. Ask them why the shape is important for that particular object. (For example, the roof of a house is often prism-shaped, so that rain will run off.)

ASSESSING STUDENT THINKING ABOUT COMPARING AND CONTRASTING

To assess this skill, ask students to write a paragraph and use a graphic organizer to compare and contrast two items like those in the application examples. If you want to use a mathematics example, ask them to compare and contrast different polygons or solid figures, and then ask them to write definitions of them, explaining the similarities and differences expressed in their definitions. Ask students to describe how they compared and contrasted the two items. Determine whether they are attending to each of the steps in the thinking map for comparing and contrasting.

Sample Student Responses • Triangles and Pyramids

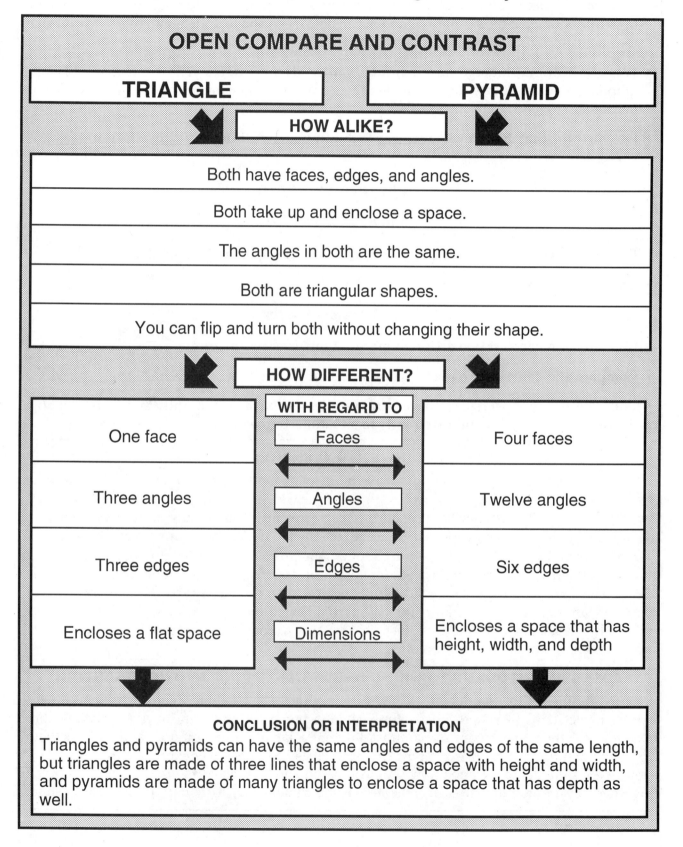

OPEN COMPARE AND CONTRAST

TRIANGLE	PYRAMID

HOW ALIKE?

Both have faces, edges, and angles.

Both take up and enclose a space.

The angles in both are the same.

Both are triangular shapes.

You can flip and turn both without changing their shape.

HOW DIFFERENT?

WITH REGARD TO

TRIANGLE		PYRAMID
One face	Faces	Four faces
Three angles	Angles	Twelve angles
Three edges	Edges	Six edges
Encloses a flat space	Dimensions	Encloses a space that has height, width, and depth

CONCLUSION OR INTERPRETATION

Triangles and pyramids can have the same angles and edges of the same length, but triangles are made of three lines that enclose a space with height and width, and pyramids are made of many triangles to enclose a space that has depth as well.

MUFARO'S BEAUTIFUL DAUGHTERS

Literature   **Grades 3–5**

OBJECTIVES

CONTENT

Students will interpret the morals of two similar stories and identify details in each story that affect its moral. Students will learn about the background and values of the cultures from which these stories come.

THINKING SKILL/PROCESS

Students will compare and contrast effectively by determining similarities and differences, by detecting patterns in significant similarities and differences, and by developing an interpretation based on them.

METHODS AND MATERIALS

CONTENT

This lesson features John Steptoe's *Mufaro's Beautiful Daughters* (Lothrop, Lee, Shephard, Books, New York, 1987), a story based on a Zimbabwe folktale. Students use illustrations in the story to clarify details. The Grimm version of the *Cinderella* story should be reviewed prior to instruction (in contrast to the Walt Disney version).

THINKING SKILL/PROCESS

Compare and contrast is guided by structured questioning and the use of a graphic organizer. (See pp. 102–107 for reproducible diagrams.) Using the Think/Pair/Share technique prompts reflection and reconsideration to promote clear expression of the conclusion.

LESSON

INTRODUCTION TO CONTENT AND THINKING SKILL/PROCESS

- **Think about a time when you heard a story that was similar to one you already knew. Write the names of the two stories. Try to recall the similarities that reminded you that you had heard a story like this before. Write down some of the similarities also.** Allow time for writing and reflection. Students usually identify incidents in the plot or descriptions of main characters that related to a story they had already heard.

- **What were some of the differences between the two stories?** Allow time for students to write down two or three differences.

- **When you noticed similarities and differences, you were "comparing and contrasting." Think about whether comparing and contrasting the stories gave you any new ideas about either story. For example, one of the stories may be more interesting now, or your ideas about one of the characters may be different. Write a few words that help you remember how your ideas changed.**

- **Describe the example to your partner. Explain how knowing a similar story affected your understanding, enjoyment, or enthusiasm for the new one.** Allow peer discussion. Briefly discuss three or four examples provided by the students.

- **We're going to read a folktale from Africa called *Mufaro's Beautiful Daughters*. A folktale is a story that people have been telling for a long time. Folktales tell us something about the customs and habits of the group of people who have been telling the story. This folktale describes how two sisters participate in a king's search to find a maiden worthy to be queen. What other stories do you know about a royal search for a wife?** Students mention *Cinderella*.

Ask the students to describe the events in the traditional *Cinderella* story, and display the illustrations in the story as they describe it.

THINKING ACTIVELY

• **As you read** *Mufaro's Beautiful Daughters***, compare and contrast it with** *Cinderella.* **Use this compare and contrast diagram. Be alert to ways that this story and** *Cinderella* **are alike. Each time you find a similarity, write it on a line in the box under "How Alike?" Also look for ways that the stories are different. Write the differences on the lines under "How Different?" Think about what that difference means and write it on the arrow under "With Regard To."** For example, *Mufaro's Beautiful Daughters* takes place in Africa; *Cinderella* takes place in Europe. What term describes that difference? *Location.* **Write the term over the arrow.** Before students start reading, explain that in *Mufaro's Beautiful Daughters,* the characters' names describe their traits. Just as Cinderella's name described her as a servant "among the cinders," in the Shona language Manyara means "ashamed" and Nyasha means "mercy." Give the students enough time to list at least three similarities and three differences on the diagram. Encourage students to examine the illustrations for additional details.

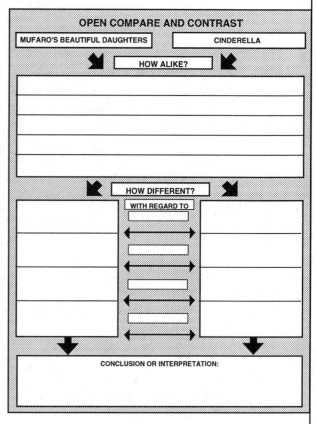

• **How are the stories alike?** After they have finished reading the story, randomly call on four or five students to report one similarity that they have found. Record their responses on an overhead transparency or on a large diagram on the chalkboard. Draw out the student's thoughts by asking for clarification or extension of the responses—the cause, effect, significance, implications, etc. POSSIBLE ANSWERS: *Both stories describe a contest between daughters, a royal marriage for the girl selected, the use of magic, kindness winning out over selfishness, a time when kings and queens were rulers.*

• **How are the stories different?** Record differences, asking what each difference describes and writing it on the arrow. Continue to ask extending questions about the cause, effect, significance, or implications of each difference. After the class diagram is completed, encourage students to add any similarities and differences they wish to their own diagrams. POSSIBLE ANSWERS: *With regard to location,* Mufaro's Beautiful Daughters *takes place in Africa,* Cinderella *in Europe. The father is the only parent in* Mufaro's Beautiful Daughters, *but the father and stepmother are the parents in* Cinderella. *In* Mufaro's Beautiful Daughters, *the sisters are natural sisters, in* Cinderella, *they are stepsisters. In* Mufaro's Beautiful Daughters, *the future queen is chosen because of worthiness and beauty; in* Cinderella, *she is selected only because of beauty. With regard to the use of magic, in* Mufaro's Beautiful Daughters, *magic is used to test a worthy character; in* Cinderella, *magic is used to help a beautiful girl unfairly treated. In* Mufaro's Beautiful Daughters, *the prince recognizes the girl selected by her responses, while in* Cinderella, *he recognizes her by her foot fitting into her slipper.*

- **Now let's think about the similarities and differences on your diagram. There are many true things that we could say about the two stories that may not be very important. For example, both stories are about people and are read to children. However, many stories that are read to children are about people. That similarity does not tell us anything important about these two stories. We want to base our understanding of the stories on factors that are important. Draw a line through any similarities and differences that are not important.** Student responses will vary.

- **Now think about something interesting that you have learned about the two stories based on your comparing and contrasting. What do the similarities and differences you have noted tell you about the stories or about the people in the stories? In the bottom box, write one sentence that expresses a conclusion or interpretation that is suggested by important similarities and differences in the stories.** Ask students to write their conclusions.

- **We're going to do an activity called "Think-Pair-Share." Each of you should pair up with a partner. One student in the pair should then read his or her statement. The partner serves as a listener to assist the speaker in expressing the conclusion clearly. The listener may only ask questions:**

    Questions of clarification: If you don't understand what a word means or the meaning of the statement, you may ask questions which help you understand what is being said. For example, you may ask, "What do you mean when you say ———?"

    Questions which extend the idea: If you think your partner is saying something interesting, but it is too brief, you can ask for more details about your partner's idea. You might say something like "What more can you tell me about ———?"

    Questions to challenge what is said: If you think the speaker is mislead or confused, you may ask questions like "Why do you think ———?" Maybe the speaker will explain why and you won't think the statement is confused anymore, or maybe the speaker will reconsider part of the statement.

After two minutes of reflection, signal students to change roles. After both partners have served as speaker and listener, allow students an opportunity to rewrite their statement in any way they see fit. Ask for volunteers to read their statements to the class. For grades four and five, ask each student to read the statement a second time so that other students can listen to each statement twice, once for content and once to identify the kind of statement the student is reading (comparison, contrast, both comparison and contrast, cause/effect, generalization, etc.). Ask the class where on the diagram the student can get supporting details if the statement was the main idea for an essay assignment. Create a composite bulletin board of students' conclusions about the two stories.

Students' conclusions often include the comment that worthy character, rather than beauty, is a more significant quality for a queen in *Mufaro's Beautiful Daughters*, in contrast to *Cinderella* where the choice is made on the basis of beauty only. The class may discuss whether some qualities are more important than a person's appearance. POSSIBLE CONCLUSIONS: *The* Cinderella *story leads people to believe that magic will help them while* Mufaro's Beautiful Daughters *leads people to believe that worthiness matters. Kind people show their kindness in many ways, even toward people who have shown them unkindness.*

- **When we study what people believe, what they think is important, what they make, and how they act, we are studying what is called their "culture." Folktales like *Mufaro's Beautiful Daughters* can sometimes tell us about the culture of the people described in the folktale. Of course, it is important to check these ideas by finding out what these people were actually like.**

Let's think about what this folktale suggests about the culture in which Mufaro and his daughters lived. With your partner, list some things about this culture that you can tell from the story. Then we'll share some of these ideas. After giving students a few minutes to discuss this with their partners, ask them to report what they've listed. POSSIBLE ANSWERS: *Some people lived in wealthy cities. Some were farmers. Kings and queens ruled these regions. This culture lived a long time ago. This culture was in Africa. People in this culture felt that being honest and doing good things were very important.*

After students have responded and their ideas have been written on the board, help them to classify these ideas into standard categories used to describe a culture. List categories like "When the culture lived," "Where the culture lived," "What occupations the people had," "How the people were governed," and "Beliefs and values of the people." Put their ideas under these categories. Discuss with them the idea that cultures are not defined simply by describing where the people live, what they wear, and how they are governed. Rather, what the people believe and value often makes a culture what it is and distinguishes it from other cultures. If the students have not suggested any ideas about the beliefs and values of the people in the story, explain that those ideas are important in understanding a culture. Ask them directly what the story suggests about the beliefs and values of the people.

THINKING ABOUT THINKING

- **Let's stop thinking about *Mufaro's Beautiful Daughters* and *Cinderella* and focus our attention on how we thought about these stories. The kind of thinking we did was called "comparing and contrasting." What did we do to compare and contrast *Mufaro's Beautiful Daughters* and *Cinderella*? What, for example, did you think about first? Next?** Prompt students to recall the steps in the process. Record their strategy on the board or use a transparency of the thinking map, uncovering each step as students identify it. Review the discussion for each step of the thinking map of open compare and contrast.

> **OPEN COMPARE AND CONTRAST**
>
> 1. How are they similar?
>
> 2. How are they different?
>
> 3. What similarities and differences seem significant?
>
> 4. What interpretation or conclusion is suggested by the significant similarities and differences?

- **How was the compare and contrast process different from just identifying similarities and differences?** Student answers should focus on thinking about the differences by asking what kind of differences they are, looking for patterns in the similarities and differences, and drawing conclusions from the similarities and differences noted.

- **Is comparing and contrasting in this way helpful in thinking about things? How?** Many students find this helpful because it allows them to consider what the similarities and differences mean and to improve their understanding about what they are comparing and contrasting.

- **How did the way that you compared and contrasted the stories differ from the way we usually read stories in class?** Students say that this strategy helps them look for important information as they read, in contrast to just attending to what happens in the story.

- **Was using the graphic organizer helpful to you in this process? How?** Students comment that using the diagram assists them in recording details that they notice and might otherwise forget. They also say that the diagram prompts them to draw a conclusion from the similarities and differences they have listed.

• **Do you think that this is a valuable way to think about two stories? Why or why not?** ANSWERS VARY.

APPLYING THINKING

Immediate Transfer

• Describe how you might use comparing and contrasting in making purchases.

• Compare and contrast two characters from stories you have read recently to understand how the two characters responded differently to conditions in the stories.

• Compare and contrast two leaders we have studied. How do you understand them differently by thinking about them this way?

Reinforcement Later

• Compare and contrast two different pieces of music or two pictures.

• Compare and contrast two plants or animals that we will be studying in science.

RESEARCH EXTENSION

By comparing and contrasting other stories that resemble *Cinderella*, students recognize the universal appeal of the story and how cultural values are expressed in the different versions. Examples include

The Egyptian Cinderella, Shirley Climo (Harper Trophy Publishers, New York, 1992) recounts the legend of Rhodopis, wife of Pharaoh Amasis in 526 B.C.

Yeh-Shen: A Cinderella Story from China, Ai-Ling-Louie (Philomel Books, New York, 1982) from the T'ang Dynasty, 618–907 A. D.

Moss Gown, William H. Hooks (Clarion Books, New York, 1987) tidewater North Carolina version of *Cinderella* mixed with a variant on *King Lear*

Aschenbradel, the German *Cinderella*

The Talking Eggs, by Robert San Souci (Dial Press, New York)

The Walt Disney version of *Cinderella* and the version by the Brothers Grimm.

The Brocaded Slipper and Other Vietnamese Tales, Ed. Lynette Dyer Young

With the assistance of the librarian, students may also locate and compare versions of other folktales in various cultures, using the thinking maps to organize their comments, and reporting orally and/or with a poster of the graphic organizer. Similar pairs include

Lon Po Po, a Red Riding Hood Story from China; *Mem Fox*, by Winifred McPherson, the Southern folk version; and the traditional *Red Riding Hood*

Doctor Coyote by John Bierholst (Macmillan: New York, 1987) and *Aesop's Fables*

Irashaniatero, the Sea King (PBS Reading Rainbow Series) and *Rip Van Winkle*

RESEARCH EXTENSION

Ask students to find books in the school library about various African cultures in the Middle Ages to verify whether their ideas about the culture described in *Mufaro's Beautiful Daughters* are accurate. Ask students to compare and contrast these African cultures with European culture in the Middle Ages, using the techniques in this lesson.

ASSESSING STUDENT THINKING ABOUT COMPARING AND CONTRASTING

To assess this skill, ask students to write an essay and use a graphic organizer to answer any of the application questions or others which you select. Ask students to describe how they compared and contrasted the two subjects. Determine whether they are attending to each of the steps in the thinking map for comparing and contrasting.

Sample Student Responses • Mufaro's Beautiful Daughters

OPEN COMPARE AND CONTRAST

MUFARO'S BEAUTIFUL DAUGHTERS	CINDERELLA

HOW ALIKE?

Both describe rivalry between daughters in a family.

Both result in a royal marriage for the girl selected.

In both stories, magic allows animals to change form.

In both stories, kindness wins out over selfishness.

Both stories occur at a time when kings and queens were rulers.

In both stories, the girl selected to be queen comes from the common people.

Both stories have a happy ending.

HOW DIFFERENT?

WITH REGARD TO

MUFARO'S BEAUTIFUL DAUGHTERS		CINDERELLA
The story takes place in Africa.	LOCATION	The story takes place in Europe.
The father is the only parent in the story.	PARENTS	There is a father and a stepmother, but the stepmother makes most of the decisions.
The sisters were natural sisters.	RELATIONSHIP	The sisters were stepsisters.
Magic is used to test the girls who would be queen.	USE OF MAGIC	Magic is used to help the girl who is unfairly treated.
The king picks his bride for her worthiness and beauty.	WHY CHOSEN	The prince picks his bride for her beauty alone.

CONCLUSION OR INTERPRETATION:

Worthiness, as well as beauty, is important in choosing a queen in the African folktale, but beauty alone is important in the European tale.

ABRAHAM LINCOLN AND FREDERICK DOUGLASS

American History   **Grades 5–12**

OBJECTIVES

CONTENT

Students will learn about the roles of Abraham Lincoln and Frederick Douglass in ending slavery in this country and will clarify the difference between being opposed to slavery and being an abolitionist.

THINKING SKILL/PROCESS

Students will compare and contrast effectively by determining similarities and differences between two leaders, by detecting patterns in the significant similarities and differences, and by developing an interpretation or conclusion based on the similarities and differences.

METHODS AND MATERIALS

CONTENT

This lesson features passages about Lincoln and Douglass used in conjunction with background knowledge about them. Guided reading, random calling, higher order questioning, and directed essay writing are employed in this lesson.

THINKING SKILL/PROCESS

Compare and contrast is guided by structured questioning and the use of a graphic organizer. (See pp. 102–107 for reproducible diagrams.) A think/pair/share activity is used to encourage the clear expression of students' conclusions about the two men.

LESSON

INTRODUCTION TO CONTENT AND THINKING SKILL/PROCESS

- Think about a time that you understood something better, or learned to do something more easily, by relating it to what you already knew. For example, when people move from one place to another, they usually note similarities and differences between their new location and their former home. Perhaps the school bus stop is within walking distance in both places but is farther away in the new location than it was where they used to live. Recognizing the difference in distance will help in planning when to leave for the bus. It should probably be earlier than in the previous location.

- When you notice similarities and differences and use that information to make a decision or judgment, you are "comparing and contrasting." Describe to your partner an example in which you learned something important by comparing and contrasting. Explain how comparing and contrasting the new thing with something you already knew helped you to understand or do things better. After peer discussion, briefly discuss three or four examples.

- In this lesson we are going to learn about the lives of two leaders—Abraham Lincoln and Frederick Douglass. Which do we know better? *Abraham Lincoln.*

- What do we know about Abraham Lincoln and the time in which he lived that might help us understand the experiences of Frederick Douglass, who lived at the same time? Students may discuss conditions in the United States prior to the Civil War, including their understanding of slavery and the legal debate surrounding it, as well as the fact that Lincoln was president during the Civil War.

THINKING ACTIVELY

- First read the passage about Abraham Lincoln. As you read the information about Frederick Douglass, be alert to ways that he and Lincoln are alike. Each time you find a similarity, write it on a line in the box of the diagram under "How Alike." Also, look for ways that Lincoln and Douglass are different. Write the differences on the lines under "How Different." Think about what that difference means and write it over the arrow. For example, Abraham Lincoln was Caucasian and Frederick Douglass was Black. What term describes that difference? *Race.* Write "race" over the arrow. Give the students enough time to list at least three similarities and three differences on the diagram. After they have finished reading the passages, call on students randomly to report similarities and differences that they have found. Ask for only one similarity or difference from each student. Record their responses on a transparency, on an overhead projector, or on a large diagram on the chalkboard. Encourage students to add any similarities or differences that they find interesting, suggested by other class members, to their individual diagrams.

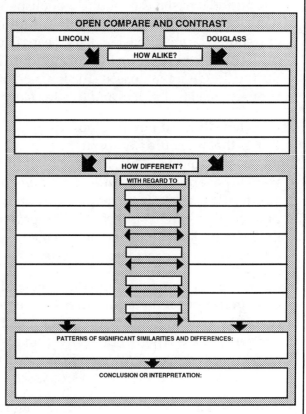

- **How are Abraham Lincoln and Frederick Douglass alike?** After they have finished reading the passages, randomly call on four or five students to report one similarity that they have found. Record their responses on an overhead transparency or on a large diagram on the chalkboard. Draw out the student's thoughts by asking for clarification or extension of the responses—the cause, effect, significance, implications, etc. POSSIBLE ANSWERS: *Both men lived in the same period, were born into very poor families, were self-educated, were intelligent, lost their mothers at an early age, spent their young adulthood on farms, and moved from border slave states to free states. Both men used language to persuade others and contributed to ending slavery in America.*

- **How are Abraham Lincoln and Frederick Douglass different?** Record differences, asking what each difference describes and writing it over the arrow. Continue to ask extending questions about the cause, effect, significance or implications of each difference between the two men. After the class diagram is completed, encourage students to add any similarities and differences they wish to their own diagrams. POSSIBLE ANSWERS: *Lincoln was Caucasian; Douglass was of African descent. Lincoln was born free with all the civil rights guaranteed to Americans; Douglass was born a slave with no civil rights, even the right to life. Lincoln was born free; Douglass purchased his freedom. Lincoln was a lawyer and a politician; Douglass was a writer and newspaper publisher. Lincoln used the war powers of the presidency to free slaves in the confederate states; Douglass used his newspaper to influence public opinion regarding rights and opportunities for blacks. Lincoln was assassinated at age 56; Douglass died of natural causes at age 77. Lincoln was primarily an orator; Douglass was both an orator and writer. Students also include among the differences that while both men opposed slavery, Douglass was an abolitionist and Lincoln was not.* To clarify the distinction between being an abolitionist and just opposing slavery, students' comments or teacher explanations may include the following factors: Abolitionists believed that the assumption that one person could own another was wrong and that slavery should be abolished by whatever means necessary. Lincoln, on the other hand, believed that while slavery was undesirable, should not be extended to new territories, and should be abandoned if legal means could be found to do so, it was nevertheless sanctioned by the right to property in the Constitution. The war powers of the president, invoked by Lincoln during the Civil War to issue the Emancipation Proclamation, allowed Lincoln to confiscate the property of slaveholders and free the slaves by legal means.

- **Now let's think about the similarities and differences on your diagram. There are many true things that we could say about the two men that may not be very important. For example, both men wore trousers. This, however, does not add to our understanding of these two men. We want to base our understanding of them on factors that are important. Draw a line through any similarities and differences that are not important.** Student responses will vary. Students may predictably ask what is meant by "important." Any information, the omission of which would limit our understanding of the two men, their characters and interests, and/or their impact on others would be considered important.

- **Are there any common ideas that you find in the important similarities and differences? For example, many of the similarities and differences mentioned describe the backgrounds of the two men. What other patterns of similarities and differences do you find? Write these in the "patterns" box.** After students have an opportunity to reflect and write, ask for three or four responses. POSSIBLE ANSWERS: *Their backgrounds, the value they placed on education, their impact on slavery, their rise from poverty to become self-supporting in distinguished professions.*

- **Now think about something interesting that you have learned about the two men based on your comparing and contrasting. What do the similarities and differences you have noted tell you about Abraham Lincoln and Frederick Douglass? In the bottom box, write one sentence that expresses a conclusion or interpretation that is suggested by important similarities and differences in the lives of the two men.** Ask students to write their conclusions.

- **We're going to do an activity called "Think-Pair-Share." Each of you should pair up with a partner. One student in the pair should then read his or her statement. The partner serves as a listener to assist the speaker in expressing the conclusion clearly. The listener may only ask questions:**

    <u>Questions of clarification</u>: If you don't understand what a word means or the meaning of the statement, you may ask questions which help you understand what is being said. For example, you may ask, "What do you mean when you say ———?"

    <u>Questions which extend the idea</u>: If you think your partner is saying something interesting, but it is too brief, you can ask for more details about your partner's idea. You might say something like "What more can you tell me about ———?"

    <u>Questions to challenge what is said</u>: If you think the speaker is misled or confused, you may ask questions that you think may prompt your partner to rethink or restate some part of his or her statement like "Why do you think ———?" Maybe the speaker will explain why and you won't think the statement is confused anymore, or maybe the speaker will reconsider aspects of the statement.

    After two minutes of reflection, signal students to change roles. After both partners have served as speaker and listener, allow students an opportunity to rewrite their statement in any way they see fit. Ask for volunteers to read their statements to the whole class. Ask them to repeat their statements so that other students can listen to each statement twice, once for content and once to identify the kind of statement the student is reading (comparison, contrast, both comparison and contrast, cause/effect, generalization, etc.). Ask the class which details from the diagram could be used to support the conclusion if the statement was the main idea for an essay assignment. Create a composite bulletin board of students' conclusions about the two stories. POSSIBLE ANSWERS: *Although Lincoln and Douglass experienced hardship and limitations as young men, they were able to rise to positions of influence and power. Abraham Lincoln and Frederick Douglass were of different races but worked for the same purpose. While Lincoln and Douglass opposed slavery for different reasons, they both contributed significantly to ending it in this country. Both men showed determination in bettering themselves and, through this achievement, bettered the lives of countless others in this country. Frederick Douglass, in contrast to Abraham Lincoln, had to win his freedom and then used its advantages to work for the freedom of Blacks and for women's suffrage.*

THINKING ABOUT THINKING

- **Let's stop thinking about Lincoln and Douglass and focus our attention on what we did to think about these two men in order to learn something important about them. The kind of thinking we did was called "comparing and contrasting." What did we do to compare and contrast Lincoln and Douglass? What, for example, did you think about first? Next?** Prompt students to recall the steps in the process. Record their strategy on the board or use a transparency of the thinking map, uncovering each step as students identify it. Review the discussion for each step of the thinking map of open compare and contrast.

OPEN COMPARE AND CONTRAST
1. How are they similar?
2. How are they different?
3. What similarities and differences seem significant?
4. What categories or pattern do you see in the significant similarities and differences?
5. What interpretation or conclusion is suggested by the significant similarities and differences?

- **How was the compare-and-contrast process different from just identifying similarities and differences?** Student answers should focus on thinking about the differences by asking what kind of differences they are, by looking for patterns in the similarities and differences, and by drawing conclusions from the similarities and differences noted.

- **Is comparing and contrasting in this way helpful in thinking about things? How?** Students comment that it allows them to think about what the similarities and differences mean.

- **How did the way that you compared and contrasted the two men differ from the way you usually study historical characters?** Students say that comparing and contrasting helps them look for important information as they read about these people, in contrast to just attending to their names and when they lived. Students often comment that this process "personalizes" these leaders in the sense that they seem like real people.

- **Was using the graphic organizer helpful to you? How?** Students comment that using the diagram assists them in recording details that they notice and might otherwise forget. They also say that the graphic organizer helps them draw a conclusion from the similarities and differences they have listed.

- **In the Think-Pair-Share activity, was writing out your statement beforehand important?** Students recognize that, for clarity and ownership, having their thoughts written down before discussion frees them to examine the meaning and implications of their conclusions.

APPLYING THINKING

Immediate Transfer

- Compare and contrast the experiences of Frederick Douglass and Josiah Henson, the escaped slave whose life is depicted as "Uncle Tom" in Harriet Beecher Stowe's *Uncle Tom's Cabin*, to illustrate life under slavery, escape, and assistance to other slaves.

- We are studying Sojourner Truth and Harriet Beecher Stowe. Compare and contrast the two women to examine how they affected public opinion about slavery.

- We have been studying conditions in the North and the South at the start of the Civil War. Compare and contrast the population, industry, food production, coastline, and railroads in the North and the South to determine their relative ability to sustain a lengthy war.

- Compare and contrast literary works about Lincoln and Douglass. What do these works tell us about the writers' views of these two men? Lincoln poems include "When Lilacs Last on the Dooryard Bloomed" and "Oh Captain, My Captain" by Walt Whitman; "What is God's Will" and "Abraham Lincoln" by Stephen Vincent Benet; and "Lincoln" by John Gould Fletcher. Douglass Poems include "I Was Frederick Douglass" by Hildegard Smith and "Frederick Douglass" by Paul Laurence Dunbar.

- Compare and contrast two characters from stories you have read recently to understand how the two characters responded differently to conditions in the stories.

- Compare and contrast two breakfast cereals in order to decide which is a better buy and which is more nutritious.

Reinforcement Later

- Compare and contrast two different pieces of music or stories.

- Compare and contrast the civil rights of blacks and whites during Reconstruction.

FOCUSED COMPARE AND CONTRAST OPTION

This lesson can be taught as a focused compare and contrast lesson. If you take this option, use the focused compare and contrast graphic organizer, and guide students to compare and contrast Lincoln and Douglass. They should define the purpose of the comparison and contrast, list the factors to consider in order to achieve this purpose, and then search in the passages for information about Lincoln and Douglass that falls into the categories they have specified. As they find information, it should be recorded under "How Alike" or "How Different," as appropriate. Sample student responses using a focused compare and contrast graphic organizer are included on page 128.

RESEARCH EXTENSION

Corroborate details in the passages about Lincoln and Douglass by consulting other works in the school library. Make sure your sources are reliable. Modify your comparison and contrast diagram, if necessary, to reflect what you find. Students may obtain more information from biographies of Lincoln and Douglass. *Two Roads to Greatness* (Macmillan Company, New York, 1967) provides biographical and literary works about the two leaders.

WRITING EXTENSION

Use your concluding statement as the main idea or conclusion for a short essay about Lincoln and Douglass. Use what you have written in the graphic organizer for your supporting details. You may include additional information about the two leaders from resources you find in the school library.

ASSESSING STUDENTS' THINKING ABOUT COMPARING AND CONTRASTING

To assess this skill, ask students to write an essay on any of the application questions or others which you select, using a graphic organizer to assist themselves. Ask students to describe how they compared and contrasted the two subjects. Determine whether they are attending to each of the steps in the thinking map for comparing and contrasting.

ABRAHAM LINCOLN AND FREDERICK DOUGLASS

Abraham Lincoln

Abraham Lincoln was born in Hardin County, Kentucky in 1809. When he was eight, the family moved to Spencer County, Indiana, where he grew up. His mother died when he was ten years old. Since his family was very poor, Lincoln began working at an early age. Although there were some schools in the Indiana territory, he had little formal schooling and was largely self-taught. He worked on a farm until he was twenty-two years old, and then in 1831 moved to Menard County, Illinois, where he worked as a clerk in a store. From 1834 to 1840, Lincoln served in the Illinois legislature, studied to become a lawyer, and moved to Springfield, Illinois, to practice law. He served one term in the U. S. House of Representatives from 1847 to 1849 then returned to his law practice.

In 1860, Abraham Lincoln was elected president of the United States. He immediately was faced with the secession of southern states from the Union and the beginning of the Civil War. Although he disapproved of slavery, Lincoln was not an abolitionist (one who believed that slavery should be done away with). He recognized that slave owners had paid for their slaves. Since slaves were considered to be property, it was believed to be unlawful to take someone's property away. Once the southern states had become enemies of the Union, President Lincoln used his war powers as Commander-in-Chief of the Army to abolish slavery in the southern states. In September 1862, Lincoln proclaimed that unless the southern states rejoined the Union by January 1, 1863, their slave property would be considered legally confiscated. Thus, Lincoln acquired the legal right to free the slaves.

Abraham Lincoln was re-elected President in 1864 but was assassinated in 1865.

Frederick Douglass

Frederick Douglass was born a slave in Tuckahoe, Maryland. Since slaves were seldom told their ages, Douglass estimated that he was born about 1818. His mother, Harriet Bailey, was hired out to a distant farmer shortly after his birth and died when Douglass was about eight years old. Like many slaves, Douglass never knew who his father was.

Frederick Douglass was taught the alphabet by Mrs. Thomas Auld until his master, Mr. Auld, discovered that she was teaching Frederick to read. It was unlawful to teach a slave to read. Frederick realized that reading was an important distinction between slaves and free men. Frederick taught himself to write by copying words in the spaces of his young master's writing book.

In 1838, Douglass bluffed his way onto a train to Delaware, a slave state, then went by boat to Philadelphia and freedom. He moved to Massachusetts and selected the name Douglass to replace his slave name.

Douglass bought his freedom from his old master. In 1847, he started a newspaper in Rochester, New York, advocating the abolition of slavery and supporting women's voting rights.

Douglass encouraged Lincoln to include black troops in the Union Army and used the power of his newspaper to encourage blacks to enlist. The first black regiment was formed in 1863, with Douglass' own sons among the first to enlist. In 1864, Douglass met with Lincoln to secure the same wages, protection, and awards for black soldiers as for white soldiers.

In 1866, Douglass was the only black delegate elected to attend the post-war convention on reconstruction. In 1877, President Hayes appointed Douglass marshal of the District of Columbia. He later served as the U. S. representative to Haiti.

Frederick Douglass died in 1895 of a heart attack.

Adapted from *Organizing Thinking Book II* by Sandra Parks and Howard Black, Critical Thinking Press & Software.

Sample Student Responses • Lincoln and Douglass

OPEN COMPARE AND CONTRAST

| ABRAHAM LINCOLN | FREDERICK DOUGLASS |

 HOW ALIKE?

Both were born into very poor families.

Both were self-educated.

Both used language to persuade others.

Both contributed to ending slavery in the United States.

 HOW DIFFERENT?

WITH REGARD TO

ABRAHAM LINCOLN		FREDERICK DOUGLASS
He was born a free citizen with all the rights guaranteed to Americans.	**CIVIL RIGHTS**	He was born a slave with none of the rights guaranteed to Americans.
His opportunities were not limited by his race.	**EFFECTS OF RACE**	Even as a free black man, his opportunities were limited.
He was opposed to slavery but was not an abolitionist.	**ABOLITION**	He was an abolitionist who believed that one person could not own another.
He used the War Powers Act to free slaves and establish military service for blacks.	**INFLUENCE**	He used his newspaper to inspire both blacks and whites to respect the rights of blacks.

PATTERNS OF SIGNIFICANT SIMILARITIES AND DIFFERENCES:
Family background, leadership, effect on ending slavery.

CONCLUSION OR INTERPRETATION:
Both men showed determination to better themselves and, through this achievement, used its advantages to better the lives of countless others in this country.

Sample Student Responses • Lincoln and Douglass • Focused Compare and Contrast

FOCUSED COMPARE AND CONTRAST

LINCOLN	DOUGLASS

GOALS: To clarify how Lincoln and Douglass contributed to ending slavery in the United States

FACTORS TO CONSIDER: Goals, priorities, attitudes towards slavery, methods, accomplishments, effectiveness

FACTORS CONSIDERED IN THIS ACTIVITY:

Goals

Methods

Effectiveness

HOW ALIKE?

They opposed slavery.

They both used language persuasively.

Both influenced a great many people to oppose slavery.

HOW DIFFERENT?

Priorities	To save the Union and uphold the Constitution while opposing slavery	Abolition of slavery
Attitudes towards slavery	Believed slavery was unacceptable, (though it was legal)	Believed that no person could own another
Methods	Legal means; the power of the presidency	Oratory and writings; any means acceptable
Accomplishments	The Emancipation Proclamation	Newspaper and his own writings
Effectiveness	Legally freed slaves in southern states.	Increased public awareness of the plight of slaves

CONCLUSION OR INTERPRETATION:

While both Lincoln and Douglass worked towards the goal of ending slavery, Lincoln was constrained by legal considerations, regarding slaves as property, that Douglass did not accept, but ultimately Lincoln used the power of the presidency to work within the law to free slaves.

COMPARING AND CONTRASTING LESSON CONTEXTS

The following examples have been suggested by classroom teachers as contexts in which to develop infusion lessons. If a skill or process has been introduced in a previous lesson, transfer activities can be designed in these contexts to reinforce it.

GRADE	SUBJECT	TOPIC	THINKING ISSUE
K–3	Reading	Mythology	Compare and contrast different versions of Pandora's Box in order to understand how each explains human character and the origin of evil.
K–3	Reading	*City Mouse and Country Mouse*	Compare and contrast the city mouse and country mouse (need for food, instincts, effects of location, type of danger, state of mind, effect of sounds, preference of food) to clarify their values.
K–3	Reading	Book characters	Compare and contrast characters in a book with characters in a movie version of the same story to understand how using different media can change the significance of characters.
K–3	Reading	Comparing fiction and nonfiction	Select two books or films about dogs, one factual and one fiction. Compare and contrast the dogs in the two stories as a basis for clarifying reality and fantasy.
K–3	Reading	"Sleeping Ugly" by Jane Yolen	Compare and contrast this story with the classic Sleeping Beauty story with regard to the story's values about inner and outer beauty.
K–3	Social studies	Jobs	Compare and contrast jobs in order to be able to draw a conclusion about their desirability.
K–3	Social studies	Communities	Compare and contrast your community with another one to decide in which you would prefer to live (considering population, climate, location, industry, cultural factors, ethnic factors, etc.).
K–3	Social studies	Transportation	Compare and contrast land, sea, air, and space vehicles in order to clarify their operation, use, comfort, fuel, distance, speed, and cargo.
K–3	Social studies	Laws	Compare and contrast rules and laws with regard to how much weight they carry and how they are made.
K–3	Social studies	Maps	Compare and contrast maps and globes (accuracy, information, map key, etc.) to clarify their use.
K–3	Social studies	Geography	Compare and contrast longitude and latitude in order to be able to read maps effectively.
K–3	Social studies	Communities	Compare and contrast characteristics of small towns and big cities regarding the quality of life.
K–3	Science	Animals	What do the footprints of ducks, bears, eagles, and deer tell you about their habitats, locomotion, and food habits?
K–3	Science	Plants/animals	Compare and contrast the characteristics of plants and animals to determine the conditions needed for life.
K-3	Science	Photosynthesis	Compare and contrast food production in leaves exposed to light and leaves kept in the dark.

COMPARING AND CONTRASTING LESSON CONTEXTS

GRADE	SUBJECT	TOPIC	THINKING ISSUE
K–3	Science	Rabbit/ hamster	Compare and contrast these animals in order to prevent confusing them.
K–3	Science	Ball/wheel	Compare and contrast a ball and a wheel to clarify their uses, properties, and movements.
K–3	Science	Earth/moon	Compare and contrast the Earth and the moon to illustrate their relative sizes and positions in relation to the sun.
K–3	Science	Energy	Compare and contrast energy and fuel to clarify that energy is not a substance that gets used up.
K–3	Science	Fruit/cones	Compare and contrast fruit and cones, especially with regard to structure, in order to evaluate their function in protecting and disseminating seeds.
K–3	Science	Soil	Compare and contrast silt, clay, and sand to decide which would be the best choice for use in a sandbox on the playground.
K–3	Science	Weather	Compare and contrast types of clouds to connect their characteristics to weather conditions.
K–3	Science	Dinosaurs	Compare and contrast the dinosaur's sizes to known objects to illustrate the diversity of size among the dinosaurs, e.g., Compsognathus, 80 cm., similar to chicken; Deinonychus, 150 cm., similar to a person; Apatosaurus, 22 meters, length of two school buses.
K–3	Science	Animals	Compare and contrast characteristics of reptiles and amphibians (metamorphosis, habitat, skin covering, etc.) in order to tell reptiles and amphibians apart.
K–3	Mathematics	Time	Compare and contrast the hands of a clock (size, what they indicate, how fast they move) to explain how to tell time.
K–3	Mathematics	Money	Compare and contrast the size, shape, color and value of various pieces of money.
K–3	Mathematics	Polygons	Compare and contrast various polygons to clarify their definitions.
K–3	Mathematics	Congruence	Compare and contrast congruent and similar figures in order to determine the meaning of congruence.
K–3	Art	Colors	Compare and contrast the use and effect of cool and warm colors.
K–3	Art	Lines	Compare and contrast the lines in two selected pictures to determine the effect of straight, curving, wavy, or zigzag lines.
K–3	Music	Rhythm	Compare and contrast the rhythm in two selected songs to illustrate the difference between accent and tempo.
K–3	Health	Drugs	Compare and contrast "good" and "bad" uses of drugs to determine any benefits in using drugs and to show the need for caution.

COMPARING AND CONTRASTING LESSON CONTEXTS

GRADE	SUBJECT	TOPIC	THINKING ISSUE
K–3	Guidance	Wants/needs	Compare and contrast wants and needs with regard to how they affect our behavior.
4–6	Language arts	Grammar	Compare and contrast adjectives and adverbs to clarify what they modify and how they are formed.
4–6	Language arts	Biographies	Compare and contrast two biographies of the same person to evaluate how the author's point of view, interpretation, and selection of information influences our understanding of the person.
4–6	Literature	*Sounder; Roll of Thunder, Hear My Cry*	In order to gain insight into how black families in the South in the 1930s dealt with adversity, compare and contrast the conflicts in these two stories and how they are resolved.
4–6	Literature	Author study	Compare and contrast "Julia of the Wolves" and "My Side of the Mountain" to understand the author's style and priorities.
4–6	Language arts/library	Media	Compare and contrast television and newspapers regarding how coverage, presentation of information, timeliness, etc. influences the user's understanding of events.
4–6	Library	Reference skills	Compare and contrast the different types of information that you would expect to find in two different reference sources.
4–6	American history	Exploration/discovery	Compare and contrast the interpretations by Native Americans and Americans of European descent of Columbus's voyages and claims.
4–6	American history	Colonial America	Compare and contrast Native Americans and colonists especially with regard to use of land and resources, beliefs, and government.
4–6	American history	Civil War	Compare and contrast population, industry, and transporation in the North and the South regarding their effects on the war.
4–6	Social Studies	Geography/global studies	Compare and contrast Great Britain and Japan to gain insight into the role that geography and the need for natural resources play in the development of an island nation.
4–6	Social studies	Latin America	Compare and contrast two countries in Central or South America to assess the impact of geography on the lives of their people.
4–6	Science	Behavior	Compare and contrast instinct, learning, and reasoning to explain human behavior.
4–6	Science	Plants	Compare and contrast conifers and flowering plants to clarify plant reproduction.
4–6	Science	Bodies in space	Compare and contrast moons, comets, meteorites, and asteroids in order to distinguish them from each other.
4–6	Science	Electricity	Compare and contrast dry- and wet-cell batteries to clarify how they operate and when they are used.

COMPARING AND CONTRASTING LESSON CONTEXTS

GRADE	SUBJECT	TOPIC	THINKING ISSUE
4–6	Science	Force	Compare and contrast force and motion in order to understand movement.
4–6	Science	Climate	Compare and contrast a tropical rain forest with tundra regarding sustaining animal and plant life.
4–6	Science	Rocks	Compare and contrast types of rocks (with regard to hardness, formation, location, etc.) to clarify characteristics that promote identification.
4–6	Science	States of matter	Compare and contrast properties of solids, liquids, and gases in order to understand their behaviors.
4–6	Science	Electricity	Compare and contrast electrical current in wall plugs with batteries to clarify types of electrical current and determine conditions for use.
4–6	Science	Planets	Compare and contrast the planets to understand the effects of location, physical features, etc.
4–6	Mathematics	Measurement	Compare and contrast the cost of sodding a specific area of the playground to the cost of seeding it.
4–6	Mathematics	Problem solving	Compare and contrast various startegies for solving a specific mathematics problem.
4–6	Mathematics	Measurement	Compare and contrast metric and English units regarding use and conversion.
4–6	Mathematiics	Fractions	Compare and contrast the greatest common factor and the least common multiple to review their uses and how they are computed.
4–6	Mathematics	Geometry	Compare and contrast how change in perimeter affects area for a variety of polygons.
4–6	Health	Drugs	Compare and contrast depressants and stimulants with regard to their effect, presence in food, health risks, & "street" names.
4–6	Guidance	Study skills	Compare and contrast the prepared student and the unprepared student with regard to test taking.
4–6	Art	Design	Compare and contrast two paintings with regard to the extent to which the elements of design contribute to communicating the artist's message.
4–6	Music	Styles	Compare and contrast a waltz and a march to determine appropriate circumstances for each.
4–6	Music	Instruments	Compare and contrast a trumpet and a clarinet in order to determine what they contribute to the orchestra and what is involved in learning to play each.
4–6	Physical education	Sports	Compare and contrast football and baseball with regard to the goals of these games and the manner in which they are played.
4–6	Physical education	Exercise	Compare and contrast types of exercise in order to determine when and how they are most useful in preparing for sports.

CHAPTER 5
CLASSIFICATION

Why is Skillful Classification Important?

Classifying things may seem like labeling them. Classification, however, carries with it much deeper significance than simply assigning a name. For example, when I identify a particular tree as an *oak tree*, I am noting that it has the specific characteristics of a tree, which distinguish it from other plants, and of an oak, which distinguishes it from other trees. When I classify it as an oak tree, I attribute to it a cluster of important characteristics: it is a living thing; it is a plant; it has a root system, branches, and leaves. Moreover, it bears acorns which fall in autumn and can grow into offspring oaks. Through the seemingly simple act of classifying, a tree that I may never have seen before now becomes much more familiar to me.

Moreover, classifying this tree as an oak tree usually attaches to it an accumulation of much more information. For example, I recognize that it makes food by photosynthesis, that it can be a haven for birds, that its wood is hard and can be used for making furniture, and that it grows very tall. Classifications are usually powerful shorthand devices for such richer meanings. Our ability to classify individual things under general concepts provides us with an elegant way of organizing and expressing more complex forms of human knowledge.

Classification and definition. At its core, classification involves putting particular things in general categories because these things have certain characteristics which we use to define those categories. The terms that we use to label these categories usually mask the variety of characteristics that define them. When I call something an oak tree, I usually do not make explicit the wealth of characteristics that I think oak trees have.

Skillful definition of the term "oak tree" makes explicit the characteristics that we attribute to particular trees when we call them "oak trees." These characteristics may include some which, strictly speaking, do not define what an oak tree

is but that nonetheless are part of our conception of an oak tree, for example, that furniture can be made from its wood. The characteristics that we make explicit are all part of what we mean by the term "oak tree."

Hence, there is an intimate connection between the thinking involved in classification and the thinking involved in defining. Classification involves putting individual things into appropriate categories based on the defining characteristics of those categories. Definition involves analyzing the meanings of category names by making the defining characteristics of the categories explicit.

The purposes of classification. Classification serves many purposes according to our needs and interests. Here are a few of the diverse purposes that classification serves:

- *To help us select something we need.* For example, the specialty of a doctor is defined by characteristics of his or her practice (e.g., the type of treatment or the portion of the body about which the doctor has special knowledge). A urologist, for example, has expertise in ailments of the kidneys, bladder, etc. Hence, when we have such ailments, we can use our knowledge of how doctors are classified to select the appropriate doctor. In other examples, some of the ways that we classify tools or books help us select items that we may need. I may need something to shovel snow or a book to provide me with information about sights to see in Paris. Looking at the items classified "shovels" or "travel guides" can help me select what I need.

- *To protect things from harm or damage.* Classifying packages as fragile signals us to handle them carefully in order to protect them. Classifying foods as frozen foods helps us to determine where to store them so that they can be protected from spoiling.

- *To help us determine important properties and/ or relationships.* Classifying people by family relationships allows us to determine various forms of entitlements, rights, and duties that are important in our society. A father and mother, for example, have certain duties towards their children, which a child who is not their son or daughter cannot claim. Classification systems used in special fields often call our attention to characteristics of things and important relationships between them. When an animal is correctly classified as a crustacean, we know that it is a shellfish that lives in water. Similarly, classifying elements in chemistry, weather patterns in meteorology, and minerals in earth science indicates certain features of these items which give us a deeper understanding of how these phenomena work.

Criteria for effective classification. There are times when it's important to determine the best way to classify certain things. Suppose I need to classify all of my financial records for 1994. I do this effectively when

1. My classification scheme indicates important features of what I am classifying so that it serves my purpose(s).

2. I understand what these features are.

3. I correctly classify things by noting that they have these features.

I may keep together all the pieces of paper that indicate how much I have paid for business expenses this year in an envelope marked "1994 Business Receipts." My purpose is to be able to locate them easily when I file my income tax return. Keeping them together in this envelope means that I won't have to sort them from nonbusiness receipts when I need them. Of course, to sort them effectively, I have to understand what a 1994 business receipt is, and I have to identify correctly that the pieces of paper I put in the envelope are such receipts.

Problems that arise in the way we classify. We can, of course, group things in any number of different ways based on their common characteristics. For example, I could group my receipts by size. This might be a good way to classify if I were concerned about papers of different sizes, but it doesn't help me find my 1994 business receipts. This illustrates one way

that a classification scheme can fail. It may not serve the purpose we have for it.

A more frequent problem with the way we classify things is that the categories may be *too broad* or *too narrow* for our purposes. If I put all of my business expense receipts in a folder but did not discriminate among different years, I wouldn't be able to use this collection easily in doing my 1994 income tax. The classification would be too broad. Or I may just keep certain 1994 business receipts together—for example, my 1994 automobile expenses. Then I have to search for other receipts to be able to figure out my overall business expenses. In this case, the way I was classifying my expense statements would be too narrow to suit my purposes.

Another problem with classification occurs when we don't put things into the appropriate categories. Incorrectly classifying a poisonous snake as a harmless one can lead to a serious problem. There are a number of reasons why we might make this kind of error. The first is that we might be confused about what specific categories entail. For example, it may not be difficult to determine whether a document is for business and whether it is for 1994. However, if I am confused about what a business receipt is and put bills as well as receipts in the folder, that may cause problems. My classification scheme may be a good one, but if I misunderstand the categories, I may misclassify the documents I put in those categories. *Misunderstanding what categories signify* is a key source of misclassification.

There are other sources of misclassification. I may understand the defining characteristics of a class of things, like 1994 business receipts, and make a mistake about whether something I am classifying has these characteristics. I may think I see "1993" on a receipt and it may be "1994." This is a matter of *misperception*. I may also make the same error through *misjudgment*. If I classify a receipt for a meal as a business receipt, but it fails to meet the requirements for a legitimate business expense, then I may have a problem with the Internal Revenue Service.

A summary of the problems with classification that makes it less effective than it could be is contained in figure 5.1.

COMMON DEFAULTS IN THE WAY WE CLASSIFY THINGS

1. The way things are classified may not fit the purposes of classifying them, e.g., the category may be too broad or too narrow.

2. We may have a superficial understanding of what makes something fall into a category. Hence, classifying it that way may lead to a superficial, rather than rich, understanding of what we classify.

3. We may not know what defines the category and may put the wrong things in it.

4. We may know what defines the category but misperceive or misjudge that an individual thing has those characteristics and, hence, misclassify it.

Figure 5.1

What Does Skillful Classification Involve?

When we classify something, we identify it as belonging to a certain category of things, and we understand the significance of its belonging to that category. We often recognize that some-things fits into a number of categories. Nothing falls into only one category. A tree is a living thing, composed of wood, cylindrical, leafy, a part of nature, and the subject of poetry. Sometimes identifying a range of different ways that a thing can be classified is called "classifying" it. However, this is not sufficient for most of the tasks that require skillful classification.

Bottom-up classification. Most natural thinking tasks involving classification are tasks in which we do more than just list ways that items can be classified. We often have to select, from among the variety of ways that we can classify something, a classification scheme that best serves our purposes. We then actively employ that classification scheme to sort things.

In the case of my business receipts, any one of the 1994 business receipts could be classified into a variety of categories; I might identify them as small pieces of paper, wood products, business receipts, 1994 business receipts, or simply receipts. There may, of course, be contexts in which classifying them as wood products serves

some purpose, but in this case, I want to use them to generate figures for my 1994 income tax return. So I can reject the categories "pieces of paper" and "wood products" because I am sorting for a business purpose. I can also reject the category "receipts" because I can't be sure that only *business* receipts are filed in this category, and I can reject "business receipts" because I can't be sure that the only business receipts filed here are from 1994. These categories are too broad. On the other hand, "1994 business receipts" seems to be a category that does serve my purpose. If I use it, I can total the receipts and arrive at a figure needed for my tax return.

This is the process of "bottom-up" classification. We initially determine many different ways that given objects can be classified by identifying a variety of their characteristics and noting the categories that these characteristics define. Then we select categories that serve our specific purposes. Figure 5.2 contains a thinking map of bottom-up classification.

BOTTOM-UP CLASSIFICATION

1. What characteristics do the given items have?

2. What classifications do these characteristics define?

3. What purpose do we have for classifying the items?

4. What way of classifying the items best serves this purpose?

5. Which items fall into each category?

Figure 5.2

Two graphic organizers can be used to guide us through this kind of thinking. The first (figure 5.3) is used after we have identified characteristics of the object(s) to be classified and we ask, "What classifications do these characteristics define?" The categories defined by these characteristics are listed on the left, and then these are grouped into broader ways to classify things. These are written on the lines in the upper right.

For example, suppose you are trying to organize items in your garage into useful categories.

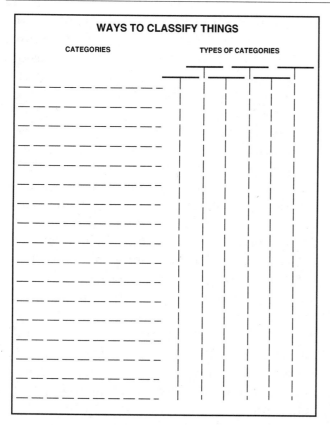

Figure 5.3

You find that some of these have the following characteristics:

- They are made of metal
- They can be used to hammer nails
- They can be used to drive screws
- They are shiny
- They are heavy
- They are under one foot long
- They are light in weight
- They are over one foot long

They could be classified into categories like the following:

- Metal objects
- Tools that hammer nails
- Screwdrivers
- Shiny objects
- Heavy objects
- Objects under one foot long
- Objects light in weight
- Objects that are over a foot long

These categories should be written on the lines on the left of the graphic organizer. Then we should determine if any of these categories are of the same type. Indeed, some are. Heavy objects and light objects are categorized by weight. "Weight" would then be written on one of the horizontal lines under "types of categories." "Heavy objects" and "light objects" should be connected to the vertical line leading to "weight." Similarly, "length," "use," and "material" can be written on the other lines for types of categories.

Determining types of categories in this way makes it easier to decide which way of classifying these objects best suits your needs or purposes. For example, you may choose "use" because you have need tools to fix things. Or you may choose "material" because you are going to take these items to the city dump for recycling.

Next, determine which, if any, additional categories and sub-categories should be added to your classification system. For example, the city dump might recycle metals and have bins for different types of metal. So you could further subdivide your categories under metal into steel, aluminum, copper, etc.

The second graphic organizer useful in classifying, a webbing diagram, shows categories and sub-categories. It appears in figure 5.4.

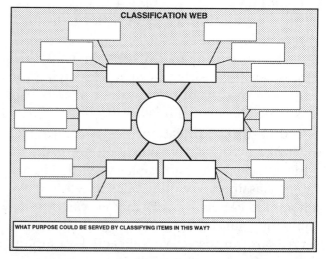

Figure 5.4

To complete our classification project, we would then sort the remaining items in the garage into the categories that we have determined. The strategy for top-down classification described in the next section provides us with a way of doing this skillfully.

We can also classify natural objects, as well as man-made products, using bottom-up classification. Animals can be classified by their body structure and functioning (e.g., quadrupeds) to help us understand life processes and evolutionary relationships. They can also be classified by habitat (e.g., animals that live in the oceans) to help us understand their environmental needs. They can be classified as predators or prey to understand the food chain and environmental balance. They can be classified by geographical area (the birds of North America) to enable us to predict what animals one might find in a given area. How we choose to classify a group of animals on a specific occasion is determined by our needs, interests, and purposes. Once we have made that choice, the webbing diagram can help us to add useful categories to the classification system.

Top-down classification. Sometimes our classification task starts after the categories for classifying given objects have been determined. I may select "1994 Business Receipts" to classify certain receipts. I know what defines the category "1994 Business Receipts": an item that falls into this category must be a receipt for money spent, but it must also be from 1994, and it must be a business-related expense. Under that category, I may also want to sort my travel expense receipts, my home office expense receipts, my receipts for professional books, etc. I also know what defines these sub-categories. To put the right items into the right categories, I must sort through them and determine which have these characteristics. Then I can label them and sort them into the appropriate category.

This form of classification is "top-down." Top-down classification assumes a pre-established classification framework, one that we have developed bottom-up, or one that someone else has developed for us to use. For example, I may use categories already provided by the Internal Revenue Service for sorting tax records. In sorting other items for other purposes, I may use other established classification systems such as the periodic table, the Dewey Decimal System, or animal phyla.

Skill at this more restricted type of classification involves two things. We must know what defining characteristics are significant or commonly used for classifying things in the given categories. We must then detect the presence of those characteristics in individual things so that we can sort them correctly.

Figure 5.5 contains a thinking map for top-down classification. The graphic organizer for top-down classification (figure 5.6) can guide the thinking.

TOP-DOWN CLASSIFICATION

1. What are the defining characteristics of the categories under which I want to classify things?

2. Which items have these characteristics?

3. How do I classify these items into the given categories?

Figure 5.5

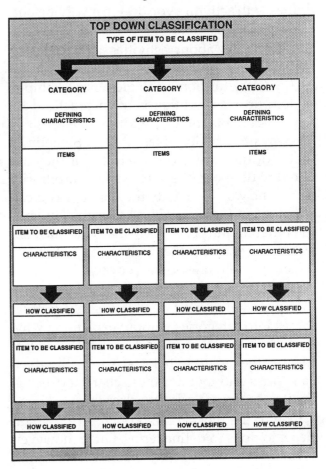

Figure 5.6

How Can We Teach Students to Classify Skillfully?

We help students develop this skill by giving them many opportunities to classify, using both bottom-up and top-down classification. We should prompt students to differentiate between the two and guide them in using each strategy while performing classification tasks until they can guide themselves.

Classification and definition activities in standard curriculum materials. Classification is one of the traditional thinking skills that has been given attention in standard curriculum materials. Students are often asked to classify things, particularly in language arts and science. Be cautious about classification activities in common curriculum materials. Top-down classification is, by far, the most common form of classification students are asked to engage in. If this is the only form of classification that students are asked to do, supplement these activities with activities you design involving bottom-up classification.

Be cautious about activities in curriculum materials that only involve students in partial use of classification strategies. For example, bottom-up classification is often practiced by having students come up with a range of different ways to classify given objects. Sometimes that's <u>all</u> they are asked to do (or, if they are asked to do more, they are asked to arbitrarily select one way to classify the objects). You can supplement these activities by asking students the different purposes that classifying such objects can serve and then helping them make a selection based on specific purposes.

Similarly, students are often asked to engage in top-down classification by merely putting things into categories without explaining why. You can extend these activities so that students identify the defining characteristics of the given categories and look for these characteristics in the items they are asked to classify.

One of the most common tasks we ask students to do is to define terms. Often, however, students are simply asked to define words without any guidance about the connection between classifying and defining.

When students *classify skillfully*, they realize that things like ducks have characteristics which differentiate them from other things in the bird category and which delimit a sub-category into which these particular objects fall (ducks). Hence, to *define a word that can be used to classify something*, like "duck," the definition should include the category the thing falls into (bird), as well as the characteristics that make it different from other things in that category (other birds). Thus, instruction in skillful classification helps students understand the information they need to include in an adequate definition.

Contexts in the curriculum for designing infusion lessons on classification. Developing infusion lessons on classification can be particularly helpful in teaching lessons with the following instructional goals:

- *It is important for students to understand and differentiate various phenomena of the same or different types.* In language arts, for example, it is important that students distinguish different types of books, forms of literature, kinds of writing, figures of speech, parts of speech, types of references, etc. In social studies, students learn about different types of buildings, weapons, land forms, artifacts, tools, architectural styles, economic or political systems or institutions, cultures, etc. In science, scientific phenomena, organisms, geographic features, astronomical phenomena, etc. are differentiated. In mathematics, students learn to differentiate geometric figures and solids, mathematical operations, units of measurement, statistics, graphs, etc.

- *Students are asked to organize various items that they are using.* For example, students often must organize topics in an outline or find reference books they use in the library. In science laboratories, students have to store equipment. In studying computers, students have to locate and retrieve information in print and electronic files.

- *Students are asked to define important concepts.* For example, students are asked to define forms of government like a democracy, a monarchy, and a dictatorship. In science, students are asked to define various types of animals, as well as processes like digestion, respiration, and reproduction.

A menu of suggested contexts for classification lessons is provided on pp. 164–167.

Tips about classification lessons. When you design lessons in one or the other of these contexts, make sure that the activities are authentic and not simply exercises in classification. Ask students to think through how to classify items in the natural contexts in which such classifications would be appropriate. One interesting type of activity involves students practicing bottom-up classification by creating files on a computer to store specific documents. You can, in fact, create a variety of analogies to classifying real objects in this way, thereby giving students valuable practice in using a computer, as well as in learning important bottom-up strategies for classification.

There are five important points to keep in mind about teaching classification:

- Always identify the thinking task as classifying;

- Encourage students to recognize the purpose of classifying in each context;

- Make sure that your students express the defining characteristic of the categories they are working with;

- Help them to relate the defining characteristic to the purpose of classifying; and

- Remind them to check the accuracy of their classifications of specific items.

Model Lessons on Classification

We include two model lesson in this chapter. The first is an elementary grade lesson in mathematics in which students engage in top-down classification of triangles by angles and sides. The second is an intermediate grade lesson in science/social studies on animals. Bottom-up classification is taught in this lesson. As you read these lessons, ask the following questions:

- How would this compare to a lesson on the same topic in which students were engaged in top-down classification only?

- Which of the graphic organizers for classification is best suited for this lesson? Why?

- What other contexts can you think of for reinforcing this skill?

Tools for Designing Classification Lessons

Thinking maps and graphic organizers for both bottom-up and top-down classification are included on the following pages.

The thinking maps (pp. 140, 143) and graphic organizers can serve as photocopy masters, transparency masters, or as models that can be enlarged and used as posters in the classroom. Reproduction rights are granted for single classroom use only.

BOTTOM-UP CLASSIFICATION

1. What characteristics do the given items have?

2. What classifications do these characteristics define?

3. What purpose do we have for classifying the items?

4. What way of classifying the items best serves this purpose?

5. Which items fall into each category?

WAYS TO CLASSIFY THINGS

CATEGORIES   TYPES OF CATEGORIES

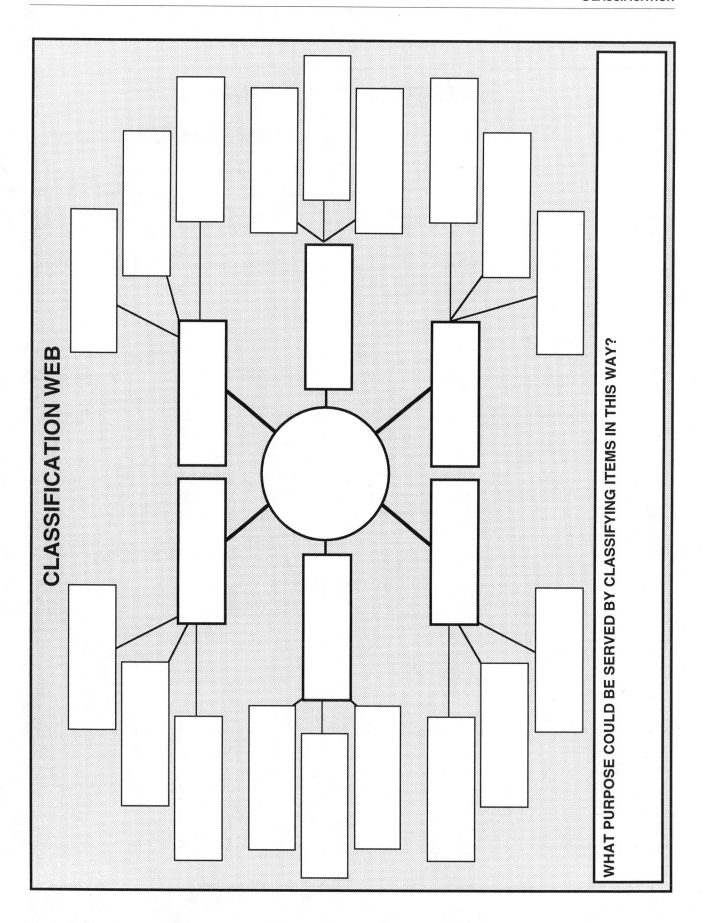

CLASSIFICATION WEB

WHAT PURPOSE COULD BE SERVED BY CLASSIFYING ITEMS IN THIS WAY?

TOP-DOWN CLASSIFICATION

1. **What are the defining characteristics of the categories under which I want to classify things?**

2. **Which items have these characteristics?**

3. **How do I classify these items into the given categories?**

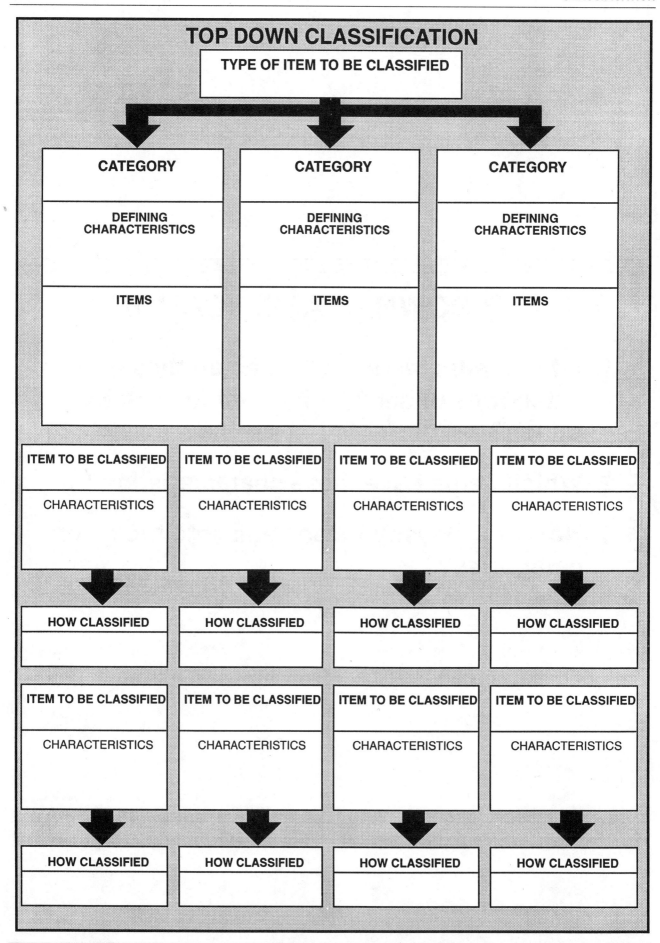

TOP DOWN CLASSIFICATION

TYPE OF ITEM TO BE CLASSIFIED

CATEGORY	CATEGORY	CATEGORY
DEFINING CHARACTERISTICS	DEFINING CHARACTERISTICS	DEFINING CHARACTERISTICS
ITEMS	ITEMS	ITEMS

ITEM TO BE CLASSIFIED	ITEM TO BE CLASSIFIED	ITEM TO BE CLASSIFIED	ITEM TO BE CLASSIFIED
CHARACTERISTICS	CHARACTERISTICS	CHARACTERISTICS	CHARACTERISTICS

HOW CLASSIFIED	HOW CLASSIFIED	HOW CLASSIFIED	HOW CLASSIFIED

ITEM TO BE CLASSIFIED	ITEM TO BE CLASSIFIED	ITEM TO BE CLASSIFIED	ITEM TO BE CLASSIFIED
CHARACTERISTICS	CHARACTERISTICS	CHARACTERISTICS	CHARACTERISTICS

HOW CLASSIFIED	HOW CLASSIFIED	HOW CLASSIFIED	HOW CLASSIFIED

DESCRIBING TRIANGLES

Mathematics **Grades 3–5**

OBJECTIVES

CONTENT

Students will review the meanings of terms related to angles (acute, oblique, and right) and terms related to the sides of triangles (equilateral, isosceles, and scalene), and will classify triangles by these characteristics.

THINKING SKILL/PROCESS

Students will learn to classify by identifying defining characteristics of classes and will recognize that the purpose for classification determines those defining characteristics.

METHODS AND MATERIALS

CONTENT

Markers, scissors for each student, and one large piece of paper for each work group are needed. Photocopy one set of pictures for each cooperative work group. Preparation of a display may take more than one session. One kiwi fruit is helpful in the demonstration.

THINKING SKILL/PROCESS

Students are guided by the teacher's questions in classifying the triangles. Students create a diagram to illustrate classification. (See pp. 140–44 for reproducible diagrams.)

LESSON

INTRODUCTION TO CONTENT AND THINKING SKILL/PROCESS

- **Think about the different ways that products are grouped in the supermarket. When we group things together because they all have something in common, we are classifying them. With your partner, list as many ways as you can think of that food and other products in the supermarket are grouped. Give some examples of each way of grouping them.** List students' responses on a chalkboard or newsprint under the heading "How things are classified in the supermarket." POSSIBLE ANSWERS: *Type of food (fruit, vegetables, beverages, mixes, pasta), utensils for the home (food preparation utensils, storage containers, cleaning tools, waste containers), beauty or health products (products to clean or protect teeth or skin, hair care products, first aid supplies, medications for minor ailments), foods that are used together (cake preparation [mixes, spices, flour, sugar], ethnic foods, foods for special diets), size and type of container (bulk or giant size packages may be grouped together on racks that are large enough to hold them), storage (food that doesn't spoil quickly is stored on shelves, perishable foods in a refrigerator, or frozen foods in a freezer), whether or not a sales person has to get you a particular amount (bakery or deli products are bought by the amount the customer wants), whether or not a sales person has to take special care of it (fruit and vegetables in the produce department must be watered and rotated and spoiled items removed each day).*

- **We always have a purpose for classifying things the way we do. Select one way of classifying things in the supermarket and describe to your partner why you think things are grouped that way.** List students' responses under the heading "Why things are classified this way." POSSIBLE ANSWERS: *Type of food (to find them easily when needed), utensils for the home (to find them easily and to display the type or size of utensil that is needed for a task), beauty or health products (to find them easily), foods that are used together (to remind us of products that are used in the same types of recipes, to show substitutes of some products, to display them the way people store them at home to find them easily), storage* *(to prevent spoilage), whether or not a sales person has to get you a particular amount (to get only the amount of food that the customer wants), whether or not a sales person has to take special care of it (to keep it fresh).* When the list is complete, add a summary statement at the bottom, for example: In the supermarket most things are classified to help us find what we want to buy and to keep the food fresh.

- Once things are classified a certain way, if we want to add other things to the same group, we have to understand what defines things in these categories. If you worked at the supermarket and stocked shelves every day, you'd have to know where to put things. Sometimes products come labeled, and it's easy. For example, when you unpack a box which is labeled McIntosh Apples, it's easy to put them in the correct bin: the one marked McIntosh Apples. However, when things don't come labeled, you have to know what characteristics products should have in order to fall into the different categories, and you have to be able to identify items that have these characteristics so that you can put them in the right bin. To define a category, we identify its *defining characteristics*: the set of characteristics that all things of that kind and only things of that kind have. For example, when we think of fruit, knowing its defining characteristics helps us identify many kinds of foods that fall into that category. With your partner, list all the defining characteristics of fruit that you can think of. After partners have had time to list characteristics of fruit, record their responses on the board. POSSIBLE ANSWERS: *Fruit grows on plants (trees, bushes, vines). It is the fleshy part of the plant that surrounds the seeds of the plant where a blossom used to be. The fleshy part can be eaten without being cooked.*

- Knowing the defining characteristics helps us identify things correctly. It may be easy to identify fruit, but where in the fruit section should you put a specific type of fruit? That depends on what defines the kind of fruit it is. Hold up the kiwi fruit. If none is available, select a fruit or vegetable that students do not commonly buy. **What is this?** *A kiwi.* **How would you describe it to someone else?** *It is a fruit that is smaller than a pear and larger than a plum. It has a thin brown skin, sometimes looks almost hairy, and has green pulp inside. It tastes mildly sweet and comes originally from the South Pacific.* **Why would it be important to know the defining characteristics of the kiwi?** POSSIBLE ANSWERS: *If you have to put new fruit out, you'd know where to put kiwis. If your mother sends you to the supermarket for one, you need to know what to look for or ask for. You also need to know which fruit the sign and the price refers to. You may also have to know what you are getting if you are trying one for the first time, so that you can make sure that it is the right fruit.* **To describe a kiwi accurately or to be sure that we are selecting the right fruit when we look for a kiwi, we must be very clear of the defining characteristics of a kiwi.**

- **This thinking map summarizes the questions to ask when you try to determine whether a specific item is classified correctly.** Show a copy of the thinking map for top down classification.

THINKING ACTIVELY

- **It isn't just in the supermarket that things are classified. We classify almost everything we know about in a variety of different ways, all for various purposes.** We've been studying mathematics, for example, and we've found that in mathematics numbers are classified in various ways, such as into whole numbers or fractions. So are the shapes that we study. They are classified in various ways for the purpose

---

TOP-DOWN CLASSIFICATION

1. What are the defining characteristics of the categories under which I want to classify things?

2. Which items have these characteristics?

3. How do I classify these items into the given categories?

---

of understanding important facts about them. As with the supermarket items, once we understand what defines the way we classify different types of triangles, we can identify individual ones that should be classified the same way. We're going to use the thinking map for top-down classification to help us understand how triangles are classified so that we can classify other triangles that we may have to work with.

- To describe different types of triangles accurately or to be sure that we select the correct triangle when one has been described to us, we must be very clear of the defining characteristics of various types of triangles. We know that triangles are found in natural and man-made things that we see everyday. We're going to identify the triangles we find in these pictures and cut them out so that we can carefully examine just the triangular shapes themselves.

  Distribute a set of the pictures (shown on pp. 153–54) to each work group and direct them to cut apart the pictures.

- **Divide up the pictures and use a black marker to trace the triangles in the pictures you get.**

- **With your group, discuss the kinds of objects within which you found triangles.** Students comment that, while some triangular forms are natural, many are found in construction and machinery.

- **What kinds of things have triangles in them?** List students' responses on the board. Ask students to identify other objects that commonly contain triangles, and add them to the list.

- **Now carefully cut out just the triangle part of the picture and turn the triangle over so that the blank side is up.** The triangles the students will be working with are shown at the right.

- **As you look at this collection of triangles, what might be the characteristics that you would describe to tell how one is different from the others?** Students describe either the angles or the sides or both.

- **Classifying triangles by their angles or by their sides may help us to group them in useful ways. It may help us identify important types of triangles and learn rules about the lengths of sides and angles. Clarifying the defining characteristics of the triangles we classify in these ways can help us be clear about the words that are commonly use to describe triangles. With your work group, examine** the triangles that you have cut out. **What characteristics related to their sides or angles do you observe? Discuss their characteristics with your work group and make a list of the characteristics you observe.** After students have listed several characteristics, ask for each group to report one characteristic and create a list of them on the chalkboard. POSSIBLE ANSWERS: *The angles may be different (right angles like corners, sharper angles like a point, or broad angles that are wider than a corner). All three sides may be the same length. Two sides may be the same. All three sides may be a different. All three angles may be the same. Two angles may be the same and the third different. All three angles may be different.*

- **Each work group should select a characteristic that seems important to use to identify and describe triangles. For example, you may choose the size of the angles or the length of the sides. When you classify triangles by the size of the angles, what small groups can you sort** them into? *Right triangles, obtuse triangles, and acute triangles.* **What are the defining characteristics of each of these types of triangles?** POSSIBLE ANSWERS: *Right triangles have one right angle; a right angle has 90 degrees. Obtuse triangles have at least one angle that is more than 90 degrees. Acute triangles have all three angles less than 90 degrees.* **When you sort them by sides, what small groups can you sort them into?** *Equilateral triangles, scalene triangles, and isosceles triangles.* **What are the defining characteristics of each of these types of triangle?** *In equilateral triangles, all three sides are the same length. In isosceles triangles, two sides are equal. In scalene triangles, no two sides are equal in length.* Students should write the appropriate term from each set of descriptors (right, acute, obtuse, or equilateral, isosceles, or scalene) on the appropriate triangle. If students have difficulty using these terms, review them in class. You can write the terms on the chalkboard, draw various triangles, and ask students to work in pairs to match these so that one specific term appears on each triangle. As they report, they should explain why they attached the term to the triangle. Then ask for comments from the rest of the class. Help them with their explanations if they are inaccurate.

- **Select one of these ways of classifying triangles, state the defining characteristics of triangles that are classified this way, pick the triangles that fit those defining characteristics, and sort them into groups: one for each defining characteristic. Label all the triangles in the small groups with the defining characteristic of that group.** After each work group has sorted and labeled each set, students should label each triangle within that group.

- **Create a display of the triangles that you have sorted. Draw other triangles in each small group.** Students may create a diagram or use a standard branching diagram or concept web to show the relationships.

- **On each display, write what you think the purposes might be for classifying triangles that way.** POSSIBLE ANSWERS: *To help us understand important facts about triangles that depend on their angles. To help us identify and select triangular objects to do certain jobs (e.g., a slide with a gradual slope so that children won't go down it too fast).*

- **What do we show about triangles by grouping them by these significant characteristics?** Students comment that there is more than one way to classify triangles, depending on whether you use sides or angles as the defining characteristic. There are two different sets of terms that are used to describe triangles: terms describing angles and terms describing sides. There are also other ways of grouping them that show important features of triangles, like area, use, or regularity.

- **Now identify each triangle on your display both by the characteristics of its angles and by the characteristics of its sides. Label each triangle with the additional terms.** This helps students understand that, if they apply only one term (such as right or isosceles), they may mistakenly believe that either sides or angles is the only important characteristic to cite. As each triangle is discussed, emphasize the use of both types of terms (angles and sides) to describe it. You can reinforce this understanding by giving students additional triangles and asking them to label them with the correct terms for sides and the correct terms for angles. You can also check for understanding by stating both characteristics and asking students to draw a triangle that fits both of them. Display the variety of triangles that are produced using the same two terms (e.g., a triangle that is isosceles and has a right angle).

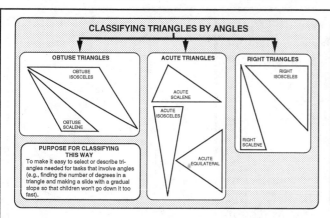

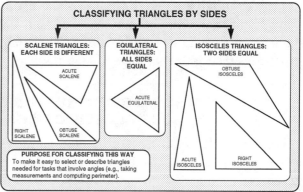

THINKING ABOUT THINKING

- **How did you go about classifying the triangles? What did you think about first, second, and third?** POSSIBLE ANSWERS: *I examined them for important characteristics, defined groups by reference to one or another of these characteristics, identified each item according to whether it had these characteristics, and put the items into the defined groups. I described what I learned about triangles by grouping them in these ways.* If students are having trouble remembering, prompt their answers by referring to their displays. Their descriptions of classifying should include the steps on the thinking map for top-down classification.

- **How does classifying triangles by different characteristics help you use words that describe triangles correctly?** POSSIBLE ANSWERS: *It reminds me that one set of words describes triangles by sides and another set of words describe them by angles. It helps me define these words. It lets me know whether the person using those terms is paying attention to sides or angles. It reminds me that the same triangle can be classified in different ways.*

APPLYING YOUR THINKING

Immediate Transfer

- Classify sets of quadrilaterals and show the relationships among the following terms: parallelogram, rectangle, trapezoid, rhombus, and square.

- Classify books by types to clarify the different purposes for reading them.

Reinforcement Later

- Classify jobs by whether they provide goods or services to show how the community needs both.

- Classify land forms and bodies of water to clarify correct terms for each.

LESSON VARIATIONS AND EXTENSIONS

Mathematics Manipulative Version: The black-line master of triangles shows the types of triangles featured in this lesson. To conduct the lesson with figures rather than with pictures, photocopy the black-line master onto colored paper as heavy as your copy machine allows. Mount the sheet on cardboard and laminate and cut out the individual triangles. Students may then write directly on the surface with crayons, and the manipulative can be reused. In this case, the triangles should be affixed to students' displays with peelable tape.

Alternative Graphic Organizer to Represent the Overlapping Classes: To illustrate that triangles can be classified both in terms of their angles and in terms of their sides, a different graphic organizer called a Venn diagram can be used. Venn diagrams show items that have characteristics of each class and items that have characteristics of both classes. The diagram at the right illustrates triangles that are acute, scalene, or both.

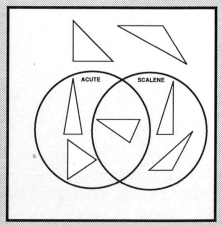

ASSESSING STUDENT THINKING
ABOUT CLASSIFICATION

To assess this skill, ask students to classify items similar to those in the transfer activities. An example includes classifying given books into fiction or non-fiction in order to clarify the different purposes for reading them. Ask them to think out loud. Determine whether they are attending to each of the steps in the thinking map for top-down classification. Encourage students to use the terms "classify" and "characteristics" and to state what the classification shows.

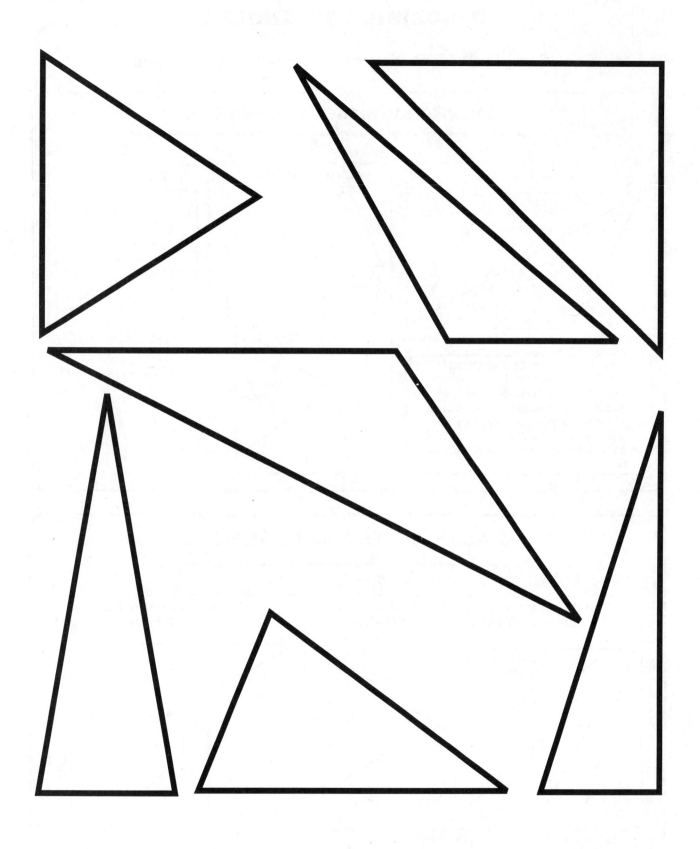

Template for Manipulative Version of Lesson on Describing Triangles

DESCRIBING TRIANGLES

Sample Student Diagrams: Classifying Triangles

CLASSIFYING TRIANGLES BY ANGLES

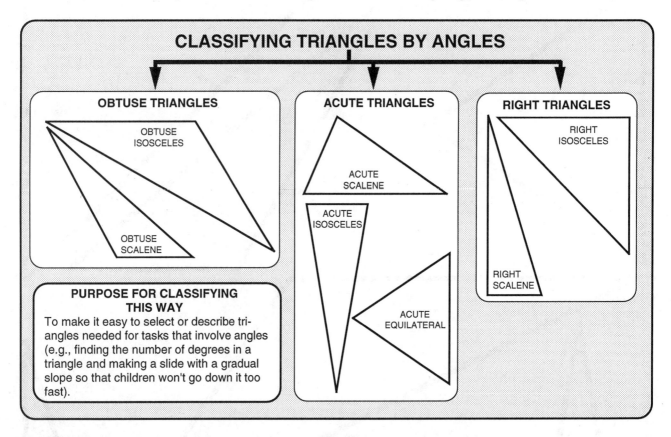

OBTUSE TRIANGLES

OBTUSE ISOSCELES

OBTUSE SCALENE

PURPOSE FOR CLASSIFYING THIS WAY

To make it easy to select or describe triangles needed for tasks that involve angles (e.g., finding the number of degrees in a triangle and making a slide with a gradual slope so that children won't go down it too fast).

ACUTE TRIANGLES

ACUTE SCALENE

ACUTE ISOSCELES

ACUTE EQUILATERAL

RIGHT TRIANGLES

RIGHT ISOSCELES

RIGHT SCALENE

CLASSIFYING TRIANGLES BY SIDES

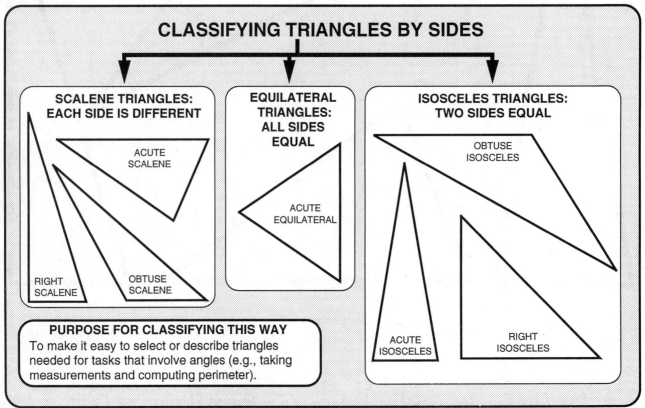

SCALENE TRIANGLES: EACH SIDE IS DIFFERENT

ACUTE SCALENE

RIGHT SCALENE

OBTUSE SCALENE

PURPOSE FOR CLASSIFYING THIS WAY

To make it easy to select or describe triangles needed for tasks that involve angles (e.g., taking measurements and computing perimeter).

EQUILATERAL TRIANGLES: ALL SIDES EQUAL

ACUTE EQUILATERAL

ISOSCELES TRIANGLES: TWO SIDES EQUAL

OBTUSE ISOSCELES

ACUTE ISOSCELES

RIGHT ISOSCELES

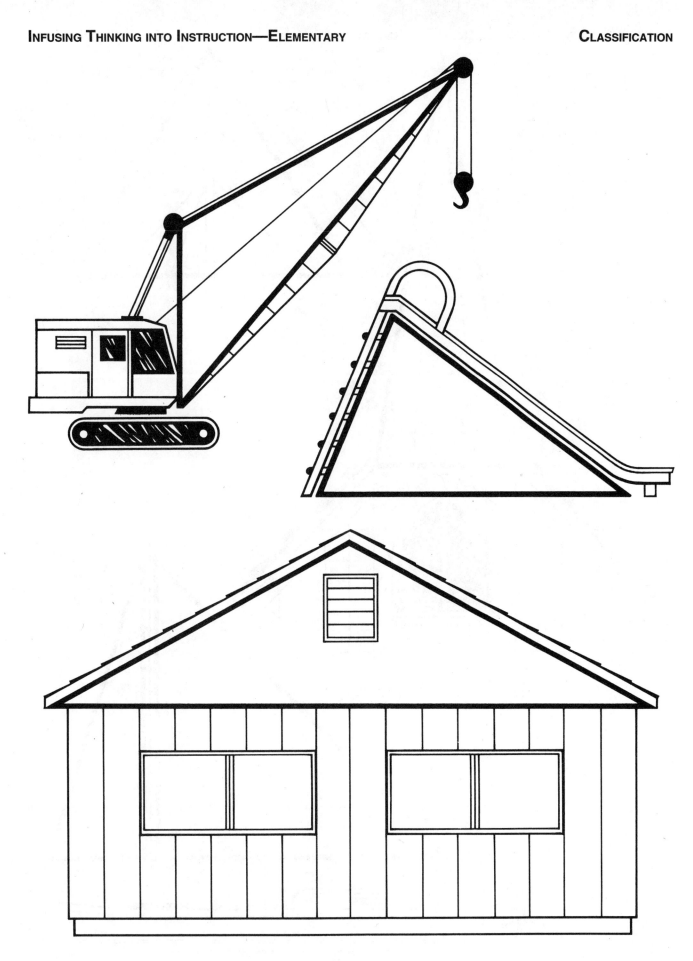

Illustration by Kate Simon Huntley

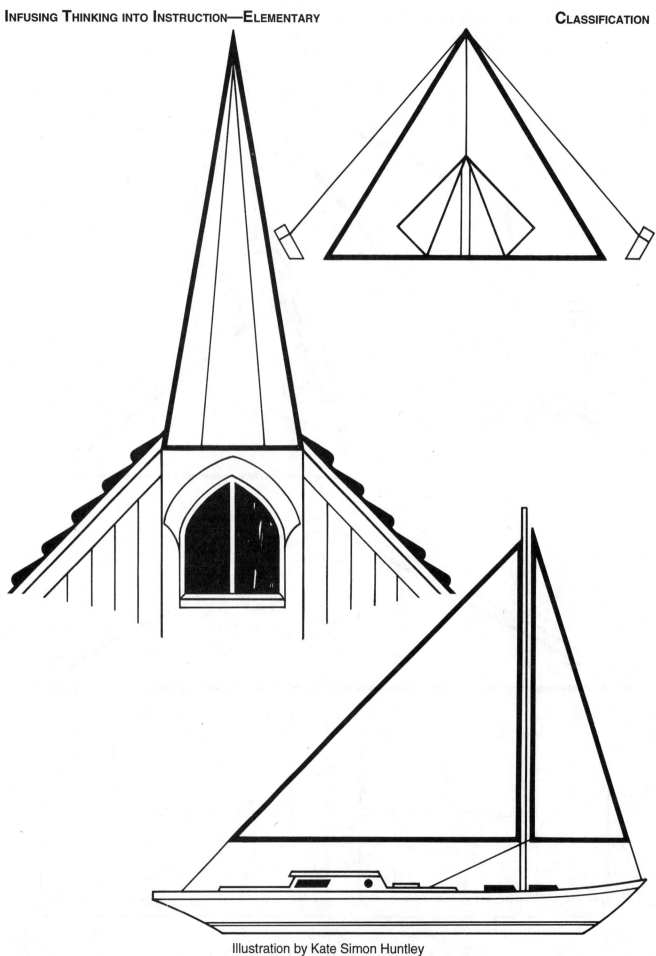

Illustration by Kate Simon Huntley

ANIMALS OF THE WORLD

Science / Social Studies   **Grades 4–6**

OBJECTIVES

CONTENT

Students will learn different ways of classifying animals and recognize that different classifications yield different information about them (e.g., body structure, needs, habitat, etc.).

THINKING SKILL/PROCESS

Students will identify defining characteristics of classes and recognize that the purpose for classification determines the defining characteristics.

METHODS AND MATERIALS

CONTENT

Students will work together in collaborative learning groups of four to six. Each group will need colored markers, a large piece of paper, index cards, and a set of animal cards or pictures (12–18 minimum) that depict a variety of animals from different phyla, habitats, and geographical locations. (See p. 163 for sample animal cards.)

THINKING SKILL/PROCESS

Students are guided by the teacher's questions and directions to classify the animals. Students create a concept map to illustrate classification. A graphic organizer guides student thinking. (See pp. 140–44 for reproducible diagrams.)

LESSON

INTRODUCTION TO CONTENT AND THINKING SKILL/PROCESS

- Think about a time when you classified or sorted various objects. Select one of these situations and describe it to your group. What was the purpose of your classification? What characteristic(s) of the things you classified was (were) important to you for that purpose? Ask each group to report one example and list several on the chalkboard. Write the example, purpose, and characteristics in each case. (See chart at right.)

EXAMPLE	PURPOSE	CHARACTERISTIC
Books	Find them easily	Type Alphabetical order
Tools	Find them easily	Type of task Where its used
Groceries	Find them easily Store properly	Perishable Locate near preparation
Hobby collection Stamps, baseball cards, figurines	Find them easily Store properly Appearance	Type Alphabetical order Color and shape
Plants for a garden	Appearance Cultivation	Color Height Growing needs (light, soil, water)

- **How did your purpose affect the characteristic you selected as a basis for your classification?** Students comment that classifying for different purposes requires paying attention to different characteristics.

- When we classify things, it is important to do it well. Otherwise we might not accomplish our purpose. We're going to learn how to classify things carefully in this lesson. We will examine the things to be classified and then determine the best way to do it.

- We've been studying animals in science. In this lesson, we will classify some animals. We're going to see how different ways of classifying these animals tell us different things about them and what different purposes might be served by classifying animals in these different ways.

THINKING ACTIVELY

- Here are some cards with information about different animals (see sample cards p. 163). **Divide the animal cards equally among the members of your group. Pick three animal cards each and look for information that you think is interesting about those animals. Write the name of the animal and one fact that you think is** important about the animal on an index card. Make a few of these information cards for each animal.

Sample Information Card
Animal's name: Information about the animal:

- Suppose that you wanted to group some of these animals together in ways that showed something important that these animals had in common. Each group should pool its information cards and discuss some characteristics that seem interesting about the animals. Group cards together that describe the same characteristic and put them in a stack or in a container. Write the type of animal that has this characteristic on an identification card on the stack or container. You can use the phrase "Animals that..." For example, you may label a container "Animals that Eat Only Meat" or "Carnivores." Then define the types of animals that you have identified by their common characteristics. For example, if you labeled a container "Carnivores" you would write what these animals all have in common: They eat only meat. Ask each student group to show the class a sample grouping and which animals are contained in this group. They should also list the other categories they have used for grouping the animals. Ask the groups to display their baskets so that other students can inspect them. POSSIBLE ANSWERS: *Animals that inhabit Europe, sea-dwelling animals, hard outer-shelled animals, animals with brown fur, carnivores, animals preyed upon by birds, scaly animals, poisonous animals, aggressive animals.* As the groups report, write the categories down the left side of the "Ways to Classify" graphic organizer on the board, on a poster, or on a transparency.

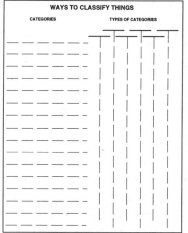

- **On the left side of the graphic organizer, we have a list of categories of animals that you have identified. Some of these categories describe the same sort of feature in the animals. For example, animals that eat only meat and animals that eat only plants both describe the kind of food the animal eats. How can we group the other categories on the list to organize them better?** Write "The kind of food the animal eats" on one of the horizontal lines at the top of the diagram. Connect the appropriate subcategories (e.g., "animals that eat only meat," "animals that eat only plants") from the list on the left to the vertical line under "The kind of food the animal eats." Use different-colored chalk or pens to show the connections. POSSIBLE ANSWERS: *Location, habitat, outer covering, what they eat, what eats them, benefit or harm to man, body structure and functioning, how they bear their young, color, size, life span, population size, species stability.*

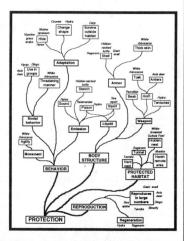

- **In your group, select a way to classify animals that shows something particularly interesting about them. Use newsprint, colored markers, and animal cards to create a display classifying the animals into categories and sub-categories, and show what is interesting about them. On the display, construct your own diagram to show how you classify the animals. Tape the animal cards**

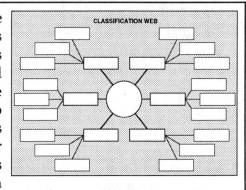

to the display in the appropriate spots. Use the cognitive map shown on the previous page to explain to students what kind of diagram they could create. After students complete this activity, ask for reports. Each group should explain their display. These displays can be taped to the wall of the classroom for future reference. An alternative to asking students to create their own classification diagrams is to have them modify the webbing graphic organizer (shown at right). It is preferable, however, to have students create their own cognitive maps of these relationships. In some cases, prepared graphics tend to restrict the number of categories and sub-categories.

- **Discuss with your group the kinds of people who might be interested in classifying animals in the way you have diagrammed. Write this at the bottom of your classification diagram.** As each group reports, write the information on a chart like the one included at the right. POSSIBLE ANSWERS: Travellers and people who hunt animals for zoos would want to be able to locate particular animals; zoo and aquarium specialists creating artificial habitats would want to know the natural conditions in which specific animals survive; doctors of sick or injured animals would want to understand the various body parts and how they function.

PURPOSES AND USES OF ANIMAL CLASSIFICATION SYSTEMS		
WAYS TO CLASSIFY	PURPOSE OF THE CLASSIFICATION	WHO WOULD USE IT AND WHY

- **Discuss with your group what you learned as you went through this classification activity.** ANSWERS VARY. Students often mention various things that they learned about the animals they studied in the lesson as well as the fact that animals can be classified in a variety of ways depending on our interests, needs, and purposes.

THINKING ABOUT THINKING

- **How did you go about classifying the animals? What did you think about first, second, and third?** ANSWERS: *Determined important information about the things to be classified. Grouped, classified, and described these things according to common characteristics. Chose a way to classify the objects that suits a specific purpose. Classified the objects by developing a system of categories and subcategories.* The thinking map should include the steps in the chart shown at the right.

BOTTOM UP CLASSIFICATION

1. What characteristics do the given objects have?
2. What ways of classifying things do these characteristics define?
3. What purpose do we have for classifying the objects?
4. What way of classifying the objects that we have identified best serves this purpose?
5. What given items fall into the categories defined by this way of classifying?

- **How is the way you classified things different from using a classification system that is provided for you? Which way do you prefer? Why?** POSSIBLE ANSWERS: *You don't just sort them into categories you are given. When you do it this way, you have to observe the things, decide what is important, and decide what categories you are going to group them in based on a purpose. I prefer this type of classification because I can decide on the best way to classify for my purposes.*

- **How did classifying animals this way help you to define the words for each category?**
  POSSIBLE ANSWERS: *I decided to group the animals together because of important characteristics, like eating only meat, that they had in common. These common characteristics define the category and can be used to define the category words (like "carnivorous animals").*

APPLYING YOUR THINKING

Immediate Transfer

- Suppose you were put in charge of a new library and were asked to arrange the books by categories that would serve the needs and interests of library users. Think through different ways of doing this using the thinking map, and recommend one, explaining why you think your classification system is a good one.

- Classify foods according to a system that highlights important their characteristics. Explain who might find it helpful to use this classification system and what purpose it would serve.

Reinforcement Later

- Suppose you were a clothing store owner. You sold every type of clothing. Develop a classification system for the clothing that will serve the purposes of making it easy for shoppers to locate clothing that they might need and will help them locate clothing in a price range that they can afford. Draw a diagram of how you would organize the clothing in the store according to this system of classification.

CONTENT EXTENSION (SCIENCE)

After students have classified the animals on the animal cards and have constructed their diagrams, ask them to go to their textbooks and/or the school library and to find other animals that fit into the categories they have established. Have them explain why they classify the new animals in the way they do.

CONTENT EXTENSION (SOCIAL STUDIES)

Ask students to classify animals by geographical regions; they should develop a system of categories that indicate in what type of geographical region the animals can be found (e.g., in rivers, mountains, plains, etc.). They should then classify the animals they have been studying using this system of categories. Students can go to the school library to gather information about other animals that can be included in their classification. Ask them to select one animal that they think would be hard to find and to write a guide for people interested in locating this animal, explaining what geographical obstacles they would have to overcome to locate the animal.

ASSESSING STUDENT THINKING ABOUT CLASSIFICATION

To assess this skill, ask students questions like the immediate transfer questions above. The situation in which the students have to arrange things (e.g., clothing, books, or food in a store) is ideal for showing whether or not the students are thinking skillfully about how they classify things. Determine whether they are attending to each of the steps in the thinking map for classification. To determine their ability to monitor their own thinking about classification, encourage students to use terms appropriate to the skill of classifying (e.g., characteristics, groups, classification, category).

Sample Student Responses • Animals of the World

WAYS TO CLASSIFY THINGS

CATEGORIES	TYPES OF CATEGORIES				
	BENEFIT/ HARM TO MAN	LOCATION	BODY STRUCTURE/ FUNCTIONING	HABITAT	WHAT THEY EAT
Animals that inhabit Europe		X			
Sea-dwelling animals				X	
Animals that have hard outer shells			X		
Animals that eat wood	X				X
Animals that eat only meat					X
Scaly animals			X		
Poisonous animals	X		X		
Animals humans eat	X				
Animals that live in the rainforest				X	
Animals with backbones			X		
Animals that live in Africa		X			
One-celled animals			X		
Animals that eat only leaves					X
Animals that have fur	X		X		
Animals that eat both plants and animals					X
Decomposers	X				X
Animals that carry diseases	X				

Sample Student Responses • Animals • A Classification System

CLASSIFICATION WEB

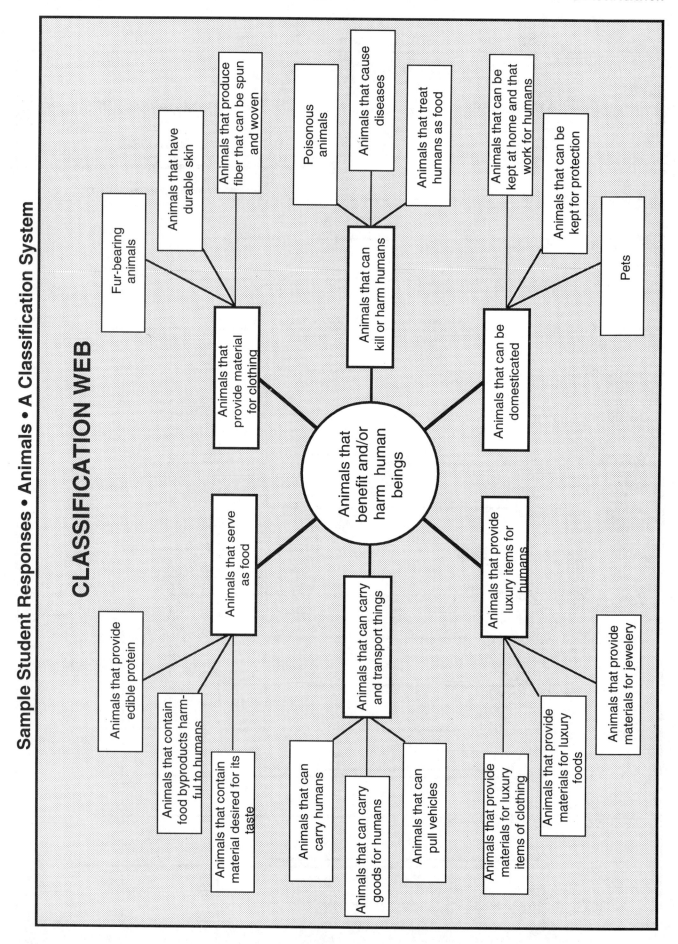

Fur-bearing animals

Animals that have durable skin

Animals that produce fiber that can be spun and woven

Poisonous animals

Animals that cause diseases

Animals that treat humans as food

Animals that can be kept at home and that work for humans

Animals that can be kept for protection

Animals that provide material for clothing

Animals that can kill or harm humans

Animals that can be domesticated

Pets

Animals that benefit and/or harm human beings

Animals that serve as food

Animals that can carry and transport things

Animals that provide luxury items for humans

Animals that provide edible protein

Animals that contain food byproducts harmful to humans

Animals that contain material desired for its taste

Animals that can carry humans

Animals that can carry goods for humans

Animals that can pull vehicles

Animals that provide materials for luxury items of clothing

Animals that provide materials for luxury foods

Animals that provide materials for jewelery

Sample Student Responses • Animals

PURPOSES AND USES OF ANIMAL CLASSIFICATION SYSTEMS

WAYS TO CLASSIFY	PURPOSE OF THE CLASSIFICATION	WHO WOULD USE IT AND WHY
Location	To indicate which animals inhabit a particular region. To indicate where in the world a particular animal can be found.	Traveler who wants to know what animals can be seen in an area. People who find animals for zoos.
Ecosystem	To indicate what kind of environment the animal needs to survive. To indicate what kinds of animals are likely to be found in a type of environment.	Environmentalists and government officials who try to preserve animals. Naturalists who want to find and observe animals in their natural environment. Zoo and aquarium workers who keep animals healthy.
Habitation (nest, den, hive, shell, etc.)	To indicate what kind of environment the animal needs to survive. To indicate in what type of home the animal can be found.	Naturalists who want to find and observe animals in their natural environment. Zoo and aquarium workers who keep animals healthy. Architects who create homes and buildings based on natural principles of design. People who cultivate animals.
Outer covering	To indicate what kind of protection the animal needs to survive.	Environmentalists who try to preserve animals. Designers who create clothing based on natural design principles.
Body structure and functioning	To provide information about the bodies of animals. To indicate how animals function in their environment.	Biologists who explain diversity and evolution of animals. Doctors who treat ill animals. Zoo and aquarium personnel who keep animals healthy.
Benefit or harm to man	To indicate which animals can be used to benefit man. To indicate how various animals can benefit man. To indicate which animals we need to protect ourselves from.	Ranchers who cultivate animals for food. People who hunt animals for food (e.g., fishermen). Travellers who are going into the wilds. People who train animals.
Population / species stability	To indicate size of population. To indicate which animals are endangered.	Environmentalists who try to preserve species of animals. People who hunt animals for food.

Sample Student Cognitive Map: Classifying Animals

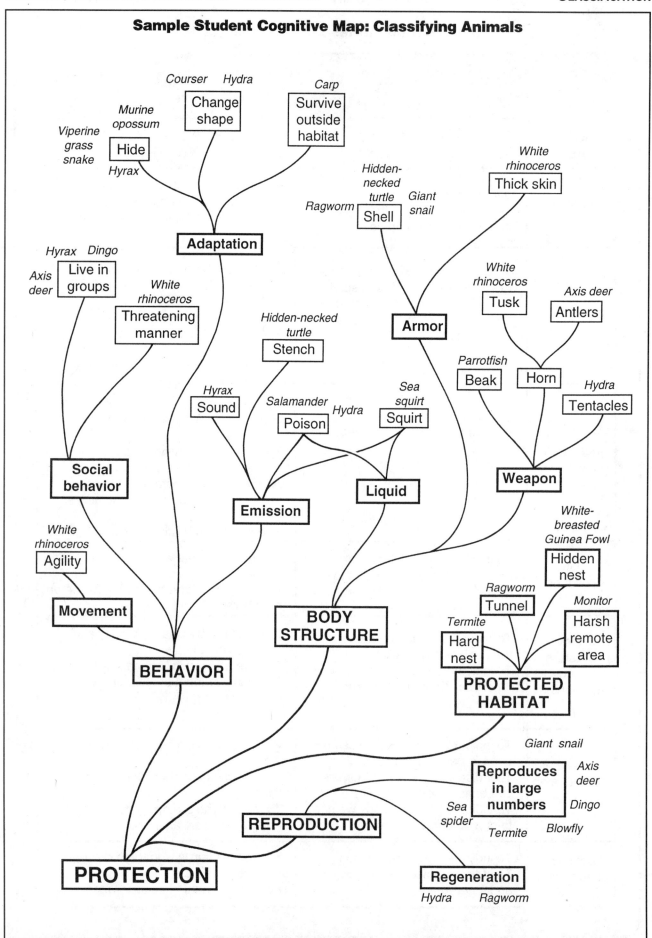

Sample Animal Cards

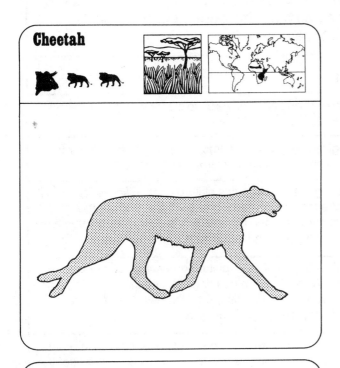

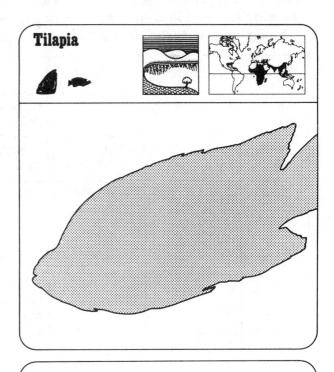

Cheetah

The fastest mammal on earth

The cheetah is the strangest of all the felines. Standing high off the ground, it has a narrow body and long tail. Its claws do not retract as do those of its cousins. It does not roar but emits an odd cry like a mewing hiss. Like a cat, it purrs to show pleasure. The cheetah is one of the rare diurnal felines. In fact it hunts by day, pursuing the antelope which it locates by means of its keen eye sight.

The cheetah lives in the open savanna and is never found in forests. It spends a large part of its time crouched on hillocks or large anthills, visually searching its territory for some kind of prey. Unlike the other big cats, which rely on surprise to take their victims, the cheetah overcomes gazelle and other antelope by running them down. Faster even than the greyhound the

cheetah can reach speeds of 90–98 km/hr (56–63 mph) which allow it to outstrip any other mammals on earth. Against this extraordinary performance must be set the fact that the cheetah has no endurance; it is exhausted after a run of 300–400 metres and has to rest for some time to get its breath back. It is a sprinter not a distance runner.

The habits of the cheetah have remained mysterious until recent years. It steadfastly refused to breed in captivity until 1967, since zoologists did not know that the presence of several males is necessary before the female will mate. It is the female who selects her partner, always the strongest member of the group.

Long ago the cheetah was used as a hunting animal in Asia and Arabia.

Gestation: 90 to 95 days Number of young: 2 to 5 Weight at birth: about 275 g (9 oz)		Adult weight: 30 to 65 kg (66 to 143 lbs) Sexual maturity: from 17 to 24 months		Longevity: 16 years Running speed: can cover 300 m (330 yards) at 70 to 90 km/hr (43 to 56 mph)
Phylum: **Vertebrata**	Class: **Mammalia**	Order: **Carnivora**	Family: **Felidae**	Genus and species: **Acinonyx jubatus**

© 1975, Editions Rencontre S.A., Lausanne

© 1975, English translation, Leisure Arts, London A   Printed in U.S.A.   Photo Wangi-Jacana   13 057 01 - 6

Tilapia

Of 'miraculous draught of fishes' fame...

The tilapia is a large fish of African origin which has gradually spread throughout the tropical and sub-tropical regions of the world, for man has taken a hand and introduced it in his diet in areas where previously it did not exist. In the beginning this fish was resident in tropical Africa, in the Nile basin and in Israel, Jordan and Syria. It lives in slow-flowing lakes and rivers, as well as in estuaries and salt-water lagoons. It acclimatizes itself well to new habitats and its resistance is absolutely incredible. For example, Graham's tilapia does well in the exceedingly alkaline waters of Lake Magadi in Kenya, where the temperature reaches 28° to 45° C (80° to 112° F). There are a hundred different species of tilapia.

Because of its ability to become used to different habitats, and above all for its

food value to populations lacking protein, the tilapia has been introduced into many areas, both voluntarily and involuntarily. Thus it appeared unexpectedly in Java in 1969, without anyone knowing how it travelled from East Africa to the East Indies. It then proceeded to spread spontaneously throughout the Indonesian islands. Recently tilapias have colonised the waters of Texas and Florida, and are becoming a serious menace to native species of fish. In 1951 the breeding of tilapia was begun in Madagascar. In several areas tilapias are kept to clean the lakes and marshland from the dangerous mosquito larvae which infest them. Even by the time of the Ancient Egyptians this fish was appreciated and it is certainly tilapias which are responsible for the Biblical 'miraculous draught of fishes'.

Oviparous Incubation: 8 to 20 days in the parents' mouth		Length: up to 45 cm (18 in) Sexual maturity: at 3 months		The tilapia can have 6 to 11 egg laying cycles per year
Phylum: **Vertebrata**	Class: **Osteichthyes**	Order: **Perciformes**	Family: **Cichlidae**	Genus and species: **Tilapia natalensis**

© 1975, Editions Rencontre S.A., Lausanne

© 1975, English translation, Leisure Arts, London   Printed in U.S.A.   Photo Albert Visage - Jacana   13 057 06 124

Safari Cards, Atlas Editions, Inc. Reprinted by permission of Atlas Editions, Inc., 33 Houston Dr., Durham, CT 06422. Cards shown are 67% of actual size. Only the outline of the animal has been reproduced. The actual animal cards show a full-color photo of the animal in its habitat.

CLASSIFICATION LESSON CONTEXTS

The following examples have been suggested by classroom teachers as contexts to develop infused lessons. If a skill or process has been introduced in a previous infused lesson, these contexts may be used to reinforce it.

GRADE	SUBJECT	TOPIC	THINKING ISSUE
K–3	Language arts	Parts of speech	Classify words as nouns or verbs to clarify their use in sentences.
K–3	Language arts	Types of books	Classify given books into a number of categories in order to distinguish books about reality from books that are fantasy.
K–3	Social studies	*We, the People*	On each page of Peter Spier's picture book, discuss the content of each picture. Write headings that classify the pictures to show that the Constitution is designed to serve all kinds of people, now and in the past.
K–3	Social studies	*The People*	Discuss the content of each picture on each page of Peter Spier's picture book. Write headings that classify the pictures to show how people from different cultures address human needs for food, shelter, clothing, love, and belonging.
K–3	Social studies	Land forms and bodies of water	Classify local land forms and bodies of water by type in order to clarify the terms and to show the interrelated features of the local ecosystem.
K–3	Social studies	Native Americans	Classify pictures of various tribes of Native American people according to the region of the country in which they live. Students will recognize that the differences in cultures indicates that there is not one view of native people that fits all tribes.
K-3	Social studies	*Bread, Bread, Bread*	Using Ann Morris's picture book, classify types of bread by appearance, ingredients, preparation, use, or culture to understand the varieties of bread (baguette, pita, pizza, bagels, chappatties, tortillas, etc.). Give additional examples.
K–3	Social studies	Goods and services	Classify various occupations regarding whether they provide goods or services in order to clarify how different people in your neighborhood make a living and to show how they are interdependent.
K–3	Science	Sounds	Classify sounds by levels (low-loud, low-soft, high-loud, and high-soft). How does this help you to describe them correctly and to identify their origin?
K–3	Science	Living things	Sort the following objects into living, nonliving, and once-living things in order to show the charactertistics of living things: balls, sun, clouds, eggs, bubbles, scarecrow, cactus, wooden objects, paper objects, dried flowers, potted plant, pine cone, carrot plant, mouse, and a river. Give additional examples.

CLASSIFICATION LESSON CONTEXTS

GRADE	SUBJECT	TOPIC	THINKING ISSUE
K–3	Science	Plants	Classify uses for plants (food, materials, oxygen, shade, beauty) in order to understand their significance in maintaining life.
K–3	Science	Observation/ Inference	Classify objects to show defining characteristics for sinking/ floating, heavy/light, and once-living/ non living things (feather, nail, lead ball, rock, balloon, cork stopper).
K–3	Science	Animals	Classify animals (meat eaters, plant eaters, or omnivores) by what they eat in order to understand their role in the food chain.
K–3	Science	Animal reproduction	To understand conditions necessary for the survival of the young, consider birth conditions (live birth, eggs with shells, and eggs without shells) in classifying the following animals: kittens, gerbils, snakes, kangaroos, whales, birds, frogs, fish, salamanders, turtles, butterflies, etc. Give further examples.
K–3	Science	Light	Classify objects according to whether they reflect or give off light in order to clarify the properties of light-generating things.
K–3	Science	Push/pull	Classify pictures to describe whether they use a pushing or a pulling motion (waterskis, tugboat, wagon, snowplow, tractor, wheelbarrow, window shade, flagpole, fishing pole). Give additional examples.
K-3	Science	Reproduction	Classify these organisms to clarify how they reproduce: bacteria, ostrich, marigold, banana, pine tree, chicken, kangaroo, cow, frog, snake, turtle, salmon, whale. Give additional examples.
K–3	Science	Food groups	Classify food into food groups (dairy, meats, fruits, vegetables, and breads/cereals) to identify elements of a balanced meal.
K–3	Science	Fruit	Classify fruits and vegetables to clarify the common and scientific term "fruit."
K–3	Science	Parts of a plant	Classify common fruit and vegetables to clarify which part of the plant we eat: root, stem, leaf, fruit, or seed.
K-3	Art	Colors	Classify color samples by whether they are warm or cool colors to describe their effect in a picture.
K-3	Music	Pitch/volume	Classify the sounds of various instruments in selected musical works to clarify the difference between pitch and volume.
4-6	English	Types of fiction and nonfiction	Classify works of fiction and nonfiction by types of narratives, periodicals, and nonprint media, or classify forms and types of poetry to clarify their characteristics and to locate them easily in the library.
4-6	English	Parts of speech	Classify parts of speech to clarify the definitions of each and to remember examples.
4-6	English	Writing	Use headings and subheadings to classify information about a topic in order to organize one's writing.

CLASSIFICATION LESSON CONTEXTS

GRADE	SUBJECT	TOPIC	THINKING ISSUE
4-6	English	Writing	Classify examples of writing by form (descriptive, expository, persuasive) to understand the key elements of each and to plan original writing accordingly.
4-6	Social studies	Colonies	Classify pictures of life in the New England colonies and life in the southern colonies to clarify differences in climate and economy.
4-6	Social studies	Local government	Given a collection of pictures of buildings in your community, classify them by local, state, and federal government services to show the functions of different levels of government.
4-6	Social studies	Geography	Classify pictures of land forms and bodies of water to clarify the defining charcteristics of each type.
4-6	Social studies	Native Americans	Given pictures of artifacts and scenes of daily life of plains, southwest, and northwest Indians, classify them to clarify how climate and environment influence their cultures.
4-6	Social studies	Pioneers	Given a collection of pictures of articles carried by pioneers on the trip across the plains, classify them to show how pioneers met basic needs.
4-6	Social studies	Industry	Classify pictures of tools from colonial times, the turn of the century, and today to reflect how industry has changed.
4-6	Social studies	Exploration	Classify items from the New World that were introduced into Europe as a result of Columbus's discoveries and subsequent exploration in order to understand the impact of the imports.
4-6	Mathematics	Factoring	Classify numbers by multiples to identify the greatest common factor.
4-6	Mathematics	Geometry	Classify pictures of objects to illustrate common polyhedra.
4-6	Mathematics	Geometry	Classify an array of triangles by size of angles (acute, right and obtuse) and reclassify by length of sides (scalene, isosceles, and equilateral) to demonstrate that we commonly describe them by either set of these attributes.
4-6	Science	Simple machines	Classify common objects that change force by the type of simple machine involved in order to demonstrate versatility and usefulness of simple machines.
4-6	Science	Ecosystem	Classify animals by the type of ecosystem they inhabit to clarify their survival needs. Who would find that kind of classification helpful?
4-6	Science	Nutrients in food	Classify foods by types of nutrients (proteins, carbohydrates, fats, minerals/vitamins, and water) to determine how much of each type of food is needed daily for good nutrition.

CLASSIFICATION LESSON CONTEXTS

GRADE	SUBJECT	TOPIC	THINKING ISSUE
4-6	Science	Simple organisms	Classify organisms by type (monerans, protists, or fungi) in order to describe their structure and functioning and by whether they are helpful or harmful. Examples may include nitrogen-fixing plant nodules, mold, yogurt-making organisms, diatoms, red tide, fungus, mildew, yeast, penicillin-producing organisms, mushrooms, and bacteria in cheese. Give additional examples.
4-6	Science	Chemical and physical changes	Classify the following examples of chemical or physical change to describe principles for such changes: campfire, smashing rocks, boiling water, adding Alka-Seltzer to water, bending a metal bar, rusting, melting, breaking glass, rising bread, breathing, digestion. Give additional examples for each type of change.
4-6	Science	Types of organisms	Classify the following organisms by type: bacteria, mold, paramecium, mushroom, grass, moss, pine trees, fruit tree, insects, spiders, frogs, snakes, kangaroo, monkeys. Give additional examples for each type.
4-6	Science	Protection	Classify the following animals to derive principles of animal protection: puff fish, chameleon, stonefish, mantid, porcupine, clams, turtles, goose, walrus, sheep, armadillo. Give additional examples for each form of animal. Who would find this way of classifying protection helpful?
4-6	Science	Protection	Classify the following plants by the way they protect themselves: cactus, rose, mesquite, bush, anemone, etc. Give additional examples of each type of plant. Who would find this way of classifying plants helpful?
4-6	Science	Status of matter	Classify these examples to illustrate changes in states of matter (melting, freezing, evaporating, condensing): making juice bars, eating juice bars, sniffing perfume, boiling fudge, puddles drying up, crayon in a hot car, fog on a windshield. Give additional examples for each type of change.
4-6	Health	Food groups	Classify common fast food items by food group to inform students whether their selections are balanced meals.
4-6	Art	Pictures	Classify selected works by their mediums (e.g., oil painting, pastel, ink drawing, collage, print, etc.) to clarify how the process affects the appearance of the work. Give additional examples of works for each medium.
4-6	Music	Musical style	Classify selected musical works by style (classical, popular, folk, religious, etc.) to clarify their origins, characteristics, and appeal. Give additional examples for each style.
4-6	Music	Musical instruments	Classify musical instruments in different ways to clarify their effect in music, the skill needed to play them, and the type of music they perform.
4-6	Physical education	Exercise	Classify various exercise activities as stretching, resistance, or aerobic to clarify their benefits: bicycling, weight lifting, playing tennis, jumping rope, step exercise, touching toes, yoga, running, and swimming. Give additional examples for each type of exercise.

CHAPTER 6
DETERMINING PARTS-WHOLE RELATIONSHIPS

Why is it Important to Determine Parts-Whole Relationships Skillfully?

Everything around us is made up of parts. Man-made things, like automobiles and TV sets, depend for their functioning on the proper operation of their parts. Many natural objects, including the bodies of animals, the solar system, and great rivers, have parts that combine and operate together for the functioning of the whole.

Things that aren't physical objects also have parts. Stories, films, and human societies have component parts which give these items their distinctive character.

Whole objects or systems are not just collections of their parts. If the parts were combined together in different ways, something different would result. The special relationship between the parts and the whole that they comprise often makes the whole object or system what it is, allows it to function as it does, and permits it to retain its integrity.

The purposes of determining parts-whole relationships. Recognizing how parts contribute to the whole and how each part functions can help us better understand the world around us. In addition, analyzing parts-whole relationships can have some immediate practical applications. If we know what function each part serves, we are better able to sustain and maintain the whole. An automobile repairman who knows the function of each part can usually fix a malfunctioning car because he knows what to repair or replace.

Indeed, our knowledge of how parts function can make us much more self-reliant. If the door sticks, we can sand or shave it. If the hinges are loose, we can tighten the screws. If we need a new lock, we know what to ask for. Being able to do these repairs efficiently ourselves depends on our knowing the parts of a door and how they function.

Knowing the function of parts can also contribute to our creativity. If we know what spe-cific components can do, we may be able to combine them in new ways to serve certain purposes. New gadgets for use around the house, new organizational systems for managing work, original stories and works of art, and new economic systems connecting independent countries are all built on knowledge of how parts can contribute to the functioning of a whole.

Problems with the way we think about parts and wholes. People often have no difficulty identifying parts of things they see before them. Parts are usually smaller than the wholes they compose, and they usually look different from each other. The knob on a TV set, for example, looks quite different from the picture tube.

Often when people think about specific parts of things that they see, they identify them only by their physical appearance. A person may see a series of controls on the front of a VCR, recognize them as parts of the VCR, but have no idea what each part does. The person may not even try to find out what the parts do as long as he or she can put a video tape in the VCR and play it. If we attend to appearance alone in characterizing a part, then our understanding of the part/whole relationship is *hasty and superficial*. Describing parts superficially blocks us from finding out how the part functions and recognizing the overall relationship between the parts and the whole they comprise.

A second problem about the way we think about parts is that we often do not consider subdividing parts into other parts in order to understand them better. This represents a *narrowness* in our conception of the parts of a whole that can limit our understanding of how the parts function. For example, I may identify the receiver on the phone as a part of the phone but need some prompting to separate it into a mouthpiece, an earpiece, and a connecting handle. Even if I did that, I would rarely go further and subdivide the mouthpiece and earpiece into their components.

A third problem is that, while we may identify many component parts of familiar things, we often think of them as *a scattered group of components* and do not consider how they may be connected to each other. I may, for example, notice that the vinyl padding on the back of a chair, its seat, the wooden chair back itself, and the arms on which my elbows rest are all parts of the chair, without thinking much about how they work together to make the chair useful and comfortable. I may not recognize, for example, that the padding, which supports my back, is held up at the right height by the chair back which also supports the arms which are positioned at the right height to rest my elbows on. Nor may I note that the arms are also supported by a strut that rests on the seat which, in turn, is supported by the legs. Although the separate parts of the chair are easily discernible, unless I think about how each contributes to the structure, function, and appearance of the chair, I may not understand their purpose or value.

Sometimes we do think in richer ways about parts and the wholes that they comprise. I may identify the receiver on the telephone as a device that transmits my voice and receives the voice of others via the telephone lines and not just as a piece of plastic with a certain shape. I may identify the keyboard on my computer as something that transmits letters to the screen and contains numerous parts: keys, a space bar, a case, and the electronic circuitry that transforms pressure on a key into an electric signal, etc. I may also be aware that the keyboard, connecting wire, and inner circuitry in my computer transmit an image onto the screen. But many of us think about parts and wholes in this way all too infrequently. Awareness of the three defaults in our thinking about parts-whole relationships can prompt us to try to think more skillfully.

Figure 6.1 contains a summary of these three common problems with the way we think about parts-whole relationships.

How Do We Think Skillfully about Parts-Whole Relationships?

Determining how parts function in relation to a whole. Determining the relationship between parts and a whole is a basic analytical

---

COMMON DEFAULTS IN OUR THINKING ABOUT PARTS-WHOLE RELATIONSHIPS

1. We define parts based only on their appearances. (Our characterization of parts is **hasty**.)

2. We don't think of subdividing parts into other parts. (Our consideration of parts is **narrow**.)

3. We don't connect parts together in relation to the whole that they comprise. (Our thinking about parts is **scattered**.)

Figure 6.1

---

thinking skill. In its most complete form, we strive to understand the basic parts of an object, an organism, a composition, or a system in terms of how the parts function together in the structure or operation of the whole. The key to understanding parts-whole relationships is understanding what the parts *do* in relation to the whole, not just their immediate appearance.

A strategy for determining parts-whole relationships. A natural way to begin thinking about the parts of a whole is to identify as many parts as possible, describing them by their common names (e.g., computer keyboard) or, if these are not known, by using a description (e.g., the light on the front of the computer monitor). This may involve a deeper investigation than just looking at the object. We may have to take the cover off, for example, and look inside. We may also need a magnifying glass or even a microscope.

We then should consider these parts one-by-one to determine their function. Sometimes this is easy. If a switch is marked "Off-On," then its function is to turn the computer on or off, presumably by opening or closing an electrical circuit. Sometimes, however, the function of a part is not clear. One important way to determine a part's function is to raise, and answer, the question, What would happen if the object didn't have this part or if the part malfunctioned? If there were no keyboard on my computer, I would not be able to type information into the computer memory banks. Therefore, I can conclude that the function of the keyboard is to transmit such data to the computer.

The thinking map in figure 6.2 guides us in determining the relationship between the parts and a whole.

DETERMINING PARTS-WHOLE RELATIONSHIPS

1. What smaller things make up the whole?

2. For each part, what would happen to the whole if it were missing?

3. What is the function of each part?

Figure 6.2

Sometimes we do not know what would happen if the object didn't have a specific part. For example, what would happen if the unmarked knob on the side of my portable radio were not there or did not function?

There are two ways to answer this question: by seeking information from a reliable source or by direct investigation. In the first instance, I can find out the function of the radio knob by consulting the radio manual or asking a radio repairman. Like other thinking skills, determining parts-whole relationships skillfully may require thinking about the reliability of sources of information.

We can also undertake some direct investigation ourselves. We could try the knob to see what happens and then remove it and see what happens. We might find that turning the knob changes the tone of the sound from the radio. When the knob is not there, it is more difficult to turn the metal rod that inserts into the knob. Therefore we realize that the function of the knob is to make it relatively easy to fine tune the tone on the radio.

If we undertake this kind of direct investigation, we try to determine possible causal connections between the functioning of the part and the operation of the whole. While determining the function of the knob on the radio is relatively straightforward, there may be occasions when it is necessary to engage in skillful causal explanation and/or prediction in order to be able to make a confident judgment about the function of a part. For example, does a specific bit of genetic material in the human body create the body's natural resistance to cancer? Although this is the same sort of question as finding the function of the knob on the radio, in this case, a simple investigation would not suffice to answer this question. Research on the function of certain components of genes in the human body may involve collecting some very sophisticated evidence before hypotheses about gene functioning can be certified as well supported.

Determining parts-whole relationships skillfully sometimes requires more sophisticated kinds of investigation, as in determining the function of specific genetic material. Fortunately, in everyday circumstances, like investigating the function of a radio knob, we can often engage in part/whole thinking skillfully without having to carry out such complex investigations.

Two graphic organizers to facilitate determining the relationship between parts and a whole. We may use graphic organizers to guide our thinking about parts and wholes and to record the results of our thinking so that we do not have to keep it in memory. The graphic organizer in figure 6.3 guides us to discriminate a number of parts and then to determine the function of *one* part that we choose to analyze further.

A similar graphic organizer in figure 6.4 can be used to record these results for all of the parts.

How Can We Teach Students to Determine Parts-Whole Relationships Skillfully?

Teaching skillful determination of parts-whole relationships explicitly. Teaching students the organized process of thinking depicted in figure 6.3 can help them improve the way they think about the parts of a whole. The approach we recommend is to teach skillful determination of parts-whole relationships *explicitly*. Explain the strategy directly and ask your students to practice it in a content lesson. As an alternative, you can guide your students to develop the strategy themselves as they examine the relationship between the parts and a whole that they are studying. In both cases this

---

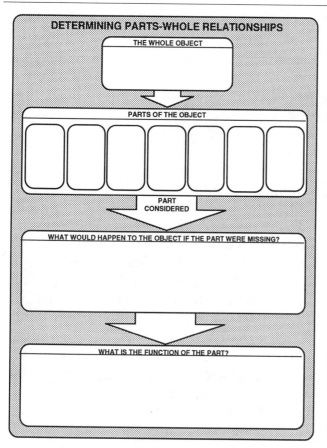

Figure 6.3

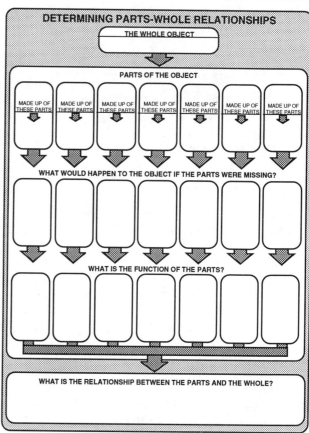

Figure 6.4

should be followed by the use of a graphic organizer (figures 6.3 and 6.4) to reinforce the strategy.

A simplified version of the graphic organizer in figure 6.3 contains cells for only five parts (see p. 175). The simplified diagram may be helpful for primary grade students and for analyzing items that have a very small number of discernible parts.

Contexts in the curriculum for lessons on determining parts-whole relationships. The curriculum offers numerous opportunities to teach students to determine parts-whole relationships skillfully. Almost everything they study has component parts: plants and animals; systems like the solar system; social and political systems; poems, novels, and short stories; paintings and musical compositions; team sports; and machines. When you choose instructional contexts in your curriculum for parts-whole lessons, make sure that there is a rich content-objective to be achieved by the lesson. In general, there are two types of contexts in which determining the relationship between

parts and wholes is important in the standard curriculum:

- *Understanding key concepts or processes depends on recognizing the function of component parts.* For example, understanding certain forms of poetry involves understanding the function of rhyming words or phrases which have a specific meter. A more concrete example involves understanding how certain machines operate by understanding the role of component parts like pulleys, gears, and levers.

- *Recognizing the function of component parts in a whole helps us understand changes in the whole.* A mass of cold air colliding with a mass of warm, moist air can bring about a severe storm like a tornado or blizzard. Understanding how these two components of a weather system function to bring about such storms is a key to predicting weather. Another example involves understanding how the interaction between various component groups in a society can bring about such events as the Russian Revolution.

A menu of suggested contexts for infusion lessons on parts-whole relationships is provided on pp. 189–91.

Reinforcing the process. Your goal in teaching these lessons is to help your students develop, remember, and internalize strategies for determining the relationship between parts and wholes so that they can guide their own thinking. This requires continued reinforcement. Make the graphic organizers for determining parts-whole relationships available in your classroom and encourage your students to use them on their own. Help them to practice this skill deliberately in curricular contexts other than the one in which you introduced it.

Help students apply the parts/whole thinking strategy in non-curricular contexts as well. Simple physical objects found around the home, such as kitchen utensils, furniture, and toys, can all be insightfully analyzed into their parts. The school building is a whole object whose smooth functioning depends on a variety of component parts: the electrical system, the plumbing, construction elements, etc.

Students may even analyze the way people in different roles contribute to the functioning of whole organizations, such as their supermarkets or schools. Families, communities, and even cooperative learning groups in the classroom are also whole systems made up of components which work together when these systems function well.

You will find that as the process of determining the relationship between parts and wholes becomes familiar, students will use the parts-whole thinking strategy without your guidance.

Model Lessons on Determining Parts-Whole Relationships

Two model lessons are included in this chapter. The first is a lesson on *Pots and Pans*, a 2nd–3rd grade hands-on science lesson in which students make use of their knowledge of heat conduction to analyze the function of the various parts of ordinary kitchen utensils. The second is a science lesson in which 4th–6th grade students analyze the parts of a bird—the American kestrel—to determine their function with regard to the whole organism.

As you review these lessons, think about the following key questions:

- How does the thinking skill instruction interweave with the content in these lessons?
- Can you clearly distinguish the four components of infusion lessons in these examples?
- What differences are there in the way determining parts-whole relationships is treated in each lesson?
- Can you identify additional transfer examples to add to these lessons?

Tools for Designing Parts-whole Lessons

The thinking map on page 174 provides focus questions to guide students' determination of the relationship between parts and wholes in infusion lessons. It can be used as represented here or modified by students.

The graphic organizers depicting part-whole relationships (see pp. 175–77) supplement and reinforce the thinking map. The first two diagrams, one for five parts (designed especially for use in the primary grades) and the other for seven, are used to determine the function of a specific part. The third diagram is used to determine how multiple parts interconnect in the functioning of a whole.

The thinking maps and graphic organizers can guide you in designing the critical thinking activity in the lesson and can also serve as photocopy masters, transparency masters, or as models that can be enlarged and used as posters in the classroom. Reproduction rights are granted for single classroom use only.

DETERMINING PARTS-WHOLE RELATIONSHIPS

1. What smaller things make up the whole?

2. For each part, what would happen if it was missing?

3. What is the function of each part?

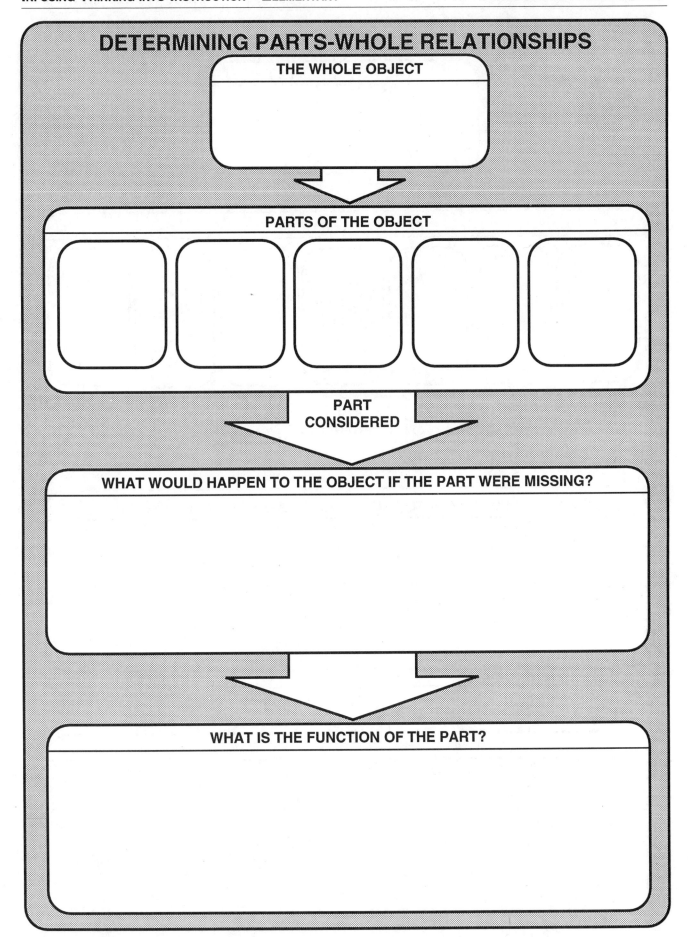

DETERMINING PARTS-WHOLE RELATIONSHIPS

THE WHOLE OBJECT

PARTS OF THE OBJECT

PART CONSIDERED

WHAT WOULD HAPPEN TO THE OBJECT IF THE PART WERE MISSING?

WHAT IS THE FUNCTION OF THE PART?

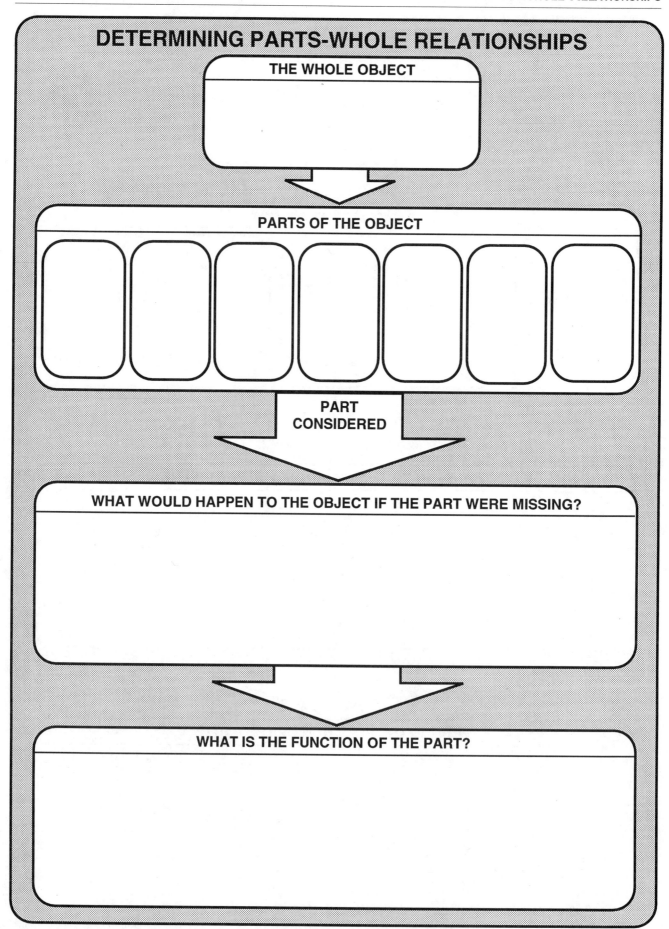

DETERMINING PARTS-WHOLE RELATIONSHIPS

THE WHOLE OBJECT

PARTS OF THE OBJECT

PART CONSIDERED

WHAT WOULD HAPPEN TO THE OBJECT IF THE PART WERE MISSING?

WHAT IS THE FUNCTION OF THE PART?

DETERMINING PARTS-WHOLE RELATIONSHIPS

THE WHOLE OBJECT

PARTS OF THE OBJECT

MADE UP OF THESE PARTS

MADE UP OF THESE PARTS

MADE UP OF THESE PARTS

MADE UP OF THESE PARTS

MADE UP OF THESE PARTS

MADE UP OF THESE PARTS

MADE UP OF THESE PARTS

WHAT WOULD HAPPEN TO THE OBJECT IF THE PARTS WERE MISSING?

WHAT IS THE FUNCTION OF THE PARTS?

WHAT IS THE RELATIONSHIP BETWEEN THE PARTS AND THE WHOLE?

POTS AND PANS

Science   **Grades 2–3**

OBJECTIVES

CONTENT	THINKING SKILL/PROCESS
Students will learn that some substances conduct heat more quickly and more efficiently than others.	Students will identify the significant parts of a whole by identifying parts and determining their functions.

METHODS AND MATERIALS

CONTENT	THINKING SKILL/PROCESS
In teams of two, students will examine pots and pans with wooden or plastic handles. If possible, there will also be a demonstration of what happens when a frying pan is heated.	A thinking map, a graphic organizer, and structured questioning prompt students to describe various component parts of a whole and to determine how these parts function with regard to the whole. (See p. 174–77 for reproducible diagrams.) Collaborative learning groups enhance student thinking.

LESSON

INTRODUCTION TO CONTENT AND THINKING SKILL/PROCESS

- If you ever put a puzzle together, did you notice how all the parts blended to make a whole picture? That's different from the mess you see in the puzzle box when the parts are all separated. When the puzzle is put together, each piece has its own place and adds something to the whole. Can you think of something else that is made of smaller parts that work together to make up the whole? POSSIBLE ANSWERS: *A car, a bicycle, a bird, a TV set, a school bus, a school building, a clock, a book, a Christmas tree, a flower, a shoe, a hand, a computer, a telephone.*

- Pick one of these and work with your partner to list as many parts of it as you can. After a few minutes, ask a few groups to report. Write the name of the whole object on the board and list the parts that the students mention. POSSIBLE ANSWERS: *Telephone: receiver, cord, push-buttons, "feet," wire. School bus: doors, seats, tires, engine, roof, driver's seat, steering wheel, windows.*

- To understand how important parts are, think about what the parts add to the whole. For example, what does a steering wheel do on a school bus? POSSIBLE ANSWERS: *When it turns, it makes the wheels turn so that the bus can go around corners. It is made to allow a person to turn it easily when he or she wants to turn the wheels of the bus.* When you describe what a part adds to a whole, you're describing the *function* of that part. The steering wheel's function is to turn the wheels of the bus. "Function" is an important word to learn so that you can use it when we are talking about parts and wholes.

- It's important to think about the parts of a whole and to figure out what they add to the whole. When something doesn't work, it is usually because one of its parts doesn't do what it's supposed to. If you know that, it's easier to fix it. For example, if the door of the school bus didn't close properly, what part might need fixing? POSSIBLE ANSWERS: *The handle, the latch, the hinges.* The reason you give those answers is because you know that these are parts of the door and that their function is to make the door open, close, and stay shut.

- Here's a thinking map that can guide you to identify the parts of a whole and what they add to the whole. Show a copy of the parts of a whole chart at the right.

THINKING ACTIVELY

- We've been studying metals in science. Let's consider what we know about metals that can help us understand why people use metal to make parts. What are some things that you've learned about metal objects? POSSIBLE ANSWERS: *Most metal things*

PARTS OF A WHOLE

1. What smaller things make up the whole?

2. For each of these parts, what would happen to the whole if it were missing?

3. What is the function of the part

---

are strong, durable, shiny, heavy, solid, and made from material that needs to be dug out of the ground; they keep their shape at normal temperatures and require a lot of heat to melt. **Can you think of some parts of things that are made of metal because metal because of these properties?** POSSIBLE ANSWERS: *The outside of a car is made of metal so that the passengers can be protected in an accident. That is because metal is strong. Nuts and bolts are usually made of metal because the strength of metal allows it to hold things together. A safe is usually made of metal because its strength makes it hard to open. It may also be too heavy to lift and carry away.*

- **Do you know what happens when you apply heat to metals? Feel it now. What does it feel like?** Ask two students to come up and feel the metal. They usually answer that it is cold. **Let's put this frying pan on a heat source like the radiator. Now what does it feel like after the pan has been on the heat for awhile?** *It is hot.* **What do the parts of the metal that aren't on the heat source feel like?** *They are hot also but not as hot as the metal right above the heat.* **Do you remember what it's called when heat spreads out in a substance?** *The substance conducts heat.* **That's why we use metals to make pots and pans for cooking things.**

- Here are some pots and pans like the frying pan we just heated. Break into teams of two. Each team should pick one of the pots or pans to examine. Use the thinking map on the board in order to determine the parts of the pot, as well as the function of each part. List the parts of the pot or pan on this graphic organizer. Show a copy of the organizer at right. After the students work in pairs, ask each team to share one of their answers with the rest of the class. Write these on a drawing of the graphic organizer on the board, on a large poster, or on a transparency. POSSIBLE ANSWERS: *The bottom, the sides, the wooden (or plastic) handle, the stem that goes into the handle, and the hook in the handle.*

DETERMINING PARTS-WHOLE RELATIONSHIPS

THE WHOLE OBJECT

PARTS OF THE OBJECT

PART CONSIDERED

WHAT WOULD HAPPEN TO THE OBJECT IF THE PART WERE MISSING?

WHAT IS THE FUNCTION OF THE PART?

- **Two of the parts of the pot or pan are the bottom and the sides. Discuss these with your partner. Write on the graphic organizer what would happen if the pot or pan didn't have a bottom and what would happen if it didn't have sides.** POSSIBLE ANSWERS: *If it didn't have a bottom, the food would fall out into the flame or onto the hot electric element on the stove. If it didn't have sides, eggs and liquids would spill.*

- **What are the functions of the bottom and of the sides? Fill these in on the graphic organizer.** POSSIBLE ANSWERS: *The bottom holds food so it can get hot and cook. The sides keep food from spilling.*

- **Now think about the wooden (or plastic) handle. What would happen if it didn't have that handle?** ANSWER: *You wouldn't be able to pick it up.* **Why couldn't you pick it up?** In class discussion, students respond that if it didn't have that handle, you couldn't pick the pot up by the sides because it would be too hot. They also say that if it had a metal stem and no handle, you could pick it up, but you would need a pot holder since the metal would be too hot.

- **Write what you think the wooden (or plastic) handle adds to the pot or pan. What is its function?** After students have written on their graphic organizer, ask for two or three responses from the class. POSSIBLE ANSWERS: *The function of the wooden (or plastic) handle is to provide something cool enough to hold on to when lifting the hot pan. Also, wood (or plastic) doesn't get so hot that it burns. It isn't on the flame.*

- **Why do you think that the wood (or plastic) doesn't get hot?** POSSIBLE ANSWERS: *The heat from the metal doesn't spread out in the wood (or plastic) as much as it does in the metal. Wood (or plastic) doesn't conduct heat as much as metal does.*

- **Now work with your partner and list some other substances from which you could make a handle that would allow you to pick up a hot pan. Discuss with your partner why these substances would or would not make good cooking pan handles.** After a few minutes, ask students to share some of their ideas about other substances that could be used for cooking pan handles and why they think so. POSSIBLE ANSWERS: *Plastic would be good because it is stiff, doesn't conduct heat very much, and probably wouldn't burn. Cloth or paper wouldn't be good because, even though it wouldn't get as hot as metal, it might burn. Wax could be molded around the handle but would melt. Soap would also melt and would be too slippery if your hands are wet.*

THINKING ABOUT THINKING

- **How did you decide what parts to write down in the "parts" boxes?** POSSIBLE ANSWERS: I looked at the pan and looked for smaller things that were different from each other that made it up. I looked at one part, like the handle, and then looked for its parts, like the ring and hook.

- **After you listed the parts, what did you think about to determine the function of each part?** POSSIBLE ANSWERS: *I imagined what the pan would be like without the part and thought about what would happen if I put something in the pan to cook. That made me realize what function the part has.*

- **What would you tell other people to think about in order to identify the parts of a whole and the function of each?** Answers usually include the steps in the thinking map for parts and wholes.

- **Sometimes we can't tell what might happen if an object didn't have a specific part. If you didn't know what would happen, how could you find out?** POSSIBLE ANSWERS: *I could try it out if it weren't too dangerous. I could watch an object that didn't have the part and compare it to one that did.*

APPLYING THINKING

Immediate Transfer

- **Identify a machine that interests you. What are its parts and what are their functions?**

- **Pick a living thing, list its parts, and determine their functions. Use your graphic organizer. Which parts are the most important for it to survive? Why?**

Reinforcement Later

Later on in the school year, introduce these additional transfer activities by saying the following:

- In social studies, we're studying communities. Pick a specific community you are familiar with, like your own, and think about its different parts. What is the function of each part in the community? Pick a specific part of the community. Write a description of what it would be like if the community didn't have that component.

- Stories are also wholes that have parts. Select a story and determine what the different parts of this story add to the whole. Discuss what the story would be like if you changed one of the parts.

ART EXTENSION

Ask the students to select one part of a pan and to draw it on a piece of drawing paper. They should write the name and function under the part. Then ask them to redesign each part so that it either functions better or serves another purpose as well. Show examples of different lids to illustrate what you mean (e.g., some sit on top of the pan, some insert into the pan, some have enamel, some have plastic knobs, some metal knobs, etc.). Discuss the differences in function for the different designs (e.g., the ones with plastic or wooden knobs are easier to lift than ones with metal knobs, which tend to get hot; the colored enamel lids are more decorative than plain metal; etc.). Each students should draw a redesigned part and write under each why it is better than the original. Then they should draw what the reassembled pan would look like.

An alternative activity involves grouping all student pictures of the same kind of part. By selecting the most interesting innovations, reassemble the best parts to create a class composite "pan" with improved features.

ASSESSING STUDENT THINKING ABOUT PARTS-WHOLE RELATIONSHIPS

To assess student thinking about parts and wholes, give them a problem about an item that is familiar to them. Explain that it doesn't work because of a malfunctioning part and ask the students to figure out what part is causing the problem. Because students in the first and second grades may find writing difficult, you may conduct this assessment orally, either individually or in small groups. In order to determine whether students are attending to each of the steps in the thinking map for parts and wholes, ask them to identify each step of the parts-whole strategy as they think about the problem.

Sample Student Responses • Pots and Pans

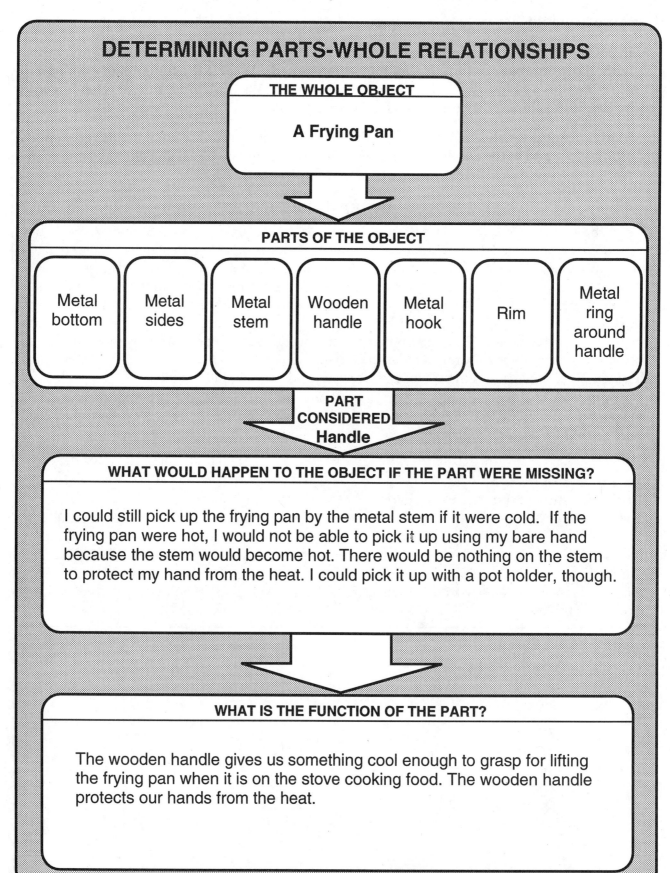

DETERMINING PARTS-WHOLE RELATIONSHIPS

THE WHOLE OBJECT

A Frying Pan

PARTS OF THE OBJECT

| Metal bottom | Metal sides | Metal stem | Wooden handle | Metal hook | Rim | Metal ring around handle |

PART CONSIDERED
Handle

WHAT WOULD HAPPEN TO THE OBJECT IF THE PART WERE MISSING?

I could still pick up the frying pan by the metal stem if it were cold. If the frying pan were hot, I would not be able to pick it up using my bare hand because the stem would become hot. There would be nothing on the stem to protect my hand from the heat. I could pick it up with a pot holder, though.

WHAT IS THE FUNCTION OF THE PART?

The wooden handle gives us something cool enough to grasp for lifting the frying pan when it is on the stove cooking food. The wooden handle protects our hands from the heat.

THE KESTREL

OBJECTIVES

CONTENT

Students will learn the importance of the structure and use of different parts of a bird of prey, the kestrel, in sustaining its ability to survive.

THINKING SKILL/PROCESS

Students will identify the significant parts of a whole by identifying parts and determining their functions.

METHODS AND MATERIALS

CONTENT

Students will read a passage about the American kestrel and will examine pictures of it. If possible, a videotape of the kestrel and its behavior will be shown.

THINKING SKILL/PROCESS

A thinking map, a graphic organizer, and structured questioning prompt students to determine parts of a whole and how the parts function with regard to the whole. (See pp. 174–77 for reproducible diagrams.) Collaborative learning enhances interchange of thinking.

LESSON

INTRODUCTION TO CONTENT AND THINKING SKILL/PROCESS

- We often notice some of the parts that make up a whole thing, for example, the engine and the body of a car. But sometimes it is important to know more about the relationship between parts and the whole. For example, when something doesn't work properly, it is usually because one of its parts doesn't do what it was designed to do. If you know what the parts are supposed to do, it's easier to fix it. For example, if the door of the classroom doesn't close properly, what part might need fixing? POSSIBLE ANSWERS: *The door knob, the latch, the hinges, or the door frame.* The reason you can figure that out is because you know that these are parts of the door and that they make the door open, close, and stay shut.

- It is usually easy to pick out the major parts that make up familiar things. Determining the relationships between the parts and the whole may be more challenging. This often means figuring out how the component parts relate to one another to define whole object or to enable it to do what it was designed to do. When we describe the relationship between a part and the whole, we usually do so in terms of the *function* of the part. For example, in addition to the engine and body, let's list some other parts of an automobile. POSSIBLE ANSWERS: *The transmission, the wheels, the frame, a radio, paint, a heater, a steering wheel, the instruments, the seats, the carpeting on the floor, and the windows.* **What are the functions of some of these parts?** POSSIBLE ANSWERS: *The engine functions to provide power for the car to move. The transmission delivers power to the wheels so that they can turn and propel the car. The body encloses the driver and passengers. The paint protects the metal and improves the appearance of the car. The radio and heater increase the comfort of the passengers.*

> **DETERMINING PARTS-WHOLE RELATIONSHIPS**
>
> 1. What smaller things make up the whole?
>
> 2. For each part, what would happen to the whole if it were missing?
>
> 3. What is the function of each part?

- **The thinking map (at right) can guide you in**

identifying the parts of a whole and their relationships to the whole. Show a copy of the chart. (See p. 174 for a reproducible thinking map.)

THINKING ACTIVELY

- **Let's try out these ideas in connection with something we've been studying in science: the predator-prey relationship. Predators depend on their prey for survival, but they also depend on their ability to capture their prey. Let's use our thinking strategy for determining parts-whole relationships to try to understand how one well-known predator, the American kestrel, has maintained a large population in both North and South America. Here is a passage about the kestrel from a guide to birds of America:**

> *American Kestrel.* The American kestrel is one of the most common birds of prey in both North and South America. Its population has flourished. It is characterized by long, narrow, pointed wings and reddish brown and slate-gray markings. It is known for its habit of hovering in one place while hunting its prey, generally consisting of snakes, lizards, large insects, and small rodents. This evolved hunting skill involves the ability to detect any small movement on the ground, the ability to hover while scanning the ground for prey, and the speed and strength to plunge onto the prey from heights of 50 feet or more. All these skills depend on the kestrel's good sense of depth perception.

If possible, show a videotape of the kestrel in flight stalking and catching its prey.

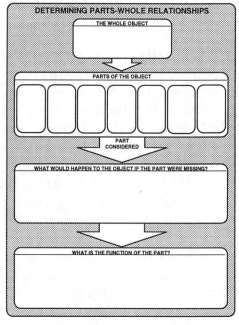

Illustration by Kate Simon Huntley

- **Use the graphic organizer for determining parts-whole relationships to compile a list of parts of the American kestrel. Break some of these parts into their components and add these to your list. Work with a partner on this activity.** After a few minutes, solicit responses from the class. Ask each team to mention only one part so that as many teams as possible can report. POSSIBLE ANSWERS: *Its beak, its head, the tip of its beak, its eye, a feather, a wing, its feet, a claw, its markings, its tail, its heart, its breast muscles, its neck, a pupil, the quill from a feather, a claw nail.*

DETERMINING PARTS-WHOLE RELATIONSHIPS

THE WHOLE OBJECT

PARTS OF THE OBJECT

PART CONSIDERED

WHAT WOULD HAPPEN TO THE OBJECT IF THE PART WERE MISSING?

WHAT IS THE FUNCTION OF THE PART?

- **Imagine what it would be like if the Kestrel were injured. Pick a part and discuss with your partner how you think the bird would be affected if that part were injured. Write your ideas in the appropriate box on the graphic organizer.** After a few minutes, ask for responses from the teams. POSSIBLE ANSWERS: *If one of its eyes were injured, it would lose depth perception and would probably not be able to judge very well how far it must dive to reach its prey. This might affect its ability to get food, and it might starve. (Some students may know that, as a bird of prey, the kestrel has stereoscopic vision, which enables* *it to see objects as three-dimensional and to judge the distance of the prey.) If the Kestrel were missing a talon, it may manage to catch its prey, since it has four talons on each foot, but it would be difficult. If the tip of the beak were injured, it would be hard for the bird to kill and eat its prey. If the Kestrel lost a feather, it could probably still fly unless the lost feather was a tail feather; in this case, the bird might not be able to dive accurately. A broken wing would be a disaster, since the Kestrel depends on rapid wing flapping to hover over its prey.*

• **Now work with your partner to complete a statement about the function of the part in relationship to the whole bird.** After a few minutes, ask for a few responses. Write them on a large version of the graphic organizer for determining parts-whole relationships. POSSIBLE ANSWERS: *The two eyes function together to give the kestrel a good sense of depth perception, allowing the bird to locate its prey accurately. The wings function to enable the kestrel to fly and to hover undetected above its prey. The claws function to enable the kestrel to grasp its prey.*

• **Using the information in the passage from the guide, describe how the different parts of the kestrel would function together in stalking and catching prey. As a pre-writing activity, fill in a new graphic organizer for determining parts-whole relationships with the responses of your fellow students in today's class work. Include it with your writing assignment.** POSSIBLE ANSWERS: *The eyes sight the prey as the bird moves its head to scan the area and moves its wings rapidly (using its muscles) to hover. After the bird detects its prey and dives to capture it, changing the motion of its wings to do so, it uses its claws to grasp the prey and its talons to kill it. The bird moves its head so that it can use its beak to peck off morsels and its jaws and tongue to swallow them.*

THINKING ABOUT THINKING

• **How did you decide what parts to write in the "parts" boxes?** POSSIBLE ANSWERS: *I first looked at the large parts, like the head, and tried to find other things that were about the same size. I looked at the smallest parts I could see, like the nails on the bird's claws, and recorded them; then I moved to bigger parts, some of which were composed of these smaller parts (for example, the claws are partly made up of the nails). I started with a big part, like one of the bird's wings, then focused my attention on the parts of this part, like the feathers and markings; then I did the same for other large parts.* A variation on this activity can occur when students are working in pairs, listing the parts of the kestrel. Ask one student to think out loud about the parts when listing them; have the other record how the first student is generating his or her list of parts. Then, the second student in each pair can report his or her observations.

• **Can you think of any other techniques for coming up with a list of the parts of the kestrel?** POSSIBLE ANSWERS: *I could find a real kestrel and look at it. I could dissect a kestrel. I could take a sample of its parts and further divide the sample; I could use a microscope.*

• **Work with your partner and describe how you thought about what would happen to the kestrel if one of its parts were injured.** POSSIBLE ANSWERS: *I imagined the kestrel trying, without the part, to do what the bird guide says it does. I then compared what I imagined to what I think happens when the kestrel has the part. That made me realize what the function of the part is.*

• **Sometimes we can't tell what would happen without a specific part if the object is unfamiliar. If you don't know what would happen, how could you find out?** POSSIBLE ANSWERS: *I could observe the object operating without the part and compare it to the object operating with the part. I could observe the operation of similar object that doesn't have the part. I could find someone who knows about kestrels and ask what would happen if the bird didn't have the part, or if the part were injured.*

• **What would you tell other people to think about to identify the part of a whole object and their**

relationships to the whole? Students should suggest questions like the ones that appear on the thinking map for determining parts-whole relationships. For a variation on this activity, ask students to draw a flow chart that can be used by others to guide their thinking about parts and wholes.

APPLYING THINKING

Immediate Transfer

- Stories are another example of wholes that have parts. For a story that you are reading, use your plan for determining parts-whole relationships to figure out how the different story parts function with regard to the whole.

- Select a machine that you are familiar with (like a washing machine) and analyze its parts and their functions.

Reinforcement Later

Later on in the school year introduce these additional transfer activities by saying the following:

- **In social studies you are studying complex societies. Pick a particular example of a society (for example, ancient Rome) to demonstrate your skill at determining parts-whole relationships. Explain the functions and roles of the different components that sustained the society over a period of time.** If students have a problem identifying components of a society such as Ancient Rome, tell them that the senate or the army are examples of such components.

- **Imagine that you are stranded on a desert island and want to make a device for signaling to passing airplanes. The only materials you have are a few long branches, a few pieces of clothing, some rocks, some matches, and a mirror. How could you put all or some of these materials together to construct a signaling device? Explain how each part would function.**

RESEARCH EXTENSION

Ask teams of students to use textbooks or school library resources to gather information from their textbooks or from resources in the school library about the parts of the kestrel (the feathers, the claws, etc.) and how they operate. Ask students to divide each of these components into parts and analyze how the sub-parts function in relation to the larger part being investigated.

ASSESSING STUDENT THINKING ABOUT PARTS-WHOLE RELATIONSHIPS

To assess student thinking about parts and wholes, give them a problem about an item that is familiar to them. Explain that it doesn't work because of a malfunctioning part and ask the students to figure out what part is causing the problem. As an alternative, you may have students construct a device from parts that you provide and ask them to explain how the parts function with regard to the purpose of the device. Ask the students to identify each step of the parts-whole strategy as they think about the problem. By attending to the questions they are asking, you may determine whether the students are attending to each of the steps in the thinking map for determining parts-whole relationships.

Sample Student Responses • The Kestrel • The Function of A Part

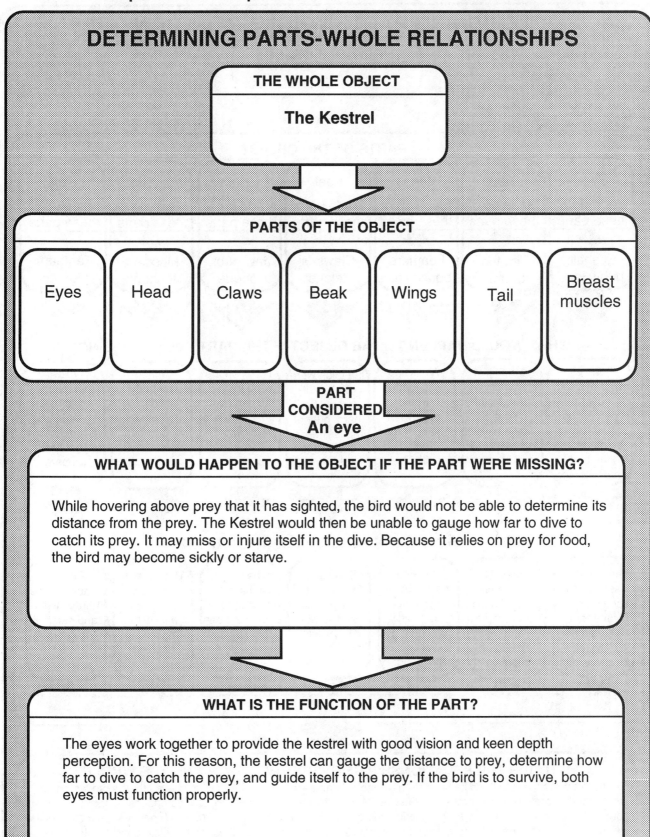

DETERMINING PARTS-WHOLE RELATIONSHIPS

THE WHOLE OBJECT

The Kestrel

PARTS OF THE OBJECT

| Eyes | Head | Claws | Beak | Wings | Tail | Breast muscles |

PART CONSIDERED
An eye

WHAT WOULD HAPPEN TO THE OBJECT IF THE PART WERE MISSING?

While hovering above prey that it has sighted, the bird would not be able to determine its distance from the prey. The Kestrel would then be unable to gauge how far to dive to catch its prey. It may miss or injure itself in the dive. Because it relies on prey for food, the bird may become sickly or starve.

WHAT IS THE FUNCTION OF THE PART?

The eyes work together to provide the kestrel with good vision and keen depth perception. For this reason, the kestrel can gauge the distance to prey, determine how far to dive to catch the prey, and guide itself to the prey. If the bird is to survive, both eyes must function properly.

Sample Student Responses • The Kestrel • Interrelationship Between Parts and Whole

DETERMINING PARTS-WHOLE RELATIONSHIPS

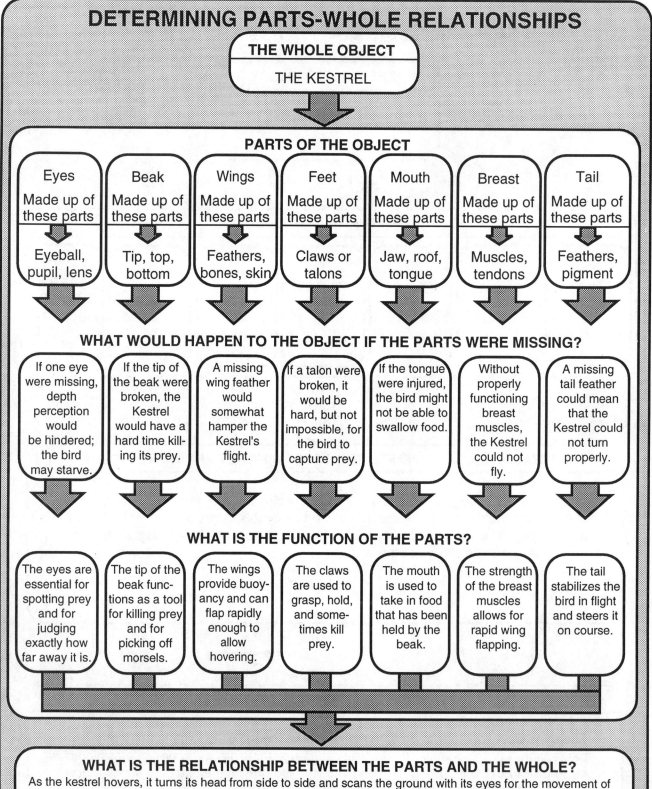

THE WHOLE OBJECT

THE KESTREL

PARTS OF THE OBJECT

Eyes	Beak	Wings	Feet	Mouth	Breast	Tail
Made up of these parts	Made up of these parts	Made up of these parts	Made up of these parts	Made up of these parts	Made up of these parts	Made up of these parts
Eyeball, pupil, lens	Tip, top, bottom	Feathers, bones, skin	Claws or talons	Jaw, roof, tongue	Muscles, tendons	Feathers, pigment

WHAT WOULD HAPPEN TO THE OBJECT IF THE PARTS WERE MISSING?

If one eye were missing, depth perception would be hindered; the bird may starve.	If the tip of the beak were broken, the Kestrel would have a hard time killing its prey.	A missing wing feather would somewhat hamper the Kestrel's flight.	If a talon were broken, it would be hard, but not impossible, for the bird to capture prey.	If the tongue were injured, the bird might not be able to swallow food.	Without properly functioning breast muscles, the Kestrel could not fly.	A missing tail feather could mean that the Kestrel could not turn properly.

WHAT IS THE FUNCTION OF THE PARTS?

The eyes are essential for spotting prey and for judging exactly how far away it is.	The tip of the beak functions as a tool for killing prey and for picking off morsels.	The wings provide buoyancy and can flap rapidly enough to allow hovering.	The claws are used to grasp, hold, and sometimes kill prey.	The mouth is used to take in food that has been held by the beak.	The strength of the breast muscles allows for rapid wing flapping.	The tail stabilizes the bird in flight and steers it on course.

WHAT IS THE RELATIONSHIP BETWEEN THE PARTS AND THE WHOLE?

As the kestrel hovers, it turns its head from side to side and scans the ground with its eyes for the movement of recognizable prey. When it spots prey, the Kestrel uses its stereoscopic vision, which depends on the co-ordination of both eyes to gauge the location and distance of the prey. The Kestrel then changes the motion of its wings, dives, and uses its tail to guide it to the prey. When the Kestrel reaches the prey, it grasps it in its claws, using its talons to immobilize and even kill the prey. The Kestrel then uses its wings to fly to a spot where it puts the prey down and pecks off morsels, which it puts into its mouth with its beak and tongue. If the prey is alive, the Kestrel kills it with the sharp tip of its beak.

LESSON CONTEXTS FOR IDENTIFYING PARTS OF A WHOLE

The following examples have been suggested by classroom teachers as contexts to develop infused lessons. If a skill or process has been introduced in a previous infused lesson, these contexts may be used to reinforce it.

GRADE	SUBJECT	TOPIC	THINKING ISSUE
K–3	Reading	Illustrations	Examine the parts of a picture book (cover, title page, text, and illustrations) to clarify how each contributes to our understanding and enjoyment of a book.
K–3	Reading	Vocabulary development	Examine common objects in order to learn the correct name, as well as the structure and purpose, of each part.
K–3	Social studies	Map reading	Identify the parts of a map (key, scale, longitude, latitude, etc.) to understand how each helps us interpret the map.
K–3	Social studies	Communities	Describe the neighborhoods that make up your community and identify what each contributes to your city. Include both business and industrial neighborhoods.
K–3	Social studies	Local government	Examine a map of your state or province. Identify its political divisions to clarify the differences between cities, counties, states or provinces, and nations.
K–3	Mathematics	Equations	Examine each part of a number statement (equation); describe why each part is necessary in expressing the value of the equation.
K–3	Mathematics/ art	Geometric shapes	Examine pictures of common objects. For a particular object, identify all the component shapes that allow you to draw it easily.
K–3	Mathematics	Measurement	Examine the markings on a ruler or measuring cup to describe how each type of mark contributes to the object's use as a measuring device.
K–3	Science	Solar system	Describe the parts of our solar system in order to explain how the system works.
K–3	Science	*Hands*	Review the many uses of hands in Jane Yolen's picture book to clarify their structure and significance.
K–3	Science	Birds	Examine the feet of different kinds of birds. What does the structure of the foot tell us about where the bird lives and how the bird meets its needs?
K–3	Science	Egg	Describe how each part of an egg protects and nourishes the developing animal.
K–3	Science	Pond	Identify the parts of a pond that provide habitats for various plants and animals. For each habitat, give several examples of associated plants and animals. Examples may include the following: edge (rooted plants, fish, frogs, ducks, ferns, cattails, lilypads), surface (frogs, mosquito larvae, water striders), bottom (worms, clams, snails, crawfish), and open water (floating plants, ducks). Add other examples.

LESSON CONTEXTS FOR IDENTIFYING PARTS OF A WHOLE

GRADE	SUBJECT	TOPIC	THINKING ISSUE
K–3	Science	Wheels	Describe how each part of the wheel (hub, spoke, axle, and rim) contributes to the wheel's function.
K–3	Science	Plants	Describe how each part of a plant contributes to the plant's growth.
K–3	Science/ health	Plants as food	For various plants, identify which parts we commonly eat (e.g., root, stem, leaves, seeds, and fruit) to clarify why it is nutritious and how it must be prepared to be edible, as well as to recognize which parts are discarded or used for some other purpose.
K–3	Art	Line	Examine pictures to identify the types of lines that make up the drawing or photograph. Describe the effects of different kinds of lines.
K–3	Music	Music notation	Identify how music symbols (bars, clefs, notes, rests, key signatures, etc.) allow us to communicate a melody.
K–3	Music	Parts of the orchestra	Identify the various parts of an orchestra and how each contributes to the sound of a musical work.
4–6	Language arts	Paragraphs	Identify the topic sentence and its supporting statements to clarify the structure of a paragraph.
4–6	Language arts	Books and letters	For a book or a letter, describe how its parts contribute to our understanding of it.
4–6	Social studies	Preamble	Examine each of the six purposes of government expressed in the preamble to the Constitution. Why is each purpose necessary for the security and growth of a country?
4–6	Social studies	Branches of the federal government	Describe each of the branches of the federal government. How does each contribute to the effectiveness of our national government? How does each provide checks and balances to other branches for distribution of power?
4–6	Social studies	Cultures	Select a dwelling, a public building, a weapon, a household article, or a tool of a given culture. Describe its parts. What do the material and the construction of the parts of the item tell you about the technology and values of that culture?
4–6	Social studies	Black history	In 1966 Maulana Ron Karenga, an African American scholar, established Kwanzaa as an African American holiday. Kwanzaa involves seven traditional African values (unity, self-determination, collective work and responsibility, cooperative economics, sense of purpose, creativity, and faith). How does each value of Kwanzaa contribute to personal pride for individuals and to community growth?

LESSON CONTEXTS FOR IDENTIFYING PARTS OF A WHOLE

GRADE	SUBJECT	TOPIC	THINKING ISSUE
4–6	Social studies	Colonial villages	Examine drawings of a New England village, a middle colonies town, and a southern plantation and identify the parts of these communities. What do the parts of each community tell us about its economics, its climate, its everyday-life activities, and its values?
4–6	Mathematics	Word problems	Examine the terms in each sentence of a word problem. How does each part of the sentence give information to show you how to solve the problem?
4–6	Mathematics	Bar graphs	Describe the parts of a bar graph and tell why the information given by each is necessary in interpreting the graph.
4–6	Science	Birds	Describe each part of a feather and explain how it protects the bird or assists it in flight.
4–6	Science	River	Describe a local river system. How does each part of the river contribute to the natural flow of the river and to the welfare of the cities around it?
4–6	Science	Eye	Describe each part of the eye and explain how each part contributes to maintaining the eye's healthy functioning.
4–6	Science	Coastlines	Describe the land and water parts of a coastline. How does each part contribute to sea life and to the needs of people living in the coastal area?
4–6	Science	Weather	Examine a weather map for your area. How do the parts of the map give you information about local weather?
4–6	Science	Plants and animal cells	Describe how the parts of a cell function to support the life of the organism and how they allow us to discriminate between plant and animal cells.
4–6	Science	Types of animal cells	Describe how the parts of nerve, blood, muscle, bone, and skin cells relate to the cell's function in the associated body part.
4–6	Science	Pollination	Explain how each part of the flower of an apple tree functions in reproduction.
4–6	Science	Digestive system	Describe how the parts of the digestive system are interrelated in helping the body process and use food.
4–6	Arts	Elements of design	Examine a given picture to describe how its component shapes and lines contribute to its composition.
4–6	Music	Instruments	Examine a musical instrument to describe how each part contributes to the instrument's musical sound.

CHAPTER 7
SEQUENCING

Why Is It Important to Sequence Things Skillfully?

Putting things and events in order is one of our most frequently practiced thinking tasks. We arrange names alphabetically in an address book in order to find an individual's address quickly. We arrange tools by size to be able to find a wrench or screwdriver that is just the right size for a particular task, to make efficient use of storage space, and to recognize quickly when a tool is missing or needed. We reconstruct a chain of events leading to an accident in order to determine who is responsible for it. We select a pet or plants for our yard based on size, the amount of care required, and the benefit that each brings to our lives and surroundings. We vote for candidates based on how well each fits our beliefs about government. In planning a work schedule, we prioritize tasks by importance and duration and fit them into time slots.

All forms of sequencing involve the same basic process—putting one thing or idea after another according to certain criteria. Any particular thing may occupy different positions in different sequences, however. Hurricane Hugo may be first on a list of the most devastating hurricanes of the decade, but it is eighth in order of hurricane occurrence in 1988. The characteristics which you select to sequence things depends on your purposes.

Types of Sequences

We commonly employ many types of sequences when we put things in order. One of the first sequences that we learn is *alphabetical order*. Putting items in alphabetical order allows us to locate them quickly (i.e., finding the telephone numbers of individuals in a telephone directory). Sequencing alphabetically simply requires accuracy in complying with the correct order of letters.

We also use *time order* frequently. Memories of past experiences, our current schedule, and our future plans are all based on the order in which things happen. Time sequences some-times involve matching data about events to a time line of given intervals. I may recall important events by relating them to other milestones, like moving to a new house or the birth of a baby in the family. Correlating national events with the leadership of particular individuals may help me understand whether or not they have been effective public officials and should be re-elected.

We commonly use three specialized types of time order: *operation analysis, causal chains, and cycles. Operational analysis* involves correctly setting up steps in a procedure. If I do not carry out the correct sequence of steps in a recipe for rolls, the bread may not rise properly. If I do not follow procedures in a given order, my word processing software may not give my computer the correct commands to check the spelling in what I am writing.

We employ time order to determine *causal chains* of events or actions leading to others. I must sequence events in the correct order to understand why something happened, who is responsible, and what I should do when similar conditions arise in the future.

Cycles are repeating sequences of events that follow in the same time order. The cycle of seasons is an example of the repetition of the same sequence of natural conditions at regular intervals. Understanding cycles allows us to predict recurring events and to realize points in the cycle in which change would affect the whole system. For example, massive rain forest cutting may interfere with the oxygen/carbon dioxide cycle in ways that affect the whole planet.

Ranking actions or things is a specialized form of sequencing. Ranking involves sequencing by quantity and/or by quality. Anything expressed in degrees can be ranked. For example, I may rank things by the *degree* to which they have certain properties (e.g., by how much sugar is included as an ingredient), by their *usefulness* for a certain task (e.g., how well various tools serve a particular purpose), and by their *value* (e.g., how beautiful they are or how well qualified specific candidates might be for a job). Ranking can also be relative to a specific property (e.g., ranking foods by calories per fixed quantity), or it can be based on combining multiple criteria (e.g., ranking foods by their overall nutritional value).

Prioritizing is a form of ranking in which the highest ranked item is the most important. We usually prioritize things that must be done. For example, I may regard paying my bills as a higher priority than going to the movies.

Problems in Sequencing

Although sequencing is a frequently used and important thinking skill, we do not always do it skillfully. Sometimes we prioritize poorly because the criterion for sequencing does not fit the purpose. To store books, I might organize them in order of color or size, which might be visually attractive. However, if my primary purpose for keeping my books is finding information, I should arrange them by type in order to locate quickly books containing certain kinds of information. If I enjoy reading books by certain authors, I may want to arrange my books alphabetically by the authors' last names so that I can easily find a number of books by the same author.

Sometimes we place items incorrectly in a sequence, either because of inaccuracy in the information or by inaccurately matching the data to the sequencing schema. For example, because of a misprint in a book, someone may think that John F. Kennedy died in 1973. If that information is placed on a time line, then subsequent events, such as Lyndon Johnson's assuming the presidency, do not make sense. On the other hand, one may have the 1963 date correct, but because of inattention, enter it incorrectly on the time line at 1973. In either case, one may mistakenly believe that Kennedy lived a decade longer than he did.

We may prioritize things poorly because we are not really clear about the criteria for ranking them. If I read "20% fat" on a box of cereal, I may mistakenly believe that this means that 20% of the weight of the cereal is fat. However, the percentage figure is really the percentage of calories provided by fat. The percentage of fat by weight may be much less than the percentage of the calories that fat provides. If I buy cereal based on the wrong criteria for percentages, I may mistakenly believe that my fat intake is lower than it actually is.

Figure 7.1 provides a summary of these defaults in sequencing.

COMMON DEFAULTS IN SEQUENCING

1. Picking a sequence that poorly fits the purpose of ordering.

2. Inadequate understanding of the criteria for putting things in a specific sequence.

3. Inaccurately matching items to a given sequence by misremembering, haste, or failing to attend to details.

Figure 7.1

How Do We Sequence Things Skillfully?

Sequencing falls into two categories: simple ordering (fitting items into a given sequence or one that we must figure out) and ranking (sequencing by degree or value), which includes prioritizing and is actually a more complex form of ordering.

Putting things in order skillfully. When I order things skillfully, I determine the purpose of the ordering and select an ordering schema that serves that purpose. If I want to find books in my collection by authors, alphabetical order is obviously a better schema to use for organizing my books than ordering them by size. I then have to place each item accurately according to the ordering schema. To organize my books, I identify the first letter of the last name of the author and put each book in the proper location.

Sometimes determining the basis for ordering items is not so obvious. If a book is co-authored, whose name do I use? I can simply decide that I will use the name of the author whose name comes earlier alphabetically. I could also decide to use the name of the primary author to alphabetize the book, even though the primary author's name starts with a letter that comes later in the alphabet.

Deciding on the ordering characteristic and

examining items carefully to determine accurately how each item fits in that order will allow me to place them properly. Skill in sequencing items involves accuracy, attention to significant details, and in some cases, sound memory.

More challenging types of sequencing activities involve sequencing the steps in a procedure according to cause-and-effect relationships (e.g., sequencing steps in a chess move, in a recipe, or in repairing electronic equipment), and reconstructing temporal sequences of events (e.g., reconstructing a crime).

The thinking map in figure 7.2 guides us through the process of sequencing skillfully.

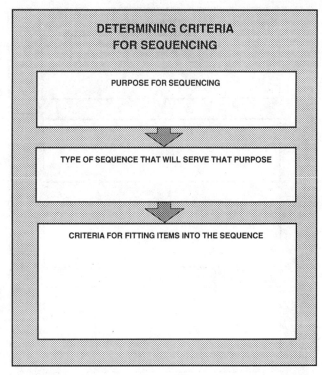

Figure 7.3

SEQUENCING

1. What is the purpose of the sequencing?

2. What type of sequence best serves this purpose?

3. What criteria should be used to fit items into this type of sequence?

4. How does each item fit into the sequence based on these criteria?

Figure 7.2

Two types of graphic organizers are used in sequencing. The first type guides us in determining and recording the criteria for fitting items into a sequence. The second type provides an organizing pattern into which items fit. We provide two different diagrams that are useful for fitting items into a sequence: a time line and a flow chart. These diagrams represent two common sequencing patterns.

The graphic organizer for determining sequencing criteria appears in figure 7.3. This graphic organizer focuses attention on the purpose of sequencing, the type of sequence that best serves that purpose, and the criteria for fitting items into that sequence.

The time line diagram in figure 7.4 contains parallel time lines so that it can either show chronological occurrence based on a given time interval or illustrate concurrent events.

The flow chart diagram in figure 7.5 (p. 196) uses arrows to mark temporal connections.

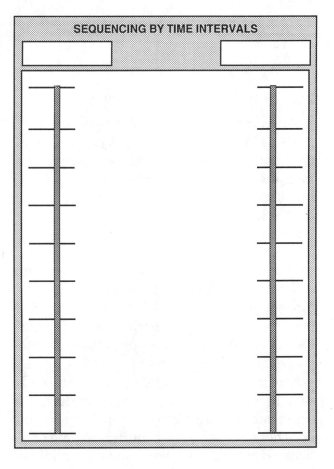

Figure 7.4

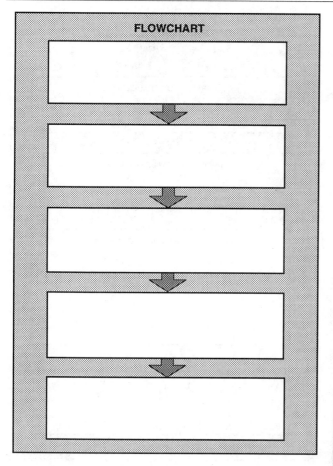

FLOWCHART

Figure 7.5

Ranking

When ranking things, we should clarify the purpose for ranking. If I am interviewing candidates for a new teaching position, I may want to rank the top five candidates. My purpose for ranking—selecting the best qualified candidate for the job—determines the criteria I will use. Experience in teaching, knowledge of the field, and personableness will be among my criteria. I may consider these qualities equally important, or I may consider one characteristic more significant than the others. If I then determine that one candidate has more experience, more expertise in her field, and is more personable than the others, she will be at the top of my list.

Ranking the job candidates may not be so easy, however. Perhaps one candidate has more experience and relates well with students but does not have as broad an understanding of his field as the other two, while another candidate has a broader base of knowledge in her field, is extremely well-liked by co-workers, and yet has

had less experience teaching. How I rank these candidates may depend on subtleties in the relative importance of these criteria.

As demonstrated in this case, ranking is often based on our values and judgments about the relative importance of the criteria we use in determining how to rank specific items. Where these judgments play a role in our ranking, we should always justify them.

The thinking map for ranking (figure 7.6) is a variation of the map for sequencing.

The graphic organizer for ranking (figure 7.7) can be varied for a different number of items.

SEQUENCING BY RANK

1. What is the purpose of the ranking?

2. What qualities must something have to serve this purpose?

3. Which of these qualities do each of the items being compared have, and to what degree do they have them?

4. Which has the largest degree of desirable qualities, the next largest, on to the least?

Figure 7.6

How to Teach Students to Sequence Skillfully

Students should learn both types of sequencing: ordering and ranking. They can develop family trees, reconstruct the major events in the plot of a story, and map out the water cycle to practice skillful ordering. They should also, however, practice ranking by engaging in activities such as ranking sources of air pollution by the amount and/or types of pollutants they put into the air or ranking United States Presidents by their accomplishments. In teaching either kind of sequencing, it is important to introduce explicitly the specific form of sequencing being taught, to guide students through the sequencing process, and to involve them in reflecting about their own thinking as they put things in sequence.

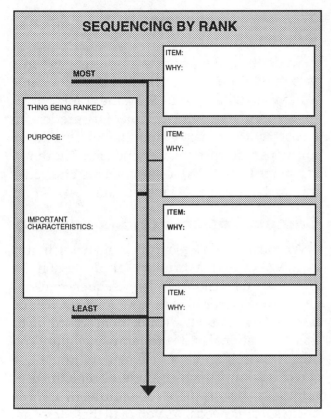

Figure 7.7

Often students make impulsive decisions about the significance or usefulness of items without taking the time to compare the merits of each. For example, in selecting foods, many students base their preferences on taste, rather than ranking foods by caloric content or nutritional value. In teaching skillful ranking, it is important to include activities in which one issue is the relative usefulness of different items in achieving a certain goal. Students should start with a list of different items and think through the pros and cons of each item, ranking the items based on their analysis.

Because sequencing plays such an important role in our lives, it is also important to provide experiences for students in carefully setting up procedures, in recognizing the sequencing of actions, and in making decisions based on contingencies. Students can develop a plan of sequenced steps to obtain good reference material from the library, to open a bank account, or to reenact pioneers' planning in the westward movement in the United States. For simple sequences, students may use the flow chart dia-

gram. When the plans involve responding to various contingencies, such as conditions encountered by a wagon train moving west, the basic flow chart diagram may be modified by adding branches.

Many sequencing exercises in textbooks involve matching items to a given order or continuing a given pattern. These exercises often provide students with information regarding the items that fall in the given sequence. For example, students are often given events in social studies texts, along with their dates, and asked to locate them on a time line. Such exercises are valuable in teaching content. However, they do not help students learn to choose appropriate sequences for ordering items or to gain practice at figuring out where various items belong in a given sequence if this information is not evident.

Contexts in the Curriculum for Lessons on Sequencing

There are several types of contexts in curriculum materials in which sequencing plays a natural role:

- *Students learn about important sequences of events or conditions.* For example, students study the chain of causes and effects leading up to important wars or to major historical events (e.g., the New Deal). Sequencing these events in a variety of ways (by their occurrence, importance, etc.) can be enlightening to students and serve as a vehicle for teaching skillful sequencing. Sequences of causes and effects studied in science can help students learn methods for controlling causal change (e.g., in nurturing the growth of plants or in understanding scientific procedures). One must clarify the order of important changes in dinosaurs and in conditions on earth to understand what might have caused the extinction of the dinosaurs. In language arts, reconstructing the sequence of interactions between characters in a novel can help students gain a deeper understanding of these characters. Such sequencing can be quite challenging because, while most narratives are told chronologically, some stories involve flashbacks or events related from another person's point of view.

- *Students use sequencing to build important skills.* For example, students learn a simple sequence of writing, reviewing, and revision in order to develop their writing skills. Planning a project in art or industrial arts classes involves developing a sequence for completing design tasks. Finally, the personal problem solving that students do in school involves sequencing. Students can learn in the elementary grades how to plan using their time and money, how to organize their possessions, and how to recognize that some things, actions, and ideas are more valuable or useful than others.

Teaching students to sequence skillfully emphasizes order and the principles and purposes behind it. Incorporating such instruction into content lessons makes the sequences we teach, like time lines, cycles, and procedures, more relevant and interesting to students.

A menu of suggested contexts for infusion lessons on sequencing is provided on pp. 219–22.

PUTTING THINGS IN ORDER

1. Why do you want to put them in order?

2. What is the best way to order them?

3. What do you have to find out about them to know where they fit?

4. Where does each item fit?

RANKING THINGS

1. Why do you want to rank them?

2. What should you find out in order to rank them for this purpose?

3. How will you rank them? Why?

Figure 7.8

Teaching Sequencing in the Primary Grades

Students in the primary grades engage in a variety of sequencing activities and in simple ranking activities. While the same graphic organizers used in the upper elementary grades can be used with primary grade students, the thinking maps require some simplification. The thinking maps (figure 7.8) for sequencing and ranking can be used in K–3 instruction.

Sample Lessons on Sequencing

We include two lessons on sequencing in this chapter. One is a primary grade lesson on children's television. Students sequence television shows according to how long they have been on the air and then rank them according to their educational and entertainment value. The other lesson is an upper elementary grade lesson on ranking in which students rank the usefulness of various pieces of equipment according to specific needs. As you read these lessons, consider the following:

- How can we help students recognize what kind of sequencing serves a specific purpose?

- What variations of sequencing can be used to reinforce this skill?

Tools for Designing Sequencing Lessons

The tools on the following pages include the thinking maps and graphic organizers for ordering and ranking. The graphic organizers include one to guide students' thinking as they choose the best sequencing schemes to fit their purposes, two information-organizing graphics for the results of sequencing activities, and a thinking-activity graphic for ranking. The thinking maps at the bottoms of pages 199 and 203 are especially designed for use in the primary grades.

The thinking maps and graphic organizers can guide you in designing the critical thinking activity in the lesson and can also serve as photocopy masters, transparency masters, or as models that can be enlarged and used as posters in the classroom. Reproduction rights are granted for single classroom use only.

SEQUENCING

1. What is the purpose of the sequencing?

2. What type of sequence best serves this purpose?

3. What criteria should be used to fit items into this type of sequence?

4. How does each item fit into the sequence based on these criteria?

PUTTING THINGS IN ORDER

1. Why do you want to put them in order?

2. What is the best way to order them?

3. What do you have to find out about them to know where they fit?

4. Where does each item fit?

DETERMINING CRITERIA
FOR SEQUENCING

PURPOSE FOR SEQUENCING

TYPE OF SEQUENCE THAT WILL SERVE THAT PURPOSE

CRITERIA FOR FITTING ITEMS INTO THE SEQUENCE

SEQUENCING BY TIME INTERVALS

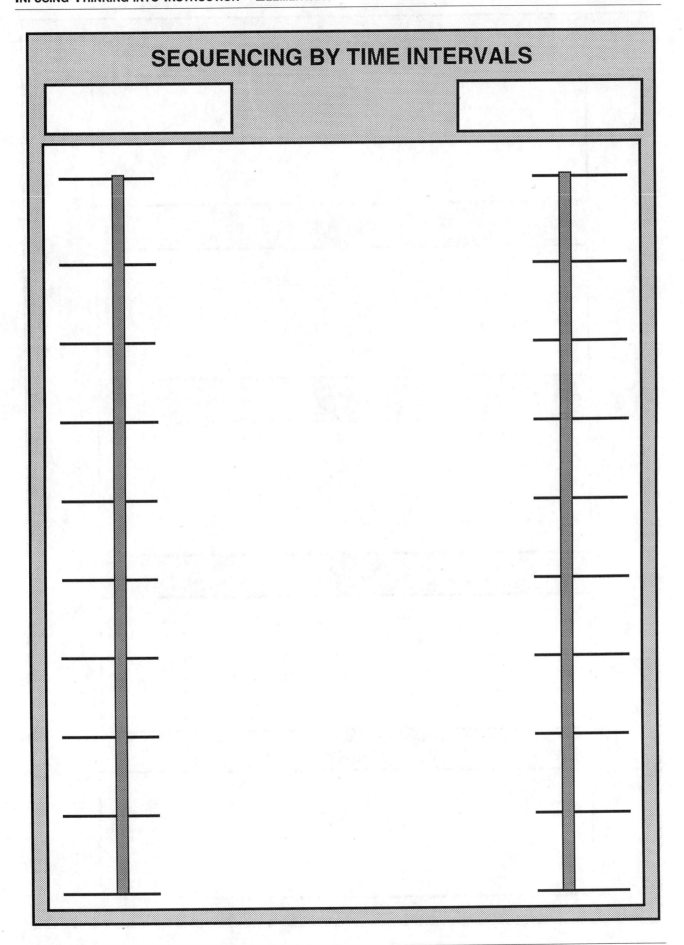

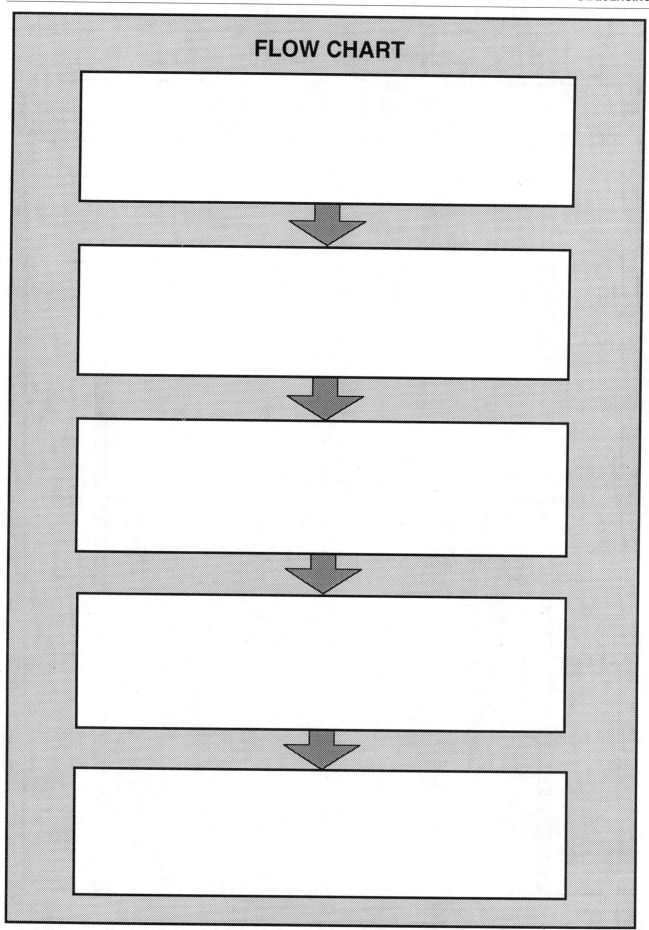

FLOW CHART

SEQUENCING BY RANK

1. **What is the purpose of the ranking?**

2. **What qualities must something have to serve this purpose?**

3. **Which of these qualities do each of the items being compared have, and to what degree do they have them?**

4. **Which has the largest degree of the desirable qualities, the next largest, on to the least?**

RANKING THINGS

1. **Why do you want to rank them?**

2. **What should you find out in order to rank them for this purpose?**

3. **How will you rank them? Why?**

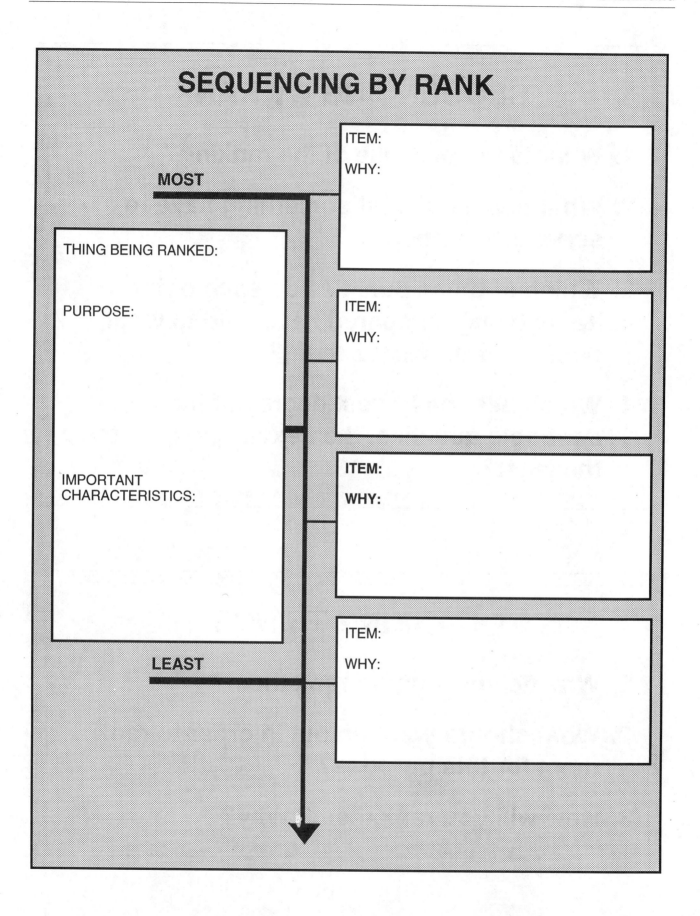

SEQUENCING BY RANK

MOST

LEAST

THING BEING RANKED:

PURPOSE:

IMPORTANT
CHARACTERISTICS:

ITEM:

WHY:

ITEM:

WHY:

ITEM:

WHY:

ITEM:

WHY:

CHILDREN'S TELEVISION SHOWS

Language Arts/Mathematics   **Grades 2–3**

OBJECTIVES

CONTENT

Students will read or listen for details to determine chronological order. Students will identify purposes and values that motivate their television viewing choices. They will apply ordinal terms and addition skills to a multi-step problem.

THINKING SKILL/PROCESS

Students will use details to put events in the correct chronological order. They will prioritize choices by selecting criteria for ranking, identifying things which meet those criteria, and explaining how items are ranked according to those criteria.

METHODS AND MATERIALS

CONTENT

Students use a time line to sequence events. Students who don't yet write discuss the correct order, while the teacher writes their comments on a transparency of the time line. When prioritizing, young students may draw their choices; older students use a ranking diagram. For young children, the lesson should be taught in three mini-lessons.

THINKING SKILL/PROCESS

Two thinking maps guide the teacher's directions in describing the tasks for two kinds of sequencing. (See pp. 199-204 for reproducible diagrams.) Time order is depicted on a time line; prioritizing is depicted on two copies of a graphic organizer for ranking.

LESSON

INTRODUCTION TO CONTENT AND THINKING SKILL/PROCESS

- **What things do we put in a particular order? With your partner, list all the things that you can remember that are organized by size (smallest to largest), by weight (light to heavy), and by height (shortest to tallest).** Give students time to think of examples of sequencing, and discuss a few of them when students report.

- **When we put things in order by one of these characteristics, we are** *sequencing* **them. In this lesson, we will sequence things in the order in which they happen. Our class schedule is the order that we do things in class each day. A birthday chart is the order in which people's birthdays occur during the year. We tell stories or explain what happened by describing the order in which things occurred. Think about events that we sequence by the order in which they happen. With your partner, list examples of things that happen in a certain order.** Make two columns on the chalkboard or newsprint. The left column should be headed "Examples of Time Order." POSSIBLE ANSWERS: *A daily schedule, directions to make something, when someone in their family was born or came to visit, a recipe or directions to prepare food, the order of students' turns to be the line leader, etc.*

- **Why would it be important to get the sequence right?** In the right column next to each example, write why the students say the order is important under the heading "Why Important." POSSIBLE ANSWERS: *People may become confused about what to do. We may not remember something that we are supposed to do. We may confuse someone who is listening to us tell about something that happened. We may mess up something that we are making.*

- **Think about one of your examples. What did you think about to sequence things correctly?**
Students' description of their thinking might include

  (1) *We thought of the first thing that happened and asked ourselves what came next.*

  (2) *We tried to remember what things in the middle could help keep track of the order.*

  (3) *We sometimes remember the end and recall what happened backward in time.*

THINKING ACTIVELY

- **In this lesson, we are going to use dates to show the sequence in which some children's television shows came on the air. Did you know that some of the television shows that young children watch today were watched by their parents and even their grandparents when they were young? Our purpose for sequencing the shows is to figure out how long they have been on the air and who in our family might have watched the show when they were little.** If needed, help students identify on the diagram (shown on this page) the present year and the year of their birth. For young children, hold up pictures from the television shows while you read aloud the information on children's television shows (see below). The pictures can be placed in order (flannel board or posters work well) as you and your students discuss when the show came on the air and as students prioritize the shows.

- **Read the information sheet on children's television shows (see p. 210). It tells when some children's television shows first started. Write the name of the show on the time line by the year when it began. Write the name between the years marked on the time line, if needed. For example, if a television show started in 1973, write it between 1970 and 1975 on the diagram. Find the first show and write it on your time line. Then read on to find the second and write it on the time line. Find the dates for all the shows. Sometimes you will need to add to figure out the year a show started.** Give this passage, on a separate sheet of paper, to the students to read. Read it aloud to younger children.

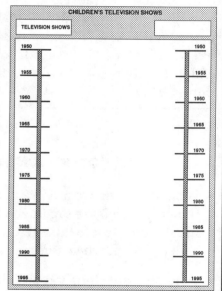

  Children's Television Shows—Many young children like to watch *Barney and Friends*. Barney and Baby Bop are friendly dinosaurs who show children how to be creative and how to get along. But *Barney and Friends*, which started in 1988, is a new show compared to other children's television shows.

  The longest-running children's show is *Captain Kangaroo*. Bob Keeshan has played Captain Kangaroo since the show began in 1956. The show taught young children numbers, letters, and important ideas. Thirteen years later, Children's Television Workshop produced *Sesame Street* to teach young children. One year later, *Mister Rogers' Neighborhood* began to be broadcast, helping kids understand their feelings and values, as well as teaching them.

- **On the right side of the diagram, write events that happened to members of your family.** Students may take the time line home and ask family members to help them remember when births, moves, or special family events occurred in order to record what the family was doing when a particular show came on the air. Discuss any questions or observations that students have about what was going on in their families when the shows came on the air. Some grandparents of today's primary students were teenagers when Captain Kangaroo started. Students find it interesting that their parents and grandparents watched shows that they identify as only their recent experiences. They wonder if a show had a similar meaning or similar entertainment value for their parents as the show does for them.

- **What seems interesting about these television shows when you see them on the time line?** Students comment that they are surprised that *Captain Kangaroo, Sesame Street,* and *Mister Rogers' Neighborhood* have been on so long. They may discuss what makes a television show successful for such a long time. They may wonder whether the actors and writers get tired of doing the show or run out of ideas. Relate the shows to the year of the students' birth and ask students to subtract to figure out how long the show had been on the air before they were born.

- **When you sequenced the shows, you carefully matched the show to the year it started and tried to get it right. Then you looked at the years in which the shows started to see if the order showed you something interesting.**

  Now let's try another kind of sequencing called <u>ranking</u>. When you put things in first, second, or third place, you rank them. This time you will rank the shows two ways: by how well they teach you and in order of how much you like to watch them. You will put them in order from best to worst.

  These shows are meant to teach children important information and to entertain them. First let's rank them according to how well they teach young children what they should know. Use a reproduction of the graphic organizer, shown at the right, on a transparency or on the chalkboard. Write the thing being ranked (children's television shows) and the purpose for ranking them (teaching children) in the box on the left. Encourage students to make a copy.

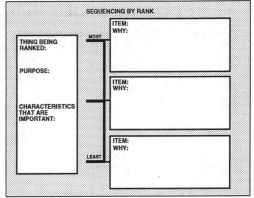

- **With your partner, decide what makes a television show educational. What qualities would you think about to rank a show by how well it teaches ideas? Write the characteristics on the graphic organizer in the box on the left under "Characteristics That Are Important."** Students commonly mention that children remember what they saw, that the show was interesting enough to hold children's attention, that lots of ideas are taught in a single show, that there are songs or special effects that help students remember the ideas, and that the ideas are important ones like they learn in school.

- **Now select three television shows that you have seen that are mentioned in this lesson. Use the graphic organizer to rank them from best to worst regarding how well you think they teach young children things that they should know. Explain your choice for the most educational show. Explain why your second choice is not quite as educational and why your third choice teaches children the least of the three shows.** Kindergarten and first grade students may draw pictures of the shows in order of how well they teach children. They should draw the most educational at the top, the second choice in the middle of the page, and the third choice at the bottom. After students have completed their ranking of the shows, ask them to report on their choices.

  Write on the board the names of all four shows discussed in this lesson, and ask for the number of students who chose a particular show as the most educational. On a transparency or the blackboard, show how the class prioritized the educational value of the shows. Write the show that gets the most "first-choice" decisions at the top, then the ones that get the second and third greatest numbers of first-choice decisions, and finally, at the bottom, the show chosen by the least number of students as their favorite. Complete a ranking diagram for the top three choices.

Discuss with students what significance they see in the way the class ranked the educational value of the shows. Why do they think that the fourth-ranked show received so few first-choice votes?

- **Did thinking of qualities that you could use to decide how well the shows teach children ideas make a difference in how you voted?** ANSWERS VARY.

- **Now let's rank the shows by how much you enjoy them. With your partner, decide what makes a television show enjoyable. What qualities determine how much you like watching a television show? Write the characteristics in the box on the left.** Students commonly mention that the content and personalities are interesting, that the show holds children's attention, that there is variety in a single show, that the songs or special effects are interesting, that the show moves at a quick pace.

- **Select three of the television shows that we have talked about that you have seen and rank them from most enjoyable to least enjoyable. Explain why you think your favorite is the most enjoyable, why your second choice is not quite as entertaining, and why your third choice is not as enjoyable as the other two.** After students have completed their ranking of the shows, ask students to report on their choices. Write the names of the four shows on the board, and ask for the number of students who chose a particular show as the most enjoyable. Write the shows with the greatest number of first choices, the second greatest number of first choices, and the third greatest number of first choices on the ranking diagram as you did in discussing the shows' educational value.

- **What does ranking the shows by how much they teach and by how much you enjoy them tell us?** ANSWERS VARY. Sometimes the shows they like are also the shows that teach them. Sometimes students prefer entertainment to learning. Comparing the ranking will alert students to the value that they assign to watching certain shows.

THINKING ABOUT THINKING

- **What did you think about to put things accurately in the order in which they happened?** The thinking map for putting things in order contains the key questions for creating a time line.

- **How does sequencing events in the order in which they happened help you understand, remember, or explain them?** Students usually comment that both knowing the questions to ask and using the graphic organizer helps them to be accurate.

PUTTING THINGS IN ORDER
1. Why do you want to put them in order?
2. What is the best way to order them?
3. What do you have to find out about them to know where they fit?
4. Where does each item fit?

- **What did you think about to rank things accurately?** The thinking map for ranking things contains the key questions in skillful ranking.

- **How was ranking different from sequencing by date?** Students usually comment that time order involves using clues to match the event to the right time. Ranking also involves order, but the criteria for how they are ranked determines the order.

RANKING THINGS
1. Why do you want to rank them?
2. What should you find out in order to rank them for this purpose?
3. How will you rank them? Why?

APPLYING YOUR THINKING

IMMEDIATE TRANSFER

• Draw or tell the events in a story that we have just read. Use the graphic organizer that helps you order them correctly. How does carefully sequencing the events help you to be clear about what happened?

• Think about a time that you and a friend disagreed about the order in which things happened. Write or tell you partner about the difference of opinion about the order things happened and explain what you would do to prevent that confusion in the future.

REINFORCEMENT LATER

• Describe a sequence that must be followed in exactly the right order. Explain why that sequence is necessary.

• Use the time line to organize events in your life so that you can write your autobiography.

MATHEMATICS EXTENSION

Students may create bar graphs of the number of students who made first, second, and third choices for each of the four shows. Encourage students to write a paragraph interpreting what the graph shows. Students may survey a kindergarten class and compare the class's findings with the opinions of students who currently watch the shows.

You may take this opportunity to teach weighted values, creating a matrix with the numbers of first, second, and third choices for each of the shows. Multiplying each number by one, two, or three produces the weighted value of each show and allows you to calculate which show got the best overall ratings.

ASSESSING STUDENT THINKING ABOUT SEQUENCING

Any of the transfer examples can be used for assessment tasks. Examples in which students prioritize items are especially suited as assessment examples. Health textbooks are especially rich in contexts for ranking the relative importance such things as foods and safety practices. Ask the students to explain why they selected a characteristic for determining rank and how they arrived at the order of items. Use the thinking map to help you determine if your students are attending to relevant matters in ranking.

CHILDREN'S TELEVISION SHOWS

Many young children like to watch *Barney and Friends*. Barney and Baby Bop are friendly dinosaurs who show children how to be creative and how to get along. But *Barney and Friends*, which started in 1988, is a new show compared to other children's television shows.

The longest-running children's show is *Captain Kangaroo*. Bob Keeshan has played Captain Kangaroo since the show began in 1956. The show taught young children numbers, letters, and important ideas. Thirteen years later, Children's Television Workshop produced *Sesame Street* to teach young children. One year later, *Mister Rogers' Neighborhood* began to be broadcast, helping kids understand their feelings and values, as well as teaching them.

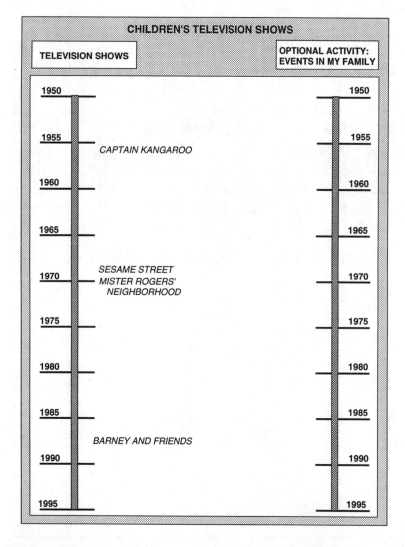

Sample Student Responses: Children's Television Shows

If students take the time line home and record family events, they will recognize what shows were on before they were born. The right side of the diagram will contain the family's history. They may add other television shows to the left column.

CHILDREN'S TELEVISION SHOWS

TELEVISION SHOWS

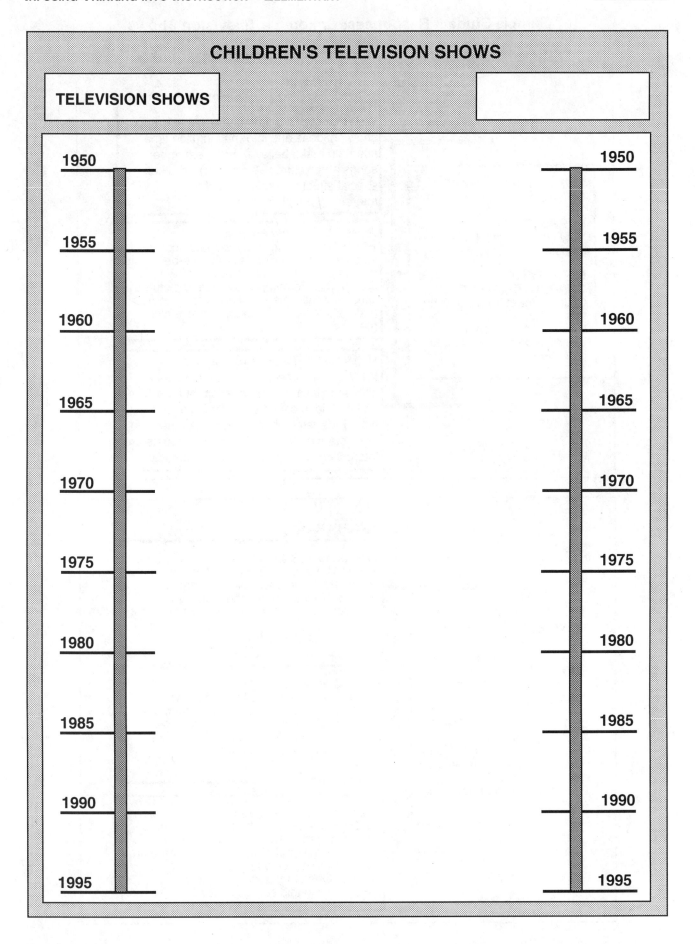

1950   1950

1955   1955

1960   1960

1965   1965

1970   1970

1975   1975

1980   1980

1985   1985

1990   1990

1995   1995

Sample Student Responses: Children's Television Shows

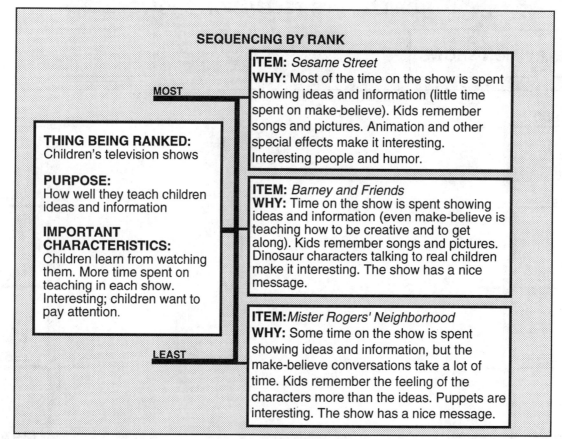

SEQUENCING BY RANK

MOST

THING BEING RANKED:
Children's television shows

PURPOSE:
How well they teach children ideas and information

IMPORTANT CHARACTERISTICS:
Children learn from watching them. More time spent on teaching in each show. Interesting; children want to pay attention.

LEAST

ITEM: *Sesame Street*
WHY: Most of the time on the show is spent showing ideas and information (little time spent on make-believe). Kids remember songs and pictures. Animation and other special effects make it interesting. Interesting people and humor.

ITEM: *Barney and Friends*
WHY: Time on the show is spent showing ideas and information (even make-believe is teaching how to be creative and to get along). Kids remember songs and pictures. Dinosaur characters talking to real children make it interesting. The show has a nice message.

ITEM: *Mister Rogers' Neighborhood*
WHY: Some time on the show is spent showing ideas and information, but the make-believe conversations take a lot of time. Kids remember the feeling of the characters more than the ideas. Puppets are interesting. The show has a nice message.

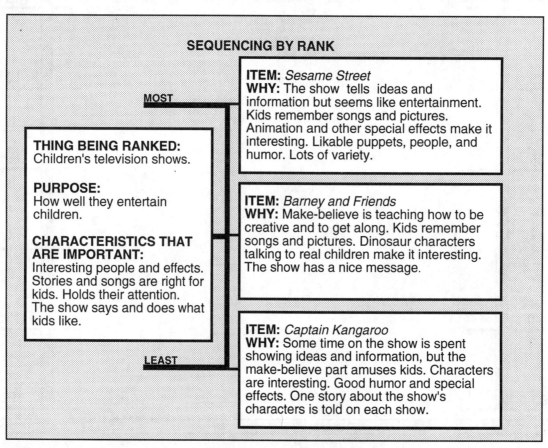

SEQUENCING BY RANK

MOST

THING BEING RANKED:
Children's television shows.

PURPOSE:
How well they entertain children.

CHARACTERISTICS THAT ARE IMPORTANT:
Interesting people and effects. Stories and songs are right for kids. Holds their attention. The show says and does what kids like.

LEAST

ITEM: *Sesame Street*
WHY: The show tells ideas and information but seems like entertainment. Kids remember songs and pictures. Animation and other special effects make it interesting. Likable puppets, people, and humor. Lots of variety.

ITEM: *Barney and Friends*
WHY: Make-believe is teaching how to be creative and to get along. Kids remember songs and pictures. Dinosaur characters talking to real children make it interesting. The show has a nice message.

ITEM: *Captain Kangaroo*
WHY: Some time on the show is spent showing ideas and information, but the make-believe part amuses kids. Characters are interesting. Good humor and special effects. One story about the show's characters is told on each show.

THE BEST WAY TO SEE IT

Science   **Grades 4–6**

OBJECTIVES

CONTENT

Students will clarify the characteristics of various types of observation instruments to decide which best fits different observation conditions or purposes. Students will differentiate between mosquitoes and flies.

THINKING SKILL/PROCESS

Students will rank objects by how well they serve certain purposes. They will select the characteristic by which the items should be ranked and will accurately place items in order.

METHODS AND MATERIALS

CONTENT

Examples of the observation equipment mentioned in the lesson or posters which show their features will remind students how each piece of equipment enhances observation. Use specimens of mosquitoes and flies, if they are available.

THINKING SKILL/PROCESS

In cooperative work groups, students discuss the purposes of ranking the items and rank them correctly for a selected purpose. The thinking map guides the teacher's directions in describing the task and the process. Three posters, drawings, or transparencies of the graphic organizer for ranking are needed. Students also need three copies of the graphic organizer. (See pp. 199–204 for reproducible diagrams.)

LESSON

INTRODUCTION TO CONTENT AND THINKING SKILL/PROCESS

- Think about things or events that we put in order. Our class schedule is the order that we do things in class each day. A birthday chart is the order in which people's birthdays occur during the year. We think about coins in order of their value. We put things on shelves in order of their size. With your partner, list as many things as you can think of that you have put in an order during the last few days. Name the characteristic that you thought about to put them in order. On the board, list several examples and characteristic for ordering.

- When we put things in order, we sequence them in certain ways. One way that we sequence things is to rank them. Ranking means putting things in order by how much of a specific quality they have or by how well they serve a specific purpose. Ask four students to stand in front of the class.

- What are some ways that we might rank these four students? Make two columns on the chalkboard or on newsprint. The left column should be headed "Characteristic." Write each characteristic under the heading. POSSIBLE RESPONSES: *Height, weight, number of people in their family.*

- Why would someone want to rank students by these characteristics? What would be the purpose of putting them in order this way? Label the right column "Why We Rank Them This Way." POSSIBLE RESPONSES: *Height (to arrange them for a picture, choir position, or game in which differences in height may be a factor), weight (to make the sides equal in organizing a tug of war), number of children in their family (to discuss sharing).* Write students' responses in the right column. Ask the four volunteers to select one of the characteristics and to arrange themselves left-to-right according to that characteristic. After the group has reassembled themselves, ask them to clarify what they thought about to do it.

- **Describe what you thought about to place yourselves in this order.**
Students' description of the thinking they used to rank themselves by height might include:

  (1) *We thought about who was the tallest and put that person on the far left.*

  (2) *We compared the heights of the others with the tallest and put the next tallest person next to the tallest.*

  (3) *We continued picking out the tallest person in the remaining group and placing that person next in order.*

  (4) *The shortest person was placed on the far right.*

  Now that the class sees the line of students in order of height, ask them for additional purposes for ranking people by height. Then ask the students to arrange themselves by birthday. Note that the order has probably changed. Again, ask students when they think this ordering would be useful.

- **Sometimes we rank things according to their usefulness. With your partner, describe things that we rank in the order of how well they help use do certain tasks. What characteristics are important in deciding which items are the most or least useful?** Discuss several student examples. POSSIBLE ANSWERS: *Tools, drawing media (pencils, markers, pastels, tempera paint), means of transportation, outerwear (coats, sweaters, jackets, parkas).*

THINKING ACTIVELY

- **In this lesson, we are going to rank various tools for use in observing insects. When studying insects, we want to learn about where they live, what their bodies are like, and what they need to survive. To make observations of flies, we must choose the best tool to use to see different things about them.** Write "Observation tools" in the box under "Thing being ranked." **Some tools for consideration are (1) a magnifying glass, often used to observe specimens in field where high magnification is not required, (2) the naked eye, which can provide more than 80 percent of the information received about the external environment, and (3) a compound microscope, which enables one to view an enlarged image of an organism by magnifying that organism up to 430 times its original size.**

- **We will be ranking these three tools according to their usefulness in observing the patterns in a fly's wing.** Under the heading "Purpose," write "To see details on the wing of an insect." **Decide what characteristics of the observation tools are important in this task.** POSSIBLE AN-SWERS: *Magnification (the wing does not need to be attached to the fly, so it can be mounted on a slide).*

- **Rank the three instruments from the most to the least useful. Write the order on the graphic organizer and explain why you ordered them this way.** After students have completed order-ing the tools, ask students to explain why they placed the equipment in this order. List their responses on a transparency or a large drawing of the graphic organizer. POSSIBLE ANSWERS: *(1)*

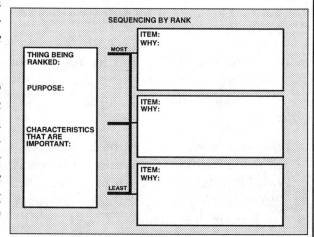

The microscope has the greatest magnification, making it best for seeing the patterns. Because the wing is thin enough to be opaque, no preparation of the wing would be necessary for viewing it under the microscope. The wing does have to be detached for viewing, however, destroying close examination of how it attaches to the body and how it works. The examination of the wing does not have to occur in the natural environment. (2) The magnifying glass offers enough magnification to see the wing but, perhaps, not in sufficient detail. It is portable and can show how the wing looks in relation to the fly's body without detaching it. The magnifying glass is easy to carry, allowing immediate examination of the specimen at the site. (3) The eye doesn't give enough magnification to see the details of patterns on the wing. The field of vision of the eye does allow the observer to see wing functioning.

- **Suppose you wanted to understand how flies behave in their natural environment.** On a new copy of the graphic organizer, write "See how the fly behaves" under the heading "Purpose." **We will be ranking the three tools according to their usefulness in observing the activity of the flies in their habitat. Decide what characteristics of the observation tools are important for this activity.** POSSIBLE ANSWERS: *Wide field of vision, little interference with the flies.*

- **Rank the three instruments from the most to the least useful. Write the order on the graphic organizer.** POSSIBLE ANSWERS: *(1) Although the eye doesn't give enough magnification to see the details on the bodies of flies, its broad field of vision does allow the observer to see flies in relation to their environment. Using the eye means that the flies and their surroundings are undisturbed by handling or preparation. The eye is always ready for use, and its acuity is as good as the vision of the observer. (2) The magnifying glass allows close-up examination with little disturbance and no dissection of the fly. It is portable and easy to use, but its field of vision limits observing the surrounding environment. (3) Using the microscope requires preparation, which must be done in a laboratory environment, even if it is a field laboratory. Little examination of the habitat can be pursued other than examining samples of substances in the flies habitat for microorganisms or chemicals. Some changes in the flies' bodies as the result of the environment might be detected, but the microscope's usefulness in understanding habitat is limited.*

- **Sometimes people mistake flies for mosquitoes. One way to differentiate them is to look carefully at their mouths. A female mosquito bites to get blood so that her eggs will develop. She pierces your skin with six little lances sheathed in a tube, interlocking to form a hollow needle. Before she sucks the blood, she injects an anticoagulant which causes the itchy, raised spot around the hole in a mosquito bite. Houseflies don't bite. Their mouthparts are spongy to absorb food. Biting flies have hard hooks above the mouth to shred its food before absorbing it. What characteristics of observation tools are helpful in examining the mouth?** POSSIBLE ANSWERS: *Some magnification; no damage to tissue in the fly's mouth.*

- **Rank the tools which would be most helpful in seeing the mouthparts of an insect in order to tell whether it is a mosquito or a fly.** POSSIBLE ANSWERS: *(1) The magnifying glass allows close-up examination with little disturbance and no dissection of the fly. Its magnification is adequate to see the details of the mouthparts of a fly or mosquito. It is portable, easy to use, and its field of vision is well suited for seeing the head area. (2) The microscope requires preparation and must be used in a laboratory environment. Preparation destroys the connection between the mouthparts. Its magnification shows more details of the structure of the mouthparts than the identification task requires. (3) Unless one has very good near vision, it is very difficult to get a good look at the mouthparts. One can, however, observe the biting behavior and its effects and tell whether the insect is a fly or a mosquito.*

- **How did ranking these tools in different ways help you understand how to use them?** Students respond that they recognize that magnification is not the only factor in observing things. More magnification limits the field around the object. Too much magnification may obscure the whole structure that one is trying to see. This lesson can be extended by asking students to analyze the utility of other tools that might be helpful in observing flies, such as a video camera, movie camera, or photographic camera with a telephoto lens.

THINKING ABOUT THINKING

- **What did you think about to rank things accurately?** This thinking map at right contains the key questions in skillful ranking.

- **What advice would you give someone about the best procedure for ranking things and ideas?** Often students make impulsive decisions about the relative usefulness of items without taking the time to compare the merits of each. In teaching the skill of ranking, it is important to have students start with a list of different items that may be useful for achieving a certain goal. In this way, students will gain practice in thinking through the pros and cons of each item and in ranking the items based on their analysis.

> ### SEQUENCING BY RANK
>
> 1. What is the purpose of the ranking?
>
> 2. What qualities must something have to serve this purpose?
>
> 3. Which of these qualities do each of the items being compared have, and to what degree do they have them?
>
> 4. Which has the largest degree of desirable qualities, the next largest, on to the least?

APPLYING YOUR THINKING

IMMEDIATE TRANSFER

- **List, in order of greater efficiency, which container would best fill a five-gallon aquarium that is five yards away from the water source: a one-gallon shallow pan, a 2 1/2-gallon plastic bucket with a handle, and a one-gallon glass jar.** Explain why you ranked them this way.

- **Rank the following items in terms of their usefulness in writing a term paper: a pencil, a typewriter, a word processor, a pen.** Explain why you ranked them this way.

REINFORCEMENT LATER

- **Find the calorie content of the snack foods available to you. Rank them by the range of their calories (0–100, 100–200, 200–300, etc.). Decide which ones fit your health goals and plan which ones you will select or reject or the frequency with which you will eat them.**

- **List all the tasks that you normally do between the time school is out and the time that you go to bed. Create a weekly schedule for yourself. Rank the five things that you do that are the least important and the five things that you do that are most important. Explain why you rank them this way. If you wanted to spend time on new things or to give more time to important things, how would you change your schedule?**

ASSESSING STUDENT THINKING ABOUT SEQUENCING

Any of the transfer examples can be used for assessment tasks. Examples in which students prioritize are especially suited as assessment examples. Health textbooks are especially rich in contexts offered to students about ranking the relative importance of such things as foods and safety practices. The children's magazine *Pennywise* is produced by Consumer Reports and features consumer information that often involves prioritizing. Ask the students to explain why they selected a given characteristic for determining rank and how they arrived at the order of items. Use the thinking map to help you determine if your students are attending to relevant matters in ranking.

Sample Student Answers: The Best Way to See It!

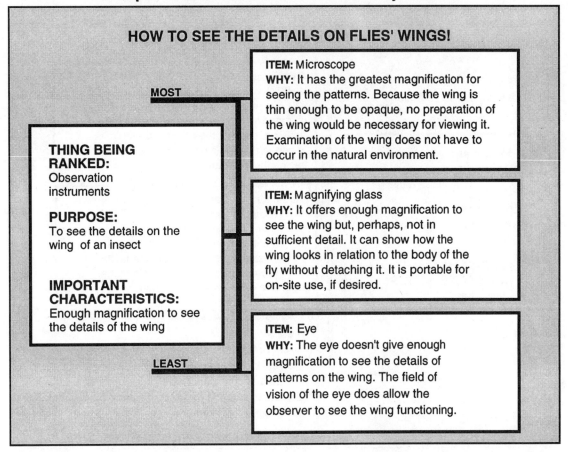

HOW TO SEE THE DETAILS ON FLIES' WINGS!

MOST

ITEM: Microscope
WHY: It has the greatest magnification for seeing the patterns. Because the wing is thin enough to be opaque, no preparation of the wing would be necessary for viewing it. Examination of the wing does not have to occur in the natural environment.

THING BEING RANKED:
Observation instruments

PURPOSE:
To see the details on the wing of an insect

IMPORTANT CHARACTERISTICS:
Enough magnification to see the details of the wing

ITEM: Magnifying glass
WHY: It offers enough magnification to see the wing but, perhaps, not in sufficient detail. It can show how the wing looks in relation to the body of the fly without detaching it. It is portable for on-site use, if desired.

ITEM: Eye
WHY: The eye doesn't give enough magnification to see the details of patterns on the wing. The field of vision of the eye does allow the observer to see the wing functioning.

LEAST

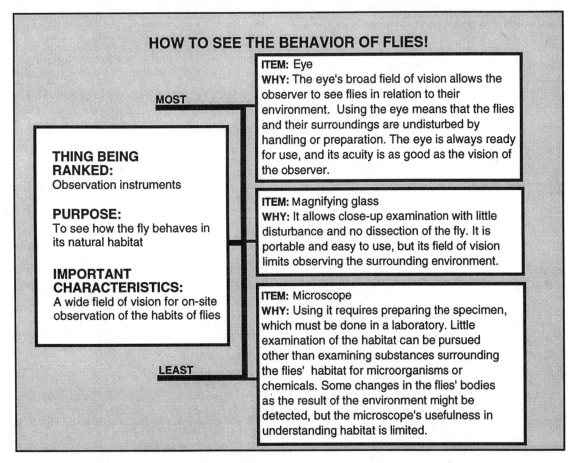

HOW TO SEE THE BEHAVIOR OF FLIES!

MOST

ITEM: Eye
WHY: The eye's broad field of vision allows the observer to see flies in relation to their environment. Using the eye means that the flies and their surroundings are undisturbed by handling or preparation. The eye is always ready for use, and its acuity is as good as the vision of the observer.

THING BEING RANKED:
Observation instruments

PURPOSE:
To see how the fly behaves in its natural habitat

IMPORTANT CHARACTERISTICS:
A wide field of vision for on-site observation of the habits of flies

ITEM: Magnifying glass
WHY: It allows close-up examination with little disturbance and no dissection of the fly. It is portable and easy to use, but its field of vision limits observing the surrounding environment.

ITEM: Microscope
WHY: Using it requires preparing the specimen, which must be done in a laboratory. Little examination of the habitat can be pursued other than examining substances surrounding the flies' habitat for microorganisms or chemicals. Some changes in the flies' bodies as the result of the environment might be detected, but the microscope's usefulness in understanding habitat is limited.

LEAST

Sample Student Answers: The Best Way to See It!

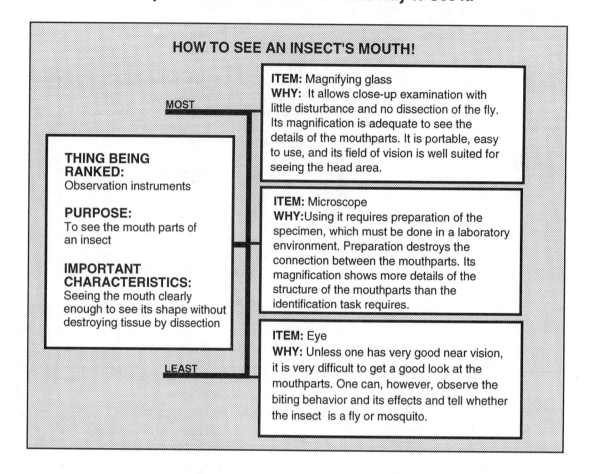

HOW TO SEE AN INSECT'S MOUTH!

THING BEING RANKED:
Observation instruments

PURPOSE:
To see the mouth parts of an insect

IMPORTANT CHARACTERISTICS:
Seeing the mouth clearly enough to see its shape without destroying tissue by dissection

MOST

ITEM: Magnifying glass
WHY: It allows close-up examination with little disturbance and no dissection of the fly. Its magnification is adequate to see the details of the mouthparts. It is portable, easy to use, and its field of vision is well suited for seeing the head area.

ITEM: Microscope
WHY: Using it requires preparation of the specimen, which must be done in a laboratory environment. Preparation destroys the connection between the mouthparts. Its magnification shows more details of the structure of the mouthparts than the identification task requires.

ITEM: Eye
WHY: Unless one has very good near vision, it is very difficult to get a good look at the mouthparts. One can, however, observe the biting behavior and its effects and tell whether the insect is a fly or mosquito.

LEAST

SEQUENCING LESSON CONTEXTS

The following examples have been suggested by classroom teachers as contexts to develop infused lessons. If a skill or process has been introduced in a previous infused lesson, these contexts may be used to reinforce it.

GRADE	SUBJECT	TOPIC	THINKING ISSUE
K–3	Literature	*Black and White*	Trace the sequence of events shown in each of the four pictures on each page of the book to show how four independent stories converge.
K–3	Literature	*The Napping House*	To predict what will happen when the flea bites the mouse, look at events in the story in reverse order.
K–3	Language arts	Writing a report	Plan your writing by identifying the steps in writing a report.
K–3	Language arts	Library instructions	To clarify the instructions for library use, sequence the steps in using the card catalog and in locating books.
K-3	Language arts	Plot	Use sequencing to show the plot of a story.
K–3	Language arts	Cumulative stories	Explain why sequencing is important in understanding and enjoying cumulative stories such as "One Fine Day," "Bringing the Rain to Kapiti Plain," or "The Green Grass Grew All Around, All Around."
K–3	Literature	*Who Has Come Down This Road?*	To clarify the changes through the centuries, trace the sequence of people and animals that came down the road.
K–3	Literature	*A River Ran Wild*	To clarify how the inhabitants around a body of water effect water pollution and to understand river renewal, trace the changes in the Nashua River from the coming of the Indians to its environmental clean-up.
K–3	Social studies	Generations in a family	Create a family tree of your parents, sisters, brothers, grandparents, cousins, aunts, uncles, and step-parents' family, as appropriate, to show the order in which your relatives were born and how they are related.
K–3	Social studies	Land forms	In order to determine what kinds of animals, agriculture, or industries one is likely to find there, sequence the following land forms by how much water is available: desert, prairie, marshland, pine forest, rainforest, riverbank, delta.
K–3	Social studies	Checking	Describe the sequence of setting up and using a checking account.
K–3	Social studies	Producers and consumers	Illustrate the circulation of money among producers, consumers, and the government to show community interdependence.
K–3	Math	Problem solving	Illustrate steps in solving multistep mathematics problems.
K–3	Math	Computer	Illustrate steps in using computer software and show why the given order is necessary.
K-3	Math	Checking computation	Describe the steps to check computations to determine whether correct procedures were followed.
K-3	Science	Water cycle	Depict the water cycle to clarify cloud formation and to illustrate the importance of responsible water use.

SEQUENCING LESSON CONTEXTS			
GRADE	SUBJECT	TOPIC	THINKING ISSUE
K–3	Science	Photosynthesis and respiration	To show the significance of oxygen production by plants, depict the photosynthesis and respiration cycles.
K–3	Science	Energy from plants	Trace energy changes from plant sources to energy uses (energy as fuel, energy as food, and energy as heat) to show how energy from the sun is transformed by plants into other forms of energy.
K–3	Science	Metamorphosis	Illustrate changes in the body of a frog to clarify the differences between amphibians and other cold-blooded vertebrates.
K–3	Science	Planets	Sequence the relative distances of planets to determine which planets the space program is likely to research most thoroughly.
K–3	Science	Trees	Compare the relative sizes of trees to clarify which types might be planted for various purposes.
K–3	Music	Rhythm	Sequence long and short beats to produce different rhythms, changing the beat in common songs: "Row, Row, Row Your Boat" (3 long, steady beats), "On Top of Old Smoky" (long-short-long), "The Itsy-Bitsy Spider" (short-long-short), "Jingle Bells" (short-short-long), "This Old Man" (long-short-long), and "Twinkle, Twinkle Little Star" (short-short).
K–3	Art	Colors	To show the relationship between primary and secondary colors, arrange colors in the order that they appear in a rainbow.
K–3	Physical education	Hopping, skip-ping & jumping	Sequence the body movements in hopping, skipping, and jumping.
4–6	Language arts	Laura Ingalls Wilder	Correlate the events in the life of Laura Ingalls Wilder with the events in her books in order to read the books in the order in which things happened in her life.
4–6	Language arts	Reference skills	Use the sequence of the Dewey Decimal System to locate books in the library.
4–6	Language arts	Debate	When planning a debate, prioritize your team's arguments and the arguments you anticipate from the opposing debate team.
4–6	Language arts	Writing a report	To show the most efficient way to write a paper, describe the steps in writing a report.
4–6	Language arts	Writing an autobiography	Use a time line to correlate your memories of things that happened to you to important local, state, national, or international events.
4–6	Language arts	Narrative writing	Use a time line to plan the events and the plot of a story that you compose.
4–6	Social studies	Colonization	Review the cycle of British stock companies investing in and profiting from the colonies in the New World to explain British attitudes toward the American colonies.
4–6	Social studies	Civil War leaders	Correlate the events in the life of Frederick Douglass with events in the life of Abraham Lincoln to show the background and achievements of these two leaders in improving conditions for African Americans.

SEQUENCING LESSON CONTEXTS

GRADE	SUBJECT	TOPIC	THINKING ISSUE
4–6	Social studies	American Revolution	To clarify the dissatisfaction of the colonists, prepare a time line showing events in the colonies and acts of the English Parliament in the period between the French and Indian War and the Declaration of Independence.
4–6	Social studies	State history	To clarify issues leading to statehood, compare events in your state's colonial or territorial period with national events during the same period.
4–6	Social studies/ science	Nuclear power	To clarify nuclear safety concerns, trace the creation of nuclear energy from nuclear fission to an electrical generator.
4–6	Social studies	World cultures	Correlate historical, sociological, economic, or political events in Mali, Mexico, and England from 800–1500 AD to illustrate the growth of cities and the development of the cultures.
4–6	Social studies	Technology	Relate social changes to changes in technology, such as the development of different forms of transportation, since 1900.
4–6	Mathematics	Fractions	Depict the relative values of common fractions.
4–6	Mathematics	Units of measure	Rank metric and British measures of length, area, volume, or weight according to size.
4–6	Mathematics	Problem solving	Use a diagram to solve word problems involving transitive order.
4–6	Mathematics	Inequality	Explain the effect of transitive order in inequality statements.
4–6	Mathematics	Flow charts	Use a flow chart to depict the order in which computer operations occur.
4–6	Mathematics	Order of operations	To confirm that the order of operations makes a difference, do a computation problem several times which contains all four operations, changing the order in which you do the operations each time.
4–6	Computer use	Computer operation	Describe the steps in starting up and shutting down your computer. Explain why it is important to do the steps in that order.
4–6	Science	*Wonders of the Deep Sea*	Analyze the accounts of ocean exploration. Select one and describe how the research might have turned out differently if another sequence of events had been followed.
4–6	Science	Acid rain	Describe the process by which acid rain forms and explain where in the process steps can be taken to reduce it.
4–6	Science	Pollution	Rank four sources of air pollution by how much pollutant they put into the air.
4–6	Science	Plants	Prioritize five uses of plants from the most to the least important.
4–6	Science	*All About Famous Scientific Experiments*	Select one of the scientific experiments that had alternative sequences for carrying it out. What difference in results would occur if a different order were followed?

SEQUENCING LESSON CONTEXTS

GRADE	SUBJECT	TOPIC	THINKING ISSUE
4–6	Science	Minerals	Compare the relative weights of minerals in order to clarify their properties and to identify them.
4–6	Science	Clouds	Compare the relative heights of clouds to describe cloud formation.
4–6	Science	Sounds	Rank various common sounds by decibel level to identify which are unsafe to our hearing.
4–6	Science	Energy changes	Identify the sequence of energy changes needed to lift a weight.
4–6	Science	Electricity	Depict the sequence in the operation of an electrical current .
4–6	Science	Internal combustion engine	Depict the gasoline engine cycle to explain common malfunctions in an automobile engine.
4–6	Science	Carbon dioxide and oxygen cycle	Use the carbon dioxide and oxygen cycle to describe how plants and animals are interdependent.
4–6	Science	Mammal gestation	List the following animals in the order the length of gestation: cat, elephant, horse, human, mouse, pig, rabbit, whale, and kangaroo. Students should realize that, with the exception of marsupials, the larger the animal, the longer the gestation period.
4–6	Science	Insects	To clarify the characteristics of different stages in the growth of a moth, describe the sequence of a moth's development.
4–6	Science	Erosion	Describe the sequence of river erosion (rain > runoff > river flooding > erosion of riverbanks) to evaluate the effects of damming a river.
4–6	Science	Decomposition	Describe how each step in the cycle of plant growth and decomposition is necessary for the health of the ecosystem. What may result if any step is altered?
4–6	Art	Printmaking	Describe the steps in making a linoleum block print. Explain why the steps must be done in this order.
4–6	Music	Musical terms	To clarify definitions, rank various terms used to describe pace or volume.
4–6	Music	Instruments	Rank string instruments by size and by tone. What does comparing the size to the tone suggest about the relationship between the two?
4–6	Art/music	Styles	Arrange selected works in chronological order to illustrate the development of that artistic or musical style.
4–6	Physical education	Games	Describe the order of events in a selected game. Explain why each event is important and should be done in the given order.

CHAPTER 8
FINDING REASONS AND CONCLUSIONS

Why is Accurately Finding a Person's Reasons and Conclusions Important?

Usually we have many reasons for accepting the views that we hold or for doing the things that we do. I may conclude that I should buy a particular make of car because a friend has one, because I like a silver one that I saw, because an automobile magazine says that this make of car has a good repair record, or because an attractive film personality in a TV commercial said it was a good car.

A basic principle of critical thinking is that we should not accept a conclusion unless the reasons for the conclusion justify believing it. When I ask myself whether my reasons for buying the car are good ones, I should be prepared to withdraw my conviction that I should buy the car if I realize that my reasons are not good ones. Unless I can make explicit what my reasons are and state my conclusion clearly, I will be hampered in making these important critical judgments.

Analyzing and evaluating arguments. Other people sometimes try to convince us to act in certain ways or to adopt views that we may not currently hold. We sometimes try to convince others to adopt views that we hold. When people try to convince others by giving them *reasons* for accepting particular actions or views, they are offering an *argument*. If we accept an idea or choice that someone else tries to persuade us to accept, we should likewise make sure that the reasons they offer justify the conclusion. When a salesperson tells me about the good features of a car in order to convince me to buy it, he or she is giving me an argument for buying this make. Before I become convinced to purchase the car, I should make sure that his reasons justify that conclusion.

Arguments occur in a multitude of contexts, including political speeches, letters to the editor, and advertising. The same standards of critical thinking apply to all of these different forms of argument. The conclusion of an argument should not be accepted unless the reasons that are offered in support of it justify believing it.

Just as in our own case, to be able to decide whether the reasons others give us are good ones, we must first clarify what those reasons are. This fundamental *analytical* skill involves first noting the *conclusion* or *main idea* that is advanced and then looking for the *reasons that are offered to support the idea*.

When we *evaluate* the reasons, we use standards of critical thinking that enable us to distinguish good reasons from weak ones. If *there is some doubt about the accuracy of the reasons* or we're not sure whether *there is additional information available that counts against the conclusion*, then the reasons are weak. They are not, in themselves, sufficient reasons for accepting the conclusion.

For example, an automobile salesman may try to convince me to buy a car by pointing out that it costs less than any of the comparable foreign imports. Am I sure that this information is accurate? Are there any hidden costs? Even if the salesman is right about the cost, I have not yet investigated either the repair record or the cost of parts. I may still find that the car has a bad repair record and that spare parts are hard to get. This additional information may convince me that I should not buy the car, even though the initial information about its price is correct. In this case, the fact that the car costs less than any of the comparable foreign imports is not, in itself, a good enough reason for buying the car.

The type of analysis involved in *finding reasons and conclusions* is usually not difficult. We are told by reliable sources that eating lots of foods high in cholesterol can cause heart attacks. This fact is often used to try to convince us to change our dietary habits, specifically that we should not eat a lot of foods high in cholesterol. It is not difficult to recognize that "Eating foods high in cholesterol can cause heart attacks" is the reason being offered for not eating such foods. Not eating such foods is the conclusion those who advance this argument want us to accept.

There is a second, but unstated, reason in this argument: heart attacks can cause death and should be avoided. It is important to make unstated reasons such as this explicit when analyzing and evaluating arguments. When this unstated reason is revealed, it is easy to grasp why we find this argument compelling. The combined reasons clearly support the conclusion.

We can determine whether there is an unstated reason in this argument, and what it is, by asking whether there is an idea that the author believes we all accept which explains why the fact that cholesterol may cause a heart attack suggests that we should avoid foods high in cholesterol. He accepts, as we all do, that heart attacks should be avoided and, hence, does not need to say so.

Difficulties in finding reasons and conclusions. It is not always easy to determine a person's reasons for his or her claims. In the cholesterol example, we are tipped off to the reason being offered by the word "because." Additionally, both the conclusion and his reason for it are stated clearly. Sometimes neither the conclusion nor the reason are present. Fiery speeches, dramatic rhetoric, the use of compelling visual images, and other appeals to our emotions often obscure the substantive reasons, if indeed there are any, that are offered to convince us of ideas or choices. Often the devices used by advertisers distract us from determining whether or not there are good reasons for buying their products. In these cases, images and rhetoric, not reasons, may convince us.

There are three common circumstances that can lead to our accepting ideas without determining whether there are reasons for accepting them. The first is that many people do not think to ask for reasons. An idea may seem like a good one because of the way it is presented, but no reasons may actually be offered. If we do not seek reasons, we may base our acceptance on how the idea is presented, not whether it is supported.

The second circumstance is that we sometimes mistake appeal for reasons. The passion of a speech or the drama of a visual image in advertising may be enough to convince us to accept an idea. These devices are usually not offered as reasons but are, instead, used to make the idea seem appealing in and of itself.

Finally, we may take only stated reasons as the reasons for accepting an idea and not look for ones that are unstated. The unstated reasons may be ideas that are problematic. Unless we search for them, we will not know whether they are credible.

Difficulties in evaluating whether reasons are good reasons for a conclusion. Often people are convinced by bad arguments because they hear some reasons which support the conclusion and do not try to find out whether there is other unstated information that counts against the conclusion. This happens frequently when people respond to advertising. You may buy a shampoo because you read in an ad that it will make your hair softer. Indeed, you find out that it does. But it also colors your hair, and you do not want that to happen. Unless you try to find out whether there are reasons against the conclusion and find that there are none, it is a mistake to take the reasons offered as conclusive.

There is a more subtle version of this problem in evaluating arguments. Sometimes we find out whether there are reasons against a conclusion but do a hasty and superficial search. For example, I may ask the salesman whether there are any reasons for not buying the shampoo, and he may say that there aren't. Thoroughness in a search for counter-reasons, however, is important. We should consult independent sources, such as *Consumer's Reports* or someone who has used this type of shampoo, before being convinced that there are no counter-reasons.

These circumstances illustrate the main defaults in recognizing the conclusions that others try to convince us to accept and in identifying and evaluating the reasons that they give to support those conclusions. Figure 8.1 summarizes these defaults.

DEFAULTS WITH REGARD TO REASONS AND CONCLUSIONS

1. We may not seek reasons for an idea someone is trying to convince us to accept.

2. We may mistake emotions or visual images for reasons.

3. We may not search for unstated reasons.

4. We may only consider the reasons in favor of a conclusion and not search for reasons against the conclusion.

5. We may not do a thorough search for reasons for and against a conclusion.

Figure 8.1

---

(1) Eating a lot of foods high in cholesterol can cause heart attacks.

(2) Heart attacks should be avoided.

Therefore

(3) We should not eat a lot of foods high in cholesterol.

Figure 8.2

What Is Involved When We Skillfully Detect Reasons and Conclusions?

Breaking out arguments. How can we develop our analytical abilities so that we can cut through rhetoric, images, and imprecision to the heart of what others try to communicate? How can we determine clearly what ideas others are trying to convince us to accept and what reasons they give us for accepting these ideas?

We "break out an argument" when we determine a person's conclusions or main ideas and the reasons offered for these conclusions. It is always helpful to try to articulate both the conclusions and reasons as clearly as possible, detaching them from a particular context in which they appear. This is commonly done by stating the reason(s) first, then stating the conclusion, using words or symbols that indicate this relationship. Figure 8.2 represents a way that the argument about heart attacks and cholesterol can be stated.

Sometimes "therefore" is replaced by three dots ($\therefore$). The reasons come before the "therefore"; the conclusion comes after it. While the reasons in an argument are often called its premises, we prefer to use the term "reasons."

Considering opposing viewpoints. One of the important dispositions of critical thinking is open-mindedness. This involves a willingness to consider all sides of an issue before making up one's mind. Often people who are convinced about something are not willing to listen to other viewpoints or to consider changing their minds. We know, however, that sometimes new information or a fresh perspective can reveal that even firmly held views may need modification. Open-mindedness counters such narrow thinking.

Seeking and assessing arguments on both sides of an issue, whether or not we are disposed towards one viewpoint or another, fosters open-mindedness. Breaking out arguments and setting them side-by-side often helps to clarify an issue and paves the way to considering whether the argument on the other side of the case has merit.

A graphic organizer and thinking map for clarifying reasons and conclusions. The graphic organizer in figure 8.3 depicts an argument. It illustrates the idea that conclusions should be supported by reasons.

The number of reason "pillars" in the graphic organizer can vary, depending on the number of reasons offered in support of the conclusion. Both stated and unstated reasons can be written on the pillars.

Note that this graphic organizer is used for one argument only. If there are multiple arguments in a passage, a number of these diagrams should be used. To depict opposing viewpoints, two of these diagrams can be used, each with a contrasting conclusion.

The thinking map in figure 8.4 prompts the reasons and conclusions that you write on the diagram.

This thinking map makes it clear that we should consider only the reasons that a specific

---

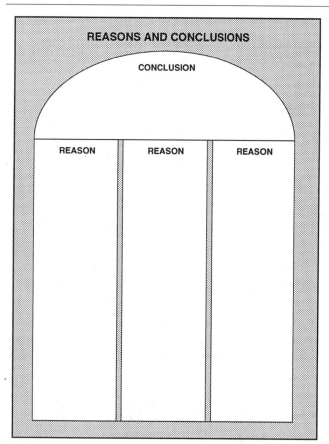

Figure 8.3

FINDING REASONS AND CONCLUSIONS

1. What is the author trying to convince us to accept or do?

2. What reasons does the author provide to support accepting or doing that?

   a. Are there any words that indicate support (e.g., "therefore," "so," "because")?

   b. Does the author provide any other indication as to why he or she concludes what he or she does?

3. Is there anything that you think the author believes is common knowledge that he or she does not state but uses to support the conclusion?

Figure 8.4

---

clusions skillfully. When someone offers reasons for an idea or action, that person often uses words like "therefore," "so," "because," etc. to indicate which statements are reasons and which are conclusions. When such signal words are not present, we can think about where we would put a "therefore" or a "because." Asking "Why does he think that?" can also lead us to the author's reasons.

Assessing whether reasons support accepting a conclusion. Finding a person's reasons for his or her conclusions is an important first step in thinking critically about whether or not a person has given good reasons to accept an idea or recommendation. To make this judgment skillfully, however, requires more thought than simply clarifying the reasons and conclusions. We must now use our critical thinking to assess whether the reasons are sufficient to support accepting the conclusion.

One way to make this assessment is to ask whether we need any other information beyond the reasons we've uncovered before we are willing to accept the conclusion. If we do, the given reasons may not be sufficient to justify the conclusion. If not, the reasons may be adequate.

In general, three basic standards should be applied in order to determine whether or not the conclusion is acceptable based on the reasons offered:

- The information stated as reasons is accurate

- The reasons count strongly in favor of the conclusion

- There is no other significant information that counts against the particular conclusion

For example, suppose a salesman tells me that I should purchase a car because it gets good gas mileage, does not cost a lot, and has the best repair record of all foreign cars. Because these are major concerns of mine, his reasons initially present a compelling case. I need much more information before I should be convinced to buy the car based on his reasons.

First, I should confirm that the information the salesman has provided is accurate. Sometimes salespeople distort the truth to sell a prod-

person gives for a judgment or conclusion. We should not try to provide our own reasons. Our reasons may not be ones that the person accepts.

It is not difficult to identify reasons and con-

uct. Is that happening in this case? Maybe it is; maybe it isn't. Having the best repair record is a good reason for purchasing a car only if that claim is accurate. I may want to confirm what the salesman says by looking at another source like *Consumer's Reports*.

Even if the information supporting an action or conclusion has proven to be accurate, the given reasons still may not be sufficient to support purchasing the car. Other factors may count against buying this particular car and override the benefits. I may find out that the car is not easily repaired and that spare parts are costly. I should not expect that a salesperson is going to tell me about these negative considerations. Until I have good reason for thinking that there is no overriding information, the salesperson's argument should be treated as inconclusive.

When a thorough and balanced argument lays out accurate reasons for and against a proposition *and* the reasons for accepting it are more compelling than the reasons against it, no additional information may be necessary. In this case, the conclusion to buy the car would be justified by the reasons.

In most cases, we more or less informally apply the standards just described for judging the viability of arguments. In some cases, however, our thinking should be more rigorous. For example, arguments about guilt or innocence in criminal matters often require more careful analysis and critical judgment. Such cases require careful evaluation involving critical thinking skills such as causal explanation or determining the reliability of sources of information.

The graphic organizer in figure 8.5 can be used to record the results of this inquiry into the soundness of an argument.

Using the argument evaluation checklist. After you have recorded reasons and conclusions in figure 8.3, you can analyze the argument using the checklist in figure 8.5. Record your response to whether you have enough information to determine that the reasons are accurate. If you do, check the "yes" box; if not, check the "no" box and list the information you need to make this judgment. In cases in which more rigor is needed in determine the accuracy of the information, you may have to determin-

Figure 8.5

ing the reliability of the sources of this information more carefully. The strategies in Chapter 12: Determining the Reliability of Sources may be used to supplement this part of the argument evaluation checklist.

The second question on the checklist presupposes that the information given as reasons is accurate and asks you to consider whether you need any more information for the argument to be convincing. This question has to do with whether the reasons alone are sufficient to justify the conclusion. In the case of the auto purchase, for example, you would check the "Yes" box and write things like "Is this car easy to repair?" "What is its repair record?" "How do other owners rate this car?" etc.

If additional information is needed, either to show that the reasons are accurate or to supplement these reasons in order to justify the conclusion, then the given reason(s) *does not justify accepting the conclusion.* The reason(s) given in this case is not a good reason(s) for accepting the conclusion, and the argument is not a viable one.

There are limitations to using the evaluation checklist, however. Answering the questions on the checklist will only enable us to make a judgment about whether a specific argument provides good reasons to justify its conclusion.

If I determine, for example, that the argument offered by the car salesman is not good enough to support buying this particular car, this does *not* show that there are not other better reasons for buying the car than those given by the salesman. There may well be. Indeed, using the checklist may help me find them. When I write the additional information that I need to be convinced of the conclusion, this can guide me in conducting further research about the car. When I do this research, I may find, for example, that people who own this type of car give it very high praise, that it has a good repair record, that it gets good mileage, etc. As I accumulate this additional information, I may be able to develop a much better argument for buying the car than the salesman gave me. If so, then, of course, when I use the argument evaluation checklist to assess this argument, it should show up as a good argument.

To summarize: Using the argument evaluation checklist helps us clarify whether or not we should acquire additional information before we accept the conclusion of an argument. As we answer the questions raised in using the checklist, we may get information that can be used to construct another, more convincing argument to resolve the issue.

Fallacies of reasoning. An alternative strategy for determining whether conclusions are well-supported by given reasons involves recognizing patterns of faulty ("fallacious") reasoning. There are specific types of fallacious arguments that occur with such frequency that they have been categorized for easy recognition. These patterns of faulty reasoning are usually called *fallacies*.

Once an argument is broken out using the strategy for finding reasons and conclusions, it may be easy to spot it as an incorrect argument if it represents one of these patterns. For example, people often argue that something happens *because* of something else only on the basis of the fact that it occurred *after* that event. This pattern of argument is fallacious because it could be a coincidence that these two events occurred after one another. The traditional name for this pattern of incorrect reasoning is the *post hoc, ergo propter hoc* ("after this, therefore because of this") fallacy. If someone offers an argument and you recognize it as an argument of this type, you can conclude that it is incorrect: the reasons are too weak to establish the conclusion.

Identifying informal fallacies is a technique used in many critical thinking textbooks, as well as in some language arts materials. While learning to identify these patterns of faulty reasoning may be helpful in spotting some fallacious arguments, many other fallacious arguments do not fit these patterns.

In contrast to recognizing fallacies, using the argument evaluation checklist guides us in assessing whether *any* argument contains reasons which support the conclusion. This strategy is employed in the lessons in this handbook because it is versatile, does not require technical language, and is easier for students to comprehend.

How Should We Teach Students to Detect Reasons and Conclusions Skillfully?

Giving students practice in analyzing arguments offered in the content they are studying and helping them to guide themselves in this process is a key to students' internalizing the strategy for finding reasons and conclusions. It is important that students extract arguments from natural contexts in which these arguments appear and restate them in a clearer form. Breaking out an argument, as represented in figure 8.2, makes an argument explicit, facilitating assessment of whether or not it is a good argument.

Contexts in the curriculum for finding reasons and conclusions. The curriculum offers many contexts for analyzing reasons and conclusions. In general, such lessons can be developed in three types of contexts:

- *Arguments are presented in textbooks for certain views or courses of action.* For example, in health instruction in elementary school, students are given reasons for brushing their teeth. Similarly, in drug education programs, reasons are given to avoid substance abuse. It is important to help students to understand these reasons and assess their significance rather than just accept the conclusions.

- *Arguments are offered by historical figures or by characters in literature in support of certain points of view.* For example, leaders offer arguments for going to war or for adopting certain national policies (like social security or graduated income tax). Such arguments are ripe for analysis, especially since opponents usually offer counter-arguments that can similarly be analyzed. The Declaration of Independence can be viewed as a complex argument for independence. Similarly, arguments that have been offered about the interaction of science, technology, and society (e.g., energy sources, pollution, genetic engineering, the rain forests) provide contexts for lessons on determining reasons and conclusions. The reasons that characters in stories give for their views and actions can similarly be analyzed and assessed.

- *Students are asked to develop their own arguments.* For example, as students learn to write persuasive prose, being clear about their reasons for their conclusions can be a valuable asset. Similarly, debating skills can also be improved when students analyze their arguments.

A menu of suggested contexts for infusion lessons on finding reasons and conclusions is provided on pp. 252–54.

Finding Reasons and Conclusions in Primary Grades

Students in the primary grades need focus only on explicit reasons; determining unstated reasons is hard for young students and can be left for grades four and beyond. The thinking map in figure 8.4 for finding reasons and conclusions can, therefore, be simplified for young children. Figure 8.6 is a version of the thinking map that can be used with primary grade students.

The graphic organizer in figure 8.3 is appropriate for all elementary students.

Open discussion of whether or not an argument is a good one is appropriate for young students. While primary grade students may be asked whether the reasons given to support a conclusion are good reasons, using the checklist for argument evaluation (figure 8.5) is more appropriate for upper elementary students.

FINDING REASONS AND CONCLUSIONS

1. What is the author trying to convince us to do?

2. What reasons does the author provide for doing this?

    a. Are there any signal words that indicate reasons and conclusions (e.g., "therefore," "so," "because")?

    b. Does the author tell us why he or she concludes what he or she does?

Figure 8.6

Tips for Teaching Lessons on Reasons and Conclusions.

Lessons which include arguments on both sides of an issue provide richer experiences for students than analyzing arguments only on one side of the case. A variety of arguments should be considered on major issues so that students can develop a sense of the variety of reasons, some weak, some not, that people have offered to support their ideas.

It is especially important to help students apply this skill to school-related extra-curricular activities and in other experiences outside of school. Helping them to analyze arguments provided in advertising, in political speeches, and on moral and social issues will put students in a much better position to assess these arguments.

Model Lessons on Finding Reasons and Conclusions

Two lesson on reasons and conclusions are included in this handbook. In the primary grade lesson, students are asked to analyze an argument for recycling garbage and then to construct their own arguments for recycling. The upper elementary lesson involves analyzing arguments offered prior to the American Revolution about whether the colonies should seek independence from Britain or remain loyal. In this lesson students are asked to analyze opposing arguments.

As you read each lesson, consider the following questions:

- How does the graphic organizer in figure 8.3 help students become aware of the structure of an argument?

- How does using that diagram help students to clarify major and minor differences in two opposing viewpoints?

- How can the graphic organizer be used in the writing extension to help students outline arguments they will present?

- What are some other examples that can be used to transfer and reinforce this skill?

Tools for Designing Reasons and Conclusions Lessons

The two thinking maps for finding reasons and conclusions can be used to help students break out any argument they are considering, whether it occurs in prose or advertising. The graphic organizer is similarly versatile. The thinking map on page 232 is designed especially for use in the primary grades.

The thinking maps and graphic organizer can guide you in designing the critical thinking activity in the lesson and can also serve as photocopy masters, transparency masters, or as models that can be enlarged and used as posters in the classroom. Reproduction rights are granted for single classroom use only.

FINDING REASONS AND CONCLUSIONS

1. **What is the author trying to convince us to believe or do?**

2. **What reasons does the author provide to support accepting or doing that?**

   a. **Are there any words that indicate support (e.g., "therefore," "so," "because")?**

   b. **Does the author provide any other indication as to why he or she concludes what he or she does?**

3. **Is there anything that you think the author believes is common knowledge that he or she does not state but uses to support the conclusion?**

FINDING REASONS AND CONCLUSIONS

1. **What is the author trying to convince us to do?**

2. **What reasons does the author provide for doing this?**

   a. **Are there any signal words that indicate reasons and conclusions (e.g., "therefore," "so," "because")?**

   b. **Does the author tell us why he or she concludes what he or she does?**

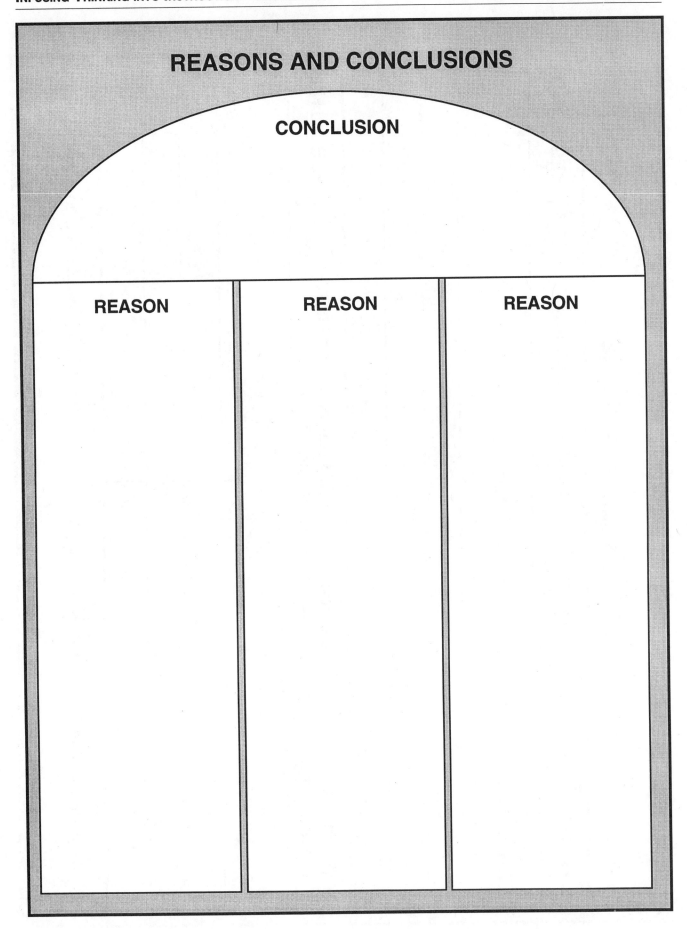

REASONS AND CONCLUSIONS

CONCLUSION

REASON

REASON

REASON

ARGUMENT EVALUATION CHECKLIST

1. Is there anything you need to find out in order to determine whether the reasons are accurate?   YES ☐ NO ☐

2. If so, what information do you need to find out?

3. Given that the reasons are accurate, is additional information needed before you can accept the conclusion?   YES ☐ NO ☐

4. If so, what information do you need?

An argument should be convincing only if you answer "NO" to questions 1 and 3 above.

GARBAGE AND TRASH

Social Studies/Science **Grades 2–3**

OBJECTIVES

CONTENT

Students will learn about the different methods of waste management and the problems with each. They will consider reasons for and against recycling as a policy.

THINKING SKILL/PROCESS

Students will develop skill at detecting the conclusions and the supporting reasons offered for these conclusions by looking for signal words like "therefore," "so," and "because."

METHODS AND MATERIALS

CONTENT

Students will read passages offering arguments for recycling. They will work together to reconstruct and assess the arguments. They will then construct their own arguments in favor of and against recycling waste in the school and will debate the issue orally.

THINKING SKILL/PROCESS

Detecting reasons and conclusions is guided by structured questioning and by the use of a graphic organizer that highlights the conclusion and its supporting reasons for an argument. (See pp. 231–34 for reproducible diagrams.)

LESSON

INTRODUCTION TO CONTENT AND THINKING SKILL/PROCESS

- **Has anyone ever tried to convince you of something important by giving you reasons why you should accept what he was saying? Write down two situations in which this has happened to you.** Ask students for a few examples. Ask them to state exactly what the other person tried to convince them of and the reasons that were offered.

- **What he was trying to convince you to do or to believe was a *conclusion* that he arrived at based on the *reasons* he gave you. The reasons together with the conclusion was an *argument* he offered to convince you to accept his position. Use one of the situations you just wrote down; state the reasons and the conclusion and write them on the reasons and conclusions diagram.** The reasons and conclusions diagram is shown at the right.

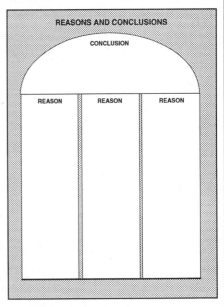

- **Sometimes people use signal words to tell us that they are stating reasons and conclusions. For example, when they state their reasons first, they may say "therefore" before stating the conclusions. Sometimes they use the word "so." What if the conclusion were stated first? Can you think of any signal words a person might use in this case? For example, if I'm trying to convince you to put on your warm coat before you go out, I might say "I think you should put on your warm coat before you go out today."** Then, to let you know I'm giving you reasons, I might say "because it's very cold out and your coat will keep you warm." What is the signal word for my reasons? *"Because."* Use the reasons and conclusion you wrote on your diagram.

Restate them to your partner using a signal word to show which is the conclusion and which are the reasons.

- Look at your diagram and think about the argument you see there. Discuss with your partner whether the reasons you have detected are good reasons for the conclusion. If so, why? If not, why not? Ask for two or three assessments of reconstructed arguments.

- In social studies, we've been studying the way people use natural resources to make things that serve our needs. We've also learned that as we use things in our society, we produce a lot of waste products. Think of our school. Work with your partner and list as many waste products as you can that are produced in the school. POSSIBLE ANSWERS: *Paper used to write on, plastic spoons and forks from the lunch room, plastic cups, paper cups, used napkins, unused food from students' plates, cans from soft drinks, bottles from soft drinks, cardboard cartons from school supplies, dirty water, juice cartons, dirt from the floor, pencil stumps, broken crayons, chalk dust, used magic markers, milk cartons, candy wrappers, plastic straws, smoke from the chimney when the heat is on, broken glass, and wood from broken furniture.*

- What do you think happens to this garbage and trash? *The janitor puts it in the dumpster and a truck comes and takes it away.*

- Usually, after the garbage is taken away, we don't think much about it. We're going to read part of a book about garbage and trash. It starts off by describing what happens to the trash when it leaves in a truck. The book is called *About Garbage and Stuff* by Ann Zane Shanks. As you listen, see if you can keep in mind the different things that might happen to the garbage after it is thrown away. We're going to chart what might happen to the garbage after it is picked up by the garbage truck. Read the first passage from *About Garbage and Stuff*. Then draw a three-branch diagram on the board. At the top, start with one box, in which you write, "The garbage truck picks it up" (see chart at right). Ask the students to describe the first place to which the garbage 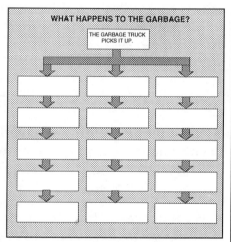 might be taken. POSSIBLE ANSWERS: *The garbage is taken to an incinerator. The garbage is burned. Black smoke comes out of the incinerator. Buildings turn black. It's hard to breathe.* Write these as a flow chart in boxes of the first branch of the diagram. If students have trouble, prompt them by asking things like, "What happens first?" "What happens right after it is burned?" Then ask them where else the garbage might be taken, and what happens when it is taken there. POSSIBLE ANSWERS FOR THE SECOND FLOW CHART: *The garbage is taken to an open dump. The garbage is dumped there. The garbage rots or is burned. There is a bad smell.* POSSIBLE ANSWERS FOR THE THIRD FLOW CHART: *The garbage is taken to a landfill. The garbage is dumped there. Tractors cover the garbage with dirt. People keep bugs or mice away. A school or park is built on top after the landfill is full.*

- What are some of the things you don't like that happen when garbage is disposed of in one of these ways? POSSIBLE ANSWERS: *A smell. Black smoke. It becomes hard to breathe.* What are some of the good things that might happen? POSSIBLE ANSWERS: *A school could be built on a landfill. A park could be built on a landfill.* Which of the three methods of getting rid of garbage seems the best? Discuss this with your partner and give two reasons why you think it is the best. After a few minutes, ask for responses. Students usually pick landfills because they don't smell as much, you can use the land to build on, and landfills don't make polluting smoke.

THINKING ACTIVELY

- **What you just stated were reasons for the conclusion that landfills are better than incinerators or open dumps. If someone wasn't sure which one was better, you would be offering that person reasons for accepting your idea that landfills are better. I'm going to write these ideas on a reasons and conclusions diagram.** On the chalkboard, on a transparency, or on a large poster, write the responses in the graphic organizer for reasons and conclusions.

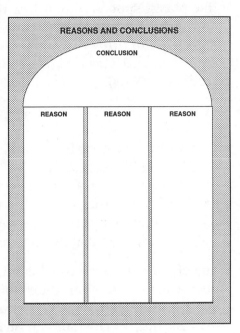

- **Even though landfills may be better than burning or open dumps, maybe landfills aren't the best way to dispose of garbage. Read the next passage in the book and discuss it with your partner. In this passage, see if there is an argument that gives you reasons to do something else with garbage. If so, use a blank graphic organizer for reasons and conclusions to pick out the conclusion of the argument and the reasons given. Remember to look for any signal words that indicate what the conclusion is and what the reasons are.** Have the students read the next two paragraphs. After a few minutes, ask them what the author is trying to convince us of that can be stated as her conclusion. Students answer that she is trying to convince us to reuse what we've already used, to recycle our garbage, or that recycling is a better than burying garbage in a landfill. Students know this because of the signal word "so" in the passage. Students may offer the following as reasons given. *There are more people and less land for landfills. If we keep using and burying cans, we'll use up all the metal, and then there will be no metal left. If we keep using and burying or burning paper, we'll use up all the trees and then there will be no trees left to make paper.* Write the conclusion and the reasons on a large reasons and conclusions diagram next to the one about landfills.

- **Now let's think about whether there are any other reasons for recycling. If so, we can add them to the reasons and conclusions diagram. Remember how you charted what happens when we burn garbage, leave it in an open dump, and bury it in a landfill? On the chart, circle some of the reasons for thinking that a landfill is better than the other two methods. As reasons against burning and open dumps, you mentioned the smell, etc., and you mentioned the fact that we could use the land. Now, I'm going to read the rest of the book, describing what happens when you recycle glass bottles, paper, and metal cans. As I read it, use a blank chart and write the reasons you hear in support of recycling. Then we'll see if there are any other reasons that can be added to the diagram.** Read the rest of the passage. After the students have finished flow charting what is described about glass, paper, and metal, ask for reports and complete a flow chart on the board. Ask the students what they see there that might be added to the argument. Students usually add that recycling produces bottles, cans, and paper that can be used again. Write these in the last column on the diagram.

- **Does this argument convince you that recycling is better than landfills? Discuss this with your partner.** After a few minutes, ask students to report. Most say they find it convincing; some say that they aren't sure because there seems to be a lot of extra land that can be used for landfills and because we can plant new trees for paper. Others say that there are lots of other things in garbage besides bottles, cans, and paper. They are not sure that these can be recycled and think that landfills may be needed for these. Have an open discussion of this question in class.

- Now let's think about our school. You listed a lot of things that are thrown away in the school, like plastic spoons and milk cartons. Each group should pick something that is thrown away and write an argument to convince the teachers and students that these items should be recycled, not thrown away. Use a blank reasons and conclusions diagram to write out your argument with reasons and a conclusion. Then put it in the form of a letter to the teachers and students. ANSWERS AND WRITING VARY.

THINKING ABOUT THINKING

- Let's think about the book and how we identified its reasons and conclusion. How did you decide what the conclusion was? POSSIBLE ANSWERS: *I thought about what the author was trying to convince us of, I looked for a signal word, found "so," and realized that what came after it was the conclusion.* How did you decide what the author's reasons were? POSSIBLE ANSWERS: I asked why she thought that recycling was a good idea. I looked at what she said before the signal word "so," and realized that these were her reasons.

- To help us determine conclusions and the reasons people offer to support their conclusions, we can use a thinking strategy. Our strategy for finding reasons and conclusions can include these steps. Read each step on the thinking map for reasons and conclusions to the students.

> **FINDING REASONS AND CONCLUSIONS**
>
> 1. What is the author trying to convince us to do?
> 2. What reasons does the author provide for doing this?
> a. Are there any signal words that indicate reasons and conclusions (e.g., "therefore," "so," "because")?
> b. Does the author tell us why he or she concludes what he or she does?

- When do you think it is a good idea to use this thinking strategy to find reasons and conclusions.? POSSIBLE ANSWERS: I can use it when someone tries to convince me to do something or when I am trying to convince someone else to do something. It helps me understand the reasons.

APPLYING THINKING

IMMEDIATE TRANSFER

- Here are some advertisements from magazines. What are the authors of the advertisements trying to convince us to do? What reasons do they offer? Fill in the diagram for reasons and conclusions and state their argument. Think about whether it is a good argument. From children's magazines, select advertisements that your students can read; provide these ads along with this activity.

- Here's a passage from a health textbook about popcorn.

   Do you like to eat popcorn? Many people like popcorn. They eat the popcorn for a snack. Popcorn can be made different ways. One way is to use oil. Popcorn kernels are put in a pan with hot oil. The hot oil makes the kernels pop. Another way is to use a hot air popcorn popper. Hot air makes the kernels pop. Many people use hot air popcorn poppers. There is a health reason why. When you eat foods fried in some oils, fats get into your blood. Too many fats are not healthful for your heart. Oil is not used in the hot air popcorn popper. There are no fats on the popcorn. This popcorn is more healthful for you.

- What conclusion are the authors trying to get you to accept? What are their reasons? Are their reasons good ones? Why or why not?

REINFORCEMENT LATER

- There are many rules for students to follow in the school. Ask a teacher to give the reasons for one of these rules. Write these on a reasons and conclusions diagram. Add any others reasons you think are important. Are these good reasons for having the rule?

- What reasons are given for checking mathematics computations? Are they good reasons? Why or why not?

ASSESSING STUDENTS' THINKING ABOUT REASONS AND CONCLUSIONS

Any of the transfer examples can be used as assessment tasks. Examples in which students analyze advertising are especially well suited, though you may wish to find others from student textbooks. Health textbooks are especially rich in arguments for what students should or shouldn't eat, etc. Ask the students to determine the author's conclusion and reasons. Have them explain why they think so. Use the strategy for finding reasons and conclusions to help you determine if your students are attending to relevant matters.

ABOUT GARBAGE AND STUFF

by Ann Zane Shanks

Dumping, Burning, and Burying Garbage

In the MacDonald house by the end of the day, there's a lot of garbage and stuff to toss out. Amy tosses out a bottle. Sam throws away a soda can. Mrs. MacDonald gets rid of the morning newspaper. Anything we are finished using is called garbage—food, clothing, rags, rugs, and toys.

Their bag of garbage and stuff is almost as big as Sam. It may even weigh more. Many families fill up a whole bag like this every day. That's a lot of garbage!

The MacDonalds leave their garbage on the sidewalk in front of their house in the city. The Sanitation Department is in charge of taking it away.

Most city garbage goes to gigantic incinerators where it is burned. But black smoke from incinerator chimneys causes pollution. Pollution means making everything dirty. Chimney pollution makes the air dirty and hard to breathe...

In many small towns garbage is brought to open dumps, where it is burned or left to rot. If the wind is blowing in your direction, you'll know how bad it smells.

Some garbage is taken to landfills. The MacDonald garbage bag may be on a truck arriving now. Men work at landfills making sure that no bugs or rats or mice move in. Landfills aren't as ugly or smelly as open dumps because men in tractors cover the garbage with layers of earth. When the fill is high enough and the earth has settled, a school might be built on this very spot. Or Sam MacDonald's box of cereal might disappear into the fill to become part of the park.

Can We Do Anything Else With Garbage?

But there are many more people than ever before. Soon there will be less space for landfills. And soon there'll be fewer places to dump garbage. Even now seagulls have to nest on garbage instead of in marshes. It's a problem for all of us.

We can't keep cutting down trees from which we make paper. Or mining metals from under the earth for tools or machines. Soon there'll be nothing left. No paper. No metal. Nothing. So we must try to use again what we've already used every day of our lives. That's called RECYCLING.

How Garbage is Recycled

What can people use over again? The MacDonalds are using some of their garbage when they remember to take their used glass bottles, metal cans and newspapers to a Recycling Center. The Center will sort and send these things back to factories for RECYCLING....

Remember when Andy tossed out a bottle? Not anymore. Now Andy's bottles go to the glass factory. Here used bottles are lifted into a grinder, where they will be ground up into tiny pieces of glass....

Machines then melt, mold, and shape the bottles from a hot liquid like the maple syrup you pour on pancakes. The sizzling bottles ride along a moving belt when they cool.

In only a few seconds, bottles—one old and used—are shaped into bottles brand new and clean. One of these bottles may really be the same one Sam brought to the Collection Center.

About Garbage and Stuff, by Ann Zane Shanks, The Viking Press, Inc., 1973. Reprinted by permission of author-photographer Ann Zane Shanks and Comco Productions, Inc., New York, and the Viking Press, New York.

Remember the morning newspaper that Mrs. MacDonald got rid of? Now it is in a factory waiting to be made into paper to be used again. Machines will beat the paper into mush called pulp.

After the pulp is washed, dried, and pressed, it comes out looking like clean bed sheets. These gigantic rolls of recycled paper can be used just like new paper....

Remember the can Sam threw away? Just like the paper and bottle, it will be used again.

Cans are mostly steel. The steel in each can is crushed into large square blocks that look like chunks of candy.

The blocks will be melted in a red-hot furnace, cooled and pressed into metal sheets. Before you know it, new cans—one way to use recycled metal. When you see an airplane, just think, part of it may be Sam's old can of soda, or Mrs. MacDonald's old can of soup, or your old can of spaghetti.

Now when the MacDonalds go to the market, they wish that all the new bottles and new cans and new paper bags they see are old bottles and cans and paper which have been recycled. And that some of them are the very ones they took to their Recycling Center.

Sample Student Responses • Flow Chart: What Happens to the Garbage?

WHAT HAPPENS TO THE GARBAGE?

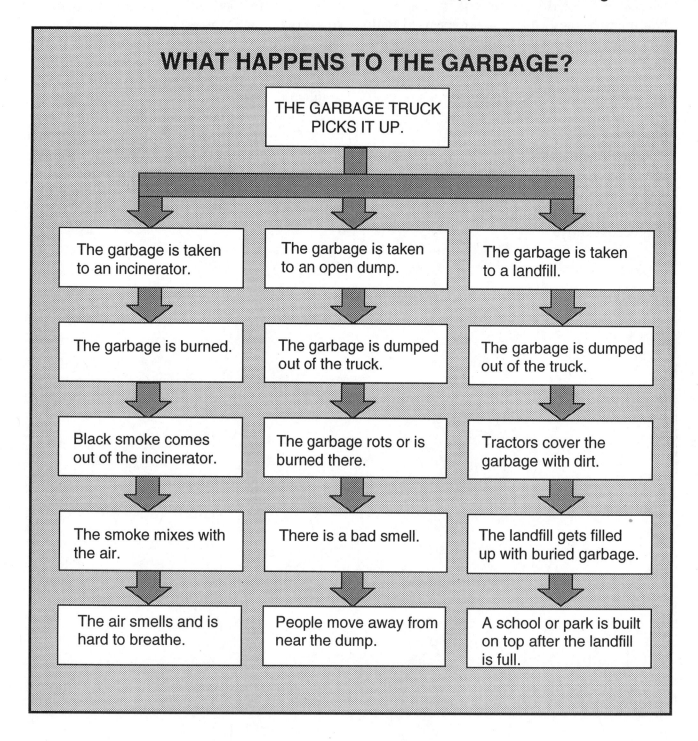

THE GARBAGE TRUCK
PICKS IT UP.

The garbage is taken to an incinerator.	The garbage is taken to an open dump.	The garbage is taken to a landfill.
The garbage is burned.	The garbage is dumped out of the truck.	The garbage is dumped out of the truck.
Black smoke comes out of the incinerator.	The garbage rots or is burned there.	Tractors cover the garbage with dirt.
The smoke mixes with the air.	There is a bad smell.	The landfill gets filled up with buried garbage.
The air smells and is hard to breathe.	People move away from near the dump.	A school or park is built on top after the landfill is full.

Sample Student Responses • Garbage and Trash

REASONS AND CONCLUSIONS

CONCLUSION

Using again what we've already used (recycling) is better than burying garbage in a landfill.

REASON	REASON	REASON
There are more and more people and less and less land for landfills.	If we keep using and burying cans, we'll use up all the metal, and then there will be none left.	If we keep using and burying or burning paper, we'll use up all the trees and there will be no trees left for making paper.

INDEPENDENCE OR LOYALTY?

American History   **Grades 5–8**

OBJECTIVES

CONTENT

Students will learn reasons that the colonists offered for declaring independence from Great Britain and reasons that loyalists gave for remaining a British colony during the period just prior to the Revolutionary War.

THINKING SKILL/PROCESS

Students will develop skill at detecting conclusions and the supporting reasons offered for these conclusions.

METHODS AND MATERIALS

CONTENT

Students will read passages from Thomas Paine's *Common Sense* and from the writings of Charles Inglis. They will work together to reconstruct the arguments offered for and against independence.

THINKING SKILL/PROCESS

Detecting reasons and conclusions is guided by structured questioning and by using a graphic organizer that highlights the conclusion and supporting reasons for an argument. (See pp. 231–34 for reproducible diagrams.)

LESSON

INTRODUCTION TO CONTENT AND THINKING SKILL/PROCESS

- Has anyone ever tried to convince you of something important by giving you reasons why you should accept what he was saying? **Write down two situations in which this has happened to you.** Ask students for a few examples. Ask them to state exactly what the other person tried to convince them of and what reasons were offered.

- **What the person was trying to convince you to believe or do was a *conclusion* he arrived at based on the *reasons* he gave you. The reasons together with the conclusion is an *argument* he offered to convince you to accept his position. Use one of the situations you just wrote down; state the reasons and the conclusion and write them on the reasons and conclusions diagram.** See the chart at the right.

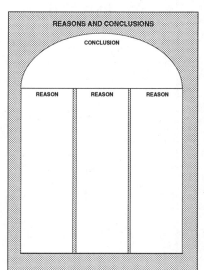

- **Sometimes people don't state some of their reasons because they think we already know them. For example, if someone says to you that you shouldn't eat a lot of sugar because it can make you gain weight, that person is presupposing that gaining weight isn't good for you. It is important to make these hidden reasons explicit and to write them on your diagram. Are there any hidden reasons in the situation you were working on?** Discuss this with your partner. If there are, please add them to your diagram.

- **Look at your diagram and think about the argument you see there. Discuss with your partner whether the reasons you have detected are good reasons for the conclusion. If so, why? If not, why not?** Ask for two or three assessments of the reconstructed arguments.

- We've been studying the period just before the Revolutionary War in what was then the thirteen colonies. People at that time thought they had good reasons for becoming independent from Great Britain. We usually take for granted that these reasons were good reasons. Did you know that there were a lot of people in the colonies who thought they had plenty of good reasons for remaining loyal to Great Britain? They are usually called "loyalists." To help us decide for ourselves which side had the best reasons, it will be important to determine the reasons some people gave for declaring independence, and the reasons others gave for remaining loyal to Britain. We're going to look at two pieces of writing that people produced to convince others to support independence, on the one hand, and loyalty, on the other. We'll extract the arguments from each by determining their conclusions and the reasons they offered in support of their conclusions.

THINKING ACTIVELY

- Imagine that you are a colonist and that you aren't sure whether independence from Great Britain is a good idea. Thomas Paine, a colonial leader, has just published his book *Common Sense* in January 1776. Already, 120,000 copies have sold. Lots of people are interested in what Thomas Paine has to say because, like you, they are not sure which position they should adopt. You've just purchased a copy of the book and are looking at the following passage. You want to see if Mr. Paine has good reasons for declaring independence from Great Britain.

    "I dare the strongest supporter of King George to show a single thing the colonies can gain by being connected with Great Britain. We do not need to trade with Great Britain alone. We can sell our corn in any Market in Europe.

    "The harm we suffer by our ties to Great Britain are without number. Thus, our duty to the world as well as to ourselves tells us to break this tie. Now our link with Great Britain draws us into European wars and quarrels. It makes enemies of countries who might otherwise seek our friendship. And whenever a war breaks out between Britain and another country, the trade of America will be ruined.

    "Everything that is right or natural begs for separation. The blood of the slain, the weeping voice of nature cries, 'Tis time to part.' Even the distance at which God has placed England and America is proof that the rule of one over the other was never the plan of heaven."

- What, overall, is the main idea of which Mr. Paine is trying to convince you? Work with your partner, formulate the conclusion he is trying to convince you to accept, and write it in the arch of a blank "Reasons and Conclusions" diagram. After students have had a few minutes to read and reflect on this passage, ask for some statements of the conclusion. POSSIBLE ANSWERS: *Mr. Paine is trying to convince his readers that we should separate from Great Britain. We should become independent of Great Britain. We should "break the tie" with Great Britain.* Write students' responses on the chalkboard. Then ask them whether any one of the ideas appears explicitly in each of the three paragraphs. The idea of separation does. Eliminate any suggestions that do not appear in each paragraph.

- Work with your partner once again, asking yourselves why Mr. Paine thinks his conclusion is a good one. Look for signal words like "therefore" that indicate reasons are being offered. Formulate the reasons he gives in your own words. Using one pillar for each paragraph, complete the diagram with Mr. Paine's reasons. Students offer three sets of reasons:

    Paragraph One: *The colonies don't gain anything by being connected with Britain. For example, we don't need to trade with Britain to sell our corn; we can sell it in any market in Europe.*

    Paragraph Two: *We suffer harm by being connected with Britain: we are drawn into European wars by allegiance with Britain, thereby making enemies of countries that would be our friends and ruining our trade.*

Paragraph Three: *Everything that is right or natural suggests separation. For example, England and America are far away from each other.*

As students suggest reasons contained in each paragraph, have the class try to reach consensus on how to state them.

- **What signal words did you find to indicate that a reason is being offered?** *"Thus" in paragraph two and "is proof that" in paragraph three.* **Can you think of other signal words that might indicate that a reason is being offered for a conclusion?** *"So," "therefore," "because."*

- **Before deciding that an argument is convincing, it is important to consider arguments for the opposite position. Here's a selection written by a minister who lived in Thomas Paine's time. As you read it, see if you can answer the question, "What is Charles Inglis trying to convince us to believe?"**

    "It is time to put aside those hatreds which have pushed Britons to shed the blood of Britons. Peace will be restored. Farming, trade, and industry will be strong again. Now they sicken while this fight goes unsettled. By our connection with Britain, our trade and our coast would again be protected by the greatest sea power in the world.

    "A few years of peace will restore everything to its former perfect state. People will come again from the different parts of Europe, filling the land and making it more valuable. By a declaration for independence, only the sword will be able to decide the quarrel. War will destroy our once happy land.

    "Americans have the manners, habits, and ideas of Britons. They are used to a similar form of government. Until very lately, America has been the happiest country in the world. Blessed with all that nature could give, she enjoyed more liberty than any other land. It is not too late to hope that matters may mend."

Ask students for their ideas about what Mr. Inglis is trying to convince us to do or to believe. Write each idea on the chalkboard. Clarify Charles Inglis's conclusion the same way that you clarified Thomas Paine's conclusion. POSSIBLE ANSWERS: *We should remain connected with Britain, we should remain loyal to Britain.*

- **Write Mr. Inglis' conclusion on a blank reasons and conclusions diagram. Think about the reasons he offers to convince us of his conclusion. Work with your partner and formulate the reasons in your own words. Ask what, in each paragraph, explains why he thinks we should be loyal. See if there are any signal words. Examine each paragraph.**

    Paragraph One: *If we reject independence and pledge loyalty to Britain, then peace will be restored and farming, trade, and industry will be strong again. The British navy (the strongest navy in the world) will protect our trade and coast.*

    Paragraph Two: *Declaring independence will lead to war and will destroy our once-happy land. Remaining loyal to Britain will bring more settlers to America and will make the land more valuable.*

    Paragraph Three: *Americans are similar to Britons in habits, manners, and customs and they are used to a similar form of government. Remaining loyal to Britain will restore happiness to this country.*

Discuss each paragraph with the class and try to reach consensus on how to state Mr. Inglis's reasons. Ask the students to write the reasons on their diagram.

- **You've now analyzed the passages and extracted the two arguments. They are each depicted on your two diagrams. Now let's decide whether either of these is a good argument. If an argument is a good one, the information in the reasons has to be accurate and adequate to** support the conclusion. To check for this, determine whether we have to find out any additional information in order to feel confident that the conclusion is acceptable. We're going to use an "Argument Evaluation Checklist" to write down our thoughts about whether each argument is a good argument. You are asked two types of questions on the checklist. First, are there any questions you need to have answered before you believe *the reasons are accurate*? Second, even if the reasons are accurate, is there anything else you would need to know before you can *accept the conclusion*? Half of the class will work on Thomas Paine's argument and half of the class on Charles Inglis' argument. Work in groups of four and try to come up with as many questions as you think are important to answer to decide about the argument. POSSIBLE ANSWERS:

> Thomas Paine's Argument: *Is it true that we can sell our corn in any market in Europe? Maybe he's just saying that to make it seem like there is no harm in being independent from Britain. Would we have to side with Britain if they fought a war with France, or could we be neutral? Even if all these things are true, could there be other more important benefits of remaining loyal to Britain?*

> Charles Inglis' Argument: *Is it true that farming, trade, and industry will be the same again if we declare loyalty to Britain? How does he know? Maybe he's just saying that to convince us. If we declare independence, is war the only way to settle our differences with Britain? Maybe there are ways to negotiate about these differences. Will we ever be happy again, once we've challenged Britain? Maybe we will, maybe we won't. Even if Mr. Inglis is right about all of these things, could there be something worth fighting for that we would lose if we remained connected with Britain? Mr. Inglis doesn't mention any negative effects of remaining loyal. Are there any?*

• For homework, try to answer these questions about the argument you worked on. Come in tomorrow with a decision about whether or not the argument is a good one and why. To defend your view, use your texts or any other source material about conditions in the colonies. Answers will vary.

THINKING ABOUT THINKING

• **What were some questions you asked that helped you figure out what the conclusions were in these arguments?** POSSIBLE ANSWERS: *What did the author want to convince me of? What was the point of what he was saying? What was his purpose in telling us all of these things?*

• **What were some of the questions you asked to help identify the author's reasons?** POSSIBLE ANSWERS: *What makes him believe that we should become independent? Why does he think his conclusion is right? What information is he giving us to try to convince us to be loyalists? Where would he put a "therefore" (whatever comes before it must be his reasons)? Are there signal words like "therefore" that show what his reasons are?*

• **To help you determine what conclusions and reasons people are offering, plan a strategy for thinking about things that people tell you.** Answers should resemble the steps on the thinking map for reasons and conclusions.

• **What do you call the result of this kind of thinking?** *An argument.*

• **Once you have extracted an author's argument from something he or she has said, what kinds of questions would you ask?** POSSIBLE ANSWERS: *Is this a good argument? Are the reasons correct? Is there anything else that I should know before I accept the conclusion?*

> **FINDING REASONS AND CONCLUSIONS**
>
> 1. What is the author trying to convince us to accept or do?
>
> 2. What reasons does the author provide to support accepting or doing that?
>
> a. Are there any words that indicate support (e.g., "therefore," "so," "because")?
>
> b. Does the author provide any other indication as to why he or she concludes what he or she does?
>
> 3. Is there anything that you think the author believes is common knowledge that he or she does not state but uses to support the conclusion?

APPLYING THINKING

IMMEDIATE TRANSFER

• You have read parts of the Declaration of Independence. Look for the reasons why the colonists who signed it supported independence. Use the same strategy for determining reasons and conclusions that you used with the passages from Thomas Paine and Charles Inglis.

• Locate an advertisement in a magazine. Determine what the authors of the advertisement are trying to convince us to do or to believe and what reasons they offer. Use the diagram for reasons and conclusions and state their argument. Think about whether it is a good argument.

REINFORCEMENT LATER

• We are studying how we elect presidents and members of congress. Find a political speech made by someone running for political office and extract any arguments you can find in it. Then think about whether or not these are good arguments.

• As we study the Civil War, consider arguments that people offered in favor of and against slavery. Extract their arguments and consider whether they are good ones.

WRITING EXTENSION

Many colonists had conflicting feelings about whether or not to support independence. What understanding of this conflict does your study of the arguments of Thomas Paine and Charles Inglis provide? After researching various other supporters of loyalty and independence, work with your partner to formulate the main pros and cons of both loyalty and independence. Then write an open letter to people in the colonies, using the best arguments you can develop, to persuade them that one of these positions is the better one and why.

READING EXTENSION

Select two novels about the colonial period, such as Johnny Tremain or My Brother Sam Is Dead, or diaries or letters of people on either side of the issue, like Abigail Adams's diaries. State the reasons and conclusions given by the characters. How are their arguments similar to or different from those given by Paine and Inglis?

ASSESSING STUDENTS' THINKING ABOUT REASONS AND CONCLUSIONS

Any of the transfer examples can be used for assessment tasks. The examples in which students analyze political speeches and advertising are especially suited as assessment examples. However, you may wish to select other controversial arguments about matters of historical significance, like the participation of the United States in the Spanish-American War or the Vietnam War, or establishing income taxes. Ask students to extract the reasons and conclusions to reconstruct the author's arguments. Ask the students to explain why they think that they have accurately stated the author's reasons and conclusions. Use the thinking map for finding reasons and conclusions to help you determine whether your students are attending to relevant matters in determining what these arguments are.

You may also want to ask your students to explore questions they would ask to decide whether or not this is a good argument. Use the lesson responses as examples by which to judge whether or not your students are asking relevant questions.

Sample Student Response • Independence or Loyalty

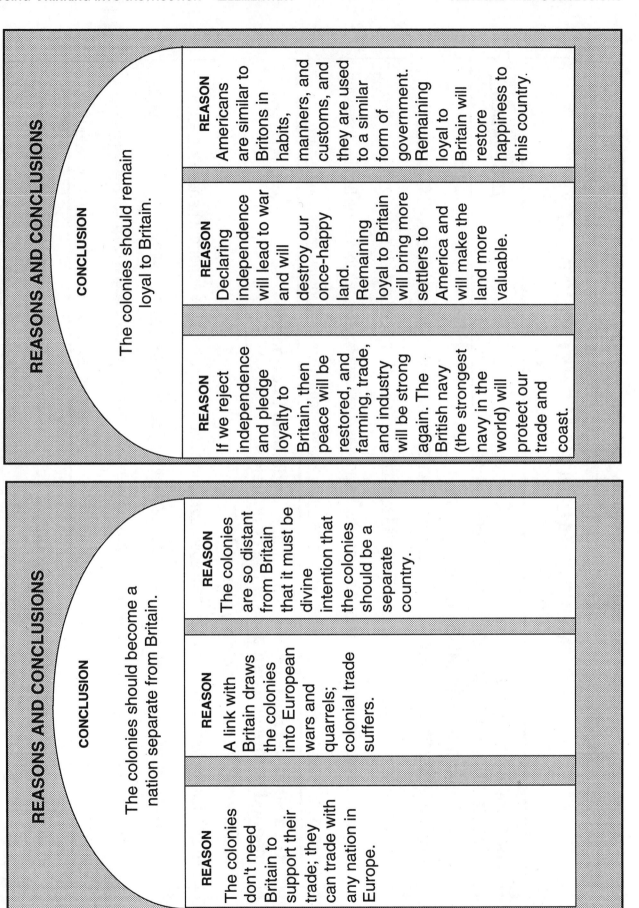

REASONS AND CONCLUSIONS

CONCLUSION

The colonies should remain loyal to Britain.

REASON

If we reject independence and pledge loyalty to Britain, then peace will be restored, and farming, trade, and industry will be strong again. The British navy (the strongest navy in the world) will protect our trade and coast.

REASON

Declaring independence will lead to war and will destroy our once-happy land. Remaining loyal to Britain will bring more settlers to America and will make the land more valuable.

REASON

Americans are similar to Britons in habits, manners, and customs, and they are used to a similar form of government. Remaining loyal to Britain will restore happiness to this country.

REASONS AND CONCLUSIONS

CONCLUSION

The colonies should become a nation separate from Britain.

REASON

The colonies don't need Britain to support their trade; they can trade with any nation in Europe.

REASON

A link with Britain draws the colonies into European wars and quarrels; colonial trade suffers.

REASON

The colonies are so distant from Britain that it must be divine intention that the colonies should be a separate country.

Sample Student Responses • Independence or Loyalty?

ARGUMENT EVALUATION CHECKLIST
THOMAS PAINE'S ARGUMENT

1. Is there anything you need to find out in order to determine whether the reasons are accurate?

YES ☑ NO ☐

2. If so, what information do you need to find out?

How do we know that we can sell our corn in any market in Europe if we gain independence? Could we be

neutral if Britain went to war with France and we were still a British Colony? If I couldn't answer the first two

questions, I would want to make sure that Thomas Paine was a reliable source of information before accepting

his reasons as accurate. For example, what is Thomas Paine's reputation in reporting facts accurately?

3. Given that the reasons are accurate, is additional information needed before you can accept the conclusion?

YES ☑ NO ☐

4. If so, what information do you need?

Even if all of the information Thomas Paine gives us is true, could there be more important benefits of remain-

ing loyal to Britain? For example, maybe British goods are inexpensive for colonists compared to their price in

independent countries. Maybe, as Charles Inglis says, the British navy will protect us if we are attacked. I would

want to know that there are not any additional benefits like these before I found the argument convincing.

An argument should be convincing only if you answer "NO" to questions 1 and 3 above.

Sample Student Responses • Independence or Loyalty?

ARGUMENT EVALUATION CHECKLIST
CHARLES INGLIS' ARGUMENT

YES ☑ NO ☐

1. Is there anything you need to find out in order to determine whether the reasons are accurate?

2. If so, what information do you need to find out?

How do we know that farming and trade will be the same if we are loyal to Britain? If we declare independence,

is war the only alternative? Could we negotiate? If I can't answer these questions, I would want to make sure

that Charles Inglis was a reliable source of information before I believed his reasons. Maybe he makes things

seem nicer than they are in order to convince us. How do we know he doesn't? What is his reputation?

YES ☑ NO ☐

3. Given that the reasons are accurate, is additional information needed before you can accept the conclusion?

4. If so, what information do you need?

Even if what Mr. Inglis says is true, could there be something worth fighting for that we would lose if we

remained connected with Britain? I read about taxation, for example. How much of a burden was that?

Would there be other burdens that Mr. Inglis doesn't tell us about? I would want to make sure there weren't

before I felt that his reasons were good reasons to accept his conclusion.

An argument should be convincing only if you answer "NO" to questions 1 and 3 above.

LESSON CONTEXTS FOR FINDING REASONS AND CONCLUSIONS

The following examples have been suggested by classroom teachers as contexts to develop infusion lessons. If a skill or process has been introduced in a previous lesson, transfer activities can be designed in these contexts to reinforce it.

GRADE	SUBJECT	TOPIC	THINKING ISSUE
K–3	Literature	*Jack and the Beanstalk*	Remember the man who traded the beans for Jack's cow. What reasons did he offer to convince Jack that the trade was a good idea? Were these reasons good reasons?
K–3	Literature	*Amazing Grace*	The children in Grace's class gave reasons why she should not try out for the part of Peter in the school play "Peter Pan." What were their reasons? Were their reasons good ones?
K–3	Literature	*Charlotte's Web*	Mr. Arable and Fern disagree about what should be done with the runt pig. What is Mr. Arable's conclusion and the reasons he offers to support it? What is Fern's conclusion and the reasons she offers to support it?
K–3	Literature	*The War with Grandpa*	What reasons did the grandson give for wanting his room badly enough to declare war on Grandpa?
K-3	Literature	*The Zax (The Sneetches and Other Stories)*	What reasons do each of the Zax give for their conclusions? Are their reasons good ones?
K-3	Literature	*The Butter Battle Book*	What reasons do the Yooks give for building a wall and arming themselves against the Zooks? Are their reasons good ones?
K–3	Social studies	The pilgrims	What reasons did the Pilgrims have for leaving England? Were their reasons good ones? What reasons did they have for coming to America? Were these good reasons?
K-3	Social studies	Money	People used to barter for things before they used money. Is it better to use money or to barter? Why? Give reasons that you think best support your conclusion.
K–3	Science	Endangered species	What reasons are given for protecting an endangered species? Are there any reasons against protecting a species? Which conclusion is supported by better reasons?
K–3	Science	Food chains	When fishermen have caught most of the herring in the ocean, what do you think will happen to birds that depend on herring for food? What reasons do you have for drawing this conclusion?
K–3	Mathematics	Arithmetic	Plan how you would set up a store to sell things that students need in the classroom, such as pencils, paper, crayons, etc. After you find out how much these items will cost you, add your expenses and draw a conclusion about how much you should sell the items for. Explain your reasons for this conclusion.
K–3	Mathematics	Plane figures	Imagine that you are going to cover the top of your desk with square tiles that have three-inch sides. Based on your calculations, what conclusion can you draw about how many tiles you will need? Explain the reasons for your conclusion.
K–3	Health	Teeth	Dentists give you lots of reasons for brushing your teeth. Discuss at least two reasons that they offer. Are these good reasons? Dentists also tell you to clean your teeth with dental floss. What reasons do they offer for doing this? Are these good reasons?

LESSON CONTEXTS FOR FINDING REASONS AND CONCLUSIONS

GRADE	SUBJECT	TOPIC	THINKING ISSUE
K–3	Health	Nutrition	What reasons are given for eating a balanced diet? Offer an argument, explaining why a person should include vegetables and fruit in his or her diet.
K–3	Health	Exercise	Describe different types of exercise. What reasons are there for engaging in each? Develop an argument to convince someone who does not want to exercise that it is a good thing to do.
4–6	Literature	*Song of the Trees*	What reasons did Mr. Andersen give the grandmother, Caroline Logan, for why she should sell him her trees? What were the threatened reasons? Were they well-founded ones?
4–6	Literature	*The Lion, the Witch, and the Wardrobe*	What reasons did the children give to justify Edmund's betrayal? What reasons would Edmund give for believing the White Witch? What reasons would the children give for not believing the White Witch?
4–6	Literature	*Sarah, Plain and Tall*	Develop an argument that you think would convince Sarah either to stay or not to stay with her new family. What are your reasons and what is your conclusion?
4–6	Literature	*Why Don't You Get a Horse, Sam Adams?*	What was John Adams trying to convince Sam Adams to do? What reasons did he give Sam for doing it? Which reason was the best reason? What was the result?
4–6	U.S. history	Colonial period	In the 1600s, what reasons were offered to people in England to convince them that they should come to America? Were these reasons accurate?
4–6	U.S. history	*Behind Rebel Lines*	According to Seymour Reit's book, what were Emma Edmond's reasons for joining the Union Army as a man, Pvt. Franklin Thompson? Were the reasons good enough to take the risks that she did? Considering that she would be considered a deserter, did she have good reasons for leaving her unit after the Battle of Vicksburg?
4–6	U.S. history	Native Americans	Some Native Americans have claimed that they should be given back the land that was taken from their ancestors in the 19th Century. Imagine that you are a lawyer for these Indians. What reasons would you use to convince a judge to give them their ancestors' land? Now imagine that you are a lawyer for the U.S. government. What reasons would you offer for not giving the land back? If you were the judge, which of these arguments would you find the most convincing? Why?
4–6	U.S. history	Women's Suffrage	Until the 19th Amendment was passed, women in this country couldn't vote. Imagine that you were in favor of allowing women to vote. What are the strongest reasons you could have offered? What reasons do you think were offered to oppose women voting? Now find out what people really said about women voting. How do your reasons compare with theirs? Which conclusion do you think is supported by the best reasons?
4–6	Science	Pollution	What are some of the reasons for and against building a landfill near homes?

LESSON CONTEXTS FOR FINDING REASONS AND CONCLUSIONS

GRADE	SUBJECT	TOPIC	THINKING ISSUE
4–6	Science	Heredity	After Mendel had sprinkled pollen on the pistil of a pea plant, he covered it so that no other pollen could reach it by insects or by wind. If you had asked him why he thought this was necessary, what reasons would he have given? Would he have been right? Why or why not?
4–6	Science	Heredity	Scientists studying genetics use fruit flies as subjects of their experiments. What reasons do they have for using flies instead of dogs, cats, or horses?
4–6	Science	Digestion	During digestion, starch is broken down into sugars. People who have diabetes suffer from too much sugar in their blood and must restrict the sugar they consume. Give an argument to support the conclusion that they must also restrict their intake of starches.
4–6	Science	Weather	When a tornado approaches houses, weather forecasters usually tell people to open their windows. What reasons do they give for doing this? Are these good reasons?
4–6	Mathematics	Arithmetic	Your friend wants an after-school job to make some spending money. He can deliver newspapers for $2.75 per hour or help unpack boxes at the supermarket for $2.25 per hour. His hours at the supermarket will be 3 hours a day after school, five days a week. Delivering newspapers, he will work only two hours a day, but he must work seven days a week. He wants your advice about which job to take. What would you advise him? What reasons would you give him to support your conclusion?
4–6	Mathematics	Measurement	What reasons are given for using the metric system when measuring distances and quantities? Are these good reasons?
4–6	Health	Food advertising	Look at two ads for breakfast cereals. What conclusion does each try to convince you to believe? What reasons are given in each to support its conclusion? Are these good reasons?
4–6	Health	Smoking	What reasons do people give for smoking? What reasons do other people give for not smoking? Which are better reasons, and why?
4–6	Art	Realism	Some people have said that, when you paint a picture, it should look exactly like the subject– like a photograph. Otherwise, they say, it isn't really art. Many artists have painted pictures that are not like photographs at all, and they think that their pictures are as much art as realistic pictures. Which of these two views about art do you agree with? Develop an argument for your view. Make sure you include what you believe are the best reasons to support your conclusion.
4–6	Music	Selecting a music class	In music class, students often must choose whether to learn to play a musical instrument or to join the chorus. What reasons are given for either choice? Are these good reasons?
4–6	Physical education / social studies	Physical exercise	The ancient Athenians thought that building strong bodies was very important for young people. What arguments would they offer for this view? What would be their reasons and their conclusion? Would this be a good argument?

CHAPTER 9
UNCOVERING ASSUMPTIONS

Why is it Necessary to Attend to Assumptions Skillfully?

When we make choices, accept information from others, or draw conclusions, we often take certain ideas for granted. When I get in my car to drive to work, I assume that the road hasn't developed huge cracks that would make it impassible. We can't think of every possible contingency and check it out.

Fortunately, most of the time we don't have to check out our assumptions. Many of the assumptions we make are perfectly reasonable. Before taking a certain route to work, I have good reason for thinking that the road hasn't developed huge cracks. It was in good condition last night, and there have been no unusual occurrences since then, like an earthquake. Our ability to assume things and act on these assumptions without bringing them to mind can make our thinking and acting very efficient.

Problems in Not Attending to Or Questioning Our Assumptions

While relying on assumptions has advantages, there are disadvantages as well. We sometimes make assumptions that we either don't have reason to believe, we have reason to believe are false, or we can check out easily and discover to be false. Because we are often unaware of our assumptions, acting on them can sometimes lead to irreparable mistakes. If I decide to make a lengthy trip to a department store to buy a television set that they have advertised, I may be assuming that they haven't sold out of them. I may not be aware of what I am assuming until I get there and find, to my dismay, that they don't have any left. If I had been aware of this assumption beforehand, that may have prompted me to call the store to determine whether it was reasonable to assume that the sets would be available when I got there.

We may, of course, be aware of what we are assuming but not consider whether our assumptions are justified. I may think that a friend whom I have lost touch with still lives in the same location. I may not think to question this. When I go to visit him, however, I find that he has moved. Then I realize that I had made an assumption. The fact that he lived there five years ago was not a good reason for thinking that he would be there now. If I had been aware that the support for this assumption was outdated, I might have checked it out.

The two main problems about assumptions that sometimes lead us to do things that are in error are recorded in figure 9.1.

COMMON DEFAULTS ABOUT ASSUMPTIONS

1. We often don't ask, Am I taking anything for granted?

2. Sometimes we are aware of assumptions that we make but don't try to find out whether they are reasonable.

Figure 9.1

A skillful approach to examining assumptions involves asking and attending carefully to both of these questions. We will never become aware of unwarranted assumptions if we don't first ask if we are making any assumptions and whether they are warranted.

Attending to Assumptions

Strategies for uncovering and testing assumptions. A simple way to uncover our assumptions is to ask, "What am I taking for granted in thinking this?" Sometimes, though, it is hard to focus on specific assumptions by asking this direct question. Another way to clarify assumptions is to ask, "If what I think is correct, what must I also believe?" If I think that I can buy a television set on sale by going to the store, asking these questions should prompt me to list assumptions like "the sale is not yet over" and "there are still TV's like the kind in the advertisement available at this price." The skill of *uncovering assumptions* helps us to become aware of assumptions that we or others make in order to decide whether these assumptions are acceptable or not.

Once we uncover these assumptions, we can try to determine which are reasonable. To do this, we should first ask, "Do I have any reasons for thinking that this assumption is correct?" Additionally we should ask whether there are any reasons for thinking the assumption is false. We may remember, for example, that this department store has a history of "bait and switch" advertising. There may be only one of the advertised television sets available, and it is likely to be sold quickly. When we find that an assumption is questionable, like in these circumstances, we should then check it out.

When we have succeeded in checking out an assumption and find that there are reasons for or against it, it ceases to be an assumption. When I call the store to inquire whether there are plenty of TV sets still available at the sale price and am told by a clerk that there are, I no longer assume that the sets are available. I know it.

When we try to uncover the assumptions of others, it may be necessary to first list possible assumptions that lie behind the person's behavior and then determine which are best supported by the circumstances. Suppose you invited a friend for dinner on Saturday evening, and he arrived on Friday evening. He might have assumed that you had invited him for Friday, not Saturday, or he might have assumed that the day he arrived was Saturday, not Friday. Both would be mistaken assumptions that explained his actions. But which did he assume? If you find that he wrote in his appointment book that the dinner date was Friday, you've got reason for thinking that he assumed that Friday was the date for your dinner.

A Thinking Map and Graphic Organizer for Uncovering Assumptions

The thinking map in figure 9.2 can guide us in detecting assumptions and in determining whether or not those assumptions are justified.

The graphic organizer in figure 9.3 can be used to record the answers to questions which help us understand whether it is reasonable to believe that assumptions are being made.

UNCOVERING ASSUMPTIONS

1. What action, belief, or conclusion of a specific person might be based on assumptions?

2. What might that person be taking for granted in performing the action, accepting the belief, or drawing the conclusion?

3. Are there any reasons for thinking that any of these possible assumptions are being taken for granted? If so, what are these reasons?

4. Are these assumptions well-founded? Explain.

Figure 9.2

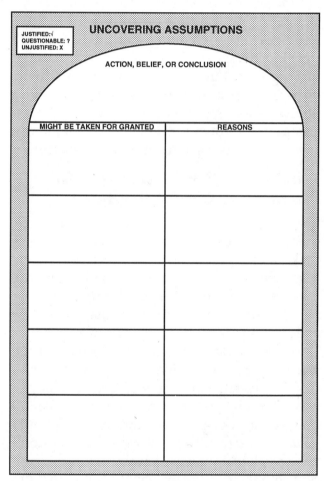

Figure 9.3

Assumptions in Arguments and Controversies

The second type of situation in which we must try to understand assumptions involves examining the reasons people give for a conclusion that they try to convince us to accept. Clarifying assumptions is especially important when people hold opposing viewpoints on an issue. When there are conflicting points of view, this disagreement is often because each side's opinion is based on different assumptions. Examining the assumptions behind each side's arguments may help us to understand clearly why they are taking opposite positions.

Uncovering assumptions can also help with conflict resolution. Once differing assumptions have been stated, the parties in a dispute can consider whether these assumptions are reasonable. This may not be so easy, especially in cases in which the assumptions are deeply held beliefs. Then the parties may at least "agree to disagree," respecting that their difference is based on differing assumptions.

Continued dialogue, even about the reasonableness of our most deep-seated beliefs, is a characteristic of good thinkers. While two parties in a dispute may agree to disagree, this should not mean that they stop inquiring about how well-founded their own assumptions are. The ideal of true Socratic questioning is especially applicable in these situations. The Socratic questioner uses probing questions to prompt others to examine the bases of their beliefs and to accept only those that are well-founded. Of course it may be that once the differing assumptions are revealed, one of the parties realizes that his or her assumptions are unwarranted, thereby resolving the dispute.

The thinking map in figure 9.4 guides uncovering assumptions in arguments.

The graphic organizer in figure 9.5 includes a "foundation" on which the speaker's reasons for the belief are based.

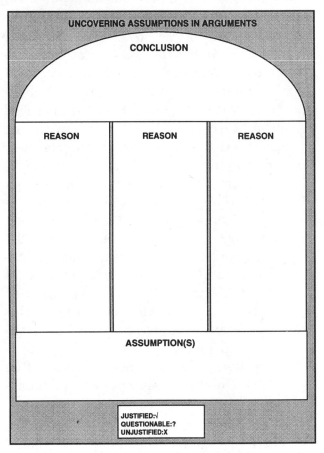

Figure 9.5

How Can We Teach Students to Attend to Assumptions Skillfully?

Tips about teaching students to attend to assumptions. In teaching students to examine assumptions, it may be easier for them to focus on the assumptions that others make before thinking about their own. When you introduce the skill, for example, you can describe situations, like the one about the sale on television sets, and ask the questions on the thinking map (figure 9.2) to guide students in uncovering and reflecting about assumptions that are made. Then, you may wish to ask students to describe some assumptions that they have made and to assess them.

**UNCOVERING ASSUMPTIONS
IN ARGUMENTS**

1. What action, belief, or conclusion is being recommended in this argument?

2. What reasons are being given for the action, belief, or conclusion?

3. Do the reasons suggest that the speaker has taken anything for granted? If so, what?

4. Are there good reasons for accepting what is taken for granted? Why?

Figure 9.4

Contexts in the Curriculum for Infusion Lessons on Uncovering Assumptions

The curriculum is ripe with opportunities for infusion lessons on assumptions. In general, there are four contexts in the curriculum for infusion lessons on uncovering assumptions:

- *Real or fictional characters that students study make assumptions in what they say or do.* Columbus' assumptions about the location of India and the Pilgrims' assumptions about life in the New World both led to crucial historical events. These assumptions can be uncovered, and students can consider whether they were reasonable assumptions at the time. Peter Rabbit's assumptions about Mr. McGregor's perceptiveness, Amelia Bedelia's assumptions that her employers language is to be taken literally, and the disagreement between Fern and Mr. Arable about the value of the life of the runt pig in *Charlotte's Web* are, likewise, rich contexts for uncovering assumptions. Humorous stories, tales of fear and superstition, and juvenile mysteries are particularly good examples because they often turn on mistaken assumptions that characters make.

- *Theories that students study rest on assumptions.* For example, the theory of spontaneous generation, long since discredited, rested on assumptions about the nature of organic matter. The Ptolemaic theory about the structure of the universe assumed the Earth as the center. Not all assumptions that lie behind theories are unreasonable, however. Democratic theory assumes that humans are educable to make rational decisions, while other theories about the best forms of social organization presuppose different conceptions of human nature.

- *Principles or practices that students learn rest on assumptions.* Generalization in science rests on the assumption of the regularity of nature, while the practice of staining and fixing specimens for observation under a microscope assumes that you can't observe specimens unless light can shine through

them. The practice of revising writing is based on the assumption that our first written expression is probably not our best one.

- *Students often base misconceptions of natural phenomena on assumptions.* Science instruction, in particular, has focused on misconceptions that students have about nature. For example, people often assume that weight determines speed, believing that heavier things fall faster than light things.

The thinking map for uncovering assumptions in figure 9.2 contains prompting questions that can be adapted for activities in each of these contexts. Once these question are raised, students should be encouraged to list as many assumptions as possible in the examples they are analyzing. Columbus assumed that India could be reached by sailing west, that the world was round, that there was no land between Europe and India, etc. Each of these assumptions gives us insight into Columbus's beliefs and behavior.

When students have mastered this skill, they will ask the questions on the thinking map themselves in appropriate circumstances without your guidance. As in other infusion lessons, transfer is enhanced by helping students to think about and plan an effective strategy for attending to assumptions and then providing opportunities for them to carry out this thinking plan.

A menu of suggested contexts for infusion lessons on uncovering assumptions is provided on pp. 283–85.

Helping Students to Uncover Assumptions in the Primary Grades

Students in grades K-3 sometimes have difficulty simply responding to questions like "What is being assumed?" or "What is taken for granted?" With these students, you may introduce this skill by posing a situation in which a person does something and is surprised because he or she makes a number of assumptions that are incorrect. Then ask the students what idea they would want to check out before they did the same thing. For example, you might pose a situation in which a student came to school on Saturday only to find no one there. If they were in that situation, what idea would they want to check out before doing the same thing? For each of the ideas they suggest, ask how they could find out whether it was true. Modelling how to respond to this question will help your students carry out this strategy.

Humorous stories that children read in the primary grades are often good vehicles for lessons on uncovering assumptions. Characters frequently make incorrect assumptions which lead to an awkward situation that often is very funny. The Curious George stories provide good material for such lessons, as do the Amelia Bedelia series.

Stories that deal with superstition or fear often provide good contexts for lessons on uncovering assumptions for primary grade students.

Figure 9.6 contains a thinking map for uncovering assumptions in the primary grades.

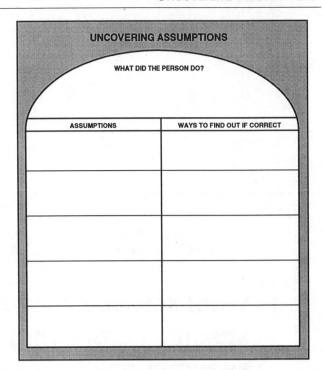

Figure 9.7

FINDING YOUR ASSUMPTIONS

1. What are you thinking about doing that might be based on an assumption?

2. What would you be assuming if you did that?

3. How can you find out whether the assumption is correct or incorrect?

Figure 9.6

The simplified graphic organizer in figure 9.7 should also be used in the primary grades.

Model Lessons on Uncovering Assumptions

Two lessons are included on uncovering assumptions. One is a primary grade lesson utilizing a humorous poem by Shel Silverstein called "Smart" in which the main character makes a number of assumptions. The second is an upper elementary grade lesson on Moctezuma's assumptions about Cortes that led to Cortes's ability to subdue and conquer the Aztecs in the sixteenth century.

As you read these lessons, consider the following questions:

- What prompting questions guide students to uncover assumptions in these lessons?

- How does uncovering assumptions build on skillfully finding reasons and conclusions?

- What other contexts can be used to reinforce this skill during the rest of the school year?

Tools for Designing Lessons on Uncovering Assumptions

The thinking maps contain guiding questions for thinking about assumptions that are made in a wide range of contexts and for assumptions upon which arguments rest. Please note that one set of thinking maps and graphic organizers is for uncovering assumptions in general, while the other is used only in contexts in which the assumptions behind an argument are being considered. The thinking map on page 262 and the graphic organizer on page 263 are designed especially for use in the primary grades.

The thinking maps and graphic organizers can guide you in designing the critical thinking activity in the lesson and can also serve as photocopy masters, transparency masters, or as models that can be enlarged and used as posters in the classroom. Reproduction rights are granted for single classroom use only.

UNCOVERING ASSUMPTIONS

1. What action, belief, or conclusion of a specific person might be based on assumptions?

2. What might that person be taking for granted in performing the action, accepting the belief, or drawing the conclusion?

3. Are there any reasons for thinking that any of these possible assumptions are being taken for granted? If so, what are these reasons?

4. Are these assumptions well-founded? Explain.

JUSTIFIED: √
QUESTIONABLE: ?
UNJUSTIFIED: X

UNCOVERING ASSUMPTIONS

ACTION, BELIEF, OR CONCLUSION

MIGHT BE TAKEN FOR GRANTED	REASONS

FINDING YOUR ASSUMPTIONS

1. What are you thinking about doing that might be based on an assumption?

2. What would you be assuming if you did that?

3. How can you find out whether the assumption is correct or incorrect?

UNCOVERING ASSUMPTIONS

WHAT DID THE PERSON DO?

ASSUMPTIONS	WAYS TO FIND OUT IF CORRECT

UNCOVERING ASSUMPTIONS IN ARGUMENTS

1. What action, belief, or conclusion is being recommended in this argument?

2. What reasons are being given for the action, belief, or conclusion?

3. Do the reasons suggest that the speaker has taken anything for granted? If so, what?

4. Are there good reasons for accepting what is taken for granted? Why?

UNCOVERING ASSUMPTIONS IN ARGUMENTS

CONCLUSION

REASON	REASON	REASON

ASSUMPTION(S)

JUSTIFIED:√
QUESTIONABLE:?
UNJUSTIFIED:X

GETTING SMART ABOUT MONEY

Language Arts/Mathematics   **Grades K–2**

OBJECTIVES

CONTENT

Students will develop listening skills, learn some of the main features of poems, and learn equivalencies between pennies, nickels, dimes, quarters, and dollars.

THINKING SKILL/PROCESS

Students will learn to uncover assumptions by considering actions that are based on those assumptions and by determining what those actions take for granted.

METHODS AND MATERIALS

CONTENT

The teacher will read aloud the poem *Smart*, by Shel Silverstein, and direct the class to listen for certain things. The class will also discuss the poem in collaborative learning groups.

THINKING SKILL/PROCESS

A thinking map, a graphic organizer, and structured questioning are used to uncover the assumptions behind a person's actions. Collaborative learning enhances the thinking. (See pp. 260–65 for reproducible diagrams.)

LESSON

INTRODUCTION TO CONTENT AND THINKING SKILL/PROCESS

- Once I read in the newspaper that a store was having a sale on television sets. I needed one, so I went to the store to buy it. When I got there, I found that the store had no more of the television sets I wanted. It had sold them out the day before and wasn't going to get new ones for another month. I was very disappointed. When I thought about it, I realized that there was something that I had believed that made me think I would find the television sets there when I arrived. What do you think it was? POSSIBLE ANSWERS: *They still had the television sets. They had not sold all the television sets. They had a lot of television sets. I would find a television set that I liked when I got there.*

- When I believe something that I haven't checked out, I am assuming something. When I assume something, I am making an *assumption.* Write the word "assumption" on the board. That's a long word, but I want you to learn it and use it. Let's try it out with another example. When you want crayons to draw with, you go to the crayon box to get them. Suppose when you got to the crayon box and opened, it you found no crayons. What assumptions would you have made? POSSIBLE ANSWERS: *There were crayons in the box. No one had taken all of the crayons out. The crayons weren't lost.* **How would you feel when you found no crayons in the box?** POSSIBLE ANSWERS: *I would feel unhappy. I would be mad. I would be surprised.* **That's how I felt when I didn't find the television sets at the store.**

- When I thought more about this, I realized that if I had known that I was assuming they still had television sets, I could have checked out this assumption by calling the store. Then I never would have gone to the store. Often we don't think about what we are assuming. If I had asked myself, "Am I making any assump-

---

FINDING YOUR ASSUMPTIONS

1. What are you thinking about doing that might be based on an assumption?

2. What would you be assuming if you did that?

3. How can you find out whether the assumption is correct or incorrect?

---

tions here?" I might have become aware of what I was assuming before I went to the store. Suppose you asked yourselves what you were assuming about the crayons before you went all the way to the cabinet. Then you would realize that you were making an assumption, and you could check out the assumption before you acted on it. Here are some questions (see thinking map previous page) **to ask that will help you whenever you think you might be making assumptions.**

THINKING ACTIVELY

- Sometimes people do things that are funny or silly because of their assumptions. **I'm going to read you a poem called** *Smart.* **It's about a little boy whose father gives him a dollar because he's so smart. As I read the poem think about what the boy does. Is he being smart?** Read the whole poem. Most students find this poem funny. If your students do, ask them why they found it funny. Accept any answer. Students usually say that he started out with a dollar and ended up with five pennies.

- **I wonder if the boy was making any assumptions that make this poem funny. I'm going to read you the first four lines of the poem again. Let's listen to see if we can tell whether or not the boy is making any assumptions. Follow the list of questions for finding your assumptions. First ask what the boy did.** Read the first stanza aloud. Ask the class what the boy did. Many will say, He traded a dollar for two quarters. Write this on the board. **Why is that funny?** Because there are four quarters in a dollar. Put a dollar bill and four quarters out on the desk, or project an image of four quarters and a dollar with an overhead projector. Write on the board, 1 dollar = four quarters. **What did the boy think when he traded the dollar for two quarters?** He thought that since he started with one piece of money and now had two pieces, he had more money. **Do you think the boy thought he had more money because he was assuming something? What might he have been assuming?** POSSIBLE ANSWERS: *That the more pieces of money he has, the greater the value. That one quarter and a dollar have the same value.* Write on the board one dollar = one quarter. **Why do you think the boy was assuming that?** *Because he thought two quarters were more than a dollar.* **Are they? Is this assumption correct or incorrect? Why?** *It is incorrect because you need four quarters to make a dollar.*

- **Here is a diagram to use when someone is assuming something.** Create a copy of the uncovering assumptions graphic organizer on the board, project a transparency of it, or use a large poster of it. **Let's fill in what the boy did that was mistaken, and what he was assuming.** Write "The boy traded a dollar for two quarters" under the dome, and "One quarter equals a dollar" in the assumptions column.

UNCOVERING ASSUMPTIONS	
WHAT DID THE PERSON DO?	
ASSUMPTIONS	**WAYS TO FIND OUT IF CORRECT**

- **There is a third question that we should ask when someone makes an assumption. Do you remember what it is?** *How can he find out if his assumption is correct or incorrect?* **Do you know if this is an incorrect assumption? Did the boy know this?** No. **How could the boy have found out?** POSSIBLE ANSWERS: *He could have asked his father, his mother, his brother, or his teacher.*

- **I'm going to read you the next three stanzas of the poem. After each one, we will ask the same questions. Let's see if the boy makes any other assumptions.** Read each of the next three stanzas. After each stanza, use the graphic organizer to record what the boy does and what the students think his assumptions were. For each exchange the boy makes, write on the board the equivalencies between the two types of money, e.g., 4 quarters = 10 dimes. Also show students these pieces of money and stack them up according to their equivalencies, so at the end of this process, you should have a stack of a hundred pennies next to the dollar. **How much money did the boy have to start with? How much did he have at the end of all of his trading?** *He started with a dollar and ended with five pennies.* **How many pennies are in a dollar?** *There are one hundred pennies in a dollar.* **That wasn't such a good trade, was it? Does the boy know this?** *No. He thinks he has more than he started with.* **That's because he doesn't know he's making an incorrect assumption. That shows how important it is to be aware of your assumptions!**

- Now I'm going to read you the last stanza of the poem again. After I finish, discuss quietly with a partner whether the boy is making any other assumptions in this stanza. Let's try to answer the first question on the thinking map: What is the boy thinking that may be based on an assumption? What does he think his father feels about him?** *He thinks his father is proud of how smart he is.* **And what do you think his father really thinks?** *The boy isn't too smart.* **At the top of the diagram, I'll write "the boy thought his father was proud of him." With your partner, try to figure out what assumption the boy makes that leads him to think this.** After a few minutes, ask two or three student groups to respond. Write their responses on the graphic organizer. POSSIBLE ANSWERS: *He was smart. His father thought he was smart. His father thought he had more money.*

- Now let's think about how the boy could have found out what his father really feels. With your partner, discuss what he could have done to find out.** After a few minutes, ask two or three student groups to respond. POSSIBLE ANSWERS: *He could have asked his father what he was thinking. He could have asked his father whether he thought it was smart to trade his dollar for five pennies.* **Just as it's important not to make assumptions about money, it's important not to make assumptions about what other people think. If you know you are making an assumption, you can check it out by asking.**

THINKING ABOUT THINKING

- **What do we call the kind of thinking we just did?** *Uncovering assumptions. Finding your assumptions.*

- **What questions did we ask as we did this kind of thinking?** POSSIBLE ANSWERS: *What did he do? Did he do it because he accepts an incorrect idea? How could he find out that it was incorrect?* Reinforce these by pointing to the thinking map of finding your assumptions or by writing it again on the board.

- **Is it a good idea to uncover assumptions? Why or why not?** POSSIBLE ANSWERS: *If we can find out what assumptions are incorrect, then we won't make mistakes. It's a good idea because we might realize that we were going to do something silly and avoid it. It's a good idea because sometimes we don't know that we are assuming something wrong.*

- **The next time you have to find out someone's assumptions, how will you do it? Will the diagram we used help you? What will you do with it?** ANSWERS VARY.

APPLYING YOUR THINKING

IMMEDIATE TRANSFER

- **Do you remember the story of Peter Rabbit? What do you think he was assuming when he went into Mr. McGregor's garden? Why do you think that?**

- When you eat food that tastes good, what do you usually assume about what the food will do for you? How can you find out if your assumption is correct?

REINFORCEMENT LATER

- Very often people buy things because they see them advertised on television. Do you think they might be assuming anything when they do this? How could they find out whether their assumptions are good assumptions?

CONTENT EXTENSION

Ask students to work together in pairs, give them the appropriate coins, and ask them to develop a plan for teaching the boy how much a penny, nickel, dime, quarter, and dollar are really worth.

ASSESSING STUDENT THINKING ABOUT ASSUMPTIONS

In the primary grades, simple examples like the ones for transfer and reinforcement can be used to assess whether students are raising questions about assumptions and how they determine what is assumed. You can also make up a story about someone who makes an assumption and ask students what they think the person in the story might be assuming. Make sure they are raising the questions on the thinking map as they uncover the assumptions in the example(s) you give them.

SMART

Shel Silverstein

My dad gave me one dollar bill
'Cause I'm his smartest son,
And I swapped it for two shiny quarters
'Cause two is more than one!

And then I took the quarters
And traded them to Lou
For three dimes -- I guess he don't know
That three is more than two!

Just then, along came old blind Bates
And just 'cause he can't see
He gave me four nickels for my three dimes,
And four is more than three!

And I took the nickels to Hiram Coombs
Down at the seed-feed store,
And the fool gave me five pennies for them,
And five is more than four!

And then I went and showed my dad,
And he got red in the cheeks
And closed his eyes and shook his head—
Too proud of me to speak!

"Smart" from *Where The Sidewalk Ends*, by Shel Silverstein. Copyright © 1974 by Evil Eye Music, Inc. Text only reprinted by permission of Harper Collins Publishers.

Sample Student Responses • Smart About Money

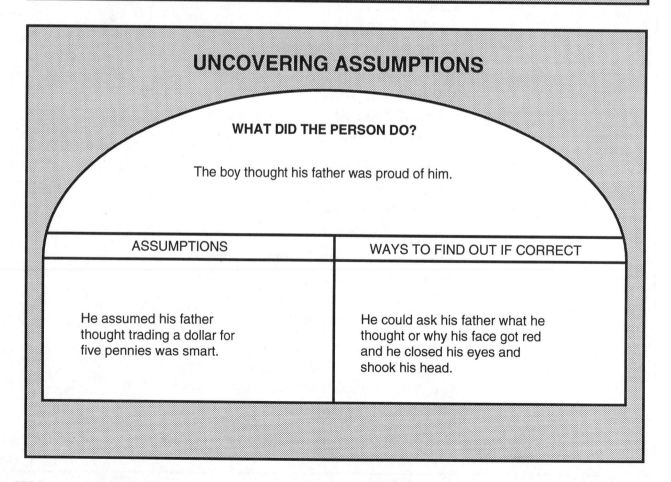

UNCOVERING ASSUMPTIONS

WHAT DID THE PERSON DO?

The boy traded one dollar for two quarters.

ASSUMPTIONS	WAYS TO FIND OUT IF CORRECT
He thought that a dollar was equal to one quarter.	He could ask his father, his mother, or his teacher, how many quarter equal a dollar.

UNCOVERING ASSUMPTIONS

WHAT DID THE PERSON DO?

The boy thought his father was proud of him.

ASSUMPTIONS	WAYS TO FIND OUT IF CORRECT
He assumed his father thought trading a dollar for five pennies was smart.	He could ask his father what he thought or why his face got red and he closed his eyes and shook his head.

MOCTEZUMA AND CORTES

World History   **Grades 4–6**

OBJECTIVES

CONTENT

Students will learn the role of cultural differences in determining the outcome of Cortes's attempt to conquer the Aztecs and take control of Mexico in 1519–1520.

THINKING SKILL/PROCESS

Students will learn to uncover assumptions and determine whether or not the assumptions are justified. They will consider actions, determine what is taken for granted in those actions, identify evidence that the person actually made the assumption, and decide whether the assumption was supported by good reasons.

METHODS AND MATERIALS

CONTENT

Students read three passages about the Aztecs and about Cortes's conquest of Mexico. They share information, using a cooperative learning "jigsaw" strategy. They write a defense of Moctezuma's assumptions about Cortes from Moctezuma's point of view.

THINKING SKILL/PROCESS

An explicit thinking map, a graphic organizer, and structured questioning are used to uncover assumptions behind a person's actions. (See pp. 260–65 for reproducible diagrams.) Collaborative learning enhances the thinking.

LESSON

INTRODUCTION TO CONTENT AND THINKING SKILL/PROCESS

• When we read about a sale at the mall, we often go to the store to buy things. But sometimes that does not work out well. Once I read in the newspaper that a store was having a sale on television sets. I needed one, so I went to the store to buy it. When I got there, however, I found that the store had no more of the television sets I wanted. It had sold out the day before and wasn't going to get new ones for another month. I was very disappointed. Then I realized that, if I had been thinking about what I was doing, I could have saved myself the trouble of travelling to the store. **What could I have thought about or done that would have saved me the trouble?** I could have called the store on the telephone and asked if they still had the television sets available.

• The reason I didn't think of calling the store was that I was making a number of assumptions of which I wasn't aware. For example, I assumed that they still had television sets of the sort I wanted to buy. An assumption is something you believe without thinking about it or checking it. Assumptions sometimes lead you to do or say certain things. Finding out what a person was assuming helps you understand why he or she did a certain thing. Assumptions might be correct or mistaken. When I set out to go to the store, **what else do you think I was assuming?** POSSIBLE ANSWERS: *That the store would be open, that my car would work, that I had enough gas in my car to get to the store, that I had enough money to buy the television set, that I needed this particular television set.* **My assumption that they still had the television sets that I wanted to buy was mistaken. Were any of these other assumptions mistaken?** ANSWERS VARY. **In this case, all of the other assumptions were correct.**

• The reason I didn't check out my mistaken assumption was that I didn't think about it. I wasn't even aware that I was making that assumption. If I had asked myself, "Am I making any assumptions here?" I might have become aware that I was assuming all of these things. If I had questioned whether these were good assumptions, I might have checked them out and saved myself a trip to the store.

• Can you think of a time when you did something based on a mistaken assumption that you could have uncovered and checked out, but didn't? Discuss it with your partner; help each other list all the assumptions that were made in this situation. Identify the ones that were mistaken and the ones that weren't. Write them down. Discuss how you could have checked out the mistaken assumptions if you had been aware of them. After a few minutes, ask for reports from the class. Ask the students reporting to identify their assumptions, those assumptions that were mistaken, and how they could have been checked.

• Everyone makes assumptions, but it's a good idea to check them out before you act on them. Leaders in history have also made assumptions. Sometimes these have been good assumptions, but sometimes they haven't. In some cases, these assumptions have led to major errors that have changed the course of history. We've been studying the Spanish conquest of the New World after Columbus. One major event during this period was Hernando Cortes's conquest of Moctezuma and the Aztecs in Mexico in 1519–1520. This brought an end to one of the greatest civilizations that had developed at that time. We're going to see if assumptions that were made by the leaders during this period played a role in this catastrophic historical event.

• Let's review what we know, what we think we know, and what we need to know about the Aztecs and the Spanish in the New World during this period. To do this, we will use a diagram with the three categories: what I know, what I think I know, and what I need to know. As you mention things that fall into these categories, I'll write them on the board in the diagram. First, we'll discuss the Aztecs, then the Spanish. Use two versions of this diagram, one with "The Aztecs" as a heading, and the other with the heading "The Spanish in the New World." Leave the completed diagram on the board. As the lesson progresses, return to the diagram periodically. Ask the students whether anything in the "I know" column should be revised and whether the class now has answers to anything in the "I need to know" column that can be added to the "I know" column.

I KNOW	I THINK I KNOW	I NEED TO KNOW

THINKING ACTIVELY

• Let's concentrate our attention on Moctezuma, the leader of the Aztecs. As Cortes invaded Mexico in 1519 to conquer the Aztecs, Moctezuma did a number of things that surprised the Spaniards. Some of these actions contributed to Cortes's success. Work in your collaborative learning groups and make a list of actions by Moctezuma that contributed to Cortes's success. Consult your textbooks for details. POSSIBLE ANSWERS: *Moctezuma sent gifts of fine robes and gold to Cortes along with the request that Cortes leave Mexico. Moctezuma invited Cortes and the Spanish to visit him in his city, Tenochtitlan. Moctezuma did not engage Cortes in battle as he approached and entered the city. He greeted and welcomed Cortes and the Spanish to Tenochtitlan. Moctezuma allowed Cortes and the Spanish to live in a palace in the city and provided slaves to feed and attend them. Moctezuma did not resist when he was captured by the Spanish nor did he call upon the Aztecs to fight Cortes and the Spanish and to drive them from the city. Moctezuma attempted to quell an uprising of the Aztecs against the Spanish.*

- **Perhaps Moctezuma made mistaken assumptions that led to a disaster he didn't want. Let's look at one of the actions—Moctezuma's not engaging Cortes in battle as he approached and entered Tenochtitlan. With the vast resources of fighting men that Moctezuma had available, it was likely he could have kept Cortes from entering the city, if not defeated him. Instead, Cortes entered the city, giving him a foothold from which he could weaken and plunder the city. List everything you think Moctezuma might have assumed that led him not to resist. Use this graphic organizer in your group to uncover these proposed assumptions.** After a few minutes, ask students to report on one proposed assumption. Write their responses on a transparency or poster version of the graphic organizer for uncovering assumptions. POSSIBLE ANSWERS: *The Spanish were friendly. Moctezuma could easily surround and destroy the Spanish force once they were in the city. Cortes might be a god. Cortes was powerful and would defeat the Aztecs in battle if the Aztecs engaged the Spanish.*

UNCOVERING ASSUMPTIONS	
JUSTIFIED:√ QUESTIONABLE: ? UNJUSTIFIED: X	
ACTION, BELIEF, OR CONCLUSION	
Moctezuma did not engage Cortes in a battle as Cortes approached and entered the city of Tenochtitlan.	
MIGHT BE TAKEN FOR GRANTED:	REASONS:

- **Here are five passages about the Aztecs, Cortes, Moctezuma, and the meeting of these two great leaders.** Divide the class into five groups and ask each group to read one of the passages. Then reassemble the class into new groups, each containing one member from the five reading groups. Students in each group will summarize and share what they have read. **As you share your information, think about whether or not your reading passage provides any support for thinking that Moctezuma was or was not making the assumptions that you wrote on your graphic organizers. Discuss the information that makes you think Moctezuma may or may not have made a particular assumption. For each assumption on your graphic organizers, write the reasons you think Moctezuma did or did not make this assumption. Circle the assumptions your group thinks Moctezuma probably made and cross out the ones you think he probably did not make.** Reorganize students for this jigsaw reading and discussion. Ask students to work with their graphic organizers and write information from various sources. POSSIBLE ANSWERS: *He probably didn't assume that the Spaniards were friendly because he knew that they were forming alliances with the Totonacs, who were enemies of the Aztecs. He probably didn't assume that he could easily surround and destroy the Spanish force once they were in the city because, if he had a plan to do so, he took no such action. He probably did assume that Cortes might be a god because of the likeness between the Spaniards and the descriptions of the followers of Quetzalcoatl, the legendary god-king of the Toltecs, and because he was a devout believer in the imminent return of Quetzalcoatl. He may also have assumed that Cortes could defeat the Aztecs in battle. He did try to bribe them to leave by offering gifts of robes and gold. He knew of the defeat of the Tlaxcalans, who fell to the superior weaponry of the Spaniards and to their own inefficiency in battle despite a superior force in numbers (30,000 men to Cortes's 2,000). However, the Aztecs had never shirked from battle before, so it isn't clear that this assumption motivated him.*

- **Many people have said that Moctezuma's mistake was in believing that Cortes might be the god Quetzalcoatl. Why might Moctezuma have made this assumption? Discuss with your**

group whether or not you think this was a reasonable assumption for Moctezuma to make, given what he believed, heard, and saw. POSSIBLE ANSWERS: *Moctezuma held deep religious beliefs that led him to think that Cortes might be Quetzalcoatl. Some things that the Aztecs had never seen before, like horses, seemed mysterious to them and could be interpreted as signs of something divine. The details describing Quetzalcoatl (bearded, plumed, arriving from the east) fit Cortes. For Moctezuma all of these beliefs made it seem quite reasonable that Cortes might be Quetzalcoatl.* Other students think that Moctezuma was jumping to conclusions and could have found out that Cortes was not a god.

Discuss with your students the idea that sometimes people believe things that seem like unjustified assumptions to us, but the assumptions are based on deeply held cultural beliefs that make these assumptions seem quite reasonable to them. Discuss with students whether or not good thinkers should accept such assumptions without question. Should good thinkers question even deeply-held beliefs? Help students understand the clash of cultures that occurred during this period of European conquest and how this clash of cultures led not to blending and assimilation but to battles for domination. Ask, "Was there any basis in these two cultures for accommodation and assimilation?"

- **What understanding of Moctezuma did you gain by examining his assumptions?** POSSIBLE ANSWERS: *Leaders who are otherwise thoughtful and well-informed may be so bound by their assumptions that they may not understand situations clearly.*

THINKING ABOUT THINKING

- **You uncovered Moctezuma's assumptions about Cortes in this lesson. What questions guided you to determine what his assumptions were?** POSSIBLE AN-SWERS: *I first asked what action by Moctezuma was unusual and might be based on assumptions. I then thought about what Moctezuma might have taken for granted that would explain why he acted as he did. Then I selected assumptions that were supported by evidence from the period. I tried to determine whether Moctezuma had good reasons for accepting these assumptions and how he could have determined whether or not they were correct.*

> **UNCOVERING ASSUMPTIONS**
>
> 1. What action, belief, or conclusion of a specific person might be based on assumptions?
>
> 2. What might that person be taking for granted in performing the action, accepting the belief, or drawing the conclusion?
>
> 3. Are there any reasons for thinking that any of these possible assumptions are being taken for granted? If so, what are these reasons?
>
> 4. Are these assumptions well-founded? Explain.

- **To guide you in uncovering assumptions in the future, construct a thinking map.** The thinking map should contain the key questions for uncovering assumptions shown at the right.

- **Is it helpful to be able to uncover assumptions? Why or why not?** Many students respond that it is helpful to become aware of their assumptions and decide whether or not they are good ones. We should ask ourselves the questions for uncovering assumptions until we know that our assumptions are well-supported. This can often keep us from acting on mistaken assumptions that we are not fully aware of. Sometimes acting on mistaken assumptions can lead to disasters, as in the case of Moctezuma.

- **How did sharing your information in a "jigsaw" help you reflect on what Moctezuma's assumptions may have been?** Students comment that the information sharing reduced the time needed to gather information so that they could concentrate on the assumptions.

APPLYING THINKING

Immediate Transfer

• We've also been studying Pizarro's conquest of the Incas in Peru. Like Moctezuma, their leader, Atahuallpa, also did things that made it easier for the conquerors. For example, he left most of his warriors behind and went to meet Pizarro with his nobles, all unarmed. This led to Atahuallpa's capture and the massacre of his nobles by Pizarro. Use your plan for uncovering assumptions to determine what Atahuallpa might have been assuming in taking this action. What could he have done to check out whether this assumption was correct?

• In science, we've been studying energy sources. What, if any, assumptions are we making in our reliance on fossil fuels as the main source of energy in this country? Are these assumptions justified? How can we check them out? Based on what you have uncovered, what would you advise that we do about our sources of energy?

Reinforcement Later

• We are studying the Pilgrims's decision to leave Europe and come to the new world. Read some of William Bradfords' passages about Plymouth Plantation. Use your plan for uncovering assumptions to find out what the Pilgrims probably assumed to be true about their life in the New World.

CONTENT EXTENSION

Ask students to research the basic belief system of the Aztecs, as well as their technological advances. Students should use resources in the school library or resources that you accumulate and bring to the classroom. A standard reference work on the topic is *Ancient America* from the Time-Life series, *The Great Ages of Man*. Students can discuss this material in collaborative learning groups and "jigsaw" what they have found. As a class project, students can develop a profile of Aztec culture that emphasizes basic religious, social, and political beliefs, as well as the technology and organization of the culture.

WRITING EXTENSION

Have students imaging that they were Aztecs who shared Moctezuma's beliefs about the Aztec gods. Ask them to write a recommendation to Moctezuma regarding how he might check out his belief that Cortes might be a god.

ASSESSING STUDENT THINKING ABOUT UNCOVERING ASSUMPTIONS

To assess student thinking about uncovering unstated assumptions, describe a significant action of a character in a story or of a historical figure. Ask students to think about what the people involved probably assumed. Ask students to make their thinking explicit. Determine whether they are attending to each of the steps in the thinking map for uncovering assumptions and whether they are using the language of uncovering assumptions.

MOCTEZUMA AND CORTES

SOURCE MATERIAL ON THE SPANISH CONQUEST OF THE AZTECS

QUETZALCOATL

Years and years ago there were beautiful cities in the high valley of central Mexico. Teotihuacan was the largest of these cities. It fell into ruins, but some of the buildings are still there. One of these was a temple built to honor a god. He had a body like a snake, or serpent. But instead of scales had red and green feathers. The people thought his feathers were like those of a long-tailed bird called a quetzal. Their word for snake was coatl. So they called their god Quetzalcoatl, or Feathered Serpent.

The people of Teotihuacan also built pyramids to the Sun and to the Moon. They used gold and silver and precious stones to make jewelry. They knew how to make clay figures and brightly decorated pottery.

Many different stories are told about Quetzalcoatl, the Feathered Serpent god. And there was another Quetzalcoatl, a king who was named for the god. The life of the man Quetzalcoatl is wrapped in the mystery of the old legends. The legends have mixed the deeds of the real person with those of the god. No two of the stories are alike. Here is one of them.

About a thousand years ago, the people of Teotihuacan left their beautiful city. We don't know whether they were conquered by an enemy or driven away because of the lack of food.

About forty miles from Teotihuacan, another great city was built. It was called Tula. Here the Toltec people built a temple with narrow flights of steps up the sides. Artists carved jaguars and eagles on the walls. There were also carvings of feathered serpents, in honor of Quetzalcoatl. The king named his baby son after the god. This little boy grew up to become king of the Toltecs. The great city of Tula was his capital. His people were happy and contented. They sang a song about their king:

In Quetzalcoatl all these Trades and arts had their beginnings.

He, the master workman, taught them

All their trades and handicraft work. Fashioned they the sacred emeralds,

Melted they both gold and silver

Other trades and arts they mastered.

But Quetzalcoatl had a wicked uncle who drove him out of Tula. His uncle's soldiers burned the city. The ruins can still be seen today.

Quetzalcoatl and his warriors marched across the valley all the way to the foot of the great volcano Mount Popocatepetl. Finally they came to another valley farther south. There Quetzalcoatl became king at a city called Cholula. The largest pyramid in the New World was built at Cholula. Deep inside the pyramid is a room. On the wall of this room is a painting of a handsome young god. He has a serpent's body and he is wearing feathers on his head—Quetzalcoatl!

A group of Toltec soldiers left this city and went to the coast. There they learned to build long canoes which held twenty men each. In these, they went by sea to the Yucatan Peninsula. After fighting with the tribes they met on the coast, the Toltecs marched inland.

They came to the town of Chichen Itza. This name means "well of the Itzas." The Itzas were descendants of the Maya. The Maya were an ancient people who had a highly developed civilization.

Today, in the ruined city that once was Chichen Itza, a tall pyramid is still standing. Here, too, is a small inside room with a wall painting. It shows warriors decorated with feathers and snakes' heads. Do you suppose King Quetzalcoatl ordered this pyramid to be built? Other buildings at Chichen Itza have carvings of

From *Fifteen Famous Latin Americans*, by Helen Miller Bailey & Maria Grijalva, Prentice-Hall, Inc., 1973. Reprinted by permission of Simon & Shuster/Prentice Hall.

jaguars and eagles, just like those on the temple at Tula.

Chichen Itza became a large city under the rule of Quetzalcoatl. The people were proud of the king, and they carved many pictures of him. Because he was the only king who ever had a beard, their name for him was "The Bearded One."

The Toltecs and the Maya people of Chichen Itza learned from each other. Quetzalcoatl and his followers taught the people how to make gold jewelry and temple bells and showed them new ways of building. On the other hand, the Mayans had a lot to teach the Toltecs. For many years they had been carving in wood and stone. They had a number system and used a kind of picture writing. They even built a high tower so they could climb to the top and study the stars. The knew the longest and shortest days of the year, and could predict an eclipse of the sun. Their weavers showed the Toltecs how to make cloth with gay designs, and how to make beautiful carvings.

But Quetzalcoatl longed to see Teotihuacan again. He promised the people of Chichen Itza that he would return. He started out, but his fleet of canoes vanished, and he was never heard from again. The Itza people lived in Yucatan for three centuries after Quetzalcoatl went away. Then for years the city of Chichen Itza lay deserted in the forest.

The people in Yucatan and the people in the central valley of Mexico never forgot Quetzalcoatl. He had been a king, a teacher, and a hero. Their memories of him were all mixed up with the old stories of the god.

Surely Quetzalcoatl, the Bearded One, was a real person. In time he became a legend. It is part of the religion of all the Indian people of ancient Mexico. His promise was never forgotten. They believed that some day he would come back. On the wings of the wind, he would come across the eastern sea. The Maya in Yucatan abandoned Chichen Itza. Hundreds of years later, people called the Aztecs came to live in the valley where Teotihuacan and Tula lay in ruins. They believed in the promise also.

At last came a day when the promise seemed to come true. A bearded one came from far across the eastern sea. Had Quetzalcoatl returned? The answer is part of another chapter in the history of these people.

MOCTEZUMA AND THE NEWS OF CORTES

In 1519 Moctezuma II, the Aztec Emperor, was about 40 years old and had ruled with a firm and skillful hand for 17 years. But recently his personality had changed. Gone was his former ability in war and diplomacy; in its place was uncertainty accompanied by spells of brooding. He seldom appeared in public but kept to the guarded interior of his enormous palace, consulting with priests and soothsayers or meditating alone.

The people of his capital, Tenochtitlan, were deeply worried too. For years the omens had been bad. Strange lights had shone in the sky. Temples had caught fire and burned uncontrollably. At night a mysterious woman was often heard in the streets crying: "O my beloved sons, now we are about to go." And fishermen brought to Moctezuma a fantastic bird with a mirror on its head. When the Emperor looked in the mirror he saw armed warriors with the triumphant air of conquerors, riding on the backs of monsters resembling deer.

What did these portents mean? Many Mexicans, including Moctezuma, suspected that they foreshadowed the second coming of Quetzalcoatl, the legendary god-king of the Toltecs who had gone into exile over five centuries before and had promised to return from the direction of the rising sun. The scheduled time for his return was now approaching, and rumors flew that he or his emissaries had actually been sighted. They were heavily bearded, as Quetzalcoatl was believed to have been, and their weapons were thunder and lightning.

MOCTEZUMA AND THE COMING OF CORTES

The news Moctezuma received from Tlaxcala was not encouraging. The Spaniards and their Tontonac allies had been heavily attacked by 30,000 plumed and painted Tlaxcalan warriors, hurling spears, swinging obsidian-edged swords and screaming their ear-piercing war cry. But the Indians had never faced such deadly things as the steel swords, crossbows, harquebuses and light artillery of the helmeted Spaniards, and these superior weapons had had a devastating and demoralizing effect on them. So had the tiny squadron of 16 cavalrymen: the Tlaxcalans, believing that each horse and rider were one creature, had been terrified.

Even more advantageous for the Spaniards than their arms and cavalry was the Indian concept of warfare. Since the Tlaxcalans and other Mexicans fought not to kill but to capture living victims for sacrifice to their gods, they tried merely to stun Spaniard and drag him away. Other Spaniards then came to his rescue, usually killing his assailants. Another weakness of the Indians was their inability to marshal their forces effectively. Though they greatly outnumbered the Spaniards, many of their soldiers never got into the fight.

In Tlaxcala the Spaniards triumphed with difficulty, but they found they had won more than a simple victory. In post-battle negotiations, during which Dona Marina distinguished herself as a diplomat, the Tlaxcalans not only surrendered to Cortes but also offered to join him in the alliance against the hated Aztecs. His plan to conquer Mexico was working magnificently.

CORTES IN TENOCHTITLAN

Cortes was now allied with his Moctezuma's most vindictive enemies, and envoys from other Aztec subject states were offering their support. Moctezuma surprised the Spaniards by inviting them to visit him in Tenochtitlan.

Loudly the Tlaxcalans warned Cortes not to accept the invitation. They described the overwhelming strength of the imperial city, the great armies that it could muster, its impregnable position in Lake Texcoco where it could be reached only by three causeways, each with bridges that could be raised to trap intruders....

Along the causeway to meet the Spaniards came Moctezuma, borne in a rich litter and accompanied by his nobles. The Emperor was tall and rather thin with a sparse black beard, and on his head he wore a plume of long green

From *Great Ages of Man: Ancient America,* by Jonathan Norton Leonard and the Editors of Time-Life Books, © 1967 Time-Life Books, Inc. Reprinted by permission.

feathers that floated down his back. He greeted Cortes and conversed with him politely through Dona Marina. No one would have judged from his dignified demeanor that the night before he had shut himself in his palace in panic and despair, praying to his gods and offering sacrifices. The gods had given no reassurance. "Of what use is resistance," Moctezuma asked his council of noble advisers, "when the gods themselves have declared against us?"

Now inside the city, the Spaniards were quartered in a commodious palace (their Indian allies camped in the courtyard) and were fed and attended by a great number of slaves. A relationship resembling friendship developed between Moctezuma and Cortes. The Emperor came to call on the Spaniard and invited him to his palace, where he lived in vast magnificence with hordes of courtiers and a thousand wives and concubines. He also arranged for Cortes a tour of the city and its grisly temples. Bernal Diaz was on this tour and vividly described what he saw in one of the twin temples on the top of the tallest pyramid. "On each altar," he wrote, "were two figures, like giants with very tall bodies and very fat, and the first, they said, was their god of war; it had a broad face and monstrous and terrible eyes, and the body was girdled by great snakes made of gold and precious stones…all the walls of the oratory were so splashed and encrusted with blood that they were black."

Through the charming lips of Dona Marina, Cortes and Moctezuma discussed their respective countries, and Cortes tried without success to convert the Emperor to Christianity. Around them the life of the city seemed to proceed normally, but Cortes was growing uneasy. He suspected that the unpredictable Moctezuma might be plotting to destroy him. Even more he feared that his rough Spanish soldiers or the wild Tlaxcalans might commit some outrage that would turn the Emperor against him.

After careful preparation he took the final, audacious step in his scheme for conquest. Entering Moctezuma's palace with 30 armed Spaniards, he took the Emperor prisoner and had him carried to the Spanish quarters in his own imperial litter. Moctezuma made no resistance; he was completely irresolute, almost as if in a trance. As the royal cortege moved through the streets, the people stood watching silently, paralyzed by their belief in the legend of Quetzalcoatl. The ancient god had returned, they told one another, to rule over their nation in the guise of the black bearded Spaniards.

THE DEATH OF MOCTEZUMA AND THE FALL OF TENOCHTITLAN

Cortes was now in complete control of the Aztec capital, but soon he had to hurry back to the coast to deal with a Spanish army of 900 men sent by Governor Velasquez of Cuba, who had heard of Cortes' growing power and was determined to curb it. The leader of the army was captured and its troops accepted Cortes as commander.

Before Cortes and greatly enlarged forces could get back to Tenochtitlan, there came the startling news that the city was in full revolt. Pedro de Alvarado, the officer he had left in charge, had invited 600 of the highest Aztec nobles into a temple enclosure to celebrate one of their religious festivals. While they were engaged in ritual dance, his soldiers had slaughtered all of them and stripped their bodies of their golden ornaments.

When this atrocity became known, the city rose in arms and a sea of furious Aztecs surged around the Spaniards. They would have been overwhelmed if Moctezuma had not partially calmed his people. Then the assault subsided to a sullen siege.

When Cortes arrived at the head of his new army, his march to the Spanish quarters was through a silent and apparently empty city. Not daring to leave the palace even though active hostilities had ceased, Alvarado's soldiers and Tlaxcalans were close to starvation and reduced to drinking brackish water from wells dug in the palace grounds.

Cortes upbraided Alvarado for his greedy savagery and through Moctezuma tried unsuccessfully to get the city under control. He sent the Emperor's brother, Cuitlahua, as a peace envoy to the hostile chiefs. This was one of his few serious mistakes. Since Moctezuma was powerless to govern, Cuitlahua was heir to the throne under the Aztec system of succession. He presently declared himself Emperor, providing the Aztecs with a leader who had no religious scruples about how to deal with the invaders.

Now that they had a leader, there was nothing hesitant about the Aztecs. The next day hordes of warriors gathered to assault their defenses and rained arrows and other missiles on them. Several bloody sallies were made against the attackers, and Bernal Diaz, who took part in them, wrote: "We noted their tenacity in fighting, but I declare that I do not know how to describe it, for neither canon nor muskets nor crossbows availed, nor hand-to-hand fighting, nor killing thirty or forty of them every time we charged, for they still fought with more energy than in the beginning."

Moctezuma mounted the roof of the Spaniards' quarters and once more attempted to pacify his people. The furious attackers fell silent when they saw him and permitted him to speak. Then the Indians discharged a shower of stones and arrows, and Moctezuma fell, seriously wounded. He refused to be tended, and soon he died.

With Moctezuma dead the Spaniards were only a handful of foreigners in a hostile city, with no magic armor to protect them from the enraged inhabitants. Cortes realized he must evacuate Tenochtitlan. Calmly he made his plans. He knew that escape would not be easy, for the Aztecs had removed the bridges from the causeways, leaving gaps that must somehow be crossed. While battle raged around them, the Spaniards with desperate haste constructed a portable wooden bridge strong enough to bear the weight of mounted men. After darkness fell and the Aztec attack had temporarily slackened, Cortes gave the order to march. All went well as far as the first of three gaps in the causeway that he had chosen, but then Aztec sentries cried the alarm. An enormous drum on Tenochtitlan's tallest pyramid boomed a deep, melancholy note; a great fleet of canoes swept close to the causeway and the warriors in them showered arrows and stones on the slow-moving column.

At the first of the gaps the portable bridge did its work, but when the Spaniards tried to carry it forward to use it again, it stuck fast between the abutments. With cries of despair the soldiers

of Cortes rushed to the second gap. Those in advance were pushed into the water by the press behind them, and many of them sank, weighted down by their own armor or by the Aztec gold that they carried. While the great drum boomed and fires flared on the pyramids, more canoes full of screaming Aztecs surged out of the darkness, and the bodies of Spaniards and Indians alike piled up in the gap, along with toppled cannon, ammunition wagons and chests of golden of treasure. At last the mound of flesh and wreckage was high enough for the rest of the army to cross. The third gap was passed in the same gory way, though the Spaniards and Tlaxcalans were fewer now. This was the *Noche Triste* , the "Sad Night" of Mexican history. When dawn came, the remnants of the army gathered on the mainland near a great cypress tree, *El Arbol de la Noche Triste,* , which still stands in Mexico City. All artillery had been lost; all muskets and many other weapons had been thrown away. It is probable that two thirds of the Spaniards had been killed or dragged off for sacrifice, and all those who remained were wounded.

The lesson of the *Noche Triste* made it very plain that to attack Tenochtitlan across the exposed causeways would be imprudent. Deciding that the water-walled city could not be taken without controlling the lake in which it stood, Cortes conceived the bold idea of constructing a demountable fleet that could be carried piece by piece to the Valley of Mexico and reassembled. The metal parts of the ships that he had ordered destroyed at Veracruz were still in storage there, and he now had them brought to Tlaxcala. Luckily he had with him a skilled shipbuilder, Martin Lopez, whom he put to work with a host of Indian helpers. About this time he also received unexpected reinforcements in men, arms and horses from several ships that put into Veracruz.

Additional help came from another ally, dreadful and unexpected. Smallpox, starting at Veracruz, swept through the country, killing friend and foe alike. The disease was unknown in Mexico, and the Indians, who had no resistance to it, died by hundreds of thousands. Among the victims was the Emperor Cuitlahua, who had so valiantly rallied his people. His death reduced the strength of Tenochtitlan while the raging pestilence further disrupted its empire.

On December 28, 1520, Cortes set out from Tlaxcala for his second march on the now weakened Aztec capital. With him marched an army of 600 well-armed Spaniards, including about 40 cavalrymen, and the flower of Tlaxcala's warriors. En route his force grew to more than 100,000, swelled by Indian recruits seeking revenge against their Aztec oppressors. Tenochtitlan was almost alone.

Cortes set up headquarters in Texcoco, where a pro-Spanish Indian faction had taken control. The demountable navy—13 small sailing vessels called brigantines—was now completed and had been carried across the mountains in pieces. While it was being assembled, the Spaniards and their Indian allies harried beleaguered Tenochtitlan. They cut the aqueducts that brought fresh water to the city and laid waste the lakeshore so that foraging parties would find no food.

Hearing that pestilence and famine raged in Tenochtitlan, Cortes allowed himself to be persuaded to try an attack across one of the causeways, but the Aztecs showed undiminished spirit and beat back the assault with heavy losses. The city now had a new Emperor, Cuauhtemoc, a 25-year-old nephew of Moctezuma, and he swore that he would fight until every Aztec warrior had been killed.

At last the brigantines were ready. They sailed out on the lake where a great flotilla of Aztec canoes was waiting for them. The unequal engagement that followed foreshadowed the end of Tenochtitlan. Maneuvering back and forth, the brigantines ran down the canoes, smashing them like eggshells. With the waters of the lake controlled by the invaders and with hostile armies lining its shores, the imperial city was cut off from all support.

Still Cuauhtemoc would not surrender or even exchange messages with the attackers. When Cortes ordered a final assault, the starving and tattered Aztecs fought as fiercely as ever while three large canoes pushed out of the city and tried to cross to the mainland. They were intercepted by the brigantines. In one canoe was Cuauhtemoc. As news of his capture spread, the few remaining Aztecs stopped fighting; they had only been trying to cover their leader's escape.

That was the end of Tenochtitlan.

Sample Student Responses • Moctezuma and Cortes

| JUSTIFIED: √ |
| QUESTIONABLE: ? |
| UNJUSTIFIED: X |

UNCOVERING ASSUMPTIONS

ACTION, BELIEF, OR CONCLUSION

Moctezuma did not engage Cortes in a battle as Cortes approached and entered the city of Tenochtitlan.

MIGHT BE TAKEN FOR GRANTED	REASONS FOR THINKING IT IS
~~The Spanish were friendly.~~	Moctezuma knew that the Spaniards had formed alliances with people like the Totanacs who were enemies of the Aztecs.
~~Moctezuma could easily surround and destroy the Spanish force once it was in the city.~~	This suggests Moctezuma had a plan to do so, yet he took no such action. Rather he gave the Spaniards a place to live.
√ (Cortes might be a god.)	The Spaniards seemed to meet the description of Quetzalcoatl, the legendary god-king of the Toltecs. Moctezuma was a devout believer in the imminent return of Quetzalcoatl.
X The Spanish were powerful and would easily defeat the Aztecs in battle.	Moctezuma tried to bribe the Spanish to leave by offering gifts. He knew of the defeat of the Tlaxcolans, who had a force superior to the Spanish. However, the Aztecs had never shirked from battle.
? Moctezuma could convince Cortes to form an alliance with him.	Moctezuma spent much time conversing with Cortes through Dona Marina after the Spaniards entered Tenochtitlan. However, Cortes had already formed alliances with the enemy.

UNCOVERING ASSUMPTIONS LESSON CONTEXTS

The following examples have been suggested by classroom teachers as contexts to develop infused lessons. If a skill or process has been introduced in a previous infused lesson, it can be reinforced with transfer activities in these contexts.

GRADE	SUBJECT	TOPIC	THINKING ISSUE
K–3	Literature	*Fables*	In Arnold Lobel's fable "The Bear and The Crow," what assumptions about Crow caused Bear's embarrassment? Why does the story suggest people would have assumptions like this one? In the fable "Madame Rhinoceros and Her Dress," what is Madame Rhinoceros's assumption about people's reactions to her dress? Why does the story suggest that she would have an assumption like this one?
K–3	Literature	*What I was Scared Of (The Sneetches and Other Stories)*	What assumption makes the main character afraid of the pale green pants with nobody inside them? Was this a good assumption? How did the character find out? How could you have found out if you were there?
K–3	Literature	*The Sneetches*	What assumption allows Fix-It-Up-Cappie to take advantage of the Sneetches? How did the Sneetches realize that assumption? What does the story suggest that people should do when they recognize that they are believing that assumption?
K–3	Literature	*The Terrible Thing That Happened at Our House*	What assumptions about the roles of parents are made in this story? How do you know that these assumptions are made? Are these good assumptions?
K–3	Literature	*Chicken Sunday*	What assumption does Mr. Kodinski make regarding who threw the eggs at this store? How do we know who he thought did it? Why did he believe that? What showed him that he was mistaken?
K–3	Literature	*Amelia Bedelia*	What does Amelia Bedelia take for granted that explains why she makes all the mistakes that she does?
K–3	Literature	*Miss Nelson is Missing*	What did the children in Miss Nelson's class assume about Miss Nelson and about Miss Viola Swamp? How do you know? Were their assumptions good ones? How do you know?
K–3	Social studies	Columbus	When Columbus landed on San Salvador, what did he assume about the land he had discovered? How do you know? Was his assumption correct? How do you know?
K–3	Social studies	*The Picture Book of Frederick Douglass*	What does Frederick Douglass assume regarding why people should learn how to read? Is his assumption a good assumption?
K–3	Science	Plants	Johnny had some nice plants in his room. The leaves on some of them started getting yellow and falling off. Johnny said that he couldn't understand why; he kept them really wet by giving them plenty of water every day. What was Johnny taking for granted about plants? Was he right? How could he have checked out his assumption?
K–3	Science	Float/sink	After students test a variety of objects, list assumptions about which will float or sink. Test their assumptions to generate a list of characteristics that are involved in floating.
K–3	Health	Food	Alice saw an ad for a new breakfast cereal on TV. It sounded really good, so she asked her mother to buy it. What was Alice taking for granted? Are her assumptions good ones to make? How can you tell?

			UNCOVERING ASSUMPTIONS LESSON CONTEXTS
4–6	Language arts	Research	Investigate the assumptions behind common superstitions or practices related to superstition (covering the mouth when yawning or saying "God bless you" when someone sneezes, etc.) to decide if there is or ever was any good reasons behind them.
4–6	Literature	*Three Strong Women: A Tall Tale from Japan*	What does this story suggest that the wrestler Forever-Mountain assumed about the women he meets? What reasons do you have for thinking that that idea is what he is assuming? Are these reasonable assumptions? What shows that his assumptions were mistaken?
4–6	Literature	*Icarus and Daedalus*	Though Icarus' father warned him not to fly too high, Icarus nonetheless flew too close to the sun. The wax on his wings melted and he fell to his death. Do you think Icarus was making any assumptions that led to this tragedy? If so, what were they and what makes you think he was making these specific assumptions? What information in the story explains why Icarus made these assumptions? If he had decided to be more cautious, how could he have checked them out?
4–6	Literature	*Maniac McGee*	In questioning Maniac about his life with the Beales, what does Grayson assume to be true about the black family's habits and lifestyle?
4–6	Literature	*Words by Heart*	What did Lena assume about the attitudes of the townspeople toward her and her family if she won the memory verse contest?
4–6	Literature	*The Gold Cadillac*	What did the black family assume would be the reactions of their relatives in the South in the 1950s when they drove to Mississippi in their gold Cadillac? Why were they surprised?
4–6	Literature	*Gilgamesh the King*	What assumptions does Gilgamesh make about the kind of person the wild man is? How do you know that he makes these assumptions? What does he find out about his assumptions? Could he have found this out earlier? How?
4–6	Literature	*The Whipping Boy*	What assumptions are made about the beliefs of the two boys? Are they good assumptions? Why or why not?
4–6	English/ world history	*The Butter Battle War*	Compare the assumptions in the Dr. Seuss story with the assumptions behind the Cold War. How well do the assumptions in the story match the rationale behind the Cold War?
4–6	Literature	*Park's Quest*	What assumption did Park make about his father's decision to return to Vietnam? What effect did this assumption have on his feelings about himself? Did he have a good reason for making this assumption? If he had been aware of this assumption, how might he have found out whether it was a good assumption to make?
4–6	Social studies	Exploration	The New World that Columbus discovered was called America in part because the mapmaker Amerigo Vespucci recognized errors in Columbus's assumptions about the lands he had discovered and the size of the world. What were Columbus's mistaken assumptions? Why did he believe them? Why didn't what he found in the New World make him question these assumptions? Why did Amerigo Vespuci not accept Columbus's ideas?
4–6	U.S. history	Immigration	At the turn of the century, what did many immigrants to the United States take for granted about the working and living conditions in this country? What were these assumptions based on?
4–6	Social studies	Colonization	European colonists were surprised at the harshness of winters in the New World. On a map, locate the settlements at Plymouth, Jamestown, and St. Augustine. What cities in Europe are on the same latitude? What mistaken assumption about climate created the colonists misjudgment?

			UNCOVERING ASSUMPTIONS LESSON CONTEXTS
4–6	U. S. history	The Westward Movement	In the middle 1800s, the Donner party made the long journey towards California by wagon train. They only made it as far as the Sierra Neveda mountains, however, where they were snowed in. Before they were rescued, many of the party died of exposure and starvation. What assumptions did the Donner party make that led to this disaster? Could they have checked out these assumptions? How?
4–6	U.S. history	Industrialization	In the 19th century, logging was a major industry in this country. By the early 20th century, most of the trees along the Ohio and Missouri rivers had been cut down. When the trees were gone, the spring flooding along these rivers and along the Mississippi got more severe than usual. Cities along the river were flooded with more frequency, and many people lost their homes and lives. What assumptions did the loggers make that contributed to these problems? How could they have checked out their assumptions? Are there any parallels to this situation today? If so, how can uncovering those assumptions help?
4–6	Science	Space	Earth-orbiting satellites are powered by sun. Probes deep into space use nuclear reactors. What assumption explains the difference?
4–6	Science	Migration	Each year Canadian geese "know" when to fly south. What can we assume about that behavior?
4–6	Mathematics	Plane and solid figures	Johnny wanted to make a frame to go around a picture that was 6 " by 9". He picked out a long piece of wood that was 1" wide and 4/3" thick. He cut two 6" lengths for the sides and two 9" pieces for the top and bottom. He nailed the top and bottom to the sides and made a rectangular frame. When he tried to put the picture in it, however, the picture didn't fit. It did fit from top to bottom, but it was 1 1/2" too long to fit from side to side. What assumption did Johnny make that led to this problem? (He assumed that the two-dimensional measurements carried over to three-dimensional objects, hence, he failed to take into account the thickness of the wood.) How should he correct his measurements next time?
4–6	Mathematics	Estimating	What assumptions do we make when we estimate? Students may discuss rounding off, averaging, considering the range of values, determining distances, areas, circumferences, and volumes, mental arithmetic, etc. How should we use those assumptions to try to make our estimates more accurate?
4–6	Mathematics/ science	Food use	A 60-pound girl ate a snack with 240 calories. To "burn" 240 calories, she would have to jump rope for 60 minutes. What must we assume to believe that a 60-pound girl jumping rope burns 240 calories per hour?
4–6	Science	Displacement	When you get into the bathtub and the level of the water goes up, what assumptions might you make about what causes the water to rise? How could you find out which assumptions are good ones?
4–6	Science	Phases of the moon	What mistaken assumptions about the moon's movement do students sometimes make by observing the phases of the moon?
4–6	Health	Teeth	Gum disease is serious. Many people don't discover that they have it until it is too late to treat it. What assumption is it easy to make that could lead a person to overlook caring for their gums? (Gums with gingevitis do not hurt; it is easy to assume that if your gums don't hurt they are healthy.) How can people be made aware of this assumption?

PART 4

SKILLS AT GENERATING IDEAS: CREATIVE THINKING

Chapter 10: Generating Possibilities

Chapter 11: Creating Metaphors

MAP OF THE THINKING DOMAIN

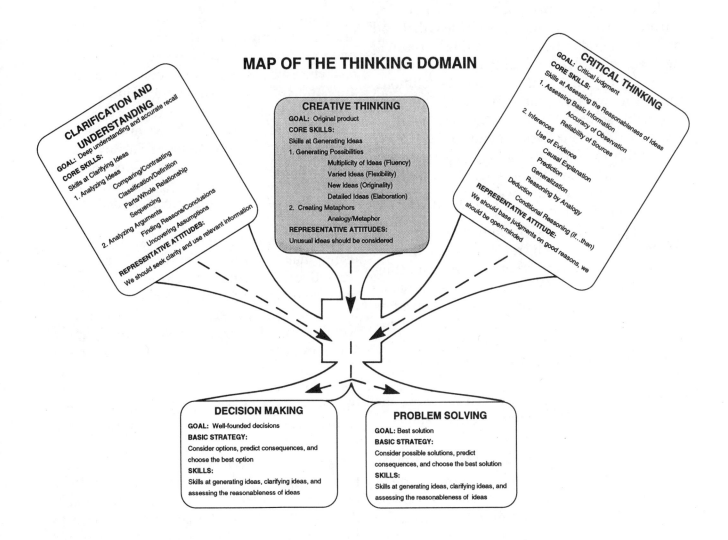

CLARIFICATION AND UNDERSTANDING

GOAL: Deep understanding and accurate recall

CORE SKILLS:

Skills at Clarifying Ideas

1. Analyzing Ideas
   - Comparing/Contrasting
   - Classification/Definition
   - Parts/Whole Relationship
   - Sequencing
2. Analyzing Arguments
   - Finding Reasons/Conclusions
   - Uncovering Assumptions

REPRESENTATIVE ATTITUDES:
We should seek clarity and use relevant information

CREATIVE THINKING

GOAL: Original product

CORE SKILLS:

Skills at Generating Ideas

1. Generating Possibilities
   - Multiplicity of Ideas (Fluency)
   - Varied Ideas (Flexibility)
   - New Ideas (Originality)
   - Detailed Ideas (Elaboration)
2. Creating Metaphors
   - Analogy/Metaphor

REPRESENTATIVE ATTITUDES:
Unusual ideas should be considered

CRITICAL THINKING

GOAL: Critical judgment

CORE SKILLS:

Skills at Assessing the Reasonableness of Ideas

1. Assessing Basic Information
   - Accuracy of Observation
   - Reliability of Sources
2. Inferences
   - Use of Evidence
   - Causal Explanation
   - Prediction
   - Generalization
   - Reasoning by Analogy
   - Deduction
   - Conditional Reasoning (if...then)

REPRESENTATIVE ATTITUDE:
We should base judgments on good reasons, we should be open-minded

DECISION MAKING

GOAL: Well-founded decisions

BASIC STRATEGY:
Consider options, predict consequences, and choose the best option

SKILLS:
Skills at generating ideas, clarifying ideas, and assessing the reasonableness of ideas

PROBLEM SOLVING

GOAL: Best solution

BASIC STRATEGY:
Consider possible solutions, predict consequences, and choose the best solution

SKILLS:
Skills at generating ideas, clarifying ideas, and assessing the reasonableness of ideas

PART 4
SKILLS AT GENERATING IDEAS: CREATIVE THINKING

Imagine facing the following problem: Winters are cold where I live and my heating bills are very high. I usually just pay the bills and don't think much about them. But is there a way to reduce them? Actually, I have no idea why they are so high. My neighbor only pays half as much as I do for heat. I've been told that the rates are going up. I can't tell what this increase will mean for my monthly budget. I don't know *what* to do.

To solve a problem ourselves without relying on others, we must come up with ideas that lead to workable solutions. Generating ideas will not, in itself, solve our problems. Unless we are able to generate a variety of possible solutions, however, we have little chance of finding a workable solution. In many ways, our ability to take charge of our lives depends on exercising this ability to generate ideas. When we can come up with no ideas about what to do, like the person described above, we are at the mercy of external circumstances.

Generating ideas is sometimes characterized as the active use of our creative imaginations. It is also described as an act of synthesis—putting thoughts together to get new ones. In either case, generating possibilities is recognized as the basic type of thinking that lies behind *creative thinking*, the generation of original ideas. Our ability to generate ideas is derived from two basic ingredients:

- Our past experience, which furnishes the raw material of creative thought; and
- Our ability to take apart and creatively combine ingredients from past experience.

Imagination plays a key role in this mode of thinking. We sometimes ask, "What would it be like if I tried to…?" For example, what would it be like if I tried to contain the heat in my house? Thinking about containing heat, I imagine a blanket. That idea may lead me to consider ways to "blanket" my house, as with weather stripping, storm windows and doors, and insulation. Using active imagination to generate ideas relies on our ability to detect insightful analogies.

Two frequent manifestations of our ability to generate ideas deserve our attention:

- Generating numerous, varied, and original ideas as possible answers to questions that arise in our personal and professional lives (generating alternative possibilities); and
- Creating analogies that can help us gain and express insight (developing metaphors).

Thinking about possible solutions to problems, generating options to consider in decision making, developing alternative hypotheses to test when we try to find out why certain things are happening, and bringing to mind the possible consequences of our actions or of the events around us are just a few of the ways in which we consider alternative possibilities. Facility in generating possibilities can be developed by techniques such as brainstorming, used judiciously and enhanced by various other explicit strategies.

Poets are not the only ones who thrive on using analogies to develop metaphorical and figurative ways of thinking. Our everyday thinking is so permeated with metaphors that learning to generate them skillfully enhances the way we understand things, as well as our ability to solve problems. Think about how often we say things like "She's a dynamo," "It's a piece of cake," and "We're up the creek." Metaphors are powerful ways of emphasizing and communicating ideas that enhance both focus and deep insight.

Generating ideas helps us to gain insight and to take charge of situations. When we have active minds full of ideas, it becomes more likely that we will find options that work. When we do find such options and act on them, we enhance the sense of our ability to manage our own lives. The positive self-concept that many people have is a function of their ability to generate their own ideas. When you teach students skills at generating ideas, improved self-concept is one important benefit that you will bring them.

CHAPTER 10
GENERATING POSSIBILITIES

Why is it Important to Generate Possibilities Skillfully?

Considering possibilities is a major ingredient in much of our thinking. Could the high incidence of violence on TV be contributing to the increased incidence of violence in the streets? Could economic and social conditions be causing the violence? Finding out the causes of this national trend is essential if we have any hope of reversing it. Considering what these causes might be is a natural first step in this process.

In general, when we are considering what caused some event, the hypotheses we generate for further testing are viewed initially only as possibilities—possible causes. Similarly, when we make decisions and try to solve problems, the options and solutions we develop are viewed as possibilities. Generating ideas and then deciding whether they work are crucial steps in engaging in more complex thinking processes such as decision making and problem solving. Unless we entertain a variety of possibilities as we wonder about causes, effects, options, and solutions, we will not be in a position to accept or reject them as good ideas.

Ideas that we consider can, of course, come to us from other people. Many times the ideas of others prompt us to think of things that we would not have considered independently. Some people, however, depend on other people for their ideas. Nevertheless, they often face challenging situations that they have to deal with themselves. Learning to generate our own ideas frees us from dependence on others and is a major step in the direction of becoming autonomous, self-reliant thinkers. It broadens our thinking in ways that maximize our chances of finding the best solution to problems, making the best choices, determining the best explanation for why things happen, and even developing innovations that improve the quality of life for ourselves and others.

Contexts in Which it is Useful to Think about Possibilities

In practical situations in which we are not sure about what to do, considering possibilities can be very helpful. Major decisions, like buying a house or changing jobs, are better made if we consider our options first. This is true also of more everyday decisions. In planning when to pay this month's bills, I may not be sure whether or not I should set time aside now to do this task. If I consider the possibility of delaying and paying them later, I may realize that such a delay would probably have adverse consequences. Since I have such a tight schedule over the next week, I probably *won't* have time to pay them after today. Because they are due in five days, it then becomes quite likely that I will have to pay additional finance charges if I delay. That's enough to make me decide not to delay any further. I would never have realized this if I had not first entertained the possibility of delaying and then asked what might result if I did delay. If we could only think about things as they are and were not able to bring to mind possibilities that may never happen, the kind of practical reasoning just described would be impossible.

In addition, many of the technological advances which enhance the quality of our lives, like radio, TV, and the automobile, would simply not have been developed unless they had first been considered as possibilities. In one way or another, the great achievements human beings have made throughout history have had their origins in ideas that people have generated for special purposes. If others had not been innovators in developing these ideas, we would not enjoy their beneficial results.

Great works of creative imagination, like Melville's *Moby Dick*, also depend on this simple ability. These works spin out and elaborate ideas that come to their creators as possibilities. Nonetheless, the same processes of thinking are involved in generating these possibilities as are involved when we ask more practical "What-If" questions like "What might happen if I delay paying my bills?"

Problems with the Way We Generate Possibilities

When someone asks what he or she can do in a specific situation, what might have caused some disturbing occurrence, or what can result if he or she does something being considered, it is rare that no possibilities occur to that person. Often, though, the possibilities we think about are very limited. If I want to meet my friend for dinner at a restaurant across town, my first impulse may be to drive the same route I took the last time I went to the restaurant. Without much thinking, I may simply go that way. What is usual, familiar, and traditional often limits what comes to mind, and we often don't think further about it.

We may think in this routine way, but it also may not serve us very well. My route to the restaurant may not be the best one and may take me much longer than a more direct route. If I never think about another way to get there, I certainly won't choose it. The idea of improving things, whether it is how we get to a restaurant, how we prepare a meal, how we express ourselves in writing, or how we teach, will never occur to us unless we break out of our ordinary ways of thinking and consider other possibilities.

Even when we consider other possibilities, they may also be limited. I realize that there are six different routes I could take to the restaurant. These alternatives allow me to choose the most desirable one, perhaps the one with the fewest traffic lights, less traffic, etc. However, when I get to the restaurant, I may find that the parking spaces are all filled and that the nearest parking garage is three blocks away. I realize that I could have taken a taxi or bus and avoided this problem. I didn't even think of that. As with other thinking processes, making decisions is often layered with assumptions. From the outset, when we spread a wide "net" for capturing ideas by considering a range of different types of possi-

bilities, we often call many of our assumptions into question.

Narrowness in thinking suggests another shortcoming in how we generate and consider possibilities. I may, indeed, consider a number of possible ways of getting to the restaurant by alternate routes. I may think about other routine ways of getting there, such as taking a bus or taxi. The best way to get there on this occasion may be among a type of possibilities that I haven't considered at all—something entirely new for me at that time. Perhaps I can borrow my son's bicycle and get there quickly, less expensively, and with easy access to the restaurant. Since I haven't ridden on a bicycle for many years, this means of transportation doesn't come to mind when I think about getting to the restaurant. Or perhaps I could call my friend and move our meeting place to another restaurant. She may not mind and may, in fact, be relieved because she's having the same problem getting there herself.

Moving from routine possibilities to novel ones is very important in considering ideas. Everyone has the ability to generate creative ideas, but few actually do. Breaking free of the constraints of routine or commonly accepted solutions to problems can lead to creative solutions. These alternatives challenge the assumptions we make in the way we typically solve problems, make decisions, and explain things that happen. Modifying aircraft hangars to make them expandable so that they can be moved around aircraft, rather than modifying an aircraft to make it fit the hangar, is a creative possibility for solving the problem of getting large jet planes into conventional hangars. This may not be the best solution to this problem, but we will never find out if we don't generate and consider this possibility.

The significance of considering unusual possibilities in such fields as medicine is also apparent. Researchers trying to isolate the cause of "Lassa fever" didn't consider the possibility that migrants from nearby urban areas were carriers transmitting the disease that was ravaging a rural African community. Believing that the source of the disease was local, they spent considerable time looking for its source in contaminated water, food, etc. within the community. While scientists were running into numerous "dead ends" in their investigation, many more people died of the disease, including some of the researchers themselves. Once the possibility that the disease was brought into the community by infected carriers occurred to them and was confirmed, they knew how to control the disease. If they hadn't thought of this possibility, many more lives would have been lost. However, if they had thought of it earlier, many more lives would have been saved.

Unusual possibilities that break away from routine ways of solving problems and explaining phenomena often provide breakthroughs that add considerably to human advancement and progress. Yet it is far too rare that people think of more than the ordinary ways of doing things when thinking about possibilities.

Finally, we often find fuzziness in people's thinking that blurs the distinction between the possible and the likely. Ideas that might work are just that: ideas that *might* work. Yet many people latch onto possibilities without realizing that they need to do more than just bring these ideas to mind in order to determine that they will work. In the restaurant example, because I think about getting there easily by driving on Elm Street, I may, without any further thought, get into my car and take the Elm Street route. This blurs the distinction between an option and a viable option. I run the risk that if I drive on Elm Street at a certain time of day, I could get caught in a rush-hour traffic jam, constantly stop and start because of the number of traffic lights, or have to take a detour because the road is blocked by construction. Taking another route may have been more satisfactory. Many people slip from "this may happen" to "this will happen" without much thought. When we fail to treat a possibility as only a possibility, we can easily make costly misjudgments.

Figure 10.1 summarizes the four major defaults in the way we bring possibilities to mind for consideration.

How Do We Generate Possibilities Skillfully?

There are strategies for generating possibili-

COMMON DEFAULTS IN THE WAY WE GENERATE POSSIBILITIES

1. We generate very few possibilities.

2. We generate the same type of possibilities only.

3. We generate only routine or ordinary possibilities.

4. We think that possibilities are desirable or likely without any reason.

Figure 10.1

---

ties that we can practice in order to develop the ability to generate a wide range of ideas as needed. The free association of ideas is sometimes mentioned as one such strategy. While free association does generate many ideas, generating a range of possibilities for consideration is not the same thing as free association. Generating possibilities is always conducted in a context and with a purpose that constrains the possibilities that we consider by requiring that they must be possible ways of solving a problem, of making a decision, of explaining an event, etc. Since we think about possibilities in specific contexts, this suggests that a more organized strategy should be used to generate possibilities skillfully.

Attention Points in Generating Possibilities Skillfully

The first important thing to keep in mind when generating possibilities is *what these possibilities are for*. What is the issue that creates the need for a consideration of possibilities?

- I may face a problem: How can I finish my work before I leave on vacation?

- I may want to anticipate what will happen in a certain context so that I can plan well: What can I expect if I introduce this new sex education program into my school?

- I may want to find out what is causing something so that I can fix it: Why does the plaster keep flaking off my kitchen wall?

Identifying the context for considering possibilities is the first step in bringing these possibilities to mind.

To generate possibilities skillfully within a specific context we should attend to four basic points: generating many ideas, generating different types of ideas, generating unusual ideas, and adding details to these ideas. We should take the time to develop a number of alternative possibilities that apply to this particular issue. But we should also make sure that we consider a range of different types of possibilities, that we strive for novel ones, and that we treat these ideas as mere possibilities not yet judged to be viable solutions.

Writers on creativity often distinguish these aspects of idea generation as involving *fluency* (generating a multiplicity of ideas), *flexibility* (generating ideas of different types), and *originality* (generating unusual ideas that have as yet not been tried in dealing with this particular issue). *Elaboration* (providing details of the ideas we are advancing) is another desirable feature of our ability to generate ideas. *Deferred judgment* (not yet taking a stand on which of these ideas is viable to meet the issue) is an attitude we should adopt about the ideas we generate in order to recognize them as possibilities and in order not to make premature judgments about which will work.

Brainstorming

Brainstorming is, of course, the technique commonly used to generate a rich set of possibilities. But research indicates that simple brainstorming is not enough. Just listing possibilities may not involve much variety or originality. Quantity of ideas does not lead automatically to quality.

To enhance variety we can deliberately make sure we have listed different kinds of possibilities. In the case of getting to the restaurant to meet my friend, I might deliberately ask myself, Have I thought about other ways to get there? A more strategic way to do this is to categorize the ideas I have come up with and ask two questions: "What other possibilities fall into these categories?" and "Are there any other categories that I might want to consider?" For example, I might classify the six routes for getting to the restaurant as ways of driving myself there. When I realize that I have not yet consid-

ered being transported by others, I then can easily come up with taking a taxi, a bus, or even asking a neighbor to drive me. Under the category of being self-propelled, I then might ask, What are other ways that I can transport myself besides using a car? A bicycle might then come to mind.

Innovation and Invention: Strategies for Generating Original Ideas

Variety may not lead to originality. Have I thought of anything new and original? Simply asking myself this question is often enough to prompt new possibilities that are, indeed, quite original. Maybe my friend can drive to my location, and we can rent a horse-drawn carriage to take us to the restaurant. If I were thinking of a romantic evening, that would add some glamour to the way we get to the restaurant.

If original ideas don't come so easily, there are techniques that can be used to bring them out. For example, listing features of some of the possibilities already generated and then combining some of these features may lead to a new possibility. A bicycle has two wheels and is powered by the action of pedals. A carriage can transport me and my friend together. Perhaps we could take a two-wheeled vehicle powered by pedals that can transport two people: a bicycle built for two.

While some novel ideas may be wild and impractical, others may not be. We will never find out unless we think of them. While we often have to dispense with original ideas because they are impractical, it only takes one good idea to achieve our goal.

In this aspect of generating possibilities, we can use the full potential of our creative imaginations to develop new and original ways of doing things and solving problems. This is why generating possibilities, as a mode of thinking, falls within the domain of creative thinking. When we search for novel ways of solving problems, we draw upon ingredients in our past experience and combine or connect them in new ways to develop new ideas. Novel solutions that work provide us with truly creative products that enrich and enhance the quality of our lives. Putting into practice original, viable ideas that serve our interests or needs is a mark of the truly creative thinker.

Emphasizing originality after working on quantity and variety in brainstorming yields the greatest potential for generating creative ideas. An effective strategy for doing this combines the ideas we have just discussed:

1. Categorize the possibilities derived from an initial brainstorming session;

2. Add new possibilities under these categories;

3. Suggest new categories; and

4. Combine categories to stimulate new possibilities that blend possibilities already on our list.

Suspending judgment during brainstorming makes brainstorming an excellent technique in carrying out this strategy.

This four-part strategy is especially useful if routine ways of doing things have their limitations. Improving products or practices that do not work well, composing and revising creative works of writing and art, as well as inventing new devices to meet needs that are not met by the present technology are common, but significant, contexts for generating new ideas. So, of course, are the more numerous opportunities for creative thinking in our own jobs and personal lives.

In generating possibilities through brainstorming, many people put a premium on original ideas. Indeed, we commonly stop short of the kind of thinking needed to create novel ideas when we are generating possibilities for consideration. However, when we decide which possibility to accept, it is inappropriate to *prefer* original ideas to routine ones just because they are original. Possibilities are only possibilities. If routine possibilities still give us the best options, these should be preferred to novel options which may not work as well. Renting a helicopter and lowering myself to the restaurant on a rope ladder may be a novel way to get a meal, but I shouldn't prefer it just because it is novel.

Assessing Possibilities

To assure that we are open to all possibilities until we have a reason for preferring one, we should think about what would make any of these possibilities preferable to others. What are the criteria for choosing one possibility among the ideas that we are considering? In the case of decision making, we should choose the option that leads to the best consequences. In the case of causal and predictive hypotheses, selection should be made on the basis of the evidence. Asking "What would make a possibility I am considering a viable one?" helps us to keep in mind that these possibilities require support to be accepted.

On the other hand, in contexts in which originality and creative elaboration are of utmost concern, creativity may be a determining criterion for choosing among the possibilities being considered. When our purpose is to develop creative products, such as stories or plays (especially fantasy) or visual works of art, seeking original ways to express ideas and insights is important. Then, all other things being equal, it is appropriate to put a premium on the more creative possibilities.

The strategy for brainstorming that we use in this chapter is effective in these contexts as well. It can help us to generate original ideas about how to express ourselves, just as it can help us to generate original ideas about our solutions to personal or professional problems. It prepares us to think through which modes of expression will be more effective.

Contexts for Brainstorming

Brainstorming can be done by individuals or in groups. Research on brainstorming indicates that ideas come faster, and with more variety, if the brainstorming is conducted within a group in an open exchange of ideas. Group members often get ideas by listening to the ideas of others in the group. If you engage in this process, generating possibilities is usually richer when carried out in a group, compared to working alone.

Thinking Maps and Graphic Organizers for the Skillful Generation of Possibilities

The thinking map in figure 10.2 shows a sequence of questions to prompt skillfully generating possibilities for consideration. Notice that the sequence of questions moves from a request for quantity to a request for variety and then to a request for originality. This sequence is important in developing viable, original possibilities.

The graphic organizer in figure 10.3 supplements the thinking prompted by the thinking map.

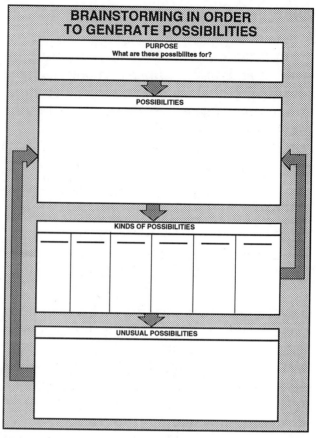

GENERATING POSSIBILITIES SKILLFULLY

1. What is the task for which you are considering possibilities?

2. What possibilities can you think of?

3. What are some other types of possibilities?

4. What original or unusual possibilities can you generate by combining possibilities already listed?

5. What information would you need in order to decide which of these possibilities is best for the task?

Figure 10.2

Figure 10.3

To use this graphic organizer, first state the purpose for the possibilities. For example, if they are for solving a specific problem, the problem should be mentioned. If they are for determining the causes of something, that should be mentioned.

As free-wheeling brainstorming occurs, every possibility that is mentioned should be put in the next box. Suspending judgment about whether these are good ideas should be explicitly advocated.

The next box is used to organize the suggested possibilities into categories, to add other categories that are missing, and to add more possibilities under new and already-established categories. Write the categories on the short horizontal lines, and list under each category the possibilities of that type. For example, if the possibilities are for getting to the restaurant, "In an internally-propelled vehicle" might be one category. Under it I would list "by car," "by taxi," and "by bus." A new category that I might add is "In a self-propelled vehicle." Under that I could add

"by bicycle." Any new additions should be circled and then added to the possibilities box.

A graphic organizer for the third step in this process is a webbing diagram, figure 10.4.

What the possibilities are for should be written in the circle. Types of possibilities already listed should be written in the boxes attached to the circle, leaving some of these free for new categories. Write possibilities that fall into these categories in the outer boxes. New possibilities should be added. All new possibilities should then be transferred to the main brainstorming diagram. The number of boxes on this diagram can be expanded as needed. A free-flowing cognitive map can also be constructed for this purpose.

The last step in using the brainstorming diagram (figure 10.3) involves generating original possibilities. We should transfer the original or unusual possibilities already listed in the top box to the lower one. Additional original ideas can be developed by combining features of other ideas from the original list and adding them to

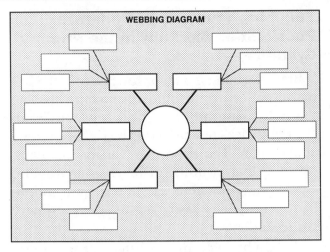

Figure 10.4

the lower box. The matrix in figure 10.5 can be used to combine ideas to develop more original and creative possibilities.

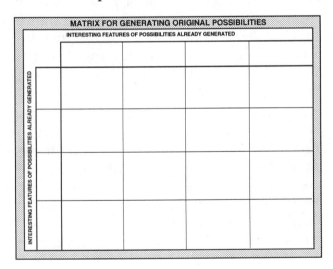

Figure 10.5

To use this matrix, list some of the categories that appear on the brainstorming diagram across the top and down the side. The ones listed down the side can be the same as or different from the ones across the top. Then, where feasible, combine them and develop a new possibility around the combination. For example, "Using a vehicle propelled by pedal action" might be one feature listed on the left and "Using a vehicle that can hold two people" on the top. Combining the two can yield "Using a bicycle built for two" in the intersecting cell.

Add the new possibilities generated in this

way to the lower box of the brainstorming diagram (figure 10.3). They, in turn, should be added to the possibilities box to create a large collection of varied possibilities, including a number of original ones, the goal of the first four steps in the strategy.

Considering what criteria we should use to determine which possibilities are feasible, reasonable, or desirable rounds out this thinking skill. These criteria will, of course, be determined by the purpose of generating the possibilities, for example, whether these are options in decision making, possible causes, or possible uses of something.

How Can We Teach Students to Generate Possibilities Skillfully?

To teach students to generate possibilities skillfully, it is not enough to ask students simply to list possibilities for something. They should attend to variety in the types of possibilities that they come up with and should suggest original or unusual possibilities. Write down their suggestions as they think of them. With this guided practice, you should prompt your students to reflect on how they develop these ideas so that they can guide themselves in this strategy.

Encouraging original ideas through brainstorming is very important in the classroom. Even though some ideas may be very imaginative, if not fantastic, and may be rejected later as not feasible, they should be both supported and encouraged. Permission to include even the most fantastic possibilities will allow students to start to develop broader, more creative habits of thought. Then, when highly imaginative ideas are needed (as in creative writing) these students will be adept at generating such ideas.

Contexts in the Content Areas for Generating Possibilities Lessons

Contexts in the curriculum in which students engage in decision making, problem solving, causal explanation, and prediction provide opportunities for teaching the strategy for generating ideas. I might design a lesson emphasizing generating options for a decision without guiding students in the whole process of decision making. What options did settlers have in making the long trip from east of the Mississippi to California in the mid-nineteenth century? Or I may embed instruction in generating possibilities in the context of finding a cause for something: What possible causes might explain the disappearance of the colonists from the lost colony of Roanoke?

Students particularly enjoy brainstorming the possible uses of something. While this is commonly practiced in artificial, decontextualized activities, it is often an effective component in working through problems that call for creative solutions. For infusion lessons, the uses of various tools in industrial arts classes or the uses of mathematical procedures are good examples of curriculum-robust contexts for this type of activity.

The curriculum contains an additional type of context for lessons on generating possibilities:

- *Students are asked directly to develop and elaborate possibilities in creative work.* For example, students are taught how to develop and structure short stories. What they write about is often a creative possibility that they elaborate in the story. Generating the idea behind the story can be an excellent context for generating an interesting and creative possibility for plot structure. In the arts, generating possibilities is basic to composition and design.

While teaching students to generate ideas skillfully is important, it rarely is useful in isolation. Encourage students to reflect on occasions when it would be useful to engage in this type of thinking. This task is easy if generating possibilities is taught in the context of a decision problem, a problem about cause, etc. If not, it is important to ask students to suggest situations in which it would be useful to engage in this kind of thinking.

A menu of suggested contexts for infusion lessons on generating possibilities is provided on pages 311-12.

Teaching Students to Generate Possibilities Skillfully in the Primary Grades

Brainstorming is a favorite activity in the primary grades. Young students quickly develop the risk-taking attitudes promoted by brainstorming ideas not judged to be right or wrong at the time. The enhanced version of brainstorming that we utilize in this chapter provides a generating-possibilities strategy in a simplified form that is easily mastered by primary grade students.

Using a brainstorming strategy prompts students to draw on their knowledge and experience. Obviously, in the primary grades, students have less background than students in the upper elementary grades. Make sure that the topic that you ask students to brainstorm about is familiar enough to enable them to draw upon an appropriate range of background knowledge. At the same time, you may be quite surprised at how much knowledge your students already have that can be brought out in brainstorming activities.

Brainstorming in a group is, therefore, especially important in the primary grades. It often leads to one student's ideas stimulating the thinking of other students—"piggybacking." In brainstorming possible uses for a brick, for example, one student may say "To hold down papers and keep them from blowing away." This may prompt another to say "To hold down my clothes at the beach to keep them from blowing away." The second student probably would not have thought of that possibility if the first student had not mentioned holding down papers. Encourage this type of cross-fertilization to enhance your students' thinking. Perhaps the most direct way to do this is to explain the idea of piggybacking to your students and then ask them to do it. They will easily.

The thinking map in figure 10.6 is appropriate for use in the primary grades to help students skillfully generate possibilities.

The same graphic organizers introduced earlier can be used in the primary grades to supplement this simplified strategy for generating possibilities.

FINDING POSSIBILITIES

1. Why do you want to find possibilities?

2. What possibilities can you think of?

3. What are some other kinds of possibilities?

4. What are some unusual possibilities?

5. How can you decide which is the best possibility?

Figure 10.6

Model Lessons on Generating Possibilities

We include one model lesson on the skillful generation of possibilities. It is an upper elementary lesson in science/social studies on the use of natural resources and recycling what are considered waste products. This lesson can easily be adapted for the lower elementary grades.

As you read this lesson, reflect on these questions:

- What specific strategies are included in this lesson to promote the generation of creative ideas by students?

- Are there other ways of helping students to recognize contexts for the use of this skill in their own lives?

- What additional examples can you find for reinforcing this skill after it is taught?

Tools for Designing Lessons on Generating Possibilities

The primary level thinking map (see p. 299) is a simplified version of the standard map for generating possibilities. The two thinking maps, as well as the graphic organizers that follow have multiple uses.

The thinking maps and graphic organizers can serve as photocopy masters, transparency masters, or as models that can be enlarged and used as posters in the classroom. Reproduction rights are granted for single classroom use only.

GENERATING POSSIBILITIES SKILLFULLY

1. **What is the task for which you are considering possibilities?**

2. **What possibilities can you think of?**

3. **What are some other types of possibilities?**

4. **What original or unusual possibilities can you generate by combining possibilities already listed?**

5. **What information would you need in order to decide which of these possibilities is best for the task?**

FINDING POSSIBILITIES

1. **Why do you want to find possibilities?**

2. **What possibilities can you think of?**

3. **What are some other types of possibilities?**

4. **What are some unusual possibilities?**

5. **How can you decide which is the best possibility?**

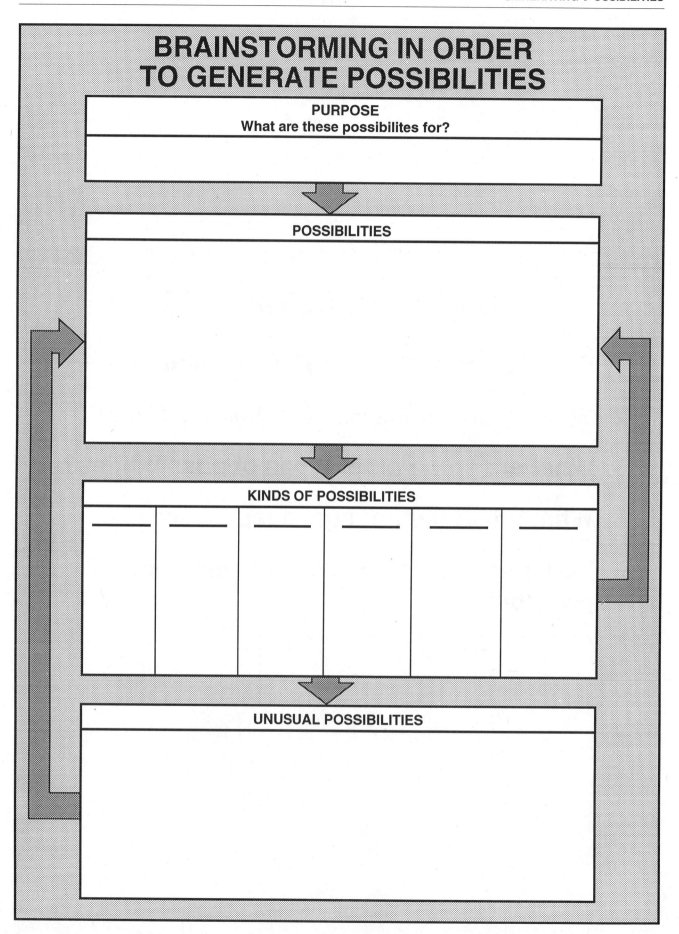

BRAINSTORMING IN ORDER TO GENERATE POSSIBILITIES

PURPOSE
What are these possibilites for?

POSSIBILITIES

KINDS OF POSSIBILITIES

UNUSUAL POSSIBILITIES

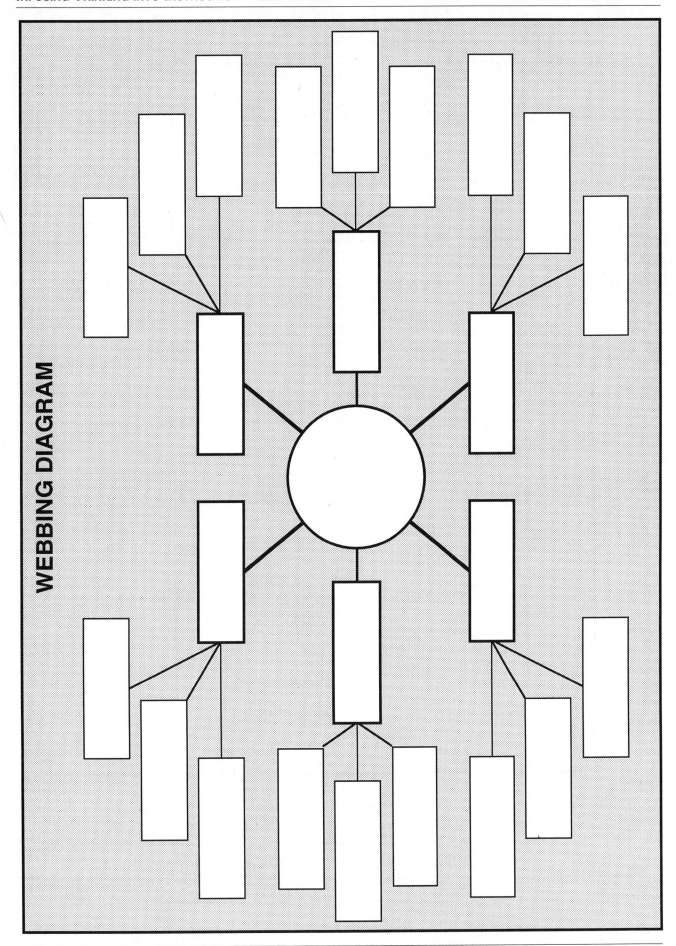

WEBBING DIAGRAM

MATRIX FOR GENERATING ORIGINAL POSSIBILITIES

INTERESTING FEATURES OF POSSIBILITIES ALREADY GENERATED

INTERESTING FEATURES OF POSSIBILITIES ALREADY GENERATED

THE PILE OF DIRT

Science **Grades 4–6**

OBJECTIVES

CONTENT
Students will learn that ordinary soil is a natural resource containing many components that have a variety of uses.

THINKING SKILL/PROCESS
Students will learn to generate possibilities skillfully in the context of solving a problem, by brainstorming a variety of ideas, and by combining ideas to generate new and original ones.

METHODS AND MATERIALS

CONTENT
Students will read in their textbooks about the composition of soil and will examine soil samples.

THINKING SKILL/PROCESS
An explicit thinking map, graphic organizers, and structured questioning facilitate a thinking strategy for generating possible uses for something. (See pp. 298–302 for reproducible diagrams.) Collaborative learning enhances the thinking.

LESSON

INTRODUCTION TO CONTENT AND THINKING SKILL/PROCESS

- Have you ever solved a problem by coming up with an unusual way of doing something? For example, I found that the window shade in my office had rolled up beyond my reach. I thought of some ways that I could get it down. I could climb up on a chair to reach it or push a broom handle through the pull loop. However, the chair wasn't sturdy enough to hold me and the broom would slip out of the loop before I could reach it. I thought for a minute, looked around my bedroom for something else that I might use, and then had an idea. I took a coat hanger, stretched it out, made a long hook out of it, and used it to pull the shade down.

- What I did was *problem solving*. I recognized that there was a problem, thought of a number of ways of solving it, thought about whether some of these solutions would work, and then figured out how to do it best. My solution was a creative solution because I used something that is not normally used for this purpose. Describe to your partner a time when you used something in a new way to solve a problem. After a few minutes, ask three or four students to describe what they had done. ANSWERS VARY.

- Whenever you come up with new ideas and put them into practice, you are doing *creative thinking*: you do something new that works that you haven't thought of before. Explain what you thought about that helped you discover a new way to use something to solve your problem. Students often say that they didn't have what they needed, so they started thinking about other things they could use or other ways to solve the problem. Some students say that they pictured using another object (like the coat hanger) altered in a way that would solve the problem. If using the object seemed to do the job, they tried it; if not, they considered another idea.

- We've discussed creative ways to solve a problem. You solved your problem because you thought of many ways to do it and picked a possible solution that worked. Whenever you come up with lots of new ideas, you are *generating possibilities*. This is a very important step in problem solving. You wouldn't solve your problem unless you thought of a good way to do it. We're going to try out a way to do this kind of thinking that will lead to many new and original ideas. These questions will guide us in this kind of thinking. Show the thinking map for generating possibilities skillfully.

• In this lesson, we're going to see if we can find new ways of using something that is very ordinary. We've been studying how people make use of natural resources around them, like minerals, wood, and water. But some natural resources aren't usually thought of as valuable. We're going to work on one such thing: the ordinary dirt that you find in vacant lots, in yards, and in the woods.

THINKING ACTIVELY

• Suppose your parents are having a new house built and the workers have dug a large hole for the foundation. They've put the soil from the hole in a pile next to it. The pile of dirt is called a "by-product" of an industrial activity. Usually a truck picks up the dirt and takes it somewhere to dump it, but you and your parents don't like to throw away things that might be useful. They ask you to help them think of different uses for the pile of dirt. Then they'll try to figure out which is the best use for the dirt.

• One way to generate ideas is called "brainstorming." When you brainstorm, you try to think of as many ideas as you can about something. At this point, you don't try to decide whether these ideas will work. You can do that later. You just let your mind go and come up with as many ideas as you can. In this case, our purpose for brainstorming is to come up with a lot of ideas about different uses for the pile of dirt. Write that purpose in the first box on the diagram for generating possibilities. Then brainstorm with a group of three other students. List the uses for dirt that you come up with in the possibilities box. Try to come up with five possibilities or more. After about five minutes, ask the students whether they are finding it easy or hard to come up with more ideas. Many say that they can't think of any more beyond the five or ten that their group has already listed on the diagram. Ask the groups to report their ideas. As they report, write their ideas on a large class diagram (on the board, on a transparency, or on a poster) for brainstorming to generate possibilities. POSSIBLE ANSWERS: *Spread the soil over the rest of the building site. Advertise it and sell it to someone who needs it to fill in a hole. Package it as potting soil for house plants. Take the worms out and sell them for bait to fishermen. Send it to schools to study life in the soil. Leave it where it is for sledding in the winter. Fill bags with it and give it to the city to use when the river is in danger of flooding.*

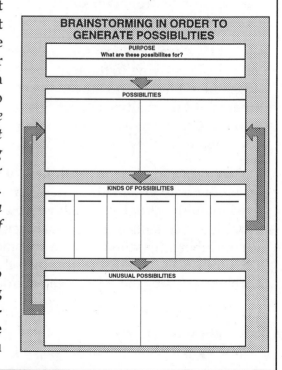

• Many of you have said that it was hard to come up with any more ideas. We're going to do something different now that will help you generate more possibilities. Work again in your groups and arrange the list of possibilities into categories. For example, you can put "Using it as a sled run" under the category "Used for Fun." Write these categories on the horizontal lines in the "Kinds of Possibilities" box. Under the horizontal lines, list the possibilities that fall into those categories. Try to think of new possibilities and add them under the appropriate categories. For example, under "Used for Fun," you might add "Bicycle run." Any new possibilities should be underlined and added to the possibilities box. After a few minutes, ask for reports on some of the students' categories, as well new possibilities that they've added. Write these on the class diagram, underlining the new ones. POSSIBLE CATEGORIES AND NEW POSSIBILITIES: *Moving the soil elsewhere (spread it over the building site, use it to fill a hole elsewhere, fill bags with it and give it to the city to use when the river is in danger of overflowing, bring it to the playground and make a hill with tunnels). Taking things out of the soil (extract the worms, have students in a science class extract the living things from the soil and study them, package the soil as potting soil for house plants, extract the rocks and use them in a rock garden). Used for fun (sled run, bicycle run, ski run, mud slide, mud castles, mud balls). Used for learning (students in a science class study the living things in the soil, test the impact of acid rain on the soil).*

• **Now work with your groups to add at least one new category. For example, a new category might be "Mixing it with other things." Next, list at least two possibilities under that category. For example, you could add "Mix it with water and make mud bricks" to this new category. What other things could you make by mixing the dirt with something else? Let's try this first in the whole class, then you add a new category to your diagram and list at least two new possibilities.** Ask students for new possibilities and add them to the diagram. Underline them. SOME NEW POSSIBILITIES: *Mix it with water to make mud balls. Mix it with compost to make good top soil. Mix it with rocks to make dirt that can be used on a dirt road.* **I've underlined these new possibilities because they weren't on the original list; I will add them to the possibilities box. You do the same when you add possibilities under your new category.** Add the new possibilities to the possibilities box. After another few minutes, ask for some reports about other new categories and possibilities and add these to the class diagram. POSSIBLE NEW CATEGORIES AND NEW POSSIBILITIES: *Used as an environment for living things (grow grass on it and make it into a grassy hill; put a fence around it, put goats inside, and feed them regularly; make it into a huge ant hill; plant trees on it). Put things in it (bury trash in it, hollow it out and store apples there to keep them fresh, bury a treasure there for a treasure hunt). Use it for building (hollow it out and use it as a club house, put it on the roof of the house that is being built and make a sod roof). Use it for health and beauty aids (extract minerals from it, make a mud pack for a facial). Use it for decoration (make terraria with it, put it in flower pots and plant bulbs in the pots).* **Notice how many new possibilities are brought out by this way of organizing your thinking. Is this a good way to add to the variety of ideas you came up with in brainstorming? Do you think you would have thought of these possibilities if we hadn't categorized them first?** Many students say that they wouldn't have thought of these new ideas if we had only brainstormed. They reiterate that they were finding it hard to add other ideas to their lists and say that categorizing helped them to come up with new ideas.

• **Now let's think about the ideas you've come up with that are unusual. These ideas involve your creative thinking. We're going to use a technique that will help you generate many more creative ideas. This time work individually with your diagram for generating possibilities. From your possibilities list, choose all of the ideas that you think are unusual or original. Write these in the last box of the diagram. Now let's generate some other unusual possibilities by using a different**

MATRIX FOR GENERATING ORIGINAL POSSIBILITIES

INTERESTING FEATURES OF POSSIBILITIES ALREADY GENERATED

INTERESTING FEATURES OF POSSIBILITIES ALREADY GENERATED

diagram. The matrix for generating original possibilities is used to combine ideas to generate new and original possibilities. Choose four of your categories and write them across the top and again down the side of the diagram. Then try to blend them together. Write in the boxes of the matrix any new possibilities that these combinations suggest. After a few minutes, ask the students to select one of the newly-developed possibilities that seems interesting or worth considering and share it with a partner. Then ask a few of the teams to report on one of their ideas. Ask them to explain why it seems worth considering. POSSIBLE ANSWERS: *Combining transporting the dirt with using it for something that is fun (take it up in a space shuttle and eject it into the upper atmosphere at night so that the particles will fall back to Earth and burn up to create a great meteoric display visible from the earth). Combining mixing the dirt with something else and using it in building (mix it with water and clay, make bricks, dry them, and use them to build a house). Combining moving it with using it for something that is fun (take it to the playground and make a hill with tunnels for children to play in).*

- **Now we've generated a list of many more interesting possibilities for using the pile of dirt. If you hadn't used this diagram for combining categories, would you have thought of these ideas?** Many students say they wouldn't have and that the diagram helped them to think of new possibilities.

- **When we began this activity, I said that people think that there is only one thing they can do with the pile of dirt left after digging a foundation: dump it. However, it just took a little thinking to come up with a large number of ideas. We have to be careful, though. Sometimes ideas that seem really great at the outset turn out to be not so good after we think about them a little. Discuss with your partner some circumstances in which it might make sense to use the soil in some of the ways now included in the possibilities box. For example, if the building site is damp and needs more fill, but fill is not easily obtainable in this region of the country, it might make sense to spread this dirt over the rest of the building site. With your partner, elaborate some circumstances for some of the other possibilities.** Ask for some reports. ANSWERS VARY. For example, some students might say that taking the soil up in a space vehicle might make sense in the following circumstances: *the Fourth of July is coming soon and it is the 50th anniversary of the first space flight; some spectacular show is needed for the celebration and 50,000 people have contributed two dollars each to pay for the event.*

- **Work with your group. To help you decide which use of the soil is best, write the various things you would want to find out about each of them. Use the descriptions of the circumstances in which these uses make sense. Jot them down so that you can share them with the class.** POSSIBLE ANSWERS: *Whether there is a need to use the soil in this way, how much it would cost, whether it would please people if the soil were used in that way, whether anyone might get hurt if the soil were used in that way, whether there was a better way to do the thing without using the soil, whether it would take a long time to use the soil that way, whether the purpose for which we would be using the soil is an important one.*

THINKING ABOUT THINKING

- **What questions were important to answer as you did this kind of thinking?** Students should mention at least the questions that are on the thinking map for generating possibilities. If they are having trouble, point to some of these questions and ask if each was a question we asked. Students identify the following questions: *What are some possible ways to use the soil? What other kinds of uses are there besides the ones mentioned? Are there any unusual or original uses? How can you decide which use is best?*

- **What kind of thinking did these questions lead you to do?** POSSIBLE ANSWERS: *Generating possible uses of something. Generating possibilities. Brainstorming possibilities.*

- **How did you think of the ideas you first listed when you brainstormed?** POSSIBLE ANSWERS: *I thought of one possible way of using the soil: by extracting the worms. Then I thought of other things that could be extracted, like seedlings for replanting. That led me to think about who does the replanting, usually a gardener. So I thought of how a gardener might use the soil, and I came up with planting a garden.*

- **Is this a good way to try to generate ideas? Why or why not?** POSSIBLE ANSWERS: *We can get a lot of ideas this way. We have a chance to develop some really original ideas that we can test out later.*

- **Consider the thinking map I showed you at the beginning of the lesson. Is this a good way to form questions to guide you for the next time you want to generate possibilities? If not, how would you change it?** Most students say that this is a good way to organize the questions.

- **In this activity, you worked in groups. Is this a good way to do brainstorming or would you rather work on your own? Why?** Most students say that they like to work in groups because they get ideas from other students. If it comes up, identify this as "piggy-backing." Some students, say, however, that they would rather work alone because other students don't let them talk or because what other students say makes them confused. If these problems come up, ask the class to treat it as a creative thinking/problem solving task: how can the group work be managed so that these problems do not arise?

- **The next time you have to generate possibilities, how will you do it? Will the diagrams we used help you? What will you do with them?** ANSWERS VARY.

APPLYING YOUR THINKING

IMMEDIATE TRANSFER

- When we studied ancient Egypt, we learned that the pyramids are a reminder of this great civilization. Imagine you are in charge of building the pyramids. The plan is to build them of massive stone blocks. These blocks must be quarried, transported to the site, and moved into place. Select one of these tasks, and do some creative thinking to generate possible ways of accomplishing it.

- Think about the long trip west to California that many people made in the 19th Century. Imagine that your class is trying to compose a musical that will represent the pioneering spirit as well as the dangers of the trip. You won't be composing any music yourselves, but you may select any popular or classical music that you think will convey the ideas and feelings of the California movement. Brainstorm different ways of starting the musical that combine music, stage setting, and a story.

REINFORCEMENT LATER

- Many wars have been fought because of disputes of different countries over territory, resources, etc. Pick a war that you have studied. Brainstorm alternatives to violence as a way of settling the dispute that caused the war. What might the countries have done to avoid fighting with each other?

- Suppose that a veterinarian has prescribed large capsules that your pet dog must swallow once a day. List as many different ways you can think of to get your dog to take the capsule.

Include lots of creative ideas. What would you need to find out in order to choose the best way to get your dog to take the medication?

ASSESSING STUDENT THINKING ABOUT POSSIBILITIES

To assess the ability to generate possibilities, select examples that challenge students to generate a wide range of ideas. Any of the transfer examples can serve as assessment items for written or oral responses. Developing multiple uses for common objects is a task that is often used to demonstrate this kind of thinking. Challenging problem-solving tasks in which you emphasize generating alternative solutions are also excellent vehicles for this type of assessment. Use the thinking map for generating possibilities as a guide to check that students are focusing their attention on the three basic factors for generating good ideas: quantity, variety, and originality.

Sample Student Responses • The Pile of Dirt

BRAINSTORMING IN ORDER TO GENERATE POSSIBILITIES

PURPOSE
What are these possibilites for?

The use of a pile of dirt left after a foundation hole is dug at a building site.

POSSIBILITIES

Spread it over the rest of the site.	Use it as a hill for a bicycle run.
Sell it to someone who needs fill.	Use it as a mud slide.
Package it as potting soil for plants.	Mix it with water to make mud balls.
Extract the worms and sell them.	Mix it with compost to make rich topsoil.
Use it in school to study life in the soil.	Mix it with rocks to put on a dirt road.
Use it as a winter sledding run.	Grow grass on it.
Bag it and use it on river banks to prevent flooding.	Make it into a fenced goat hill.
Dump it in a vacant lot.	Make it into a huge ant hill.
Extract the rocks for a rock garden.	Plant trees on it for a shady knoll.
Bury a treasure in it for a treasure hunt.	Bury trash in it.
Hollow it and use it as a club house.	Store apples in it.
Use it for a sod roof.	Use it for a meteoric display in the atmosphere.
Use it for mud packs for facials.	Mix it with water and clay to make bricks.
Make terreria with it.	Make a hill with tunnels for children in the playground.
Put it in flower pots and plant bulbs in the pots.	Make a travelling mud-wrestling show.

Moving elsewhere	Extracting Things	Used for fun	Used for learning	Mixed with something
Spread over site.	Sell worms.	Winter sled run.	Study living things.	Water for mud balls.
Fill hole elsewhere.	Study living things.	Bicycle run.	Test impact of acid	Compost for top soil.
Bags for flooding.	Potting soil.	Winter ski run.	rain.	Rocks for dirt for
	Rocks for garden.	Mud slide.		road.
		Mud balls.		

Habitat	Putting things in	Health & Beauty	Decoration	Building
Grow grass.	Bury trash.	Minerals for health.	Make terraria.	Hollow for club
Goat hill.	Store apples.	Mud pack for facials.	Put in pots and plant	house.
Ant hill.	Bury treasure.		bulbs.	Sod roof.
Plant trees.				

UNUSUAL POSSIBILITIES

Extract and sell worms.	Send it up in the space shuttle and eject it into the atmosphere for a meteoric display.
Hollow it for a club house.	Mix it with water and clay and make bricks for building.
Use it for mud packs for facials.	Take it to the playground and make a hill with tunnels for children to play in.
Bury a treasure for a treasure hunt.	Put it in the back of a truck, mix it with water, and have a travelling mud-wrestling show.
Extract rocks for a rock garden.	
Make it into a fenced goat hill.	

Sample Student Responses • The Pile of Dirt • Original Possibilities

MATRIX FOR GENERATING ORIGINAL POSSIBILITIES

INTERESTING FEATURES OF POSSIBILITIES ALREADY GENERATED	Move It Elsewhere	Use it for Fun	Use it in Building	Mix with Something
Move It Elsewhere	✕	Take it up in the space shuttle and eject it into the atmosphere for a great meteoric display visible from Earth.	Use it to build a ramp that cement trucks can drive on to pour cement into a form for a new, high, prison wall.	Mix it with fertilizer and move it to a place on the property where it can be used to start a garden.
Use it for Fun	Take it to the playground and make a hill with tunnels for children to play in.	✕	Build a dirt model of the castle at Disney World.	Mix it with water, put it in the back of a truck, and make it into a travelling mud-wrestling show.
Use it in Building	Move it to a river that has to be dammed up and use it to build a dam. Add large rocks to hold it in place.	Hollow it out and make it into a haunted house that people can visit on Haloween.	✕	Mix it with grass seed and use it to make the sod roof of your new house.
Mix with Something	Move it to a road construction site, mix it with more dirt from other building sites, and use it to build up the road bed.	Mix it with water, put it in an empty swimming pool, and use it for mud wrestling.	Mix it with water and clay; make bricks, dry them, and use them in building.	✕

(Header column label: **INTERESTING FEATURES OF POSSIBILITIES ALREADY GENERATED**)

LESSON CONTEXTS FOR GENERATING POSSIBILITIES

The following examples have been suggested by classroom teachers as contexts to develop infused lessons. If a skill or process has been introduced in a previous infusion lesson, transfer activities can be designed in these contexts to reinforce it.

GRADE	SUBJECT	TOPIC	THINKING ISSUE
K–3	Literature	*The Lorax*	What are some creative possibilities for the Lorax to make thneeds without causing the problems described in the book?
K–3	Literature	*On Beyond Zebra*	Describe what the speaker did to come up with letters beyond our alphabet. Do same thing and come up with other letters that you can add to his list.
K–3	Literature	*What Mary Jo Shared*	What could Mary Jo show to her class that no other student would have? Brainstorm some possibilities.
K–3	Literature	*Josephine's Imagination*	How might Josephine get a doll? What are some possible ways to get a doll? How would you decide which is the best way?
K–3	Literature	*Oh, The Thinks You Could Think*	How does Dr. Seuss say that we can create new ideas from old ones? Why does that make the book likeable? Create some new ideas yourself the same way Dr. Seuss does.
K–3	Social Studies	Colonial America	The Thanksgiving feast was a way that the British settlers showed gratitude to the Native Americans who occupied the land where they settled. In what other ways could the settlers have shown friendship to the Indians?
K–3	Social Studies	Neighborhoods	One of the problems faced by a neighborhood is litter. With your partner, brainstorm ways that the people in your neighborhood could keep your neighborhood clean.
K–3	Science	Dinosaurs	Select three dinosaurs that have characteristics that you believe would help them survive and that you would like to see in animals today. Create a new dinosaur that combines these qualities. Draw and name your dinosaur. Describe its needs and habits.
K–3	Health	Ears	List a number of possibilities that let you enjoy the music at a concert while keeping your ears from getting damaged.
K–3	Health	Diet	What foods could you add to those you usually eat to make a balanced diet? Include some original possibilities.
K–3	Health	Pollution	Pollution can occur in school as well as outside school. Select one type of pollution you notice in school. Generate many possible ways of preventing it. Include some original possibilities.
K–3	Art	Murals	Brainstorm several ways that you can enlarge a drawing to create a mural.
K–3	Music	Musical effects	What are some ways to get the effect of animal sounds into a piece of music?
K–3	Guidance	Television viewing	Suppose that you realize that you should watch television less often. What can you and your family do to ensure that you spend your viewing time on the shows that you most want to see? How can you break the habit of just turning on the television set?

LESSON CONTEXTS FOR GENERATING POSSIBILITIES

GRADE	SUBJECT	TOPIC	THINKING ISSUE
4–6	Literature	Greek myths	Create a new god for Mt. Olympus that combines some of the traits of the traditional Greek gods. Explain how the new god got those traits and how the new god would relate to others.
4–6	Literature	Greek myths	Suppose that a thirteenth labor was required of Hercules. Create this new task based his other labors.
4–6	Social studies	Slavery	Find other ways to rescue slaves and help them get to freedom. Compare your ideas to some that were tried.
4–6	Mathematics	Computers	What application not currently used could computers have in the future?
4–6	Science	Asteroids	How might we use asteroids?
4–6	Science	Space exploration	How might orbiting observatories be used in ways not yet undertaken?
4–6	Science	DNA	Create an amphibian/reptile that results from research on recombinant DNA. Give the advantages and disadvantages of the new creature as compared to the two original species.
4–6	Science	Fumeroles	To what new uses could the energy from fumeroles be put?
4–6	Science	Plankton	Brainstorm new uses for plankton and/or seaweed.
4–6	Science	Weather	Brainstorm possible ways of making Antarctica habitable by humans by making the weather less severe.
4–6	Science	Dinosaurs	Imagine that some dinosaurs survived. Select a specific dinosaur and brainstorm possible ways of keeping it as a pet.
4–6	Science	Robotics	For each of the following situations, brainstorm different ways that robots can be used to save time and/or to diminish risk or danger to humans: food production, automobile manufacture, home maintenance, school use, space travel.
4–6	Health	Pollution	Brainstorm possible ways of making your community aware of pollution problems.
4–6	Health	Smoking	What are some possible ways to help people make good choices regarding smoking?
4–6	Art	Monuments	Brainstorm possible monuments you might construct to commemorate or memorialize one of the following people or events: a person you admire, a disaster, a significant human triumph.
4–6	Music	Key	What are some different ways to play a melody in a key higher than that in which it was written?
4–6	Guidance	Conflict resolution	What are some possible ways to deal with other students who insult you?
4–6	Library use	Returning books	At the end of the school year, school libraries often find that many books taken out during the year have not been returned. Brainstorm ways to get the books back into the library.

CHAPTER 11
CREATING METAPHORS

Why Is It Important to Create Metaphors Skillfully?

Metaphors accentuate characteristics of objects, people, and events using an image of something analogous that highlights those characteristics clearly and dramatically. If a co-worker is described as a "loose cannon," that metaphor suggests that this individual is directionless, unguided by purpose or principle, unfocused, and capable of doing great harm with one impulsive, unexpected discharge. The image of an unsecured cannon on the rolling deck of a ship, primed and ready to go off, communicates these ideas very effectively.

The economy of language in using metaphors is striking. Two words, "loose cannon," call up an image that communicates several important perceptions about the co-worker. Comprehending and discussing those perceptions depends on the background of the person hearing the metaphor. Only if the listener knows what a cannon is will that image communicate its meaning effectively.

Developing effective metaphors is a form of creative thinking, connecting together two things that are not ordinarily associated to give us a new insight. Using metaphors is common in creative expression and is especially important in creative writing and the visual media.

In problem solving, creating metaphors is also effective for suggesting new ideas for unusual problem solutions. By creating a metaphor for the problem, solutions that may not be initially apparent may emerge. Creative problem solving based on metaphoric thinking can help people solve personal, professional, and technical problems.

Uses of Metaphors

Images in poetry often communicate ideas through various types of metaphor, such as figures of speech or allusions. In saying "All the world's a stage and all the men and women merely players," Shakespeare used the stage as a metaphor to give us insight into key relationships and actions in different periods of life. In "Dream Deferred," Langston Hughes used five metaphors in eleven short lines, one of which is "a raisin in the sun," to express the frustration of African-Americans in continually postponed justice and opportunity. In William Blake's "To See A World in a Grain of Sand," the poet used four metaphors in four lines to describe how understanding significant ideas is found in observing small things.

Metaphors communicate images and insight in other forms of literature, as well. Plato's cave allegory, Aesop's fables, the parables of Jesus of Nazareth, the African trickster tales of Anansi the Spider, the humor of Abraham Lincoln and Will Rogers, and the homilies of Ben Franklin employ metaphors to express spiritual, moral, or political principles.

Metaphors are sometimes used to persuade. Roosevelt used the metaphor of an epidemic to support resisting the expansion of the Nazi movement and lending a garden hose to a neighbor whose house was on fire to justify the lend-lease policy. Churchill's metaphor of an "Iron Curtain" became the common term to describe the division of Europe after World War II, an image that conveyed a "we-they" relationship of threat and impenetrability. "The rising tide of Communism" during the early 1950s suggested that political leaders should take precautions against a destructive and uncontrollable flood.

Metaphors also convey humor in jokes or puns. The Volkswagon ads of the '60s used humorous visual metaphors to draw attention to the special features of the "beetle." Soon after the 1969 moon landing, Volkswagon used a picture of the lunar landing module in its ad with the caption, "It's ugly, but it gets you there." Poking fun at itself and the charges that the "beetle" was ugly, Volkswagon also called upon American pride in the moon landing to sell its cars. Political cartoons similarly rely on metaphors for meaning and humor.

Metaphors may help people not familiar with

certain objects, actions, and functions understand new information more easily. The computer industry uses metaphors like "virus," "mouse," "trash," "file," "byte," etc. to convey abstract, technical ideas or operating procedures in language that people not familiar with computer technology can understand.

Metaphors are also used in scientific investigation to develop and express sometimes complex and abstract scientific principles. Mendeleev's dream of a table on which all elements had a place or Kekule's image of the benzene ring as a snake with its tail in its mouth expressed ideas that these scientists had been incubating. Scientific models, like the DNA double-helix, serve as metaphors for abstract structures, properties, or complex causal relationships.

Problems in Creating Metaphors

Although metaphors can communicate ideas well, sometimes poorly selected metaphors can be misleading and or confusing. One limitation in the way that people create metaphors involves using a metaphor that is too narrow to communicate what we are trying to convey, making the message superficial. To describe a starched table cloth as "stiff as a board" is a fairly useful description. Both are materials that have a rigid appearance and do not bend easily. To describe someone as "stiff as a board" suggests that the person seems inflexible, but does not convey the person's behavior or characteristics very meaningfully. Does the person have an overly polite or inexpressive manner, a rigid posture, dogmatic views, a stilted way of expressing ideas, or unimaginative ways of thinking? This metaphor is too thin to convey the complexity of human personality.

Metaphors may also convey incorrect ideas about something. We must be sure that the metaphor suggests what we want to describe and does not convey unintended meanings. If I notice how a person walks and comment that he is "squirrelly," I may be trying to convey that he makes scampering movements like a squirrel. I may be unintentionally communicating that he seems fearful, easily distracted, or that he hides things away. In this case, the metaphor is not effective because it carries ideas that suggest misimpressions, rather than insight. Most of us can think of a time that we used a metaphor jokingly and offended someone, either because it didn't fit the situation in a humorous way or because it carried some other message that was offensive.

Metaphors may also create confusion, rather than clarification. Mixed metaphors, for example, often confuse us or seem humorous because they convey conflicting ideas. Consider the mixed metaphors in this advice, "To get ahead, keep your nose to the grindstone, your shoulder to the wheel, your ear to the ground, and your eye on the ball." The resulting image is one of motionless contortion, rather than progress.

Malapropism sometimes result from mixing metaphors, an error that the speaker often does not intend. If a pessimistic friend comments "Do not count your chickens before they come home to roost," the speaker is mixing a proverb about not expecting something good before you know it with a proverb about bad things always coming back to their origins. The listener does not know whether the speaker is confused, starting to say one thing and ended up in another proverb, is trying to make a joke, or is suggesting that the outcomes can only be bad ones. Malapropisms confuse the listener because the mixed metaphor blurs together several sets of connections, some of them conflicting.

Figure 11.1 summarizes these problems in creating metaphors.

DEFAULTS IN CREATING METAPHORS

1. We select metaphors with narrow meanings or that have only superficial connection with what they stand for.

2. We select metaphors without thinking about ideas that they convey that are inaccurate or misleading.

3. We mix metaphors in ways that convey conflicting or contradictory ideas.

Figure 11.1

Two additional problems arise in using metaphors: inappropriateness and overuse. A metaphor must fit the background of the listener for its communication to be complete. We are sometimes "put off" by "inside jokes" used in a group in which others share a common language and experience. We may feel slightly ignorant if we must look up allusions to understand a writer's metaphors or confess that we do not know what a speaker is referring to. We may be critical of a person using an obscure metaphor, believing that the speaker is being insensitive or "showing off" by using an analogy that excludes us from enjoying the humor or sharing the insight.

The esoteric metaphors of T. S. Eliot or Ezra Pound may not mean much to readers unfamiliar with the allusions. Since these metaphors are profound to those familiar with the background, the insights of these authors warrant the research that might be necessary to comprehend what the metaphors are supposed to convey.

Overuse also detracts from the effectiveness of metaphors. Skill in creating and using metaphor lies in connection with what we are expressing and in originality. Overuse of the same metaphor or using only hackneyed ones adds little interest or insight to our ideas. Poets and writers poke fun at themselves and others in overusing metaphors. Sylvia Plath's poem "Metaphors" and Ogden Nash's poem "Very Like a Whale" satirize overuse and misuse of metaphors. Shakespeare's Sonnet "Shall I compare thee to a summer's day..." describes the limitations of using them.

How Do We Create Metaphors Skillfully?

When we draw an analogy between two things of different types, we recognize that they have important similarities. We use analogies for a number of purposes. When we reason by analogy, we extend something we know about one of the two things to another, based on the analogy. In creating metaphors, analogies are used to convey something we already know about one thing by using an image of something else that is literally quite different from the original object. Creating metaphors is a creative thinking activity because metaphors clearly express ideas or insights by matching two things that are not ordinarily associated.

Creating metaphors is not just free associa-tion, although it almost seems to be that intuitive when we hear people who are good at metaphoric thinking spinning off metaphors. While some individuals hear and express metaphors spontaneously, we can all create metaphors skillfully with some careful, organized thought: determining what you want to say with a metaphor, identifying the characteristics that suggest that meaning, and selecting a metaphor which is analogous enough to convey the same image or meaning effectively.

Creating metaphors can be facilitated by using a variety of creative thinking techniques. Visualization or imagery prompts analogies that are used to create solutions to business or technical problems. Free association techniques that awaken stored memories or sharpen observation can generate metaphors for creative expression or practical problem solving.

In whatever way we get ideas for metaphors, it is important to think about whether these metaphors communicate what we intend, offer deep understanding or original expression, and do not carry with them misleading associations. The strategy described in this chapter is based on explicitly using analogies between things to give us ideas for metaphors and then analyzing whether or not the metaphors are a good fit. It is a strategy that we all can use, regardless of our background or experience with other creative thinking techniques.

Attention Points in Creating Metaphors Skillfully

We set the stage for creating new metaphors by asking, *"What is the purpose of this metaphor? What am I trying to communicate that a metaphor would express?"* Identifying the context for creating the metaphor is the first step in bringing possibilities to mind for consideration.

Next we should list the key characteristics that explain what we want to communicate about the given object. These important characteristics are the "idea bridges" that allow us to search our memory to find something else that expresses in a new way the idea that we are working with. Clarifying these key characteristics allows us to put forward connections to a new object that is analogous. For example, I may want to communicate that a co-worker is dedicated to her job, very hard working, and quite productive. Key characteristics that express these ideas include that she is always active, puts out a lot of energy, and accomplishes many tasks.

A metaphor will work only if a number of characteristics connect it to the given object. We should consider a range of different types of characteristics related to the ones we start with so that the metaphor is a rich and useful one. Thinking about the details that elaborate each characteristic of the given object helps us to be very clear about what we are trying to convey.

With a variety of characteristics before us, we are ready to brainstorm a number of images, objects, or ideas that have these key characteristics. For example, when thinking about many types of characteristics of my co-worker, I think of a locomotive, an army, a dynamo, and a basketball player.

From this metaphor menu, we can select the ones that have the most significant characteristics in common with the given idea. When one object, person, or event seems most promising for our purpose, we can check how well the key characteristics of one fits the other, noting whether any significant differences might interfere with the effectiveness of the metaphor. A basketball player is similar, but there are too many breaks in the action in a basketball game. A locomotive is too overbearing. An army suggests a complex of individuals working together. A dynamo, on the other hand, does not have similar disadvantages.

The last step in creating metaphors is determining whether the characteristics and details between the two things are strong enough to make the metaphor a good one. "She's a dynamo" seems to convey what we wanted to describe about her very well.

The thinking map for creating metaphors (figure 11.2) summarizes these steps.

The graphic organizer for creating metaphors in figure 11.3 is an adaptation of the compare/contrast graphic, redesigned for the creative development of metaphors.

Add any additional characteristics boxes that may enhance the richness of your metaphor.

CREATING A METAPHOR

1. What do I want to describe about an object, person, or event that a metaphor would express?

2. What are the details of the key characteristics of what I am trying to describe?

3. What other things (objects, people, or events) have these key characteristics?

4. Which of these things might make a good metaphor?

5. What details of the metaphor fit the characteristics of what I am trying to describe?

6. Are there differences that make the metaphor misleading? If so, why?

7. Is this metaphor a "good fit"? Why?

Figure 11.2

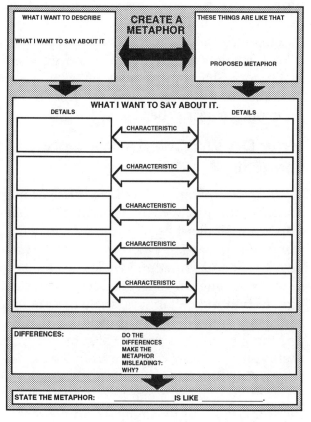

Figure 11.3

The graphic organizer follows the questions on the thinking map, moving vertically down the diagram. After writing in the upper-left box what you want to describe about the thing or idea, write these characteristics on the arrows in the middle of the box. Think about whether there are other related characteristics of the given object that occur to you as you consider the key characteristics. For example, I may want to describe my co-worker as active, energetic, and able to do many tasks. Then I realize that she is also forceful. I add this somewhat related characteristic to the list of things that I want to say about her and to the arrows in the middle of the diagram.

To have a clear image of what you want to convey, brainstorm details about the given object and write them in the "Details" boxes. Figure 11.4 shows how the diagram may look at that point in the process.

After surveying the details and the characteristics of the thing that you wish to describe,

suggest several things that have many of the same characteristics and write the list of possible metaphors in the top box on the right. From this list, select an object that seems like a good fit for many of the characteristics on the left, and write it in the "Proposed Metaphor" section of the same box.

Now brainstorm details of each of the characteristics as that characteristic applies to the "Proposed Metaphor." Add characteristics that are important in describing the proposed metaphor to find out whether there are any similar features in the original object that we may have overlooked earlier. For example, a dynamo keeps on going for long periods of time without breaking down and so does my co-worker. I now add "keeps on going" to the characteristics and think of details about how both my co-worker and a dynamo keep on going. Figure 11.5 shows how the graphic organizer may look.

Some differences between the metaphor and what you are trying to describe give richness to

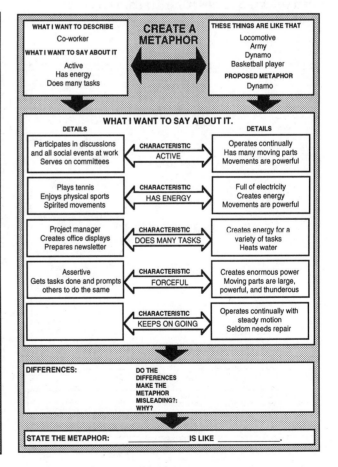

Figure 11.4

Figure 11.5

the metaphor. The difference in the degree of energy, power, and productivity between a dynamo and my co-worker adds desirable meaning to the metaphor. Using the metaphor of a dynamo exaggerates those qualities in her in a complimentary way. However, I must check to see that the image of the dynamo does not carry with it some undesirable connotation that I do not want to ascribe to her.

Seeing the details and characteristics side-by-side, I can now decide whether the proposed metaphor has enough of the characteristics of the thing that I wish to describe to convey that thing's important characteristics. Then I write the metaphor: My co-worker is like a dynamo. I may then use information in the "Characteristics" and "Details" boxes of the diagram to write about my co-worker as if she were a dynamo. Figure 11.6 shows how the completed graphic may look.

The metaphor web diagram in figure 11.7 is used to summarize the metaphors that have been selected to describe the same object or idea. This activity shows that many metaphors can be

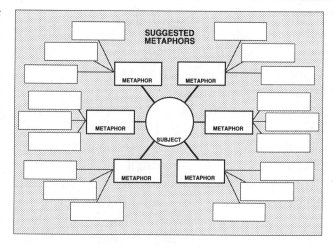

Figure 11.7

used to describe the same thing, each adding different understanding and emphasizing different characteristics. The web diagram can be used by an individual to compare metaphors that he or she has developed or in a group activity to summarize the metaphors developed by several group members.

Extended uses of metaphors in writing. To use a metaphor in a poem or persuasive prose, one should ask, *What details about one thing can I use to describe details about another?* In describing a co-worker as a "loose cannon" or as a "dynamo," the metaphor is a focused one and need not be elaborated. However, the force of the metaphor can be extended in continued dialogue by using details about a loose canon or a dynamo to further describe the co-worker. I might say of her, "She never shuts down," or "She's full of electricity." This is an important device in poetry. In creating a metaphor like the cat in Carl Sandburg's poem "Fog," details are very important to express and extend the image of the cat to convey meaning about fog. The fog is described as creeping in "on little cat feet," for example. The details boxes in a completed graphic organizer like that in figure 11.6 contains the "raw material" from which a poem, some other literary work, or a pictorial representation can be created. The next step in the creative process is executing the images, poetry, or prose for which the metaphor is created.

Fluency and originality are important in any form of creative thinking. The three steps in this strategy that involve brainstorming (listing char-

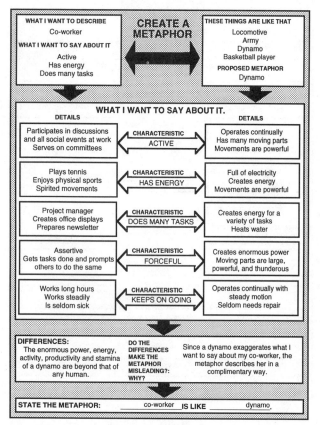

Figure 11.6

acteristics, creating a menu of possible metaphors, and generating many details for expressing the connection) should provide original material that can be used in the creative expression of the metaphors developed.

How Can We Teach Students to Generate Metaphors Skillfully?

It is not enough to ask students to "be creative" in developing and using metaphors. The strategy outlined in the thinking map helps students who may not view themselves as creative thinkers become skillful and confident about generating metaphoric images. Emphasize the importance of the purpose of the metaphor to give students a sense of why we develop and use metaphors and to establish a clear set of standards for selecting good metaphors from among the possible ways of expressing their ideas.

Creating metaphors reduces students' insecurity and confusion when asked to interpret symbols, figures of speech, or analogies in prose. In addition to its cognitive value, creating metaphors promotes self-esteem by confirming for students that they are creative thinkers who can suggest workable, original ideas.

As in the case of teaching other thinking skills and processes, you should guide students' practice and prompt them to reflect about how they developed these ideas so that they can guide themselves in using this creative thinking strategy.

Contexts in the Curriculum for Lessons on Creating Metaphors

Metaphors that students are exposed to as well as contexts in which students can create their own metaphors appear throughout the curriculum. In general, there are three contexts in which infusion lessons on creating metaphors can be developed and taught.

- *Students read literature and study works of art in which metaphors are used.* Poetry is, of course, rich with metaphors. Students can reflect on whether these metaphors "work" and what they convey. Similarly, metaphors used in short stories and novels can be

analyzed and students asked to evaluate their effectiveness. In *Fantastic Voyage*, Isaac Asimov's metaphor of a trip through the body as a submarine voyage provides the details that suggest action in the narrative. Similarly, in the visual and performing arts, metaphors suggest designs or themes. The use of metaphoric images in art and music also provides such contexts.

- *Students are asked to compose works which contain metaphors.* Creative writing is a prime context for activities in which students develop their own metaphors. For example, students can develop a metaphor as the basis for a story. For example, students may create images to illustrate human traits like heroism, friendship, etc. They can also create metaphors for major historical events, for example, settlers making the trip from the Mississippi to California in the 1800s.

- *Students engage in creative problem solving.* Students may modify the possible uses of something based on its similarity to something else, a problem-solving application of metaphor. For example, creating a metaphor to stimulate use of the library might entail using fast-food restaurants as a metaphor. Examining what makes fast-food restaurants appealing and successful can suggest ideas to encourage students to use the library more often and more effectively.

A menu of suggested contexts for infusion lessons on creating metaphors is provided on pp. 335–336.

Teaching Students to Create Metaphors Skillfully in the Primary Grades

Creating metaphors draws on background knowledge and experience. Obviously, students in the primary grades have less knowledge than students in the upper elementary grades do. Encourage students to select metaphors that are familiar enough to enable them to draw upon what they know. Teachers are frequently surprised at how much already accumulated information their students express when creating metaphors.

The stage in the strategy in which students generate details for the key characteristics presents a good opportunity for "piggybacking" on other students' responses. Encouraging this type of cross-fertilization will enhance your students' thinking. Perhaps the most direct way to introduce piggybacking to young children is to explain the idea directly, and then ask them to do it in cooperative groups, followed by large group discussion. They are usually surprised and excited by what they have added to each other's ideas.

The thinking map in figure 11.8 may help primary grade students to create metaphors.

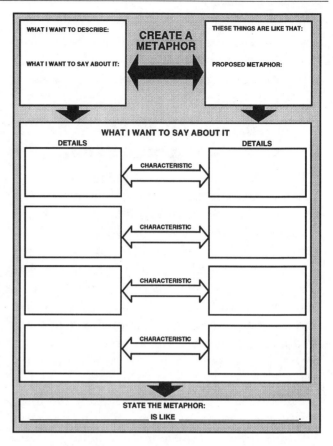

Figure 11.9

MAKING A METAPHOR

1. What do I want to say with a metaphor?

2. What are some details about what I want to say about it?

3. What other things have the same characteristics?

4. Which of these things might make a good metaphor? What are some of its details?

5. Is it a good metaphor? Why?

Figure 11.8

The graphic organizer for creating metaphors in figure 11.3 can be simplified slightly, as shown in figure 11.9, for students in the primary grades.

Model Lesson on Creating Metaphors

The model lesson on creating metaphors skillfully includes both a primary and an upper elementary poem. As you read the lesson, reflect on these questions:

• What specific strategies promote creating metaphors?

• How do the graphic organizers promote understanding, as well as creating, metaphors?

• What additional examples can you identify to reinforce this skill?

Tools for Designing Lessons on Creating Metaphors

The tools on the following pages include thinking maps and graphic organizers that can be used in designing infusion lessons on creating metaphors for primary or intermediate classes. The thinking map on page 323 is designed especially for use in the primary grades.

The thinking maps and graphic organizers can guide you in designing the critical thinking activity in the lesson and can also serve as photocopy masters, transparency masters, or as models that can be enlarged and used as posters in the classroom. Reproduction rights are granted for single classroom use only.

CREATING A METAPHOR

1. **What do I want to describe about an object, person, or event that a metaphor would express?**

2. **What are the details of the key characteristics of what I am trying to describe?**

3. **What other things (objects, people, or events) have these key characteristics?**

4. **Which of these things might make a good metaphor?**

5. **What details of the metaphor fit the characteristics of what I am trying to describe?**

6. **Are there differences that make the metaphor misleading? If so, why?**

7. **Is this metaphor a "good fit"? Why?**

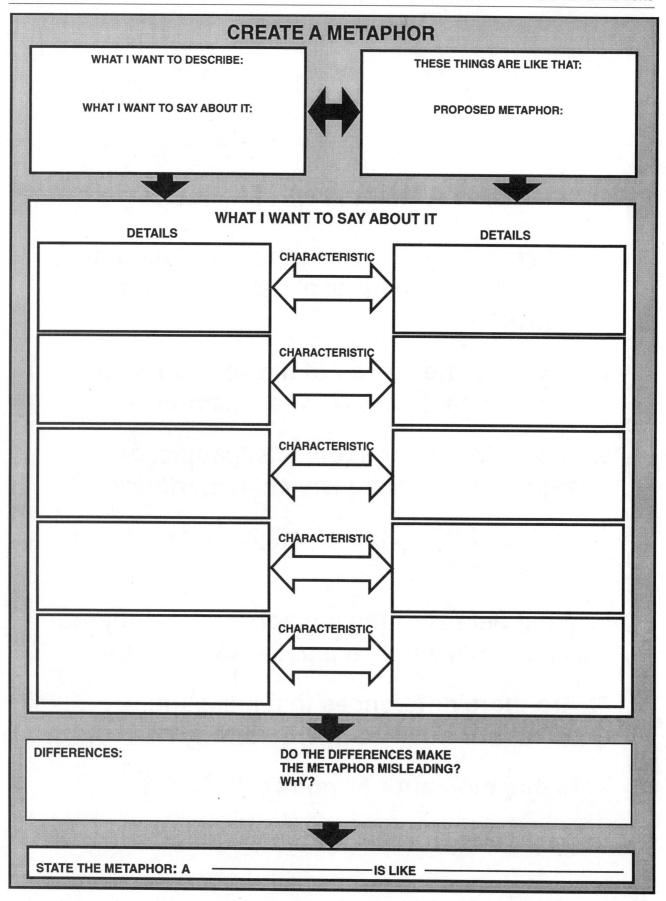

CREATE A METAPHOR

WHAT I WANT TO DESCRIBE:

WHAT I WANT TO SAY ABOUT IT:

THESE THINGS ARE LIKE THAT:

PROPOSED METAPHOR:

WHAT I WANT TO SAY ABOUT IT

DETAILS   CHARACTERISTIC   **DETAILS**

CHARACTERISTIC

CHARACTERISTIC

CHARACTERISTIC

CHARACTERISTIC

DIFFERENCES: **DO THE DIFFERENCES MAKE THE METAPHOR MISLEADING? WHY?**

STATE THE METAPHOR: A ————————— IS LIKE —————————

MAKING A METAPHOR

1. What do I want to say with a metaphor?

2. What are some details about what I want to say?

3. What other things have the same characteristics?

4. Which of these things might make a good metaphor? What are some of its details?

5. Is it a good metaphor? Why?

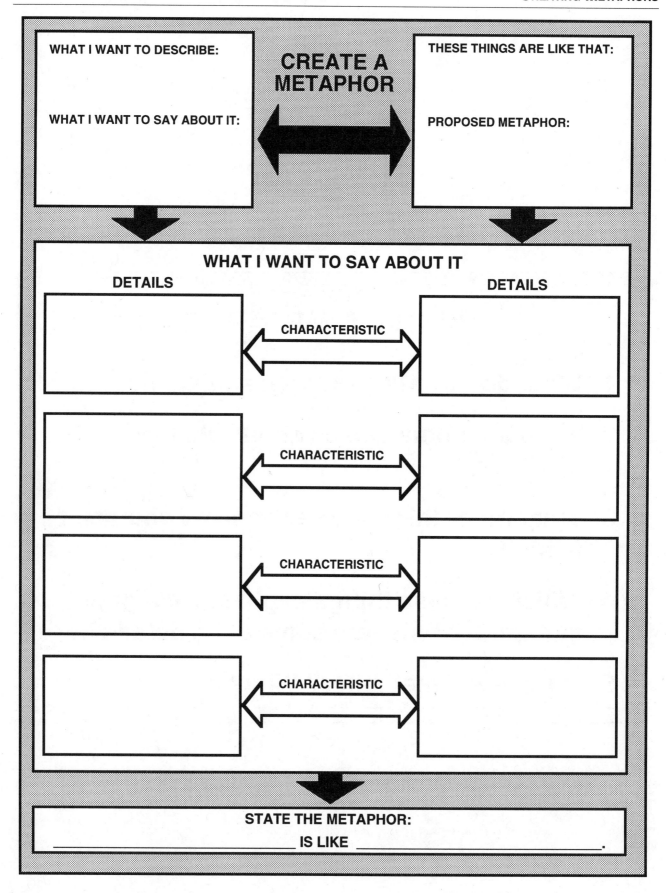

WHAT I WANT TO DESCRIBE:

WHAT I WANT TO SAY ABOUT IT:

CREATE A METAPHOR

THESE THINGS ARE LIKE THAT:

PROPOSED METAPHOR:

WHAT I WANT TO SAY ABOUT IT

DETAILS　　　　　　　　　　　　　　　　　　　　DETAILS

CHARACTERISTIC

CHARACTERISTIC

CHARACTERISTIC

CHARACTERISTIC

STATE THE METAPHOR:

_____ **IS LIKE** _____ .

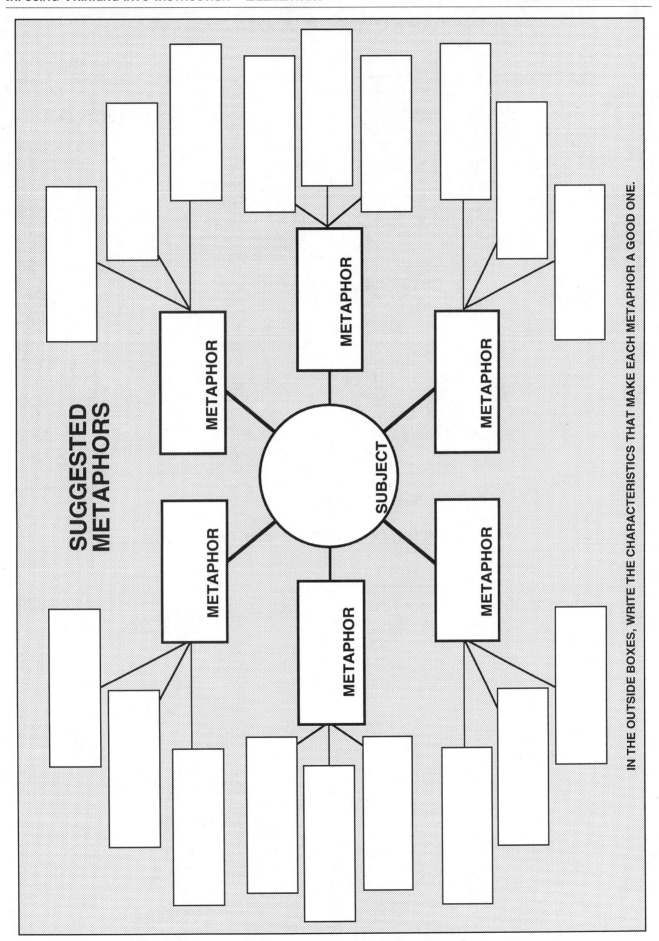

SUGGESTED METAPHORS

IN THE OUTSIDE BOXES, WRITE THE CHARACTERISTICS THAT MAKE EACH METAPHOR A GOOD ONE.

A METAPHOR FOR A DINOSAUR

WRITING   **GRADES 2–6**

OBJECTIVES

CONTENT

Students will analyze a figure of speech and develop a metaphor to be used in a poem or descriptive writing.

THINKING SKILL/PROCESS

Students will create metaphors effectively by performing the following steps: stating the idea that the metaphor will convey, listing the characteristics of the thing being described, brainstorming other things which have important similarities, and selecting an item whose details convey the idea well.

METHODS AND MATERIALS

CONTENT

Transparencies of the comparison diagram, the graphic organizer for creating metaphors, and a webbing diagram are used to record class discussion. Distribute one graphic for creating metaphors to each pair of students. Carl Sandburg's poem "Fog" should be read prior to instruction.

THINKING SKILL/PROCESS

Creating metaphors is guided by structured questioning and the use of a graphic organizer. Brainstorming is featured twice in the lesson: first, to suggest possible metaphors and, second, to generate details to express them. For primary-grade students the simplified thinking map and graphic organizer should be used. (See pp. 321–336 for reproducible diagrams.)

LESSON

INTRODUCTION TO CONTENT AND PROCESS

- **In Carl Sandburg's poem, "Fog," what does the poet use to tell us about fog?** *A cat.* **When a writer or speaker uses one thing to tell us about another, he or she is using a metaphor. Let's show how certain characteristics of a cat describe fog.** Use the transparency of the comparison graphic organizer for understanding metaphors to record responses as students examine the similarities between a cat and fog.

- **In what ways are the cat and fog similar?** On the central arrow, write each type of similarity between a cat and fog. Prompt students to identify many adjectives, nouns, and verbs that describe each similarity between cats and fog. POSSIBLE ANSWERS: *Attitude, sound, motion, texture, appearance, position, and intention.*

- **What are some words that we use to describe these characteristics in a cat?** For each similarity, ask for students' responses and write them in the boxes on the left side of the graphic organizer. POSSIBLE ANSWERS: *Attitude (aloof, impersonal, disinterested, watchful), sound (pad-*

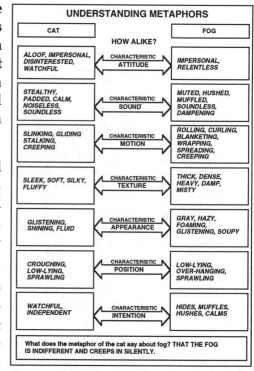

UNDERSTANDING METAPHORS

CAT	HOW ALIKE?	FOG
ALOOF, IMPERSONAL, DISINTERESTED, WATCHFUL	CHARACTERISTIC ATTITUDE	IMPERSONAL, RELENTLESS
STEALTHY, PADDED, CALM, NOISELESS, SOUNDLESS	CHARACTERISTIC SOUND	MUTED, HUSHED, MUFFLED, SOUNDLESS, DAMPENING
SLINKING, GLIDING STALKING, CREEPING	CHARACTERISTIC MOTION	ROLLING, CURLING, BLANKETING, WRAPPING, SPREADING, CREEPING
SLEEK, SOFT, SILKY, FLUFFY	CHARACTERISTIC TEXTURE	THICK, DENSE, HEAVY, DAMP, MISTY
GLISTENING, SHINING, FLUID	CHARACTERISTIC APPEARANCE	GRAY, HAZY, FOAMING, GLISTENING, SOUPY
CROUCHING, LOW-LYING, SPRAWLING	CHARACTERISTIC POSITION	LOW-LYING, OVER-HANGING, SPRAWLING
WATCHFUL, INDEPENDENT	CHARACTERISTIC INTENTION	HIDES, MUFFLES, HUSHES, CALMS

What does the metaphor of the cat say about fog? THAT THE FOG IS INDIFFERENT AND CREEPS IN SILENTLY.

ded, stealthy, calm, soundless), motion (slinking, gliding, stalking, creeping), texture (sleek, silky, soft, fluffy), appearance (glistening, shining, fluid), position (crouching, low-lying, sprawling), and intention (watchful, independent).

- **What are some words that we use to describe these characteristics of fog?** Record the students' details about fog in the boxes on the right side of the graphic organizer. POSSIBLE ANSWERS: *Attitude (impersonal, relentless), sound (muted, hushed, muffled, soundless, dampening), motion (rolling, curling, blanketing, wrapping, spreading, creeping), texture (thick, heavy, damp, misty), appearance (gray, glistening, hazy, foaming, soupy), and intention (hides, muffles, hushes, calms).*

- **Because the poet used the cat to describe it, we get certain ideas about fog. What are the main ideas about fog that we get in this poem?** POSSIBLE ANSWERS: *Aloof, indifferent, silent.*

- **Is using a metaphor like this a good way to describe something?** POSSIBLE ANSWERS: *You can't really know what the poet meant, but you get some good ideas. A metaphor says a lot about something in a few words.* Students note that "playing" with the metaphor makes reading the poem interesting. Some students like that ambiguity; more literal-minded students may be somewhat troubled by it.

- **To understand a metaphor, we have been looking at similarities between two things. In this case, we wanted to try to uncover all the things that the poet could be saying about fog based on its similarity to a cat. Suppose you wanted to create a metaphor to tell something important about a person or things that you want to describe. By slightly changing the procedure we used in discussing "Fog," we can make our own original metaphors.**

THINKING ACTIVELY

- Suppose that you wanted to create a metaphor to describe a dinosaur. Let's pick a common dinosaur that we all know: the brontosaurus, more recently called the apatosaurus. Since a brontosaurus is the subject, write that in the top part of first box on your graphic organizer "Create a Metaphor." Discuss with your partner what you want to say about it. Write what you want your metaphor to tell about a brontosaurus in the bottom part of the first box on your graphic organizer. Students usually want to describe the size, antiquity, appearance, power, or disappearance of dinosaurs. Students may also suggest their thunderous sound, their variety, their fossil remains, their role in the formation of oil or coal, or some modern-day appearance of a *brontosaurus*, as in *The Dinosaur Who Lived In My Backyard*. POSSIBLE ANSWERS: *Long neck and flat head, massive body and legs, eats plants.*

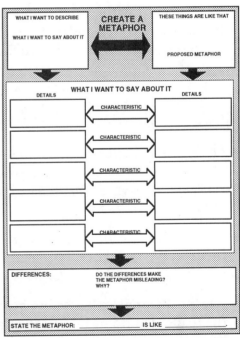

- To describe a brontosaurus, the metaphor you pick must tell these important characteristics of the dinosaur. Write these characteristics on the arrows in the middle of the diagram. These are the "idea bridges" that carry the similarities between a dinosaur and your metaphor. Write any additional things that you want to say about a dinosaur on the arrows. POSSIBLE ANSWERS: *Swinging motion of its head.*

- Next to each characteristic write all the details that you and your partner can think of that describe that characteristic of a brontosaurus. Writing down these details helps you bring to mind what this characteristic of the dinosaur really seems like to you. POSSIBLE ANSWERS: *Long neck and flat head (large, square, flat head with a wide jaw at the end of a long, thick neck that can reach up many stories), massive body and legs (large, thick body with sturdy legs), eats plants (reaches high in trees for leaves or grazes on low grass), and swinging motion of its head (the swinging movements of a large head on a long neck, side-to-side and from treetops down to the ground).*

- What other things have many of the same characteristics as the ones you have identified? With your partner, brainstorm a list of things that might be enough like a brontosaurus that they can be used as metaphors for a dinosaur. Write your list in the box at the top right. POSSIBLE ANSWERS: *Steam shovel, dragon, lizard, and giraffe.* After students have completed their own diagrams, ask for six things that various groups have suggested, and write them in the metaphor boxes on the webbing diagram (shown at the right). For each idea, write three characteristics that students believe describe both the suggested metaphor and a dinosaur. Encourage students to write on their own diagrams any suggested metaphors that they think fit what they want to say about a dinosaur. POSSIBLE ANSWERS: *Cherry picker, tractor-trailer truck.*

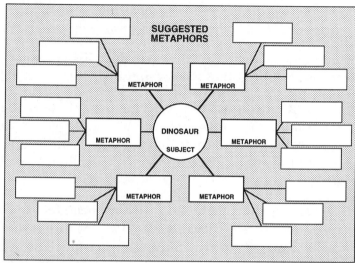

- Now decide with your partner which suggested metaphor on your list best describes a brontosaurus. Pick one that you think has the most important connections. Write the details of your suggested metaphor in the boxes on the right next to each arrow. POSSIBLE ANSWERS: *The shape of its head and body (large, square, flat scoop with a wide mouth at the end of a long boom that can reach up many stories), massive body and legs (square cab on top of wide tread), eats plants (scoops up dirt and grass), and swinging motion of its head (the swinging movements of a large scoop on a long boom, side-to-side and from high in the air down to the ground).*

- Does your metaphor suggest characteristics of a brontosaurus that you didn't think of earlier? Add any additional characteristics and details to the arrows and boxes on your diagram. POSSIBLE ANSWERS: *The steam bursting from the steam shovel seems like the snorting bursts of the breathing of a large animal.*

- If there are any significant differences between a brontosaurus and your metaphor, write them on the lower box. POSSIBLE ANSWERS: *The brontosaurus was a living animal; the steam shovel is a machine. The dinosaur lived in ancient times; the steam shovel is modern.*

- Are the differences between a brontosaurus and your suggested metaphor so significant that the reader would be misled? Explain why or why not in the lower box. *The differences between an ancient animal and a modern machine make the metaphor more interesting rather than distorting what I want to say about a brontosaurus.* If the differences are too misleading, pick another possible metaphor and find out whether its characteristics and details are better suited for describing a dinosaur.

- Write your metaphor in the box at the bottom of the diagram. Explain whether you think that your metaphor is an effective and original one to describe a brontosaurus.

THINKING ABOUT THINKING

- **What did you think about to come up with your metaphors?** Prompt students to recall the steps in the process. Record their strategies on the board or use a transparency of the thinking map "Creating a Metaphor," uncovering each step as students identify it. Discuss each step.

- **Do you think that this is a valuable way to think when you try to find one thing to describe another? Why or why not?** Most students comment that using this strategy is more organized than using the first idea that comes into your mind. It helps them carry out the process of finding a metaphor.

- **How does listing the characteristics of the dinosaur on the graphic organizer help you "see" the traits it shares with the metaphor?** POSSIBLE ANSWERS: *Listing the characteristics of a dinosaur reminds me of details that I can use later to write or draw. Writing them down jogs my memory about other details or characteristics and makes selecting and using a metaphor easier.*

> ### CREATING A METAPHOR
>
> 1. What do I want describe about an object, person, or event that a metaphor would express?
>
> 2. What are the details of the key characteristics of what I am trying to describe?
>
> 3. What other things (objects, people, or events) have these key characteristics?
>
> 4. Which of these things might make a good metaphor?
>
> 5. What details of the metaphor fit the characteristics of what I am trying to describe?
>
> 6. Are there differences that make the metaphor misleading? If so, why?
>
> 7. Is this metaphor a "good fit?" Why?

APPLYING THINKING

IMMEDIATE TRANSFER

- **Examine some of the Dr. Seuss books. Select a metaphor from one of them. What is the metaphor describing? Create another metaphor to describe it. Draw your metaphor.** Examples may include *Yertle the Turtle* (metaphor for Hitler), The *Lorax* (metaphor for environmental pollution), *The Butter Battle Wars* (metaphor for the arms race).

REINFORCEMENT LATER

- **Use the same strategy to create ideas for a holiday picture. Select an object associated with the holiday and create a metaphor for the object. Draw a picture of your metaphor representing the holiday.**

- **Select a joke that contains a metaphor. Use this strategy to create another metaphor that is funny.** Answers may take the forms of puns, cartoons, commercials, greeting cards, or political speeches.

- **Select a figure of speech (a simile, a personification, or a hyperbole). Use the strategy for creating metaphors to create another metaphor that says the same thing.**

WRITING EXTENSIONS

Any of the following writing assignments will extend the understanding of metaphors developed in this lesson.

- **Poems are expressive because the poet conveys so much meaning in so few words. In Sandburg's "Fog," how does the image of the cat suggest fog to you? Write a similar poem, an extended description, an essay about the effectiveness of the metaphor, or a journal entry describing the effect the poem had on you.**

- **Write an essay explaining why you think metaphors are useful or interesting to read. What purposes do metaphors serve in language? Why would you use a metaphor rather than a literal description?** Metaphors can richly express ideas; they act as analogies that help us understand a thing by showing its similarity to something else. Objects or organisms that have many similar characteristics can be used to describe each other in very few words.

- **If your metaphor is a good one for a dinosaur, you could probably use a dinosaur as an image for describing the thing you picked as a metaphor. With the information on your graphic organizer, write a poem using a dinosaur to describe what you picked for a metaphor.**

- **Use the information on our first graphic organizer to write a cat poem using the descriptors of fog, or write a second verse to Sandburg's poem, showing another characteristic of a cat.**

CONTENT EXTENSIONS

Students may wish to discuss the metaphor of a steam shovel used to describe dinosaurs in the following poem. To interpret the metaphor in the poems, students can use the comparison graphic organizer for understanding metaphors or the graphic organizers of students who used a steam shovel as a metaphor.

The Steam Shovel
by Lynn Marie Skapyak

Dinosaurs are not in books
with necks that do not swing,
flat, monster beast, who merely looks
like he could eat up anything.

I saw a hungry one, just yesterday,
loudly chomping his steel jaws
as he ate, downtown by the bay
huffing as he moved, on rubber claws.

He threw dirt and rocks to the side
scooping earth loads in his iron head,
leaving a hole, oh so wide.
Chugging white smoke puffs as he led.

The Steam Shovel
by Charles Malam

The dinosaurs are not all dead
I saw one raise its iron head
To watch me walking down the road
Beyond our house today.
Its jaws were dripping with a load
Of earth and grass that it had cropped.
It must have heard me where I stopped,
Snorted white steam my way,
And stretched its long neck out to see.
And chewed and grinned quite ami-
ably.

ASSESSING STUDENTS' THINKING ABOUT CREATING METAPHORS

To assess the skill of creating metaphors, ask students to answer any of the application questions or others which you select. Ask students to describe how they created the metaphor. If they write a poem using metaphors, ask them to show how they selected their metaphors. Determine whether they are attending to each of the steps on the thinking map.

Reprinted by permission of the author, Lynn Marie Skapyak.

From *Upper Pastures: Poems by Charles Malam*. Copyright 1930, © 1958 by Charles Malam. Reprinted by permission of Henry Holt and Company, Inc.

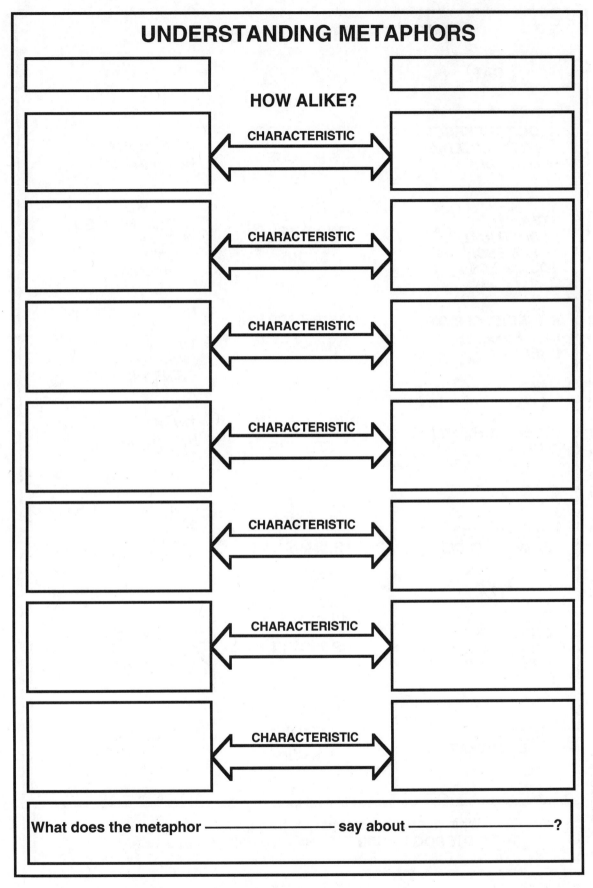

UNDERSTANDING METAPHORS

HOW ALIKE?

CHARACTERISTIC

CHARACTERISTIC

CHARACTERISTIC

CHARACTERISTIC

CHARACTERISTIC

CHARACTERISTIC

CHARACTERISTIC

What does the metaphor ——————— say about ———————?

Comparison graphic organizer adapted from *Organizing Thinking II*, Howard and Sandra Black, Critical Thinking Press and Software, 1990

UNDERSTANDING METAPHORS

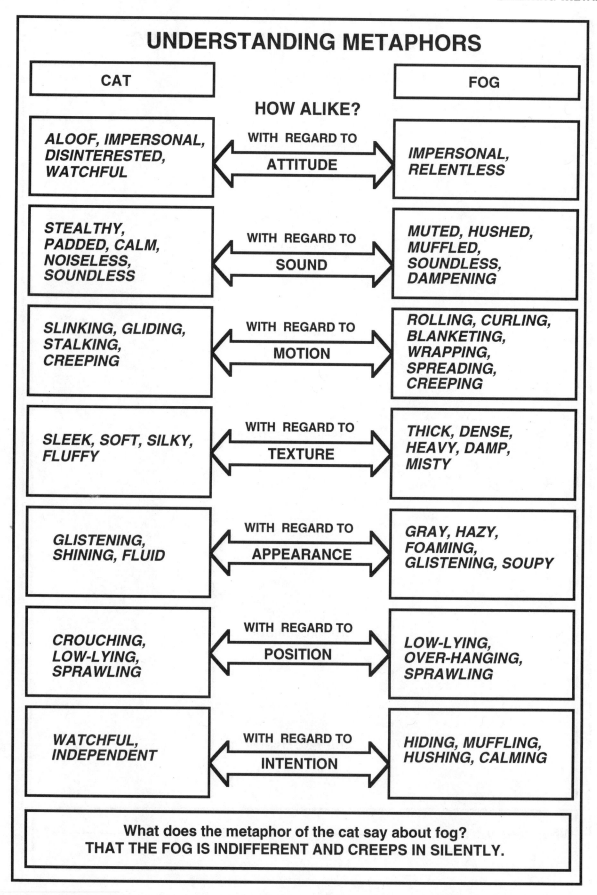

CAT		FOG

HOW ALIKE?

	WITH REGARD TO	
ALOOF, IMPERSONAL, DISINTERESTED, WATCHFUL	⟷ ATTITUDE	IMPERSONAL, RELENTLESS
STEALTHY, PADDED, CALM, NOISELESS, SOUNDLESS	⟷ SOUND	MUTED, HUSHED, MUFFLED, SOUNDLESS, DAMPENING
SLINKING, GLIDING, STALKING, CREEPING	⟷ MOTION	ROLLING, CURLING, BLANKETING, WRAPPING, SPREADING, CREEPING
SLEEK, SOFT, SILKY, FLUFFY	⟷ TEXTURE	THICK, DENSE, HEAVY, DAMP, MISTY
GLISTENING, SHINING, FLUID	⟷ APPEARANCE	GRAY, HAZY, FOAMING, GLISTENING, SOUPY
CROUCHING, LOW-LYING, SPRAWLING	⟷ POSITION	LOW-LYING, OVER-HANGING, SPRAWLING
WATCHFUL, INDEPENDENT	⟷ INTENTION	HIDING, MUFFLING, HUSHING, CALMING

What does the metaphor of the cat say about fog?
THAT THE FOG IS INDIFFERENT AND CREEPS IN SILENTLY.

Sample student responses as they appear in *Organizing Thinking II*, Howard and Sandra Black, Critical Thinking Press and Software, 1990

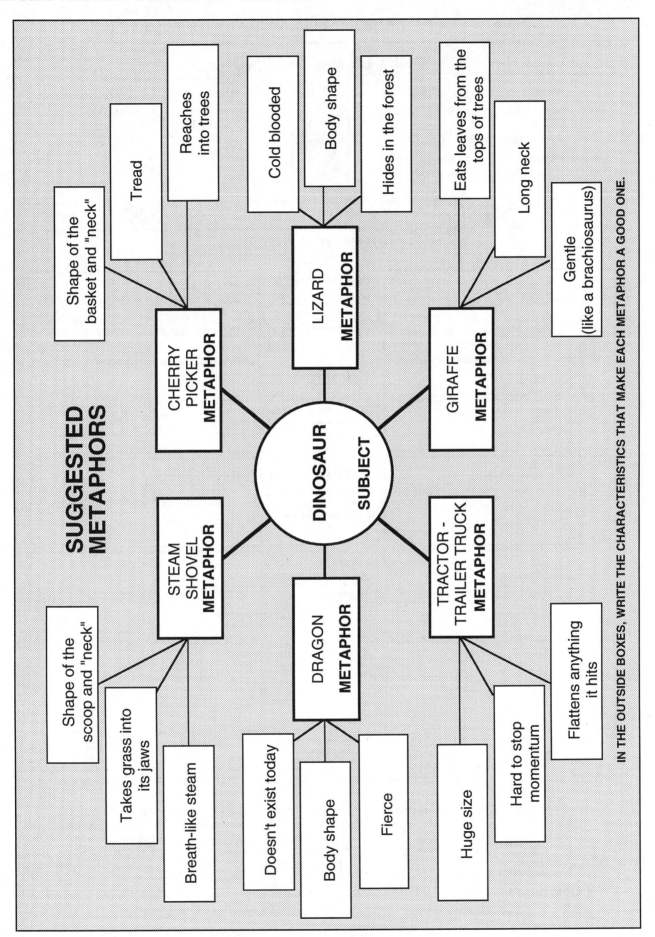

SUGGESTED METAPHORS

CHERRY PICKER METAPHOR
- Shape of the basket and "neck"
- Tread
- Reaches into trees

LIZARD METAPHOR
- Cold blooded
- Body shape
- Hides in the forest

GIRAFFE METAPHOR
- Eats leaves from the tops of trees
- Long neck
- Gentle (like a brachiosaurus)

DINOSAUR SUBJECT

STEAM SHOVEL METAPHOR
- Shape of the scoop and "neck"
- Takes grass into its jaws
- Breath-like steam

DRAGON METAPHOR
- Doesn't exist today
- Body shape
- Fierce

TRACTOR-TRAILER TRUCK METAPHOR
- Huge size
- Hard to stop momentum
- Flattens anything it hits

IN THE OUTSIDE BOXES, WRITE THE CHARACTERISTICS THAT MAKE EACH METAPHOR A GOOD ONE.

Sample Student Responses • Metaphor for a Dinosaur

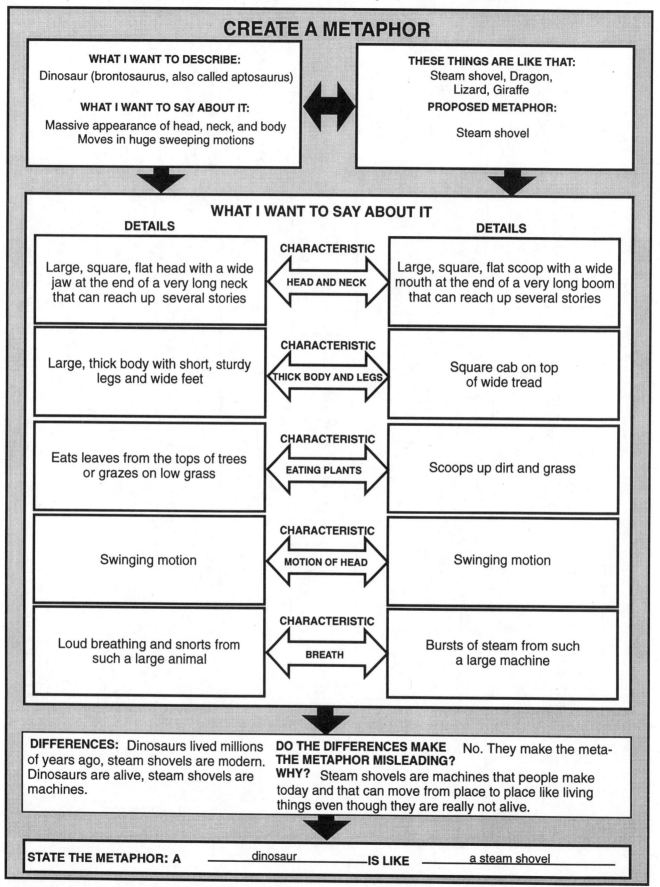

CREATE A METAPHOR

WHAT I WANT TO DESCRIBE:
Dinosaur (brontosaurus, also called aptosaurus)

WHAT I WANT TO SAY ABOUT IT:
Massive appearance of head, neck, and body
Moves in huge sweeping motions

THESE THINGS ARE LIKE THAT:
Steam shovel, Dragon,
Lizard, Giraffe

PROPOSED METAPHOR:
Steam shovel

WHAT I WANT TO SAY ABOUT IT

DETAILS **DETAILS**

DETAILS	CHARACTERISTIC	DETAILS
Large, square, flat head with a wide jaw at the end of a very long neck that can reach up several stories	HEAD AND NECK	Large, square, flat scoop with a wide mouth at the end of a very long boom that can reach up several stories
Large, thick body with short, sturdy legs and wide feet	THICK BODY AND LEGS	Square cab on top of wide tread
Eats leaves from the tops of trees or grazes on low grass	EATING PLANTS	Scoops up dirt and grass
Swinging motion	MOTION OF HEAD	Swinging motion
Loud breathing and snorts from such a large animal	BREATH	Bursts of steam from such a large machine

DIFFERENCES: Dinosaurs lived millions of years ago, steam shovels are modern. Dinosaurs are alive, steam shovels are machines.

DO THE DIFFERENCES MAKE THE METAPHOR MISLEADING? WHY? No. They make the meta-phor misleading? Steam shovels are machines that people make today and that can move from place to place like living things even though they are really not alive.

STATE THE METAPHOR: A _____ dinosaur _____ **IS LIKE** _____ a steam shovel _____

LESSON CONTEXTS FOR CREATING METAPHORS

The following examples have been suggested by classroom teachers as contexts to develop infused lessons. If a skill or process has been introduced in a previous infused lesson, these contexts may be used to reinforce it.

GRADE	SUBJECT	TOPIC	THINKING ISSUE
K–3	Language arts	Greek myths	Create a modern monster based on one from Greek mythology. Use the strategy for creating metaphors to decide what it should be like. Draw your monster.
K–3	Language arts	Folk tales	Create a present-day metaphor for Johnny Appleseed. Write a story or draw a picture of your modern Johnny Appleseed.
K–3	Literature/science	Folk tales/weather	Read a folk tale that compares a weather condition (wind, thunder, rain, snow, etc.) to a person. Note how the weather condition acts in the story. Create a metaphor of a different weather condition and write a story or poem with that weather condition as a character.
K–3	Reading	Folk tales	Read a folk tale that explains how an animal got its colors. Note how the animal acts in the story. Create a metaphor for another animal and write a story or poem about how that animal got its colors.
K–3	Social studies	Colonies	Create a metaphor to show how the thirteen colonies were related to England. Create a poster or write a story to show that metaphor.
K–3	Mathematics/science	Computer	Many of the parts of a computer have names that are metaphors for how they look or what they do (mouse, file, trash, etc.) Think about a part of the computer that you have a hard time remembering or understanding. Create a name or icon to show that part.
K–3	Social studies	Westward movement	Create a metaphor for the experiences of pioneers moving west. Draw one picture of the pioneers and one of your metaphor. How are they related?
K–3	Social studies	Neighborhood	Create a metaphor for your neighborhood. Use your metaphor to describe your neighborhood.
K–3	Social studies	Economics	Create a metaphor for barter so you can explain the concept to someone unfamiliar with it.
K–3	Science	Earth formation	Create a metaphor for how the layers of the earth were formed and write a story or draw a mural to show it.
K–3	Science	Amphibian	What are some of the important characteristics of an amphibian? Create a metaphor to show those ideas to someone else. Draw a picture of your amphibian metaphor beside the amphibian on which it is based.
K–3	Science	Seeds	Select one way that seeds travel and create a metaphor for it. Using your metaphor, draw or write a story about a seed's journey.
K–3	Art	Printing	Create a metaphor for making a print. Use it to write the directions for making a print.
K–3	Music	Rhythms	Identify which names for rhythms are metaphors. Select a type of rhythm and create a metaphor to explain how it was created or what it is like (i.e., "beat:" like the regular rhythms of heartbeat).
K–3	Physical education	Relay race	Create a metaphor for a relay race to explain why teamwork is important.
4–6	Language arts	Advertising	Select an ad that you think is particularly effective in promoting an event. Based on that ad, create a metaphor to advertise a school project.

GRADE	SUBJECT	TOPIC	THINKING ISSUE
4–6	Language arts	Writing/ Greek myths	Create a modern day metaphor for Persephone. Use your metaphor to create a short story.
4–6	Language arts	Writing/ Roman myths	Using the legends of Greek heros as a model, create an original Greek legend.
4–6	Language arts	Writing	Create a metaphor for a clone. Write a short story describing the experiences of a plant or animal that is a clone.
4–6	Social Studies	Frontier life	Many pioneers came from other countries and didn't read English. Many people on the frontier had not gone to school to learn to read. In frontier towns businesses, doctors, and dentists hung signs outside their shops that frequently contained pitures or symbols of what they did. Select a business or profession that would be found in a frontier town and create a symbol that would convey to a passersby what that business offered.
4–6	Social Studies	Pilgrims	Examine the reasons that the Pilgrims gave for leaving Holland to come to New England. Select an immigrant group today in similar circumstances and use the Pilgrims as a metaphor to describe their immigration. Create a story, poster, or persuasive essay.
4–6	Social Studies	American Revolution	Create a four page newspaper using current newpaper features to show a modern version of the events of July 4, 1776.
4–6	Social studies	American Indians	Draw a totem pole in the style of Northwest Indians to depict the ideas in Chief Seattle's speech.
4–6	Social Studies	Ancient Egypt	Create a cartouche or obelisk that shows the life of an Eqyptian farmer or the life of a famous Egyptian that you admire.
4–6	Mathematics	Fractions	Create a metaphor for the greatest common factor and the least common multiple that will help you remember the difference.
4–6	Mathematics	Computer use	Create icons for computer commands and assemble several as a poster.
4–6	Science	Volcanoes	Create a myth that would show how ancient people would explain volcanoes.
4–6	Science	Oceans	Create a myth or mural to show how the oceans were created.
4–6	Science	Crusteceans	The names given to crustaceans often fit their appearance, such as the horse shoe crab. Select three mollusks that you are just learning about and give them a name based on their appearance.
4–6	Science	Animal protection	Many animals have unusual means of disguising themselves. Create a metaphor based on disguise, that you can use to remember how various animals disguise themselves.
4–6	Art	Poster design	Create a metaphor for television violence and use it as a theme for a poster.
4–6	Music	Musical style	Identify which names for musical styles are metaphors. Select a type of musical style and create a metaphor to explain how it was created or what it is like.
4–6	Physical education	Soccer	Create a metaphor for soccer that describes the action of the game.

PART 5

SKILLS AT ASSESSING THE REASONABLENESS OF IDEAS: CRITICAL THINKING

ASSESSING BASIC INFORMATION

Chapter 12: Determining the Reliability of Sources

WELL-FOUNDED INFERENCE

USE OF EVIDENCE

Chapter 13: Causal Explanation
Chapter 14: Prediction
Chapter 15: Generalization
Chapter 16: Reasoning by Analogy

DEDUCTION

Chapter 17: Conditional Reasoning

MAP OF THE THINKING DOMAIN

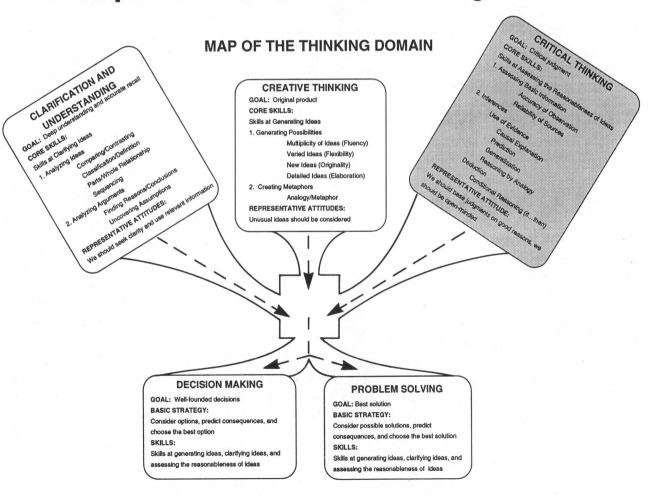

CLARIFICATION AND UNDERSTANDING
GOAL: Deep understanding and accurate recall
CORE SKILLS:
Skills at Clarifying Ideas
1. Analyzing Ideas
  Comparing/Contrasting
  Classification/Definition
  Parts/Whole Relationship
  Sequencing
2. Analyzing Arguments
  Finding Reasons/Conclusions
  Uncovering Assumptions
REPRESENTATIVE ATTITUDES:
We should seek clarity and use relevant information

CREATIVE THINKING
GOAL: Original product
CORE SKILLS:
Skills at Generating Ideas
1. Generating Possibilities
  Multiplicity of Ideas (Fluency)
  Varied Ideas (Flexibility)
  New Ideas (Originality)
  Detailed Ideas (Elaboration)
2. Creating Metaphors
  Analogy/Metaphor
REPRESENTATIVE ATTITUDES:
Unusual ideas should be considered

CRITICAL THINKING
GOAL: Critical judgment
CORE SKILLS:
Skills at Assessing the Reasonableness of Ideas
1. Assessing Basic Information
  Accuracy of Observation
  Reliability of Sources
2. Inferences
  Use of Evidence
    Causal Explanation
    Prediction
    Generalization
    Reasoning by Analogy
  Deduction
    Conditional Reasoning (if...then)
REPRESENTATIVE ATTITUDE:
We should base judgments on good reasons, we should be open-minded

DECISION MAKING
GOAL: Well-founded decisions
BASIC STRATEGY:
Consider options, predict consequences, and choose the best option
SKILLS:
Skills at generating ideas, clarifying ideas, and assessing the reasonableness of ideas

PROBLEM SOLVING
GOAL: Best solution
BASIC STRATEGY:
Consider possible solutions, predict consequences, and choose the best solution
SKILLS:
Skills at generating ideas, clarifying ideas, and assessing the reasonableness of ideas

PART 5
SKILLS AT ASSESSING THE REASONABLENESS OF IDEAS: CRITICAL THINKING

Should I accept the idea that eating red meat regularly is a health hazard, or should I believe that it is risk free? Should I endorse site-based management as a way of improving the quality of education, or should I reject it as ill conceived? Should I embrace the idea that teaching thinking is important, or should I concentrate on just teaching students the facts? Accepting ideas and acting on them is the primary way we progress through our lives and in our professional work. Unless we can assess which ideas are reasonable and which are not, we run the risk of acting on ideas that are incorrect, often leading to personal, professional, and even social harm.

When we engage in critical thinking we assess the reasonableness of ideas. Critical thinking is crucially important to insure that the judgments we make are more likely to be correct than incorrect. We cannot expect to make sound judgments if we accept everything we hear and read or every idea that pops into our heads.

Critical thinking has been described in different ways: as the evaluation of reasoning and argument; as reasonable, reflective thinking directed at deciding what to believe or do; and as the application of standards to our judgments. What these conceptions of critical thinking have in common is that before we accept a judgment, we should be sure that it is supported by good reasons. If it is not, we should not accept it.

Skillfully assessing the reasonableness of ideas requires that we utilize acceptable standards. For example, when we appeal to the views of experts and well-respected authorities about matters we know little about, we use standards that are generally acceptable. However, a critical thinker does not just accept standards that are in vogue but subjects the standards themselves to critical thinking. For example, when you reflect on appealing to an expert, you realize that even experts are sometimes wrong. While there are reasons to trust experts, getting a sec-

ond opinion may be more acceptable than trusting the word of one authority.

Critical thinking also involves important *attitudes and dispositions.* Critical thinkers search for reasons. They do so with open minds, looking for all of the reasons, both pro and con, before accepting an idea as feasible. They are willing to suspend judgment if they can find no reasons that support or counter an idea. They are willing to change their minds if they get new evidence. They are willing to submit even the most basic beliefs to critical scrutiny; for critical thinkers, everything they believe and do should be based on good reasons.

Critical thinking is as much a way of life as it is a set of abilities. Teaching for critical thinking must address the attitudinal and dispositional aspects of critical thinking, as well as the skills and abilities in good judgment that critical thinking involves.

The critical thinking skills in this handbook are the most frequently needed skills in our personal and professional lives. They fall into two categories:

- Skills related to *basic information* that we get from a variety of sources, including media, textbooks, other people, and even our own observations (determining the accuracy of observation, determining the reliability of sources); and

- Skills related to *inferences* in which we draw conclusions that we do not verify directly from information offered as *evidence to support* them (causal explanation, prediction, generalization, and reasoning by analogy), or inferences in which we *deduce conclusions* (conditional reasoning).

Each type of critical thinking skill involves the common theme of searching for reasons that support ideas and only accepting those ideas if they are based on good reasons. However, different types of supporting reasons are needed depending on the type of ideas being considered. For example, the support needed to determine whether or not a source is reliable (usual reliability, possible bias, expertise, etc.) is different from the type of evidence needed to support a prediction about tomorrow's weather, a generalization about voters' tendencies, an explanation of the causes of an accident, or a judgment about humans based on information about how mice behave in a laboratory. Critical thinkers can discriminate these different types of critical thinking and engage in each of them well.

Thinking skillfully about causal explanation, prediction, generalization, reasoning by analogy, conditional reasoning, and the reliability of sources of information is essential in our lives and professional work. Students will quickly develop the habits of mind necessary to become good critical thinkers when these thinking skills are taught across the curriculum and suitably reinforced.

CHAPTER 12
DETERMINING THE RELIABILITY OF SOURCES

Why is Evaluating Sources Skillfully Important?

We find out about many things without witnessing them ourselves, i.e., we rely on others as sources of information. We read about things in newspapers and magazines that we did not observe ourselves. We hear about events on television. Other people tell us about things that they've witnessed directly, but we didn't.

We also rely on other sources for more specialized information. We sometimes consult sources for technical and/or general information that we may not be in a position to verify ourselves, like the usefulness of certain medications in treating illnesses or the correct translation of a foreign language passage.

The reliability of such information is extremely important to us. We often make key decisions based on it. We get certain medications for illnesses based on what a physician says. We make travel plans based on information we get from others. Misinformation in these contexts can be costly indeed. People are often surprised to find out how much information we get from other sources and how much we depend on its being reliable.

Problems about Sources of Information

Unfortunately, we sometimes do get misinformation from others. Deliberate deception or distortion is one source of misinformation. However, sometimes well-meaning people who are unaware of the inaccuracy of their information pass it on to us. They may make hasty judgments themselves, or their sources may not be sufficiently reliable. Sometimes a person's biases transform what they hear into subtle changes of meaning that are then unwittingly communicated from person to person. Rumors are extreme examples of misinformation transmitted by a number of people who are often influenced by such factors.

Problems about How We Think about Sources

One common problem in the way we handle information is that we often don't question our sources. Even if we do question a source, we may rely on just one or two factors to establish the source's credibility. In some instances, we accept a person as a reliable source because he or she seems honest. In other cases, if the source has expertise in a field, we assume that the information he or she provides must be accurate. However, we know that people who seem honest, or who have expertise in a field, may have biases or vested interests. They may be uncritical themselves in accepting information which they pass on to us. Often if a witness describes an event at which he or she was present, people accept that witness as credible. An account published in a newspaper or book is considered reliable by some people just because it appears in print. These reasons for accepting reliability are risky oversimplifications.

These defaults in our thinking about sources of information are summarized in figure 12.1.

COMMON DEFAULTS IN OUR THINKING ABOUT SOURCES OF INFORMATION

1. We accept information from sources without asking whether they are reliable.

2. We use information about only a small number of factors to make judgements about the reliability of sources.

Figure 12.1

To gather accurate information, we must exercise skillful discrimination about the information we are given. We can try to do this by confirming the information ourselves. However, when we have no direct access to the information, we must judge the credibility or reliability of the sources of the information in order to be able to judge its accuracy. Evaluating a source can, indeed, be done with care and skill.

How Do We Determine the Credibility of a Source Skillfully?

Types of Sources. Any person, publication, or other medium of communication can be a source of information. When the information we receive is important, we should take note of who or what the source is. The source could be a family member, a friend, a teacher, a salesperson, someone who witnessed an event, a newspaper article, an encyclopedia, a new book, an advertisement, or a TV show.

There are basic ways we classify such sources that have bearing on their credibility. The information may be secondhand (secondary), or it may be firsthand source (primary). Generally, we tend to trust primary sources more than secondary sources. This, however, does not mean that secondary sources are untrustworthy. If the source is a secondary source, we should also find out where he or she got the information and try to trace it back to its primary origins. Then we should inquire about the primary source.

Determining Reliability

What else can we find out that would support or count against a source's credibility? Important factors include reputation, past history in providing reliable and accurate information, the person's expertise, the datedness of the information, the procedures used in gathering it, and the vested interests of those relating the information.

Eyewitness accounts are a special case of primary source information based on direct observation. In this instance, the conditions of observation, the use of observation-enhancing instruments, the person's expectations of what he or she is seeing, and when the report was recorded are all important.

We should apply the same principles to ourselves as sources of information. When we intend to communicate information to others, we can and should plan out how we acquire the information to be sure of its accuracy. When we plan and prepare observation reports, for example, we should be concerned with the same factors we take into account when we assess the reliability of others as sources of information. While we may attend to some of these factors naturally, like putting our glasses on before we observe things, we should also think about other factors that we often don't consider. For example, we should make sure that we know enough about what we are observing beforehand so that we don't misname or misdescribe it. We should also make sure that we write down or otherwise record what we observe at the time, rather than waiting until later when we might misremember.

Others develop confidence in us as reliable sources when we explain how we acquire our information. Describing how we make our observations or explaining any experimental procedures we use helps others to judge our reliability as observers. References to other reliable sources from whom we got our information also builds credibility. Indeed, these are standard procedures in the natural and social sciences for establishing a source's credibility.

Sometimes we get information about one of the factors that influence credibility. We may find out, for example, that an individual who provides some important information on a current matter may have not given accurate information in the past. His past record casts some doubt on whether he is a reliable source for the information he is providing now. However, it would be a mistake to conclude that he is an unreliable source of the present information and that his report is inaccurate. An error in the past is not sufficient support for unreliability in the present.

Similarly, it is a mistake to think that because someone is an expert in a field, his or her judgment must be accurate. Experts often disagree and may have vested interests or biases, whether or not they acknowledge these biases, which can color and distort the information they provide. To have good reasons for thinking that a source is reliable or unreliable on a specific occasion, all factors must be weighed and a pattern of support for or against a source's reliability must be established.

When all factors have been considered and

the credibility of a source remains uncertain, one way to elevate the credibility of the source is to seek out other sources. If these additional sources are reliable and independently corroborate what the initial source tells us, that consensus can raise the credibility of the information.

Even without independent corroboration, we can still make judgments of relative reliability. If there were five witnesses to an automobile accident, determining which factors were present and which were not may suggest that one of these witnesses is more likely to give us accurate information than the others. One person may have been close to the accident and in full view of it, while others may have had an obstructed view or have been attending to something else at the time. While this may not guarantee that the first person is giving us an absolutely accurate description of what happened, there is a better chance that his or her account is more accurate than the others, all other things being equal. Of course, corroboration by additional witnesses can provide further support for the credibility of one or another of these accounts.

Tools for Determining the Reliability of Sources

A good way to make informed judgments about the reliability of sources is to develop a checklist of important factors to guide our search for information about the source. To exercise care in our judgments of reliability, we should think about all the factors on our checklist. Such a checklist can also be used to plan what we ourselves should do to become a reliable source of information.

The thinking map in figure 12.2 for evaluating the reliability of sources contains a checklist of this sort. It is useful when we don't know much about the source. If the information is an observation report, the more specialized map for determining the accuracy of an observation, depicted in figure 12.3, can be used.

These thinking maps can guide us in making judgments about sources in any field. This, however, does not imply that if you are a good source of information or a good observer in one field, you'll be a good source or observer in others. You wouldn't expect a person with ex-

---

EVALUATING THE RELIABILITY OF SOURCES SKILLFULLY

1. What is considered the source of the information being considered?

2. List the factors present that are relevant to the reliability of the source in the following categories:

    Published?
        Date?
        Reputation of publication?
        Kind of publication (e.g., report, fiction)?
    Author?
        Expertise?
        Bias or distorting point of view?
        Special interest?
        Primary or secondary?
            If secondary, the reliability of any other sources the information is derived from?
            If primary, the other relevant factors, e.g., equipment used?
    Corroboration/confirmation?

3. Weigh the factors present and make a judgement of reliability based on them.

Figure 12.2

---

pertise in medicine to be able to observe a malfunction in an automobile engine with the reliability of an auto mechanic, unless the medical expert is also knowledgeable about automobile repair. Expertise in a field is a criterion of accuracy and reliability as a source and can vary from field to field. In using the checklists on these maps, interpret "Expertise" and "Background" to mean "in the field within which the information is contained."

The graphic organizer in figure 12.4 can be used to assess either secondary or primary sources of information. Write relevant questions from the thinking map in the boxes under "Questions" to guide you in searching for information about the source. The items that you put in the "Questions" boxes can be derived from either the reliable sources or accuracy of observation checklists, depending on whether or not the source is an observer.

**DETERMINING THE ACCURACY
OF AN OBSERVATION**

1. Which of the following features of the observer, observation, and report are present in this case?

   Observer:
   Background?
   Qualifications?
   Usual reliability?
   Free of bias?
   State of mind?
   Physical ability to observe (eyesight, etc.)?
   Capacity to observe (proximity, direction, free of distraction)?
   Expectations/point of view?
   Vested interest in having audience believe the report?

   Conduct of the observation:
   Frequency?
   Equipment?
      Strength or accuracy?
      Condition?
      How operated?
   Date and location?
   Replicated?
   Observation conditions?

   Report:
   How soon after the observation?
   Details (drawings, photographs, graphs)?
   Language and findings expressed objectively?

   Corroboration:
   By others?
   By me?

2. When you weigh these factors, how reliable would you judge the observation to be?

Figure 12.3

As you gather information about the source, write it in the "Information" box. Put a plus or minus next to it, depending on whether the information counts in favor of or against reliability. This process creates an informed profile of the source. Based on this profile, make your determination of the reliability of, unreliability of, or your uncertainty about the source. Usually, lack of information about corroboration and a mixture of other relevant information

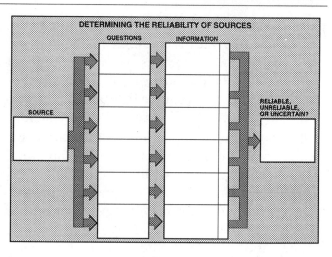

Figure 12.4

about the source, some of which counts for and some of which counts against reliability, should lead you to be uncertain about a source's credibility. Corroboration by an independent source of good repute can eliminate this uncertainty. On the other hand, in cases of such uncertainty, if other credible sources conflict with the one you are considering, this should lead you to judge that the source is not reliable.

How Can We Teach Students to Evaluate Sources Skillfully?

The goal of teaching students to evaluate sources skillfully is to encourage them to raise questions about reliability when appropriate and then to attend to the significant factors in judging reliability. It is not enough simply to ask students which sources among a given sample are most reliable. Challenge students to articulate their reasons for accepting or rejecting a source's reliability in the context of their understanding of the kind of information they need to make that judgment. Make the process of evaluating sources explicit through the frequent use of the language of the skill, the thinking map, and explicit graphic organizers to guide your students as they respond to these challenges.

Contexts in the Curriculum for Lessons about the Reliability of Sources

Textbooks, teachers, and other resource people that your students learn from are sources of information. However, the best contexts for lessons on the reliability of sources are those in which an authentic issue about reliable information relates to curricular content. In general, there are four sorts of instances which provide rich contexts for reliable sources lessons:

- *Sources disagree about information students are learning.* For example, different texts may give different accounts of historical events. Sources may also disagree about whether or not certain foods have nutritional or medicinal value or whether certain chemicals are harmful to the environment.

- *Observation reports and measurements sometimes conflict, reflect questionable procedures, or reveal something surprising.* For example, laboratory reports from students in science classes or measurements made in mathematics often differ widely. Observation accounts of social conditions in texts also sometimes vary.

- *There is a variety of sources of differing quality available for student writing, reference, or research (e.g., in the school library).* For example, the library may contain popularized, outdated, and more recent information on topics you ask your students to write about.

- *People or fictional characters students learn about have relied on certain sources to make decisions.* For example, various controversial historical events may involve problematic information (e.g., "Custer's last stand," Columbus' observation reports of "Indians"). Characters in children's stories often act hastily without thinking about their sources (e.g., in *Hansel and Gretel* or *Henny Penny*).

Numerous specific contexts in the K–6 curriculum for such reliable sources lessons are provided in the menus at the end of this chapter (pp. 382–84).

Two Approaches in Teaching Students to Determine the Reliability of Sources

You may choose to use a direct approach in teaching this skill. For example, you can give students the thinking maps for reliable sources

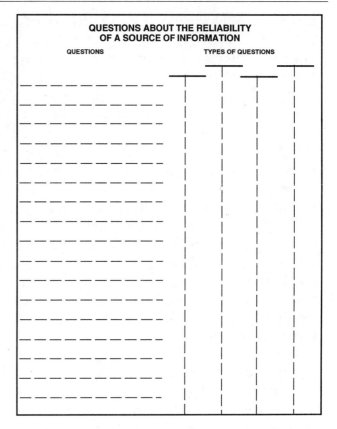

Figure 12.5

and accurate observation and ask them to use these as a guide, making a list of relevant factors they discover about a particular source. You can prompt students' consideration of these factors by direct questions about the source, which you formulate yourself based on these maps.

Whenever possible, however, we recommend deriving maps for determining the reliability of sources from the students' own comments about a specific example. This inductive approach to learning the skill is featured in the sample lessons in this handbook. In conducting a lesson in this way, the teacher asks students to generate questions they would ask about sources and to categorize the questions into types of questions that one would ask about any source. This checklist can then be transformed into a thinking map for the skill. The graphic organizer in figure 12.5 is useful in conducting an inductive lesson of this sort.

On the left side of this graphic organizer students should list questions they would want to have answered in order to determine the reliability of the source. For example, to assess the accuracy of information in an article from a science magazine, students may list such questions as "What is the background and training of the author?" "Is the author usually reliable in giving information?" and "What is the reputation of the magazine in which the article appeared?"

Next, the students should group the questions into types, which they label on the short horizontal lines. They then connect the lines that the questions are on with the vertical line under the label. For example, "About the Author" might be listed on the first horizontal line under "Types of Questions." Then all of the questions about the author, including the questions about the author's background and usual reliability, can be connected to the first vertical line leading to this heading. When complete, the types of questions can be reorganized into a checklist to develop a thinking map like the one we have included. If you use this technique for making the skill explicit, you should use the thinking map that the students generate, rather than the one we have presented.

Teaching Reliability of Sources in the Primary Grades

We recommend introducing this skill in the primary grades. Grade-appropriate material should, of course, be used, and the skill should be simplified for students this age. We include a reliable sources lesson that illustrates how this skill can be taught in kindergarten and first grade. The simplified thinking map in figure 12.6, more appropriate for primary grade students, is used in this lesson.

Reinforcing the Skill

After students have worked through a curricular example and have developed a checklist for the reliability of a source, you should give them more practice in using this checklist. When you ask them to apply the checklist to new examples, prompt students to use the terms from their checklist often and appropriately. Science, current events, mathematics, and art offer plentiful contexts for evaluating the reliability of sources. Evaluating sources is particularly useful in resolving student conflicts. Your

RELIABILITY OF SOURCES

1. To find out whether a source is reliable ask whether the source

   Knows the subject?
   Found out from someone else who is reliable?
   Found out by careful investigation?
   Has a reason for wanting you to believe him?
   Is known and trusted by others?

2. Also ask whether anyone else thinks the same thing.

Figure 12.6

goal is to encourage students to use this skill deliberately whenever appropriate.

Model Lessons on Determining the Reliability of Sources of Information

We include three model lessons on this skill: a primary language arts lesson, an upper elementary science lesson, and an upper elementary general science lesson. Each illustrates a different variation on teaching this skill mentioned in the commentary. The primary language arts lesson uses a simplified thinking map for the primary grades. The elementary science lesson guides students in making judgments about the reliability of resources in a school library. The other science lesson focuses on the accuracy and reliability of an observation report. As you review these lessons try to answer the following questions:

- How is the importance of determining the reliability of sources of information introduced to students in these lessons?

- What techniques are used to prompt an inductive development of students' understanding of these skills?

- What are the near and the far transfer activities introduced in these lessons?

- Can you think of other ways of reinforcing students' skillful determination of the reliability of sources of information after these lessons have been completed?

Thinking Maps and Graphic Organizers for Determining the Reliability of Sources

The thinking maps provide questions to guide students' thinking in evaluating the reliability of sources of information skillfully. They can be used as stated or modified by students as they reflect on how they engage in evaluating sources skillfully. One thinking map is for determining the reliability of any source, the second is for determining the reliability of an observer as a source of information.

Tools for Designing Lessons on the Reliability of Sources

There are two graphic organizers included. The first is for generating and categorizing questions to be asked in gathering information relevant to the reliability of a source or the accuracy of an observation. The second is for evaluating specific sources and reinforces the sequenced questions on the thinking maps. The thinking map on page 348 is designed especially for use in the primary grades.

The thinking maps and graphic organizers can guide you in designing the critical thinking activity in the lesson and can also serve as photocopy masters, transparency masters, or as models that can be enlarged and used as posters in the classroom. Reproduction rights are granted for single classroom use only.

RELIABILITY OF SOURCES

1. To find out whether a source is reliable, ask whether the source

   Knows the subject?

   Found out from someone else who is reliable?

   Found out by careful investigation?

   Has a reason for wanting you to believe him or her?

   Is known and trusted by others?

2. Also ask whether anyone else thinks the same thing.

EVALUATING THE RELIABILITY OF SOURCES SKILLFULLY

1. What is the source of the information being considered?

2. List the factors present that are relevant to the reliability of the source in the following categories:

   a. Published?
      Date?
      Reputation of publication?
      Kind of publication? (e.g., report, fiction)?

   b. Author?
      Expertise?
      Bias or distorting point of view?
      Special interest?
      Primary or secondary?
        If secondary, the reliability of any other sources the information is derived from?
        If primary, other relevant factors, e.g., equipment used?
      Corroboration/confirmation?

3. Weigh the factors present and make a judgement of reliability based on them.

DETERMINING THE ACCURACY OF AN OBSERVATION

1. Which of the following features of the observer, observation, and report are present in this case?

   Observer:

   Background?

   Qualifications?

   Usual reliability?

   Free of bias?

   State of mind?

   Physical ability to observe (eyesight, etc.)?

   Capacity to observe (proximity, direction, free of distraction)?

   Expectations/point of view?

   Vested interest in having audience believe the report?

   Conduct of the observation:

   Frequency?

   Equipment?

   Strength or accuracy?

   Condition?

   How operated?

   Date and location?

   Replicated?

   Observation conditions?

   Report:

   How soon after the observation?

   Details (drawings, photographs, graphs)?

   Language and findings expressed objectively?

   Corroboration:

   By others?

   By me?

2. When you weigh these factors, how reliable would you judge the observation to be?

QUESTIONS ABOUT THE RELIABILITY
OF A SOURCE OF INFORMATION

QUESTIONS

TYPES OF QUESTIONS

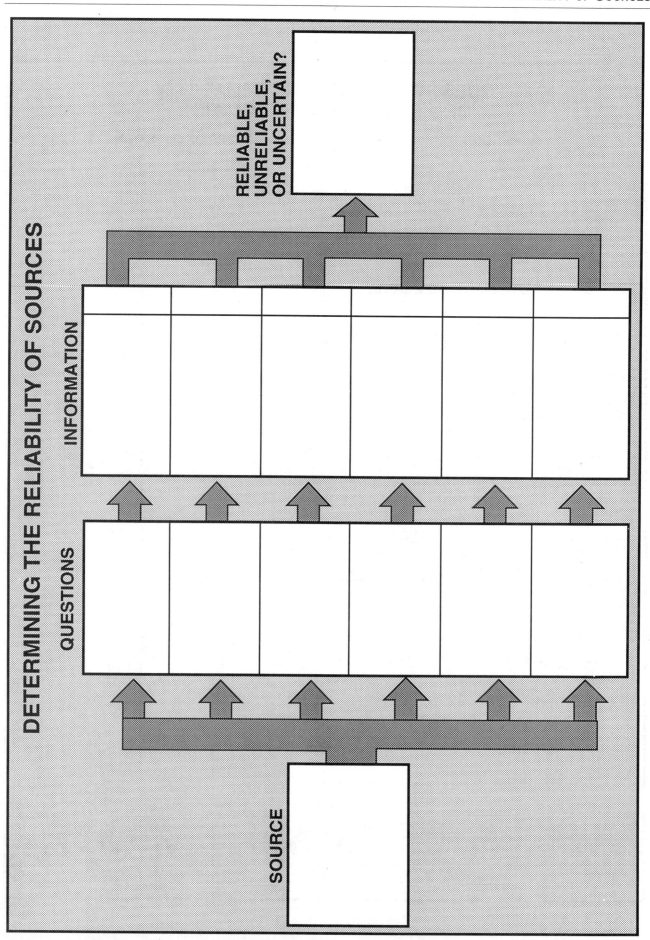

DETERMINING THE RELIABILITY OF SOURCES

RELIABLE, UNRELIABLE, OR UNCERTAIN?

INFORMATION

QUESTIONS

SOURCE

COCKY LOCKY

Language Arts **Grades K–2**

OBJECTIVES

CONTENT

Students will develop good listening skills, identify a sequence of occurrences in a story, and learn how to state the moral of a story.

THINKING SKILL/PROCESS

Students will learn how to make judgments about the accuracy and reliability of sources of information based on the presence or absence of relevant factors.

METHODS AND MATERIALS

CONTENT

The teacher reads the story of Henny Penny aloud to the students. The students repeat parts of the story.

THINKING SKILL/PROCESS

This lesson uses structured questioning to help students identify factors which influence the reliability of sources of information. (See pp. 348–352 for reproducible diagrams.) Collaborative learning strategies are also employed.

LESSON

INTRODUCTION TO CONTENT AND THINKING SKILL/PROCESS

- We can't discover everything ourselves. Other people often tell us about things that we don't find out ourselves. These people are called "sources of information." Can you think of times when other people have been sources of information for you? Mention some people who are sources of information. Sources may include teachers, parents, friends, people who have shows on television, people in television commercials, and clerks in stores.

- Often the information we get from others is correct. Sometimes it isn't. It's important to be sure that we get good information when we have to depend on other sources. Can you think of a time when you got information from someone else and it turned out to be wrong? Discuss this with a partner. Ask for some examples from the class. ANSWERS WILL VARY.

- In order to get information that we can depend on from other sources, we should check the sources of the information. Sometimes what we find out about the source makes us wonder whether the information is dependable, or reliable. This means that we have to think about things like who the source is, how much he or she knows, how the source knows about what he or she is telling us, how the source feels about it, and when the information was obtained by the source. Sometimes we should even evaluate whether we ourselves are good, reliable sources of information. When we have answered these questions and believe that we can depend on a source to give us correct information, we have determined that the source is reliable.

- Suppose someone told you that the best cereal to eat was called "Double O Breakfast Cereal." What would you want to find out to decide whether this person was a reliable source? POSSIBLE ANSWERS: *Did the person try the cereal himself or herself? Did the person learn about it from a magazine advertisement? Did the person learn about it from another person who had tried the cereal? Was the information from an ad for the cereal? Does the person have a good memory?* **If you ask these** questions and decide not to believe the source until you have answered them, you're a good thinker.

- I'm going to read you a story. Listen for the times when someone gets information from someone else in the story. We're going to think about what we can find out about some of the characters who are sources of information. Then we can decide whether they are reliable sources. This is the story of Henny Penny. Let's listen to find out what happens. Read the story of Henny Penny. Every time a new animal comes along prompt students to repeat what the animal asks: "Where are you going in such a hurry?" Then try to get them to repeat what Henny Penny and the other animals say: "The sky is falling and we're going to tell the king." Read through to the end of the story when the animals are led into the fox's den and become a meal for the fox's family.

THINKING ACTIVELY

- **Which of the animals were sources of information for someone else?** *Henny Penny for Cocky Locky; Henny Penny and Cocky Locky for Ducky Lucky; Henny Penny, Cocky Locky, and Ducky Lucky for Goosey Loosey; Henny Penny, Cocky Locky, Ducky Lucky, and Goosey Loosey for Turkey Lurkey; and Henny Penny, Cocky Locky, Ducky Lucky, Goosey Loosey, and Turkey Lurkey for Foxy Loxy.* **What information did the animals who were sources tell the others?** *The sky was falling. They were going to tell the king that the sky was falling.*

- **How many animals told Turkey Lurkey that the sky was falling?** *Four.* **How many animals told Cocky Locky that the sky was falling?** *One.*

- **Does it matter that there were more animals who told Turkey Lurkey? Does that make the information more reliable? Why?** *No. They all got the information from Henny Penny.* **When a lot of people tell you something they heard from one person, it may seem to be true because so many people tell you the same thing. However, it is only as reliable as the person they heard it from.**

- **Was Cocky Locky a good thinker? Why or why not?** *Cocky Locky was not a good thinker because he didn't ask any questions. He just believed what Henny Penny told him without knowing whether or not she was a reliable source.* **Let's call it "Cocky Locky" thinking when a person just believes what a source says and doesn't ask questions or find out whether or not the source is reliable.**

- Rumors are similar. When one person tells another something that he is not sure about and that person tells another person who also repeats it to someone, it may seem true. However, the story may get changed as different people repeat it. If it wasn't certain to begin with, you shouldn't consider it reliable, no matter how many people believe the story.

- **Make believe that you are Cocky Locky. Suppose that Henny Penny just came rushing along and you asked her where she was going in such a hurry. She says that the sky is falling and she is going to tell the king. You want to be a better thinker than Cocky Locky in the story. Talk to your partner and figure out what questions you could ask to find out whether or not she is a reliable source. List four questions that you would ask.** Write students' questions on the board. POSSIBLE ANSWERS: *Is Henny Penny a scientist? Does she lie? Did anyone else see a piece of the sky fall on her head? Did anyone see something else fall on her head? Did anyone see her talking to Foxy Loxy? Does she jump to conclusions often? Is she careful about what she reports to other people? Is she a newspaper reporter? Did she look around to see what hit her on the head or did she quickly say that it was a piece of the sky without looking?*

- **Let's look at these questions and make a list of things that you should ask about a source to decide whether or not it is reliable. What should be on the list?** Write a blank thinking map on the board with the heading "RELIABILITY OF SOURCES" and, as students mention things to ask about, fill it in. It may include the items on the thinking map.

- **Work together with your partner and use the thinking map to help you decide whether you have any reason to think that Henny Penny is or is not a reliable source of information.** Ask the students to report and to explain why they think Henny Penny may or may not be a reliable source. Write students' responses on a

> ## RELIABLITY OF SOURCES
>
> 1. To find out whether a source is reliable ask whether the source
>
>   Knows the subject?
>   Found out from someone else who is reliable?
>   Found out by careful investigation?
>   Has a reason for wanting you to believe him?
>   Is known and trusted by others?
>
> 2. Also ask whether anyone else thinks the same thing.

transparency or poster of the graphic organizer. POSSIBLE ANSWERS: *Henny Penny is probably not reliable because she didn't investigate. Henny Penny is probably not reliable because no one else saw a piece of the sky hit her on the head.*

- **If Cocky Locky had done some good thinking about Henny Penny, like you just did, do you think he would have been eaten up by the fox?** *No, because he probably wouldn't have gone along.*

- **What can we learn from what happened to Cocky Locky? What is liable to happen if you don't do good thinking?** *We might get into trouble. We might get hurt.* **What should you do to avoid getting into trouble or getting hurt when someone gives you information?** *Make sure that person is a reliable source by asking good questions and finding out the answers. We should ask the questions on the thinking map.*

- **When we learn something, from a story, about what we should do, that's called the "moral" of the story. What moral did we learn from Henny Penny?** POSSIBLE ANSWERS: *Don't accept information from someone unless you are sure that person is a reliable source. Think before you do things. You should make sure you know what has happened before you tell other people about it.*

THINKING ABOUT THINKING

- **How did you figure out whether Henny Penny was a reliable source of information? What did you think about?** POSSIBLE ANSWERS: *I asked questions about Henny Penny. I found out that she didn't investigate what hit her on the head.*

- **Is this a better way to think about what Henny Penny said than "Cocky Locky Thinking?" Why?** POSSIBLE ANSWERS: *Yes, because you can find out whether to believe her. Yes, because if you don't ask questions, you may not find out whether she is a reliable source until it is too late. Yes, because Cocky Locky got into trouble.*

- **Plan what you would do to decide whether someone who you don't know and who gave you information is a reliable source.** POSSIBLE ANSWERS: *I would ask that person how they know. I would ask someone else whether or not they think that person is a reliable source. I would try to find out whether other people who didn't get their information from this person think the same thing.*

APPLYING YOUR THINKING

Immediate Transfer

• Think about something you might like to buy. What sources would you go to in order to get the most reliable information about it? Why?

• We've been studying healthy foods in science. Decide who, among the following people, would give you the most reliable information about which foods are healthy and why:

The school nurse	The grocer
The crossing guard	The person who sits next to you in school
A television commercial	The school bus driver

Reinforcement Later

When the class studies the following topic later in the school year, ask these questions:

• We're going to be looking at some story books with pictures of what it was like in Plymouth, Massachusetts when the Pilgrims lived there. What will you want to find out to decide whether these pictures are reliable sources of information about the Pilgrims?

ASSESSING STUDENT THINKING ABOUT RELIABLE SOURCES

Any of the transfer examples can serve as an assessment item. The examples about a new purchase, healthy foods, and the Pilgrims are good ones for this purpose. The example about a new purchase is particularly suited to be used as pre- and post- tests on this skill. Decide beforehand which items from the reliable sources thinking map a student should mention in the post-test in order to show improvement.

HENNY PENNY

One day Henny Penny was pecking corn in the barnyard when—whack!—something hit her on the head. "Goodness gracious me!" she said, "The sky is falling. I must go and tell the King."

So she went along, and went along, and went along until she met another animal on the road, Cocky-Locky. "Where are you going in such a hurry, Henny-Penny?" said Cocky-Locky.

"The sky is falling! I'm going to tell the King," said Henny Penny.

"That's important. May I come with you?" said Cocky Locky.

"Certainly," said Henny Penny. So Henny Penny and Cocky Locky continued on the road to tell the King that the sky was falling.

They went along, and went along, and went along till they met another animal, Ducky Lucky. "Where are you going in such a hurry, Henny Penny and Cocky Locky?" said Ducky Lucky.

"We're going to tell the King the sky is falling," said Henny Penny and Cocky Locky.

"May I come with you?" said Ducky Lucky.

"Certainly," said Henny Penny and Cocky Locky. So Henny Penny, Cocky Locky, and Ducky Lucky continued on the road to tell the King the sky was falling.

So they went along, and went along, and went along until they met another animal who was there on the road, Goosey Loosey. "Where are you going in such a hurry, Henny Penny, Cocky Locky, and Ducky Lucky?" said Goosey Loosey.

"The sky is falling! We're going to tell the King," said Henny Penny, Cocky Locky, and Ducky Lucky.

"That sounds very important. May I come with you?" said Goosey Loosey.

"Certainly," said Henny Penny, Cocky Locky, and Ducky Lucky. So Henny Penny, Cocky Locky, Ducky Lucky, and now Goosey Loosey continued on the road to tell the King the sky was falling.

So they went along, and went along, and went along until they met yet another animal on the road, Turkey-Lurkey. "Where are you going in such a hurry, Henny Penny, Cocky Locky, Goosey Loosey and Ducky Lucky?" said Turkey Lurkey.

"We're going to tell the King the sky is falling," said Henny Penny, Cocky Locky, Ducky Lucky and Goosey Loosey.

"May I come with you?" said Turkey Lurkey.

"Certainly," they said. So Henny Penny, Cocky Locky, Ducky Lucky, Goosey Loosey and Turkey Lurkey all continued on the road to tell the King the sky was falling.

So they went along, and went along, and went along until they met another animal who also was there on the road. It was Foxy Loxy. Foxy Loxy said to Henny Penny, Cocky Locky, Goosey Loosey, Ducky Lucky and Turkey Lurkey, "Where are you going to in such a hurry, Henny Penny, Cocky Locky, Goosey Loosey, Ducky Lucky and Turkey Lurkey?"

And Henny Penny, Cocky Locky, Goosey Loosey, Ducky Lucky and Turkey Lurkey said to Foxy Loxy "We're going to tell the King the sky is falling."

"That sounds important. May I join you?" said Foxy Loxy.

All the animals said "Certainly," and Foxy Loxy joined them as they continued on the road to tell the king that the sky was falling.

Soon, however, Foxy Loxy stopped and said to the other animals, "Oh, but this is not the way to the King, Henny Penny, Cocky Locky, Goosey Loosey, Ducky Lucky and Turkey Lurkey. You're going the long way. I know a short cut. Shall I show it to you?"

"Oh certainly Foxy Loxy," said Henny Penny, Cocky Locky, Ducky Lucky, Goosey Loosey and Turkey Lurkey. So Henny Penny, Cocky Locky, Ducky Lucky, Goosey Loosey, Turkey Lurkey and Foxy Loxy all went to tell the King the sky was falling.

Adapted from an English folktale

They went along and they went along, till they came to a small, dark hole. Now this was the door of Foxy Loxy's cave. So Foxy Loxy said to Henny Penny, Cocky Locky, Goosey Loosey, Ducky Lucky and Turkey Lurkey, "This is the short way to the King's palace. You'll soon get there. Follow me. I will go first, and you come after, Henny Penny, Cocky Locky, Goosey Loosey, Ducky Lucky and Turkey Lurkey."

"Why, of course, certainly," said Henny Penny, Cocky Locky, Goosey Loosey, Ducky Lucky and Turkey Lurkey.

So Foxy Loxy went into his cave, and he didn't go very far. He turned around to wait for the other animals.

First Turkey Lurkey went through the dark hole into the cave. He hadn't got far when "Hrumph," Foxy-Loxy snapped off Turkey Lurkey's head and threw his body over his left shoulder to feed his family.

Then Goosey Loosey went in, and "Hrumph," off went her head, and Goosey Loosey was thrown beside Turkey Lurkey.

Then Ducky Lucky waddled in, and "Hrumph," snapped Foxy Loxy, and Ducky Lucky's head was off and Ducky Lucky was thrown alongside Turkey Lurkey and Goosey Loosey.

Then Cocky Locky strutted down into the cave, and he hadn't gone far when Foxy Loxy took a bite at Cocky Locky. But Foxy Loxy had been so busy that he missed Cocky Locky, and before he took a second bite at Cocky Locky and got him, Cocky Locky had time to call out to Henny Penny to run away. So Henny Penny turned around, ran off, and never did tell the King that the sky was falling.

SAMPLE STUDENT RESPONSES • COCKY LOCKY

DETERMINING THE RELIABILITY OF SOURCES

QUESTIONS   **INFORMATION**

RELIABLE, UNRELIABLE, OR UNCERTAIN?

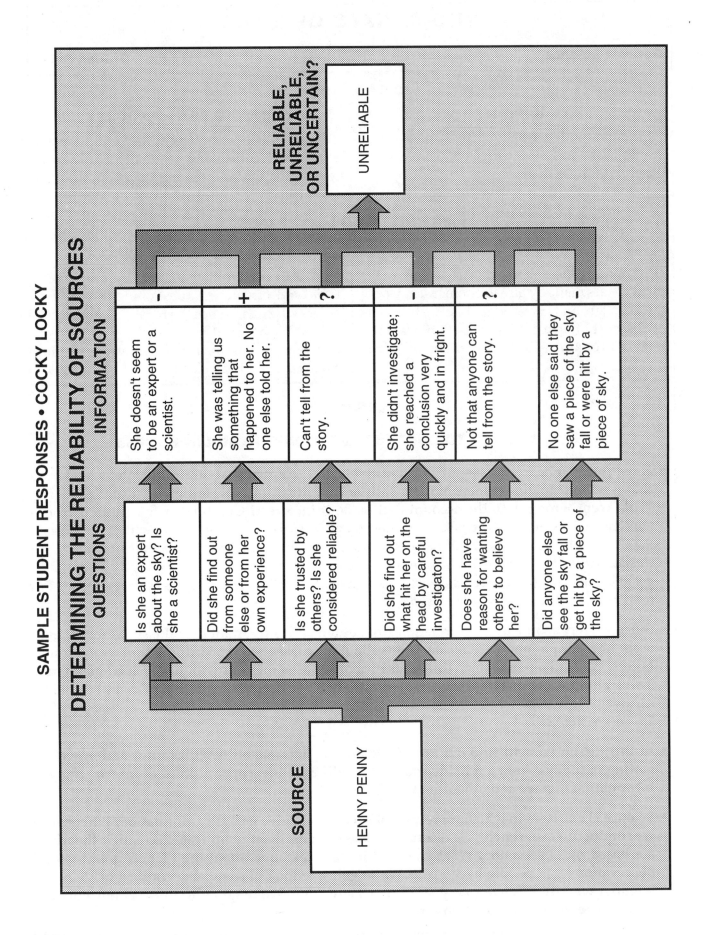

SOURCE

HENNY PENNY

QUESTIONS

- Is she an expert about the sky? Is she a scientist?
- Did she find out from someone else or from her own experience?
- Is she trusted by others? Is she considered reliable?
- Did she find out what hit her on the head by careful investigaton?
- Does she have reason for wanting others to believe her?
- Did anyone else see the sky fall or get hit by a piece of the sky?

INFORMATION

- – She doesn't seem to be an expert or a scientist.
- + She was telling us something that happened to her. No one else told her.
- ? Can't tell from the story.
- – She didn't investigate; she reached a conclusion very quickly and in fright.
- ? Not that anyone can tell from the story.
- – No one else said they saw a piece of the sky fall or were hit by a piece of sky.

UNRELIABLE

THE CANALS OF MARS

General Science   **Grades 6–11**

OBJECTIVES

CONTENT

Students will learn about the surface of the planet Mars and will learn how astronomical observations are made.

THINKING SKILL/PROCESS

Students will learn how to make judgments about the accuracy and reliability of observations based on the presence or absence of relevant factors.

METHODS AND MATERIALS

CONTENT

Students read an observation report about the planet Mars made by an astronomer. They pool their background knowledge about instruments of observation in astronomy, in particular telescopes. They also read other reports about Mars.

THINKING SKILL/PROCESS

An explicit thinking map, a graphic organizer, and structured questioning emphasize factors which influence the reliability and accuracy of an observation. (See pp. 348–352 for reproducible diagrams.) Collaborative learning enhances the thinking.

LESSON

INTRODUCTION TO CONTENT AND THINKING SKILL/PROCESS

- **Have you ever heard an account of an event that you accepted as accurate, but later found out that it wasn't? Jot down some of the details of that situation. Now tell your partner about it. What went wrong with the account that made it incorrect?** Get three or four reports from students and write on the chalkboard their diagnoses of what went wrong with the reports. POSSIBLE ANSWERS: *It was based on rumors. It was a deliberate distortion for some ulterior motive. It was advertising to sell something. It was in a sensationalistic newspaper. The person who gave the account got information that was inaccurate from someone else and didn't know it. The person made a mistake in what he thought he saw because he was distracted.*

- **Since we rely so much on information from others, it is important to make sure that we get accurate information. We make decisions about purchases based on information we get from others. We find out how to do things, as in sports, based on information we get from others. Think about all the different sources of information you use. Jot down a few of them.** POSSIBLE ANSWERS: *Newspapers, TV news, textbooks, teachers, salespeople, friends, dictionaries, telephone books, TV documentaries.*

- **In this lesson we will find out how to determine beforehand whether information we're getting is coming from a reliable source. We will examine a special kind of information—information that we and others get from observation.**

- **Science is one field in which we rely on observation to give us basic information. Whenever we conduct an experiment, we record our observations. Even complicated scientific theories are based on observation. What you read in your textbook about the planets is based on observations that people have made. We're going to look at some observations made by a scientist who drew some pretty startling conclusions. We're going to think about how to decide whether the observations are accurate.**

THINKING ACTIVELY

- **Read the following illustrated description written by someone who was interested in the planets and who decided to observe them to find out what they were like. This is his description of what he saw when he looked at the planet Mars.**

  15 July—I was amazed to see dark areas of blue-green that exactly typify the distant look of our own forests. Only a few months ago this area was pale yellow in color, suggesting the seasonal changing color of leaves. A projection stood out from the planet's surface, but it was clearly not a mountain peak, since the projection was not fixed in place, but suggested a cloud formation. The most startling observation of all was that of miles and miles of parallel lines, so geometrically regular that I am at a loss to show their ruled effect in my drawing. I'm certain that these bizarre parallel features are canals, laid down with as much precision as railway metals on Earth. Only intelligent life could have constructed such canals!

- **What reaction do you have to this?** POSSIBLE ANSWERS: *I didn't know there was life on Mars. I wonder what the canals do. This must be science fiction. This is dumb.*

- **Let's think about this. Sometimes great discoveries sound fantastic. On the other hand, sometimes reports like this are wrong. How can we tell? It's clear that what this person is telling us about life on Mars is not something he observed directly. Rather, he is saying this because of his observation of canals on Mars, something he thinks only intelligent beings could construct. So let's think about this observation. How can we tell it is accurate? Work together in groups of three or four to make a list of questions you would like to have answered to help you decide whether this report is accurate and reliable. List questions you would ask about the source and circumstances, as well as question about the report. Use the diagram for questions about the reliability of sources for your list of questions. Write them on the dotted lines on the left.** When the students have worked for about five minutes, ask them to report. Ask each group to mention one question, so that all the groups respond. List the questions on a large "class" diagram which you construct on the board or on a transparency. Then ask if there are any other questions that haven't been mentioned. Add those to the diagram.

QUESTIONS ABOUT THE RELIABILITY OF A SOURCE OF INFORMATION		
QUESTIONS	TYPES OF QUESTIONS	

- **We could try to answer these questions one by one, but perhaps there is a more organized way to do this. If we group questions, we can make a checklist of types of things we want to find out about the source. This will help us decide whether or not he or she is a reliable and accurate observer. Group these questions together into a few basic categories, such as questions about**

From *The Search for Life on Mars: Evolution of an Idea*, by Henry S. F. Cooper, Jr. (Holt, Rinehart and Winston, 1976)

the observer. **Write these categories on the short lines on the top of the diagram and connect the appropriate questions to the dotted line that leads to it.** Call for responses and write them on the class diagram. POSSIBLE ANSWERS: *The observer, how the observation was conducted (including the equipment and its condition), the report itself, corroboration.*

- **Let's try to organize these types of questions and construct a thinking map that we can use to determine the accuracy of an observation. We can use the map as a checklist for making these kinds of judgments. Add relevant subcategories under each major heading.** The list that students develop may resemble the thinking map shown at the right.

- **Now let's go back to the report on the canals of Mars and try to answer some of these questions. Here's the title page of a book that the observer wrote about the canals of Mars and some additional biographical data about the observer.** (Make available copies of pages 366–67). **What information does this material provide that answers questions on your list? Record your results on this graphic organizer, "Determining the Reliability of Sources."** Ask students to read some of the recorded answers to their questions. POSSIBLE ANSWERS: *The observer had the background and training to be a good astronomical observer. He was well qualified (professor at M. I. T.). He won many prizes, hence probably had a good reputation as an astronomer. He wrote Mars and Its Canals in 1906—before scientists had the sophisticated technology that we do now for observing planets. He used a large telescope for his time. He made many observations. He wrote this passage in his journal while he made the observation. He believed that there were canals before he looked through his telescope, perhaps creating a predisposition to believe this. There is no evidence of drinking or psychological disorder.*

- **Try to reach agreement in your groups about whether or not you believe that this is an accurate and reliable observation. Explain why. In the box on the right side of your graphic organizer, write whether the observation report is reliable, unreliable, or uncertain.**

- **Use your textbooks and other sources for more information about the surface of the planet Mars. What would this information show about the credibility of Lowell's account? Is there any information that corroborates Percival Lowell's observations? Is any of this information more acceptable than Percival Lowell's report? Why?** If you want to extend this

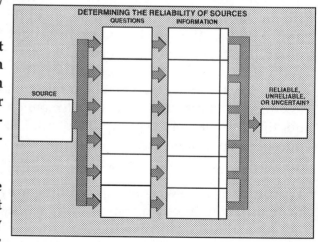

DETERMINING THE ACCURACY OF AN OBSERVATION

1. Which of the following features of the observer, observation, and report are present in this case?

    Observer:
        Background?
        Qualifications?
        Usual reliability?
        Free of bias?
        State of mind?
        Physical ability to observe (eyesight, etc.)?
        Capacity to observe (proximity, direction, free of distraction)?
        Expectations/point of view?
        Vested interest in having audience believe the report?
    Conduct of the observation:
        Frequency?
        Equipment?
            Strength or accuracy?
            Condition?
            How operated?
        Date and location?
        Replicated?
        Observation conditions?
    Report:
        How soon after the observation?
        Details (drawings, photographs, graphs)?
        Language and findings expressed objectively?
    Corroboration:
        By others?
        By me?

2. When you weigh these factors, how reliable would you judge the observation to be?

activity, show students some of the Mariner photographs of Mars. These are contained in the book *MARS, As Viewed by Mariner 9*, published by NASA in 1976 and in other sources that are available at most libraries. Discuss with your students the differences in the technology and its reliability for the following circumstances: when a person observes Mars through a telescope on Earth, when photographs of Mars are taken through a telescope on Earth, and when a spacecraft near Mars sends back to Earth computer-enhanced pictures.

- **Prepare a report about what you think the surface of Mars is like. Illustrate this report. Explain why you think this is an accurate description. What unanswered questions do you have about the surface of the planet?** Discuss with students the planet's surface features that might have made Percival Lowell think he was seeing canals.

THINKING ABOUT THINKING

- **Let's put aside these questions about Mars now. Think about how you developed your checklist of things to consider in determining the reliability and accuracy of an observation report. What did you think about first, and how did you proceed so that you had a good checklist?** Answers should refer to listing the questions, categorizing them, and then transforming the categories into a checklist. Some students may also comment on the collaborative nature of the activity.

- **Is that a good way to develop a checklist? Can you think of other situations for which this strategy would be helpful?** Answers may refer to checklists for making purchases. *You could make a list of questions you would want answered to help you decide what to buy and a list of sources to consult to answer these questions.*

- **Is the checklist you developed for judging the reliability and accuracy of an observation report a helpful one to use for this purpose? Why?**

- **What advice would you give to another person about how to make sure that his or her observation reports are as accurate and reliable as possible?** Good advice includes using the checklist to plan how you are going to conduct and report on an observation.

APPLYING YOUR THINKING

Immediate Transfer

- **Suppose you were going to visit a nearby pond in order to make observations about the natural behavior of animals that lived in and around the pond. Plan your observation so that you will bring back the most accurate observation reports you can. Write out your plan.** Students should use the checklist and apply it to this specific observation.

- **Suppose that there has been an automobile accident in which a car collided with the side of a truck. There were a number of witnesses. Which of the following witnesses do you believe would give you the most accurate and reliable account? Which the least? Why?**

    A man getting into a car on the other side of the street

    A policewoman directing traffic at the next intersection

    The driver of the truck that was hit

    A three-year-old passenger in the back seat of the car that collided with the truck

    A man looking out of his window from a third-story window on the other side of the street

Reinforcement Later

When the class is studying the following topic later in the school year, ask the given questions.

• **We are now studying the effects of diet on health. We're going to look at various reports about diet and health in advertising, from health clinics, on milk cartons, etc. Apply your checklist to try to determine which of these is likely to be more reliable and accurate than others. What might you do to verify the information contained in these sources?**

• **We are studying the way of life of the American Indians. Find four sources of information about the American Indians. Use your checklist to decide which of these sources is likely to provide the most accurate and reliable information. Explain why. Compare these descriptions to your textbook and to a movie you've seen about the Old West. Describe two important things you've found out about the American Indians in the Old West that you didn't know before and that you think are accurate. List some things that you think are not accurate. Explain.**

• **Think about a purchase you will be making over the next few months. What sources would give you the best information for making a good decision? Why?**

ASSESSING STUDENT THINKING ABOUT RELIABLE SOURCES

Any of the transfer examples can serve as an assessment item. The example about the pond is particularly suited for this purpose. It can be used as pre- and post-tests to see whether the students have changed the way they make judgments about accuracy and reliability. Decide beforehand how many additional items from the checklist the student should mention in order to show improvement.

Here is an example of pre- and post-test responses that can be used as a paradigm for judging student improvement. In the pre-test, students were asked to plan an observation of animal behavior in and around a nearby pond. Student responses were predominantly like the following:

I would plan to look at things.

I would go there.

In the post-test given a few months after the *Canals of Mars* lesson, their responses included plans like the following, none of which were mentioned in the pre-test:

I would bring binoculars.

I would make sure I could get close enough to get a good view.

It would have to be daylight.

I would read up on what I was going to be observing beforehand so I knew what I was going to be looking at.

I would bring a pad and pencil and write down what I saw when it was happening.

I would bring someone along who would also take note of these things.

The post-test responses are more articulate than the pre-test responses. In this case, the scoring criteria for substantial improvement was that a student's plans must include mention of one or two factors from each of the major categories on the thinking map. These responses clearly show improved judgment about determining the reliability of an observation.

SAMPLE STUDENT RESPONSES • THE CANALS OF MARS

QUESTIONS ABOUT THE RELIABILITY OF A SOURCE OF INFORMATION

QUESTIONS

TYPES OF QUESTIONS

OBSERVATION — OBSERVER

REPORT — CORROBORATION

What is his background?

What is his scientific reputation?

For whom was the report written?

What kind of equipment did he use?

Did he use the same equipment for all sightings?

What was his state of mind? Was he clear-headed?

Where was he when he made his observation?

Did other accounts corroborate his report?

In what form or publication did the report appear?

Was the report a translation or his own words?

What were the weather conditions?

In what year did he make the observation?

When did he write the report?

Did he have normal sight?

Was the equipment appropriately maintained?

Was he typically trustworthy?

What did he expect to see?

Did he know how to use the equipment?

How often did he observe it?

Is the lens scratched?

How long did he observe it?

Did he believe in life on Mars prior to the observation?

Did he make accurate observations of other planets?

Was he drinking before he made the observations?

Was a model made to verify how formations should look?

Was he paid for this account? If so, by whom?

MARS

AND ITS CANALS

BY

PERCIVAL LOWELL

DIRECTOR OF THE OBSERVATORY AT FLAGSTAFF, ARIZONA; NON-RESIDENT PROFESSOR
OF ASTRONOMY AT THE MASSACHUSETTS INSTITUTE OF TECHNOLOGY; FELLOW OF
THE AMERICAN ACADEMY OF ARTS AND SCIENCES; MEMBRE DE LA SOCIETE
ASTRONOMIQUE DE FRANCE; MEMBER OF THE ASTRONOMICAL AND
ASTROPHYSICAL SOCIETY OF AMERICA; MITGLIED DER ASTRO-
NOMISCHE GESELLSCHAFT; MEMBRE DE LA SOCIETE BELGE
D'ASTRONOMIE; HONORARY MEMBER OF THE SOCIEDAD
ASTRONOMICA DE MEXICO; JANSSEN MEDALIST OF
THE SOCIETE ASTRONOMIQUE DE FRANCE,
1904, FOR RESEARCHES ON MARS;
ETC., ETC.

ILLUSTRATED

New York

THE MACMILLAN COMPANY

LONDON: MACMILLAN & CO., Ltd

1906

THE CANALS OF MARS

Lowell's interest in Mars had begun late in the last century, when he became interested in reports of observations made in 1877 by Giovanni Schiaparelli, an Italian astronomer. Schiaparelli said he had seen faint lines on Mars, and he referred to them as *canali*. The popular British and American interpretation of the word *canali* was that it meant canals—which are, of course, man-made—rather than channels, which need not be. Nor did Schiaparelli make any attempt to clarify the interpretation; indeed, he once remarked; "I am very careful not to combat this suggestion, which contains nothing impossible"—a use of the double negative still favored by seekers after extraterrestrial life, particularly Sagan. (It is, of course, a not ungrammatical use of the double negative.) Schiaparelli, whose eyesight was failing, continued to observe Mars on its close approaches to the Earth until about 1890. (Mars and the Earth pass each other in their orbits about every 2 years. At these times, they are said to be in opposition; exceptionally close approaches occur every 16 years.) Lowell, who had exceptionally good eyesight and was proud of it, took up the watch in 1894, when he set up an 18 inch telescope on a hill, which came to be called Mars Hill, outside Flagstaff, Arizona; this was the genesis of the Lowell Observatory, one of the first in this country to be situated in a remote spot for good visibility, and today a major astronomical institution. Then, as now, Mars watching had its difficulties. When the planet was low in the sky, so that the telescope's eyepiece was high off the ground, Lowell had to hang from a ladderlike scaffold that lined the observatory walls like the stall bars of a gymnasium. On a drawing board hooked to a convenient rung, Lowell made sketches of his observations. In color, Mars was a brilliant, splotchy orange red, though there were some darkish blue-green splotches as well. In 1659 the Dutch astronomer Christiaan Huygens—the first man to study Mars telescopically—had discovered white splotches at either pole, which he deduced to be polar caps. The markings looked fuzzy and ill-defined, and they varied from time to time, the way a nearsighted man might view the image in a kaleidoscope; Mars had, in fact, the shifty splotchiness of a Rorchach inkblot, in which people are sometimes asked to tell what they think they see.

Over the next 20 years, Lowell concluded that Mars was laced with an elaborate webbing of canals, which, because of their extreme length, precision, and straightness, could have been created only by a highly advanced civilization. Lowell, who was as literate as Sagan (the poet Amy was his sister and his brother Abbott Lawrence was president of Harvard), recorded his observations in three very persuasive books. "Suggestive of a spider's web seen against the grass of a spring morning, a mesh of fine reticulated lines overspreads (the planet)," he wrote in *Mars and Its Canals*, which was published in 1906. "The chief difference between it and a spider's web is one of size, supplemented by greater complexity, but both are joys of geometric beauty. For the lines are of individually uniform width, of exceeding tenuity, and of great length. These are the Martian Canals."

From *The Search for Life on Mars: Evolution of an Idea*, by Henry S. F. Cooper, Jr. (Holt, Rinehart and Winston, 1976)

SAMPLE STUDENT RESPONSES • CANALS OF MARS

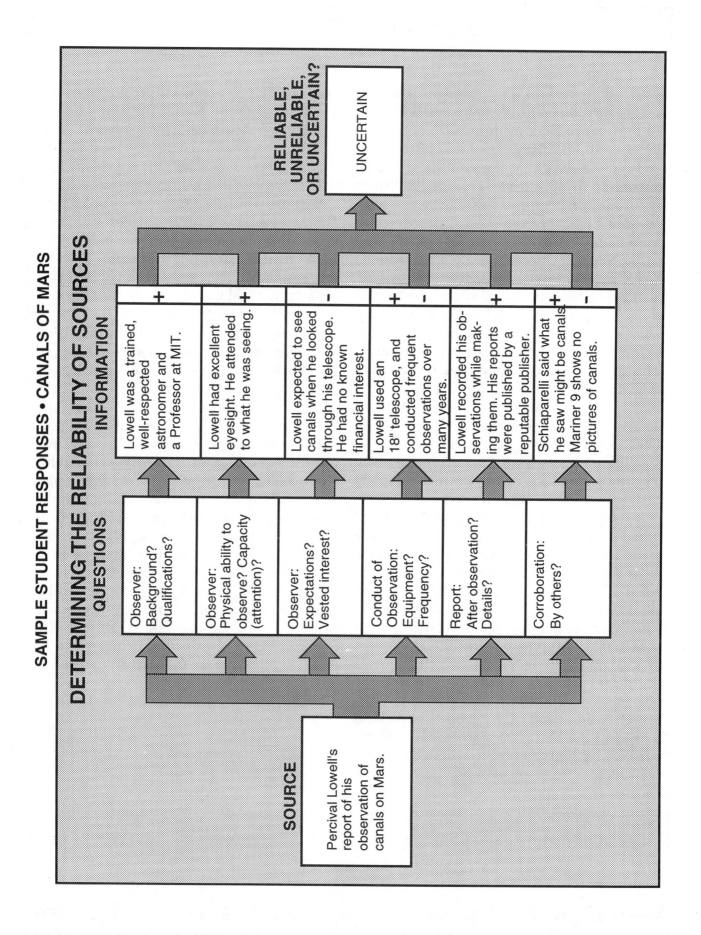

DETERMINING THE RELIABILITY OF SOURCES

RELIABLE, UNRELIABLE, OR UNCERTAIN?

UNCERTAIN

INFORMATION

+ Lowell was a trained, well-respected astronomer and a Professor at MIT.

+ Lowell had excellent eyesight. He attended to what he was seeing.

– Lowell expected to see canals when he looked through his telescope. He had no known financial interest.

+ – Lowell used an 18" telescope, and conducted frequent observations over many years.

+ Lowell recorded his observations while making them. His reports were published by a reputable publisher.

+ – Schiaparelli said what he saw might be canals. Mariner 9 shows no pictures of canals.

QUESTIONS

Observer: Background? Qualifications?

Observer: Physical ability to observe? Capacity (attention)?

Observer: Expectations? Vested interest?

Conduct of Observation: Equipment? Frequency?

Report: After observation? Details?

Corroboration: By others?

SOURCE

Percival Lowell's report of his observation of canals on Mars.

THE BOTTOM OF THE OCEAN

Science/Library   **Grades 5–8**

OBJECTIVES

CONTENT

Students will learn how to select references for scientific topics. They will also learn about the ocean floor and about deep sea exploration.

THINKING SKILL/PROCESS

Students will learn how to make judgments about the accuracy and reliability of sources of information based on the presence or absence of relevant factors.

METHODS AND MATERIALS

CONTENT

Students read information about authors and publications that describe the bottom of the ocean. They interpret charts and read descriptions of the ocean floor. Library research is part of this lesson.

THINKING SKILL/PROCESS

This lesson makes use of structured questioning and a graphic organizer to aid students in identifying factors which influence the reliability and accuracy of sources of information. (See pp. 348–352 for reproducible diagrams.) Collaborative learning enhances the thinking.

LESSON

INTRODUCTION TO CONTENT AND THINKING SKILL/PROCESS

- **We can't discover everything ourselves. To find out important information, we often have to rely on what other people tell us. Can you think of times when you have relied on other people for information?** Sources may include teachers, textbooks, radio talk shows, television documentaries, television commercials, parents, friends, salespeople, advertisements, and the movie page in the newspaper.

- **Sometimes the information we get from others is accurate. Sometimes it is not. It's important to be sure that we get good information when we have to rely on others. Can you think of a time when you got information from someone else and it turned out to be inaccurate? Discuss one with your partner.** Ask for a few examples from the class.

- **Finding information that we can rely upon depends on how well we check out our sources of information. This means that we have to think about the many factors that involved: who the sources are, how much they know, how they know about what they are telling you, what they believe about it, when they found it out, etc. Sometimes we even have to evaluate whether we ourselves are good, reliable sources of information.**

- **Suppose a friend told you that the best bike to buy was a "Fantastic Flyer." What would you want to find out to decide whether this was reliable information?** POSSIBLE ANSWERS: *Did the friend learn it from a magazine or another person who owned a Fantastic Flyer? Was the information taken from an ad for the bicycle? Was it from an article about bicycles written by someone who didn't favor one particular brand? Does the friend have a good memory? Can you read the same article yourself?*

- **We've been studying the oceans in science. Much of the Earth's surface is covered by the oceans. We get food from the oceans. That's why it is important to us to find out as much as we can about the oceans.**

- Did you ever wonder what the *bottom* of the ocean was really like? You can't go there yourself, and an ocean map doesn't tell you much. Let's think about what you might find at the bottom of the ocean. In order to think about this in an organized way, I'm going to ask you to respond to three questions: What do you know about the bottom of the ocean, what do you think you know, and what do you need to know? As you respond, I will write what you say in three columns under each of these headings. On the chalk board or a transparency, draw a diagram like the one shown. Ask for responses to the questions, one by one, from the class, and write student responses in the columns. Students often comment that they *know* things like the following: *It's very dark. It's very cold. There is a lot of pressure from the water. There are deep ravines.* Students say they *think they know* things like the follow-

I KNOW	I THINK I KNOW	I NEED TO KNOW

ing: *There are sunken ships. The animals will be very small because of the pressure. There will be debris thrown overboard from ships. It will be hard to see anything. The bottom of the ocean is miles from the surface.* Students often say that they *need to know* things like the following: *What kind of animals live there? How deep is it? Can humans survive there? Exactly how cold is it? Has anyone ever been there? Can we get food there?*

THINKING ACTIVELY

- Suppose you went to a library and found a number of books and articles about the oceans. You might want to use them to find out whether the class's ideas about the bottom of the ocean are accurate and to answer some of our questions. Here are some examples of books and articles:

  "Man's New Frontier," by Luis Marden, from the *National Geographic Magazine*, April 1987.

  The Sea and Its Living Wonders, by Dr. G. Hartwig, 1860.

  Twenty Thousand Leagues Under the Sea, by Jules Verne, 1870.

  "Monsters Under the Sea," in *Great Science Fiction Stories*, 1955.

  "Incredible World of Deep Sea Rifts," by Robert Ballard and J. Frederick Grassle, from the *National Geographic Magazine*, November 1979.

- Is there anything about these works that might suggest that some of them are more reliable than others? What? POSSIBLE ANSWERS: *Since one of them is a science fiction story, perhaps its descriptions of what lives in the ocean are fiction, not fact. However, maybe the science fiction story is based on science facts.* Twenty Thousand Leagues Under the Sea *and* The Sea and Its Living Wonders *came out in the 1800s. They didn't have submarines then and may not have had any way to see what was at the bottom of the ocean. Also, wasn't* Twenty Thousand Leagues Under the Sea *a science fiction novel? The* National Geographic Magazine *has articles about real explorations. The articles written in the 1970s and 1980s were at a time when we could see what was there. Robert Ballard discovered the* Titanic *by going to the bottom of the ocean in a small submarine with lights and windows.*

- What other questions would you want to have answered to help you decide which sources are likely to give you the most accurate and reliable information about the bottom of the ocean? Work in your groups. Use the graphic organizer for questions about the reliability of a source. Write your questions on the dotted lines on the left. Compile a class list of questions on the chalkboard or on a transparency of the diagram by asking for one or two questions at a time from each group. POSSIBLE ANSWERS: *Was the article written by a person who actually explored the ocean? Does the magazine have a reputation for accurate information? Are the authors experts on the oceans? If the authors explored firsthand, what equipment did they use? Why did they write these articles? Are there photographs in the articles that show the bottom of the ocean?*

QUESTIONS ABOUT THE RELIABILITY OF A SOURCE OF INFORMATION

QUESTIONS   TYPES OF QUESTIONS

- **We could try to answer these questions one by one, but perhaps there is a more systematic way to do this. If we group them, we can make a checklist of types of things we want to find out to decide whether a source is reliable and accurate. Group these questions together into four or five basic categories, such as questions about the author. Write these categories on the short lines at the top of the diagram and connect the appropriate questions to the dotted line that leads to it.** Call for responses and fill them in on the class diagram. POSSIBLE ANSWERS: *Questions about the author (whether or not he was there, his expertise about the oceans), about the publication (its reputation, special interests), about the article (when the article was published, corroboration by photographs).*

- **In order to create a checklist for making these kinds of judgments, let's use these categories as part of a thinking map for determining the reliability of a source. The first question we should have on our thinking map is, "What is the source we are using?" The next question has to do with factors that count in favor of or against the source's reliability. Then we should have a list of the factors we should attend to. You should fill in these factors yourselves. For example, one of your question categories concerned the author. Put "Author?" on your checklist of factors relevant to reliability. That will guide you to find out things about the author that are relevant to his or her reliability as a source of information. A subcategory you mentioned was the author's expertise about the oceans. That is something specific about the author that you'll want to find out. If he's an expert on the oceans, that will count in favor of his reliability; if not, that will count against it.** What the students develop should resemble the thinking map shown.

EVALUATING THE RELIABILITY OF SOURCES SKILLFULLY

1. What is the source of the information being considered?

2. List the factors present that are relevant to the reliability of the source in the following categories:

   a. Published?

   Date?
   Reputation of publication?
   Kind of publication? (e.g., report, fiction)?
   b. Author?

   Expertise?
   Bias or distorting point of view?
   Special interest?
   Primary or secondary?
     If secondary, the reliability of any other sources the information is derived from?
     If primary, other relevant factors, e.g., equipment used?
   Corroboration/confirmation?

3. Weigh the factors present and make a judgement of reliability based on them.

- **Where can you get information to answer some of these questions?** You or the school librarian should show students where they can find the date on books and magazines and how they can find out about the author from the dust jacket of books, the title page, and biographical sketches in magazines, etc. Ask the students to make a list of these research strategies and add any others they find.

- **Let's take a close look at one of the sources. Use your checklist to gather relevant information about whether or not it is a reliable source of information. Write your results on the graphic organizer for determining the reliability of sources. Make a judgment about how reliable the source is for accurate information about the bottom of the ocean. Each group should explain their judgment to the class.** Use the article "The Incredible World of Deep Sea Rifts," find one or two others, or ask the students to go to the library and work there. The two *National Geographic* articles are usually identified

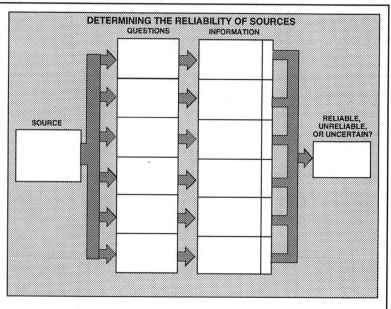

as very reliable. When students explain why, their explanations should be thorough and should show an awareness of how relevant information indicates reliability. For example, the authors of "The Incredible World of Deep Sea Rifts" are identified in the magazine as "a marine geologist and biologist" from the Woods Hole Oceanographic Institution. They are firsthand observers. Their submersible (the *Alvin*) is described in detail in the article as having observation ports, lights, mechanical arms, and the capability of travelling to the deepest parts of the ocean. There are many colored photographs accompanying the article. The *National Geographic* has a reputation for publishing scientific works of discovery and exploration. The article does not indicate whether the authors have a reputation as good researchers or whether they have any vested interests or scientific biases. Endorsement of them as reliable sources is justified, but with the understanding that these questions remain unanswered. As each group reports, discuss with the class what the information on their graphic organizer reveals about the reliability of the source being considered.

- **Each group should also make a list of the interesting information it has gathered about the bottom of the ocean.** Ask each group to report one interesting piece of information it has found. As the groups report, circle information in the "I know" column of the original diagram if the information is confirmed. If it is not there, add it. Cross out any information it conflicts with, and if it answers any questions in the "I need to know" column, cross these out. POSSIBLE ANSWERS: *There are worms six- to eight-feet long in some of the deep-sea trenches at the bottom of the ocean. There are foot-long clams with red blood in these trenches. Crabs and other sea life live near these trenches. The water is hot around these trenches because of lava, which is being ejected into the water. The water is rich in food for the plants and animals that live there. The pressure is very great. Man can explore these deep-sea trenches in specially designed submersible craft like the* Alvin.

THINKING ABOUT THINKING

- **Let's put aside these questions about the bottom of the ocean and think about how you developed your checklist for determining the reliability and accuracy of a source of information. What did you think about first, and how did you proceed so that you had a good checklist?** Answers should refer to listing the questions, categorizing them, and then transforming the categories into a checklist. Some students may also comment on the collaborative nature of the activity.

- Is that a good way to develop a checklist? Is the checklist you developed for judging the reliability and accuracy of a source of information a good and helpful one to use? Why?

- **Plan out how you will gather the most reliable information on the next topic you have to research. Describe what you will attend to, how you will get the information you need about the sources, etc.** Students should indicate that they will use their checklist to guide their search for relevant information about reliability and accuracy. They should also describe where they will seek relevant information and mention the school librarian as a resource.

APPLYING YOUR THINKING

Immediate Transfer

- **Think about something you might like to buy. Plan what sources you will use to get the most reliable information about it. Why will you use those sources?** School libraries may feature *Penny Wise*, the *Consumer Report* magazine for children, designed to provide consumer information. If they use this periodical, make sure they explain why they believe it to be reliable. Discuss other sources such as advertising, a salesperson, and someone who owns the item.

- **We've been studying ocean pollution. Gather information about the kinds of pollution you find in the oceans, the problems the pollution causes, and what people have been trying to do about it. Explain where you got the information and why you think it is reliable.**

Reinforcement Later

When the class studies the following topics later in the school year, use the given dialog.

- **We are now studying the effects of diet on health. We're going to look at various reports about diet and health in advertising, from health clinics, on milk cartons, etc. Apply your checklist to determine which of these is likely to be more reliable and accurate than others. What might you do to verify the information from these sources?**

- **We are studying the movement west in this country. One of the topics you study is the way of life of the American Indians. Go to the school library and gather four sources of information about the American Indians. Use your checklist to decide which of these sources is likely to provide the most accurate and reliable information. Explain why. Compare these descriptions to your textbook and to a movie you've seen about the Old West. Describe two important things you've found out about American Indians in the Old West that you didn't know before and that you think are accurate. List some things that you think are not accurate. Explain.**

ASSESSING STUDENT THINKING ABOUT RELIABLE SOURCES

Any of the transfer examples can serve as an assessment item. The examples about a new purchase, ocean pollution, diet, and the American Indians are good ones for this purpose. The example about a new purchase is particularly suited to be used as pre- and post-tests on this skill. Decide beforehand which items from the checklist a student should mention in order to show improvement.

If your students are collecting information on a topic over a period of time, you can use portfolio assessment techniques to supplement other forms of assessment. You can ask students to develop a research plan and to keep a portfolio of references they research, each with an explanation of why the references are or are not reliable sources. You can also ask them to keep a journal in which they record information from the sources they think are reliable. This can be used in a future writing assignment.

IT IS EASY to become jaded these days, but there is a powerful antidote to that feeling. I experienced it last June in France as I witnessed the excitement and jubilation that followed the successful flight of *Gossamer Albatross*. That flimsy dragonfly made of graphite tubing, plastic, and tape, designed by aeronautical engineer Dr. Paul B. MacCready and driven by a wiry young biologist named Bryan Allen, had crossed the English Channel on Allen's leg power alone. The flight won not only £100,000 prize but also the plaudits of a world waiting to thrill to such exploits.

A few weeks later I talked with a group of our editors who had been huddled around scientists at the Jet Propulsion Laboratory in California when the spacecraft Voyager 2 began sending back its breathtaking portraits of Jupiter's moons (pictures that will appear in our January 1980 issue). Again high excitement was in the air, as a new frontier was unveiled by a superb team effort.

While Voyager 1 and 2 probed the outer world of our solar system, a manned deep-sea research vehicle named *Alvin*, using image-making equipment of high sophistication, brought back startling scenes from the inner world far below the surface of the Pacific Ocean. There, along rifts where earth's crustal plates are separating, were revealed life forms and geologic processes never seen before. As the scientists reported their findings to the National Geographic, which helped support the exploration, they were equally excited and jubilant.

Such moments of achievement and discovery have been occurring all during the 91 years we have been publishing, and they will continue as long as human beings find challenges to meet. Those on the vast scale of the planet have given rise to vast accomplishment. When we read Rick Gore's report on worlds desertification in this issue, we should remember that the earliest civilizations grew out of the deserts, that both advanced technology and societies were formed in response to their challenge.

It is not time to become jaded, when man had probed only the innermost fringe of the universe, and when he had seen only one mile in a thousand of the seafloor rift system. We expect to be publishing great adventures for a long time to come.

Gilbert M. Grosvenor

NATIONAL GEOGRAPHIC

THE NATIONAL GEOGRAPHIC MAGAZINE VOL. 156. NO. 5 COPYRIGHT© 1979 BY NATIONAL GEOGRAPHIC SOCIETY WASHINGTON, D.C. INTERNATIONAL COPYRIGHT SECURED

November 1979

COVER: *Dressed for the desert in Upper Volta, a Bella tribesman combines sunglasses and turban to shield against sun and sand.*
Photograph by George Gerster.

Scientists explore rifts in the seafloor where hot springs spew minerals and startling life exists in a

STRANGE WORLD WITHOUT SUN

ACROSS THE BOTTOM of the four oceans of the world runs the largest feature on the face of this planet, a mountain range and rift system some 40,000 miles long. Man has seen with his own eyes scarcely forty miles of this Mid-Oceanic Ridge.

But along those few miles in the past six years, scientists in tiny submarines such as *Alvin* have found, in those utterly dark nether depths of the sea, animals and mineral factories unlike any seen before.

In 1979 the latest in a series of expeditions went out into the Pacific to study spreading centers of the ocean floor. These are places where the thin, rigid plates that form the hard crust of our planet are pulling apart, separating as much as eight inches a year. In the cracks molten magma wells up, meets cold seawater, and solidifies into a contorted landscape of black lava.

In such regions the scientists have been witnessing the all but believable. They have seen:

- Huge blood-red worms protruding from forests of white plasticlike tubes.

- Clams far larger than most shallow-water types, their meat scarlet with hemoglobin.

- Strange dandelionlike creatures moored by threads near fountains of warm water.

- Plumes of even hotter water—350° C (650° F) or more—spewing black clouds of minerals from seafloor chimneys.

Since William Beebe's bathysphere dives in the 1930s and the descents of Jacques-Yves Cousteau, Jacques Piccard, and others in the 1950s and 1960s, the National Geographic Society has participated in and reported on many historic ocean explorations.

In May 1975 NATIONAL GEOGRAPHIC carried a full report on Project FAMOUS, man's first look at the Mid-Atlantic Ridge. In August 1976 we described dives into the yawning Cayman Trough in the Caribbean. In October 1977 the GEOGRAPHIC reported the astonishment of geologists who descended to the Galapagos Rift in the eastern Pacific and first discovered warm-water vents teeming with life. Rich in hydrogen sulfide and bacteria, these oases apparently attract larval organisms drifting in the currents.

This discovery set the stage for further dives in the Pacific. In 1978, French U. S., and Mexican scientists using the French submersible *Cyana* explored the East Pacific Rise as 21° North, off the mouth of the Gulf of California. They found inactive vents and huge dead clams, similar to those discovered on the Galapagos Rift in 1977.

Then, in back-to back expeditions beginning in January 1979 and continuing this fall, funded by the National Science Foundation and the Office of Naval Research, scientists returned to the Galapagos Rift and 21° N with *Alvin* and its support ships. On the pages that follow, two of the leaders report on expedition findings.

WE ARE PROUD that the National Geographic Society has played a part in these explorations. By a major research grant, as well as by providing cameras, film, and photographic experts and by operating color laboratories abroad the surface ships, the Society has markedly extended science's ability to see and record phenomena in the abyss.... — THE EDITOR

Diagram of Alvin submersible, © The National Geographic Society, reprinted by permission of NGS Art Division. Photographs of scientists on the Alvin, © Al Giddings, reprinted by permission of The National Geographic Society.

RETURN TO OASES OF THE DEEP

By ROBERT D. BALLARD and J. FREDERICK GRASSLE

BOTH WOODS HOLE OCEANOGRAPHIC INSTITUTION

THE SCENE a few feet outside *Alvin's* view port overwhelms. A riot of red-tipped worms, some of them 12 feet tall, grow around the organic-rich vents. Crabs and mussels are everywhere. These creatures that greeted geologists diving in 1977 now meet us, a group of biologists, chemists, and geologists returning to study the living oases of the Galapagos Rift.

The extraordinary worms have not eyes, no mouth, no gut, no anus. Laboratory dissections reveal they do have separate sexes, and most likely broadcast eggs and sperm into the water. Hemoglobin—red blood pigment—accounts for their bright color. Covering the solid spongy plume, more than 300,000 tiny tentacles arranged on flaps, or lamellae, absorb molecules of food and oxygen form the water. The blood carries this nourishment throughout the body.

The concentration of suspended food available at the vents is amazing. By one estimate, it is 300 to 500 times greater than just outside vent areas and four times greater than in productive surface waters.

Fountains of Life in the Abyss

WE LOOK directly into the heart of an active vent as *Alvin's* heat probe, at left, registers up to 13° C (55° F), much warmer than the usual deep-sea chill of 2° C. Yet heat is not the main lure for the flowerlike sea anemones, brown mussels, curling serpulid worms, and blind crabs gathered here, 2.5 kilometers below the surface. Sparse populations of similar animals survive the cold even at the sea's deepest point, 11 kilometers, existing on whatever organisms drift down from the sunlit surface.

Animals congregate at vents because of the enormous food supply based on bacteria. The bacteria, sulfur, and heat give the vent water its milky blue shimmer. Microbes exist everywhere in the sea, often in a state similar to suspended animation. Some types can metabolize hydrogen sulfide; when they find that nourishment here in vent water, they proliferate, providing food for clams, worms, and mussels.

We find that the mussels have a long larval stage. Such larvae, drifting great distances in ocean currents like plant seeds riding the wind, could start a community whenever a vent opens up. Then dead mussels, in turn, become food for scavengers, such as crabs.

The white brachyuran crabs—of a crustacean family not previously known—scramble into our fish-baited traps. In insulated containers kept at 2° C, dozens survive decompression on the hour-and-a-half ascent with *Alvin*. So we select this animal as the best living subject for studies on the relationship of temperature and pressure to metabolism, investigations pursued in a laboratory at the University of California at Santa Barbara.

When kept at sea-surface pressure of one atmosphere, the crabs did not live long. But those placed in a pressure vessel set at 250 atmospheres, the same as their home environment, behave normally and easily tolerate changes in temperature. The last survivor lived for more than six months.

New Ways to Study a New World

A JOURNEY to the deep sea is a little like going to the moon. We spend months preparing for an unknown realm, but can stay only a few hours on the spot. And we have not just a new geology but also a complex, unfamiliar ecosystem to investigate.

Biologists are especially curious about respiration and growth rates at the vent, since elsewhere in the abyss metabolism slows down. Using *Alvin's* claw, we place mussels for 48 hours in a chambered respirometer to check oxygen uptake; others we leave in wire cages to test when we return this fall. The grenadier fish—common in the depths—may be attracted by *Alvin's* lights.

Everywhere we look for new life forms. Microbiologist Holger W. Jannasch searches for bacteria in water samples, on rocks, and here on a mussel shell. Later a scanning electron micrograph of the mussel's shell raises questions. The strings are stalks of bacteria. But what are the strange protuberances? Geologists thought they might be minute manganese nodules. Dr. Jannasch has found they are bacteria cells coated with manganese and iron.

Filtered vent water yields solid evidence that bacteria multiply rapidly within the vents by metabolizing hydrogen sulfide, carbon dioxide, and oxygen. Bacteria grow in mats and clumps in the subsurface spaces of porous rocks until the flowing water peels them off. The bacteria count is high, up to a million per cubic centimeter (less than a quarter teaspoonful). More than 200 different strains of bacteria are being kept alive at Woods Hole. The pink fish that we observed head down in vents may be feeding on bacterial masses.

FIELDS OF FOOT-LONG CLAMS, overrun by galatheid crabs, populate active vents along the rifts. A smooth-shelled individual from 21° N proves slightly larger than an eroded Galapagos specimen. Radiochemical dating at Yale University shows vent clams grow four centimeters a year, 500 times faster than a small deep-sea cousin which can live as long as a century. Galapagos clams have numerous large and yolky eggs, but we have not yet found how the clams disperse.

The meat inside is startlingly red, a rare sight in clams. Their hemoglobin has an unusually high affinity for oxygen, possibly an adaptation to periods of low oxygen.

A Marvelous Multitude

TO MARINE BIOLOGISTS, vent communities are as strange as a lost valley of prehistoric dinosaurs. The "dandelion," first spotted suspended by filaments above the seafloor during the 1977 Galapagos expedition, proved to be a new siphonophore. Related to the Portuguese man-of-war, it consists of a gasbag for buoyancy, surrounded by hundreds of members with specific functions—some capture food, others ingest it, still others handle reproduction. Brought to the surface, the fragile animal started to fall apart, so we quickly put it in a fixative.

Another unusual animal, a small worm, forms a tube from minerals in the water, cementing

itself near the chimneys at 21° N that spew solutions hotter than 350° C. This effluent cools so quickly on meeting the seawater that the worms don't actually live in the hottest water. Geologists dubbed them Pompeii worms, since they must survive a constant rain of metal precipitates. They turn out to be bristle worms, or polychaetes, which probably consume bacteria with feeding tentacles.

Among hundreds of specimens collected, we discover even more new species of whelks, barnacles, leeches, and a red-blooded bristle worm. While dissecting mussels, invertebrate zoologist Carl Berg finds the worm living in the mantle cavity.

On videotape from the CCD camera we can see such worms leaving the mussels we collect.

On board *Lulu*, geologist-author Ballard examines the largest tube worm brought to the surface; its body fills more than half of the 2.5-meter tube. Several juveniles had cemented themselves to this adult. We also find on such tubes a new variety of filter-feeding limpet, a living representative of fossils from the Paleozoic era.

Lava Lakes and Frozen Pillars

THE SEAFLOOR near the vents gives us a big surprise. Geologists had believed that lava underwater always flowed slowly, forming bulbous pillows. Instead, we find, lava lakes fill depressions, much as on land. This means molten magma rushed up with such ferocity that cold seawater could not immediately harden it. The flow swirled and coiled before solidifying, a few hundred to a few thousand years ago, only yesterday in geologic time.

As it advanced across the cold seafloor, the lava capped water-filled cracks. This water heated and rose in a jet, hardening the lava it touched. After the lava lake drained, the hollow pillar—the mold of a water column—remained, with ledges like bathtub rings. Similar ledges line the lake edge three meters beyond.

On top of the pillar we see animals, perhaps tube worms. Sediments begin to collect, snowing down at the rate of five centimeters every 1,000 years, eventually blanketing the bottom as it moves away from the rift.

INFUSING THINKING INTO INSTRUCTION—ELEMENTARY

Quiet for now, the ocean-floor crust will undergo intermittent rifting and eruption on a cycle of about 10,000 years. With time the lava cracks, and water circulates down and up again, creating new vents. When cracks go deep enough, magma will again be released, and the cycle will repeat.

Our findings clear up major mysteries about the composition of ocean water. We once assumed all its minerals had to come from river runoff. Yet the elements in the ocean were out of balance—not enough magnesium and too much manganese. Direct sampling of vent water proves that during circulation deep in the ocean crust, seawater drops off magnesium and picks up manganese. John Edmond, geochemical leader of the Galapagos II expedition, calculates that all the world's oceans circulate through the crust once eery ten million years.

Minerals Erupt at Hot Spots

LIKE A FACTORY at full throttle, a submarine chimney at 21° N belches hot mineral-laden water that rises through cold seawater pressing down at nearly two tons per square inch. As the solution mixes with the near-freezing water, it precipitates yellow, ocher, and reddish brown deposits of iron, copper, and zinc sulfides. When *Alvin* breaks off and retrieves a fragment, we learn its dull interior is sphalerite, a zinc sulfide, while its bright interior is chalcopyrite—fool's gold.

With *Alvin's* claw, we insert a temperature probe vertically into a "black smoker." The readout inside the sub spins off scale. Later we determine that the water must be hotter than 350° C (650° F) But only one end of the plastic rod has melted. The far end is unaffected, showing that the solution cools instantly as it mixes with seawater.

As Mid-Oceanic Ridge exploration has shifted from relatively quiet spreading centers in the Atlantic to the Pacific's more active rifts, our anticipation has grown. Will we finally actually see molten lava erupting, and more exotic animals thriving, when we dive to the fastest spreading center known, off Easter Island on the East Pacific Rise?

378   ©1994 CRITICAL THINKING PRESS & SOFTWARE • P.O. BOX 448 • PACIFIC GROVE, CA 93950 • 800-458-4849

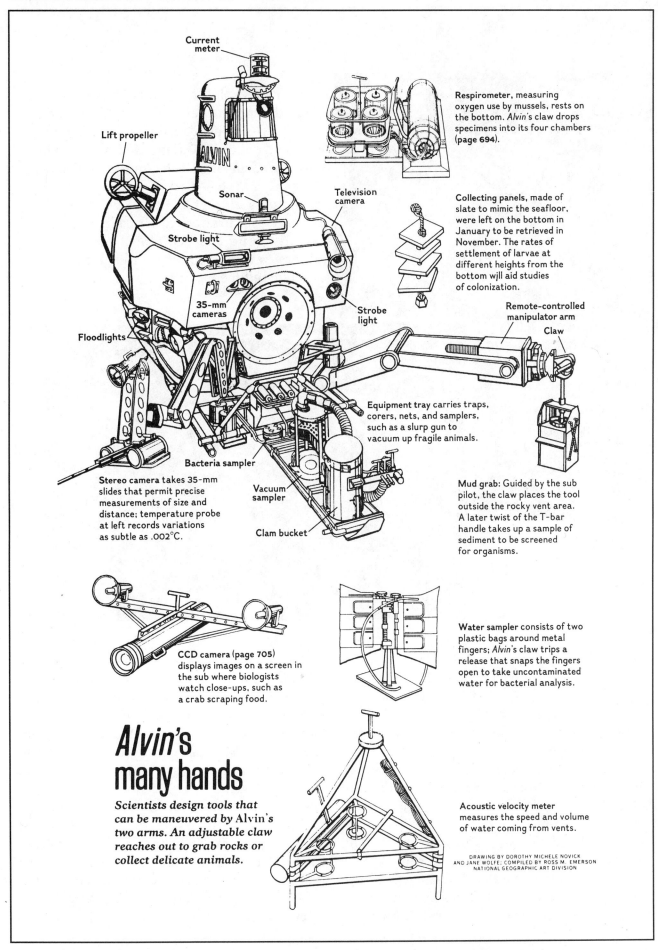

Current meter

Lift propeller

Sonar

Television camera

Strobe light

35-mm cameras

Floodlights

Strobe light

Respirometer, measuring oxygen use by mussels, rests on the bottom. *Alvin*'s claw drops specimens into its four chambers (page 694).

Collecting panels, made of slate to mimic the seafloor, were left on the bottom in January to be retrieved in November. The rates of settlement of larvae at different heights from the bottom will aid studies of colonization.

Remote-controlled manipulator arm

Claw

Equipment tray carries traps, corers, nets, and samplers, such as a slurp gun to vacuum up fragile animals.

Bacteria sampler

Vacuum sampler

Clam bucket

Stereo camera takes 35-mm slides that permit precise measurements of size and distance; temperature probe at left records variations as subtle as .002°C.

Mud grab: Guided by the sub pilot, the claw places the tool outside the rocky vent area. A later twist of the T-bar handle takes up a sample of sediment to be screened for organisms.

CCD camera (page 705) displays images on a screen in the sub where biologists watch close-ups, such as a crab scraping food.

Water sampler consists of two plastic bags around metal fingers; *Alvin*'s claw trips a release that snaps the fingers open to take uncontaminated water for bacterial analysis.

Alvin's many hands

Scientists design tools that can be maneuvered by Alvin's two arms. An adjustable claw reaches out to grab rocks or collect delicate animals.

Acoustic velocity meter measures the speed and volume of water coming from vents.

DRAWING BY DOROTHY MICHELE NOVICK AND JANE WOLFE; COMPILED BY ROSS M. EMERSON NATIONAL GEOGRAPHIC ART DIVISION

Seafloor explorers: Geologist Robert D. Ballard (left) has descended in Alvin to all the deep-sea spreading centers so far explored—the Mid-Atlantic Ridge, Cayman Trough, Galapagos Rift, and East Pacific Rise at 21° N—and described those adventures in the GEOGRAPHIC. Marine biologist J. Frederick Grassle (below) usually conducts ecological studies of diverse animal communities living in Atlantic sediments.

For the 1979 Galapagos expedition, other biological investigators were Carl J. Berg and Ruth D. Turner, Harvard University; James J. Childress, University of California at Santa Barbara, UCSB; Judith P. Grassle, Marine Biological Laboratory; Robert R. Hessler, Kenneth L. Smith, and George N. Somero, Scripps Institution of Oceanography, SIO; Holger W. Jannasch, Howard L. Sanders, and Albert J. Williams III, WHOI; David M. Karl, University of Hawaii; Richard A. Lutz and Donald C. Rhoads, Yale University; Jon H. Tuttle, University of Texas. Other geologists were Robin Holcomb and Tjeerd H. van Andel, Stanford University; Kathleen Crane, WHOI. Geochemists included John Edmond, MIT; John B. Corliss and Louis I. Gordon, Oregon State University; Michael L. Bender, University of Rhode Island. On the subsequent U.S.-French- Mexican geological expedition to 21° N, the principal scientists were Fred N. Spiess and Kenneth C. Macdonald, co-leaders, and John A. Orcutt, all of SIO; Bruce P. Luyendyk, UCSB; William R. Normark, U.S. Geological Survey; Jean Francheteau and Thierry Juteau, Centre National pour L'Exploitation des Oceans; Arturo Carranza, Diego A. Cordoba, Victor Dias, Jose Guerrero, and Claude Rangin, Universidad Nacional Autonoma de Mexico.

SAMPLE STUDENT RESPONSES • THE BOTTOM OF THE OCEAN

DETERMINING THE RELIABILITY OF SOURCES

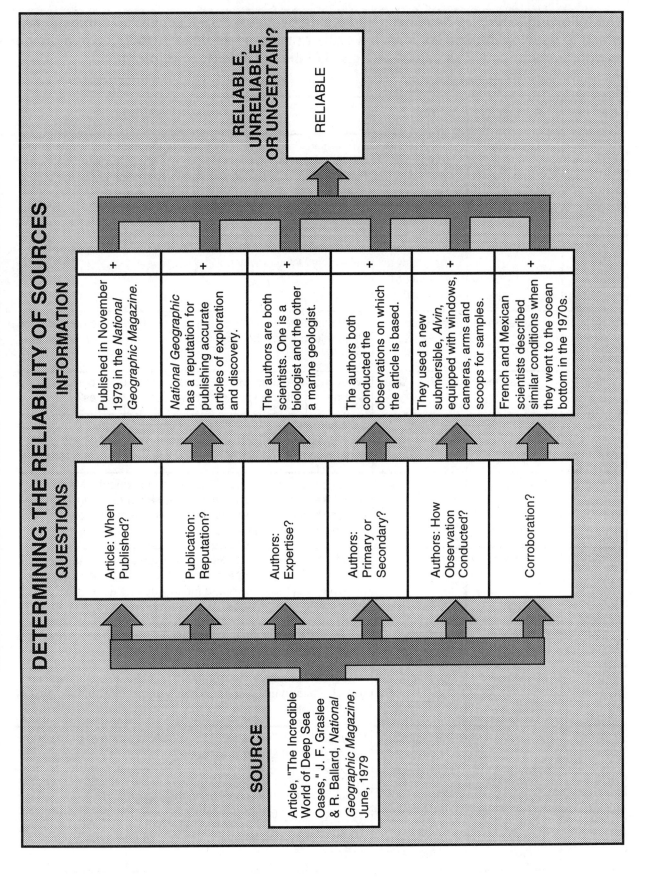

SOURCE

Article, "The Incredible World of Deep Sea Oases," J. F. Graslee & R. Ballard, *National Geographic Magazine*, June, 1979

QUESTIONS

Article: When Published?

Publication: Reputation?

Authors: Expertise?

Authors: Primary or Secondary?

Authors: How Observation Conducted?

Corroboration?

INFORMATION

Published in November 1979 in the *National Geographic Magazine*. +

National Geographic has a reputation for publishing accurate articles of exploration and discovery. +

The authors are both scientists. One is a biologist and the other a marine geologist. +

The authors both conducted the observations on which the article is based. +

They used a new submersible, *Alvin*, equipped with windows, cameras, arms and scoops for samples. +

French and Mexican scientists described similar conditions when they went to the ocean bottom in the 1970s. +

RELIABLE, UNRELIABLE, OR UNCERTAIN?

RELIABLE

RELIABLE SOURCES LESSON CONTEXTS

The following examples have been suggested by classroom teachers as contexts in which to develop infused lessons. If a skill or process has been introduced in a previous lesson, transfer activities can be designed in these contexts to reinforce it.

GRADE	SUBJECT	TOPIC	THINKING ISSUE
K–3	Literature	*Jack and the Beanstalk*	What might Jack try to find out about the man who wants to trade the beans for Jack's cow? How may Jack determine how likely it is that the man is a reliable source of information about the beans?
K–3	Literature	*Henny Penny*	When the fox tells the animals his hole is a short-cut to the king, what should they consider in order to decide whether to trust him?
K–3	Literature	*And To Think That I Saw It On Mulberry Street*	Is the person's account of what he saw on Mulberry Street believable? Why or why not?
K–3	Literature	*The Emperor's New Clothes*	What might the emperor think about to decide whether the people who make comments about his new clothes can be trusted as reliable?
K–3	Literature	*Freckle Juice*	What should Andrew Marcus consider in order to decide whether Sharon is a reliable source on how to make freckles?
K–3	Social studies	Cities	Let's say you were visiting another city and wanted to bring back to your classroom a report about that city. What would you do to make sure that you would bring back an accurate and reliable?
K–3	Social studies	The Pilgrims	Today, people at Plymouth Plantation in Plymouth, Massachusetts dress like and re-enact the lives of the Pilgrims in the 1600s. What can you find out that will show whether you can believe that the Pilgrims really lived like this?
K–3	Science	Animals	Which of the following is likely to give you the best information about how to keep a hamster alive in your classroom: the school principal, a pet store owner, a friend who has a hamster, or a person who sells pet food? Why did you select whom you did?
K–3	Science	Food	Where can you get the most reliable information about how healthy a breakfast cereal is? Why?
K–3	Mathematics	Measurement	What factors make a measurement reliable? (Care in measuring, use of standard units, use of a measurement instrument, time of recording, etc.)
K–3	Art	Representational art	What could you find out about a specific drawing or painting to decide if what it shows is accurate?
K–3	Guidance	Conflicts	What should you consider to determine the accuracy of reports about fighting in the school or on the playground?
4–6	Literature	*Be a Perfect Person in Just Three Days*	What should Milo Crinkley find out about Dr. K. Pinkerton Silverfish before trying his recommendations about how to be a perfect person?

RELIABLE SOURCES LESSON CONTEXTS

GRADE	SUBJECT	TOPIC	THINKING ISSUE
4–6	Literature	*Wizard of Oz*	What made Dorothy initially think that the Wizard of Oz was a reliable source of information? What did she find out later that made her think that he wasn't? What did she learn from this experience about how to determine whether a source is reliable?
4–6	Literature	*Alice in Wonderland*	Choose one of the following characters from "Alice in Wonderland": the rabbit, the Mad Hatter, the March Hare, or the Red Queen. Ask what sorts of things Alice should try to find out before assuming that information from the character is reliable.
4–6	Literature	*Alice*	What questions should Alice ask about the "winner" letter before travelling to Manhattan to collect the prize?
4–6	Language arts/social studies	Ghost stories	What should you consider in order to determine whether specific accounts of seeing ghosts are accurate?
4–6	Social studies	Columbus	Several sources may give accounts of what happened aboard ship when Columbus's sailors were getting discouraged. Which of the following are most likely to be accurate ones: a story book about Columbus, a cartoon about Columbus, Columbus's diary, a textbook that children used 50 years ago, or your textbook? Why?
4–6	Social studies	Media/news sources	What should you consider in deciding which of the following news sources is the most reliable: the nightly TV news, the Weekly Reader, specific newspapers, specific magazines, or your neighbor?
4–6	Social studies	Africa	A map of Africa may give us information about the borders and names of its various countries. What can you find out to determine whether the map is accurate?
4–6	American history	Custer's Last Stand	What accounts of Custer's last battle are likely to be the most reliable? Why?
4–6	American history	Industrial revolution	Read various accounts of conditions in the Lowell textile mills of Lowell, Massachusetts in the mid-nineteenth century. Some possible sources are advertisements by the mill owners, accounts by the mill maids, accounts by the local townspeople, stories about life at the mills, etc. Which would you judge to be the most reliable and accurate source? Why?
4–6	Foreign language	Speaking the language	Who could give you the most reliable information about how to speak a language such as Spanish? Why is it the most reliable?
4–6	Geography/ mathematics	Speed/time/ distance	What is the most accurate way to calculate how long it will take you to travel across the country? Explain how you will determine the accuracy of any information used to make these calculations.
4–6	Science	Food ingredients	How would you evaluate a label to judge whether its product information is reliable and accurate?
4–6	Science	Energy	Compare various sources of information about the risks and benefits of nuclear power. Determine which is likely to be most accurate. Explain why.
4–6	Science	Data collection	Suppose you were going to observe and gather data about the feeding habits of animals that live in and around a nearby pond. Plan how you would conduct your obsrvation to be sure you bring back the most reliable information.

RELIABLE SOURCES LESSON CONTEXTS

GRADE	SUBJECT	TOPIC	THINKING ISSUE
4–6	Science	Environment	How can you decide whether information about "natural foods" or "environmentally safe products" is reliable?
4–6	Mathematics	Estimation/ distance	What is the best way to estimate distances? Why is this way better than other ways?
4–6	Art	Shirt design	What is the most reliable source of information about shirt styles that consumers prefer? Why is it the most reliable source? Why are the other sources less reliable?
4–6	Media	TV	How can you determine whether TV ratings are reliable?
4–6	Music	Popular music	If you were a disc jockey, how would you get reliable information about which recordings your audience would like to hear? Explain why you think this is a reliable source.
4–6	Health	Drugs	What would you consider to determine whether someone's remarks on the risks and benefits of various drugs were reliable?
4–6	Physical education	Team sports	What sources of information about a specific team sport would be reliable to help you decide whether you should try out for it? Why do you think these sources would be reliable?
4–6	Guidance	Purchases	Where could you get the most accurate information about a purchase in order to decide whether it will serve your needs? Explain why you think the source you select is reliable.
6–8	Literature	*Where the Red Fern Grows*	Determine whether Mr. Benson is a reliable source of information for Billy about Billy's dogs. Explain why or why not.
6–8	Literature	*Lydde*	What should you consider to determine whether the picture of life at the Lowell Mills presented in "Lydde" is accurate?
6–8	Social studies	The Ancient Egyptians	What are some ways of getting reliable information about living in Ancient Egypt? Why do you think this information is reliable?
6–8	U.S. history	Colonial period	What would you consider to make a judgment about the reliability of accounts of the "New World" in order to advise John White whether to undertake a colony at Roanoke?
6–8	U. S. history	Slavery	Read various accounts of conditions in this country under slavery (e.g., by slaveholders, by slaves, by abolitionists, by slaves interviewed many years later). What would you want to find about the authors and about these accounts that can help you decide whether they are reliable?
6–8	U.S. history	Kennedy assassination	Make a judgment about the reliability and accuracy of each of the following accounts of Kennedy's assassination, and explain why you rate its reliability as you do: video tape of a spectator, Jackie's story, Governor Connelley's story, the Secret Service Report, the Warren Commission Report, the film "JFK."

CHAPTER 13
CAUSAL EXPLANATION

Why is There a Need for More Skillful Causal Explanation?

When we try to prevent something we don't want (like a disease) or try to produce something we do want (like better crops or higher grades), we usually try to find the causes of these things. We can then try to alter causal conditions in order to block undesirable results or to foster desirable ones.

Knowing the causes of events or conditions can also enable us to predict them, although we may not be able to prevent them. Then we can try to avoid or minimize harmful effects. We know, for example, that certain conditions can cause severe weather. Predicting a storm based on knowledge of the presence of these conditions can give us time to find shelter.

The variety of contexts for causal explanation. Scientific investigation often involves trying to determine the causes of things. Knowing the cause of AIDS allows us to avoid conditions which lead to the spread of the disease. Understanding the causes of global warming allows for informed policies to prevent its serious consequences.

We also make causal judgments in other fields of study. When we try to explain what led to the Civil War, we are offering a causal explanation. When we attribute a specific motivation to a character or leader, we are offering a causal explanation of that person's behavior. When we explain why stock prices tumbled, we are offering a causal explanation of an economic trend. We also make causal explanations about everyday matters. When we try to figure out why the car didn't start, we are searching for a cause.

Problems regarding the way we think about causes. We can seldom find causes by direct inspection. Once the effect occurs, the cause is usually gone. In such situations, causal explanation is a matter of inference.

If we don't think carefully about what is causing something, we may jump to hasty conclusions which can create serious consequences. A hasty judgment about the cause of an illness may lead us to spend effort and money on the wrong treatment. A hasty judgment about a person's motive may cost that person his or her job or, in a murder case, his or her life.

There are two sources of hasty conclusions about causes. We often accept the first causal explanation that comes into our minds and become convinced that it is the correct one. Often, being anxious or fearing a situation or condition that has caused harm in the past, we become convinced that some current difficulty was brought about by the same cause. When the *Challenger* disaster occurred, many people believed immediately that it was sabotage. Like them, we sometimes don't consider other possibilities before making up our minds.

The second source of hasty judgments about causes is that, while we might think about other possibilities, we may not consider all of the relevant evidence to decide which explanation is the best one. The first bit of evidence we get for one possible cause sometimes leads us to accept it. Good detective story writers exploit this. It is all too easy to get us to think that a shady character committed the crime simply because someone saw him running from the scene.

The two basic problems with the way people usually think about causes are summarized in figure 13.1.

If you find that you are limiting your causal judgment in either of these ways, you can learn to make more careful judgments about causes.

**COMMON DEFAULTS IN
OUR THINKING ABOUT CAUSES**

1. We consider only one possible cause and affirm it without thinking about other possibilities.

2. We take account of only a small sample of the relevant and available evidence in determining a cause.

Figure 13.1

How Do We Engage in Skillful Causal Reasoning?

Tips for Determining Causes Skillfully. We can guard against selecting a cause hastily by considering many possible explanations of an event. Then it is easy to avoid affirming the first explanation that pops into our minds. Before we knew the actual cause of the *Challenger* disaster, many people speculated about a number of things that might have caused the tragedy. While the explosion could have been caused by sabotage, it could also have been caused by ruptured "O" rings or a malfunctioning engine. Realizing that there are usually many possible causes reduces the tendency to jump to a quick conclusion about causation.

Thinking about what we can find out that would make one or another explanation plausible can help us avoid making a causal judgment on too little evidence. Often it is helpful to list the kind of evidence that would be needed to justify selecting one possible explanation as the most reasonable one. Knowing what kind of evidence we need prompts us to search for information that we might otherwise overlook. For example, if my car doesn't start and my lights don't work, I may realize that I should not rule out the possibility that there is a broken wire, rather than a dead battery. This realization may then prompt me to check whether the wires are intact. When I find that they are, then a dead battery becomes a likelier cause.

Thinking carefully about what may be causing something can guide well-planned research in which we rule out various possibilities until the weight of evidence points to one causal explanation as the most plausible one. Conducting controlled experiments to gather necessary evidence is one of the more sophisticated techniques commonly used in scientific and medical research.

Skillful thinking about causes, therefore, involves four important matters:

- Generating ideas about possible causes
- Considering what evidence would be necessary to show which is the probable cause
- Considering the evidence we have or gathering additional evidence that we need
- Making a judgment about the cause based on the evidence

When we find that we have sufficient evidence to justify selecting one possible explanation, we are ready to affirm it. The investigation into the *Challenger* disaster is a case in point. Only after the investigating commission had sufficient evidence to rule out other possible explanations in favor of the rupture of protective rings did it advance this explanation as the most reasonable one.

We may attend to these four points and still find that we don't have sufficient evidence to make a causal judgment. Trying to determine what caused the extinction of the dinosaurs is this kind of causal issue. Nevertheless, even in this case, skillful thinking about what caused the extinction pays off. When we realize that we cannot determine a probable cause, we can defend that judgment by showing that there are a variety of possible causes yet insufficient evidence to pick one out as the clear explanation.

Tools for determining causes skillfully. Considering these four factors (possible causes, necessary evidence to support causes, actual evidence, and judging whether a cause is warranted by the evidence) can help us make better causal judgments. The thinking map of causal explanation in figure 13.2 summarizes these key points. By asking and answering these questions carefully, we avoid the common defaults in determining causes.

As we think about what caused something,

SKILLFUL CAUSAL EXPLANATION

1. What are possible causes of the event in question?

2. What could you find that would count for or against the likelihood of these possibilities?

3. What evidence do you already have, or have you gathered, that is relevant to determining what caused the event?

4. Which possibility is rendered most likely based on the evidence?

Figure 13.2

---

we can use the graphic organizer in figure 13.3 to focus our attention on the evidence for a specific possibility. Using the diagram is particularly helpful when the evidence is complex. By recording the evidence on the diagram, we don't have to hold it all in memory and can turn our attention to evaluating what it shows about the possible cause. The number of boxes can be expanded depending on specific needs.

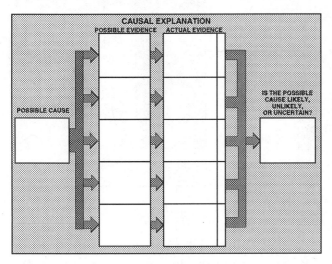

Figure 13.3

To use this graphic organizer, first brainstorm a list of possible causes of the event you are seeking to explain and record these on a piece of paper. You can then pick the ones that seem, initially, to be lively possibilities and explore them more fully using the graphic organizer. To do this, write one from your short list of lively possibilities in the "Possible Cause" box. Then brainstorm possible evidence that would support this as a likely cause. This evidence should be listed in the boxes under "Possible Evidence."

Then, using what you have projected as possible supporting evidence to guide you, try to determine whether such evidence exists. This may mean just looking around (Do I see any footprints near the scene of the crime?). It could call for more extensive investigation (Are there any witnesses?) or even an experiment (If I test his hands for powder burns, will they show up?). You might even remember something that you already know that is relevant (Did I see him at the scene of the crime yesterday?).

When you find that there is such evidence, write it in the appropriate boxes under "Actual Evidence." Each time you enter some evidence you should indicate, with a plus or minus, whether it counts in favor of or against the possibility you are considering. Then, when you've done a satisfactory search for evidence, look at the weight of the evidence you've recorded and make a judgment about whether the possibility is likely, unlikely, or uncertain based on the evidence. Write this in the final box.

Causal chains. In some cases, we may wish to examine the remote causes of an event, as well as the immediate ones. We can then try to map a causal chain that leads to an event. In many cases, an important cause may be many steps back along the chain. If my car does not start, it may be because the spark plugs don't work well. The spark plugs may be faulty because the auto mechanic didn't install them properly and, over months of use, they have weakened.

Explaining past events in a causal chain can help us make better judgments about responsibility. We may find that people's past actions were involved in some of the causes that appear in the chain. If the automobile mechanic didn't install the spark plugs properly, the repair shop may be responsible for repairs resulting from their malfunction.

The graphic organizer in figure 13.4 can be used to record causal chains. It can be expanded as needed. The diagram can be used to depict a chain of possible causes prior to investigating whether this chain of events is likely to have occurred. It can also be used to record the results of such an investigation, i.e., what you have determined is the most reasonable chain of causes leading to the event in question.

Multiple causal factors. Another consideration in determining causes lies in the fact that

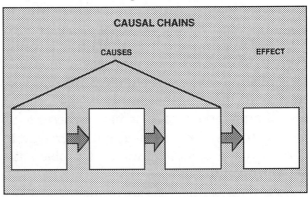

Figure 13.4

usually no single factor causes related effects. Usually a cluster of factors blend together to bring about effects. Lighting the match isn't, by itself, the cause of an explosion. Gas from a leak, in the right mixture with the oxygen in the air, is also necessary to create the explosion. The latter are sometimes called "standing conditions" since they are constants and the former "differential conditions" since they are new events that make the difference.

Standing and differential conditions work together to bring about an effect. Each of them alone is not sufficient, but each seems necessary. Neither the gas nor the oxygen nor the lit match were sufficient in themselves for the explosion. Together, along with the other relevant standing conditions like the temperature, they are sufficient. Each is necessary; without one of them, the explosion would not have occurred.

The graphic organizer in figure 13.5 can help us explore what factors blend together to bring about a specific event. In this case also, the graphic organizer can be used to record the results of speculation about a possible blend of causal factors leading to an effect or the most reasonable explanation supported by evidence.

When should we think about causal chains and about multiple causes? When considering questions of human responsibility for events, we should extend our thinking beyond immediate causes and develop a causal chain that led up to an event. This can pinpoint places in the chain where human beings were involved. We've already discussed an example of this—the brakes failed on a car, and the basic responsibility lies in faulty work done earlier by an auto mechanic.

Similarly, when we're interested in finding out what caused some event in order to prevent a similar situation in the future, we may want to identify a variety of different factors that blended together to bring about an undesirable result. Perhaps some causes are more easily modified than others. Maybe it's better to fix the gas leak than to stop lighting matches. If we just focus on the differential condition, it may not occur to us that there may be an easier and safer way to correct the problem by altering problematic standing conditions.

Both in cases when you are trying to construct

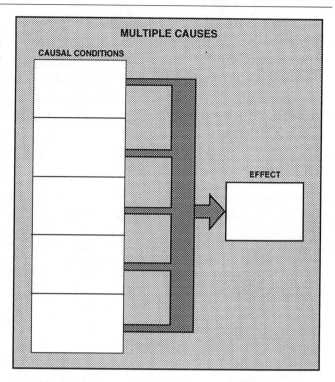

Figure 13.5

a causal chain and in cases when you are trying to determine multiple causes, you can use the same basic strategy outlined in the thinking map (figure 13.2) in order to make reasonable judgments. For causal chains, consider possibilities one-by-one in backwards order until you've constructed a plausible chain of causes. For multiple causal conditions, consider all the factors that may be present and together contribute causally to the effect, investigating evidence for each factor. In each of these cases, it is important to consider alternatives, rule out the implausible ones, and accept the plausible ones based on real evidence.

How Can We Teach Students Skillful Causal Explanation?

Asking students to identify already specified causes and effects, such as "identify the cause and the effect" activities in many instructional materials, is not yet engaging them in causal explanation. The students might be reading a story in which they are told that one effect of the main character's reassuring comments was to make her friends feel less anxious about a task they were about to perform. At the end of the chapter, a typical "cause and effect" question might be "Identify the cause of the group's feeling less anxious about their task." This is nothing more than a straightforward recall question which emphasizes identifying the reassuring comments of the main character as a cause.

There may, of course, be value in asking students to identify causes that are already specified. This does help to clarify the language of cause and effect and to make students more aware of the variety of causal relationships we experience in our lives. Such preliminary thinking about causes, however, is no substitute for causal explanation. Causal explanation involves trying to determine a cause when *we are aware of an effect and don't know what caused it.*

Even when students don't know what caused something, it is not enough to simply ask students what the cause is. "Why did the plague spread so rapidly in medieval Europe?" typically prompts quick answers, many of which don't involve much thought. Asking these sorts of "higher-order questions" doesn't teach students skillful causal reasoning.

Teaching causal explanation explicitly. Instruction in skillful causal explanation should help students internalize the pattern of thinking specified on the thinking map of causal explanation in figure 13.2. We want students to ask questions about possible causes and relevant evidence spontaneously when trying to figure out what caused something and to recognize whether they have answered those questions adequately.

The pattern of instruction in skillful causal explanation should follow the same structure we use in all infusion lessons.

- Introduce the skill explicitly.

- Guide students through an activity in which they use the skill by asking them about alternative explanations and evidence and by helping them to use the graphic organizer for causal explanation.

- Help them to reflect on what causal explanation involves and whether it is valuable to use the strategy on the thinking map to do it.

- Provide them with plenty of good opportunities to practice the same kind of thinking in other contexts.

Initially you will guide your students through this practice; eventually they will guide themselves. The result will be that they will explain causes carefully and confidently.

Contexts in the curriculum for causal explanation lessons. The K–12 curriculum is replete with examples of causal explanation. The causes of wars, eclipses, population changes, miscommunication, and characters' actions described in stories are among the many applications throughout the curriculum. In general, there are two types of contexts in which it is natural to develop causal explanation lessons.

- *Causal explanations are important to learn in order to understand basic ideas and concepts in the curriculum.* In science, it is important for students to learn the causes of various phenomena, e.g., the weather, earthquakes, and plant growth, in order to understand these phenomena better. The same is true in the study of the American Revolution or the Civil War. Students can be guided to determine what the causes are in these examples by using skillful causal thinking.

- *Causal explanations are important when either there is a controversy about the causes of important events studied in the curriculum or no one yet knows what caused these events.* For example, lessons on the extinction of the dinosaurs, like the one we have included in this handbook, can help students gain a deeper understanding of dinosaurs and their worlds, as well as of scientific investigation. When reading *Sarah, Plain and Tall*, students may interpret why Sarah left her home in New England to travel to the Midwest to take care of children she did not know. Clarifying what causes characters to make choices can bring students insight about human motivation as well as an understanding of how to make reasonable judgments about why people do what they do.

By locating significant contexts like these, you have numerous opportunities to develop robust infusion lessons on causal explanation.

The menus we provide at the end of this chapter (p. 411–412) illustrate some of the specific examples that teachers have found in their curriculum causal explanation lessons.

Teaching causal explanation in the primary grades. There are significant contexts for infusion lessons on causal explanation in the primary grades. The lesson example on Henny Penny shows how easily common stories can be used to teach this kind of thinking. When you choose a context to teach this skill in the primary grades you should, of course, use grade-appropriate material. Also make sure that your students have sufficient background knowledge to be able to generate a robust list of possible causes for the event you ask them to think about. The key notion to stress with primary grade students is the need for clues or evidence to be able to tell what caused something.

The language used in the thinking map and graphic organizer require modification for use with primary grade students. A simplified thinking map for causal explanation in figure 13.6 can be used in grades 1–2.

FINDING CAUSES

1. What are some possible causes?

2. What possible clues could you find?

3. What real clues do you have?

4. What do the clues show about the cause?

Figure 13.6

The standard graphic organizer can be used with students at this grade level to emphasize evidence and what it shows. Substituting "Possible Clues" and "Actual Clues" for "Possible Evidence" and "Actual Evidence" may make using this diagram more comfortable for students in the primary grades. Kindergarten students should draw or manipulate pictures of possible causes and evidence when they use the diagram, rather than writing on it.

Model Lessons on Causal Explanation

We include two lessons which infuse instruction in skillful causal reasoning into content area teaching. The first is a first grade language arts lesson on the story of Henny Penny—the lesson

we commented upon in Chapter One. The second is an upper elementary science lesson on the extinction of the dinosaurs.

Each lesson illustrates the way structured questioning derived from the thinking map, together with a graphic organizer, can guide students through a process that leads to a well-founded critical judgment. The simple thinking map for causal explanation is used in Henny Penny. In addition, the graphic organizer for causal chains is employed in the lesson on the extinction of the dinosaurs.

As you read each lesson, ask yourself the following questions:

- How does the graphic organizer facilitate a careful look at what the evidence shows about causes?

- What metacognitive strategies are employed to help students take charge of their own thinking?

- Are there alternative metacognitive strategies you could use?

- Are there other ways of reinforcing this kind of thinking besides the application examples mentioned in the lesson?

Tools for Designing Lessons on Causal Explanation

The thinking maps provide focus questions to be integrated into causal explanation lessons to guide student thinking. The thinking map below is used in grades 3 and above; the second thinking map is simplified for use in the primary grades.

The graphic organizer for causal explanation supplements and reinforces the sequenced questions on the thinking map. Graphic organizers for causal chains and for multiple factors show how many caused contribute to a specific effect.

The thinking maps and graphic organizers can guide you in designing the critical thinking activity in the lesson and can also serve as photocopy masters, transparency masters, or as models that can be enlarged and used as posters in the classroom. Reproduction rights are granted for single classroom use only.

SKILLFUL CAUSAL EXPLANATION

1. What are possible causes of the event in question?

2. What could you find that would count for or against the likelihood of these possibilities?

3. What evidence do you already have, or have you gathered, that is relevant to determining what caused the event?

4. Which possibility is rendered most likely based on the evidence?

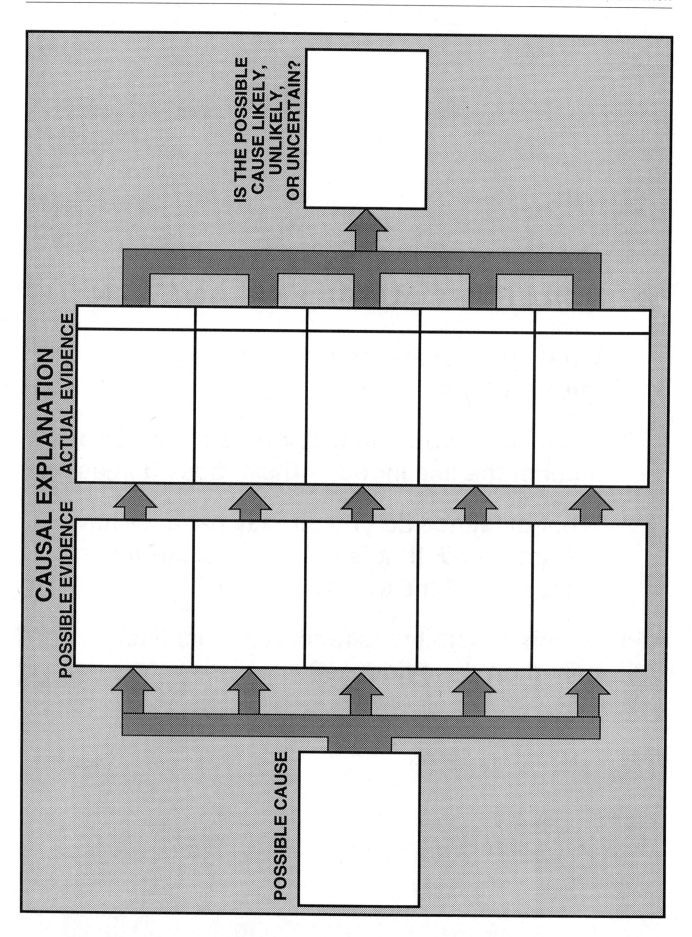

CAUSAL EXPLANATION

POSSIBLE EVIDENCE

ACTUAL EVIDENCE

IS THE POSSIBLE CAUSE LIKELY, UNLIKELY, OR UNCERTAIN?

POSSIBLE CAUSE

FINDING CAUSES

1. What are some possible causes?

2. What possible clues could you find?

3. What real clues do you have?

4. What do the clues show about the cause?

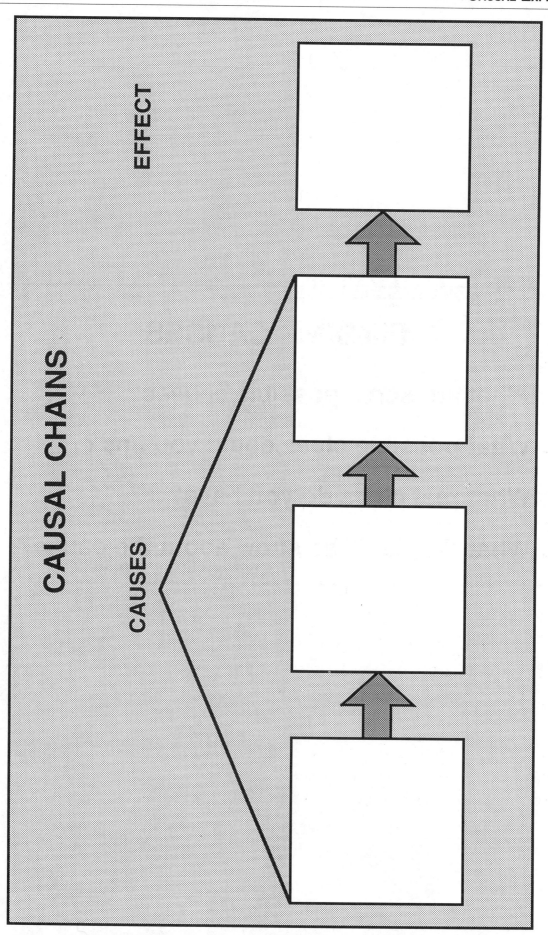

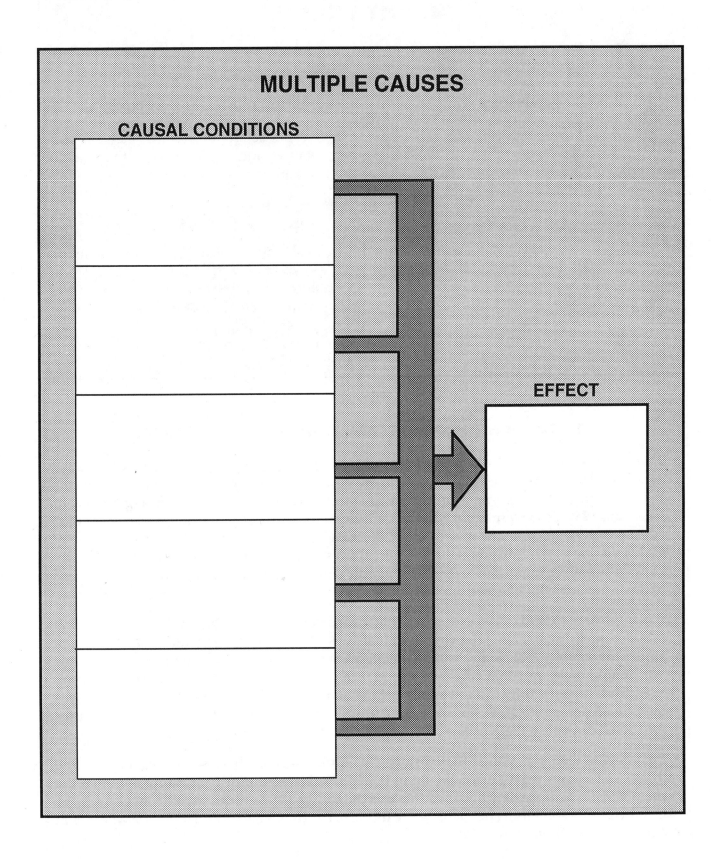

HENNY PENNY

Language Arts   **Grades K–2**

OBJECTIVES

CONTENT

Students will develop good listening skills and will learn to identify the moral of a story.

THINKING SKILL/PROCESS

In trying to determine the most likely cause of a situation, students will learn to think about possible causes and evidence.

METHODS AND MATERIALS

CONTENT

The story of Henny Penny is read aloud to the students. The students repeat parts of the story. An art activity requiring crayons and drawing paper is optional.

THINKING SKILL/PROCESS

In collaborative learning groups, students are guided by structured questioning to brainstorm possible causes and possible evidence. Students follow a thinking map of causal explanation. (See pp.391–395 for reproducible diagrams.) An optional hands-on investigation of actual evidence is included.

LESSON

INTRODUCTION TO CONTENT AND THINKING SKILLS/PROCESS

- Think about a time when something happened and you wondered why it happened. POSSIBLE ANSWERS: *I had a stomach ache and I wondered why. I got sick and I wondered why. My dog was barking and I wondered why.* When you wonder why something is happening, you are trying to find out what caused it. Did you find out what caused some of the things you were wondering about? POSSIBLE ANSWERS : *I ate a lot of green apples. My mom had a cold and I had one too. A noise in the yard made my dog bark.* What do you call all of these things? *Causes.* To make sure something doesn't happen again, it's important to find the cause. If you found out that you have a stomach ache because you ate a lot of green apples, you wouldn't want to eat a lot of green apples again.

- It is important to find causes correctly. That means you've got to think carefully about what makes something happen. You shouldn't just guess. If you don't know that it was the green apples that caused your stomachache, you might eat them again and get another stomachache. You should make sure that you have a good reason for believing what the cause is. Did you ever think that one thing caused another thing and then found out that something else was the cause? Accept students' answers. Let's think about how to find out what really causes things to happen, so that we don't make mistakes about it.

- I'm going to read you a story. In this story, something happens to one of the characters. She thinks she knows what caused the thing to happen. Listen carefully to figure out what the characters do because they believed this was the true cause. Remember, whenever we try to figure out why something happens, we're trying to find out what caused it. This is what we're going to think about in the story.

- The story is the story of Henny Penny. If you already know the story, don't tell us what happens. Let's find out what happens by listening. Read the story of Henny Penny as it appears on page 400. Every time a new animal comes along, prompt the students to repeat what the animal asks: "Where are you going in such a hurry?" Then encourage them to repeat what Henny Penny and the other animals say: "The sky is falling and we're going to tell the King." Read to the end, where the animals get led into the fox's den and become a meal for the fox's family.

• **What caused the animals to get eaten by the fox's family?** *They went into the fox hole and the fox's family was hungry.* **What caused them to go into the fox's hole?** *The fox told them that it was a shortcut to the king.* **Why were they going to see the king?** *They thought the sky was falling.* **Why did they think the sky was falling?** *Henny Penny told them.*

THINKING ACTIVELY

• **Now let's think about Henny Penny herself. What did she think caused the bump on her head?** *A piece of the sky.* **Do you think she found the right cause?** ANSWERS VARY: *It must have been something else because the sky can't hit you on the head.* **Do you think she figured that out in a good way?** ANSWERS VARY: *She didn't look for reasons. She just guessed. She just said it was the sky and didn't try to find out.* **Let's call the way she decided that the sky caused the bump on her head "Henny Penny Thinking." Is that very good thinking?** *No.*

• **Let's see if there's a better way to think about what happened to Henny Penny. First, instead of just saying that it must be a piece of the sky, let's think about what it might be. Let's think about possible causes.** Write "Possible Causes" on the board. **Talk with your neighbor and, together, see if you can come up with a list of five possible causes. Write them down.** Wait a few minutes. **Now tell the class about one of your possibilities.** Ask students from each group to respond with one possibility and repeat, asking each group until the class creates a long list of possible causes. Write their possible causes on the board. Clarify that these are possible causes and that we don't know yet what the real cause is. POSSIBLE ANSWERS: *Hail, an acorn, an apple, a rock, a piece of corn pecked up by another chicken, a coke bottle, something that fell off the roof of the barn, another animal pecking Henny Penny, a dream, satellite debris, bird or squirrel droppings, an object thrown from the hayloft, a rock thrown by the fox, an egg thrown by a child, a farmer sowing seeds, a shingle, an insect bite, Henny's imagination, a golf ball, a piece of the space shuttle, a clam that a bird dropped, Henny fell, a rock kicked up by her own pecking, a meteorite.*

• **Each group should pick one possible cause. List what you might find if you did some investigation like a detective. A detective looks for clues to try to find out which of the possible causes was the real cause. If the cause you are working on is the real cause, what clues do you think you might find?** POSSIBLE ANSWERS: *If it were an apple, then we might find apples on the ground. Henny Penny might be under an apple tree, and it might be autumn when the apples are ripe. If it were hail, maybe other animals saw hail fall. Maybe we could find out from the weather reporter that there was a hail storm, and maybe there would be hail or water on the ground.*

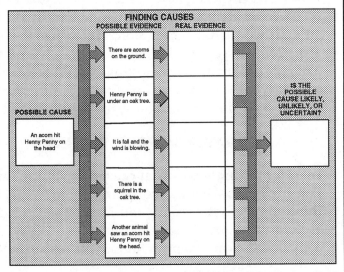

• **The clues you have just listed are called "evidence." If you find them, you have evidence that the possible cause is what really caused Henny Penny's bump on the head. You should only say you know what the cause is if you have evidence like this. I'm going to use this diagram for**

finding causes and fill in some possible causes and some of the possible evidence you listed. It can guide you to look for real evidence for what hit Henny Penny on the head. Fill in two or three of the "Possible Evidence" boxes on the chalkboard or on a large poster. The graphic organizer might look like the one shown on the previous page.

- **Now look in the story. See if you can find some of the things that you mention. Look at the pictures. Is there anything that looks like evidence that can show us what really hit Henny Penny on the head?** POSSIBLE ANSWERS: *It says she was in the barnyard pecking up corn, so there is evidence that it was corn.* Ask the students to look at the illustrations as well as the text to identify evidence. For example, if there is a picture of Henny Penny under a tree and there are pictures of the leaves, ask the students what kind of tree it is. If it is an oak tree, ask them which possible cause (e.g., an acorn, a branch) might be likely from the evidence.

- **Now I'm going to add to our diagram the real evidence you found.** Use student answers to fill in some of the "Real Evidence" boxes of the diagram for finding causes. If the evidence in the story is scanty, however, you should supplement it with the following hands-on activity.

- **Suppose that when Henny Penny looked around this is what she found.** Show a bag full of things that you might find in a barnyard. It may include some acorns, oak leaves, twigs, grass, feathers, etc. Spill it out on the table and tell the students that this is what Henny Penny found. **What would these things show about what really caused the bump on Henny Penny's head?** Let them sort through the items. Ask them to work together in groups to try to decide what possible cause this supports and why. Ask each group to report to the class. Use their answers to fill in the "Real Evidence" boxes of the diagram.

- **Now let's think about how well our real evidence supports our possible cause.** Read aloud the evidence in the first box. **Is this evidence a clue that makes you think our cause is the real cause?** For each box, ask the students whether the real evidence works in favor of or against the possible cause; add a "+", a "−", or a "?" to the right of each, accordingly.

- **Now we can decide whether our possible cause is likely, unlikely, or uncertain. If we have lots of plus marks, we have lots of evidence to think our cause is likely to be the real one. Lots of minus marks would mean that our cause is unlikely to be the real cause of Henny Penny's bump. Do you think an acorn hitting Henny Penny's head is likely or unlikely to be the real cause?** *Likely.* Write a summary statement in the final right-hand box as to whether the cause is likely or unlikely. (Example: It is fairly likely that an acorn hit Henny Penny on the head.)

- **If Henny Penny had thought about the situation and realized it was just an acorn that hit her on the head, do you think she would have rushed off to the king?** *No.* **Do you think the other animals would have come along if they had thought about it and found out that it was just an acorn?** *No.* **Do you think all those animals would have been eaten up by the fox's family if they had not rushed off to see the king?** *No.* **What do you think we should learn from the story?** *That we should think about things before we decide what happened.* **When we learn something important from a story, like we did here, that's called the "moral" of the story.**

THINKING ABOUT THINKING

- **In order to figure out what caused the bump on Henny Penny's head, what did you think about? What did you think about first, second, and third?** *Possible causes, evidence (or clues), and then what the real cause was.* On the board, copy the thinking map for finding causes as the students

FINDING CAUSES
1. What are some possible causes?
2. What possible clues could you find?
3. What real clues do you have?
4. What do the clues show about the cause?

come up with these answers. Prompt their answers if they have trouble remembering. The thinking map for finding causes should resemble the one shown on the previous page.

- **How is our way of thinking about causes different from "Henny Penny Thinking"?** POSSIBLE ANSWERS: *Henny Penny didn't look for clues, Henny Penny guessed, Henny Penny jumped to a conclusion.*

- **Think about how you played detective for Henny Penny's problem. Is this a better way to think about a cause than the way Henny Penny thought? Why?** POSSIBLE ANSWERS: *I looked for clues and Henny Penny didn't. I thought about it and Henny Penny didn't. My way is better because I found out the real causes and Henny Penny didn't.*

APPLYING YOUR THINKING

Immediate Transfer

- **Suppose you couldn't find your pencil. Why do you think this might have happened? How could you find out?**

- **Suppose you find a puddle of water on the floor near the window of your kitchen. What could have caused it? How could you find out?**

Reinforcement Later

- When you teach about communities, ask the students to think about what might cause people to want to live together in a community.

- When you teach about plants, ask the students to think about what might be causing the plants in the classroom to grow.

ART EXTENSION

Ask the students to draw a picture that could be used to illustrate the story of Henny Penny, showing a possible cause for the bump on Henny Penny's head. Ask them to make sure they include the evidence.

ASSESSING STUDENT THINKING ABOUT CAUSES

To assess the skill of causal explanation, ask students questions like the immediate transfer questions. Additionally, you may ask the following: If one of the students in the class is in a bad mood, how could we find out what is causing the problem? Ask the students to think out loud. Determine whether they are attending to each of the steps in the thinking map for finding causes. Encourage students to use the terms "clues," "causes," and "evidence."

HENNY PENNY

One day Henny Penny was pecking up corn in the barnyard when—whack!—something hit her on the head. "Goodness gracious me!" she said, "The sky is falling. I must go and tell the King."

So she went along, and went along, and went along until she met another animal on the road, Cocky Locky. "Where are you going in such a hurry, Henny Penny?" said Cocky Locky.

"The sky is falling! I'm going to tell the King," said Henny Penny.

"That's important. May I come with you?" said Cocky Locky.

"Certainly," said Henny Penny. So Henny Penny and Cocky Locky continued on the road to tell the King that the sky was falling. They went along, and went along, and went along till they met another animal, Ducky Lucky.

"Where are you going in such a hurry, Henny Penny and Cocky Locky?" said Ducky Lucky.

"We're going to tell the King the sky is falling," said Henny Penny and Cocky Locky.

"May I come with you?" said Ducky Lucky.

"Certainly," said Henny Penny and Cocky Locky. So Henny Penny, Cocky Locky, and Ducky Lucky continued on the road to tell the King the sky was falling.

So they went along, and went along, and went along until they met another animal who was there on the road, Goosey Loosey.

"Where are you going in such a hurry, Henny Penny, Cocky Locky, and Ducky Lucky?" said Goosey Loosey.

"The sky is falling! We're going to tell the King," said Henny Penny, Cocky Locky, and Ducky Lucky.

"That sounds very important. May I come with you?" said Goosey Loosey.

"Certainly," said Henny Penny, Cocky Locky, and Ducky Lucky. So Henny Penny, Cocky Locky, Ducky Lucky, and now Goosey Loosey continued on the road to tell the King the sky was falling.

So they went along, and went along, and went along until they met yet another animal on the road, Turkey Lurkey. "Where are you going in such a hurry, Henny Penny, Cocky Locky, Goosey Loosey and Ducky Lucky?" said Turkey Lurkey.

"We're going to tell the King the sky is falling," said Henny Penny, Cocky Locky, Ducky Lucky and Goosey Loosey.

"May I come with you?" said Turkey Lurkey.

"Certainly," they said. So Henny Penny, Cocky Locky, Ducky Lucky, Goosey Loosey and Turkey Lurkey all continued on the road to tell the King the sky was falling.

So they went along, and went along, and went along until they met another animal who also was there on the road. It was Foxy Loxy. Foxy Loxy said to Henny Penny, Cocky Locky, Goosey Loosey, Ducky Lucky and Turkey Lurkey, "Where are you going to in such a hurry, Henny Penny, Cocky Locky, Goosey Loosey, Ducky Lucky and Turkey Lurkey?"

And Henny Penny, Cocky Locky, Goosey Loosey, Ducky Lucky and Turkey Lurkey said to Foxy Loxy "We're going to tell the King the sky is falling."

"That sounds important. May I join you?" said Foxy Loxy.

All the animals said "Certainly," and Foxy Loxy joined them as they continued on the road to tell the king that the sky was falling.

Soon, however, Foxy Loxy stopped and said to the other animals, "Oh, but this is not the way to the King, Henny Penny, Cocky Locky, Goosey Loosey, Ducky Lucky, and Turkey Lurkey. You're going the long way. I know a short cut. Shall I show it to you?"

"Oh certainly Foxy Loxy," said Henny Penny, Cocky Locky, Ducky Lucky, Goosey Loosey and Turkey Lurkey. So Henny Penny, Cocky Locky, Ducky Lucky, Goosey Loosey, Turkey Lurkey and Foxy Woxy all went to tell the King the sky was falling.

They went along and they went along, till they

Adapted from an English folktale

came to a small, dark hole. Now this was the door of Foxy Loxy's cave. So Foxy Loxy said to Henny Penny, Cocky Locky, Goosey Loosey, Ducky Lucky and Turkey Lurkey, "This is the short way to the King's palace. You'll soon get there. Follow me. I will go first, and you come after, Henny Penny, Cocky Locky, Goosey Loosey, Ducky Lucky and Turkey Lurkey."

"Why, of course, certainly," said Henny Penny, Cocky Locky, Goosey Loosey, Ducky Lucky and Turkey Lurkey.

So Foxy Loxy went into his cave, and he didn't go very far. He turned around to wait for the other animals.

First Turkey Lurkey went through the dark hole into the cave. He hadn't got far when "Hrumph," Foxy Woxy snapped off Turkey Lurkey's head and threw his body over his left shoulder to feed his family.

Then Goosey Loosey went in, and "Hrumph," off went her head, and Goosey Loosey was thrown beside Turkey Lurkey.

Then Ducky Lucky waddled in, and "Hrumph," snapped Foxy Loxy, and Ducky Lucky's head was off and Ducky Lucky was thrown alongside Turkey Lurkey and Goosey Loosey.

Then Cocky Locky strutted down into the cave, and he hadn't gone far when Foxy Loxy took a bite at Cocky Locky. But Foxy Loxy had been so busy that he missed Cocky Locky, and before he took a second bite at Cocky Locky and got him, Cocky Locky had time to call out to Henny Penny to run away. So Henny Penny turned around, ran off, and never did tell the King that the sky was falling.

Sample Student Responses • Henny Penny

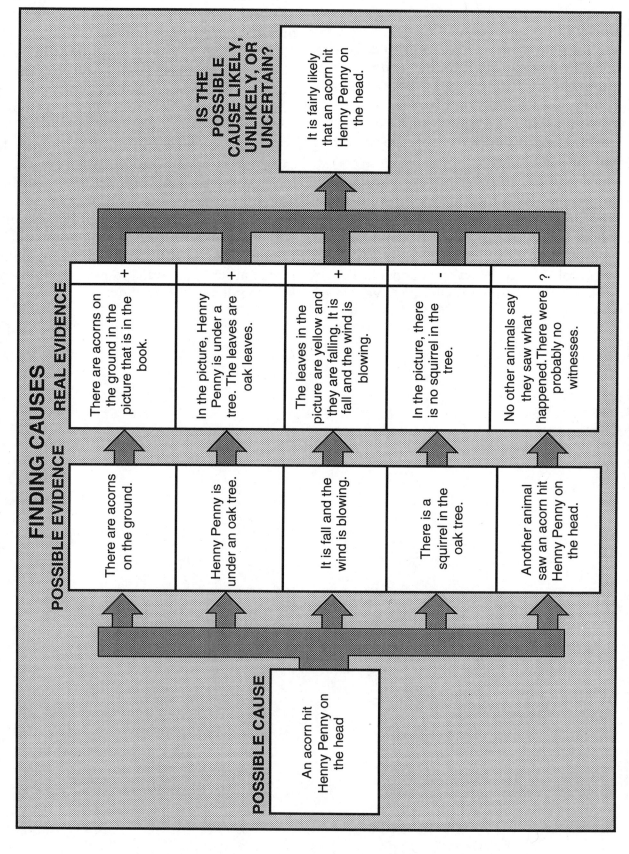

FINDING CAUSES

POSSIBLE EVIDENCE — **REAL EVIDENCE**

IS THE POSSIBLE CAUSE LIKELY, UNLIKELY, OR UNCERTAIN?

It is fairly likely that an acorn hit Henny Penny on the head.

Real Evidence	+/-/?
There are acorns on the ground in the picture that is in the book.	+
In the picture, Henny Penny is under a tree. The leaves are oak leaves.	+
The leaves in the picture are yellow and they are falling. It is fall and the wind is blowing.	+
In the picture, there is no squirrel in the tree.	-
No other animals say they saw what happened. There were probably no witnesses.	?

Possible Evidence:
- There are acorns on the ground.
- Henny Penny is under an oak tree.
- It is fall and the wind is blowing.
- There is a squirrel in the oak tree.
- Another animal saw an acorn hit Henny Penny on the head.

POSSIBLE CAUSE

An acorn hit Henny Penny on the head

THE EXTINCTION OF THE DINOSAURS

Science **Grades 5–6**

OBJECTIVES

CONTENT

Students will learn that there are different theories about the extinction of the dinosaurs and that fossils and other prehistoric dinosaur remains that we have today can provide us with evidence about what caused their extinction.

THINKING SKILLS/PROCESS

Students will learn to develop alternative hypotheses and consider present evidence when trying to make a judgment about what caused something to happen.

METHODS AND MATERIALS

CONTENT

Students draw upon their prior knowledge about dinosaurs, fossils, and food chains from their texts or other sources. They collaborate to examine the content. Writing is used to elaborate details.

THINKING SKILLS/PROCESS

Structured questioning that follows the thinking map for the skill and a specialized graphic organizer are used to guide students through the thinking. (See pp. 391–395 for reproducible diagrams.) Collaborative learning enhances their thinking.

LESSON

INTRODUCTION TO CONTENT AND THINKING SKILL/PROCESS

- When things happen that we don't like, we often try to find out what is causing them. If we find the cause, we can sometimes fix it. If the picture on your TV is fuzzy and you know it's because the antenna is pointing in the wrong direction, you can fix it by moving the antenna. If that's not the cause, you may not be able to fix the picture until you find the real cause. It won't help to guess. That may only waste your time. Trying to find a cause requires some careful critical thinking.

- Finding out what caused something is called "causal explanation." This involves thinking about possible causes and then deciding which is the likeliest cause based on evidence. Scientists do this all the time. To cure a disease, scientists first try to find out what causes it. That may help them find a cure. When there is a natural disaster like a flood, scientists try to find out why it occurred in order to prevent it in the future.

- Scientists are not just interested in things that happen today. They are also interested in major changes that happened on the Earth a long time ago. One thing that has puzzled scientists for a long time is what happened to the dinosaurs at the end of the Mesozoic Era. No one knows why they became extinct, but scientists continue to think about what could have caused their extinction and how we can find out.

- In this lesson, we're going to think about what might have caused the extinction of the dinosaurs and see what we can find out about this topic. But first, let's think about what we know about the dinosaurs themselves. Dinosaurs lived on the Earth a very long time. Even though there were lots of them and many were huge animals, not one survives today. Some ate only plants; others ate meat and hunted other animals. What other things do you know about the world of the dinosaurs? Are there things that you aren't sure about? Are there other things that you don't know but would like to find out? In conducting class discussion, use the graphic organizer at the right to help students organize their ideas.

I KNOW	I THINK I KNOW	I NEED TO KNOW

Show the students drawings and photographs of dinosaur bones that illustrate some of the commonly-accepted facts about dinosaurs and ask them whether these answer some of their questions about dinosaurs. Modify the graphic organizer accordingly.

THINKING ACTIVELY

• **Now let's consider the fact that the dinosaurs disappeared from the earth some time ago. That's quite amazing, when you think about it. What could have caused this change? Before we try to decide about what caused the extinction of the dinosaurs, we should think about some possibilities. What are some different conditions that might have caused the dinosaurs to disappear from the earth?** Ask collaborative learning groups to brainstorm and list as many possibilities as they can identify. Encourage different and unusual possibilities. Ask each group to mention one of their possibilities, then allow any group to add others. List these on the board under "Possible Causes." Accept all responses; later, they will be subject to the test of evidence. POSSIBLE ANSWERS: *Disease, drastic depletion of the food supply (e.g., plants died), genetic changes that caused problems getting food, abduction by aliens, major changes in the climate, a catastrophic event (meteor impact or volcanic eruption which caused massive fires), a great flood, conflict with warm-blooded animals, limited agility, egg predators, evolution into something else, fiercer animals killed them.*

• **Suppose you looked for clues about which of these possibilities was the likeliest explanation. What might you find today that could give you evidence for or against each possibility? How could you go about finding out these things?** Ask each group to pick one of these possible causes and to make a list of the possible evidence, using the graphic organizer for causal explanation shown on the next page. Ask each group to report, displaying their diagram. If other students in the class have ideas about additional evidence, it should be added. POSSIBLE ANSWERS: *We could find dinosaur remains in the ice and do medical tests for disease-causing viruses (disease). We could find dinosaur fossils in rocks and notice changes that cause problems, e.g., with teeth (genetic changes). We could find craters from large meteors (meteor impact).*

• **Imagine that, while looking for clues, you find the following evidence in various sedimentary rocks:**

  • **Lots of dinosaur tracks at one level, fewer at another, and then none.**

  • **Fossilized leaves and plants at one level and then very few.**

  • **More mammal tracks and bones in some levels than in others.**

When the rocks are dated, you find that the plants and leaves coincide with a lot of dinosaur tracks. The layers with fewer plants came just before there were fewer and then no other dinosaur tracks. The number of mammal bones increased as the dinosaur tracks diminished.

• **What possible explanation does this evidence support?** Ask the students to discuss this in their groups and return with their responses. RESPONSE: *Drastic reduction in the food supply: the plants died, causing the plant eaters to starve, which in turn caused the meat eaters to starve.* **Scientists shouldn't accept an explanation until they have sufficient evidence to be sure of it. Otherwise, it is just a theory. Are the clues we just discussed sufficient evidence?** *No.* **Why?** POSSIBLE ANSWERS: *They are only from one location. Other explanations are still possible: maybe only the dinosaurs in this one location didn't have enough food, but something else killed the dinosaurs living in other parts* *of the earth, or maybe something caused both the plants and the dinosaurs to die out at the same time.* **What other evidence would you need to be sure that this was the best causal explanation?** Draw a graphic organizer for causal explanation on the chalkboard or use a transparency or large poster. Write "Drastic depletion of the food supply" in the box for the possible cause. Then add what the students suggest to the boxes for "Possible Evidence." The graphic organizer should look like the sample at the right. POSSIBLE ANSWERS: *Similar but more extensive evidence from sites all over the world (decreasing fossils of plants as fossils of plant eaters decrease), other animals that ate plants also disappearing from the fossil records, evidence about conditions that caused the plants to die, evidence of malnutrition in the bones of plant-eating animals that lived at the time, evidence against other possible explanations.*

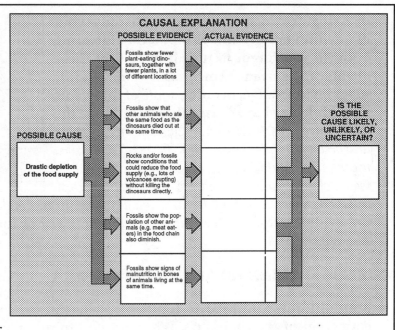

- **Work in your groups again and, in the "Possible Evidence" column on your graphic organizers, add any possible evidence that you think would be needed to be sure of the causal explanation.**

- **What actual evidence about the extinction of the dinosaurs can you get from your text or from other sources? What possible cause(s) does this evidence support? What possibilities does this evidence count against? Each group should return to the graphic organizers in which they wrote down possible evidence that would support one of the alternative causal explanations. Look for evidence of the sort that you mention. Write the actual evidence you find for or against those possible explanations in the boxes marked "Actual Evidence" on your diagram. Rate the evidence by putting a plus next to it if it counts in favor of the possibility, a minus if it counts against, and a plus and a minus if it is neutral.** Students usually find their text books very limited in actual evidence about the extinction of the dinosaurs. Provide additional sources from the school library, or ask the students to go to the library and find additional information. Each group should display their graphic organizer on a bulletin board or copy it on the chalkboard. Students usually find that there is little evidence to support some theories (e.g., disease), but more to support others (drastic reduction in the food supply). They also realize that what killed the dinosaur could have been a combination of factors. Nonetheless, they realize that there is not enough evidence to be sure that any of the possibilities are correct.

  Discuss with students the differences among the following: 1) speculation about what caused something based on no evidence, 2) theories about causes that have some support but are not yet proven because other possibilities have not been eliminated, and 3) theories about causes that have been proven by supporting evidence and evidence that rules out alternatives (e.g., about what causes certain diseases).

- **When you are trying to find out what caused something, you will often realize that the cause of the event was, in turn, caused by something else. That may be important. For example, you may get to school late because you missed the bus. You may have missed the bus because you** overslept. You may have overslept because your alarm didn't ring. Perhaps the alarm didn't ring because you forgot to turn it on. All of these events can be arranged in a *causal chain.* Use this diagram to arrange, in order, some of the events you think may have caused the extinction of the dinosaurs. POSSIBLE ANSWERS: *The meat eaters died because the plant eaters died; the plant eaters died because the plants died; the plants died because there was a cloud of dust around the earth; the dust was*

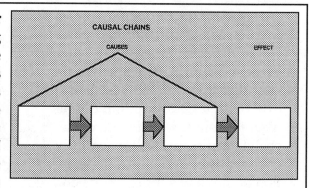

caused by a meteor hitting the earth and throwing up dust and debris into the atmosphere. **Does any of the evidence that you've uncovered support any of these causal chains more than others?** ANSWERS VARY.

THINKING ABOUT THINKING

- **Map out how you tried to figure out what caused the extinction of the dinosaurs. What did you think about first, next, etc.?** Ask students to work together in collaborative learning groups. Put their maps on the board. Try to reach consensus about what they did. The standard thinking map of causal explanation is shown at the right.

> **SKILLFUL CAUSAL EXPLANATION**
>
> 1. What are possible causes of the event in question?
>
> 2. What could you find that would count for or against the likelihood of these possibilities?
>
> 3. What evidence do you already have, or have you gathered, that is relevant to determining what caused the event?
>
> 4. Which possibility is rendered most likely based on the evidence?

- **Compare the way you thought about the causes of the extinction of the dinosaurs to the way you ordinarily think about causes. Which do you think is the better way to try to find causes? Why?** Encourage students to reflect on what they thought caused some personal situation and how their understanding of what caused that situation would have been different if they had used this process.

- **Think about situations in which you wonder about causes, like what caused an illness or what is causing problems around the house. Plan what you might think about the next time one of these situations arises so that you can find the most likely cause.** Ask students to keep this plan in their notebooks, so that they can refer to it next time they have to use it.

APPLYING YOUR THINKING

Immediate Transfer:

- **We have studied other animals that are classified as endangered species. Make a list of these animals and pick one that you'd like to study further. Use your plan for causal explanation to determine what is causing this animal to be endangered. Based on this determination, make some suggestions as to what we might do to help these animals.** You can ask students to write a short analysis of the problem for the animal they choose, along with their suggested remedies. If you use a portfolio assessment plan in your classroom, suggest to your students that they may wish to include these writings in their portfolios along with comments about the quality of the thinking that they represent.

- **There are a number of things that happen at school that many students and teachers are concerned about: lots of noise in the cafeteria, a great many library books getting lost every year, etc. Select something that could be changed to make our school better. Try to find out the cause(s) of some of these situations, so that you can recommend some remedies.**

Reinforcement Later

- Use the strategy for causal explanation to figure out the cause of the increase in the population of mammals after the Mesozoic Era.

- As we study early civilizations, we can find causes for changes in their way of life. When we studied ancient Egypt, we saw that the early Egyptians changed from being nomads to living in settlements along the river Nile. Try to figure out what caused this change and map out the causal chain that led to the development of the great civilization of the Egyptians.

WRITING/ART EXTENSION

Pick one of the possible causes of the extinction of the dinosaurs and write a story about how this could have happened. Draw some pictures to illustrate your story. Ask four or five students to show their pictures and explain their stories to the whole class.

THINKING SKILL EXTENSION: EVALUATING OTHER CAUSAL EXPLANATIONS

Ask students to use the school library and find books or articles in which people have discussed the extinction of the dinosaurs. Ask them to record the explanations that they find for extinction and the evidence that is offered to support them. Students should recognize that the different views about what happened to the dinosaurs are also scientific theories and that, for theories to be accepted, they must be well supported by evidence. They should report to the class on these different theories and discuss whether they are well supported and the evidence used to support them. The following recent articles summarize current research:

"Rewriting the Book on Dinosaurs," *Time Magazine*, Apr. 26, 1993.

"New Theories & Old Bones Reveal the Lifestyles of the Dinosaur" *Newsweek*, Oct. 28, 1991.

"Dinosaurs," *National Geographic*, January 1993.

"The Road to Extinction," *National Geographic*, June 1989.

"What Dinosaurs Were Really Like," *Discover*, March 1987.

Available videotapes about the dinosaurs and their characteristics include "The Death of the Dinosaurs," an animated work on various theories for extinction (WHYY Inc. 1992 Distributed by the Pacific Arts Corp, Nesmith Enterprises, 11858 LaGrange Ave., Los Angeles, CA 90025).

THINKING SKILL EXTENSION: MULTIPLE CAUSES

Ask students to explore the possibility that multiple causes brought about the extinction of the dinosaurs. Provide them with copies of the "Multiple Causes" graphic organizer and ask them to put together the causes that, based on their research, might have blended together to cause the dinosaurs to become extinct. Ask them to blend together the causes that there is evidence to support and that could have worked together to cause the disaster for the dinosaurs. The result might look like the graphic organizer at the right.

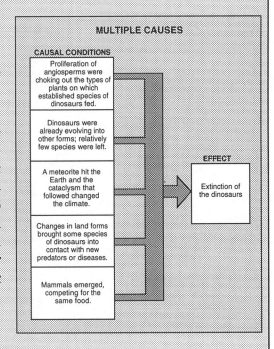

MULTIPLE CAUSES

CAUSAL CONDITIONS

- Proliferation of angiosperms were choking out the types of plants on which established species of dinosaurs fed.
- Dinosaurs were already evolving into other forms; relatively few species were left.
- A meteorite hit the Earth and the cataclysm that followed changed the climate.
- Changes in land forms brought some species of dinosaurs into contact with new predators or diseases.
- Mammals emerged, competing for the same food.

EFFECT

Extinction of the dinosaurs

ASSESSING STUDENT THINKING ABOUT CAUSES

To assess the skill of causal explanation, ask students to write an essay to answer any of the application questions or similar ones that you develop. They may critique someone else's causal explanation of some event or find a causal explanation for something that has happened (e.g., the plants in the classroom have all died; find out why). You can supplement their writing with interviewing. In all these assessment tasks, students should make their thinking explicit. Determine whether they are attending to each of the steps in the thinking map of causal explanation.

You can also use a portfolio assessment plan to gather information about your students' mastery of skillful causal explanation. For example, ask your students to continue to gather information about the extinction of the dinosaurs and to cull any additional evidence they find that supports or counts against the various hypotheses that they are exploring. Students may record their own progress in gathering such evidence (e.g., by using a research log). Their consideration of possible causes, possible evidence and actual evidence, and their judgments about the plausibility of the various possible causal explanations will reveal how well they have internalized the thinking involved in skillful causal explanation.

Sample Student Responses • The Extinction of the Dinosaur

CAUSAL EXPLANATION

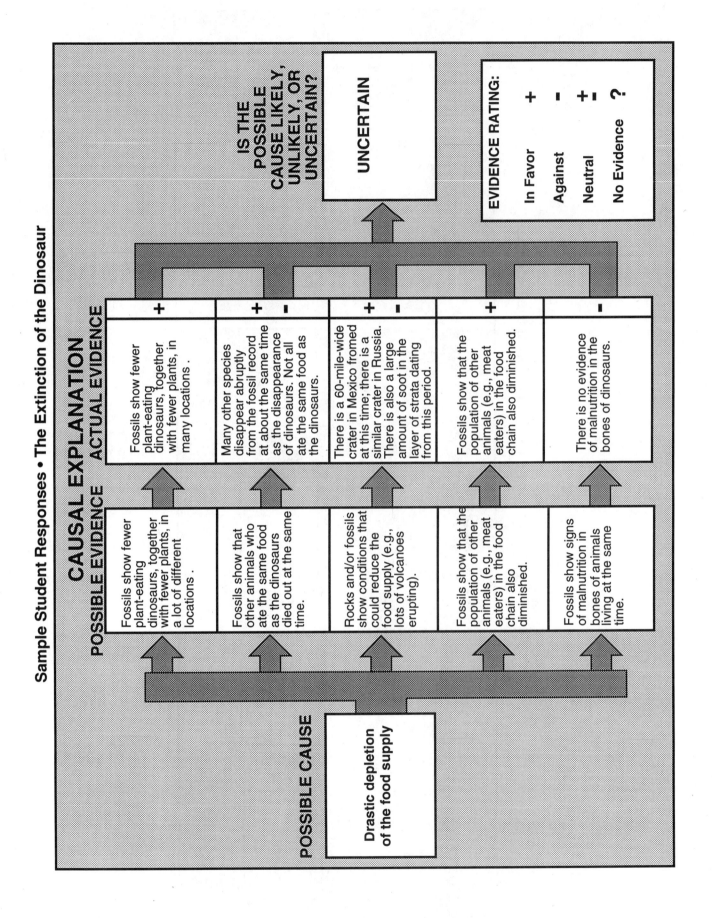

IS THE POSSIBLE CAUSE LIKELY, UNLIKELY, OR UNCERTAIN?

UNCERTAIN

EVIDENCE RATING:

In Favor	+
Against	-
Neutral	+-
No Evidence	?

ACTUAL EVIDENCE

Rating	Evidence
+	Fossils show fewer plant-eating dinosaurs, together with fewer plants, in many locations .
+ -	Many other species disappear abruptly from the fossil record at about the same time as the disappearance of dinosaurs. Not all ate the same food as the dinosaurs.
+ -	There is a 60-mile-wide crater in Mexico fromed at this time; there is a similar crater in Russia. There is also a large amount of soot in the layer of strata dating from this period.
+	Fossils show that the population of other animals (e.g., meat eaters) in the food chain also diminished.
-	There is no evidence of malnutrition in the bones of dinosaurs.

POSSIBLE EVIDENCE

- Fossils show fewer plant-eating dinosaurs, together with fewer plants, in a lot of different locations .
- Fossils show that other animals who ate the same food as the dinosaurs died out at the same time.
- Rocks and/or fossils show conditions that could reduce the food supply (e.g., lots of volcanoes erupting).
- Fossils show that the population of other animals (e.g., meat eaters) in the food chain also diminished.
- Fossils show signs of malnutrition in bones of animals living at the same time.

POSSIBLE CAUSE

Drastic depletion of the food supply

Sample Student Responses • The Extinction of the Dinosaur

CAUSAL CHAINS

CAUSES

EFFECT

| Large meteor hits the earth. | → | Dust thrown up by the meteor obscures the sun for many years. | → | Much plant life dies. | → | Plant-eating dinosaurs die off. | → | Meat-eating dinosaurs die off. | → | Dinosaurs become extinct. |

CAUSAL EXPLANATION LESSON CONTEXTS

The following examples have been suggested by classroom teachers as contexts in which to develop infused lessons. If a skill or process has been introduced in a previous lesson, transfer activities can be designed in these contexts to reinforce it.

GRADE	SUBJECT	TOPIC	THINKING ISSUE
K-3	Literature	*Alexander and his Terrible, Horrible, No Good, Very Bad Day*	What really caused Alexander to have such a bad day? Can you find any information in the story that gives you a clue?
K-3	Literature	*Freckle Juice*	From the story, what can you find out about Andrew that helps you figure out why he was misled about making freckles? What really causes freckles?
K-3	Social studies	Cities	Why might cities grow up in some places rather than others? Pick a specific city. What can you find out about it that helps you figure out why this city grew where it is?
K-3	U.S. history	Westward expansion	What might have caused pioneers to travel west in the 1800s in this country? Study a particular pioneer (like Daniel Boone) or group of pioneers (like the people who settled Colorado) to try to determine why they travelled west.
K-3	Science	Sinking/floating	Why do things sink or float? Why do some things that sink in fresh water float in salt water? Examine shape, weight, area, and material for clues.
K-3	Science	Plants	Perform the following experiment over several weeks: give one plant sun and water; give one plant water, but no sun; give one sun, but no water. What evidence do you get about what plants need to stay alive and to grow?
K-3	Science	Birds	What can you find out about birds to help you figure out what causes them to migrate?
K-3	Science	Oceans	Why are oceans salty and lakes not salty? What could you find out about oceans and lakes that will help you understand what causes this difference?
K-3	Science	Wind	Sometimes the air is very still; sometimes it's windy. What could cause this difference? How can you find out?
K-3	Science	Animals	Suppose that the ants in an anthill died. What clues would you look for to find out why they died?
K-3	Mathematics	Arithmetic	Suppose you set up an apple stand in your school. Each apple costs you 10¢. For the space, weekly rental is $5.00, which you can pay at the end of the week. You have $4.00 to spend, which you use up to buy apples. You decide to sell them for 20¢ each. After selling apples for a week, you have $4.00. You realize you didn't make enough to pay the rent for the table. What might have caused this problem? What could you do to prevent it from happening next week?
K-3	Health	Dental health	Why do people get cavities? Do you have any evidence to support your explanation?
K-3	Health	Diseases	What are some causes for the spread of diseases? What could prevent you from getting diseases? Do you have any evidence that these preventions work?

CAUSAL EXPLANATION LESSON CONTEXTS

GRADE	SUBJECT	TOPIC	THINKING ISSUE
4-6	Literature	*Bridge Over Tarabathia*	In the story, what would you look for to determine why Jess left a note on Janice Avery's desk?
4-6	Literature	*Little House in the Big Woods*	What can you find out from the story that explains what caused the family to move west?
4-6	Literature	*Sarah, Plain and Tall*	What would you consider to determine why Sarah responded to the ad?
4-6	Literature	*Pandora's Box*	What does the story tell you about Pandora that helps you to explain why she opened the box, thereby letting the evils out into the world?
4-6	Literature	*Sounder*	From this book, what do you find out that helps to explain the treatment of Blacks in the South during the given time period?
4-6	U.S. history	Jamestown	What can we find out about the people who settled the Jamestown colony and their circumstances that helps us understand what caused the successes and problems of the colony?
4-6	U.S. history	Lost Colony	What caused the Roanoke Colony to disappear? Explain the evidence you used to make your judgment. What does the colony's failure tell us about conditions necessary for European colonization to succeed in the New World?
4-6	U.S. history	Urban history	What contributed to the spread and devastating effects of the Chicago fire? Explain your reasons.
4-6	U.S. history	Immigration	What might have caused people from other countries to come to the United States? Study a specific group of immigrants (e.g., the Irish in the late 19th Century) to determine the best explanation for their coming to this country. Explain your reasons.
4-6	Science	Sound	People's voices often sound quite different. What could be causing the differences? What kind of experiment could provide you with data to determine whether your explanation is reasonable?
4-6	Science	Rocks	Even though they are hard and solid, some rocks that we find today contain fossils. What do the rocks' locations and characteristics show about what caused them to contain fossils?
4-6	Science	Endangered species	Pick one of the endangered species you have read about and identify the factors contributing to the problem.
4-6	Science	Electricity	Suppose the light in your room went out. What could be the cause and how could you find out?
4-6	Science	Air	What might cause a candle in a jar to go out? How could you determine which possibility is the actual cause?
4-6	Mathematics	Bar graphs	Suppose that, when each student constructed a bar graph of the heights of students in the class, some bar graphs were quite different from others. What might cause the differences? How could you find out what explains the difference in specific cases?
4-6	Guidance	Self esteem	What could cause students to have low self confidence in their abilities in school? How could you find out which of these possibilities was a cause in a specific case? For each cause, suggest something that might help to develop better self esteem.

CHAPTER 14
PREDICTION

Why is Skillful Prediction Needed?

Whenever we expect something to happen, we are making a prediction. If we like what we expect to happen, we may take action that will enable us to experience it. If we do not like it, we try to avoid it. I may expect that it will rain this afternoon. If my prediction is right, bringing an umbrella will prevent me from getting wet.

Types of Predictions

What will the weather be like next week? What will the economy be like next year? Will I keep my job? Will global warming occur? Will global warming happen in my lifetime? These are all direct questions about trends or general conditions in the future. To answer them well, we have to make predictions.

We also make predictions when we are concerned about the effects of an event that is occurring now or that we think might occur. For example, if we hear of an approaching hurricane, we may prepare for the effects of wind or water.

In other situations, we might be wondering about the results of something that might occur but hasn't yet. We might, for example, be considering specific options in making a decision and want to predict the consequences of adopting one or another. I may want to take a trip to a ski resort on a vacation. There are factors about doing so that I may need to consider. How much will it cost? What will the food be like? Does the terrain allow the kind of skiing I enjoy? Predicting likely outcomes minimizes my chances of being disappointed and allows me to choose more carefully. In this case, skillful prediction is an important subskill of decision making.

The three types of predictions include

- Predicting trends or general conditions
- Predicting the effects of a particular event
- Predicting the consequences of options

Problems about the Way We Make Predictions

The most common problem about predicting is that sometimes we do not take time to think about what might happen in the future. We do not ask questions like, "What might it be like tomorrow?" or "What might happen as a result of what's going on today?" If we do not ask such questions, we may experience situations that we do not expect and may not like.

Even when we do consider what might happen in the future, we may develop unrealistic expectations that result in unnecessarily costly disappointments. Often we let our hopes or fears lead us to anticipate opportunities, rewards, or difficulties that we do not have a good reason to expect. I may go to a movie theater early because I'm worried that I won't be able to get a ticket. If I have no good reason to think the movie is popular, I may unnecessarily cut my meal short and rush to the theater to find that few other people are interested in the movie. We take a risk in making hasty predictions that are no more than guesses about what is going to happen.

There is another more subtle problem with the way we make predictions. Sometimes we have reasons for thinking that something will happen but do not attend to significant information that can change our predictions. I may rush to meet a friend who has said that he will join me at a local restaurant at 6:00 P.M. However, I may forget that my friend has never been on time in the past. Not taking account of all the available relevant information that has bearing on our predictions is another default in the way we develop expectations about the future.

It is important to make sure that our predictions are well-founded. Skillful prediction involves thinking carefully about what we expect and how likely it is to happen.

The three main defaults in prediction are summarized in figure 14.1.

```
COMMON DEFAULTS IN THE WAY
WE MAKE PREDICTIONS

1. We don't raise questions about what might
   happen as the result of a particular circum-
   stance.

2. We don't consider how likely our predictions
   are.

3. We don't take into account all the relevant
   evidence in determining how likely our predic-
   tions are.
```

Figure 14.1

How Do We Make Skillful Predictions?

Tips on making predictions skillfully. Because predictions are always made before what is predicted happens, they are always inferences. As such, predictions require good support to be well-founded. Only then are we justified in feeling confident that our predictions are likely to happen. Basing predictions on good support is the crux of skillful prediction.

The same pattern of skillful prediction is helpful in each of the three types of prediction identified earlier. To make predictions skillfully, it is important to think first about what *might* happen—about possible future occurrences and when they might happen. These could be trends (like a recession next year), results we might expect of some natural occurrence (like the increased risk of skin cancer because of the thinning of the ozone layer), or consequences of some action we are considering (like an enjoyable evening at the movies). These are not yet predictions because they are tentative. But it is important to be aware of these possible outcomes in order to determine whether we should affirm them as predictions. In effect, they serve as hypotheses that we are considering about the future.

Predicted occurrences may or may not happen. People sometimes mistakenly believe that *possible* occurrences are *likely* occurrences without any real basis for doing so. What are good reasons for believing that an occurrence is likely to happen?

Generally we have to look for available evidence in order to determine whether a prediction is likely. This usually involves information about similar events in the past. If many trees have been blown down when hurricanes have hit coastal towns, it is likely that trees will be blown down in a coastal town in the path of an impending storm of the same magnitude.

Sometimes we have more exact information about likelihood. If, in 80% of the cases in the past when conditions in the atmosphere have been as they are now, it has rained within a few hours, then we have evidence that now there is an 80% chance of rain. Frequencies of past occurrences provide the type of evidence many people rely upon to make quantitative predictions of likelihood. Statistical evidence provides strong support for the likelihood that an event will occur.

This evidence, however, may not be enough to make the outcome likely. We should also think about evidence that might count against our predictions. If there is some important difference between the event you are considering and what you are comparing it to in the past, that discrepancy may provide evidence against the likelihood of a consequence. Although most hurricanes cause trees to fall, storms with winds under 65 miles per hour seldom uproot trees. If an approaching storm has winds under 65 miles an hour, then we have evidence against the likelihood that trees will be blown down.

Making skillful predictions about trends or general conditions, rather than specific events like a hurricane, operates the same way. Will a current economic recession continue? What will the economy be like next year? If factors are present that are frequently correlated with an economic trend continuing, like increasingly high unemployment and a decline in business productivity, then we can predict the economic consequences with some confidence.

Sometimes frequencies are summarized in general statements. I might be planning a trip to London in September. When I find out that Septembers are rainy in London, I can plan to bring appropriate clothing. The information that Septembers are rainy in London is based on the frequency of past occurrences of rain in London in September. That frequency makes it a pretty good bet that it will rain again this September.

We must recognize, however, that predicting trends is, in general, more tenuous than predicting the results of an event like a hurricane. A broad and complex range of factors can affect things like economic trends. Gathering information about them is often difficult.

When we consider all of the relevant information that counts for and against the likelihood of something we predict, we should weigh the evidence in order to judge whether the prediction is likely, unlikely, or uncertain. If, based on the evidence, it is likely, then the prediction is well-founded and we can explain why by referring to the evidence that supports it.

If we can't get evidence about these past frequencies, there is another way to get good reasons for thinking that an occurrence is likely. We may get information from a reliable source who we believe has consulted the primary evidence about such situations. We judge whether a weather reporter who predicts rain is reliable by knowing of his or her "track record." How often have this person's predictions been right? Asking about evidence of past effectiveness is another good way to decide whether or not a prediction that someone makes is well-founded.

A Thinking Map and Graphic Organizer for Making Skillful Predictions

How can these ideas help us to make better predictions? The thinking map in figure 14.2 contains a sequence of important questions to ask in making skillful predictions. We can also use a graphic organizer to supplement the thinking map and to write down information in response to these questions.

The graphic organizer in figure 14.3 illustrates the important points in skillful prediction highlighted on the thinking map.

In using this graphic organizer, write what you need to know to confirm the likelihood of your prediction in the "Possible Evidence" column before writing available information in the "Actual Evidence" column. Then, when you've accumulated the available evidence in the "Actual Evidence" column, you can compare it to

SKILLFUL PREDICTION

1. What might happen?

2. What evidence might you get that would indicate that this prediction is likely?

3. What evidence is available that is relevant to whether the prediction is likely?

4. Based on the evidence, is the prediction likely, unlikely, or uncertain?

Figure 14.2

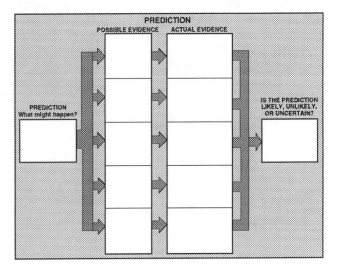

Figure 14.3

what you put in the "Possible Evidence" column to determine whether you have enough evidence to judge whether or not the prediction is likely.

Multiple effects. There are times when it isn't just one possible future occurrence that concerns us, but many. For example, if you were a public official in a town on the east coast of the United States and were concerned about the hurricane bearing down on the town, you would want to make an accurate judgment about the range of effects of the hurricane so that you could be adequately prepared. Trees blown down might be one of these effects, and you would want to make sure that everyone knew of this danger. If you expected significant coastal flooding, you would certainly plan to evacuate people from their homes in coastal regions. The flooding is a function of the tides as well as the storm, so in assessing the likelihood of such flooding, this additional information will be necessary. And, of course, depending on the strength of the winds, you could expect lots of debris being blown about, some potentially life threatening. Similarly, possible power outages, pollution of the water supply, blockage of roads, and looting may also be consequences you will want to attend to if there is a likelihood of their occurrence. Taking the time to remind yourself that these things might happen is an important first step in skillful prediction.

The simple but important graphic organizer in figure 14.4 encourages a systematic approach to listing the varied potential effects.

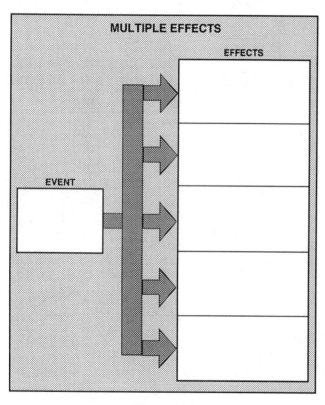

Figure 14.4

In listing predicted consequences under "Effects," we should recognize that these, too, have the status of *possible* consequences until we have sufficient evidence to judge them to be likely. Developing such a list is taking the first step in ascertaining what is likely to happen. Each consequence listed should, therefore, be subjected to a search for supporting evidence of likelihood before we affirm that it will happen.

Predicting the consequences of options skill-

fully. Decision making provides a specialized context in which it is important to predict a range of consequences well. We want to determine the positive and negative consequences of different courses of action we are considering— their risks and benefits. The thinking maps for prediction (figure 14.2) and for decision making (chapter 2, figure 2.2) are modified and blended to produce the thinking map in figure 14.5 which stresses predicting the consequences of options.

PREDICTING THE CONSEQUENCES OF OPTIONS

1. What consequences might result from a specific option?

2. Does each consequence

   a. count for or against the decision?

   b. rank as important?

3. How likely is the consequence?

   a. Is there evidence that counts for or against the likelihood of the consequence?

   b. Based on all the evidence, is the consequence likely, unlikely, or is its likelihood uncertain?

4. Is the decision advisable in light of the significance and likelihood of the consequences?

Figure 14.5

The "Multiple Effects" diagram in figure 14.4 is modified to produce the graphic organizer in figure 14.6 for considering the likelihood of consequences predicted as the outcomes of options. This prediction strategy can supplement the decision-making strategy provided in Chapter 2.

Notice that steps (1) and (3) in the thinking map (figure 14.5) for predicting the consequences of options (and the "consequences" and "evidence" columns in the graphic organizer, figure 14.6) relate to prediction but prompt us to assess the likelihood of consequences somewhat differently from the way likelihood is assessed using the standard prediction strategy. In the

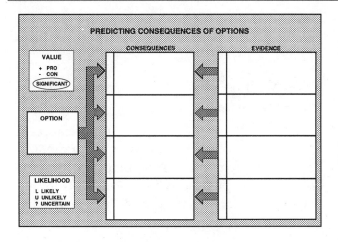

Figure 14.6

standard prediction strategy, we take time to consider what evidence would show that the predicted outcome is likely before we search for actual evidence. In this form of predicting the consequences of options, one dispenses with considering possible evidence that may need to be researched and attends directly to the actual evidence that is available. We can then more efficiently blend our judgments about the likelihood and significance of the consequences in order to determine whether the option is an advisable one.

How Should We Teach Students to Make Skillful Predictions?

Just asking students to make predictions will not teach them strategies for skillful prediction. For example, students are often asked to predict how a story they are reading will end. They are then asked to read the story to see if they predicted the right ending.

To teach skillful prediction, students should, in addition, be asked to attend carefully to what is in the story in order to make a *well-founded* prediction that can be backed up with reasons. Teaching students to attend to evidence in an organized way when they make predictions is lacking in activities in which they are just asked to tell what they think will happen.

Teaching Skillful Prediction Explicitly

Both the thinking maps and the graphic organizers are valuable tools for constructing infu-

sion lessons on prediction. They can guide students in their thinking as they make predictions so that they get in the habit of asking the right questions and confirming that their answers support their judgments.

Following the guidelines for infusion lessons used in this handbook, such lessons should introduce students to skillful prediction explicitly, involve them in an activity in which they engage in skillful prediction, and provide them with opportunities to both reflect on how we can make skillful predictions and apply this way of thinking to a variety of important predictions. This is how students will come to internalize the thinking process involved in skillful prediction.

Contexts in the Curriculum for Lessons on Skillful Prediction

There are a myriad of natural contexts in the curriculum into which instruction in skillful prediction can be infused. Predicting how characters in a story or novel will behave or predicting how historical characters will react to important events both provide such contexts, as does predicting broader outcomes in science and in history. The curriculum contexts in which decisions are studied also provide opportunities for lessons in which predicting consequences skillfully, as an important ingredient in good decision making, can be emphasized.

In general, there are three basic curriculum contexts in which prediction lessons can serve the purpose of teaching students skillful prediction while enhancing content learning:

- *The outcome of events or actions is thought-provoking.* In *Jack and the Beanstalk,* what can Jack predict will happen if he attempts to steal the goose that lays the golden egg? In the *Wizard of Oz,* what could Dorothy predict that the scarecrow, the tin woodsman, and the lion would do when faced with danger? These questions from children's books are thought provoking for students. Similarly, the study of history contains many dramatic moments that provoke us to wonder what the outcome will be. What could Rosa Parks predict would happen as a result of her staying seated on the bus? What could the colonists predict would happen if they declared independence from Britain? Notice that, in contrast to decision-making activities in which we ask students what these people or groups *should* do, when we teach prediction lessons, we are asking what we can reasonably expect that they *would* do, given what we know about them and their circumstances. It becomes quite clear that prediction is about what will happen, rather than what should happen, when the outcomes we are curious about are natural events. What impact on people will global warming have? How well does the body operate in space? What will happen if the rain forests are destroyed? These, too, provide robust contexts for prediction lessons.

- *The consequences of important decisions studied in the curriculum require careful thought.* In these contexts, prediction lessons become ways of fine-tuning the strategy for skillful decision making (Chapter 2). The difference is that predicting the likelihood of consequences of choices is the main emphasis in prediction lessons. Risky and heroic decisions make good contexts for prediction lessons and can accentuate qualities of character that students should become aware of. In *Little House on the Prairie,* Laura Ingalls Wilder's family decides to leave their home in Wisconsin in winter to travel to South Dakota. What hazards can they predict they will face? What insight do we get about their motivation since they were willing to make the trip despite the hazards? The Pilgrims' decision to sail to the New World provides a similar context for a prediction lesson in elementary social studies.

- *Students have to make certain predictions themselves as part of their learning.* When students compose pieces of writing and create works of art, they often want to have a certain impact on their audience. For example, how readers will respond to a story (e.g., a horror story) can provide a context to learn skillful prediction and enhance writing style. Students also must make predictions in science activities, in physical education, and in arts and crafts activities. These, too, provide viable contexts for prediction lessons.

A menu of suggested contexts for infusion lessons on prediction is provided on pp. 441–442.

Teaching Skillful Prediction in the Primary Grades

For primary level students, a simplification in the language of prediction is appropriate, but basically the same thinking map and graphic organizer can be used. The simplified thinking map for prediction in figure 14.7 can be used in grades K–2.

PREDICTING WHAT WILL HAPPEN

1. What might happen?

2. What clues could show whether that will happen?

3. What real clues are there?

4. Do the clues show that it will happen?

Figure 14.7

Similar changes in language on the basic graphic organizer for prediction are appropriate.

Model Lessons on Skillful Prediction

We include two prediction lessons in this handbook. One is an upper elementary lesson which combines geography and mathematics. Students predict the amount of time a trip will take using map skills and applying the rate/distance/time equation. The second is an upper-elementary language arts lesson in which students predict the outcome of a risky but heroic decision that a character makes to save the lives of others.

Each of these lessons uses the thinking map and graphic organizer appropriate for the kind of prediction being made. In *The Trip*, the basic prediction graphic is used. *The Wave* demonstrates how prediction can be handled using the more complex strategy for predicting the consequences of options. Each lesson helps students develop a habit of skillful prediction by guiding them to think about what might happen as the result of some event or circumstance and then to weigh the evidence about the likelihood of these possible results. As you examine these lessons, ask yourself the following questions:

- How are students introduced to the need for skillful prediction?

- How is the need for evidence to support predictions emphasized?

- What content objectives are enhanced by the predictions the students make?

- What additional contexts are there for reinforcing skillful prediction after the lesson has been completed?

Tools for Designing Prediction Lessons

The thinking maps that follow provide questions to guide student thinking in prediction lessons. The primary grade level thinking map on page 421 is for grades K–2. The others can be used in grades 3 and higher. These maps can also be used to help students reflect on how to engage in skillful prediction.

The graphic organizers that follow each thinking map are included for your use in prediction lessons. They supplement and reinforce the guidance in critical thinking provided by the sequenced questions derived from the thinking map.

The thinking maps and graphic organizers can guide you in designing the critical thinking activity in the lesson and can also serve as photocopy masters, transparency masters, or as models that can be enlarged and used as posters in the classroom. Reproduction rights are granted for single classroom use only.

SKILLFUL PREDICTION

1. **What might happen?**

2. **What evidence might you get that would indicate that this prediction is likely?**

3. **What evidence is available that is relevant to whether the prediction is likely?**

4. **Based on the evidence, is the prediction likely, unlikely, or uncertain?**

PREDICTING WHAT WILL HAPPEN

1. What might happen?

2. What clues could show whether that will happen?

3. What real clues are there?

4. Do the clues show that it will happen?

PREDICTING THE CONSEQUENCES OF OPTIONS

1. What consequences might result from a specific option?

2. Does each consequence

    a. count for or against the decision?

    b. rank as important?

3. How likely is the consequence?

    a. Is there evidence that counts for or against the likelihood of the consequence?

    b. Based on all the evidence, is the consequence likely, unlikely, or is its likelihood uncertain?

4. Is the decision advisable in light of the significance and likelihood of the consequences?

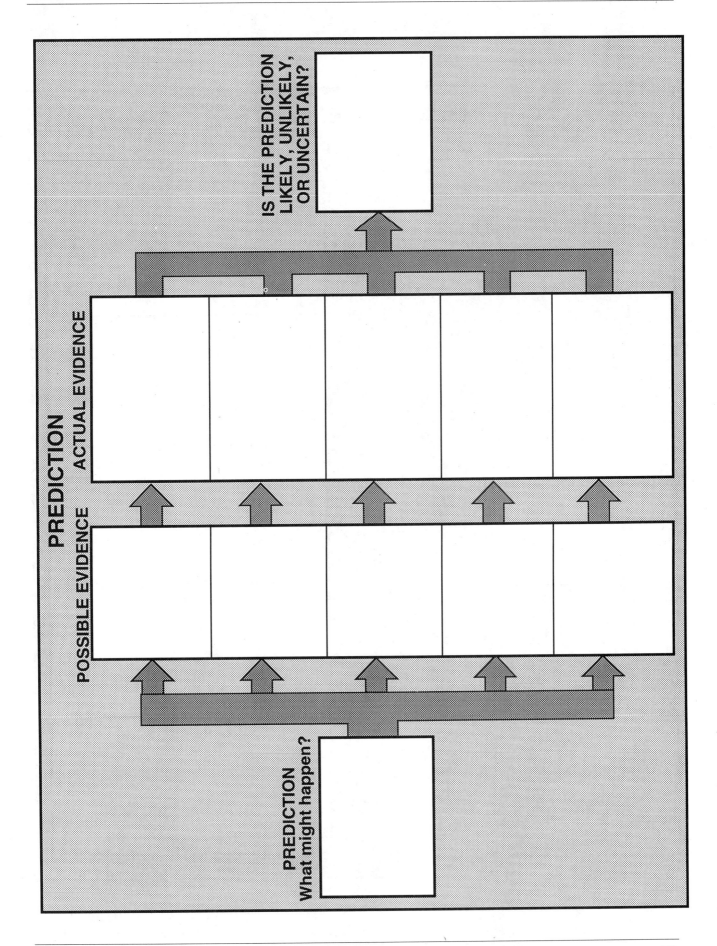

PREDICTION

POSSIBLE EVIDENCE

ACTUAL EVIDENCE

IS THE PREDICTION LIKELY, UNLIKELY, OR UNCERTAIN?

PREDICTION
What might happen?

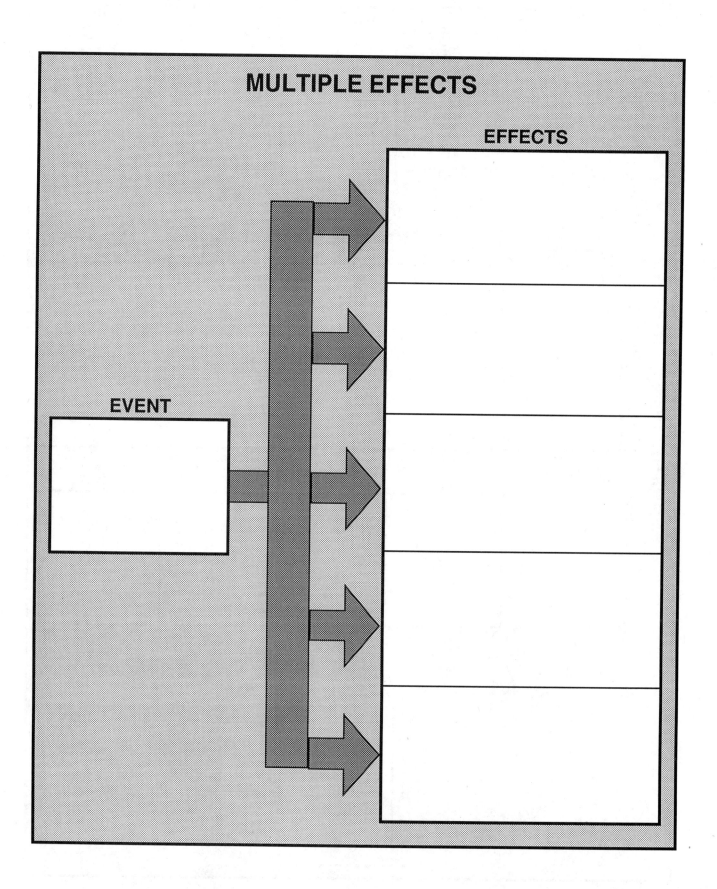

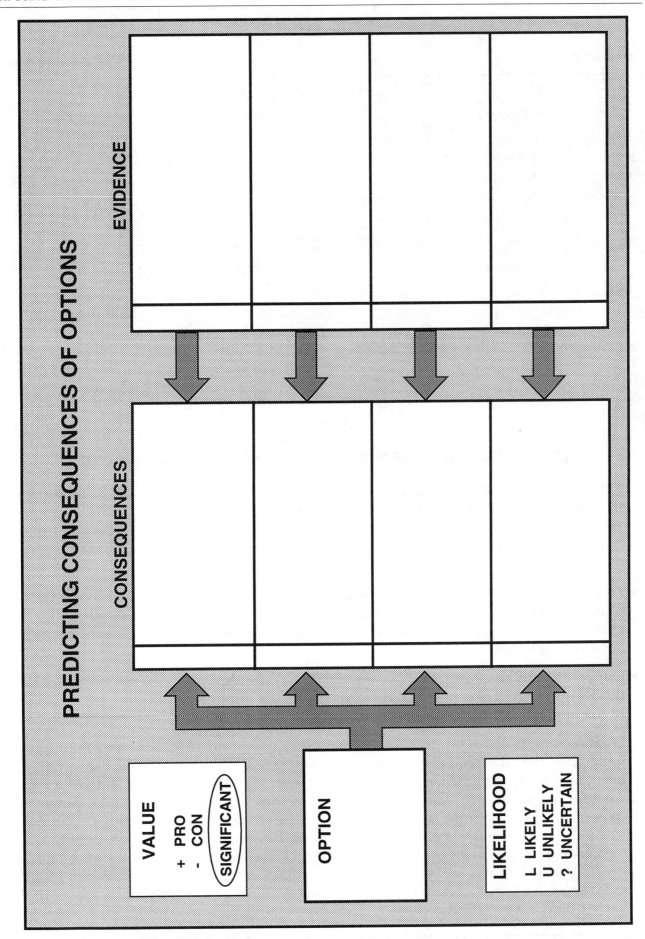

PREDICTING CONSEQUENCES OF OPTIONS

EVIDENCE

CONSEQUENCES

VALUE
+ PRO
- CON
SIGNIFICANT

OPTION

LIKELIHOOD
L LIKELY
U UNLIKELY
? UNCERTAIN

THE WAVE

OBJECTIVES

CONTENT

Students will interpret character traits by analyzing the significance of the main character's actions. They will read for details to gather evidence for interpreting the actions and motivations of characters.

THINKING SKILL/PROCESS

Students will develop skill at predicting and evaluating consequences by weighing their significance and considering evidence of their likelihood.

METHODS AND MATERIALS

CONTENT

Students will read or listen to the first portion of the short story "The Wave." After the prediction activity, they will finish reading the story to examine the character in light of his decision.

THINKING SKILL/PROCESS

Predicting consequences is guided by structured questioning and a graphic organizer that highlights key points in skillful prediction. (See pp. 420–425 for reproducible diagrams.) Collaborative learning promotes discussion of options, consequences, and evidence.

LESSON

INTRODUCTION TO CONTENT AND THINKING SKILL/ PROCESS

- **Think about a decision that someone you know or have read about has made that was risky, wise, or courageous in light of the person's understanding of the possible consequences. Write down what that person had to decide.** After students write what made the decision risky, wise, or courageous in light of conditions in the incident, they may discuss the example with partners.

- **Prediction is important in making decisions because the choice that we make may depend on consequences that we can predict, some of them unpleasant ones. What do you think the person predicted might happen as the result of his or her decision?** Give students time to list a few consequences.

- **Our predictions about the consequences aren't just guesses, hopes, or fears, but judgments that we make based on evidence. What might the person you selected have known that helped him or her predict the possible consequences?** Give students time to write a few consequences.

- **What does the decision tell you about that person? In that situation, how important is it to understand the likelihood that certain consequences would happen?** Briefly discuss three or four examples with the whole group. Students often say that it is very important to know whether certain consequences of their choices are likely because if it has very dangerous consequences, the choice may not be a wise one. On the other hand, some students say, you have to take certain risks sometimes. For example, if someone is injured and you can save him or her, then your decision may be a brave one, even if you know that there is a chance you might get injured yourself. However, if you know it is likely that you would be seriously injured and not save the person, then your decision would be unwise. Therefore, it is important to find out how likely dangerous consequences are.

- **We're going to read part of a story about a person who faces something dangerous and who must make a decision about what to do. Think about the choices this person could make and the consequences that are likely. Look for evidence that these consequences might, indeed, occur.** Give students the first selection of "The Wave" (p.431 only).

- **What do you think is the danger that Ojiisan fears threatens the village?** Students usually recognize the threat of a tidal wave. **What details in the passage lead you to believe that?** ANSWER: *The retreat of the sea following an earthquake suggests that the two events are related. Ojiisan trusts the accounts of similar events told by his grandfather.*

THINKING ACTIVELY

- **What might Ojiisan do in this situation?** Solicit responses from the whole class. List Ojiisan's options on the chalkboard. SAMPLE RESPONSES: *Yell loudly, send Tada, panic, signal a warning (mirror, horn, bell, flag, mirror, smoke), set fire to his house, set fire to the rice fields, pray, go down to the village himself, start a landslide, do nothing, get a message to leaders or a network of messengers, call the police, seek higher ground.*

- **Let's think about one of these options: setting fire to his rice fields. Let's try to decide whether or not this would be a wise thing to do. With your partners, make a list of all the consequences you can think of that might occur if Ojiisan set fire to his rice fields.** Ask each group to mention one consequence until all groups have reported. Then ask for volunteers to add other consequences; list them on the chalkboard. POSSIBLE RESPONSES: *The fire may spread rapidly and the village rice crop may be destroyed. Rushing up the mountain to put out the fire may save the people. Ojiisan's rice crop will be destroyed. The villagers may starve. He or Tada may be injured by fire. The fleeing villagers may be injured by fire. People may not see the fire. The villagers may run toward the ocean to get water or flee the fire. Rushing up the mountain to put out the fire may not save the old people and the children. The villagers may be upset and angry. His house may also be destroyed. The people would praise him as a hero. It would create air pollution. Ojiisan will feel satisfied that he did what he could to save the villagers. The fire might get out of control and cut off the people's escape route up the mountain. Ojiisan would be disgraced if there was no tidal wave.*

- **Now let's think about whether or not it is likely that the rice crop will be destroyed if Ojiisan sets fire to the rice fields. We're going to use a graphic organizer to guide us so that we can keep everything clear in our minds as we think about it.** Guide students through the thinking skill using the graphic organizer for predicting the consequences of options. Draw it on newsprint or the chalkboard or use a transparency. Write "Burn his rice fields" in the option box and write "The fire will spread rapidly and the village rice crop will be destroyed" in the first box under "consequences."

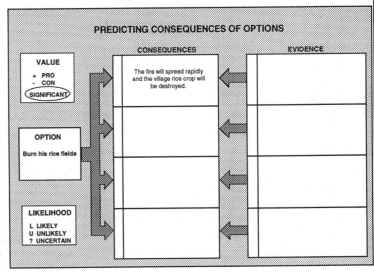

- **Does the possibility of destroying the rice crop count for or against setting fire to the rice fields?** Most students indicate "against." Put a "-" in the space to the left of the box containing the words, "The fire will spread rapidly and the village rice crop will be destroyed."

- **Is the possibility that the whole crop may be destroyed significant?** *Yes.* Circle "Rice crop will be destroyed."

- **What evidence does Ojiisan have to help him determine whether or not it is likely that the crop will be destroyed?** *The rice is dry.* Write "The rice is dry" in the top right box under "evidence."

- **Does the dryness of the rice count for or against the likelihood that the crop will be destroyed if he sets fire to the rice fields?** Most students respond that the dryness of the rice supports the likelihood that the fire will spread quickly. Write (L) next to the words, "The rice is dry." Ask for additional evidence concerning whether the fire would spread rapidly and destroy the rice crop. Ask whether the evidence is for or against the likelihood that the fire will spread rapidly. For each item of evidence, enter "L" or "U" to indicate whether it makes crop destruction likely or unlikely. Enter a "?" if it is not clear. POSSIBLE ANSWERS: Ojiisan's fields are high up on the mountain (L). There is no wind (U). The rice fields are terraced (U). Rice grows in moist soil (U).

- **When we look at all the evidence, is it likely, unlikely, or uncertain that the village crop will be destroyed if Ojiisan sets fire to the rice fields?** Most students agree, given weather conditions, the terraced design of the fields, the position of Ojiisan's rice fields (high up on the mountain), and the significance of the crop to the villagers, that it is questionable to unlikely that the rice crop of the village would be destroyed, though they agree that Ojiisan's rice would probably be destroyed. On the arrows pointing toward the consequence, enter a "U" for unlikely or a question mark for uncertain.

- **Each group should select another consequence and follow the same procedure.** If students seem uncertain about the procedure, repeat it with another consequence. Because the negative consequences are so significant, some students may not understand why anyone would set fire to the food supply. They may interpret the action as impulsive, foolish, or ill-conceived. Therefore, it is important to make sure that some groups consider significant positive consequences, such as "saving the people." If no positive consequences appear on the list, point this out to students and ask them to add consequences that are positive or beneficial.

  Ask each group to designate one member to act as recorder. The recorder will to report the group's decision regarding whether the consequences of burning the rice fields are likely, unlikely, or uncertain. Record each group's report on the chalkboard or on a transparency. After each group reports, decide as a class whether unlikely or uncertain consequences are so significant that they should, nevertheless, be taken into account.

- **Would you advise Ojiisan that setting fire to the rice fields is a good way to help the people avoid the disaster? Why?** Ask students to discuss this issue in their groups and to report their decision to the class. Most students say that although setting fire to the rice fields is risky, the likelihood that the villagers will come up the mountain to put out the fire makes it worth trying in spite of the risk.

- **Now read the rest of the story. As you do, think about what Ojiisan's decision suggests to us about his priorities and his character.** Discuss what the story tells us about Ojiisan's character and about Japanese values. POSSIBLE RESPONSES: *Ojiisan was brave, self-sacrificing, willing to risk harm to himself in order to help the villagers, and confident in the account of a tidal wave told to him by his grandfather.*

THINKING ABOUT THINKING

- **In this activity, how did we think about decisions in a new way?** Students usually respond by saying that they often don't think about consequences and rarely, if ever, take the time to figure out how likely the consequences are. Ask students to recall the questions they asked as they thought about Ojiisan's option of burning his rice fields. Write these on a thinking map for predicting the consequences of options, which you might put on a poster for future reference. The result should resemble the chart shown at the right.

> **PREDICTING THE CONSEQUENCES OF OPTIONS**
>
> 1. What consequences might result from a specific option?
> 2. Does each consequence
>   a. count for or against the decision?
>   b. rank as important?
> 3. How likely is the consequence?
>   a. Is there evidence that counts for or against the likelihood of the consequence?
>   b. Based on all the evidence, is the consequence likely, unlikely, or is its likelihood uncertain?
> 4. Is the decision advisable in light of the significance and likelihood of the consequences?

- **When would you use this way of thinking? In what circumstances might you not use it?** Some students say that this way of thinking should be used for important decisions when we have the time to think about things. Other students agree that we should use it for important decisions, but say that even if there isn't enough time to gather all of the information needed, we should always do as much as we can to think about these decisions in this way.

- **Is it valuable to take the importance and likelihood of consequences into account in making decisions? Explain.** Students usually respond that it is valuable because we can tell how much danger there is in doing certain things and how likely it is that our decisions will have good consequences.

- **How would using this process affect your confidence in your decisions?** Students usually respond that they would feel very confident since they would have a better idea ahead of time about what was going to happen.

- **Regarding Ojiisan's decision and his character, what insight did we gain by evaluating consequences?** POSSIBLE ANSWER: *Ojiisan was smart and did some quick thinking.*

APPLYING THINKING

Immediate transfer

- **Identify examples of decisions you are making that require careful prediction of consequences. Use this prediction strategy to think through one of them.** Students can do this assignment as homework and share their results the next day.

- **Select another story in which a character has to make a risky or serious decision. Use the strategy for predicting consequences of options to see what it tells us about him or her. Decide whether you would make the same decision.**

- **We are studying Pearl Buck's story "The Big Wave." Use the strategy for predicting consequences to decide whether the young man made the right decision staying with his relatives. If you think he did, why do you believe that his decision was a good one? What does this strategy tell us about his character? What does this story tell us about Japanese values that is similar to or different from what is presented in "The Wave?"**

Reinforcement Later

- **Use the strategy for predicting consequences to think through Rosa Parks' decision to stay seated on the bus in Montgomery, Alabama in 1955. What does predicting the likelihood of** her actions tell you about her? Do you think she make the right decision?

- Predict the consequences of signing the Declaration of Independence to see whether or not you would have made the decision to sign it.

WRITING EXTENSION

Before discussing the advisability of Ojiisan's setting fire to the rice fields, students may write a persuasive essay recommending to Ojiisan whether or not his decision to set fire to the rice fields is advisable in light of the evidence of the likelihood of the consequences. Their essays should include a discussion of the likelihood of significant consequences in light of the evidence.

ASSESSING STUDENTS' THINKING ABOUT CONSEQUENCES

To assess how skillfully students predict the likelihood of consequences and to evaluate how well they have learned the importance of predicting likely consequences in a decision-making context, ask them to write an essay on a controversial topic calling for a decision. Ask students to make their thinking explicit. Determine whether they use each step in the thinking map for predicting consequences in making their decisions about the best course of action.

THE WAVE

by Margaret Hodges

Long ago in Japan a village stood beside the sea. When the water was calm, the village children played in the gentle waves, shouting and laughing. But sometimes the sea was angry and waves came tearing up the beach to the very edge of the town. Then, everyone, children, fathers, and mothers, ran from the shore back to their homes. They shut their doors and waited for the storm to pass and for the sea to grow calm again.

Behind the village there rose a mountain with a zigzag road that climbed up, up through the rice fields. And these rice fields were all the wealth of the people. There they worked hard, drenched by the spring rains that made the mountainside green and beautiful. They toiled up the steep, zigzag road in the heat of the summer to care for the rice fields. When the stalks turned gold and dried in the sun, the villagers bent their backs to gather in the heavy harvest, rejoicing that they could eat for another year.

High on the mountain, overlooking the village and the sea, there lived a wise old man, Ojiisan, a name that in Japan means Grandfather. With him lived his little grandson, whose name was Tada.

Tada loved Ojiisan dearly and gave him obedience, due to his great age and great wisdom. Indeed, the old man had the respect of all the villagers. Often they climbed up the long, zigzag road to ask him for advice.

One day when the air was very hot and still, Ojiisan stood on the balcony of his house and looked at his rice fields. The precious grain was ripe and ready for the harvest. Below he saw the fields of the villagers, leading down the valley like an enormous flight of golden steps.

At the foot of the mountain he saw the village, ninety thatched houses and a temple stretched along the curve of the bay. There had been a very fine rice crop and the peasants were going to celebrate their harvest by a dance in the court of the temple.

Tada came to stand beside his grandfather. He too looked down the mountain. They could see strings of paper lanterns festooned between bamboo poles. Above the roofs of the houses festival banners hung motionless in the heavy warm air.

"This is earthquake weather," said Ojiisan.

And presently an earthquake came. It was not strong enough to frighten Tada, for Japan has many earthquakes. But this one was queer—a long, slow shaking as though it were caused by changes far out at the bottom of the sea. The house rocked gently several times. Then all became still.

As the quaking ceased, Ojiisan's keen old eyes looked at the sea shore. The water had darkened quite suddenly. It was drawing back from the village. The thin curve of the shore was growing wider and wider. The sea was running away from the land!

Ojiisan and Tada saw the tiny figures of villagers around the temple, in the streets, on the shore. Now all were gathering on the beach. As the water drew back, ribbed sand and weed-hung rock were left bare. None of the village people seemed to know what it meant.

But Ojiisan knew. In his lifetime it had never happened before. But he remembered things told him in his childhood by his father's father. He understood what the sea was going to do and he must warn the villagers.

There was no time to stand and think. Ojiisan must act. He said to Tada, "Quick! Light me a torch!"

Tada obeyed at once. He ran into the house and kindled a pine torch. Quickly he gave it to Ojiisan.

The old man hurried out to the fields where his rice stood, ready for the harvest. This was his precious rice, all of his work for the past year, all of his food for the year to come.

He thrust the torch in among the dry stacks and the fire blazed up. The rice burned like tinder. Sparks burst into flame and the flames raced through Ojiisan's fields, turning their gold to black, sending columns of smoke skyward in one enormous cloudy whirl.

Tada was astonished and terrified. He ran after his grandfather, crying, "Ojiisan! Why? Ojiisan! Why? Why?"

But Ojiisan did not answer. He had no time to explain. He was thinking only of the four hundred lives in peril by the edge of the sea.

For a moment Tada stared wildly at the blazing rice. Then he burst into tears, and ran back to the house, feeling sure that his grandfather had lost his mind.

Ojiisan went on firing stack after stack of rice, till he had reached the end of his fields. Then he threw down the torch and waited.

Down below, the priests in the temple saw the blaze on the mountain and set the big bell booming. The people hurried in from the sands and over the beach and up from the village, like a swarming of ants.

Ojiisan watched them from his burning rice fields and the moments seemed terribly long to him.

"Faster! Run faster!" he said. But the people could not hear him.

The sun was going down. The wrinkled bed of the bay and a vast expanse beyond it lay bare and still the sea was fleeing toward the horizon.

Ojiisan did not have long to wait before the first of the villagers arrived to put out the fire. But the old man held out both arms to stop them.

"Let it burn!" he commanded. "Let it be! I want all the people here. There is a great danger!"

The whole village did come—first the young men and boys, and the women and girls who could run the fastest. Then came the older folk and others with babies at their backs. The children came, for they could help to pass buckets of water. Even the elders could be seen well on their way up the steep mountainside. But it was too late to save the flaming fields of Ojiisan. All looked in sorrowful wonder at the face of the old man. And the sun went down.

Tada came running from the house "Grandfather has lost his mind!" he sobbed. "He has gone mad! He set fire to the rice on purpose. I saw him do it!"

"The child tells the truth. I did set fire to the rice," said Ojiisan. "Are all the people here?"

The men were very angry. "All are here." They said. They muttered among themselves. "The old man is mad. He will destroy our fields next!" And they threatened them with their fists.

Then Ojiisan raised his hand and pointed to the sea. "Look!" he said.

Through the twilight eastward all looked and saw at the edge of the dusky horizon, a long, dim cone like the shadow of a coast where no coast ever was. The line grew wider and darker. It moved toward them. That long darkness was the returning sea, towering like a cliff and coming toward them more swiftly than the kite flies.

"A tidal wave!" shrieked the people. And then all shrieks and all sound and all power to hear sounds were ended by a shock, heavier than any thunder, as the great wave struck the shore with a weight that sent a shudder through the hills.

There was a burst of foam like a blaze of sheet lightning. Then for an instant, nothing could be seen, but a storm of spray rushing up the mountain side, while the people scattered in fear.

When they looked again, they saw a wild, white sea raging over the place where their homes had been. It drew back, roaring and tearing out the land as it went. Twice, thrice, five times the sea struck and ebbed, but each time with less strength. Then it returned to its ancient bed and stayed, still raging, as after a typhoon.

Around the house of Ojiisan no word was spoken. The people stared down the mountain at the rocks hurled and split by the sea, where the houses and temple had been.

The village was no longer there, only broken bamboo poles and thatch scattered along the shore. Then the voice of Ojiisan was heard again, saying gently, "That was why I set fire to the rice."

He, their wise old friend, now stood among them almost as poor as the poorest, for his wealth was gone. But he had saved four hundred lives.

Tada ran to him and held his hand. The father of each family knelt before Ojiisan and all the people after them.

"My home still stands," the old man said. "There is room for many." And he led the way to the house.

Sample Student Responses • The Wave

PREDICTING CONSEQUENCES OF OPTIONS

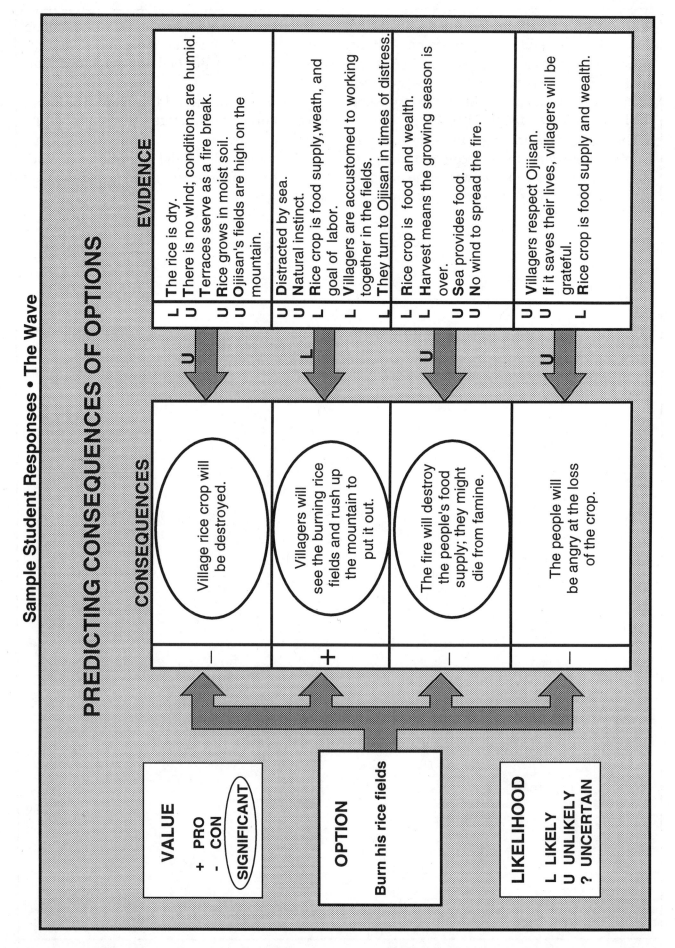

EVIDENCE

- L The rice is dry.
- U There is no wind; conditions are humid.
- U Terraces serve as a fire break.
- U Rice grows in moist soil.
  Ojiisan's fields are high on the mountain.

- U Distracted by sea.
- U Natural instinct.
- L Rice crop is food supply, weath, and goal of labor.
- L Villagers are accustomed to working together in the fields.
- L They turn to Ojiisan in times of distress.

- L Rice crop is food and wealth.
- L Harvest means the growing season is over.
- U Sea provides food.
- U No wind to spread the fire.

- U Villagers respect Ojiisan.
- U If it saves their lives, villagers will be grateful.
- L Rice crop is food supply and wealth.

CONSEQUENCES

U → Village rice crop will be destroyed. —

L → Villagers will see the burning rice fields and rush up the mountain to put it out. +

U → The fire will destroy the people's food supply; they might die from famine. —

U → The people will be angry at the loss of the crop. —

VALUE

+ PRO
- CON
(SIGNIFICANT)

OPTION

Burn his rice fields

LIKELIHOOD

L LIKELY
U UNLIKELY
? UNCERTAIN

THE TRIP

Mathematics/Geography   **Grades 5–6**

OBJECTIVES

CONTENT

Students will learn to estimate speed, time, and distance and apply map-reading skills to maps of the United States.

THINKING SKILL/PROCESS

Students will develop skill at predicting by considering evidence for the likelihood of their predicted consequences.

METHODS AND MATERIALS

CONTENT

Students will examine maps and other resource material and use a calendar to plan a trip. This lesson will take more than one class session.

THINKING SKILL/PROCESS

Predicting consequences is guided by structured questioning and the use of a graphic organizer which highlights key points in skillful prediction. (See pp. 420–25 for reproducible diagrams.) Students will work together in collaborative learning groups on this activity.

LESSON

INTRODUCTION TO CONTENT AND THINKING SKILL/PROCESS

• Think about a time when something took longer than you or your family thought it would. Why did it take longer? Make a list of the circumstances that caused your estimate to be wrong. List students' responses on the chalkboard or on newsprint.

• When you think ahead of time that something will happen or that it will happen at a particular time, you are making a prediction. All of the things you mentioned interfered with the accuracy of your predictions. Predicting accurately is very important. Otherwise, you may make plans and then be disappointed. To make an accurate prediction, you should try to find out in advance if anything might cause your prediction to be mistaken. When you do this, you are looking for evidence that your prediction may or may not turn out as you think. For example, think about the circumstances you just discussed. What could you have found out that would have indicated that the event would take longer? List the sources or examples of information in a separate column.

• Let's put together some of these ideas about how to make skillful predictions. We'll make a thinking map that can guide us to make more accurate predictions. The thinking map contains questions to ask and to answer carefully as you are making a prediction. The map helps you think critically about your predictions. If, as you use this strategy, you find that your prediction is not accurate, you should then modify it according to the evidence you have.

SKILLFUL PREDICTION

1. What might happen?

2. What evidence might you get that would indicate that this prediction is likely?

3. What evidence is available that is relevant to whether the prediction is likely?

4. Based on the evidence, is the prediction likely, unlikely, or uncertain?

• Let's use these ideas to think about a really simple prediction. If you are going outside and it's sunny, you may predict that it is not going to rain and decide not to take your raincoat.

When you see that it's sunny, that is your evidence for thinking that it will not rain. Is that a good reason? Why? *No. Lots of times when it's sunny it gets cloudy and rains.*

- **If you hear on the radio that thunderstorms will move into your area before you get back from school, how might that influence whether or not you take a raincoat? Why?** Students often respond that the report would change their minds and that they might decide to wear their raincoats. They sometimes say that they remember times when they got wet in an unexpected storm. **Whose prediction is more reliable: yours or the weatherperson's? What reasons might you have for reconsidering your prediction of sunny weather?** POSSIBLE ANSWERS: *Weather reports are based on records and observations with equipment that we don't commonly have. The weather service bases its predictions on conditions in a larger area than we can see. All of this usually provides evidence that is better than just noticing that it is sunny.*

- **What information might help the weather service to predict precisely <u>when</u> it is going to rain?** POSSIBLE ANSWERS: *Information about the speed of an approaching front, the differences in barometric pressure on either side of a front that may influence its intensity or speed, records of the speed of approaching storms based on past ones.*

THINKING ACTIVELY

- **People often make poor predictions in planning trips. Often, they just think about the distances they will travel and don't consider things that could affect the time required for the trip. For example, someone might be planning a holiday trip to the next town to visit relatives. Because it isn't too far, this person might think it will only take an hour to get there; however, another person on the trip may like to stop and look at beautiful scenery. Suppose you had to travel across town for a doctor's appointment. What things should you and your parents take into account in deciding when to leave for the appointment?** POSSIBLE ANSWERS: *How far it is, how long it usually takes to get there, whether anyone wants to (or needs to) stop anywhere on the way, whether the traffic will delay you or allow you to get there in less time than usual, the type of road (expressway, residential street, etc.), road conditions (construction, poor surface, snow, etc.), the time of day or day of the year (if there are special events), the speed limit, comfort conditions (how long one drives easily or whether one needs to eat), the terrain (winding roads around lakes or mountains), etc.*

- **Even when people take these things into account, their estimates for travel time are sometimes inaccurate. How did the person estimate that the holiday trip would take only an hour?** Maybe that was just a guess. The driving time might actually be much longer, and the person might be really late for dinner. We've been studying a way to figure out how long something will take if you know the *rate* at which it will be done. A rate tells you how much of something happens in a given period of time. **For example, suppose you can run across the school yard in two minutes. What would be the rate at which you can run across the school yard?** *Once across the yard in two minutes.* **Someone else might cross the yard at a different rate. Perhaps it takes that other person three minutes. Once you know this, you can tell how long it will take you to run across the school yard five times at the same rate. How long will that take?** *Ten minutes.* **How did you figure that out?** *If one time across takes two minutes, then five times across takes five times two, or ten minutes.* Review this idea with your students so that they will be clear about it. If they are having trouble with the concept of rate, you may engage them in an activity in which their task is to figure out certain rates. For example, you might introduce them to the idea of a reading rate—how long it takes them to read one page of a book. Ask them to determine their reading rates by timing themselves or other students. Have them record these rates, then ask them to plan enough time to read a ten-page book. Once they've figured out everyone's reading rate, you can ask them to calculate the class average.

- In this country, for travel over long distances, the rate of speed is measured as the number of miles you can travel in one hour. When a car travels at twenty-five miles per hour (abbreviated mph), what does that mean? *In one hour, the car will travel the distance of twenty-five miles.* Can you formulate a statement that tells you how to calculate the amount of time it will take to travel a specific distance at a certain rate of speed? *You divide the distance by your speed to compute the time it will take to get to where you are going.* Of course, to use this equation, you have to judge your speed accurately. Let's see if this can help us make good predictions.

- Suppose that you and your parents want to make a trip by car to Boston or Los Angeles. You need to leave enough time to get back for the start of school. You want to spend a week at your destination. Let's plan a route and predict how long the trip will take so that you can help your parents decide when to leave. We will use the distance/rate/time equation to estimate how long certain portions of the trip will take. We will also use information about the geography of the area to predict how that might affect travel time. We will also take into account the various times you will want to stop. We will record all this information on a graphic organizer so that we will not forget any of it while we think about our prediction.

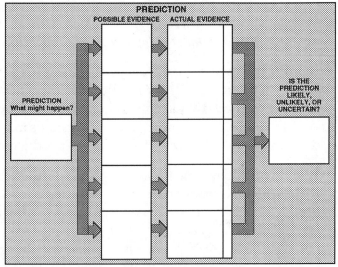

- With your work group, select one of the two destinations that is at least 750 miles away. Map out a route and predict, as accurately as possible, how long the trip will take. Examine the road map to estimate how many miles the trip will be. Make use of the legend on the map to make your estimates. Assume that the speed limit is 55 miles per hour on major highways and 25 miles per hour in cities; make sure you calculate the average speed, taking into account traffic lights, etc. When you estimate the time for all or a part of the trip, write it in the left box on the graphic organizer.

- Now think about what possible information you would need in order to decide whether this is an accurate prediction. Write the type of information you would need in the boxes marked "Possible Evidence." POSSIBLE ANSWERS: *Special road conditions (e.g., snow, repairs, narrow winding road, bridges), traffic conditions (e.g., rush-hour traffic, holiday traffic, tolls), need or interest in stopping (e.g., for sightseeing, for meals, for an overnight hotel room), condition of the car (e.g., likelihood of breakdowns, working properly for highway driving), number and ages of family members (affecting stamina, need for rest stops, special supplies).*

- Now carefully check the road map and any other sources for the actual information you need to be sure your prediction is right. Assume that the car is in working order and has recently been serviced. Write information from your research in the boxes marked "Actual Evidence." When you have discussed the best information you can get for all the possible conditions that might affect your estimate, decide with your group whether your predicted time is likely, unlikely, or too uncertain to trust. Determine whether it should be changed and by how much. Students may start with a "guesstimate" about the time of the whole trip based on a similar one. They may, instead, do a more detailed analysis, dividing the trip into segments in which travel conditions are similar, analyzing each segment, and adding up the segments. Encourage students to use as much detail as possible to predict stops or delays. For example, one group of students noticed that there was an antique auto museum only a few miles from the highway in Kansas, so they factored in a trip to the museum.

• **Use your predictions about how long the trip might take to create a daily plan for the trip. Using a calendar, create a travel schedule presuming that the trip will begin early in the morning and must be finished by evening on September 8. Allow one full week at your destination.** After student groups have arrived at a prediction about the travel time and created their schedule, each group should report. Keep a record on the chalkboard or on newsprint of the time, conditions, and dates each group reports, as well as a brief description of how they addressed the problem. After all groups have reported, compare the reports to discuss common predictions and conditions and decide as a class what the likeliest time prediction would be.

THINKING ABOUT THINKING

• **What did we do in this activity that is different from the usual ways you make predictions?** POSSIBLE ANSWERS: *Usually I don't think about whether my predictions are accurate, I just make them. I rarely ask whether there is any evidence for my predictions when I make them. I never compare my reasons for my predictions with the information I think I would need to make a good prediction.*

• **In your own words, construct a thinking map of skillful prediction that you can use in the future to be sure that your predictions are as accurate as possible.** Discuss with your students how the methods they sketch in their thinking maps produce predictions that aren't just guesses. Ask the students to write their thinking maps in their notebooks for future reference. If there are differences between what the students produce, ask them to discuss these differences.

• **When would you use this strategy for prediction? In what circumstances might you not use it? Discuss this with a partner.** Ask students for some of their ideas. POSSIBLE ANSWERS: *I would use it when something dangerous might happen, when what I am predicting is important to me, and when I have the time to get evidence. Only rarely would I not use it: when there is no time to get the information I need, and when the prediction is not important; however, if there was no time to get a lot of information and the prediction was important, I would do the best I could.*

• **How would using this process affect your confidence in your predictions? How would using this process affect your confidence in your decisions?** Usually students say that it makes them feel more confident in both their predictions and the decisions they base on these predictions because they've looked for evidence and can back up their predictions with reasons.

• **By predicting how long something would take, what insight did we gain that we might otherwise have missed?** Students typically say that they now realize that they can plan their use of time in a much more organized way than they had thought they could.

APPLYING THINKING

Immediate Transfer

• Apply the skillful prediction strategy to plan doing your homework.

• **Scientists are warning us about the possibility of "global warming"—an increase in the temperature of the Earth due to industrial gasses acting as a blanket in the atmosphere. They project that the planet's average temperature could increase by approximately 5 degrees over the next fifty years. Use skillful prediction to determine the impact of this increase in temperature on how we live.**

Reinforcement Later

- Apply the plan for predicting time to a current class or school project.

- Apply skillful prediction to decide whether a currently-endangered species, such as the Florida panther, is likely to become extinct.

- Apply skillful prediction to a recent historical event that we have studied or to some current news event to determine what its consequences are likely to be.

LESSON EXTENSION

- **We're going to study weather prediction. We often hear a weather report to the effect that there is a 50% or a 70% chance of rain, for example. Determine what evidence the weather service uses to make predictions of this sort. What other kinds of predictions can be made with this degree of specificity? Gather relevant information about graduating seniors in your high school and make a numerical prediction concerning some important outcome, for example how many will go to college.** The weather predictions are based on statistical data about how often, in similar circumstances in the past, it has rained. If it has rained in 7 out of 10 occasions on which the weather conditions have been like they are now, then there is a 70% chance of rain, all other things being equal. Similar statistical predictions have been made about earthquakes, chances of getting into auto accidents, and about chances of contracting certain diseases.

ASSESSING STUDENT THINKING ABOUT PREDICTIONS

Any of the transfer examples in this lesson can serve as assessment items for determining the extent to which students are thinking about their predictions skillfully. Make sure information is available for students to use in supporting their predictions. Determine whether students are thinking about possible evidence, making use of actual evidence, and considering how likely the predictions are based on the evidence used.

A variation on this approach is to ask students to critique predictions made by others. Give them examples of predictions and ask them to determine whether these predictions are well-founded. They should demonstrate a sensitivity to the same aspects of skillful prediction that you want them to display when they make their own predictions.

Sample Student Responses • The Trip

PREDICTION

PREDICTION
What might happen?

The trip will take 11 days (2 days to get there, 7 days in Boston, 2 days to return).

EXAMPLE:
A trip from Charlotte, NC to Boston, MA on Route I-95: approx. 850 miles.

POSSIBLE EVIDENCE

Normal driving conditions for 50 mph average speed for 17 hours.

Special conditions: No significant rush hour traffic, holiday traffic, fog, snow, etc.

Family drivers can cover 425 miles per day for eight and a half hours of driving.

No stopovers for sightseeing.

Terrain: No mountains with winding roads, narrow bridges across rivers, etc.

ACTUAL EVIDENCE

Everyday traffic in New York City, Richmond, Baltimore, Philadelphia, and Washington, D.C. is significant. (−)

Labor Day traffic in metropolitan areas is intense. Travelers' demands for services cause delays in gas stations, restaurants, and motels. (−)

Two drivers may take turns to reduce fatigue. Several people traveling require more comfort stops. (+) (−)

Members of the family are likely to want to stop to see special sites at one or more cities along the way. (−)

No mountains, but tunnels and bridges in Baltimore and New York may cause congestion. (−)

IS THE PREDICTION LIKELY, UNLIKELY, OR UNCERTAIN?

UNLIKELY

MODIFICATIONS IN PREDICTIONS:

Add two or more days of travel time, or consider taking the I-77, I-81, I-84 route both ways or for the return trip to avoid Labor Day traffic in big cities.

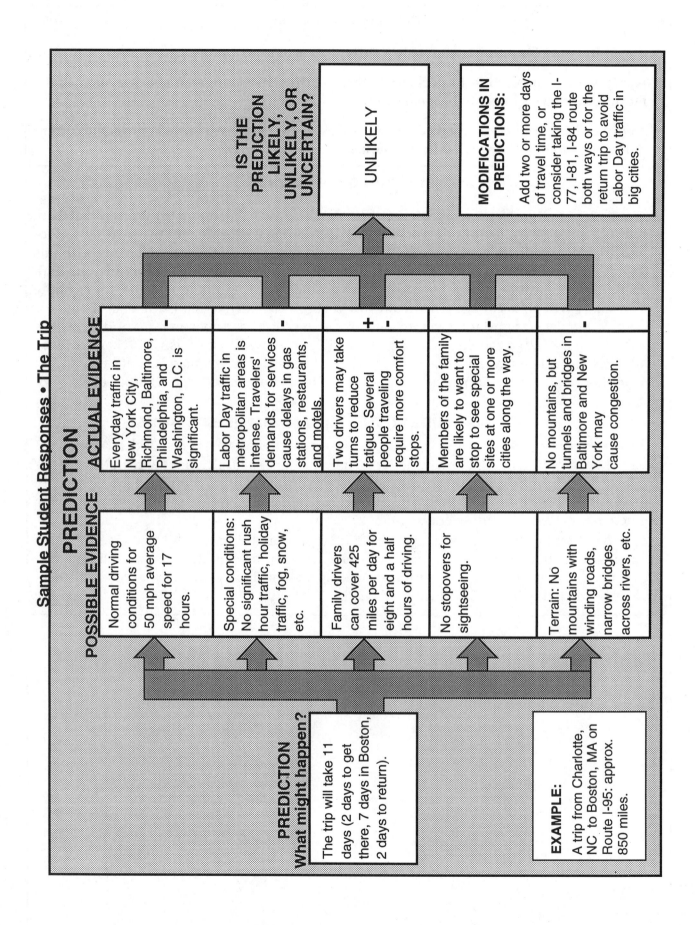

PREDICTION LESSON CONTEXTS

The following examples have been suggested by classroom teachers as contexts in which to develop infused lessons. If a skill or process has been introduced in a previous infused lesson, transfer activities can be designed in these contexts to reinforce it.

GRADE	SUBJECT	TOPIC	THINKING ISSUE
K–3	Literature	*Arthur's Glasses*	What will happen if Arthur doesn't wear his glasses? What are your reasons for your prediction?
K–3	Literature	*Peter Rabbit*	What could Peter Rabbit predict would happen if he disobeyed? Why? What was likely to happen when Peter Rabbit stole the carrots? Why?
K–3	Literature	*Little Boy Blue*	What does the nursery rhyme suggest would happen if Little Boy Blue didn't wake up?
K–3	Literature	*Sadako and the Thousand Cranes*	What can you find out from the story that would suggest how Chizuko's gift of the paper cranes would affect Sadako?
K–3	Literature	*Boxcar Children*	Predict the consequences of remaining in the boxcar. Explain why.
K–3	Social studies	City planning	How would your city have developed differently if it was located 50 miles farther inland? What reasons do you have for your predictions?
K–3	Social studies	Recycling	What do you think would happen if we did not recycle? Why?
K–3	Social studies	Being lost	What would happen if you got lost in the mall? Explain why you think that would happen.
K–3	Science	Effects on plants	What would happen to the living things in a pond if it dried up? Explain why.
K–3	Science	Plant life	What would happen to people and animals if all the plants died? Explain why.
K–3	Science	Trees	What is likely to happen if we do not plant trees? Why do you think that will happen?
K–3	Science	Weather	What can you predict about a coming storm by observing clouds? Explain what it is about the clouds that helps you predict.
K–3	Science	Magnets	Predict what will happen when various common items (e.g., a pencil, a frying pan, a hammer) are put near a magnet. Explain why you make these predictions. Test the predictions.
K–3	Science	Hatching eggs	What will the chicks look like when the eggs hatch? Will they all look alike? What will happen if the electricity goes off? Why?
K–3	Health	Fire Safety	If the school had a fire, what would you predict that you and others in your class would do? Why do you predict this?
K–3	Guidance	Social skills	Predict what would happen if you could bring your own toys to recess. Explain why you predict that. How could you prevent problems?
4–6	Literature	*Trouble With Tuck*	Predict whether Tuck is likely to regain his eyesight. Why do you think so?

PREDICTION LESSON CONTEXTS

GRADE	SUBJECT	TOPIC	THINKING ISSUE
4–6	Literature	*Sarah, Plain and Tall*	Predict whether Sarah is likely to stay with her new family. Explain what reasons you have for your prediction.
4–6	Literature	*Journey Home*	What might Yuki and her family predict will happen to them when they are released from the Topaz internment camp? What reasons do they have for this prediction?
4–6	Literature	*Bridge to Terabithia*	What would have happened if Leslie had gone to Washington with Jess? Why?
4–6	Writing	Style and genre	Write a story that you predict will be scary when it is read. Explain what it is about the way you have written it that makes you think people will react that way. Then give the story to someone else to read and test your prediction. Is it scary?
4–6	Social studies	The Pilgrims	Imagine that you are a Pilgrim in Holland. Predict what the trip will be like aboard the Mayflower. Explain your predictions.
4–6	U.S. history	Westward Expansion	What conditions could you expect to find along the way if you were in a wagon train heading west from St. Louis in the 1850s? Explain what you would base your expectations on. Would this provide enough evidence for you to be confident in your expectations? How would you prepare to meet the challenges of the trip that you planned?
4–6	U.S. history	The Industrial Revolution	What would you expect your daily life to be like if you took a job in the textile mills in the 1840s? How much could you expect to earn, how long would you work, etc. What are your reasons for these expectations?
4–6	U.S. history	Texas	How would United States history have been affected if Texas had remained a republic? Explain why.
4–6	Science	Water pollution	Predict how your life would change if your community found that its water supply was polluted. Why do you think these changes would take place?
4–6	Science	Environment	Use information about population growth, energy use, global warming, and waste disposal to predict what a day in your community might be like in 2020. Explain how this information leads to your predictions.
4–6	Science	Food chains	Predict what will happen to the population of Ospreys that feed on herring off the coast of Chile if the herring fishermen overfish the area and the herring population becomes very low. Explain why.
4–6	Science	Food chains	Predict the impact on black-footed ferrets if farmers continue killing prairie dogs. Explain why.
4–6	Science	Solutions	Predict the outcome of adding a variety of substances to water (e.g., salt, sugar, oil). Why do you think these things will happen?
4–6	Science	Ecology	What is likely to result in the biosphere from the destruction of rain forests? Explain why you predict these results.
4–6	Mathematics	Probability	After teaching laws of probability, set up a problem situation. After students predict outcomes based on laws of probability, they perform experiments to verify their predictions. Adjust conditions (what if...) and ask students to predict how results would change. Ask them to explain why they make their predictions.

CHAPTER 15
GENERALIZATION

Why Is Skillful Generalization Necessary?

We often get to know someone better by learning more about that individual. I may find out that a friend is planning a trip to Hawaii because she is interested in birds, and Hawaii is noted for exotic birds. This knowledge may enrich our relationship. If I, too, have an interest in birds, I know that she is someone with whom I can share this interest.

As important as learning such new things about my friend may be, what I learn is limited. It informs me only about an individual. If I want to know if there are other individuals with whom I can also share this interest, what I have just learned doesn't help much. I have to learn about other people's interests individually.

Sometimes, though, we expand what we know by learning something about *types* of things. Roses smell sweet. Antelope run fast. Diamonds are hard. These are generalizations that apply to *all* things of a certain sort (roses, antelope, or diamonds), not just to one individual. While we learn things about specific individuals, we can also learn generalizations that inform us about all individuals of a certain type without having to investigate each of these individuals separately.

The Importance of Generalizations in Our Thinking

Using generalizations makes our thinking much more efficient. I know that roses smell sweet. On the basis of this general knowledge, the next time that I want to buy sweet-smelling flowers, I can decide quickly that I will buy roses. I do not have to sniff around until I find an individual flower that smells sweet. Accepting the general statement licenses me to be confident that *any new* individual rose I get will smell sweet.

Our knowledge of general statements can help us avoid danger too. I know that certain kinds of jellyfish have a poisonous sting. If I recognize the distinctive crown of a Portuguese man-of-war jellyfish floating on the surf, I can be confident of its harmful nature because of my general knowledge about this kind of jellyfish.

Common Problems about the Way We Generalize

Because of their efficiency, generalizations run through much of our thinking. We learn many generalizations from others but also develop them ourselves.

Our tendency to generalize, however, can lead ourselves and others astray. It is risky to accept uncritically all generalizations that occur to us or that we hear from others. Not all generalizations are well-founded. If the large, juicy grapes in a grocery store advertisement look wonderful, I may think that all the grapes at the supermarket are large and juicy. While they may be, often we find that the quality of what was advertised isn't as good as it appeared in the ad. It is easy to make hasty generalizations.

Stereotyping and various forms of bias and prejudice also revolve around faulty generalizations. On my first visit to a school, I may find that there is a group of students in the corridors being rowdy. Because of this, I might say to myself, "The students in this school are rowdy and poorly behaved." This is a generalization that could affect my attitudes about this school. Indeed, this could be a case of stereotyping. I might carry this belief with me and think of anyone who came from that school as rowdy and poorly behaved.

This generalization may well turn out to be inaccurate. Such a small sample is not adequate support for this generalization. The supporting evidence is too narrow. These could be the only rowdy students in the school. Are they representative of the rest of the students? If they are not representative, then the sample is too narrow. If we are going to use generalizations in our thinking, we should make sure that they are well-founded.

Generalizing in either of these circumstances (based on a small sample or based on a narrow sample which does not represent the whole) is often called the fallacy of "hasty generalization." Figure 15.1 contains a list of these defaults in generalizing.

```
┌─────────────────────────────────────────┐
│         COMMON DEFAULTS IN THE           │
│           WAY WE GENERALIZE              │
├─────────────────────────────────────────┤
│                                         │
│  1. We often generalize based on a small │
│     number of individuals.               │
│                                         │
│  2. We often generalize based on a sample│
│     of individuals without knowing       │
│     whether or not it is representative  │
│     of the whole group.                  │
│                                         │
└─────────────────────────────────────────┘
```

Figure 15.1

What Does Skillful Generalization Involve?

Usually generalizations are supported by studying a number of individuals (a "sample") that fall under the generalization. This is why generalizing is often characterized as "inductive" reasoning. We start with knowledge about individuals and infer general conclusions.

A Strategy for Determining Whether a Generalization is Well-founded

Since most generalizations are about all things of a certain type, like all roses or all Portuguese man-of-war jellyfish, we can't hope to support most of them completely. Still, the better the sample we do study, the more likely the generalization will be correct.

Before we generalize, we should make sure we gather information about a number of individuals. How large a number is needed to support a generalization? This depends on the selection procedure used. What is really important is that we should make sure that these individuals are *representative* of the whole group. This involves not just the size but also the selection of the group of individuals that we use as a basis for the generalization.

Using a nonrepresentative, or skewed, sample is one of the most common mistakes in generalization. If I think that my state favors a certain political candidate because everyone in my neighborhood does, I am making this mistake.

Maybe my neighborhood has some special reason for preferring this candidate, and people in other communities do not.

Choosing a large number of individuals *at random* from the total population is one way to minimize mistakes from misleading samples. Doing this effectively, however, requires that we sample a relatively large number. If, on the other hand, we pick individuals *at random from representative groupings* (e.g., some from each of the different areas of the city), we may not need such a large number. If we do not use either method, the sample may be biased.

Whichever method of selection we choose, before we can support a generalization sufficiently, we should have reasons for thinking that our sample is representative of the whole group. Attending to the sample size and its selection allows us to judge the strength of support it provides for the generalization. This is what makes generalizing skillful.

The thinking map for generalization in figure 15.2 prompts reflection on the adequacy of a sample for well-founded generalization.

```
┌───────────────────────────────────────────┐
│ ╔═══════════════════════════════════════╗ │
│ ║        SKILLFUL GENERALIZATION        ║ │
│ ║                                       ║ │
│ ║  1. What generalization is suggested? ║ │
│ ║                                       ║ │
│ ║  2. What sample is needed to support  ║ │
│ ║     that generalization?              ║ │
│ ║                                       ║ │
│ ║  3. Is the sample being used large    ║ │
│ ║     enough?                           ║ │
│ ║                                       ║ │
│ ║  4. Is the sample being used like the ║ │
│ ║     whole group?                      ║ │
│ ║                                       ║ │
│ ║  5. Is the generalization well        ║ │
│ ║     supported by the sample?          ║ │
│ ║                                       ║ │
│ ║  6. If not, what additional           ║ │
│ ║     information is needed to support  ║ │
│ ║     the generalization?               ║ │
│ ╚═══════════════════════════════════════╝ │
└───────────────────────────────────────────┘
```

Figure 15.2

A Graphic Organizer for Skillful Generalization

The graphic organizer in figure 15.3 provides spaces for writing a description of the sample used to support a generalization and for assessing the characteristics of the sample.

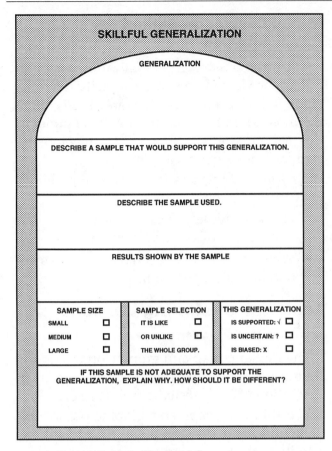

SKILLFUL GENERALIZATION

GENERALIZATION

DESCRIBE A SAMPLE THAT WOULD SUPPORT THIS GENERALIZATION.

DESCRIBE THE SAMPLE USED.

RESULTS SHOWN BY THE SAMPLE

SAMPLE SIZE	SAMPLE SELECTION	THIS GENERALIZATION
SMALL ☐	IT IS LIKE ☐	IS SUPPORTED: √ ☐
MEDIUM ☐	OR UNLIKE ☐	IS UNCERTAIN: ? ☐
LARGE ☐	THE WHOLE GROUP.	IS BIASED: X ☐

IF THIS SAMPLE IS NOT ADEQUATE TO SUPPORT THE
GENERALIZATION, EXPLAIN WHY. HOW SHOULD IT BE DIFFERENT?

Figure 15.3

How Can We Teach Students to Generalize Skillfully?

Teaching this skill should involve having students work with examples of specific generalizations. They should be prompted to think about the sample that the generalization is based on and to determine its size and representativeness. On the basis of this determination, they should be given an opportunity to reflect about the support the sample provides for the generalization. The goal of your teaching should be to help students raise these questions and gather information to answer them when they consider accepting a generalization.

In situations in which generalizations are not founded on an adequate sample, students can use the descriptions that they wrote of what an adequate sample would be like as a basis for an investigation. This may lead to additional support that may make the generalization well-founded. For example, students can develop a polling strategy which they believe creates an adequate sample. On the basis of this sample,

they can legitimately generalize about students' attitudes regarding recycling.

Constructing Lessons to Teach Students Skillful Generalization

Using the graphic organizer for skillful generalization will help your students evaluate generalizations. In addition, though, you should use the thinking map to make the strategy explicit. You should also provide opportunities for students to reflect on the process and to use it in different contexts. When you combine the thinking map and the graphic organizer in the infusion lesson format, you can teach students skillful generalization.

Contexts in the Curriculum for Lessons on Skillful Generalization

Generalizations appear in almost every subject students learn. Science instruction relies heavily on generalizations: hot air rises, hummingbirds migrate in the winter, and acid is corrosive to metals. Generalizations about social groups and societies appear in social studies (e.g., there is a division of labor in functioning communities, industrialization raises the standard of living). Students make generalizations about people as they read stories, poems, and novels in language arts. In art, generalizations students learn about materials guide their use (clay can be shaped by the pressure of our fingers but retains its shape if left undisturbed). That bats, baseballs, footballs, and basketballs behave in certain ways is the basis for decisions that students continually make in playing sports.

There are two types of contexts in the curriculum in which students can become engaged with generalizations:

- *Generalizations others have made are presented directly to students.* For example, in science students are told the properties of certain materials, e.g., metals. They also read fiction in which the characters make certain generalizations.

- *Students are asked to make their own generalizations based on information provided or that they gather.* For example, many hands-on science activities involve students in situations in which they are asked to draw general conclusions from their own observations. Student writing, based on studies in history or the reading of a work of literature, often feature generalizations that are supported by the details of what they are studying.

Planning a research project is a particularly useful way to help students develop skill at generalization. In the primary grades, they can gather information about objects in the classroom. The project can involve gathering data to test a generalization that someone else has made, to test one that they develop, or to provide data from which generalizations might be suggested.

In the upper elementary grades, students may develop a profile of the likes and dislikes of the student body. They may design a questionnaire that provides them with information on which they can draw general conclusions. If you help them determine how many and which students to sample, you will be helping them with skillful generalization. This activity can either be an initial lesson or be used to reinforce the skill after you introduce it in a more standard curricular context.

A menu of suggested contexts for infusion lessons on generalization is provided on pp. 454–55.

Model Lesson on Skillful Generalization

The model lesson on generalization is a grade 3–4 science lesson on static electricity in which students make generalizations and then critique them based on the need for a good sample. In this lesson, students themselves develop the standards for a good sample.

As you read this lesson, consider the following focus questions:

- How can this lesson be a vehicle for explicit instruction in scientific methodology?
- What other examples can reinforce instruction in skillful generalization?

Tools for Designing Lessons on Generalization

The thinking map and graphic organizer for skillful generalization guide students in their evaluation of a suggested generalization.

The thinking maps and graphic organizers can guide you in designing the critical thinking activity in the lesson and can also serve as photocopy masters, transparency masters, or as models that can be enlarged and used as posters in the classroom. Reproduction rights are granted for single classroom use only.

SKILLFUL GENERALIZATION

1. What generalization is suggested?

2. What sample is needed to support that generalization?

3. Is the sample being used large enough?

4. Is the sample being used like the whole group?

5 Is the generalization well supported by the sample?

6. If not, what additional information is needed to support the generalization?

SKILLFUL GENERALIZATION

GENERALIZATION

DESCRIBE A SAMPLE THAT WOULD SUPPORT THIS GENERALIZATION.

DESCRIBE THE SAMPLE USED.

RESULTS SHOWN BY THE SAMPLE

SAMPLE SIZE		SAMPLE SELECTION		THIS GENERALIZATION	
SMALL	☐	IT IS LIKE	☐	IS SUPPORTED: √	☐
MEDIUM	☐	OR UNLIKE	☐	IS UNCERTAIN: ?	☐
LARGE	☐	THE WHOLE GROUP.		IS BIASED: X	☐

IF THIS SAMPLE IS NOT ADEQUATE TO SUPPORT THE GENERALIZATION, EXPLAIN WHY. HOW SHOULD IT BE DIFFERENT?

STATIC CLING

Science   **Grades 3–4**

OBJECTIVES

CONTENT

Students will generate static electricity by rubbing certain objects together and will apply the concepts of positive and negative electrical charges.

THINKING SKILL/PROCESS

Students will learn to base generalizations on an adequate number of representative samples.

METHODS AND MATERIALS

CONTENT

Students will read text explanations of static electricity. Students will generate static electricity by rubbing balloons on wool fabric. Each group will need balloons and fabric samples.

THINKING SKILL/PROCESS

An explicit thinking map, graphic organizers, and structured questioning emphasize a thinking strategy for well-founded generalization. (See pp. 447–48 for reproducible diagrams.) Collaborative learning enhances the thinking.

LESSON

INTRODUCTION TO CONTENT AND THINKING SKILL/PROCESS

- When I was shopping at a market, I noticed a sign above the grapes: *These Grapes Are Delicious: Sample a Few Before You Buy Them.* **So I tasted one that was on the top. It was sweet and seedless. I decided that all the grapes would be tasty, so I bought some. Do you think that was a good way to decide that they all were tasty?** While some students say that this is a good way to decide, most say that one grape isn't enough ("Maybe you tasted the one good grape.") and that one from the top is from only one place ("Maybe the grocer put the sweet ones on the top."). **If you think this isn't a good way, work with a partner and figure out a better way to decide.** After a few minutes, ask for two or three of the plans. POSSIBLE ANSWERS INCLUDE: *Try about five grapes. Pick them from different places in the bin. Make sure you try some from underneath, and from the back. Don't eat them all from one bunch: make sure you try a grape from a lot of bunches.*

- **What you've been doing is planning how to make a good *generalization*. A generalization is a statement that begins with an "all" and says that something is true of all things of a certain sort. "All the grapes in the bin are tasty" is the generalization we've been discussing. With your partner, list three more generalizations that you think you know.** Write six to ten of these on the board as the groups respond. POSSIBLE ANSWERS: *All the students in this school are nice. All the people in this country are Americans. All heavy objects sink in water. All candy is sweet. All water is wet.*

- **When deciding whether a generalization is one you should accept, you usually can't look at every individual. It would probably not be possible to find out about every person in this country before you could say whether or not they were all Americans. Usually we base our generalizations on a smaller *sample*, like the grape that I tasted. In order to generalize about all of the things in the group, like all of the grapes, you suggested the kind of sample needed. Let's review what you said about the kind of grape sample required.** ANSWERS: *You need more grapes and from different bunches and locations so that you get a better idea that the ones you tasted were like all of them.*

- What ideas about samples should we think about whenever we need to make a generalization? POSSIBLE ANSWERS: *A sample should not be too small, and it should be like the whole group, or from many parts of the whole group.* To be sure that our generalizations are based on a good sample, let's use these ideas for a thinking map of skillful generalization.

SKILLFUL GENERALIZATION

1. What generalization is suggested?

2. What sample is needed to support that generalization?

3. Is the sample being used large enough?

4. Is the sample being used like the whole group?

5 Is the generalization well supported by the sample?

6. If not, what additional information is needed to support the generalization?

- We make generalizations in science based on studying a sample of things. For example, if we've studied turtles and list things that we learned, some of you might write that turtles have shells, that they travel slowly, and that they lay eggs. These are generalizations. They are about all turtles. We're also studying electricity. We're going to conduct an experiment and see what generalizations we can make about electricity based on the experiment.

THINKING ACTIVELY

- I'm going to do an experiment with this balloon. Watch what happens when I rub this balloon against this cloth. Rub the balloon on the wool fabric and then put it against the wall. What do you see? *The balloon clings to the wall.* Let me do the same thing with another balloon. What do you think will happen? *The balloon will stick to the wall.* Let's see. Pick a balloon of a different shape and color and rub the balloon on your wool fabric. Put it on the wall next to the first balloon. You were right. Now let me try a third balloon. Pick another balloon of a different shape and color and do the same thing.

- To try to figure out why these balloons stick to the wall, it may be helpful to look at other examples of the effects of rubbing things. What happens when you put a comb through long hair? Why? *Because when you move the comb through the hair, the hair rubs against the comb, creating friction.* Watch what happens when I put the comb over little bits of paper. What happens? Why? *The bits of paper move toward the comb. Friction with the hair produces an electrical charge. The comb becomes charged like one of the ends of a magnet. This small charge changes the neutral charge in small pieces of paper just enough so that the paper is attracted to the opposite charge in the comb.*

- If the small electrical charge on the comb is negative, then the paper will display a positive charge. Negative and positive charges attract. Positive and positive charges repel, as do negative and negative charges. Demonstrate these points with a comb and small pieces of paper and with two magnets. Draw a diagram in which you use a "+" and a "-" to indicate the charges. Then draw a diagram of what happens when the balloon stuck to the wall. The friction caused by the fabric on the balloon produces a negative charge that is attracted to the positive charge on the wall.

- Here are a lot of balloons. Based on what you learned, try to make these balloons stick to one of the walls of the classroom. The students will rub the balloons on their clothing. When they do this, some balloons will stick, others will not. Some will stick, but soon fall off.

- What happened? *Most of the balloons didn't stick.* Why did you think that the balloons would stick? What generalization did you make? On a transparency of the graphic organizer (shown on the next page), write this generalization in the dome of the diagram. POSSIBLE ANSWER: *Any time you rub a balloon on cloth, it will stick to the wall.* What was the sample that made us believe

that generalization? *The class demonstration in which three balloons were rubbed on wool fabric. Write that in the sample box on the diagram.*

- **With your partner, discuss two questions to decide whether it was a good sample: Was the sample large enough? Was the class experiment similar to all others in which you might rub a balloon with cloth?** After a few minutes ask the groups to report. Most students say that the sample was not a good sample. **Was the sample large enough?** POSSIBLE ANSWERS: *Three balloons may be too small a sample. There wasn't any difference in the sizes of balloons that did cling and those that didn't, so the size of the balloons didn't seem to matter. Three tries with the same cloth may not be enough to generalize about all types of cloth.* Mark "small" on the graphic organizer. **Was the class experiment similar to all others in which you might rub a balloon with cloth?** *When the balloons did cling, you rubbed them all on the same thing, the wool fabric. Maybe other pieces of cloth don't affect the balloon the way the wool fabric does. To generalize, maybe we need a lot of different pieces of clothing.* Mark "unlike" on the graphic organizer. In the box at the bottom, write "The balloon was rubbed only on the wool fabric. Rubbing the balloon on another fabric might not make it cling to the wall. "

- **If the sample was not adequate, how should it be different?** ANSWERS VARY. A typical answer student is, *The sample should be different by rubbing the balloons on different kinds of cloth fabrics. Perhaps the balloons should also be rubbed at different speeds.*

- **With your partner, develop a plan for testing balloons and pieces of cloth so that you can make some good generalizations regarding when they will or will not cling. Then use your plan to get information, and make a generalization you think is well-supported. Fill in a blank generalization graphic to show your generalization, what your sample was, and why you think it was a good sample.** Students' work varies. Review their plans with each team and coach them on what information they might get to support their proposed generalization. Provide several pieces of fabric and balloons for them to work with. Discuss the results with the class. They usually support the idea that static electricity through friction is only generated by certain sorts of natural fabrics, e.g., wool and silk. Write the well-supported generalizations on the board. Display the graphic organizers on the wall of the classroom.

THINKING ABOUT THINKING

- **What do we call the kind of thinking we just did?** *Generalization.*

- **What questions did we ask as we did this kind of thinking?** Students should mention the questions on the thinking map for skillful generalization. If they are having trouble, point to some of the questions and ask if each was considered. Students identify the following questions: *What is the generalization that is being considered? What is the sample? Is the sample large enough? Is it like the whole group (representative of the whole group)?*

- **Is it a good idea to support generalizations in this way? Why or why not?** POSSIBLE ANSWERS: *If you can't test all of the things the generalization is about, then you have to use a sample. The generalization could be wrong if the sample is too small or unlike the group as a whole. If we make sure that the sample is a good one, we will probably make a good generalization.*

- In the lesson, we did not think about the kind of sample that would be needed to support the generalization until after we had decided that the sample we used was not a good one. Is this the best time to think about what kind of sample would be a good sample? If so why? If not, why not? Most students respond that it is better to think about this question before taking the sample so that we can avoid making mistakes in relying upon too small or nonrepresentative a sample, like we did in the balloon example.

- What advice would you give a friend about making good generalizations? Would you advise your friend to use the diagram we used? Why? If you think the diagram is a good idea, how would you advise your friend to use it? ANSWERS VARY.

APPLYING YOUR THINKING

IMMEDIATE TRANSFER

- School elections come up every year. Suppose you had to predict for whom the majority of students in the school would vote but couldn't ask every student. Design a way of getting information that would allow you to generalize from your sample.

- When we were studying the planets in the solar system, we learned where they were, their size, etc. What generalizations can you make about planets from your study of our solar system?

REINFORCEMENT LATER

- Draw a picture of a Native American family as they lived in the 1800s. Compare your drawings with others in the class. What are the objects and customs pictured by students in your class? Now compare your drawings with pictures of five different tribes from different parts of the country in the 1800s. Were your drawings good samples of what Native Americans were like? Why or why not? If your drawings were not good samples, what additional information would you need and how could you get it?

- List some school rules. What generalizations can you make about the purposes of these rules?

CONTENT EXTENSION

Relate principles of static electricity to how lightening works. (There's a strong negative charge in thick clouds. The ground is charged positively, so a giant spark jumps to the ground from the clouds.) Draw a diagram explaining what happens in a lightning storm when the lightning hits something. Use pluses and minuses to show the charges. Relate these principles to the danger involved in Ben Franklin's kite experiment.

ASSESSING STUDENT THINKING ABOUT GENERALIZATION

Ask students to select one of the generalizations that they thought was true at the beginning of the lesson. They should write or discuss with a partner whether the generalization was based on a good sample. If not, what would one do to get a good sample? As they try to solve the problems, confirm that in their writing or discussions the students are raising the questions on the thinking map.

Sample Student Responses: Static Cling

SKILLFUL GENERALIZATION

GENERALIZATION

Any time you rub a balloon against cloth, the static electricity will make the balloon stick to the wall.

DESCRIBE A SAMPLE THAT WOULD SUPPORT THIS GENERALIZATION.

In this particular lesson, this matter is deferred until after students have discussed the sample used so that students can figure out why the sample was not adequate and then construct a better one based on their critique of the sample.

DESCRIBE THE SAMPLE USED.

Several sizes and colors of balloons rubbed on wool fabric.

RESULTS SHOWN BY THE SAMPLE

Three balloons of different colors and sizes stuck to the wall when rubbed on wool fabric.

SAMPLE SIZE		SAMPLE SELECTION		THIS GENERALIZATION	
SMALL	☑	IT IS LIKE	☐	IS SUPPORTED: √	☐
MEDIUM	☐	OR UNLIKE	☑	IS UNCERTAIN: ?	☐
LARGE	☐	THE WHOLE GROUP.		IS BIASED: X	☒

IF THIS SAMPLE IS NOT ADEQUATE TO SUPPORT THE GENERALIZATION, EXPLAIN WHY. HOW SHOULD IT BE DIFFERENT?

The balloon was rubbed only on the wool fabric. Rubbing the balloon on another fabric might not make it cling to the wall. The sample should be different by rubbing the balloons on different kinds of cloth fabrics. Perhaps the balloons should also be rubbed at different speeds.

LESSON CONTEXTS FOR GENERALIZATION

The following examples have been suggested by classroom teachers as contexts to develop infused lessons. If a skill or process has been introduced in a previous infused lesson, these contexts may be used to reinforce it.

GRADE	SUBJECT	TOPIC	THINKING ISSUE
K–3	Literature	Animals in Fairy Tales	List some animals that appear in fairy tales. Name the characteristics that the stories suggest about these animals. (Wolves- mean or predators; spiders- smart and creative; rabbits- quick and clever; snakes- evil, etc.) Are these generalizations based on good support? What else could you do to find out about these animals to decide whether the generalizations are good ones?
K–3	Literature	*I Had Trouble in Getting to Solla Sollew*	Based on his experiences in getting to Solla Sollew, what generalization does the main character make about finding places where there are few, if any, troubles?
K–3	Social studies	Behavior	Suppose someone visited your school, saw some students running and making noise, and then told people that all of the students at your school were noisy and ill-behaved. How would you convince him that his generalization was not based on good support?
K–3	Social studies	Rules	List twenty school rules. Ask students to write some generalizations about the purpose of school rules and how they are made.
K–3	Mathematics	Rectangles	Ask students to check several squares to confirm whether or not all squares are rectangles. How many squares would you need to check to accept that generalization?
K–3	Science	Mass and volume	If a student weighs several items that are about the same size and finds out that they weigh about the same, should he accept the generalization that things that are the same size generally have the same weight?
K–3	Science	Running	Categorize the following animals by speed (fast runners, slow movers): turtle, inchworm, alligator, snail, cheetah, deer, ostrich, horse. Identify characteristics that may explain their speed. Assess the generalization that animals with the longest legs compared to its body size are usually the fastest runners.
2–4	Science	Planets	How are the planets near the sun alike? (Made of rock, smaller, few or no moons). How are the planets away from the sun alike? (Made of frozen gases, larger than earth, some have more than a dozen moons). What might we generalize about the effect of distance from the sun?
K–3	Art	Warm and cool colors	What colors seem to have a cool effect? What other effects do these colors seem to show? Find other cool colors in pictures. Can you expect that cool colors will usually have these same effects? Is your generalization well-supported? Why?
4–6	Language arts	Selecting books	If you have read a book that you liked, can you generalize that you will like others by the same author? What additional information, if any, would you need to make this generalization?
4–6	Literature	*Maniac McGee*	What generalization does Grayson suggest about black families? Was his generalization well supported? What doubt do Maniac's comments raise in Grayson's mind?

LESSON CONTEXTS FOR GENERALIZATION

GRADE	SUBJECT	TOPIC	THINKING ISSUE
4–6	Social Studies	American Indians	Draw a picture of a Native American family as they lived in the 1800's. Compare your drawing with those of other students in your class. Do many students draw the same objects or customs? Now compare your pictures with pictures of northwestern tribes, Navajo tribes, and Iroquois. What differences do you find? On what samples of Indian culture did you base your view of Native American tribes? Are these good samples on which to base generalizations? Why or why not?
4–6	Social Studies	Gender roles	Identify generalizations that have been made about men and women. How can you determine whether or not these are good generalizations? Do you have any information that supports or counts against these generalizations? Explain.
4–6	Mathematics	Probability	What is the probability of rolling a "one" when throwing a single die? (One in six) How many throws do you need to make to confirm that probability?
4–6	Science	Revolution and rotation	Is the generalization that all planets, moons, and asteroids revolve around another body a well-supported generalization? Explain. Do all planets, moons, and asteroids rotate on an axis? Is that a well-supported generalization? Explain.
4–6	Science	Galaxies	Many "stars" seen at night are really galaxies containing millions of stars. Consider the generalization that all of the "stars" we see at night are really galaxies. What would be wrong with this generalization if it was based on pictures of a dozen galaxies that look like stars at night?
4–6	Science	Animals	Suppose that you were observing the behavior of humpback whales so that you could learn something about their food and migration patterns. Sketch out how you would conduct this observation so that you would have enough data to make some well-supported generalizations.
4–6	Science	Reproduction	Fish may produce millions of eggs; mammals often produce only one or a few eggs at a time. What generalization might you draw from that? How might you confirm it?
4–6	Health	Smoking	"Smoking is hazardous to your health" is a warning that cigarette manufacturers have to put on their cigarette packages. Is this warning a generalization? What would it have to be based on to be well supported?
4–6	Health	Medication	If a child weighs one fourth what an adult does, should the child get one fourth of the adult dosage of medication? Explain what generalization you would be making if you thought so. Is that a good generalization?
4–6	Art	Styles	Many artists create natural scenes rather than abstract pictures. Some people think that only realistic pictures can be works of art. Is this a well-supported generalization? Explain.
4–6	Music	Classical Music	Suppose that, when you tell a friend that you are going to a classical music concert, she says, "Ugh, all classical music concerts are boring!" What questions would you ask her in order to help her determine whether her generalization is well founded?

CHAPTER 16
REASONING BY ANALOGY

Why is There a Need for Skillful Reasoning by Analogy?

We sometimes raise questions about familiar things that we can't answer. For example, I may wonder how computer programs work, but I don't know enough about them to understand the technical language involved in answering this question. I could take the time to find out directly by taking a computer course. Sometimes, however, an analogy helps us learn more quickly. Someone may suggest that using a computer program is like using a code. If I know about codes, I can use this knowledge to understand how computer programs work.

When we note that two different kinds of things are alike in various ways, we draw an analogy between them. If, on the basis of that analogy, we think that what we know about one thing is also true of the other, we are *reasoning by analogy*.

Uses of Reasoning by Analogy

People appeal to analogies to justify drawing various conclusions about one thing based on its similarity to another. For example, many draw an analogy between the president of the United States and the captain of a ship. This comparison creates an image of leadership and authority. Most of us learned about atoms by using the analogy of the solar system. This comparison creates the image of powerful forces binding the atom together into a single system of particles revolving around a nucleus. More recently, the Persian Gulf War was compared to World War II in that one country was invaded by another. On the basis of this analogy, it was argued that our intervention was justified.

A special case of reasoning by analogy may arise if we have a question about something, and finding an answer directly would be risky. Can a bridge withstand extreme stress? How do humans react if they eat only a certain diet? If these issues can't be determined by conducting research directly with the bridge or with hu-

mans because of the risks involved, research using something analogous may help. Engineers may simulate the stresses on the bridge with a model. Researchers might try the diet on an animal.

Other Uses of Analogies That Do Not Involve Reasoning by Analogy

Recognizing that two things are analogous can serve other purposes besides allowing us to form conclusions about one thing based on our knowledge of another. Analogy is the basis for similes, metaphors, and personifications. When Shakespeare said, "My love is like a red, red, rose," he meant to highlight certain characteristics that his love exhibits that are also manifested in a beautiful rose. The speaker is not drawing or affirming a conclusion about his love based on the analogy. Rather, the analogy communicates the author's perception that his beloved is lovely, soft, and fragile. In using analogous objects metaphorically, we highlight the characteristics that the two objects have in common; in analogical reasoning, we infer something new about one of the objects based on the fact that they have characteristics in common.

Problems with the Way We Use Analogical Reasoning

The problem with reasoning from simple analogies, like comparing guinea pigs to human beings, the president to the captain of a ship, or the Persian Gulf War to World War II, is that sometimes they mislead us into drawing incorrect conclusions. The analogy between the president and the captain of a ship may mislead one to expect that the president is the sole authority in this country. This is a mistake: the congress and the judiciary put constraints on absolute presidential power.

When we don't think critically about using analogies to draw such conclusions, the mere fact that the two items compared are alike may be enough for us. Yet often, as in the case of the power of the president, the similarities are superficial and not strong enough to support analogical reasoning.

Comparing the Persian Gulf War to World War II in order to justify our fighting against Iraq presents a different problem. These wars were, indeed, similar in significant ways. There was an important difference between them, however. In World War II, the United States was attacked by the Japanese. In the Persian Gulf War, Kuwait was attacked by Iraq. This difference is crucial and makes the analogy a poor one to use in supporting the intervention of the United States. This is, of course, not to say that there aren't better analogies or reasons to justify such intervention.

Figure 16.1 contains a summary of the two main problems that lead to faulty analogical reasoning.

**COMMON DEFAULTS IN
REASONING BY ANALOGY**

1. We note that two things are alike but don't ask whether they are enough alike to support the conclusion we wish to draw.

2. We note that two things are alike but don't ask whether there are differences between them that weigh against drawing the conclusion we wish to draw.

Figure 16.1

Analogical reasoning in which these questions are not asked is tenuous and incomplete.

What Does Skillful Reasoning by Analogy Involve?

Skillful reasoning by analogy involves initially searching for things that are similar to what we are trying to understand. Then we must decide whether any of these similar things yield good analogies. Even if someone else suggests an analogy, we still have to determine whether it is a good analogy for our purposes.

To decide whether we can use a suggested analogy, *we must first determine how the two things are alike and whether their similarities are significant.* The likenesses may be too superficial to

extend what we know about one to the other. I may wonder which of the following is a good analogy to help students understand how blood carries nutrients to various parts of the body: a conveyor belt, water in a pipe, or the postal service. The postal service is similar in that its members carry things around, but there are no deeper similarities between the two. Water in a pipe seems to be more analogous to the blood in the body. Both are liquid, move in tubular enclosed vessels, and carry substances that are dissolved. This image is clearly better for helping students understand how the blood provides nourishment to the body.

When we ascertain that two things are significantly alike, we usually describe them as analogous. *Determining whether there are any significant differences between analogous objects is the next important step in skillful reasoning by analogy.* The similarities between humans and guinea pigs are not superficial. Similarities in body functioning are significant. But we should not draw conclusions about humans from studies of guinea pigs on the basis of similarities alone. There may be basic differences between guinea pigs and humans that weigh against drawing these conclusions. Not every difference is important, however. But some may be. For example, we may find that guinea pigs are genetically different from humans in their ability to fight certain diseases. However similar they are, this difference would be quite significant in determining whether the analogy supports drawing conclusions about the risk of disease for humans because certain substances cause disease in guinea pigs.

There are two ways to try to find out whether significant differences between the things compared make drawing a specific conclusion tenuous. First, we may list as many of the differences as we can discover and then ask whether any are significant. When we compare guinea pigs and humans, we find, of course, that there are many differences. None of the differences, however, may be known to block in guinea pigs the effects of an experimental drug being developed for humans. In that case, the conclusion that if the drug is effective in guinea pigs, it will work in humans is supported by the analogy because differences that would interfere are not known to exist.

The second strategy is to identify what factors would block the effectiveness of the treatment and find out whether humans and guinea pigs function alike regarding that factor. If we find no such differences between guinea pigs and humans, we can reasonably extend to humans similar effects to those found in guinea pigs.

Both strategies for evaluating differences should be used in a careful application of reasoning by analogy. This will assure thoroughness in this type of thinking and will counter the tendency we have to ignore differences or treat them as unimportant.

A Thinking Map and a Graphic Organizer for Skillful Reasoning by Analogy

The thinking map in figure 16.2 can be used to guide us through skillful reasoning by analogy. Note how it begins by having students generate analogies and then has students use the analogies to support conclusions. The corresponding graphic organizer for reasoning by analogy is shown in figure 16.3.

In using the graphic organizer in figure 16.3, we should, of course, make explicit the basis for the analogy by writing the significant similarities at the top. Then we make explicit potential conclusions that might be drawn from this analogy by indicating information we have about the second item that we think might be true of the first. This can guide us in searching for significant differences. The two strategies for finding significant differences will make this a thorough search. We should write any significant differences we find in the spaces provided for differences. Finally, we reaffirm the tentative conclusion in the box at the bottom if there are no significant differences. If there are significant differences, we should write "None" in the box at the bottom.

How Forceful is Reasoning by Analogy?

We may develop a line of analogical reasoning fairly quickly by using information that we already have about one thing to suggest an-

REASONING BY ANALOGY

1. What things are similar to the object or idea that you are trying to understand?

2. Which are similar in significant ways?

3. What do you know about these things that you don't know about the thing you are trying to understand?

4. Are there any differences between the two that could affect whether what you are trying to understand has these features?

5. What can you conclude regarding what you are trying to understand based on this analogy?

Figure 16.2

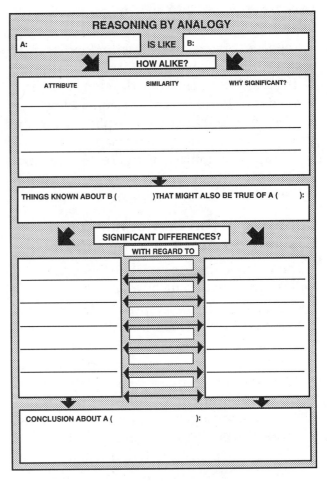

Figure 16.3

swers to the questions we have about another. We should be cautious about reasoning by analogy, however, even if it is conducted skillfully. At most, the conclusions we draw using this kind of reasoning are supported only by indirect evidence. They are at best well-supported suggestions that should never substitute for getting the information we need to answer our questions more directly.

How Can We Teach Skillful Reasoning by Analogy?

In teaching reasoning by analogy, it is not enough to ask students to draw analogies between something they are studying and something they already know. This stops short of *reasoning* by analogy. They should also be asked to note why the two items are analogous, what conclusions or insights they might draw about one from their knowledge of the other, and whether there are significant differences between the two things that might make such inferences problematic.

Repeated practice using this thinking strategy with a variety of analogies will reinforce the use of this skill. Students can develop their own analogies or critique analogies offered by others. Make sure that you are explicit about the strategy by using the thinking map in figure 16.2 and graphic organizer in figure 16.3. Prompt students to reflect on the strategy and use it deliberately when appropriate.

Contexts in the Curriculum for Lessons on Reasoning by Analogy

There are two main contexts in the curriculum for lessons in reasoning by analogy:

- *Explicit analogies are used to help students understand important concepts or ideas.* For example, in science, the atom is often compared to the solar system, electricity to water flowing through a pipe, and the human body to a machine. In history and social studies, analogies are drawn between historical events ("Gettysburg was the South's Waterloo"), historical figures and social roles ("the founding fathers"), and different social phenomena ("Your school rules are like the U. S Constitution.").

- *Students are asked to construct analogies, simulations, or models to help them understand important concepts and ideas.* For example, in science, students construct models to understand the structure of molecules. Social studies concepts are often simulated in school when students set up a store in their classroom. In history, students can be asked to compare the exploration of space to analogous events in our history, like the pioneers' movement west in the 1800s, in order to draw insight from this analogy about the prospects of future colonization of the planets. In science, students are sometimes guided to draw analogies between the way white blood cells work and how protective devices used in industry operate.

A menu of suggested contexts for infusion lessons on reasoning by analogy is provided on pp. 478–80.

Reasoning by Analogy in the Primary Grades

Students in the primary grades have little difficulty thinking of analogies once they recognize that similarities between two things makes them analogous. Introduce them to the word "analogy" in this way. Pictures of analogous objects can also help them to recognize why they are analogous.

Once students in the primary grades understand what an analogy is, you can help them with analogical reasoning. It is sufficient to work with them on determining what the analogy suggests that might be true about the first item. They can learn the more sophisticated strategy for assessing whether the analogy supports drawing this conclusion as they move into grades 3-6. Figure 16.4 is a simplified thinking map for the primary grades.

REASONING BY ANALOGY

1. What is similar to the object?

2. How are they similar?

3. What do you know about the second object that might be true of the first?

Figure 16.4

The graphic organizer for analogical reasoning in the primary grades is a modified version of the basic diagram in figure 16.3. It is represented in figure 16.5.

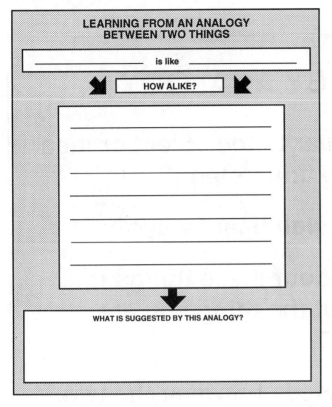

LEARNING FROM AN ANALOGY BETWEEN TWO THINGS

_____ is like _____

HOW ALIKE?

WHAT IS SUGGESTED BY THIS ANALOGY?

Figure 16.5

Model Lessons on Reasoning by Analogy

There are two lessons on reasoning by analogy included in this booklet. A language arts lesson for grades 2–4 based on a passage from *Charlotte's Web* involves analogies between animals and people that are relevant to how we treat animals. The second lesson is an upper-elementary/middle school science/social studies lesson on ocean farming in which students develop analogies and determine what conclusions they can derive from them about methods of cultivating and harvesting food from the sea. The following questions can be helpful as you read these lessons:

- How is reasoning by analogy different from simply comparing and contrasting two things?

- Are there alternative ways of introducing the thinking skill in the lesson introduction?

- What additional examples are there for reinforcing this skill?

Tools for Designing Lessons on Reasoning by Analogy

We include the basic thinking map for reasoning by analogy (p. 462), a modified thinking map for the primary grades (p. 463), and two graphic organizers for teaching this skill.

The first graphic organizer (p. 464) is used in the primary grades. It focuses on finding analogies and drawing out suggested conclusions. The second (p. 465) is for full-blown reasoning by analogy in which students explore differences to see whether or not they weaken the conclusion.

The thinking maps and graphic organizers can guide you in designing the critical thinking activity in the lesson and can also serve as photocopy masters, transparency masters, or as models that can be enlarged and used as posters in the classroom. Reproduction rights are granted for single classroom use only.

REASONING BY ANALOGY

1. **What things are similar to the object or idea that you are trying to understand?**

2. **Which are similar in significant ways?**

3. **What do you know about these things that you don't know about the thing you are trying to understand?**

4. **Are there any differences between the two that could affect whether what you are trying to understand has these features?**

5. **What can you conclude regarding what you are trying to understand based on this analogy?**

REASONING BY ANALOGY

1. **What is similar to the object?**

2. **How are they similar?**

3. **What do you know about the second object that might be true of the first?**

LEARNING FROM AN ANALOGY
BETWEEN TWO THINGS

_____ is like _____

HOW ALIKE?

_____

_____

_____

_____

_____

_____

_____

WHAT IS SUGGESTED BY THIS ANALOGY?

REASONING BY ANALOGY

A: **IS LIKE**   **B:**

HOW ALIKE?

ATTRIBUTE	SIMILARITY	WHY SIGNIFICANT?

THINGS KNOWN ABOUT B (   ) THAT MIGHT ALSO BE TRUE OF A (   ):

SIGNIFICANT DIFFERENCES?

WITH REGARD TO

CONCLUSION ABOUT A (   ):

©1994 CRITICAL THINKING PRESS & SOFTWARE • P.O. BOX 448 • PACIFIC GROVE, CA 93950 • 800-458-4849

PIGS AND PEOPLE

Language Arts   **Grades 2–4**

OBJECTIVES

CONTENT

Students will learn that personification is a literary device used in works of fiction. They will also clarify different points of view about the status of animals.

THINKING SKILL/PROCESS

Students will learn what an analogy is, how to specify the ways in which analogous things are similar, and to determine whether ideas suggested by the analogy are accurate by noting whether there are important differences.

METHODS AND MATERIALS

CONTENT

Students will read part of *Charlotte's Web.* They will work in collaborative learning groups to share information from the story and record it on a graphic organizer.

THINKING SKILL/PROCESS

Structured questioning, the use of a graphic organizer, and a thinking map guide students through reasoning by analogy. (See pp. 462–65 for reproducible diagrams.) Students also work in collaborative learning groups.

LESSON

INTRODUCTION TO CONTENT AND THINKING SKILL/PROCESS

• **How is reading a book like listening to someone talk to you? Think of some ways they are alike and discuss them with your partner. See if you can come up with at least four ways.** Ask each group to report. Write their responses on the board on the following diagram: POSSIBLE ANSWERS: *Books use words and so do people who talk to you. Words in books make you think of things they are about; so do words people use when speaking. Books are written by people who use them to tell you their ideas; listening to people lets you know their ideas.*

• **When two things are alike in important ways, we say that there is an analogy between them. We make analogies by comparing things. There is an analogy between reading a book and listening to someone talk. See if you can think of things that are analogous to one of the following: watching TV, going to a restaurant, going to school. Use a blank diagram for learning from an analogy to list the ways in which the two are alike.** ANSWERS VARY.

• **Sometimes you can learn more about something by using analogy to compare it to something else. For example, think about the analogy between reading a book and listening to someone tell you something. Though you usually wouldn't think of asking questions**

LEARNING FROM AN ANALOGY
BETWEEN TWO THINGS

Reading a book _____ **is like** ____ listening to someone talk.

HOW ALIKE?

WHAT IS SUGGESTED BY THIS ANALOGY?

when reading a book, you know that, when listening to someone, you can ask them questions. From the analogy, you might get the idea to ask the author for more information about the book. When you find out something new because of an analogy you make, that's called reasoning by analogy. Can you think of other things that you can learn about reading a book from this analogy? What is suggested by the analogy?

• We have to be careful in using reasoning by analogy. Sometimes there are important differences between the two things that make it wrong to accept something about one based on its analogy to another. You may think that because reading a book takes a long time (days or many hours) listening to someone talk will also take a long time. However, there is a big difference between a book and a talk. Books usually contain much more information than a person can say in one conversation. This difference shows that one idea suggested by the analogy is not a good one. It's always important to find out if there are important differences before you accept the suggestions made by an analogy.

THINKING ACTIVELY

• I'm going to read the beginning of *Charlotte's Web* by E. B. White. Listen for analogies that are used to draw conclusions.

"Where is Papa going with that ax?" said Fern to her mother as they were setting the table for breakfast.

"Out to the hoghouse," replied Mrs. Arable. "Some pigs were born last night."

"I don't see why he needs an ax," continued Fern, who was only eight.

"Well," said her mother, "one of the pigs is a runt. It's very small and weak, and it will never amount to anything. So your father has decided to do away with it."

"Do away with it?" shrieked Fern. "You mean kill it? Just because it's smaller than the others?"

Mrs. Arable put a pitcher of cream on the table. "Don't yell, Fern!" she said. "Your father is right. The pig would probably die anyway."

Fern pushed a chair out of the way and ran outdoors. The grass was wet and the earth smelled of springtime. Fern's sneakers were sopping by the time she caught up with her father.

"Please don't kill it," she sobbed. "It's unfair."

Mr. Arable stopped walking.

"Fern," he said gently, "you will have to learn to control yourself."

"Control myself?" yelled Fern. "This is a matter of life and death, and you talk about controlling myself." Tears ran down her cheeks and she took hold of the ax and tried to pull it out of her father's hand.

"Fern," said Mr. Arable, "I know more about raising a litter of pigs than you do. A weakling makes trouble. Now run along!"

"But it's unfair," cried Fern. "The pig couldn't help being born small, could it? If I had been very small at birth, would you have killed me?"

Mr. Arable smiled. "Certainly not," he said, looking down at his daughter with love. "But this is different. A little girl is one thing, a runty pig is another." "I see no difference," replied Fern, still hanging onto the ax. "This is the most terrible case of injustice I have ever heard of."

• **What analogy does Fern use to draw a conclusion about the runt pig?** *Fern compares the runt pig* *to herself.* **Write "Runt pigs are like little girls" at the top of this diagram for reasoning by analogy.** The diagram is shown at the right.

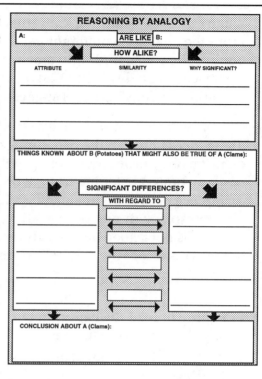

- **What conclusion does Fern draw based on this analogy?** *It's unfair to kill the runt pig just because it was born small.* **Write this in the box at the bottom of the diagram.**

- **What would you expect that Fern has observed about runt pigs that they have in common with little girls like her? For example, they look alike: both have bodies, legs, heads, eyes, and ears. Write "Both have bodies, legs, heads, eyes, and ears" under "How Alike" on the diagram. In what other ways are Fern and the runt pig alike? Write these similarities in the box.** Ask the class to respond, but for each student to mention only one similarity. Call on as many different students as you can. Write the responses on a graphic organizer on the chalkboard or on a transparency. POSSIBLE ANSWERS: *Mothers gave birth to them. Their mothers feed them when they are young. They are both living things. They both can see, hear smell, taste, and feel. Both can feel pain. They can't help their size at birth. People care about them and value them.*

- **What does Fern believe about little girls that might be true about the runt pig?** *It isn't fair to kill a little girl just because she was born small.* **Write this in the box below the similarities on the diagram.**

- **What important difference does Fern see between a pig and a little girl?** *Fern believes that there are no important differences between a runt pig and a little girl.* **Write "No important differences" in the first set of difference boxes.**

- **How does the analogy help her draw this conclusion?** ANSWER: *Because Fern doesn't believe that there are differences and because she thinks it is unjust to kill a little girl just because she was born small, she believes that it is unjust to kill the pig because it was born small.*

- **Now let's look at what Mr. Arable thinks about Fern's analogy between little girls and runt pigs. Use another diagram for Mr. Arable's reasoning and write "Runt Pigs" in box A and "Little Girls" in box B.** Draw a new graphic organizer on the chalkboard (or on a transparency) and also write "Runt Pigs" and "Little Girls" in the boxes at the top. **Would Mr. Arable agree with Fern about what she and the runt pig have in common? For example, would he agree that both have bodies, heads, legs, eyes, and ears?** *Yes.* **Write "Both have bodies, legs, heads, eyes, and ears under "How Alike" on the diagram.** Do the same on the diagram on the board. **What other similarities from Fern's diagram do you think he would also agree with? Write these similarities in the box on the diagram for Mr. Arable's analogy.** Students usually agree that all of the similarities on the diagram for Fern's analogy should be put on the graphic organizer for Mr. Arable's analogy. **Would he also agree that it isn't fair to kill little girls just because they were born small?** *Yes.* **Why? Because he says "Certainly not" when Fern asks if he would kill her if she was born small. Write "It isn't fair to kill little girls just because they were born small" in the box below the similarities on the new diagram.** Also write this on the graphic organizer for Mr. Arable that you have drawn on the chalkboard.

- **Does Mr. Arable agree with Fern that it isn't fair to kill runt pigs just because they were born small?** *No.* **Why?** POSSIBLE ANSWERS: *He thinks that there is a big difference between runt pigs and little girls. He would probably say that because there are important differences between animals and people we don't have to treat animals the way we treat humans.* **What differences does Mr. Arable think there are between a pig and a little girl? Discuss this with your partner and make a list of these differences.** After a few minutes, ask the teams to mention one of their differences. Write these on the graphic organizer on the chalkboard. POSSIBLE ANSWERS: *Mr. Arable raises the pigs to sell for food, but he raises his daughter to become a loving, healthy, good person. The value of the pig lies in how much money it makes for the family; his daughter is valuable because she is a human being who can think and feel. He would say that pigs don't have feelings, can't think about things, aren't intelligent, and can't speak, read, or write, while humans can do all of these things.* **Write these in the boxes for differences on the diagram for Mr. Arable and write what you think his conclusion would be in the box at the bottom.**

- **Now let's read more of the story and see what the animals are really like in the story.** Read *Charlotte's Web* through the end of the second chapter so that the students can identify the human-like characteristics that Wilbur and the other animals display. **Which view about the runt pig is correct according to the story, Mr. Arable's or Fern's?** *Fern's.* **What characteristics do Wilbur and the other animals display that are like Fern?** POSSIBLE ANSWERS: *They have feelings, are loyal, are intelligent, use language, think about things, care about each other, help each other.*

- **What other stories have you read about animals given human characteristics? List two or three with your partner.** After a few minutes ask students to mention some of these other stories. They mention stories like *Winnie the Pooh, The Three Little Pigs, Goldilocks and the Three Bears*, and *Peter Rabbit*. **When authors give animals human characteristics, it's called "personification." If animals were really like that, would you agree with Fern that they should be treated the same way as humans? Discuss this with your partner. Explain why you think as you do.**

- **Now discuss the real differences between animals and humans with your partner. Decide if any of the similarities are important enough to suggest that animals should be treated like humans, or if you agree with Mr. Arable that it's all right to raise and kill animals like pigs for food.** Students often disagree about this. Some say that humans and animals are different in enough important respects that it is all right to kill them for food. Others say that while animals and humans are different in that animals can't speak, animals can still feel things, and that makes a difference. Still other students raise questions about animals like chimpanzees, dolphins, and whales, which seem to be able to communicate with each other, and they wonder whether that makes them enough like humans to deserve better treatment. Allow open discussion, including concerns about other animals raised for food.

- **Use a new diagram for reasoning by analogy to indicate what similarities and differences there are between animals and humans; include any conclusions you can reach about animals based on these similarities and differences using reasoning by analogy.** STUDENT ANSWERS VARY, REFLECTING THE DIFFERENCES IN VIEWS EXPRESSED ABOVE.

THINKING ABOUT THINKING

- **What do we call the kind of thinking we just did?** *Reasoning by analogy.*

- **How did you do that kind of thinking? What did you think about first, second, etc.?** POSSIBLE ANSWERS: *I thought about how two things, a pig and a human being, were alike, and then I thought about whether they were so different that Fern's conclusion was a poor one.*

- **Is there anything you have to be careful about when you learn new things by analogy?** POSSIBLE ANSWERS: *Yes. The analogy could make me think that everything true of one thing in the analogy is true of the other, and that could be misleading. I should always look for important differences that may show that my conclusion is a poor one.*

- **What questions would a thinking map for reasoning by analogy include?** Student responses should suggest the ideas on the thinking map for reasoning by analogy.

> **REASONING BY ANALOGY**
>
> 1. What things are similar to the object or idea that you are trying to understand?
> 2. What are the significant similarities between them?
> 3. What do you know about these things that you don't know about the thing you are trying to understand?
> 4. Are there any differences between the two that could affect whether what you are trying to understand has these features?
> 5. What can you conclude regarding what you are trying to understand based on this analogy?

APPLYING YOUR THINKING

IMMEDIATE TRANSFER

- **You've been learning about different kinds of animals in science. One type of animal has a shell. Can you think of any animals that have shells?** POSSIBLE ANSWERS: *Clams, snails, turtles, crabs, lobsters, mussels, and oysters.* **People sometimes say that the shells of such animals are analogous to houses. Using the questions on the chart, think about this analogy the way we thought about Fern's analogy. What can you learn from the analogy?**

- **You've learned that many people came from other countries to live in the United States. How is this analogous to a new student entering your school? From this analogy, what can you learn about how these people felt when they came to the United States and how other people felt about them?**

REINFORCEMENT LATER

Later in the school year when you cover the following topics ask students to draw analogies and explain what they can learn from them.

- **What analogies can be drawn between industrial pollution and things that happen in the school or at home? What can you learn from these analogies?**

- **What analogies can be drawn between reading stories and watching TV? What can you learn from these analogies?**

ASSESSING STUDENTS' REASONING BY ANALOGY

Any of the application examples can serve as assessment items to demonstrate whether students are reasoning by analogy skillfully. Remember, it is not enough to ask them to find analogies. They should also be able to formulate new ideas about one thing suggested by its analogy to another. In addition, they should be able to support or show reason for rejecting claims based on analogies by citing similarities or differences that verify or count against these ideas. Ask the students to make their thinking explicit to show how well they are considering whether two things are really analogous and whether they can support their judgment that the analogy does or does not provide them with accurate ideas. Use the thinking map as a checklist to make sure they are following all of the steps in using this skill.

REASONING BY ANALOGY

A: RUNT PIGS   **ARE LIKE**   **B:** LITTLE GIRLS

HOW ALIKE?

Both are living beings.	People care about each of them and value them.
Both have bodies, heads, legs, eyes, and ears.	Their mothers feed them when they are young.
Mothers gave birth to both of them.	Both can feel pain.
Neither of them can help their size when they are born.	Both can see, hear, smell, taste, and feel.

THINGS KNOWN ABOUT B (Little girls) THAT MIGHT ALSO BE TRUE OF A (Pigs):

IT'S UNFAIR TO KILL A LITTLE GIRL JUST BECAUSE SHE WAS BORN SMALL.

SIGNIFICANT DIFFERENCES?

WITH REGARD TO

No significant differences.		No significant differences.

CONCLUSION ABOUT A (Runt Pigs):

IT'S UNFAIR TO KILL A RUNT PIG JUST BECAUSE IT WAS BORN SMALL.

Sample Student Responses • Pigs and People • Mr. Arable's Argument

REASONING BY ANALOGY

A: RUNT PIGS   ARE LIKE   **B:** LITTLE GIRLS

HOW ALIKE?

Both are living beings.	People care about each of them and value them.
Both have bodies, heads, legs, eyes, and ears.	Their mothers feed them when they are young.
Mothers gave birth to both of them.	Both can feel pain.
Neither of them can help their size when they are born.	Both can see, hear, smell, taste, and feel.

THINGS KNOWN ABOUT B (Little girls) THAT MIGHT ALSO BE TRUE OF A (Pigs):

IT'S UNFAIR TO KILL A LITTLE GIRL BECAUSE SHE WAS BORN SMALL.

SIGNIFICANT DIFFERENCES?

WITH REGARD TO

Mr. Arable raises pigs for sale as food.	WHY HE RAISES THEM	He raises his daughter whom he loves to become a loving, healthy, good person.
Pigs don't have human qualities (intelligence, use of language, humor, caring, love and other emotions).	HUMAN QUALITIES	People have special qualities (intelligence, humor, caring, love and other emotions).
The value of the pig is based on how much money its weight brings to the farm family.	VALUE	Little girls have value just because they are human beings who think and feel.

CONCLUSION ABOUT A (Runt Pigs):

A RUNT PIG AND A LITTLE GIRL ARE TOO DIFFERENT FOR OUR TREATMENT OF ONE TO BE THE BASIS FOR THE WAY WE SHOULD TREAT THE OTHER. IT IS ACCEPTABLE TO KILL A RUNT PIG BECAUSE ITS LIFE DOESN'T HAVE THE SAME VALUE AS HUMAN LIFE.

FARMING THE OCEAN

SOCIAL STUDIES/SCIENCE   **GRADES 4–6**

OBJECTIVES

CONTENT

Students will learn about the various types of food that people get from the ocean and the conditions needed to cultivate some of these types of organisms.

THINKING SKILL/PROCESS

Students will learn to skillfully reason by analogy by finding analogies, determining which are significantly alike, determining whether there are any significant differences, and drawing conclusions about one based on the other.

METHODS AND MATERIALS

CONTENT

Background information is needed about animals that live in the sea, as is information about farming and raising livestock on land. If this information is not in student texts, supplementary material on these topics will be needed.

THINKING SKILL/PROCESS

Structured questioning, a graphic organizer, and a thinking map guide students through reasoning by analogy. (See pp. 462-65 for reproducible diagrams.) Students also work in collaborative learning groups.

LESSON

INTRODUCTION TO CONTENT AND THINKING SKILL/PROCESS

- Sometimes we can understand something better by comparing it to something else that we know. For example, to help someone understand how food provides energy for our bodies, you might say that food is like gas in a car. This comparison is an *analogy*. It can lead to the conclusion that food is used in the body to provide energy just as gas is used in an automobile engine to provide energy. When you draw a conclusion like this you are *reasoning by analogy*. Think of some analogies that you have used or heard that help you understand something better. Write them down by completing sentences like the following (write on the board or on a large piece of paper):

  _____ is like _____

- Discuss with your partner what conclusion(s) you can draw about the first thing based on what you know about the second. Write your conclusion.

- Sometimes analogies can fool you. Cars run on one type of fuel: gasoline. That does not mean that we need only one type of food. In reasoning by analogy, you need to be sure that the differences between the things you compare do not lead to false conclusions. Check out your conclusions by thinking about whether there are differences between the two things that could make you draw false conclusions. What are some of the false conclusions you might draw?

- We've been studying food, food production, and the population explosion in social studies and science. Can we use reasoning by analogy to understand these topics better? Maybe this story will give us some ideas to think about.

  The other night, Clyde and Barbara were very excited. They had been talking about what they were going to have for dinner. Both found that their parents were planning a fish meal. They had just been reading about starvation in Africa and realized how lucky they were to be living in a country where people have plenty of food. But they wondered how more food could be available so that people wouldn't starve. Then they had a great idea. They had just talked about how people travel all over the ocean to get fish for food. That reminded them about how people once had to hunt on the land for food. Clyde said to Barbara: "Suppose that we could turn part of the ocean into a big garden or even a farm, like people did when they started to cultivate and grow crops for food. Then we could plant and feed the things they were growing, just like people do in gardens and farms on land." Barbara said, "That could increase the amount of food we get; we would know exactly how much food we would be getting and where to go to get it. Gathering food in the ocean would be much easier than hunting for it." Clyde said, "It would be just like on a regular farm. Maybe we'd be able to get so much more food this way that there would be plenty for everyone."

Clyde thought about this. They wanted to discuss this idea in their class. "Would we really be able to use the ocean as a farm?" Clyde wondered. "Does comparing it to a farm on land really help? Maybe there are some differences between the two that would make it harder—or impossible—to use the ocean as a farm." Barbara agreed with Clyde. They had to think about how it would all work before they suggested this idea in class.

THINKING ACTIVELY

- **Discuss with your partner what things that live in the ocean people eat. Make a list of these.** After a few minutes, ask students to read a few items from their lists. Write them on the chalkboard. POSSIBLE ANSWERS: *Lobsters, shrimp, clams, tuna, oysters, seaweed, swordfish, crabs, squid, mackerel, scallops, mussels, and other fish and shellfish.* If students mention other food items of which the class does not have a general knowledge (like seaweed used for food), ask the student who mentioned it to elaborate on how it is used as food. If your students have practiced skillful classification, ask them to categorize the seafood items listed on the board.

- **Let's think about Clyde and Barbara's analogy. Suppose you were to try to raise food in the ocean. With your partner, pick three of these items and identify food sources that we raise on land that would be analogous to each of them. For each one, complete the sentence, putting one of the food sources from the ocean in the left blank and a source raised on the land in the right blank.**

_____ is (are) like _____.

Write on the board or on a large piece of paper.

Ask each group to report on one of their analogies. POSSIBLE ANSWERS: *Swordfish are like cattle. Tuna are like sheep. Clams are like potatoes. Muscles are like broccoli. Lobsters are like chickens. Crabs are like ducks. Oysters are like peas in a pod. Seaweed is like lettuce.*

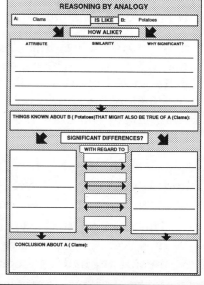

- **Let's work with the analogy between clams and potatoes. Use the graphic organizer for reasoning by analogy to determine whether this is a good analogy. Can we learn something about how people could raise clams in the ocean from the way people raise potatoes on land? First see if you can find important similarities between the food sources with regard to how they live and grow.** Break students into groups of five. Each group should use a graphic organizer like the one at the right. POSSIBLE SIMILARITIES: *They both live and grow underground. They absorb their nourishment from their immediate environment. They don't need*

to be in the open air. *They are eaten regularly as a food all over the world. They are small enough to hold in your hand.* Ask the students whether these are significant similarities (they are) and why (their habitats are similar, they feed on nutrients from their environment in similar ways, and they are both easily accessible to humans).

- **What do you know about growing potatoes on farms that you might be able to apply to raising clams in the ocean? Write these in the box marked "Things known about B (potatoes) that might also be true of A (clams)."** POSSIBLE ANSWERS: *You can plant a lot of them in a small space. You can harvest them easily by digging them up when they grow big enough. You can feed them to make them grow and be healthy.*

- **Are there some differences between clams and potatoes that make it harder to farm clams in the ocean than to grow potatoes on land? Work in your groups and write these differences in the space provided on the graphic organizer under "Significant Differences."** POSSIBLE ANSWERS: *Clams are living animals and potatoes are roots. Clams can move; potatoes can't. Seagulls eat clams; potatoes aren't eaten by birds. Clams have hard outer shells; potatoes don't. Clams live underwater (though the sand they live in is exposed when the tide goes out) while the ground that potatoes live in is always exposed. Clams grow from eggs while potatoes grow from the "eyes" of live potatoes.*

- **Based on the similarities and differences you've listed for clams and potatoes, what conclusions can you draw about farming clams in the ocean? Discuss this in your group and write your conclusion in the box at the bottom of the diagram.** Ask students to share their conclusions with the rest of the class and to explain why they think these conclusions are supported by the analogy. SAMPLE CONCLUSION: *Clams could be cultivated in sand that is covered at high tide and exposed at low tide (or in shallow water) by "planting" them in the sand. We could feed them what they need to grow at low tide. A wire enclosure could be built to keep the birds away, or maybe we could develop a "scare-sea-gull" that's like a scarecrow. They could be dug up like potatoes, but people would have to do this with rakes or shovels. Perhaps it would be hard to use a tractor. They should be harvested quickly so that they couldn't move away.*

- **Each group should pick one of the other analogies between foods from the ocean and foods from the land. Use reasoning by analogy to give your ideas about how to cultivate other things living in the ocean for food.** ANSWERS VARY.

THINKING ABOUT THINKING

- **How did you think about this analogy to make sure it was a good analogy? What did you think about first, next, etc.? Develop a thinking map containing these questions for reasoning by analogy.** Answers should refer to finding important similarities in cultivating and growing the two things for food, describing things we know about farming one of the two that might be a good way to farm the other, determining any significant differences between the two that had a bearing on how the second one could be cultivated in the ocean, and then drawing a conclusion about ways of farming the second based on these similarities and differences. The thinking map should look like the figure on the right.

REASONING BY ANALOGY

1. What things are similar to the object or idea that you are trying to understand?

2. What are the significant similarities between them?

3. What do you know about these things that you don't know about the thing you are trying to understand?

4. Are there any differences between the two that could affect whether what you are trying to understand has these features?

5. What can you conclude regarding what you are trying to understand based on this analogy?

- **How did going through this process help you with your reasoning by analogy?** ANSWERS

VARY. Many students say that they can think about whether the analogy is a good analogy. It also makes them feel more confident that the conclusions they are drawing are good ideas.

- **Develop a checklist of things to find out when someone else draws a conclusion from an analogy.** This could be the thinking map developed above, or some variation of it that the students put in their own words.

APPLYING YOUR THINKING

IMMEDIATE TRANSFER

- **When scientists test a new drug for people, they usually test it first on mice. If the drug works on mice, they sometimes conclude that the drug is good for people. What is the analogy? Use your set of rules to decide whether or not the scientists' conclusion is a good.**

- **What analogy would you use to help a first or second grade student understand how blood carries nutrients to various parts of the body? Check to see if it's a good analogy. What would you expect the student to learn from this analogy? Explain.**

REINFORCEMENT LATER

Later in the school year, when the students are studying these topics, ask them the following:

- **Suppose someone suggested that Columbus crossing the Atlantic Ocean in 1492 is a good analogy to the pioneers moving west in this country in the 19th Century. Is this a good analogy? Check it out using your plan for good reasoning by analogy. What can we learn about the pioneers by comparing them to Columbus?**

- **In what ways are music and art analogous? What can we learn about each by comparing them in this way?**

RESEARCH EXTENSION

After completing the thinking actively part of this lesson, ask the students to use the school library to research some of the techniques of ocean farming. Ask students to compare these techniques to what they had suggested using reasoning by analogy. If there is a difference, ask them to think about why the actual farming is conducted as it is, considering the differences between cultivating food in the ocean and cultivating food on land.

ASSESSING STUDENT THINKING WHEN THEY REASON BY ANALOGY

Any of the application examples can serve as assessment items to determine whether students are reasoning by analogy skillfully. Remember, it is not enough to ask them to find analogies. They should also be able to determine whether the analogies are good ones and whether certain conclusions are supported by the analogy on the basis of similarities and differences. Ask them to make their thinking explicit so that you can ascertain how well they are considering significant similarities and differences before declaring that the analogy is or isn't a good one. Use the thinking map as a checklist to make sure they are covering all of the steps in the use of this skill.

SAMPLE STUDENT RESPONSES • FARMING THE OCEAN

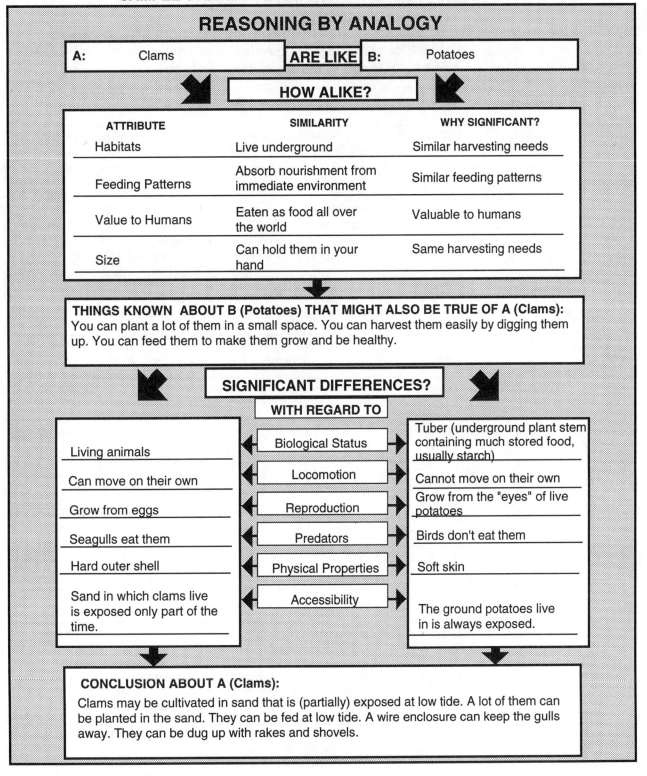

REASONING BY ANALOGY

| **A:** | Clams | **ARE LIKE** | **B:** | Potatoes |

HOW ALIKE?

ATTRIBUTE	SIMILARITY	WHY SIGNIFICANT?
Habitats	Live underground	Similar harvesting needs
Feeding Patterns	Absorb nourishment from immediate environment	Similar feeding patterns
Value to Humans	Eaten as food all over the world	Valuable to humans
Size	Can hold them in your hand	Same harvesting needs

THINGS KNOWN ABOUT B (Potatoes) THAT MIGHT ALSO BE TRUE OF A (Clams):
You can plant a lot of them in a small space. You can harvest them easily by digging them up. You can feed them to make them grow and be healthy.

SIGNIFICANT DIFFERENCES?

WITH REGARD TO

Living animals	Biological Status	Tuber (underground plant stem containing much stored food, usually starch)
Can move on their own	Locomotion	Cannot move on their own
Grow from eggs	Reproduction	Grow from the "eyes" of live potatoes
Seagulls eat them	Predators	Birds don't eat them
Hard outer shell	Physical Properties	Soft skin
Sand in which clams live is exposed only part of the time.	Accessibility	The ground potatoes live in is always exposed.

CONCLUSION ABOUT A (Clams):
Clams may be cultivated in sand that is (partially) exposed at low tide. A lot of them can be planted in the sand. They can be fed at low tide. A wire enclosure can keep the gulls away. They can be dug up with rakes and shovels.

LESSON CONTEXTS FOR REASONING BY ANALOGY LESSONS

The following examples have been suggested by classroom teachers as contexts to develop infused lessons. If a skill or process has been introduced in a previous infused lesson, transfer activities can be designed in these contexts to reinforce it.

GRADE	SUBJECT	TOPIC	THINKING ISSUE
K–3	Literature	*Peter Rabbit*	How is Peter Rabbit's going into Mr. McGregor's garden analogous to things that you do? What can you learn from this analogy?
K–3	Literature	*On Beyond Zebra*	What insights about symbols (abbreviations, logos, etc.) is suggested by the analogy between creating letters and creating symbols?(Letters are generated in the story for a variety of reasons: they stand for the beginning sounds or repeated sounds in names, the shape or sound of the letter suggests what it stands for, the letter marks some unusual characteristic or use).
K–3	Literature	*I Had Trouble in Getting to Solla Sollew*	What is the analogy between the events in this story and people's belief that they would have fewer or no troubles if they were someplace else?
K–3	Literature	*The Green Stone*	What does the green stone stand for?What understanding of himself should the boy get from the green stone?
K–3	Literature	*Cornrows*	What does the analogy between cornrow braids and pieces of African sculpture tell Sister about family background and pride?
K–3	Literature	*The Giving Tree*	What does the analogy between the tree and parents tell us about giving?
K–3	Literature	*Mei Ling's Tiger*	How does Mei Ling's cat resemble a tiger? Why does the analogy make the last line funny?
K–3	Social studies	Division of labor	How can we understand how different people work together in a community by drawing an analogy to the way a bicycle works?
K–3	Social studies	Local government	What does the analogy between a mayor's being the head of a city government and a president's being the head of our national government suggest about what a mayor can do? What are some things that a president can do that a mayor can't do?
K–3	Social studies/ science	Social insects	How are bee hives analogous to human communities? What can we learn about bees? (They must communicate in some way. etc.)
K–3	Science	Seasons	In winter the northern hemisphere is tipped away from the sun and the weather in that part of the world is cold. During this time, what are the seasons like in the southern hemisphere?
K–3	Science	Human hand and a bat wing	How is a bat wing like a human hand? Can we learn anything about bat wings from this analogy? Why or why not?
K–3	Science	Body Parts	The ear is sometimes compared to a funnel. Is this a good analogy?
K–3	Science	Body Parts	Describe how similarities between a bird beak and a grasping tool like pliers inform us about how birds eat. (Both have parts that can pivot and can close together to hold an object, have sharp peices for cutting, and can be used in small spaces).

LESSON CONTEXTS FOR REASONING BY ANALOGY

GRADE	SUBJECT	TOPIC	THINKING ISSUE
K–3	Science	*The Dinosaur Who Lived in My Backyard*	How does comparing the needs and size of dinosaurs with everday things we know help us understand them?
K–3	Science	Dinosaurs	What do reptiles need to survive? Dinosaurs have important similarities to reptiles alive today. What might have caused the dinosaurs to die out?
K–3	Science	Spreading germs	Illustrate how germs are spread by having a group of children wet their hands. One child should dip wet hands into sand, pick up a cracker, and pass it to others. Student will correlate the sand on their hands with germs.
K–3	Science	Respiration	Demonstrate that when someone breathes on a mirror, water droplets form. Use this information to explain why campers sometimes find water on the inside of their closed watertight tents. Why would there be moore water if there are more compers in the tent?
K–3	Health	White blood cells	People often draw an analogy between white blood cells and soldiers. What does this analogy help you to understand about the way white blood cells function?
K–3	Art	Cool colors	If light blue and gray are analogous to cool temperatures, what are other colors analogous to? What effect would you expect from using these colors in a painting?
4–6	Literature	*Park's Quest*	What ideas about his own family does Park's analogy between the King Arthur legend and his family's circumstances lead him to accept? What implications does this have for Park's ability to accept his father's situation? Is this a good analogy?
4–6	Literature	*The Sneetches*	Is the story of the Sneetches a good analogy for racism or sexism? What solution does the story suggest?
4–6	Literature	*The Hundred-Penny Box*	What connection between the aunt's life and the hundred-penny box leads us to believe that if the box was gone she would stop living?
4–6	Literature	*An Angel for Solomon Singer*	How does Solomon Singer use analogies about things he loves about his home in Indiana and things he sees in New York City to cure his homesickness?
4–6	Literature	*Brother Eagle, Sister Sky*	How does the analogy stated in Chief Settle's farewell between the Earth and a family show Indian reverence for nature? Is this a good analogy? What meaning might this analogy have for us today?
4–6	Literature	*Lydde*	Why was Lydde troubled by the comparison that the runaway slave made between his situation and hers?
4–6	Social studies	China	Confucius described a good government as a good family. "Let the ruler be as a ruler ought to be. Let the official be as the official ought to be. Let the father be as the father ought to be. Let the son be as the son ought to be." What rules of conduct within a family would also show how citizens, officials, and rulers should act? According to this analogy, how would people develop good governments?

LESSON CONTEXTS FOR REASONING BY ANALOGY

GRADE	SUBJECT	TOPIC	THINKING ISSUE
4–6	Social studies	Ancient Egypt	The river Nile in ancient Egypt has been compared to a major highway in the 20th century. Is this a good analogy? If so, what can you learn from it; if not, why not?
4–6	U.S. history	Westward expansion	What analogies can you draw that can help to understand why people moved west in this country in the 19th century? What can you learn from these analogies?
4–6	Mathematics	Scale drawing	How are proportions analogies? How can the analogy help you decide how to double the size of adrawing (using a larger grid, doubling units, using a opaque projector, etc.?
4–6	Science	Nuclear fission	Evaluate the analogy between nuclear fission and falling dominos.
4–6	Science	Convection and currents	How is the convection of air circulating in a room analogous to the way that oxygen dissolved in water at the surface of a lake reaches the bottom of the lake? What can you learn from this analogy?
4–6	Science	Bubbles	Cook bread without yeast and with yeast to illustrate that bubbles from yeast cause bread to rise. If we don't use yeast in cookies or biscuits, which ingredients might create the bubbles?
4–6	Science	Bones and muscles	How are the actions of arm bones and muscles like the operation of a lever? What analogies can you think of for fixed joints, pivot joint, ball and socket joints, hinged joints?
4–6	Science	Plants	The freezing point of antifreeze is below 0°C, so it remains liquid below the freezing point of water. If the anemone plant is analogous to antifreeze, what conclusions might you draw about its survival at temperatures below 0°C?
4–6	Science	Cancer	Use an analogy to explain how cancer grows and spreads.
4–6	Science	Cells	How is cell respiration like burning fuel? Is this a good analogy to help us understand important features of cells in the body?
4–6	Science	Cells	Use information about cell functioning to describe how one cell can be analogous to a whole living organism.
4–6	Science	Electricity	How is electricity in a wire analogous to water flowing in a pipe? What can you learn about electricity from this analogy?
4–6	Science	Neutralization	Use the analogy of baking soda and stomach acid to suggest ways to minimize the damage of acid rain on a pond. What might be limitations on your plan?
4–6	Health	Disease	Is AIDS analogous to the bubonic plague? What can we learn from this analogy? Are there any significant differences between AIDS and the bubonic plague that suggest that we should be cautious about drawing too much from this analogy?
4–6	Health	Smoking	Some people have drawn an analogy between smoking and a time bomb. Is this a good analogy? If so, what can we learn from it? If not, why not?
4–6	Art/ Music	Rhythm	Rhythm in music is the beat; rhythm in art is repeating shapes, lines, or colors. Would making the beat more rapid in a piece of music have an effect similar to adding more of the same shapes, lines, or colors in a picture?

CHAPTER 17
CONDITIONAL REASONING

Why Is It Necessary to Engage in Skillful Conditional Reasoning?

Whenever we draw a conclusion based on information in the form of "if…then" (a "conditional" judgement), we are engaging in *conditional reasoning*. For example, suppose that you know that if a person you are rooting for in the tennis match wins *this* game, she wins the championship. When she wins this game, you have every right to celebrate; you draw the conclusion that she's won the championship. Someone who does not put these ideas together may not realize that this player has won the championship even if he finds out that she has won this game. Conditional reasoning is one way that we combine information to extend our knowledge.

Conditional reasoning pervades our thinking. It is involved in both our everyday activities and our professional work. In fact, we engage in conditional reasoning with such frequency that we often are not even aware that we are doing it. I know that if I buy something, I own it. I know that if I drive more than 55 miles per hour on the highway, I'm breaking the law. We carry with us a multitude of information about conditions under which a variety of things happen and use this information to advance our knowledge every day of our lives.

Conditional reasoning is a form of deductive reasoning. Conditional reasoning is different from causal explanation, prediction, generalization, and reasoning by analogy in which *we use evidence to support the likelihood of a conclusion*. Reasoning based on evidence is often called "inductive" reasoning. The fingerprints of the alleged murderer on the murder weapon and his footprints near the body strongly support the hypothesis that he was the murderer, but his guilt isn't *proven* with 100% certainty.

In contrast, when you conclude that the person you are rooting for has won the tennis championship, the reasoning you are engaged in is an example of *deductive* reasoning. The conclusion that you draw from the two pieces of information isn't just made highly likely by that information. *It follows from it with 100% certainty.* If the information is accurate, it cannot turn out that she did not win the championship.

The caveat in the last sentence is important. Like reasoning based on evidence, the information we start with in deductive reasoning has to be accurate if we are to have confidence in the accuracy of the conclusions we draw. If it is inaccurate, there is no guarantee that the conclusion is accurate. An environmental scientist may know that if there are certain chemicals in a community's water supply, the water isn't safe to drink. There is some indication that these chemicals may be present, but he isn't sure. He realizes that he must investigate further. Until he does, he cannot affirm the conclusion that the water is not safe to drink based on conditional reasoning. But if he finds that the information about the chemicals *is* accurate, you'd better not drink the water!

Conditional reasoning is only one type of deductive reasoning. Other types involve reasoning with statements containing "all" and "some" ("categorical" statements) and, especially, drawing conclusions by combining two such statements ("syllogisms"). Still other types of deductive reasoning involve combining statements containing "and," "or," and "not" to draw conclusions ("propositional reasoning"). If I know that all mammals are warm-blooded and that all warm-blooded creatures have hearts, and I draw the conclusion that all mammals have hearts, I am engaging in categorical or syllogistic reasoning. If I reason that I must have left my car keys at the restaurant because I know that either I left them there or in the bookstore, and I've found out that they aren't at the bookstore, I'm engaging in propositional reasoning.

The study of arguments in which categorical statements are used is called "syllogistic" logic. The study of arguments in which "and," "or," and "not" statements are used is called "propositional" logic. Propositional logic also is the branch of logic in which conditional arguments are studied.

Problems we encounter when we engage in conditional reasoning. Sometimes we make mistakes in conditional reasoning. Suppose I am the environmental scientist who is investigating the water supply of a community for traces of certain chemicals. I am conducting this investigation because of rumors that a chemical plant had illegally dumped this chemical nearby. I am quite concerned because I know that if these chemicals are in the water, the water is unsafe to drink. As I am conducting this investigation, a colleague informs me that she has just completed her investigation of the same water supply and determined that it was, indeed, unsafe to drink. I would be making a mistake to conclude that it was polluted with the same chemicals that I was investigating and then to recommend action against the chemical company. There are many ways that a water supply can become polluted.

Likewise, if I found out that the water supply *does not* contain any traces of the chemicals produced by the company, it would be premature to conclude that the water *was* safe to drink. It could be polluted in some other way.

We can see the errors in these two examples if we make the reasoning explicit. The sequence below represent the reasoning in the first example:

1. If the chemicals are in the water, then it is not safe to drink.

2. The water is not safe to drink.

Therefore

3. The chemicals are in the water.

This conclusion clearly does not follow.

The following sequence makes the reasoning in the second example explicit:

1. If the chemicals are in the water, then it is not safe to drink.

2. The chemicals are not in the water.

Therefore

3. The water is safe to drink.

This conclusion doesn't follow either. Traditional deductive logic—the study of the forms of valid and invalid deductive reasoning—catego-

rizes these fallacious types of deductive reasoning. They are called "affirming the consequent" and "denying the antecedent," respectively. (The antecedent is the part of the conditional that comes after the "if," and the consequent is the part of the conditional that comes after the "then.") It is not as important, however, to learn the *names* for these fallacies as it is to understand *why* they are fallacies—the patterns of faulty reasoning they represent.

Figure 17.1 contains a summary of the common problems people experience in conditional reasoning.

COMMON DEFAULTS IN THE USE OF CONDITIONAL REASONING

1. We do not think to draw conclusions by combining conditional statements with other relevant information.

2. We draw a conclusion to the effect that the antecedent is true because we have information that the consequent is true (the fallacy of Affirming the Consequent).

3. We draw a conclusion to the effect that the consequent is not true because we have information that the antecedent is not true (the fallacy of Denying the Antecedent).

Figure 17.1

What Does Skillful Conditional Reasoning Involve?

Much of the time our conditional reasoning is sound. Sometimes, however, our conditional reasoning misleads us into accepting conclusions that are not justified by the information we start with. Skillfulness in our reasoning can allow us to avoid these mistakes.

In skillful conditional reasoning, we combine information with a conditional statement and accept only conclusions that follow from this combination. Skill in conditional reasoning involves discriminating between conclusions that can and cannot be drawn from such given information. When we make such discriminations, we are determining the *validity* of inferences from the given information to the conclusion that is drawn.

Contexts for using skillful conditional reasoning. In practice, there are a number of different situations in which we use the skills involved in conditional reasoning. One such situation involves *someone else* presenting a conditional argument to you. Others involve *your* use of the skills of conditional reasoning to try to find information needed to draw a specific conclusion which you think follows from that information.

The first type of situation occurs, typically, when another person tries to convince you of something using a conditional argument. You should then reflect on whether or not their reasoning is correct (valid) and whether or not the information it is based on is accurate. This involves a *reactive* assessment of the arguments of others. It is a special case of the type of argument evaluation we discussed in Chapter 8: Finding Reasons and Conclusions.

For example, a Realtor might be trying to convince you to buy a particular house. You like the house and are interested in buying it but find that you cannot because the interest rates are too high and the mortgage will take too much of your monthly income. Suppose your Realtor shows you that if interest rates fall to below 7%, then you will be able to keep up with your monthly payments. A few weeks later she calls you with good news. She tells you that she's found out that the interest rates have gone down to 6.75%. "You should buy now," she says. Should you change your mind? You are now in a position to assess whether her reasoning is sound. The three lines below make her reasoning explicit:

1. If the interest rates go down to below 7%, you can afford the house.

2. The rates have gone down to 6.75%.

Therefore

3. You can now afford the house.

You agree with the Realtor about statement (1) and verify statement (2). Since the amount of the monthly payments was all that was deterring you from buying the house, her advice is good advice. The conditional reasoning above is quite correct.

Political speeches, letters to the editor, and advertising usually involve conditional reasoning. Once an argument is extracted from one of these contexts, it can be assessed to determine whether the conclusion follows from the given information.

In the second type of situation, we use conditional reasoning in our own thinking. Instead of reacting to the arguments of others, we actively draw and affirm conclusions which extend our knowledge. While this dynamic is quite different from the more reactive assessment of arguments offered to us by others, at its roots we use the skills of conditional reasoning in the same way; we have to determine the validity of the conditional argument on which the conclusion is based.

One typical situation of this sort is when we select various conditional statements from our own ideas and gather relevant information to enable us to affirm conclusions that we previously only tentatively advanced. I might know that if I have driven over 3000 miles since my last oil change, my car is due for another oil change. So I seek information about when I had the oil changed last. When I find that it was more than 3000 miles ago, I know I should make an appointment for an oil change. In this case, I did not have some of the information that I needed in order to draw a conclusion and had to seek the needed information. When I get that information, I can draw the conclusion. The three lines below represent this example of conditional reasoning:

1. If I have driven over 3000 miles since my last oil change, my car is due for another oil change.

2. My last oil change was 3500 miles ago.

Therefore

3. My car is due for another oil change.

My recognition that the reasoning in the above lines is valid conditional reasoning helps me realize that if I find out statement (2), I can determine whether I ought to take my car in for another oil change. This leads me to investigate when I had my last oil change.

Assessing conditional reasoning: can you legitimately draw the conclusion? As we have seen, for conditional reasoning to lead to an acceptable conclusion, two conditions must be satisfied:

- The conclusion follows from the information we combine to generate it; and

- The information we start with—the "premises" of the argument we develop—is acceptable.

Conditional reasoning can lead us to new insights; if one or both of these conditions fail, however, it can also lead us to accept conclusions which are quite false.

The first of these conditions relates to the validity of the conditional reasoning. How can we decide whether this condition is satisfied? In general, there is an informal strategy that can be used to determine whether the conclusion follows from the premises in any deductive argument. If the conclusion of a deductive argument follows, then *the conclusion cannot be false if the premises are true.*

If it is true that my friend won last night's game and it is also true that if she won the game she became the champion, then it *has to be true* that she became the champion. It could not be otherwise. As we saw earlier, on the other hand, if I find out that my friend *did not* win last night's game and I conclude that she lost the championship, this would be invalid reasoning. Maybe she has two chances to win—if she wins tonight she could also win the championship. So there *is* a circumstance in which the conclusion would be false and yet the original premises true. It is, therefore, not legitimate to conclude that she did not win the championship because she did not win last night's game.

To summarize: When we engage in conditional reasoning we can ask, "Could there be circumstances in which the conclusion is false and yet the information on which it is based true?" If the answer to this question is "Yes," the reasoning is not valid; if the answer is "No," the reasoning is valid.

This strategy (trying to imagine a situation in which the information given could be true and the conclusion be false) is helpful in assessing many straightforward conditional arguments.

If you can imagine such a circumstance then the conclusion does not follow. Not finding an exception, however, does not guarantee that the conclusion does follow. Maybe you simply cannot think of an exception now. But if you spend some time trying to imagine an exceptional situation and cannot, chances are that there is none. So at least you've got a good reason for thinking that the conclusion follows.

Assessing conditional reasoning: are the premises acceptable? When we assess conditional reasoning in the way described, we are assessing the reasoning only—whether or not we can legitimately put together the two ideas and draw the conclusion in question. In many cases, however, we have to ask whether the information we use or the information given in the premises of someone else's argument is, in fact, accurate and acceptable. If it is not, then even though the reasoning may be valid, the conclusion won't be acceptable. You can start with the most outlandish conditional statements and add false information that the antecedent is true and then use valid conditional reasoning to draw false conclusions. Only if the information you start with is acceptable will the conclusion be acceptable.

It is, therefore, important to ask ourselves whether or not we have good reasons for accepting both the conditional statement and the additional information provided in the premises of a conditional argument, even if it is a valid argument. If either of the premises is problematic, we should note what information we need to be able to accept it. Perhaps the person who gave you the information about the winner of last night's game is a well-known trickster. Then you may have to ask someone else or read the newspaper about the game. Or maybe you aren't sure you have correctly calculated the number of games needed to win the championship. Then you can recalculate or consult an official to corroborate your own calculations.

To determine whether the information we start with is acceptable, we often have to make use of other critical thinking skills, like determining the reliability of sources. If, when you do, you are satisfied that the premises are acceptable and that the argument is valid, you can accept the conclusion.

The diagram in figure 17.2 can help us record our thinking about the soundness of conditional arguments.

CONDITIONAL ARGUMENT EVALUATION CHECKLIST

1. Are there circumstances in which the premises could be true while the conclusion is false?   YES ☐ NO ☐

2. If so, describe that situation.
_____
_____
_____

A deductive argument is valid only if there are no circumstances in which the premises are true and the conclusion false.   YES ☐ NO ☐

3. Is there any additional information needed to determine whether the conditional and/or the additional information is acceptable?   YES ☐ NO ☐

4. If so, what information is needed?
_____
_____
_____
_____

The conclusion of a deductive argument is acceptable only if the argument is valid and the premises are acceptable.   ACCEPTABLE? YES ☐ NO ☐

Figure 17.2

This graphic organizer, like the corresponding one used in Chapter 8 on reasons and conclusions in arguments, serves two purposes. It provides us with a record of why we judge that a particular conditional argument is valid, invalid, sound, or unsound. It can also remind us what additional information to seek to make the conclusion more acceptable.

Alternative methods for assessing conditional reasoning. We can also assess validity in conditional reasoning by identifying the pattern of reasoning and comparing it to patterns of valid and invalid conditional reasoning. Many logic programs teach this method. Generally, there are two common types of valid conditional reasoning and two common invalid types. We have explored examples of some of these already. The valid types include

- Additional information affirms what is stated in the antecedent of a conditional statement, and we conclude that what is stated in the consequent of the conditional is true. (The traditional name for this type of reasoning is "modus ponens.")

- Additional information denies the consequent, and we deny that what is stated in the antecedent is true. (The traditional name for this type of reasoning is "modus tollens.")

The example about the tennis championship represents the first of these. You know that if your friend wins tonight's game, she will win the championship, and you find out that she won the game. Therefore you know that she has won the championship.

The second is exemplified by a situation in which you find out that your friend did not win the championship. Then you can conclude that she did not win the game last night.

The invalid types are the fallacies of affirming the consequent and denying the antecedent. Concluding that she lost the championship because she lost the game last night is an example of denying the antecedent. The example in which a person concludes that she won the game last night because she won the championship is an example of affirming the consequent.

The chart in figure 17.3 provides a checklist of these patterns of valid and invalid conditional reasoning.

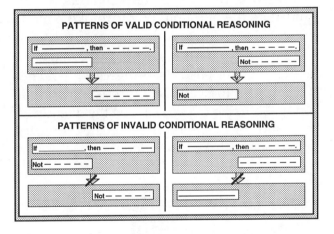

Figure 17.3

There is a third type of valid conditional reasoning which is worth noting, though it is not as common as the previous types:

- We combine two conditional statements in which the consequent of the first conditional statement appears in the antecedent of another conditional statement and conclude that the antecedent in the first conditional statement is a condition for the consequent in the second one. (The traditional name for this type of reasoning is "hypothetical syllogism.")

This type of conditional reasoning is exemplified by the following reasoning: Suppose we have information that the person who wins the championship in this tennis match will be given a free trip to Paris. We can combine the information we have so far (if my friend wins tonight's game, then she will win the championship) with this new information (if my friend wins the championship, then she will receive a free trip to Paris) to conclude that if she wins tonight's game, she will win a free trip to Paris.

Tools for engaging in skillful conditional reasoning. We can learn to engage in sound conditional reasoning and avoid the fallacies by adopting some specific thinking strategies. The thinking map in figure 17.4 can guide us in making our conditional reasoning explicit and in assessing it. The graphic organizer in figure 17.5 can be used along with the thinking map.

Note that this graphic organizer is useful for recording someone else's conditional argument or our own conditional reasoning as we are guided by the questions on the thinking map.

After the conditional reasoning is made explicit on the graphic organizer, we can use the strategy suggested to assess the reasoning. Then we can either indicate that the reasoning is valid or invalid using the markers on the diagram. If it is valid, a "V" should be put in the arrow; if it is invalid, a stroke across the arrow will mark this.

How to Teach Students to Engage in Skillful Conditional Reasoning

In teaching conditional reasoning, it is important to provide students with activities in which they consider examples of each of the main types of conditional arguments (modus ponens, modus tollens, affirming the consequent, and denying the antecedent). They should be asked to both analyze and assess arguments given by others as well as engage in their own conditional reasoning.

Many conditional-reasoning exercises in logic textbooks involve exercises in which students are only given examples of conditional arguments that others have offered and are asked to

---

CONDITIONAL REASONING

1. What topic are you trying to get information about?

2. Formulate a conditional statement that you know about that topic.

3. What information do you have about the components of the conditional statement?

4. What conclusion are you considering?

5. Is it valid to reason from the conditional statement and the given information to the conclusion?

   a. If the conditional statement and the given information could be true but the conclusion false, then the reasoning is invalid.

   b. If the conditional statement and the given information couldn't be true but the conclusion false, then the reasoning is valid.

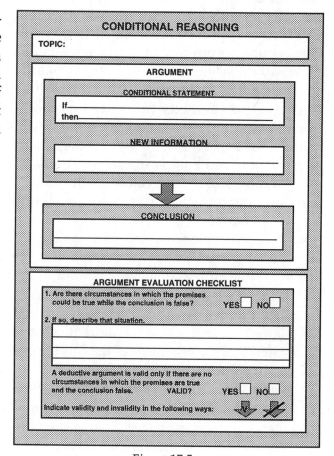

Figure 17.5

determine whether or not they are valid. Because the active use of conditional reasoning plays such an important role in our lives, it is important not to overlook generating such examples as well. The lesson in this handbook does both.

Contexts in the curriculum for lessons on conditional reasoning. It is easy to construct examples of conditional reasoning in everyday situations as we have done in this commentary. Such examples are somewhat harder to find in curriculum materials. Nonetheless, there are two types of contexts in which conditional reasoning plays a natural role and that provide good contexts for infusion lessons:

- *Conditional reasoning is used in the dialogue of stories that students study or in historical and scientific nonfiction.* For example, characters in stories often employ conditional reasoning, either explicitly or implicitly, as they engage in dialogue or think about hard choices. *Alice in Wonderland* often contains examples of explicit conditional reasoning, while in children's stories like *The Cat in the Hat* the use of conditional reasoning is present, but the conditional statements remain implicit. The Declaration of Independence begins with a conditional statement and suggests an important conclusion—that the authors explain why they have decided to become independent.

- *Students learn conditional statements and engage in inquiry to determine whether there is any information which combines with the conditional to enable them to draw legitimate conclusions.* For example, students learn a variety of principles in mathematics in the form of "if...then" statements (if the length of one of the sides of a rectangle is doubled, then the area will be doubled). In mathematical calculations, students often are given or have to gather information that they combine with these principles to draw specific mathematical conclusions. Similarly, in science, students learn principles such as "If the volume of water an object displaces is the same weight as the object, then the object will float." Then they often gather data about what is in the antecedent

(e.g., how much the water that an object displaces weighs). When they get this data, they can draw a conclusion using conditional reasoning (e.g., about whether or not the object will float).

One technique for constructing infusion lessons about conditional reasoning is to construct a vignette in which characters reason conditionally about the topic that students are studying, such as in the lesson "Growth and Digestion," an upper elementary science lesson. There we include a dialogue between two students who use various types of conditional reasoning as they think about what they are learning. The students who are taught this lesson are asked to determine what this reasoning involves and whether it is good conditional reasoning. Guiding students through such activities by using the thinking map and graphic organizer for conditional reasoning will begin to fix this strategy in their minds.

To confirm students' understanding of conditional reasoning, you can ask students to try to figure out the rules for the valid and invalid types of conditional reasoning and then develop a plan for using these rules when they are thinking about conditionals. As they think about their thinking in this way, you can give them other examples in which they can use their thinking maps to monitor their own use of conditional reasoning.

Continued practice in which students reflect on, identify, and certify the conditional reasoning of others, together with examples in which the students themselves have to engage in conditional reasoning, will reinforce their skillful use of this type of reasoning.

A menu of suggested contexts for infusion lessons on conditional reasoning is provided on pp. 502–03.

Sample Lessons on Conditional Reasoning

We include one lesson on conditional reasoning in this chapter. It is an upper elementary science lesson on growth and digestion. This lesson provides students with samples of conditional reasoning and asks them to determine whether these are valid or invalid forms of this type of reasoning. As you read these lessons, consider the following:

- For the activities in these lessons, can you construct alternative examples in which students react to the arguments of others, on the one hand, and develop their own conditional reasoning, on the other?

- What additional examples of conditional reasoning can be used to reinforce this skill?

Tools for Designing Lessons on Conditional Reasoning

The thinking map for conditional reasoning is provided on page 489. The first graphic organiz-

ers (p. 490–91) can be used to record conditional arguments that others offer as well as conditional arguments that we develop ourselves. The chart of patterns of valid and invalid conditional arguments can serve as a checklist against which specific conditional arguments can be compared.

The thinking maps and graphic organizers can guide you in designing the critical thinking activity in the lesson and can also serve as photocopy masters, transparency masters, or as models that can be enlarged and used as posters in the classroom. Reproduction rights are granted for single classroom use only.

CONDITIONAL REASONING

1. **What topic are you trying to get information about?**

2. **Formulate a conditional statement that you know about that topic.**

3. **What information do you have about the components of the conditional statement?**

4. **What conclusion are you considering?**

5. **Is it valid to reason from the conditional statement and the given information to the conclusion?**

   a. **If the conditional statement and the given information could be true but the conclusion false, then the reasoning is invalid.**

   b. **If the conditional statement and the given information couldn't be true but the conclusion false, the reasoning is valid.**

CONDITIONAL REASONING

TOPIC:

ARGUMENT

CONDITIONAL STATEMENT

If _____

then _____

NEW INFORMATION

_____

CONCLUSION

_____

ARGUMENT EVALUATION CHECKLIST

1. Are there circumstances in which the premises could be true while the conclusion is false?

YES ☐   NO ☐

2. If so, describe that situation.

_____
_____
_____

A deductive argument is valid only if there are no circumstances in which the premises are true and the conclusion false.   **VALID?**   YES ☐   NO ☐

Indicate validity and invalidity in the following ways:

CONDITIONAL ARGUMENT EVALUATION CHECKLIST

1. Are there circumstances in which the premises could be true while the conclusion is false?

☐ YES   ☐ NO

2. If so, describe that situation.

_____

_____

_____

A deductive argument is valid only if there are no circumstances in which the premises are true and the conclusion false.

☐ YES   ☐ NO

3. Is there any additional information needed to determine whether the conditional and/or the additional information is acceptable?

☐ YES   ☐ NO

4. If so, what information is needed?

_____

_____

_____

The conclusion of a deductive argument is acceptable only if the argument is valid and the premises are acceptable.

ACCEPTABLE?

☐ YES   ☐ NO

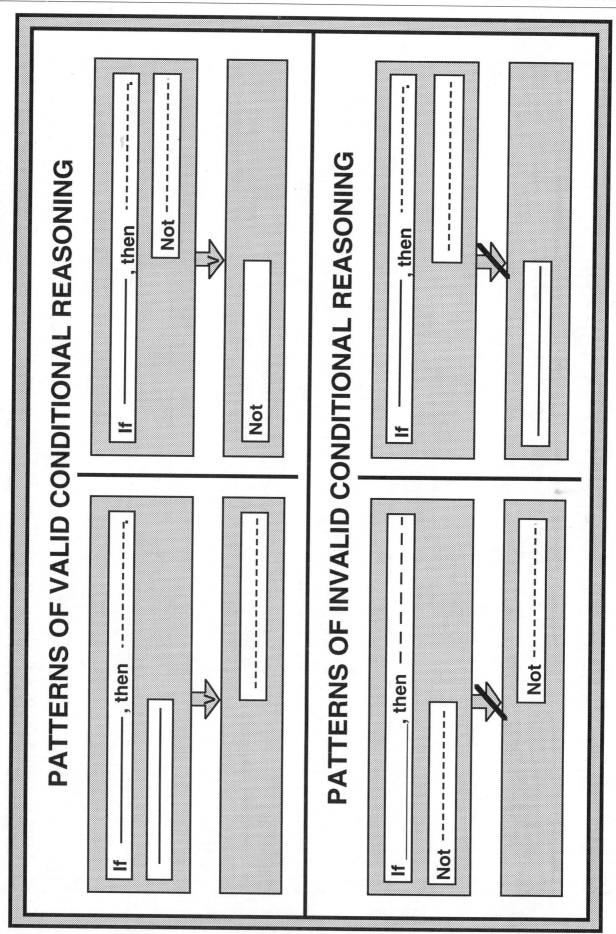

PATTERNS OF VALID CONDITIONAL REASONING

If ——— , then - - - - -

Not - - - - -

→ Not ———

If ——— , then - - - - -

———

→ - - - - -

PATTERNS OF INVALID CONDITIONAL REASONING

If ——— , then - - - - -

- - - - -

↛ ———

If ——— , then - - - - -

Not ———

↛ Not - - - - -

DIGESTION AND GROWTH

Science

Grades 4–6

OBJECTIVES

CONTENT

Students will learn about the role of the pancreas and pituitary glands in regulating growth and digestion. They will learn about the effects that various diseases of these glands have on growth and digestion and how these diseases can be treated.

THINKING SKILL/PROCESS

Students will learn to combine information that is conditional in character (information expressed by "if...then" statements) with other relevant information to draw conclusions.

METHODS AND MATERIALS

CONTENT

Students will gather information about the glands in the human body from their textbooks and outside reading. They will organize this information on a matrix indicating where each gland is, what it does, its disorders, and treatments of these disorders .

THINKING SKILL/PROCESS

Students will be guided to engage in conditional reasoning by structured questions and a graphic organizer. (See pp. 489–92 for reproducible diagrams.) They will also work together in collaborative learning groups to develop rules for conditional reasoning.

LESSON

INTRODUCTION TO CONTENT AND THINKING SKILL/ PROCESS

* If you follow sports, you know that there is a point in the season at which, if one of the teams wins just one more game, that team will win the championship. If you're a fan of that team and you find out that they have won that game, you've got reason to celebrate. You know your team has just won the championship!

* The kind of thinking you've done is called "conditional reasoning." You put two ideas of certain sorts together and drew a conclusion from them.

    One of these ideas was the conditional statement

    <u>If your team wins the next game</u>, <u>it will win the championship</u>.

    You found out that

    <u>Your team has won the game</u>.

    The conclusion you drew was

    <u>Your team has won the championship</u>.

If someone did not know the first of these ideas, but found out that your team won the game, that person wouldn't know what you know—that your team has won the championship. If someone knows that if your team won the next game, it would win the championship, but didn't know what happened in that game, that person also would not know what you know— that your team has won the championship. You know this because you combined these two ideas and drew a conclusion. That's one important way we can learn about things—by drawing good conclusions from things we already know. Can you think of another example in which you came to know something by conditional reasoning? Ask students to discuss the example with a partner and to write down the examples. Have two or three students tell the class about their examples. Write them on the board in the same form as the example about winning the championship. STUDENT ANSWERS VARY.

- These examples of conditional reasoning all have something in common. Notice the first statement. It is an "if...then" statement. That sort of statement is called a "conditional" statement because it tells us that something will happen on the condition that something else happens. That is why this kind of thinking is called "conditional reasoning." Also notice that the second statement tells us that the condition has occurred. When you put these two ideas together you can draw the conclusion that the result has occurred. When you engage in conditional reasoning and you draw a conclusion that does follow from the information you start with, the reasoning is called "valid." There is a specific pattern to this type of valid conditional reasoning. It looks like this chart. Show a larger copy of the conditional reasoning chart at the right.

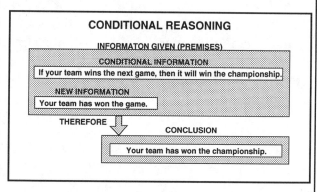

- Work with your partner and write down some more conditional statements. Also, under "New Information," write a second sentence that describes the condition that you'd have to check out before concluding that the result will happen. Then write the statement of what you would be able to conclude under the other part of the conditional statement with an arrow pointing to it from the first two statements. Then discuss with your partner how you might find out whether the condition actually existed. Write "If ___ then ___" on the board and ask the students to fill in the blanks to produce a group of conditional statements that they know are true. Get one example of a conditional statement from the students and write it on the board. Then write the rest of the argument on the board in the same form as the sports example. Under the argument write, "If I can find out ___ I will be able to conclude ___," filled in appropriately. Ask the students to write similar sentences after they have constructed their arguments.

- Conditional reasoning is an example of <u>deductive reasoning</u>. If the reasoning is valid and the information you put together to draw the conclusion is true, this doesn't just make the conclusion likely or probable. The conclusion has to be true. That's what's special about deductive reasoning. Now you can see why this kind of thinking is so important. If you know a conditional statement and you find out that what comes after "if" is true (the condition is satisfied), then what comes after "then" will also be true.

- While conditional reasoning can be a great help to us in putting ideas together and finding out new things, we can also make mistakes in conditional reasoning. Suppose you don't know how your team did in the last game they played, but someone tells you that they won the championship. Can you conclude that they won the last game? Write this reasoning on the board starting with "If your team wins the game, they'll win the championship," and "Your team won the championship," and put a question mark after "Your team won the last game" as the conclusion. This conclusion does not necessarily follow from the information you start with. Your team might have won the championship because the second place team lost the game it was playing and was eliminated, not because your team won its game.

- When the conclusion doesn't follow from the given information, called the premise, the reasoning is "invalid." Here is how to find out if conditional reasoning is invalid. Imagine a situation in which the information you start with could be true and the conclusion false.

That's what we just did when we imagined that the second-place team lost its game. Then, even though your team also lost, it could have won the championship because the second-place team was eliminated. Draw a diagram that represents the pattern of this invalid type of conditional reasoning. Put a slash through the arrow to indicate that the reasoning is invalid. See the diagram at the right.

CONDITIONAL REASONING

INFORMATON GIVEN (PREMISES)

CONDITIONAL INFORMATION

If your team wins the next game, then it will win the championship.

NEW INFORMATION

Your team has won the championship.

THEREFORE

CONCLUSION

Your team has won the game.

- We've been learning some things about our glands—the endocrine system—in science that can be stated conditionally. I'm going to tell you a story about two students—Bob and Sandy—who were studying the endocrine system and described some of the things that they were learning about conditional statements.

THINKING ACTIVELY

- This is a story about two students who had just worked together on a science project in which they had made a chart of the endocrine system. They were fascinated with the idea that tiny glands in various parts of the body can control so many things, such as the way we grow. The chart helped them organize the information they were learning so that they could see it all clearly. They made a column down the side of the chart and listed the glands in the endocrine system in each box. Across the top, they listed different things they were learning that they thought were important about these glands . In the cells under

ENDOCRINE SYSTEM MATRIX

GLAND	IMPORTANT INFORMATION			
	LOCATION Where it is in the body	FUNCTION What it does for people	DISORDERS Possible problems with it	TREATMENT Cures for disorders

each of the headings, they wrote specific information they had gathered about the glands. Use your textbook or library resources to fill in the cells as Bob and Sandy might have. You can also gather supplementary material about the glands and make it available in the classroom.

- Bob became very concerned when he started writing the disorders of the various glands in the disorder column.

    "I didn't realize how important glands were," he said. "If your pancreas doesn't function properly, for example, you can't digest food properly. If your pituitary gland doesn't function properly when you're young, there's a danger that you won't grow."

    Sandy thought about this for a minute. "You know," she said, "I remember my mother telling me that one of the children in the new family that moved in down the street had a problem with his pituitary gland and that's why they were going to the hospital all the time. I didn't realize what that meant then, but I do now. That's scary!"

- Let's think about this to see what would be so scary about what Sandy remembered. What does Bob say that reminds Sandy about the child down the street? *If your pituitary gland doesn't function properly when you're young, there's a danger that you won't grow.*

- **What kind of statement is that?** *A conditional statement.*

- **Let's fill in the steps in Sandy's thinking so that we can determine what she thought about the child down the street that was scary to her. This time we're going to use a graphic organizer that will allow us to state her reasoning. Write the condition you just identified in the top box marked "Conditional Statement."** Students should write "your pituitary gland doesn't function properly when you're young" after the "If" and "there's a danger that you won't grow" after the "then." Ask them what condition they wrote in the diagram and remind them of the conditional statement they just identified if they are having trouble. **What new information did Sandy recall when she heard Bob's conditional statement? Write it in the box for "New Information."** Students should write "A child down has a pituitary gland that doesn't function properly" in the box for new information. If they have a problem with this, ask the students what Sandy remembered about the child who just moved in down the street that has to do with the pituitary gland. **What conclusion do you think she drew based on these two pieces of information? Write the conclusion in the box for "Conclusion."** The conclusion is that there is a danger that the child who moved in down the street may not grow. If they write statements like "Something scary will happen," ask them what was scary. Tell them that sometimes people don't state their conclusions, but they make them all the same.

- **Is this good conditional reasoning—was Sandy right to be concerned? Does the conclusion *follow from* the information she started with? Fill in the argument evaluation checklist on the graphic organizer and explain to your partner why you think the conclusion does or doesn't follow.** Ask for explanations from the students. POSSIBLE ANSWERS: *Yes, it follows, because if the first two statements are true, the conclusion must be true. Yes, because the new information tells us that the condition in the conditional statement is satisfied. The condition is that he has a problem with his pituitary gland, so what it is a condition for (that his growth may be stunted) must be true.* Students may also write out the argument in the form that was used in the team championship example (see p. 493) and show that it falls into the same pattern.

- **Now let's continue the story.**

    While Bob and Sandy were talking, Bob suddenly remembered something. The night before, his mother said she was having a bad case of indigestion. What she ate for dinner was just lying in her stomach like a lump, she said, and it didn't feel good. Bob got worried. "There must be something wrong with my mother's pancreas gland," he said. "And that's serious." He explained to Sandy what his mother had said. Sandy got concerned for a moment, too. But what Bob had said didn't seem quite right.

- **Can you help Sandy figure this out? Use the conditional reasoning graphic organizer to state**

Bob's reasoning. Then discuss with your partner whether this was valid reasoning. Use the form for checking the validity of conditional arguments to explain why you think it is or isn't valid. After a few minutes, ask students to report on how the graphic organizer should be filled in to represent Bob's reasoning.

In this case, the conditional statement is

<u>If your pancreas doesn't function properly</u>, <u>you can't digest food properly</u>.

The new information obtained from Bob's story about his mother is

<u>Bob's mother couldn't digest her food properly last night</u>.

The conclusion is

<u>Bob's mother's pancreas is not functioning properly</u>.

Students usually indicate that the above isn't valid conditional reasoning. POSSIBLE REASONS: *Maybe her indigestion had nothing to do with her pancreas; maybe it was because she ate too much. Maybe she had indigestion because the food was too spicy, not because of her pancreas. This isn't a good conclusion to draw because in the conditional statement we are not told that poor digestion is a condition of the pancreas not functioning properly. Rather, it is the other way around.*

• **As you can see with Bob and Sandy, it is sometimes very easy to get misled: you might think that a conclusion follows from a conditional statement and a new piece of information that appears in the wrong place in the conditional. When we make a mistake like this it is called a "fallacy of reasoning." A fallacy is invalid reasoning in which you think a conclusion follows, but it really doesn't. Who committed the fallacy here, Bob or Sandy?** *Bob did.*

• **Let's think about the child who lives down the street from Sandy. What sorts of things can be done to help someone who has problems with their pituitary gland?** Remind the students that they have just drawn up a matrix that may have this information on it. If it doesn't, ask them to do some research in their textbooks or in the school library to try to see if there is anything that can be done for pituitary disorders and what that might be. Ask them to write their findings in their matrices and to report what they found to the class.

THINKING ABOUT THINKING

• **Let's think about your thinking now. What did you think about to be sure that valid conditional reasoning was used to draw conclusions? List what you thought about and draw up a thinking map to reflect these ideas.** POSSIBLE ANSWERS: *I thought about the conditional statement used to draw the conclusion about the boy who had a problem with his pituitary gland. I identified which part stated a condition and what the result would be if the condition occurred. I then thought about whether or not the condition had occurred. When I found out that the boy had the pituitary problem, I knew the conclusion that he wouldn't grow had to be true. If the statement, "If you have a problem with your pituitary gland, then you don't grow properly," is true and you find out that you have a problem with your pituitary gland, then it must be true that you won't grow properly.*

CONDITIONAL REASONING
1. What topic are you trying to get information about?
2. Formulate a conditional statement that you know about that topic.
3. What information do you have about the components of the conditional statement?
4. What conclusion are you considering?
5. Is it valid to reason from the conditional statement and the given information to the conclusion?
a. If the conditional statement and the given information could be true but the conclusion false, then the reasoning is invalid.
b. If the conditional statement and the given information couldn't be true but the conclusion false, then the reasoning is valid.

I thought about Bob's conclusion that his mother had a problem with her pancreas and wondered if you could really get that conclusion from the information given in the story. I then identified the conditional statement on the topic of glands and the new information Bob added to it to get his conclusion. I tried to imagine a situation in which the information he started with could still be true and yet the conclusion false. When I realized Bob's mother could have had indigestion because she ate too fast, I realized that Bob's reasoning was not valid. The thinking map should resemble the conditional reasoning map on the preceding page.

• **In this lesson, we drew two diagrams of patterns of valid and invalid conditional reasoning. Can you formulate rules about conditional reasoning based on these patterns that will help you to draw valid conclusions from information and avoid committing fallacies?** POSSIBLE ANSWERS: *If the stated condition is true, then you can draw the conclusion that what it is a condition for is true. If what comes after the "then" in a conditional statement is true, you still can't say that the condition is satisfied.*

• **What advice would you give to someone who is having trouble with conditional reasoning to help them avoid making mistakes in their reasoning?** POSSIBLE ANSWERS: *Be clear about the conditional statement that you start with and any other information corresponding to the components of the conditional. Before accepting the conclusion, check your reasoning for validity, and make sure that the information you start with is acceptable.*

APPLYING YOUR THINKING

Immediate Transfer

• **Suppose a record store were selling records at 50% off their regular price. Let's say the sale started last Saturday and was going to last a week. It is now Wednesday and you're in school. You know that on Thursday and Friday you have practice after school and can't get to the record store before it closes. You really want to get a particular record at the sale price. When is the only time you can go to the store to get the record at the sale price?** *Today after school (Wednesday).* **Explain how you used conditional reasoning to conclude this.** POSSIBLE AN-SWERS: *There are two pieces of conditional reasoning that lead to this decision. The first conditional statement can be formulated in the following way: "If I am to buy the record at the sale price, I have to go to the store before Saturday." Since I do want the record at the sale price, I can conclude that I have to go to the record store before Saturday. The second conditional statement is "If I am to go before Saturday, then I have to go on Wednesday, Thursday, or Friday." I can't go on Thursday or Friday, and today is Wednesday, so if I am to go before Saturday, I can only go today (Wednesday). The conditional statement combines with the fact that I do have to go before Saturday to yield my conclusion that I have to go today.* Ask students to fill in the graphic organizer for conditional reasoning as they explain these pieces of reasoning. Then ask them if these are good pieces of reasoning. They should refer to the rules they have formulated for conditional reasoning.

• **Go back to your matrix about the endocrine system. Formulate any conditional statements you can based on the matrix. For example, you could formulate a different conditional statement about the pituitary: If a child grows normally, then that child's pituitary is functioning properly. After you've formulated some conditional statements, pick one and construct a story like the one I just told you. It should involve some conditional reasoning that is good and some conditional reasoning that contains a fallacy.**

Reinforcement Later

Later in the school year, when your students are studying the following topics, prompt their use of conditional reasoning with the given dialog.

• **We've been studying diet and nutrition. Formulate some conditional statements about the results of certain eating habits based on what you've learned. Based on these statements and** what you know about your own eating habits, can you draw some conclusions about the results of how you eat?

• In *Alice in Wonderland*, after Alice went down the rabbit hole, she found a little bottle with a paper label tied around its neck saying "DRINK ME." Here's what happened next:

> It was all very well to say "Drink Me," but the wise little Alice was not going to do that in a hurry. "No, I'll look first," she said, "and see whether it's marked 'poison' or not." She had read several nice little stories about children who had got burned, and eaten up by wild beasts, and other unpleasant things, all because they would not remember the simple rules their friends had taught them. But Alice did remember the rules she had learned. She knew that a red-hot poker will burn you if you hold it too long; and that, if you cut your finger very deeply with a knife, it usually bleeds. And she also never would forget that, if you drink from a bottle marked "poison," it will almost certainly be harmful for you sooner or later. However, this bottle was not marked "poison." Alice decided to taste it....She very soon finished the whole bottle off.

What kind of reasoning leads Alice to drink what is in the bottle? Is this good reasoning? If you were there with her, what would you advise her to do, and why?

THINKING SKILL EXTENSION

You can build on what is taught in this lesson to teach your students other aspects of conditional reasoning. There are two important additional principles that deal with denying the consequent and denying the antecedent. You can use negative information about the consequent of a conditional (what comes after the "then") to draw a negative conclusion indicating that what is stated in the antecedent (what comes after the "if") is false. Suppose that if your team is to win the championship, then it has to win the last two games, and suppose your team didn't win the last two games. It is valid to conclude that your team didn't win the championship. On the other hand, suppose that your team doesn't win the championship. Then you can't conclude that it didn't win the last two games. It could have won the last two games and yet come in second to a team that won its last three games. All the conditional statement tells us is that if the team doesn't win the last two games, it will be eliminated. It doesn't tell us that if it wins those games that guarantees that it will win the championship. You can teach students these forms of conditional reasoning by using these examples, the example from *Alice in Wonderland*, or by constructing examples similar to the ones used in this lesson but representing these types of reasoning. A good way to bring this extension to a close is to ask your students to categorize the four patterns of reasoning represented by the two in the lesson and these additional types. The diagram at the right represents one way to do this.

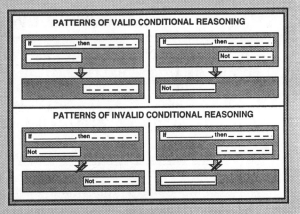

ASSESSING STUDENTS' CONDITIONAL REASONING

You can assess how well students engage in conditional reasoning by using any of the transfer or reinforcement examples and judging whether the students have followed the strategy outlined in the map for conditional reasoning. Make sure you ask students to explain their reasoning when you use these examples. They should use the correct terms (like "conditional") when they explain their reasoning.

Sample Student Responses • Growth and Digestion

CONDITIONAL REASONING

TOPIC: The pituitary gland.

ARGUMENT

CONDITIONAL STATEMENT

If your pituitary gland doesn't function properly,

                                  then there's a danger you won't grow.

NEW INFORMATION

A child down the street has a pituitary gland that doesn't function properly.

CONCLUSION

There is a danger that the child down the street won't grow.

ARGUMENT EVALUATION CHECKLIST

1. Are there circumstances in which the premises could be true while the conclusion is false?
2. Explain.   YES ☐ NO ☒

> It has to be true that the boy down the street is in danger of not growing if
>
> it is true that he has a problem with his pituitary and it is also true that if
>
> someone has a problem with their pituitary, there is a danger he won't grow.

A deductive argument is valid only if there are no circumstances in which the premises are true and the conclusion false.

VALID? YES ☒ NO ☐

Indicate validity and invality in the following ways:

Sample Student Responses • Growth and Digestion

CONDITIONAL REASONING

TOPIC: The pancreas gland.

ARGUMENT

CONDITIONAL STATEMENT

If your pancreas gland doesn't function properly,

then you can't digest food properly.

NEW INFORMATION

Bob's mother couldn't digest her food properly last night.

CONCLUSION

Bob's mother's pancreas is not functioning properly.

ARGUMENT EVALUATION CHECKLIST

1. Are there circumstances in which the premises could be true while the conclusion is false?   YES [X]   NO [ ]

2. Explain.

Bob's mother could have had indigestion because she ate too much. In that case, it might not be true that she has a problem with her pancreas even though the conditional statement and the information about her indigestion are true.

A deductive argument is valid only if there are no circumstances in which the premises are true and the conclusion false.

VALID?

YES [ ]   NO [X]

Indicate validity and invality in the following ways:

LESSON CONTEXTS FOR CONDITIONAL REASONING

The following examples have been suggested by classroom teachers as contexts to develop infused lessons. If a skill or process has been introduced in a previous infused lesson, these contexts may be used to reinforce it.

GRADE	SUBJECT	TOPIC	THINKING ISSUE
K–3	Literature	*How the Grinch Stole Christmas*	Explain whether you believe that the Grinch's conditional statement is something we should be concerned about: If the Whos don't have presents and the decorations of Christmas, then they won't have Christmas at all. If the statement were true, what would happen if the Whos didn't have presents?
K–3	Literature	*Jack and the Beanstalk*	Jack thought that if he stole the goose that laid the golden egg, the giant would get angry. Was he right? Why or why not? He also believed that if he was quiet, he could get away easily. Was he right? Why or why not?
K–3	Social studies	Thanksgiving	The Pilgrims believed that if they shared their food with the Indians, it would help them keep friendly relations with the Indians. What conclusion did they draw about the first Thanksgiving? Were they right? Why?
K–3	Social studies	Settlers in the West	Formulate some "If, then" statements that the settlers believed. Were they right? Why or why not?
K–3	Mathematics	Arithmetic	Suppose that your mother is shopping and she adds three apples to the two she already has in her bag. How many does she have? What conditional statement helped you draw this conclusion? (If you add three to two, that equals five.) Suppose she also has five plums in another bag. Does that mean that she added three plums and two plums together like she did with the apples? Why?
K–3	Mathematics	Geometry	A cube has six square sides. Suppose you are painting a cube and you know that it takes a can of paint to paint one side. What can you conclude about how many cans you will need to paint the whole cube? Explain what "If, then" statement helped you draw this conclusion.
K–3	Science	Food	In the winter when it snows, the snow covers the grass that cattle feed on. What danger can you conclude the cattle are in when this happens? State your reasoning using "If, then" statements. What can people do to help the cattle? Explain your reasoning using "If, then" statements.
K–3	Science	Rain	Students should list many responses about dress, activity, and conditions to the question "If it is raining, .." Ask them whether, if you reverse the order of the parts in the conditional statements, the results say the same thing.
K–3	Science	Water	What "If, then" statement explains why people expect puddles after a snow storm when the weather gets warm? Are they right to expect this?
K–3	Health	Teeth	Eating too much sugar can cause cavities in your teeth. If you don't have many cavities, then you don't have to go to the dentist as much as you would if you had more cavities. What can you conclude about the amount of sugar you eat and how often you may have to go to the dentist?

LESSON CONTEXTS FOR CONDITIONAL REASONING			
GRADE	SUBJECT	TOPIC	THINKING ISSUE
4–6	Literature	*Race Against Death*	In this story by Irma H. Taylor McCall, certain conditional statements are mentioned ("If [the diphtheria epidemic] were not stopped now, it could easily carry hundreds of miles," and "If he could give serum to all the people who were well, they would not get sick.") Identify all of the conditional statements that appear in the story. What inferences can we make from these statements and additional information that we get in the story? How do these inferences carry the drama of the story along?
4–6	Literature	*Paul Revere's Ride*	What inferences does Paul Revere make based on the famous line, "One, if by land, and two, if by sea," in Longfellow's poem? Does he have enough information to make these inferences?
4–6	Literature	*Alice in Wonderland*	When Alice falls down the rabbit hole, she finds a bottle that says "Drink Me" on it. She drinks it because she reasons that it isn't marked poison and if it were marked poison, it would harm her. Is that a wise inference? What are the consequences of this inference? What would she have to find out to be justified in drinking what is in the bottle?
4–6	Social Studies	Ancient Egypt	When the ancient Egyptians settled along the river Nile, they drew the conclusion that they could survive and flourish in this region without having to go back to a nomadic way of life. Formulate the conditional statements that they must have believed when they drew this conclusion (e.g., if they irrigated the land near the river with river water, they could grow crops). Was their reasoning good reasoning?
4–6	Social Studies	Columbus	Columbus believed that if you sailed west from Spain, you would reach Asia. What role did this conditional statement play in his reasoning and in his actions? Was his reasoning sound?
4–6	Mathematics	Geometry	Suppose that you want to locate only right triangles. What can you conclude about a triangle that you know has one obtuse angle? What can you conclude about a triangle that has two acute angles? What can you conclude about a triangle that has two 45-degree angles? Formulate the conditional statements that allow you to draw your conclusions from this information.
4–6	Science	Plants	You know that if you fertilize your plants, they will grow more rapidly. What information would you need to be sure that they will grow more rapidly? What could you conclude if you didn't fertilize your plants?
6	Science	Pollution	Write these facts on the board and ask students to construct a series of conditional arguments based on them, supporting the ban against burning coal in humid regions: 1) Some coal is high in sulphur content. 2) Sulfur reacts with oxygen to make sulfur dioxide. 3) Oxygen in the air is used when coal is burning. 4) Sulfur dioxide irritates the lungs. 5) Sulfur dioxide released into the air can form sulfur trioxide. 6) Sulfur trioxide reacts with water to form sulfuric acid. 7) Sulfuric acid is harmful to plants and animals.
4–6	Health	Smoking	What conclusion can you draw about the risk of cancer if you smoke a pack of cigarettes a day? What conditional statement allows you to draw this conclusion? Is the conditional statement acceptable? Suppose you find out that a person on your street has lung cancer. What conclusion can you draw about his smoking?

PART 6

DESIGNING AND TEACHING INFUSION LESSONS

Chapter 18: Instructional Methods

Chapter 19: The Role of Metacognition

Chapter 20: Selecting Contexts for Infusion Lessons

INFUSION LESSON PLAN EXPLANATION

TITLE:

SUBJECT: GRADE:

OBJECTIVES

CONTENT	THINKING SKILL OR PROCESS
Statement of content objectives from curriculum guide or text outline	Description of the thinking skill/process the students will learn

METHODS AND MATERIALS

CONTENT	THINKING SKILL OR PROCESS
Use of instructional methods to teach the content effectively	Use of instructional methods to teach the thinking process effectively
Expository methods · Using manipulatives Inquiry methods · Discourse/Socratic dialog Co-operative learning · Integrated arts Graphic organizers · Directed observation Advance organizers · Advance organizers Higher order questions · Higher order questions Specialized software · Specialized software	Structured questioning strategies Specialized graphic organizers Collaborative learning, including Think/Pair/Share Direct or inductive explanation of thinking processes Learner-generated cognitive maps (diagrams and pictures)

LESSON

INTRODUCTION TO CONTENT AND THINKING SKILL/PROCESS

Teacher's comments to introduce the content objectives
The lesson introduction should activate students' prior knowledge of the content and establish its relevance and importance.

Teacher's comments to introduce the thinking process and its significance
The lesson introduction should activate students' prior experience with the thinking skill/process, preview the thinking skill/process, and demonstrate the value and usefulness of performing the thinking skillfully. The introduction serves as an anticipatory set for the thinking process and should confirm the benefits of its skillful use.

THINKING ACTIVELY

Active thinking involving verbal prompts and graphic maps
The main activity of the lesson interweaves the explicit thinking skill/process with the content. This is what makes the content lesson an infused lesson. Students are guided through the thinking activity by verbal prompts (e.g., questions) in the language of the thinking skill/process and by graphic organizers.

INFUSION LESSON PLAN EXPLANATION

THINKING ABOUT THINKING

Distancing activities that help students think about the thinking process
Students are asked direct questions about their thinking. The metacognition map guides the composition of these questions. Students reflect about what kind of thinking they did, how they did it, and how effective it was.

APPLYING THINKING

Transfer activities that involve student-prompted use of the skill in other examples
There are two broad categories of transfer activities: (1) near or far activities that immediately follow the substance of the lesson and (2) reinforcement later in the school year. Both types of transfer involve less teacher prompting of the thinking process than in the Thinking Actively component of the lesson.

Immediate transfer

Near transfer: Application of the process within the same class session or soon afterward to content similar to that of the initial infusion lesson. Decrease teacher prompting of the thinking.

Far Transfer: Application of the process within the same class session or soon afterward to content different from that of the initial infusion lesson. Decrease teacher prompting of the thinking.

Reinforcement later Application of the process later in the school year to content different from that of the infusion lesson. Decrease teacher prompting of the thinking.

OPTIONAL EXTENSION ACTIVITIES
(Can occur at any time during the lesson)

REINFORCING OTHER THINKING SKILLS AND PROCESSES: Working on additional thinking skills/processes from previous infusion lessons which can play a role in this lesson.

RESEARCH EXTENSION: Gathering additional information which may be useful in reaching a conclusion or an interpretation in this lesson.

USE OF SPECIALIZED ASSIGNMENTS TO REINFORCE THE THINKING: Assigning written or oral tasks or projects which may further illustrate students' thinking about the content in this lesson.

ASSESSING STUDENT THINKING

Extended written or oral assignments or performance assessments of the effective use of the thinking skill or process

CHAPTER 18
INSTRUCTIONAL METHODS IN INFUSION LESSONS

Instructional Methods That Prompt Student Thinking

Infusion blends explicit instruction in thinking skills and processes with content instruction, using methods which enhance students' thinking and comprehension of the content. Understanding how these methods affect students' thinking enables you to select, combine, and vary instructional techniques in order to create rich and effective infusion lessons.

Various instructional methods are used in infusion lessons for different purposes: to teach the thinking skills and processes, to foster thinking collaboratively, to prompt students to learn content thoughtfully, and to promote thoughtful habits of mind. Instructional methods to achieve the first and second purposes are featured in all infusion lessons and give them their special character. Methods that promote thoughtful content learning will vary from discipline to discipline based on effectiveness in teaching objectives within a field. Techniques to promote thoughtfulness and a thinking disposition are featured in all infusion lessons.

Direct instruction strategies to teach thinking skills and processes. All infusion lessons feature an array of instructional strategies to promote clarity and reflection about the thinking skill or process and to guide students in developing patterns of skillful thinking. These strategies—structured questioning and using specialized graphic organizers—make explicit what is involved in skillful thinking. These methods distinguish infusion lessons from other approaches for prompting thinking in content learning. Modifications in using each of these methods make lessons varied and developmentally appropriate.

Thoughtful discussion of thinking and content through guided collaborative tasks. In infusion lessons, students carry out their thinking in a social context. A variety of collaborative and cooperative learning strategies are used in these lessons as students are given thinking challenges. These strategies encourage student thinking by prompting interaction with other students. In addition, each lesson varies small-group work with thinking tasks for individual students and class discussion. Blending individual thinking and group interaction shows students how the interplay of ideas enhances the ideas of each individual.

Instructional methods that prompt thoughtful content learning. The selection of instructional methods to teach content thoughtfully in infusion lessons varies based on appropriateness to the content and the level of cognitive development of students. Such methods include guided reading, asking higher order questions, prompting writing for reflection, directed essay writing, using standard graphic organizers or student-generated cognitive and concept maps, employing Socratic dialogue, engaging students in "hands-on" investigation, using mathematics manipulatives, prompting student questioning, and using whole-language techniques. Selecting such methods carefully and using them in developmentally appropriate and thoughtful ways promotes students' responsiveness to the explicit thinking instruction that occurs in these lessons as well as enhancing their deep understanding of the content.

General teacher behaviors that model good thinking dispositions. One of the goals of thinking instruction is to demonstrate the habits of mind that good thinkers are disposed to use—their thinking dispositions. Certain behaviors that teachers engage in model the thinking dispositions that we seek to foster in students. These habits of thoughtful interaction with students in any instructional context should occur regularly in infusion lessons as well. Practices that encourage the thinking dispositions we seek to foster in students include allowing wait time; prompting reconsideration; asking clarifying questions; responding with acceptance; listening with empathy and in order to clarify understanding; using precision in language and promoting precision of expression; and requesting evidence.

Selecting instructional methods. Instructional methods from each category can blend to design lessons that are varied in form, robust in fostering students' thinking, rich in deep understanding of the content, and supportive of a classroom culture of thoughtfulness.

The outline in figure 18.1 summarizes how information on instructional methods is organized in this chapter.

Instructional Methods for Teaching Thinking Skills and Processes in Infusion Lessons

Using thinking maps. The key element of an infusion lesson is the use of a thinking map to clarify and organize skillful thinking. A thinking map (also called a thinking map) is a structured list of key questions phrased in the language of the thinking skill or process which leads to an informed judgment. These are questions that thoughtful people ask when they engage in skillful thinking. They are sequenced in a natural order to represent effective ways of organizing one's thinking but may be reconsidered and raised again at any time during the process in order to give more depth and thoroughness to the thinking.

Thinking maps provide visual reminders in making the thinking skillful. They may be written on the blackboard, displayed on a poster,

---

INSTRUCTIONAL METHODS FEATURED IN INFUSION LESSONS

INSTRUCTIONAL METHODS TO TEACH THINKING DIRECTLY (FEATURED IN ALL INFUSION LESSONS)

   Using thinking maps
   Using specialized graphic organizers to guide thinking
   Structured oral questioning

INSTRUCTIONAL METHODS TO FOSTER THOUGHTFULNESS AS STUDENTS ENGAGE WITH THE CONTENT (VARY IN INFUSION LESSONS)

   Using graphic organizers to depict information
   Higher-order questioning
   Whole-language techniques
   Guided reading
   Reflective writing
   Essay writing
   Using manipulatives

INSTRUCTIONAL METHODS TO FOSTER THOUGHTFULNESS AS A SOCIAL ENDEAVOR (FEATURED IN ALL INFUSION LESSONS)

   Pooling background information
   Collaborative engagement with thinking tasks
   Cooperative learning strategies
   Think/Pair/Share
   Varying individual, small group, and class discussion

TEACHER BEHAVIORS WHICH PROMOTE THOUGHTFULNESS AND THINKING DISPOSITIONS (FEATURED IN ALL INFUSION LESSONS)

   Allowing wait time
   Prompting reconsideration
   Using precision in language and promoting that in students' responses
   Asking clarifying questions about students' responses
   Asking for reasons for students' judgements

Figure 18.1

---

projected on a screen using a transparency, or photocopied for each student.

Whenever possible, derive the thinking map from students' understanding of the thinking skill or process. In the decision-making lesson on *Mr. Arable and the Runt Pig*, students' comments are organized and transcribed to produce the thinking map of skillful decision making. In the *Canals of Mars*, student's questions about the reliability and accuracy of the observer's report are categorized, producing a thinking map to guide making well-considered judgments about the reliability of any observation.

In some lessons, however, written thinking maps are displayed or shown to students in the lesson introduction, and the students are asked to use them. This is especially appropriate with primary grade students. In these cases, the language and complexity of the maps is revised to make them appropriate for young students. For example, the thinking map for decision making used in *Horton and the Hunters* is provided directly to primary grade students to guide their thinking about what Horton should do. Its language is a simplification of the more sophisticated thinking map for decision making that is used in lessons like *Alternative Energy Sources*.

Whether or not these maps are derived inductively, their use prompts students to raise and answer a series of questions in order to make an organized and careful judgment. Wherever possible, students' own wording of the thinking map should be used in your initial lesson and in transfer activities.

Thinking maps, not necessarily expressed in the terms students will use, have a second role in the methodology of direct instruction. Teachers may follow the thinking maps to keep their own thinking focused as they guide discussion.

By posting the thinking maps in the classroom, students are reminded of the guiding questions for skillful thinking when called upon to use that kind of thinking in the future. The steps on the displayed thinking map serve as a checklist for key points in the thinking activity.

Using thinking maps promotes skillful thinking directly by

- Providing key questions that students answer as they engage in a thinking activity

- Demonstrating to students that they have insight and capability at thinking

- Promoting recall of the thinking skill or process

- Modeling reflection about one's thinking

- Promoting students' confidence and competence in skillful thinking

Structured oral questioning. Questions prompt thinking. The kind of thinking prompted, however, is primarily a function of the type of question asked, the context in which it is asked, and students' background knowledge. Using structured questioning in a classroom is the oral equivalent of using a thinking map to guide students through a process of thinking. In structured questioning, the teacher or the students identify the type of thinking being done (e.g., decision making). The questions focus students on the key attention points in doing this type of thinking skillfully. Thus, as they are thinking about Mr. Arable's decision to kill the runt pig, the teacher asks students to put themselves in Mr. Arable's position and to suggest what options he has. When they have had a chance to explore this, she asks them to select an option and to answer the question, "What will the consequences of this option be?"

Structured questioning is an important ingredient in the direct instruction of thinking incorporated into infusion lessons. The repetition of these questions not only prompts students' thinking but also gets students used to these questions as they engage in the thinking activity. Thus, students will get used to hearing "What are the options?" as they go through a process of decision making or "What possible evidence would show that this was the cause?" as they go through a process of causal explanation.

This type of questioning goes hand-in-hand with the thinking maps. Together they form the first step in internalizing these questions as students engage in these thinking activities.

Using structured questioning promotes skillful thinking by

- Identifying a sequence of important questions to ask in skillful thinking

- Providing auditory cues that prompt students' organized thinking

- Helping students to recall important questions to ask as they engage in a specific type of thinking

Use of specialized graphic organizers to guide the thinking process. This handbook provides graphic organizers that are specially designed for the thinking skills and processes that are taught in the lessons. These graphic organizers serve as visual guides to involve students in active thinking about the content.

The graphic organizers in this book serve four purposes. Their most important feature is that they visually guide the process of thinking about a variety of factors. They are "graphic maps" of the thinking process, guiding students through the thinking by using diagrams, symbols, and the language of the thinking skill or process. Students "picture" the questions raised by the thinking maps. Using the graphic organizers also allows students to "download" information so that they can use it meaningfully, not relying on remembering large quantities of data. In addition, the graphic organizers depict and organize complex information so that relationships among pieces of information are made clear and can be easily managed.

Graphic organizers that guide us through a process of skillful thinking are different from graphic organizers that merely depict information and its relationship. The data matrix used in the *Growth and Digestion* lesson helps us to organize information and to understand relationships but does not guide our thinking.

On the other hand, in *The Wave* lesson, the graphic organizer prompts students to think systematically about evidence of the likelihood of the consequences of Ojiisan's decision to burn his rice fields. The graphic organizer not only holds details about conditions in the story but also visually represents how the likelihood of the consequences is weighed and incorporates terms like "prediction," "possible consequence," "evidence," and "likelihood."

Graphic organizers can be used in two different ways in infusion lessons: (1) individual students or collaborative learning groups use them to *guide* their thinking and (2) individual students, a collaborative group, or an entire class can use them to *record* their thoughts.

Both in individual and small group work, the primary purpose of using a graphic organizer is to guide students' thinking. Graphic organizers lose their effectiveness if individual students use them only to record the results of someone else's thought, such as copying comments. Teachers may, however, record students' responses on a transparency or drawing of the graphic organizer *after* the students have worked on their own diagrams.

When collaborative learning groups work on different issues (for example, when each group is working on a different problem solution using problem-solving diagrams), students can write their deliberations on a transparency of the graphic organizer or a large poster of the diagram and then display the group report. These completed graphics can then serve as the basis for the class to form its judgment on the issue.

After an infusion lesson, the graphic organizers can be posted as a bulletin board display to remind students of the thinking activity. The completed diagram of the initial thinking activity becomes a metacognitive tool to prompt students' recall of the process and to transfer the thinking skill to other contexts.

The goal in using graphic organizers is to demonstrate the usefulness of "drawing out one's thought" and not to make students' thinking conform to any given design. Ask students to critique graphic organizers used in lessons and to design other diagrams to represent their skillful thinking. Some diagrams, such as the cognitive maps used in the classification lesson on animals, are completely user-generated and follow no given form.

Using graphic organizers promotes skillful thinking by

- Guiding students to organize their thinking
- Utilizing figural/visual learning style to organize verbal information
- Serving as a visual outline of relationships between pieces of information (particularly useful as a pre-writing tool)
- Promoting retention of the thinking process, as well as a deep understanding of the content

Summary of instructional strategies used for direct instruction in skillful thinking. In infusion lessons, two instructional strategies (structured questioning using thinking maps and specialized graphic organizers) blend to incorporate direct instruction in thinking into content lessons. These strategies may be used in a variety of ways to guide students' thinking, to prompt them to use the language of the thinking skill, and to help them recall and guide their own thinking in other situations.

Instructional Methods Used to Foster Students' Collaboration with Others

All infusion lessons involve collaborative learning experiences: discussion with one or more partners, working independently, and whole-class consideration of thinking issues. When accompanied by thinking prompts (e.g., questioning strategies), cooperative learning techniques help students reason together as a social endeavor and foster a variety of dispositions of good thinking, such as the willingness to listen to and respect the ideas of others.

Collaborative group thinking: open small-group work on a thinking task. When students in small groups brainstorm possible causes of the extinction of the dinosaurs in the lesson on *The Extinction of the Dinosaurs,* they discuss ideas and generate possible explanations. Similarly, when they work together in small groups to make a judgment about the function of a specific part of the kestrel in the lesson on *The Kestrel,* they think together in a more convergent task. In both of these cases, students are prompted by the teacher to engage in a specific thinking task, but their group work is not structured for any other instructional or social purpose.

In such collaborative work, students' discussion stimulates ideas that they might not otherwise have developed. Prompted by the ideas of other students, they may modify their ideas in ways that they might not have considered if working on their own. Engaging students in metacognitive reflection on using the thinking strategy helps students to clarify their own thinking and learning processes.

Cooperative learning: organized small-group work for thinking. Cooperative learning refers to specific procedures to achieve a variety of goals related to group interaction.

One popular method of cooperative learning involves using techniques to teach group functioning (face-to-face interaction, individual accountability, the development of social skills, positive interdependence, and group processing regarding how they work as a team). Others are more content focused, including teacher-assisted individualization involving mixed-ability groups working in teams on a mathematics task, cooperative reading, group demonstration of mastery, games and tournaments, and student teams' analysis of given answers. A third approach involves content-free "structures" that can be applied to content: answering in a prescribed order like "round robin," using a "jigsaw" in which each member teaches another a part, or "match ups" that make students partners. Other models involve group investigation which stresses problem solving and reports.

You can use different cooperative learning systems in the same infusion lesson. Gathering information on energy sources in *Alternative Energy Sources* can serve as a context for teaching team functioning and social skills. Mixing ability groups and helping students demonstrate their understanding in a game-like presentation can enhance content learning, resulting in a lesson that is especially motivating and beneficial for low-ability students. A jigsaw activity allows students to teach each other the information they have gathered. Using group investigation procedures that incorporate problem-solving strategies can enrich students' research about energy sources.

Think/Pair/Share as a cooperative learning strategy. "Think/Pair/Share" commonly means any activity in which two students discuss what they are learning and reflect on how they think through or comprehend some new concept or process. A technique called "paired problem solving" involves one student listening and asking reflective questions as the partner talks about how he or she is working a mathematics problem. The listener prompts clarification of the partner's strategy for solving the problem.

In *Lincoln and Douglass,* Think/Pair/Share takes the form of a directed-listening activity in which students working in pairs take turns assisting each other to express their ideas as clearly as possible. The listener raises questions to assist the partner to reconsider, refine, modify, or extend his or her answer.

In this highly structured, collaborative activity, one partner reads and clarifies a statement, interpretation, or conclusion that he or she has thought about and written out. In order not to impose his or her own ideas on the speaker's, the listener may only ask questions:

> Questions of clarification: If the listener does not understand what a term means or does not follow the meaning of the statement, he or she may ask questions to clarify what is being said.

> Questions which extend the idea: If the listener thinks the partner is suggesting something important but that it needs elaboration, the listener may ask the partner for more details.

> Questions to challenge what is said: If the listener thinks the partner is misled or confused, the listener may ask questions to prompt the speaker to reconsider aspects of the statement.

After two minutes of reflection, the teacher signals students to change roles. After both partners have served as speaker and listener, students have the opportunity to reread, reconsider, or restate their statements.

Think/Pair/Share demonstrates the value of wait time, clarification, and reconsideration. It allows deliberate or uncertain students to review their responses and to express their ideas in their best choice of words.

Using collaborative and/or cooperative learning promotes thinking by

- Prompting ideas through student interaction
- Engaging students in reflective collaboration
- Promoting self-correction and confidence in expressing ideas
- Confirming the value of students' own words and understanding

- Engaging students in reflective understanding of information
- Demonstrating active listening for another's ideas

Pooling information. Model infusion lessons usually involve a class discussion in which information about the content is pooled to provide a common knowledge base for the thinking activity. As students share what they know individually or after working in small collaborative learning groups, the teacher writes all responses on the board or on a transparency. In the lesson on creating metaphors, student responses create an array of attributes and details which other students may use to develop their own metaphors.

A more structured version of this strategy involves asking students what they know, think they know, and need to know about a subject and then recording what they say on a special information-organizing diagram. In the lesson on *The Bottom of the Ocean,* students' responses are listed on a Know/Think You Know/Need to Know organizer. This technique creates a class composite of significant information and research in order to conduct subsequent examination of an issue or concept.

This form of collaborative learning promotes thinking by

- Identifying and utilizing students' prior and current knowledge to establish a common knowledge base for examining an issue or concept
- Promoting retention
- Validating students' understanding of concepts and information

Varying individual, small group, and class discussion of the thinking skill or process. Infusion lessons involve individual reflection (often as writing or drawing activities), small group discussion, and engagement in a thinking activity through discussion in the whole class. This progression from individual to group consideration affirms the value of individual perspective, small group work for creativity and refining ideas, and whole-class participation to consider important information and processes.

Varying levels of interaction foster responses

from students who are reluctant to volunteer responses and is often more time efficient than waiting for individual students' responses in whole-group discussion.

In many infusion lessons, after a skill or process is demonstrated the first time, it is repeated with a smaller group, which reports its findings. In *Mr. Arable and the Runt Pig*, students work in collaborative learning groups on the consequences of an option and then pool their results with the rest of the class. They repeat the process with another option, transferring the process to another context immediately.

After students have practiced a thinking process with sufficient guidance to do it skillfully, small groups may repeat the process by considering additional options, consequences, or evidence. After the whole class reviews the small group reports, the collected analysis helps students make an informed judgment in a time-effective manner. This practice provides immediate transfer of the thinking skill or process.

Providing many opportunities for individual, small-group, and large-group consideration promotes thinking by

- Demonstrating the role and value of individual reflection in the larger context of group discussion
- Demonstrating the value of small-group discussion in an individual's thinking and learning
- Demonstrating to students that they have background about the content and insight about the process

Other Instructional Methods Used in Infusion Lessons to Foster Thoughtfulness

Higher order questioning. Asking higher order questions commonly refers to posing questions which prompt students to be analytical, creative, or evaluative about the content that they are learning. This type of questioning contrasts with asking question which basically require only recall.

While questions which ask why, how, and what-if are sometimes identified as higher order questions, context also determines the type of thinking a student does. A "Why" question asked after students have read a passage which explains why something happens requires only simple recall.

Higher order questioning typically seeks to extend or clarify students' understanding of information by asking questions about relationships, by seeking new ideas about a subject, or by requesting support for judgment about the content. With these goals in mind, a broad range of questions beyond simple why, how, and what-if questions can be formulated to prompt these kinds of thinking. For example, expanding a why question into a "Why do you think..." question, or asking more directly, "What reasons do you have for thinking..." makes it clearly a request for reasons. We recommend that teachers who wish to improve the quality of their questions use the original outline provided by Benjamin Bloom and his colleagues rather than relying on the simplified question stems often presented as expressions of the Bloom model.

In *Lincoln and Douglass*, higher order questions clarify and extend students' responses in comparing and contrasting the two leaders. The teacher asks questions about the cause, effect, significance, or implications of information that students cite. Since the compare/contrast process leads to an interpretation or conclusion about the two leaders based on their similarities and differences, such questioning brings out deeper understanding of the implications of the information that students have identified.

When you ask higher order questions, you model how thoughtful people interact with information that they are presented. While asking higher order questions prompts thoughtfulness about the subject, students do not learn a strategy for skillful thinking unless the thinking process is made explicit. Because including higher order questions in infusion lessons enhances understanding of the content, when students learn the thinking strategy, they gain more insight about the issue.

Using higher order questions in infusion lessons promotes thinking by

- Requesting student responses about relationships, new ideas, and reasons for judgments

- Modeling how thoughtful people interact with information

Using manipulatives. Manipulatives refers to concrete objects that the learner examines, moves, or operates as he or she is learning concepts or processes. Manipulatives usually prompt curiosity and can lead to discoveries in which students make use of various forms of thinking.

While manipulatives are commonly used to illustrate concepts in mathematics and science, it is students' own manipulation of specimens, artifacts, or models that brings out their thinking. Where this is not possible, detailed pictures or sentence strips may also used as semi-concrete manipulative tools.

Using manipulatives appeals to visual and tactile learning styles and to the developmental readiness of elementary students. While using manipulatives is essential in teaching young children, they are helpful in any instruction in which observing characteristics is required. Presenting the content in developmentally appropriate ways frees the child to engage in active thinking about it.

One may conduct *Henny Penny*, for example, as a hands-on activity by giving primary grade students a bag full of artifacts that they sort and think about in order to find evidence about what hit Henny Penny on the head. Seeing actual objects prompts more questions about these clues than engagement with the story alone will do and often provides students with more authentic contexts for learning.

In the *Animals of the World* lesson, detailed photographs are arranged on a cognitive map which learners design as a group. The pictures illustrate details about the animals that elementary students would have to read long passages to discover. Matching details visually prompts asking what those similar characteristics mean. Moving the picture around the cognitive map prompts consideration of the most appropriate classification of the animal.

While manipulatives are important in teaching small children, they are helpful in any instruction in which observing characteristics is required.

Using manipulatives brings out student thinking by

- Prompting students' curiosity about the concrete objects they are working with

- Allowing students to perceive characteristics of objects in detail

- Enriching interpersonal interaction in small group discussion

Whole-language techniques. A whole-language approach to reading, as defined in the professional literature, involves four basic ingredients. Students read *whole works* of children's literature, as compared to reading passages in basal readers designed to teach word attack skills. Instruction focuses on the *whole range of language experiences* (writing, speaking, drama, puppetry, choral reading, etc.) to increase students' comprehension and appreciation of a work. Students are encouraged to bring their *whole life experiences* (background, feelings, values, etc.) to interact with what they are reading. Finally, students also *examine a story holistically*, considering how all elements of the work (illustrations, background, format, style, etc.) affect its meaning. This is the approach used when infusion lessons are developed in language arts or involve reading in the content areas.

In *Henny Penny*, for example, students listen to the story, often viewing large illustrations of it as well. Students are encouraged to repeat the order in which the animals joined the group that was going to warn the king that the sky was falling. To determine what caused the bump on Henny Penny's head, students must examine the illustrations for clues. Similarly, in *The Wave*, students interact with the story by integrating their background knowledge of Japan with details in the text to predict the consequences of the main character's actions and also to gain insight about his character.

Using whole-language techniques promotes thinking by

- Prompting a search for meaning in what is read

- Appealing to a variety of learning styles

- Examining children's literature and nonfiction in ways that are developmentally and socially appropriate

- Confirming the value of students' own understanding and appreciation of a text

Guided reading. Guided reading involves prompting students to think about what they are reading in certain ways. For example, students may be asked to read for specific patterns or topics within a passage. In *Lincoln and Douglass*, they are asked to pick out and record similarities and differences between Lincoln and Douglass as they read and compare two texts. Often guided reading prompts students to interact with the text by "downloading" information onto a graphic organizer as they read the passage.

Guided reading promotes thinking by

- Identifying a common knowledge base for examining an issue or concept

- Prompting students to search a text for specific items

Engaging students in writing for reflection. Writing for reflection includes a variety of writing experiences in which students "think on paper." They are asked to reflect on their analyses, conclusions, or interpretations by writing both their thoughts and the thinking involved in developing that understanding. The writing may be in journals, double-entry records, or short essays. Writing for clarification before discussion is especially helpful for students who are uncertain about their ideas. As the "hard copy" of a student's thinking, reflective writing is a valuable addition to thinking or writing portfolios. Such writing helps to confirm to students that they have sound ideas before they respond in class, allowing deliberate learners to gather their thoughts before expressing them in class discussion.

At any stage of an infusion lesson, students may write to reflect about their thinking, as well as about the content they are learning. They can write to recall prior experiences with the thinking skill or process in the lesson introduction, to clarify the thinking activity in the lesson as it happens, to record their metacognition retrospectively, or to preview when the thinking process might be helpful again.

An example of how writing helps students to reflect on the content occurs in the *Lincoln and Douglass* lesson. Students write out their conclusions or interpretations before discussing it with

a partner. Writing out their thought clarifies meaning, promotes students' ownership and confidence in their conclusions, and provides a record for reconsideration and restatement. Then, after discussing their statement with a partner, they rewrite their statement to make their ideas clearer.

In *Mr. Arable and the Runt Pig*, students write about decisions they made in the past along with ideas about how to improve their thinking. Then, after trying some of these ideas out, they write a plan for decision making that they can use in the future based on their metacognitive reflection of previous experience.

Writing for reflection promotes thinking by

- Providing a vehicle for clear expression of one's thinking

- Promoting self-correction and confidence in expressing ideas

- Confirming the value of students' own words and understanding

- Modeling the reflective understanding of information

Essay writing. Essay writing, as a follow up to an infusion lesson, can extend student thinking about the content studied in the lesson. In *Moctezuma and Cortes* and in *Loyalty and Independence*, students propose a recommendation for action, drawing upon the thinking they've done in the lesson. They should always be asked to support the thesis of the essay with reasons or details, as appropriate. Essays offer an extended consideration of the reasons for decisions, conclusions, or interpretation.

Follow-up essays should be of appropriate length to address the thinking issue in the lesson. The essay should confirm that the thinking process featured in the lesson is reflected in the student's writing.

Essays may also be used as a tool for personal reflection in the introduction to an infusion lesson. For example, students write about their decisions and what they might do to improve them in *Mr. Arable and the Runt Pig* as a prelude to developing a thinking map for skillful decision making. Any of the thinking skills and processes featured in this handbook can be addressed in essays.

Essay writing promotes thinking by

- Applying thinking processes in writing
- Promoting self-correction and confidence in expressing ideas
- Confirming the value of students' own words and understanding
- Allowing extended response and fully developed expression of students' thought.

Using content-oriented graphic organizers. A variety of graphics (matrices, Venn diagrams, flow charts, branching hierarchical diagrams, story maps, web or fishbone diagrams) depict how information is related. In contrast to the specialized graphics to guide thinking, these graphic organizers prompt students to think about and to organize the content they are learning. Many such graphics stimulate analytical forms of thinking.

In *Alternative Energy,* a data matrix is used to record students' findings and to guide additional research. These matrices promote systematic investigation of the content and summarize information to assist students in forming generalizations about the material. By examining the energy information in rows, one summarizes the pros and cons of a particular source. By examining the columns, one compares various types of energy in light of a particular variable, such as ease of production or effect on the environment.

In *A Metaphor for a Dinosaur,* a comparison graphic organizer is used in the introduction to show students how metaphors work. The purpose of the graphic organizer is to record ideas that express similarities between a cat and fog, thereby addressing what the metaphor of a cat communicates in the Robert Frost poem "Fog." The graphic organizer for the process of creating metaphors, also used in this lesson, is a thinking-skill graphic and functions quite differently. It, like other thinking-oriented graphics used in infusion lessons, guides students to follow the strategy for creating metaphors.

For some information-oriented graphic organizers, a standard design outlines information visually. Venn diagrams, flow charts, and matrices are common forms for showing relationships among data.

Some graphic organizers, on the other hand, like concept maps or cognitive maps are user-generated to reflect the perceptions of its creator. Concept maps are web-like diagrams with many branches and "bubbles." They are used to record metaphors in creative thinking or to depict attributes in analytical thinking. In *Animals of the World,* the shape of a cognitive map depends on how the student classifies an array of organisms.

Information-oriented graphic organizers promote student thinking by

- Providing a structure which organizes information in relation to other information
- Depicting types of relationships among pieces of information
- Prompting drawing conclusions or interpretations by comparing pieces of information depicted on the graphic

Additional instructional methods for teaching the content in infusion lessons. Selecting the best fit of instructional methods for content improves the quality of instruction in infusion lessons, as it does in any classroom context. The outline shown in figure 18.1 summarizes some, but not all, instructional methods to improve thoughtfulness and understanding of content. We recommend that when teams of teachers work together to plan infusion lessons, careful attention be given to using a variety of well-researched instructional strategies that can promote student thinking.

Teacher Behaviors That Model Thinking Dispositions in the Classroom

One goal of thinking instruction is to help students develop the habits of mind of effective thinkers and to become disposed to demonstrate these thinking habits when needed. Some teaching behaviors, whatever the activity, promote a classroom climate of thoughtfulness. These behaviors model important thinking dispositions and should be employed in infusion lessons as well.

Using sufficient wait time. Research indicates that teachers commonly give students too little time to formulate thoughtful answers. Often teachers ask students questions and then, when no one responds, they answer the question themselves. In addition, many teachers acknowledge student responses too quickly and don't give other students time to think about their answers.

Both practices suggest that the teacher values facility over depth, short responses over rich consideration, and quick reply over careful reflection. Students who are deliberate thinkers and who take time to reflect about the richness or accuracy of their responses are sometimes characterized as "slow," suggesting lack of ability rather than speed of response. We as a society tend to misconstrue speed as capability.

Good thinkers take time to think things through carefully when time is available. Deliberate consideration is a valued disposition in sound thinking. Varying the pace of instruction demonstrates that some kinds of tasks warrant quick responses and others require careful thinking. Students begin to recognize that thinking tasks which require judgment also require more time. Practice "wait time," time for thinking which may involve several minutes of silence. Cooperative group work on a thinking issue can also extend the time in which students arrive at a reflective response. Writing for reflection, if only jotting down preliminary ideas, improves the quality of students' responses.

Using wait time promotes thinking by

- Modeling reflective thinking
- Promoting students' confidence in expressing ideas
- Confirming the value of students' own words, understanding, and ideas
- Valuing differences in thought processing and learning style

Asking several questions to clarify and extend a student's responses. Students often expect that they will only have one chance to explain their ideas before the teacher must give others a chance to respond. Teachers' habit of accepting one-sentence answers limits students' processing time to the few seconds before they reply, as well as limiting the amount of time that students expect to take to express their ideas.

Asking additional questions to clarify and extend a student's response models other important dispositions of thinking: continuing to develop and elaborate one's thought and resisting impulsivity.

Often higher order thinking skills are involved in follow-up questions: requesting reasons, possible causes or results, inquiring about why certain information seemed important, asking what inferences can be drawn from what the student has reported, etc. As students realize that the teacher's additional questions about their ideas allow them to give richer answers, they curb their impulsivity, refraining from giving quick "sound bite" answers.

Asking several clarifying questions improves thinking by

- Modeling taking time for the elaboration and development of one's ideas
- Modeling the resisting of impulsivity
- Modeling a reflective understanding of information and active listening
- Promoting students' confidence in expressing ideas by demonstrating that questions are not just "tests" for right answers but the means of understanding
- Confirming the value of students' own words, understanding, and ideas

Prompt reconsideration. An extension of the previous technique is to ask the student directly to take time to reconsider and restate any conclusions or previous understanding of an issue. Reconsideration could be based on acquiring new information, using the thinking process in class, or arriving at new insight through collaborative discussion. Reconsideration of previously held views demonstrates open-mindedness and personal responsibility for one's views and actions.

Teachers may explicitly add time in writing activities for students to reread and reconsider what they have written and restate their ideas if necessary. Students must believe that there is more respect in reconsideration than in persisting to hold mistaken ideas. Acknowledge such intellectual maturity and be willing to share your own reconsideration of ideas.

Prompting reconsideration promotes thinking by

- Modeling open-mindedness
- Promoting self-correction and confidence in expressing ideas
- Confirming the value of students' own words and understanding
- Modeling reflective understanding of information

Using precision in language and promoting precision of expression. Critical thinking both requires and promotes precision in the use of language. Being disposed to seek clarity is an important disposition of critical thinkers. Often when students are unclear or ambiguous in oral and written responses, they are also unclear and ambiguous about the language of thinking. For example, adults and students often say "I feel" for "I believe." Whether confused about whether an idea is well-supported or is intuitive, or unwilling to take the stronger stand of stating a belief rather than a hunch, the speaker is expressing an idea in a misleading way.

The habit of defining terms, concepts, and issues clearly is the mark of a critical thinker. Acknowledge and value responses in which a student restates for clarity or raises respectful questions about the clarity of others. Rethink and restate your own descriptions or explanations to demonstrate that you believe that clarity is important.

Demonstrating and valuing precision in language

- Models the desirability of clarity
- Promotes self-correction and confidence in expressing ideas
- Confirms the value of students' own words and understanding
- Models reflective understanding of information

Requesting evidence. Seeking reasons for ideas is an important thinking disposition. Not accepting an idea as true until we are convinced that it is well-supported is a mark of a critical thinker. Often students develop beliefs without support for those views. Continuing to ask students for their reasons when they advance ideas, especially controversial ones, models this search for good reasons to support our judgments.

Often when students request evidence to support or reject an idea, it is in a spirit of challenge or disagreement. When students realize that critical thinkers base their understandings, judgments, and actions on evidence, they recognize that requesting evidence is natural, commonly practiced, and essential in order to understand and evaluate what we learn. Model, acknowledge, and value students' open, curious, and respectful requests for evidence.

In addition to asking for reasons, you can model this disposition by citing information as evidence when you explain or describe content or offer reasons for your ideas. Requesting evidence

- Models the importance of having reasons for our judgments and beliefs
- Confirms value of inquiry
- Models reflective understanding of information
- Demonstrates respectful, responsible discourse

Using instructional methods which promote thoughtfulness models the thinking dispositions and learning-to-learn skills that we want to promote in our students. They create a classroom climate that supports thinking, understanding, and growth. Often the media and student's surroundings offer misleading views of how people come to believe what they do. Instructional methods to promote careful thinking and learning are more than devices to improve student performance. They set a climate and tone of careful thinking and demonstrate the value of thought. They are essential if schools are to become "a home for the mind," our classrooms workshops of thought, and the lessons we teach vehicles to provide students with a variety of tools and techniques for thinking and learning.

CHAPTER 19
THE ROLE OF METACOGNITION

Why is Metacognition Necessary?

Skillful thinkers reflect on and manage their own thinking. For example, when a decision is needed, skillful thinkers stop themselves from making hasty decisions and guide themselves through more careful decision making. Even after they've made a decision, they remain open to new information which may change their minds. In effect, skillful thinkers have developed strategies for good thinking and manage their own thinking by using these strategies when needed.

The defaults in thinking described in this handbook result when people do not manage their thinking very well. Impulse, association, and emotional appeal often determine their thoughts and judgments. Many of these thoughts and judgments do not serve them well.

Everyone, however, can learn to manage their thinking in more productive ways. One of the great insights growing out of recent work to improve thinking is that our thinking is as much within our own control as our actions are. Metacognition plays a key role in this. We have to be able to think about our thinking if we are to take charge of it.

To take charge of our actions, we have to know what we are doing, how we can act differently to do things in better ways, and what we can do to modify our behavior so that we do what we think is best. To take charge of our thinking, we similarly have to understand what kind of thinking we are doing, how we do it, and how it can be done differently to improve it. We are then in a better position to change it according to our conception of what more skillful thinking is like. Metacognition is the internal managing process that we use to take charge of and direct our own thinking so that it is no longer determined by impulse and association but by what we should do to be skillful thinkers.

What is Involved in Thinking about Our Thinking Skillfully?

What kind of thinking is metacognition? Some writers describe metacognition as a special kind of thinking skill or process different from the types of thinking we use to think about things, people, and events around us. On the contrary, metacognition is no different from certain types of thinking we use regularly.

We can, of course, think about our thinking in any number of ways. What *is* special about metacognition is that it involves certain ways of thinking about our thinking that are involved in our ability to manage things well. In metacognition

- We have to be able to *identify what kind* of thinking we are doing or plan to do. We should be able to tell that we are engaged in decision making, comparing and contrasting, determining the reliability of a source, etc.

- We also have to be able to *analyze* how we presently do this kind of thinking in order to determine whether it needs improvement. For example, I may realize that I usually decide to do the first thing that comes into my mind and sometimes miss opportunities for better choices. Or I may realize that I often notice differences between things but rarely think about what the differences mean and, hence, do not gain much understanding of what I am comparing. Or I may realize that I usually accept as reliable anything in print and sometimes end up accepting things that are false or one-sided.

- We also should be prepared to *distinguish component subtasks* that we usually do not engage in but that we think might be included in the thinking we have been performing. For example, I may wonder whether it is important to consider evidence for consequences when I make a decision, to draw conclusions from the similarities and differences I note, or to consider whether the publication in which an article appears is usually reliable.

- We should be ready to *evaluate* how we carry out our thinking and any new thinking strategy that we may be considering.

How effective are these likely to be? For example, in making a decision, will my decisions be better if I consider consequences than if I do not consider them? If I consider the consequences, perhaps I can avoid being surprised by results that will affect me adversely and reject options that lead to problems. If I draw a conclusion from similarities and differences in the nutritional value of two foods, perhaps I can understand much better how my body benefits from eating them. If I consider whether a publication is usually reliable, perhaps I can avoid being misled into believing things that may not be true.

The thinking involved in these tasks is similar to the kind of thinking we do when we try to manage and improve any kind of performance. To improve my tennis performance, for example, I should be able to tell how I am handling the racket and moving my arm as I swing. I can then try to determine if I am using my racket effectively. Do my shots go where I want them to? Do they hook to the right more than I would like? If my playing is not as effective as I would like, I can develop a plan to play differently. Perhaps I should hold the racket a little higher or lift my elbow. Then I can execute this plan and see if it makes a difference.

Such management tasks are similar to metacognition, except that in metacognition, what we manage is our own thinking, not a physical performance. What is different about metacognition is *what we think about*—our thinking—and not *the kind of thinking we do* when we think about it.

The thinking map in figure 19.1 describes metacognitive thinking that aims at improving our

performance in situations in which our thinking is what we are concerned about.

Notice the kinds of component thinking skills that are involved in skillful metacognition. When you are asking yourself about the type of thinking you are doing, you *classify* it. When you ask how you do it, you are *analyzing* it into its component parts. Both are ways of *describing* your thinking. Often in thinking skills programs, when students are asked to think about their thinking, they are only asked to engage in one or the other of these types of thinking.

If students are to manage their own thinking, however, the way they think about their thinking must involve more than just these types of thinking. Students must also be able to *evaluate* and *plan* their thinking. When you ask if your thinking strategy was effective or how you might improve it, you are *evaluating* your thinking. When you ask yourself how you will do it next time, your goal is a *decision* about how you will think in the future. You are *planning* your thinking.

Each of the four types of metacognitive thinking is essential for managing and planning our thinking effectively. When we blend them together to think about our thinking, they become a powerful strategy for self-directed thinking.

The graphic organizer in figure 19.2 provides spaces to jot down answers to the questions that we should ask ourselves to engage in skillful metacognition.

When do we engage in skillful metacognition? The wording of the thinking map of skillful metacognition (figure 19.1) indicates that metacognition sometimes occurs *after* we engage in some type of thinking. For example, after I have made a decision, I may realize that it was not a good one. I may have decided to go to a mountain resort for my vacation. After getting there, however, I discover that certain "hidden" costs that I did not know about made the daily cost of the vacation almost double. I never would have gone to that resort if I had known in advance about these additional costs. I note that when I made my decision about where to go, I did not gather all of the relevant information I could have. I can't change my vacation now, but I must remember next time to gather all relevant information before I decide where to go. To do this carefully, I also decide that

---

THINKING ABOUT THINKING SKILLFULLY

1. What type of thinking did you engage in?

2. How did you do the thinking?

3. Was that an effective way to do this thinking? Why or why not? If not, what can you do to improve this way of thinking?

4. How will you do this kind of thinking next time it is needed?

Figure 19.1

METACOGNITION LOG

What was the thinking skill you used in this lesson?

What questions or directions prompted you to engage in this thinking in the lesson?

How did you carry out this thinking? (What steps did you go through in your thinking as you did the lesson?)

Describe how this way of thinking compares with other ways you might have thought about the issues in the lesson. Which do you prefer and why?

If you use this thinking in another situation, how would you plan to do it? Pick a specific example and describe what you would think about in some detail.

Figure 19.2

I should take some time to think about what information I will need before I try to get it.

In this case, I am reflecting on how I engaged in a certain kind of thinking that has already occurred, but I use these reflections to develop a plan that would modify the way I expect to engage in this type of thinking in the future.

I can also *monitor and correct* my thinking while I am doing it. This means shifting my attention back and forth from what I am thinking about to the thinking itself. For example, while trying to make a decision about where to go on my vacation, I may be tempted to go to the mountain resort, but I may step back from thinking about the vacation and ask myself, Am I considering all that I should to make a really well-informed decision? I may then realize that I am just considering a few important factors and that there may be more information I need. So I switch my strategy and decide to take time to gather more relevant information before I decide.

Being metacognitive before, during, and after we think maximizes the degree to which we can manage our own thinking.

Prerequisites for metacognition. What makes metacognition seem like a new and mysterious type of thinking is that, in order to do it well, we have to be able to distinguish different types of thinking as well as different elements in our thinking. To do this, we have to know and use the language of thinking and apply it to ourselves by attending to episodes of our own thinking. When I remark that I considered a number of options and then examined the consequences, searching for reasons why I should or should not choose one of my options, I am using the ordinary language of thinking that we all use, not a new technical language. I am using this language to describe my own thinking.

While we are familiar with and use the language of thinking, we do not describe our thought processes as frequently or insightfully as we might. We attend to events and things around us, but while our own thinking is constantly occurring, we rarely attend to it. Shifting our attention to our own thinking and applying the ordinary concepts and language of thinking to it, however, is necessary for skillful metacognition.

Learning to use precise language to describe our thinking is no different from other situations in which we learn and apply a new conceptual framework and language to differentiate things around us. When we teach students to distinguish the parts of an automobile and to understand how they work, we teach them to apply and use automotive concepts and language. ("The carburetor is skipping and needs repair, but the spark plugs are in good working order.") Practice in using these concepts and words helps students identify the parts of automobiles with some facility. Discriminating and describing a variety of aspects of our thinking is, likewise, the result of getting used to attending to our thinking and applying the concepts and language of thinking to it.

This is why teaching thinking explicitly, as we do in infusion lessons, is so important in helping students develop and use their metacognitive abilities well. Explicit instruction uses the language of the thinking skills being taught to guide students' thinking and hence prompts application of this language to their own thinking. This is the first step in helping them to develop the habit of thinking about their thinking.

Teaching Students to Engage in Skillful Metacognition

Because metacognition is an essential ingredient in all forms of skillful thinking, there are no separate lessons on metacognition in this handbook. Rather, metacognition is introduced in infusion lessons as a key component in learning to manage *any* type of thinking. An organized process of metacognitive questioning based on the thinking map in figure 19.1 appears in every infusion lesson.

The following summary of the dynamics of an infusion lesson makes it clear why it is important to include such organized metacognitive activities in each lesson:

- In infusion lessons, the teacher makes thinking strategies explicit and guides students in their use as they think about what they are learning in the curriculum (e.g., what to do about the runt pig in *Charlotte's Web*, the similarities and differences in the experiences of Lincoln and Douglass and their significance, the reliability of observation reports about the surface of the planet Mars).

- Then students are asked to extract the strategy they used from the specific context of the lesson as they reflect on whether this strategy is one that is effective.

- The students then create a plan in their own words for the thinking they have just done.

- They will then use this plan the next time they must do the same kind of thinking.

With repeated applications, guided by their thinking plans, students develop the habits of thought that make them skillful thinkers. Metacognition plays a key role in the transition from teacher-guided thinking to students' using thinking strategies on their own. Without metacognition, students' transfer and use of skillful thinking in other appropriate contexts will be minimal.

Becoming more metacognitive is not difficult. When you are learning to play tennis, it is initially hard to monitor and evaluate your playing yourself. Your instructor gives you feedback, suggestions, and support. As you develop more expertise, you increasingly guide yourself. The same is true of skillful thinking. Your instructor guides you in doing it *and* in thinking about it so that you learn to guide yourself.

There are four basic practices used by teachers to teach metacognition in infusion lessons:

- Distancing activities in which students are prompted to shift their attention to their thinking and away from what they have been thinking about

- Structured questioning to prompt students to think skillfully about their thinking

- Prompted practice in which students use specific thinking strategies to guide their own thinking

- Reflective writing to express students' thinking about their thinking

Distancing students from what they have been thinking about and shifting their attention to their own thinking. In the critical thinking activity in infusion lessons, students often get deeply involved in thinking about the content-related topic of the lesson. This could be what Mr. Arable should do, what caused the extinction of the dinosaurs, what assumptions Moctezuma made about Cortes, etc. A common strategy in distancing students from what they have been thinking about and shifting their attention to their thinking process is to ask them directly to do so. You might say, "Let's stop thinking about the dinosaurs now and focus our attention on how we thought about what caused their extinction" or "We're going to shift our attention away from the dinosaurs now and think about how you tried to figure out what caused their extinction." If students have become accustomed to doing this, your comments may be all that is needed to shift their attention.

If, on the other hand, students are not used to doing this, you may have to explain what you mean. You might say, "When you think about the dinosaurs, you remember many things about them: what they ate, etc. When you shift your attention to your thinking, you will be thinking about something different: what went through your mind as you were thinking about the dinosaurs? What questions did you ask? Did you remember things? That's thinking about thinking."

With younger children, you can draw a diagram in which you show the dinosaur and a bubble for their thoughts about what caused the extinction of the dinosaurs. You can then point to each picture as you talk about thinking about thinking. This will help to shift their attention.

Structured questioning to prompt students to think skillfully about their thinking: kinds of questions to ask. When a teacher asks a student how he or she conducted a certain type of thinking, the teacher's question prompts the student to *describe the strategy used* for the thinking. After a decision-making activity, for example, the teacher's goal is to help the student become aware of and identify the degree to which options were considered, information about the consequences was considered, etc. If the student has difficulty doing this, the teacher can ask more specific questions about the process. She might even ask, "Did you think about options at all?" "What did you think about to weigh the consequences?" Guidance using prompting questions helps students to become familiar with their thinking, to learn how to describe it using the language of thinking, and to learn the kinds of questions they should ask themselves when they recall their own thinking.

Similarly, teachers use different types of questions to prompt students to *assess the effectiveness of their thinking*. Recurring questions like "Was that an effective way to make a decision?" and "How well did that strategy help you to assess the reliability of sources of information?" prompt students to evaluate their thinking and teach them questions they should ask themselves when they independently seek to evaluate how effectively they are engaging in a thinking task.

More specific evaluative questions can also be asked. For example, this is a question sequence from the *Henny Penny* lesson: "Is this a better way to find out what caused something than Henny-Penny thinking? Why?" Such comparative questions are usually easier to answer than simply asking whether the kind of thinking students did was effective.

Guiding students even more specifically in evaluative metacognition may be necessary. A teacher might ask, "For example, do you think that developing a list of possible causes increases your chances of finding out what the cause really was? How?" or "Is thinking about options and consequences a way to avoid some of the defaults in decision making? How does using this way of making decisions help to avoid these defaults?"

Planning how we will engage in skillful thinking again is the culminating metacognitive activity in infusion lessons. Asking students to write out a plan or to create a flow chart which can guide them in doing the same kind of thinking again is a common practice. This creates ownership of these thinking plans since students can put their plan in their own words. Soon students become accustomed to planning how they will carry out their thinking in a variety of thinking tasks.

Students may also work together to develop a class plan for a specific thinking skill then post it on the wall of the classroom. This, of course, blends cooperative work with metacognition.

Structured questioning to prompt students to think skillfully about their thinking: when to ask metacognitive questions. The main organized metacognitive activities in infusion lessons occur after the students have engaged in a well-developed thinking activity like deciding what the best thing is for Mr. Arable to do with the runt pig. The diagram in figure 19.3 shows the order in which activities typically occur in infusion lessons.

INFUSION LESSON

Introduction

Thinking Actively

Thinking about Thinking

Applying your Thinking

Figure 19.3

At the same time, the more that metacognitive prompts are peppered throughout infusion lessons, the more practice students will get with the varied kinds of metacognition that are important for them to engage in as skillful thinkers. For example, there are numerous opportunities to prompt students to engage in metacognitive monitoring and reflection *while* the thinking activity is still going on. After they have generated a list of options, asking students a question like "What is it important to think about next?" can distance them enough from thinking about Mr. Arable and the runt pig to prompt their thinking about the importance of thinking about consequences. That question allows them to focus on the consequences of the options they have generated.

A more sustained and subtle practice is to move from group to group as students are engaged in cooperative thinking tasks and ask the students if they are having any difficulties with the thinking they are doing. Are they finding anything hard? If so, what? When students describe the problems they are having, you can then discuss ways of overcoming these difficulties. You can also ask the group to help.

For example, as they move from group to group during a decision-making activity, teachers commonly find that some students have problems generating many options. Sometimes teachers suggest ways of overcoming these, like piggybacking on the ideas of other students. Or they may ask other students who are generating many options how they generate so many ideas. For example, in the lesson about *Mr. Arable and the Runt Pig*, a student may respond that she asks herself, "What kind of option is this?" about an option that another student has mentioned. The option of giving the pig to a 4-H club, which another student has raised, involves giving the pig away, she notes. This prompts her to raise the question, "Who are some others that the pig might be given to?" She then thinks of other possibilities: the farmer next door, the butcher, a science class, a zoo, and another sow. Hearing this account, the teacher may suggest that the student who is having difficulty may also try this technique.

Helping students to monitor their thinking and overcome problems they are having while the thinking activity is going on is an excellent way to give students practice at thinking about their thinking. The more we couple monitoring thinking while we are doing it with retrospective metacognition and advanced planning, the more we help students become disposed to managing their own thinking.

The diagram in figure 19.4 contains important question stems that can be used to prompt skillful metacognition in students whether it occurs before, during, or after the main thinking activity. It is arranged to move from identifying a type of thinking to evaluating the strategy used in the thinking and planning how to do it again next time.

Prompting students to manage their own thinking. Describing, evaluating, and planning one's thinking are important stages in thinking

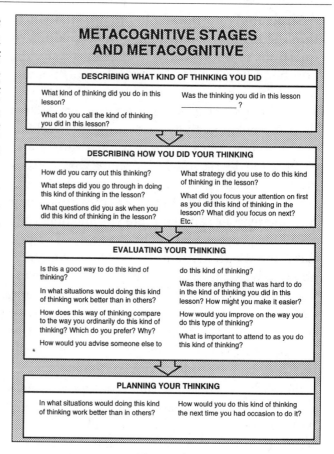

Figure 19.4

about thinking skillfully. The questions teachers ask to guide students through these stages help students to learn how to do this kind of metacognition, and their continued use by teachers gets students accustomed to them. When the teacher does this, she is providing a supporting structure for students' metacognition. This "scaffolding" should be gradually removed, however, to allow students to take over this task themselves. Specific questioning strategies that you can use to accomplish this are featured in the application section of infusion lessons, part of the general strategy in these lessons to teach for the transfer and reinforcement of the thinking skills.

For example, after students have thought about Lincoln and Douglass and engaged in metacognitive reflection about ways of comparing and contrasting effectively, the teacher may introduce a transfer activity by saying, "Go back to your plan for skillful comparison and contrast and use it to compare and contrast fractions and decimals." With less scaffolding, the teacher might say, "Pick the thinking plan and graphic organizer that you think should be used here. Use it to be sure you understand fractions and decimals." Students will begin to guide their own thinking as they respond to these more general metacognitive prompts.

Thinking about thinking through writing. Reflective writing is an excellent vehicle for stimulating sustained thinking. Its use in infusion lessons provides an opportunity for students to do sustained thinking about the content they study in these lessons. It can also be used to support students' ongoing reflections about their thinking.

You can use one of two strategies for reflective writing about thinking. The first is to simply ask students to write about their thinking. For example, you can ask students to write out how they will try to solve a problem before they do it. After working on decision making, for example, students can be asked to write a more extensive essay about the differences between the way they used to make decisions and the way they do now. They can write a recommendation for an effective decision-making strategy for people who make impulsive decisions. There are a multitude of other possible situations in which students can write about their thinking.

The second strategy relates to situations in which students keep journals as a regular writing activity. You can ask your students to use a second column in their journals to enter their thoughts or notes about their thinking as they do content-oriented writing in the first column. You can suggest that they ask themselves questions like "Was this idea easy to understand? Was it hard to solve that problem? Why? Could I have improved on the way I tried to solve it?" Using double-entry journals can help students become accustomed to thinking about their thinking as they do it.

Metacognition in the primary grades. In general, primary grade students have, at best, primitive concepts of the various types of thinking that we commonly engage in. They also have little understanding of the important questions to ask in thinking skillfully.

Because the way we describe thinking is often unclear to young children, you should first concentrate on helping them to understand the language of thinking and then to apply it to their own thinking. For example, explain directly to your students that what they are about to do is to *make a decision,* to think about *options,* etc. Write these words on the board. After doing this, ask: "What was the kind of thinking that we did?" If they are having trouble, point to the board, and ask them if this is what they did. Soon, they will respond to your metacognitive questions with ease.

In some cases, you should use simpler language to describe thinking than you might use with upper elementary students. Instead of "evidence" use the word "clue." Decision making can be "choosing." Your students can always learn the standard terminology later.

Summary: Teaching to Internalize Skillful Thinking

Figure 19.5 illustrates the role of metacognition as we move from highly scaffolded lessons with a significant amount of teacher guidance to students' management of their own thinking.

The diagram in figure 19.5 summarizes the way infusion, as an instructional strategy, makes good thinking stick with our students.

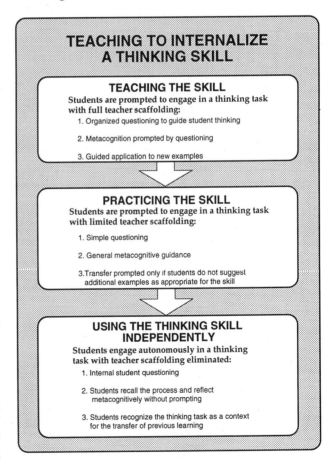

Figure 19.5

Tools for Designing Metacognition Sections of Lessons

The thinking map of sequenced questions for skillful metacognition on page 527 can be used to guide you in designing the section of infusion lessons in which students think about their think-ing. The thinking map and the graphic organizer can be used to supplement the Thinking About Thinking section of the lessons included in this handbook.

Both can be made into transparencies, photo-copied, or enlarged as posters for display in the classroom. Reproduction rights are granted for single classroom use only.

THINKING ABOUT
THINKING SKILLFULLY

1. **What type of thinking did you engage in?**

2. **How did you do the thinking?**

3. **Was that an effective way to do this thinking? Why or why not? If not, what can you do to improve this way of thinking?**

4. **How will you do this kind of thinking next time it is needed?**

METACOGNITION LOG

What was the thinking skill you used in this lesson?

How did you carry out this thinking? (What steps did you go through in your thinking as you did the lesson?)

What questions or directions prompted you to engage in this thinking in the lesson?

Describe how this way of thinking compares with other ways you might have thought about the issues in the lesson. Which do you prefer and why?

If you use this thinking in another situation, how would you plan to do it? Pick a specific example and describe what you would think about in some detail.

METACOGNITIVE STAGES AND METACOGNITIVE QUESTIONS

DESCRIBING WHAT KIND OF THINKING YOU DID

What kind of thinking did you do in this lesson?

What do you call the kind of thinking you did in this lesson?

Was the thinking you did in this lesson _____ ?

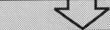

DESCRIBING HOW YOU DID YOUR THINKING

How did you carry out this thinking?

What steps did you go through in doing this kind of thinking in the lesson?

What questions did you ask when you did this kind of thinking in the lesson?

What strategy did you use to do this kind of thinking in the lesson?

What did you focus your attention on first as you did this kind of thinking in the lesson? What did you focus on next? Etc.

EVALUATING YOUR THINKING

Is this a good way to do this kind of thinking?

In what situations would doing this kind of thinking work better than in others?

How does this way of thinking compare to the way you ordinarily do this kind of thinking? Which do you prefer? Why?

How would you advise someone else to

do this kind of thinking?

Was there anything that was hard to do in the kind of thinking you did in this lesson? How might you make it easier?

How would you improve on the way you do this type of thinking?

What is important to attend to as you do this kind of thinking?

PLANNING YOUR THINKING

In what situations would doing this kind of thinking work better than in others?

How would you do this kind of thinking the next time you had occasion to do it?

CHAPTER 20
SELECTING CONTEXTS FOR INFUSION LESSONS

Guidelines for Selecting Contexts

Selecting good contexts for infusion lessons is crucial in designing effective instruction. To accomplish the dual objectives of infusion lessons (teaching skillful thinking and improving students' understanding of the content), one should select contexts in which the thinking process relates naturally to the content being taught. For example, Mr. Arable's being challenged by Fern about killing the runt pig is a natural situation for skillful decision making. If there is similar biographical information about two leaders of the same period, such as Abraham Lincoln and Frederick Douglass, it is natural to compare and contrast them.

The key to choosing appropriate contexts is finding examples that offer rich development of the thinking process and rich instruction of the content objective. For example, in the lesson *Independence and Loyalty*, students examine colonists' reasons just prior to the Revolutionary War for and against seeking independence from Britain. This important conflict in U.S. history offers a rich context for teaching the thinking skill of finding reasons and conclusions because of the clarity and drama of the arguments. Making the thinking skill explicit by posting the thinking map for reasons and conclusions and using the corresponding graphic organizer prompts students to examine details of the debate and to realize how controversial and personal this important issue was for the colonists.

If the content is too complex, however, there is a danger that the subject may overshadow the thinking activity to the extent that students remember the content but not the thinking process. For example, if you use an initial lesson on global warming as a context to introduce skillful decision making, the complexity of the topic and length of the unit may overshadow the decision-making process. Unless students are reminded of the decision-making strategy repeatedly, they may learn about global warming but remember little about decision making.

At the other extreme, students may understand the thinking clearly but learn little information about the subject. The content should be well-developed in the thinking lesson, not just a topic that is superficially touched on to provide a vehicle for teaching thinking. For example, if you use a real school incident as a context for a lesson on the reliability of observation reports, students may learn how to evaluate an observation report but do not, unless prompted, apply the thinking skill to curriculum examples.

While the curriculum abounds in opportunities for teaching all the thinking skills and processes featured in this handbook, some thinking skills are taught more effectively in some disciplines than in others. For example, in foreign language instruction, teaching compare/contrast or classification may be helpful in teaching basic language usage, but there may be fewer contexts for lessons on reliable sources or uncovering assumptions lessons.

Designing effective infusion lessons often depends on the clarity with which the content objective is stated. For example, "compare two folktales" does not focus on the purpose of the comparison. Stating general similarities and differences adds interest but prompts little understanding of the two stories. Sometimes teachers suggest that students compare two aspects of a story (characters, morals, setting) but do not relate them to a purpose or kind of conclusion that they expect students to draw. As you state the content objective, try to be as clear as possible about the kind of insight that you expect as the outcome of comparing and contrasting the two stories. For example, in *Mufaro's Beautiful Daughters*, the content objective is stated in terms of contrasting cultural values. This content emphasis yields a more robust lesson than would result if the lesson were a more general comparison and contrast.

In the commentary that introduces each thinking skill or process, there are suggestions for contexts which are rich examples for improving students' understanding of both the content and the thinking. The lesson menus at the end of each chapter list examples of contexts which teachers have suggested or used to design infusion lessons.

Sometimes planning teams designate specific thinking skills and processes for particular grade levels. This practice conveys the idea that students are not ready for or capable of certain types of thinking in the early grades. If instructional methods are developmentally appropriate, students from kindergarten through the elementary grades can skillfully demonstrate the thinking skills and processes featured in this handbook. While it may take more than one year to design and gather lessons in all the skills and processes, our goal should be a full range of instruction in skillful thinking at any grade level.

Finding contexts by reviewing curriculum guides and texts is particularly important if instruction is assessed by procedures designed to indicate higher order thinking. If the school, district or state assessment tests include extended writing or performance tasks which evaluate the quality of student's thinking, students should have sufficient practice to be competent and confident in carrying out the thinking required in such activities. Offering teachers a broad selection of contexts increases the likelihood of sufficient instruction for the transfer of the thinking skills and processes to become evident in students' performance.

Three Procedures for Finding Contexts for Infusion Lessons

We recommend three procedures for locating contexts for infusion lessons: creating menus of lesson ideas as you review demonstration lessons, scanning the curriculum for good opportunities to teach an infusion lesson, and reviewing curriculum guides and texts to identify many significant contexts. Using one or more of these procedures will depend on

- The number of teachers working together to design infusion lessons;
- How much experience you have in designing infusion lessons;
- How much thinking instruction you want to infuse;
- Whether you are designing infusion les-

sons for your own classes or as part of a district team on thinking skills instruction;
- The amount of available planning time for review and curriculum planning; and
- Whether procedures for assessing students' thinking beyond those provided in the model lessons are used in the school or district.

Menus

We use the term "menu" to describe a list of suggested contexts for infusion lessons. The menus in this handbook contain the grade level, subject, topic, and thinking issue for contexts which offer a rich opportunity to teach or reinforce a thinking skill or process. These topics have been suggested by teachers and have been reviewed by the authors.

Creating your own menus of lesson ideas as you become familiar with infusion lessons is a good way to apply the principles of designing infusion lessons. As you first read a chapter about a thinking skill or process, identify contexts in your curriculum in which to develop your first lessons. Take some time after reading each model lesson to suggest thinking instruction contexts. Use the menus at the end of the chapter as idea starters for developing your own lessons.

Creating menus as you first review the model lessons offers several lesson-planning advantages:

- Immediate application. Immediately applying the thinking skill or process to your own teaching fosters confidence and confirms the instructional relevance of the thinking instruction.

- Versatility. Menus demonstrate the usefulness and versatility of the thinking skills and processes in a variety of instructional uses across the curriculum.

- Increased likelihood of use. Creating menus while the thinking skill or process is fresh in your mind allows you to apply it to content objectives right away.

- Significant contexts come to mind first. Teachers' first ideas about good contexts for infusion lessons have often proven to be effective ones. Weeding out less effective ideas or restating them for clarity may be necessary.

The disadvantages of selecting contexts by developing menus include

- First responses. These contexts are initial ideas which may or may not prove to be effective ones as you develop a lesson. Sometimes a lesson suggestion may not be suitable because it does not work well for explaining the thinking skill or process clearly.

- Not comprehensive. Other significant contexts to which the thinking skill or process would be better suited may be overlooked.

- Not sequential. Although thinking skills and processes may usually be taught in any order, there are a few cases in which it is desirable, but not necessary, to teach some skills or processes before others. For example, compare and contrast involves classification and analogy. Identifying reasons and conclusions plays a role in uncovering unstated assumptions.

Suggesting menu ideas does not take into account when in the school year the lesson will be offered. The initial lesson on a particular thinking skill should occur early enough in the school year to allow time for transfer examples.

Looking for contexts and predicting how the thinking process may work in the lesson allows you to "replay" the thinking skill or process almost immediately and apply it to content you teach. During the first year that you use this handbook, using the menus provided in the handbook or developing lessons from your own menus is sufficient to begin teaching thinking.

Scan the Curriculum for a Few Examples that Illustrate the Thinking Process Well

If you are the only teacher in your school or grade who is designing infusion lessons and have limited planning time, you can search your texts and curriculum guides for a few examples that "showcase" a particular thinking skill. You then locate a few topics for transfer lessons to provide sufficient classroom practice. The goal in scanning the curriculum for rich contexts for thinking instruction is to identify key topics in your curriculum in which to implement the thinking instruction, followed by a few good transfer lessons.

Scanning the curriculum often produces a list of lesson ideas that addresses more significant curriculum objectives than generating menus from the first topics we identify. Even a quick survey of texts often prompts teachers to recognize key concepts that can be effective infusion lesson topics, examples that may not occur to us when we read these lessons for the first time.

The advantages of scanning the curriculum for contexts which best fit the thinking activity include

- Creating powerful examples of using the thinking skill or process;

- Designing a few good lessons which demonstrate the thinking skill well; and

- Selecting contexts that teach significant curriculum objectives.

Disadvantages of this approach include

- Lesson suggestions are not comprehensive; and

- The thinking skills and processes may appear less versatile or relevant. Since you are looking for only a few good examples, you may not realize how often using the thinking skill or process might be beneficial or how important it can be in helping students understand issues.

If you want to assure that you are offering adequate thinking instruction in the fewest lessons, you may find the "best fit" approach helpful. Teacher educators or staff development personnel who must demonstrate infusion lessons for other teachers may want to pick only the most dramatic uses of the thinking processes for clarity and to add interest in their lessons.

As you begin to teach infusion lessons, you may recognize in the middle of a lesson that this would have been a rich opportunity for teaching an infusion lesson. While the idea is fresh, highlighting with markers or using tabs to mark these contexts in the teacher's manual provides a reminder for planning next year's lessons. You are "scanning the curriculum for contexts" by being alert to good opportunities.

A Comprehensive Review of Curriculum Guides and Texts

After you have practiced writing infusion lessons and have some experience locating rich contexts, you may serve on a planning team to review local or state curriculum guides and textbooks to locate a variety of other topics well suited for infusion lessons. Given sufficient planning time, reviewing the curriculum for the best contexts for teaching the thinking skills and processes results in well-articulated thinking instruction and effective content instruction.

The matrix for integrating content objectives by thinking skills (figure 20.1) serves as a worksheet for each planning-team participant to identify contexts for one grade. Teachers write district or state codes for curriculum objectives or topics from texts in each square. Suggested contexts are then reviewed with other teachers in the same field or at the same grade level. Then teachers from several grade levels may combine their contexts grade-by-grade, producing a collection of lesson contexts for thinking instruction across grade levels and subjects. Contexts from all grades and subjects can be combined using an extended form of the same diagram. Indicate which contexts seem best suited for initial lessons and transfer examples, taking into account the order in which content objectives are usually taught in the school year.

Advantages of this systematic review process include the following:

- Comprehensive. The review process identifies an array of contexts to which the thinking skill or process is well-suited.

- Serves as a basis for integrating the curriculum. There are many ways of integrating the curriculum: by cross-indexing topics around common themes, using district goals, or by featuring a thinking skill or process as a principle for unifying the curriculum. Developing interdisciplinary units around a thinking skill or process correlates concepts and emphasizes transfer of the thinking process.

- Demonstrates the relevance of the thinking skill or process to a wide range of content objectives. Teachers recognize the versatility of the thinking skills and processes and

the wide range of content objectives in which improved student thinking will result in more effective learning of the content.

- Creates a larger pool of contexts. Selecting the best examples from many topics promotes a well-designed thinking program. Having many contexts allows teachers to schedule initial lessons and transfer examples systematically in the school year.

- Identifies concepts and thinking processes featured on tests and other assessment procedures. The review process allows teachers to select topics about which students' understanding and thinking will be evaluated. As extended response writing and alternative assessment procedures are commonly used, demonstrating organized thinking, as well as thorough knowledge, becomes increasingly important.

- Articulation across grade levels. Teachers recognize topics that other teachers at earlier and later grade levels teach, confirming the significance and continuity of their efforts to design infusion lessons.

- Lasting. While curriculum reforms come and go, the core concepts of the curriculum are constant. The curriculum guides for teaching thinking that grow out of this review process will be useful, regardless of other curriculum initiatives. The school's or district's commitment of time for curriculum review and planning demonstrates its recognition that improving students' thinking is an on-going priority.

- Reduces planning time for individual teachers. A grade, school, or district compilation of content objectives allows each teacher to select identified contexts, rather than spending time looking for good topics.

- Available to new teachers coming into the school or district. As new teachers become familiar with designing infusion lessons, an array of curriculum contexts is already available to them.

- Addresses state and local instructional priorities and testing practices. Teaching thinking addresses the school improvement stra-

Continued on page 537.

INTEGRATING CONTENT OBJECTIVES BY THINKING SKILL OR PROCESS

SKILL	LANGUAGE ARTS	MATHEMATICS	SOCIAL STUDIES	SCIENCE/ HEALTH	ART/MUSIC/GUIDANCE PHYSICAL EDUCATION
Comparing/ contrasting					
Classifying					
Parts/whole					
Sequencing					
Uncovering assumptions					
Reliable sources/ accurate observations					
Reasons/ conclusions					
Causal explanation					

Figure 20.1

INTEGRATING CONTENT OBJECTIVES BY THINKING SKILL OR PROCESS

SKILL	LANGUAGE ARTS	MATHEMATICS	SOCIAL STUDIES	SCIENCE/ HEALTH	ART/ MUSIC/GUIDANCE PHYSICAL EDUCATION
Prediction					
Reasoning by analogy					
Generalization					
Conditional reasoning					
Generating possibilities					
Generating metaphors					
Decision making					
Problem solving					

Figure 20.1 continued

Continued from page 534.

tegic plans of many individual schools and school districts. Relating thinking contexts to specific content objectives demonstrates that the thinking program is being addressed systematically.

Disadvantages of reviewing curriculum guides and texts include the following:

- Lack of planning/curriculum development time. Preparing a systematic guide for infusing thinking skills and processes requires significant planning time for thoughtful review of curriculum guides and texts.
- Training and/or experience of planning team staff. The curriculum review process should begin after teachers have had considerable experience designing and teaching infusion lessons. After designing infusion lessons, teachers understand more fully what is entailed in skillful thinking and how thinking instruction adds to students' understanding of content.
- Less ownership and involvement by individual teachers. Teachers who did not participate in the review process may not utilize a curriculum guide that is "handed to them." Many curriculum guides are not used because teachers either do not know they exist or are familiar with them.

As the effectiveness of teaching thinking prompts schoolwide implementation, groups of teachers may help each other write lessons and edit the curriculum for contexts. However, school or district commitment to this instruction merits sufficient review time to allow teachers to plan systematic implementation.

Using any of these techniques for locating contexts, teachers recognize the versatility of the core thinking processes and the heightened understanding that teaching thinking adds to content learning. These approaches represent the stages that individual teachers experience as they design infusion lessons.

Integrating Instruction by Infusing the Teaching of Critical and Creative Thinking

The significance of infusing thinking skills

and processes into instruction becomes more apparent as one recognizes how the curriculum can be unified by common threads of thought. Using the thinking maps and graphic organizers demonstrates to students the relatedness of thinking in one subject to the same kind of thinking in another. As teachers become more aware of the interconnectedness within the curriculum, they may integrate learning by using either of two organizing principles:

1. The thinking skill or process itself may be a unifying theme for a given period of instruction.
2. The kinds of thinking involved in an interdisciplinary theme adds to student's understanding of that theme.

Thinking skills or processes to unify curriculum for a given period of instruction. In this approach to unifying curriculum, the thinking skill or process is stated and displayed as an instructional focus for a given period. This can be done at the individual classroom level, for all the classes at a given grade level, or for the whole school.

For example, for a period of about four weeks, teachers in an elementary school taught infusion lessons on decision making. The thinking map and graphic organizers for decision making were displayed as posters in the halls, on bulletin boards, and in parent communications. In each class, there were reminders that good decision making is important and that students in that school were learning to do it well.

Students recognized that decision making in different subjects involves the same strategy. They also recognized the variety of opportunities for skillful decision making and the significance of doing it well. The graphic organizers and student products, including their writing about decisions, were displayed. The parents' night featured skits showing parents the decision-making strategy their children were learning. Teacher-prepared webbing displays showed parents the many contexts in which their children were learning decision making.

This approach can be enhanced by studying the strategies used by important decision makers and by considering specialized kinds of decisions. Case studies may include decisions made by presidents, by scientists, by artists, and by athletes. Students recognize both the common strategy and the important factors that can make decision making somewhat different in different disciplines or contexts.

The goal in using this approach was to demonstrate transfer, relevance, and versatility of the thinking skill or process; thematic connection between disciplines was of little concern. The summary of the goals, curriculum modification, and planning process on the next page explains this way of unifying instruction. The graphic organizer in figure 20.1 serves as a guide for this kind of planning. The outline in figure 20.2 summarizes the goals, curriculum modifications, and planning process to integrate curriculum by a selected thinking skill or process. The sample webbing organizer in figure 20.3 illustrates this curriculum integration for teaching decision making in a fifth grade class.

Teaching the thinking skills or processes involved in a theme that has been selected for instruction across disciplines. In this case, the goal of curriculum integration is for students to develop a deep understanding of the theme

Continued on page 540.

INTEGRATING CURRICULUM:
THINKING SKILL ➡ SUBJECT AREA ➡ TOPIC

Goals of Integrating Content by Thinking Skill or Process

- Emphasize thinking skills and processes as a curriculum goal.
- Transfer teaching thinking skills and processes systematically and with frequent use.
- Demonstrate curricular and noncurricular examples of thinking skills and processes schoolwide, including displays of the thinking maps and graphic organizers.
- Convey the goals of thinking instruction to parents and the community.
- Demonstrate students' interpersonal and individual behaviors based on skillful thinking.
- Demonstrate the versatility, usefulness, and variations in the skillful use of the thinking skill or process in different contexts.

Instructional Modifications to Integrate the Curriculum by Thinking Skills or Processes

- The school/district desires curriculum integration, but teaching themes is not the primary goal. Teaching thinking is an organizing principle of curriculum integration.
- Schoolwide commitment to infusing thinking instruction into the total curriculum
- School climate that values thinking and makes it a priority

Planning Process

- Identify versatile thinking skills and processes.
- Identify significant contexts for teaching thinking skills or processes meaningfully.
- Identify periods in the school year in which most teachers can easily implement their lessons on this skill, and plan to offer all lessons on the selected thinking skill at that time.
- After thinking skills and processes have been scheduled, check that all curriculum objectives have been addressed in units based on thinking skills and processes.
- Prepare classroom displays of webbing diagrams showing how the thinking skill or process was implemented in various subjects.
- Rotate the total list of thinking skills and processes on a two-to-three-year cycle.

Figure 20.2

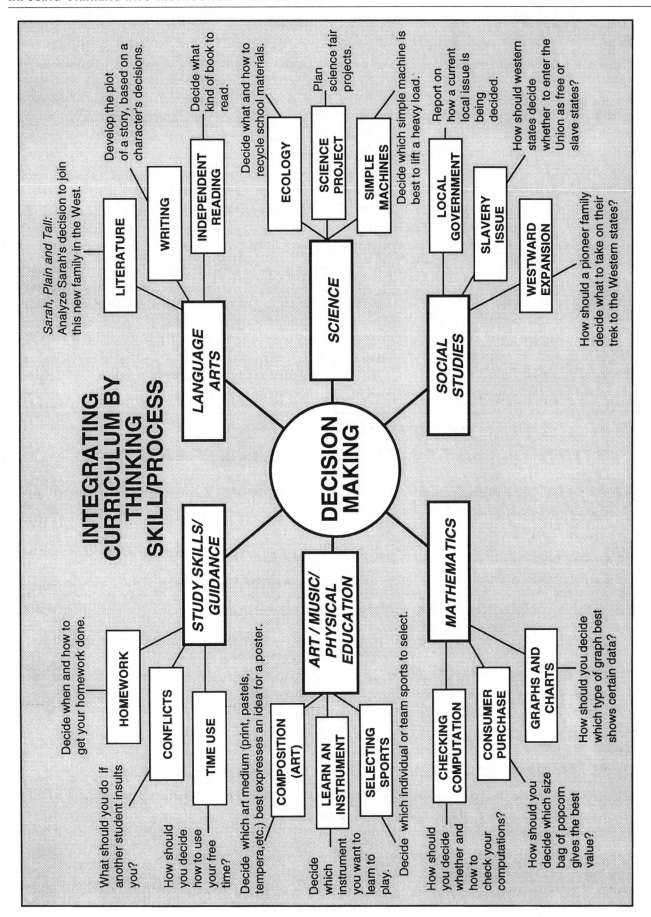

Figure 20.3

Continued from page 538.

selected for interdisciplinary instruction. For example, if the theme is "change," the teacher planning the unit would ask, "What kinds of thinking will help students understand change meaningfully?" The student may need to know what causes change in a variety of situations, to predict what may happen as the result of change, to understand how decisions affect change, to understand common patterns of change, to compare and contrast different forms or indicators of change, and to suggest ways to bring about change. Then one selects topics from various subjects that offer good examples of both the theme and the thinking process.

The outline in figure 20.4 summarizes the goals, curriculum modifications, and planning process to integrate curriculum by teaching selected thinking skills or processes involved in an interdisciplinary theme.

The webbing diagram in figure 20.5 shows the topics of lessons by which a fifth grade class may study change. They think skillfully about causal explanation, prediction, decision making, sequencing, comparing and contrasting, and generating possibilities as they gain insight into the thinking involved in different forms of change.

Themes that are as versatile as change can be meaningfully implemented across the curriculum. However, all academic subjects should not necessarily be included in a single integrated unit. Some themes, such as relationships, responsibility, rules, families, or cities, involve general principles of individual or social behavior and can be developed in social studies, science, and literature. Some themes, such as functions, systems, planning, or proportions, relate to science, mathematics, or information processing. Some themes, such as seasons or animals, are more limited topics that involve only a few subjects but still apply thinking skills and processes effectively.

INTEGRATING CURRICULUM:
THEME ➡ THINKING SKILL ➡ SUBJECT AREA ➡ TOPIC

Goals of Integrating Content around the Significant Thinking Skills and Processes Involved in Selected Themes

- Enhance students' insight about the theme selected for curriculum integration.
- Implement thinking instruction within an interdisciplinary unit plan.
- Demonstrate and frequently transfer thinking skills and processes.

Instructional Modifications to Integrate Curriculum

- School- and/or districtwide commitment to integrated curriculum, expressed in connecting some, but not necessarily all, curriculum to each interdisciplinary theme.
- Common themes have already been identified in curriculum objectives that serve as organizing principles for scheduling thinking instruction.
- Schoolwide commitment to thinking instruction

Planning Process

- Identify significant themes and key ideas that students should understand .
- Identify thinking skills and processes that offer insights about these key ideas.
- Examine curriculum objectives for significant contexts in which selected thinking skills or processes can be meaningfully taught.
- Schedule each theme in the school year when it most naturally falls.
- Check that the introductory lesson on each thinking skill or process occurs early enough in the school year to allow sufficient transfer lessons.

Figure 20.4

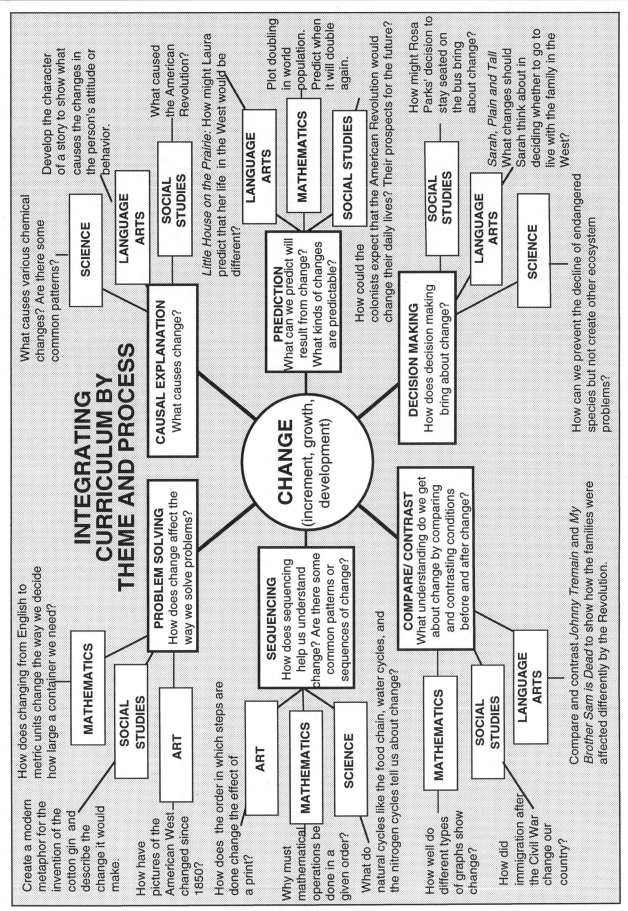

INTEGRATING CURRICULUM BY THEME AND PROCESS

CHANGE (increment, growth, development)

CAUSAL EXPLANATION What causes change?

SCIENCE — What causes various chemical changes? Are there some common patterns?

LANGUAGE ARTS — Develop the character of a story to show what causes the changes in the person's attitude or behavior.

SOCIAL STUDIES — What caused the American Revolution?

PREDICTION What can we predict will result from change? What kinds of changes are predictable?

LANGUAGE ARTS — *Little House on the Prairie:* How might Laura predict that her life in the West would be different?

MATHEMATICS — Plot doubling in world population. Predict when it will double again.

SOCIAL STUDIES — How could the colonists expect that the American Revolution would change their daily lives? Their prospects for the future?

DECISION MAKING How does decision making bring about change?

SOCIAL STUDIES — How might Rosa Parks's decision to stay seated on the bus bring about change?

LANGUAGE ARTS — *Sarah, Plain and Tall.* What changes should Sarah think about in deciding whether to go to live with the family in the West?

SCIENCE — How can we prevent the decline of endangered species but not create other ecosystem problems?

PROBLEM SOLVING How does change affect the way we solve problems?

MATHEMATICS — How does changing from English to metric units change the way we decide how large a container we need?

SOCIAL STUDIES — Create a modern metaphor for the invention of the cotton gin and describe the change it would make. How have pictures of the American West changed since 1850?

ART — How does the order in which steps are done change the effect of a print?

SEQUENCING How does sequencing help us understand change? Are there some common patterns or sequences of change?

ART — Why must mathematical operations be done in a given order?

MATHEMATICS —

SCIENCE — What do natural cycles like the food chain, water cycles, and the nitrogen cycles tell us about change?

COMPARE/ CONTRAST What understanding do we get about change by comparing and contrasting conditions before and after change?

MATHEMATICS — How well do different types of graphs show change?

SOCIAL STUDIES — How did immigration after the Civil War change our country?

LANGUAGE ARTS — Compare and contrast *Johnny Tremain* and *My Brother Sam is Dead* to show how the families were affected differently by the Revolution.

Figure 20.5